"Bernd Janowski (University of Tübi ... to English-speaking readers. He will be n ... no has written a world-class book that will promptly become the benchmark for theological interpretation of the Psalms. Janowski, in a dense, complex, genuinely inviting book, combines acute theological sensibility, close exegetical alertness, and attention to the large human questions now before us concerning life and hope in a failed world. The result of his work is a study that will reward close, careful, sustained reading. We may be grateful to Westminster John Knox for bringing this fresh and judicious book into English translation."

—**Walter Brueggemann,** William Marcellus McPheeters Professor Emeritus of Old Testament, Columbia Theological Seminary

"Bernd Janowski's *Arguing with God* combines masterful exegetical knowledge of ancient Near Eastern literature with pastoral theology. The result is a superb resource for understanding the Psalms as a distinctively human-centered portion of Scripture. Perhaps most significantly, Janowski moves psalms of lament to their rightful place—to the forefront of conversation about the nature of the human being in relation to God. We are fortunate now to have this important work available in English."

—**Jerome F. D. Creach,** Robert C. Holland Professor of Old Testament, Pittsburgh Theological Seminary

"There has not been a book like this since Hans Walter Wolff's famous *Anthropology of the Old Testament*. Janowski offers both insightful analyses of individual psalms and a comprehensive framework for biblical anthropology. The result is a subtle exploration of the Old Testament's understanding of human existence in the presence of the living God."

—**Andreas Schuele,** Professor of Old Testament and Director of the Institute of Judaic Studies, University of Leipzig.

"Only in a few books of the Bible is the human condition picked up as such a central theme as in the book of Psalms, even though it is God, and not humankind, that is the center of interest. In this book, Bernd Janowski pays close attention to the anthropological issues of these prayers, showing not only the usual topics like the social context of lament and praise in Old Testament times, but also familiarizes contemporary readers with uncommon topics like the fluid border between life and death, the desire for vengeance, and the anthropological and theological backgrounds of such concepts. He includes not only iconographic documents for better understanding of rites, worldview, and metaphors, but also presents examples of reception of the 'psalm' genre in poetry and contemporary arts. This is a very important exegetical and theological book, which will be very helpful for teaching and preaching."

—**Irmtraud Fischer,** Professor of Old Testament Studies at the Catholic Theological Faculty of the University of Graz

"Bernd Janowski offers a comprehensive account of theological anthropology of the Psalms within the wider context of the Old Testament and the ancient Near East. Conversant with past studies, and especially the seminal work of H. W. Wolff, Janowski also incorporates the more recent work in the social sciences and the study of the ancient Near East that have expanded our understanding of the self in recent decades. Painstakingly researched, this volume is full of thoughtful insights that will surely enlighten scholars and others interested in the biblical vision of human identity."

—**Jacqueline E. Lapsley,** Associate Professor of Old Testament, Princeton Theological Seminary

"Bernd Janowski has written a masterful study of the Psalms from the perspective of its anthropology. He uses his wide knowledge of psychology, philosophy, art, and Near Eastern studies to great benefit as he reads individual psalms. Sensitive to the book's literary quality and theological depth, he provides great insight not just into the meaning of the text but also into the significance of the Psalms as a 'mirror of the soul.'"

—**Tremper Longman III,** Robert H. Gundry Professor of Biblical Studies, Westmont College

"Finally translated into English, this monumental treatment of psalmic prayer is part theology, part anthropology, part psychology, and part reception history. Janowski brings to bear his wide-ranging knowledge of ancient Near Eastern literature, Hebrew poetry, and European scholarship. He also exhibits in his writing a deep pastoral sensitivity that will make his work eminently useful in the church."

—**William P. Brown,** William Marcellus McPheeters Professor of Old Testament, Columbia Theological Seminary

Arguing with God

Arguing with God

A Theological Anthropology of the Psalms

Bernd Janowski

Translated by Armin Siedlecki

Translated by Armin Siedlecki from the German *Konfliktgespräche mit Gott: Eine Anthropologie der Psalmen*, third edition, published in 2009 by Neukirchener Verlag, and including additional revisions from the author to the German fourth edition.

See p. v–vi, "Acknowledgments and Permissions," for other permission information.

Scripture quotations are English renderings of the author's German translations. Verse numbering is for English versions, with different Hebrew numbers added after a slash (for one verse) or within parentheses or brackets.

13 14 15 16 17 18 19 20 21 22—10 9 8 7 6 5 4 3 2 1

Book design by Drew Stevens
Cover design by Dilu Nicholas
Cover illustration: Abstract portrait © Tudor Catalin Gheorghe/shutterstock.com

Library of Congress Cataloging-in-Publication Data

Janowski, Bernd, 1943–
[Konfliktgespräche mit Gott. English]
Arguing with God : a theological anthropology of the Psalms / Bernd Janowski ; translated by Armin Siedlecki.—First [edition].
pages cm
Includes bibliographical references and indexes.
ISBN 978-0-664-23323-5 (alk. paper)
1. Bible. Psalms—Criticism, interpretation, etc. I. Title.
BS1430.52.J3613 2013
223'.206—dc23

2013019672

♾ The paper used in this publication meets the minimum requirements of the American National Standard for Information Sciences—Permanence of Paper for Printed Library Materials, ANSI Z39.48-1992.

Acknowledgments and Permissions

Page 200, Figure 25
PAUL KLEE
***Angstausbruch II* [Outbreak of Fear II], 1939, 110 (L 10)**
66.5 x 48 cm
Ink on paper on cardboard
Schenkung LK, Klee-Museum, Bern

Page 206, Figure 26
PAUL KLEE
***Das Tor zur Tiefe* [The Gate to the Abyss], 1936, 25 (K 5)**
24 x 29 cm
Ink and watercolor on grounding on gauze on cardboard on stretcher frame
Private collection, Switzerland

Page 332, Figure 41
PAUL KLEE
***Ecce . . .* , 1940, 138 (T 18)**
29.7 x 21.1 cm
Zulu grease pencil on Bieber paper with glue on cardboard
Schenkung LK, Klee-Museum, Bern

Contents

List of Figures

Preface to the U.S. Edition

As my book *Konfliktgespräche mit Gott: Eine Anthropologie der Psalmen*, which was first published ten years ago in German and is now available in its fourth expanded edition as well as in French translation (*Dialogues conflictuels avec Dieu: Une anthropologie des Psaumes*, Genève 2008: Labor et Fides), is now being published in an American edition, I would like it to be accompanied by a word of thanks and a request. I am grateful in particular to Daniel Braden, Managing Editor at Westminster John Knox Press, for his interest in my book and for his strong support of its translation and publication. This is not to be taken for granted. I am therefore especially happy that my anthropology of the Psalms is now being released by one of the leading theological publishers in the United States.

I then ask American readers to be lenient about the fact that they are presented with the results of European and in particular German research in ways that may be unusual to them and which may even appear one-sided. In my defense I can only point to the fact that research on the Psalms has undergone a remarkable resurgence in Germany in the past twenty-five years, which is evident in many new perspectives. This includes the combination of critical and canonical exegesis of the Psalms (*Psalmen*exegese and *Psalter*exegese), the study of metaphors in the Psalms, the comparison with ancient Near Eastern devotional literature, and the consideration of the reception history of the Psalms. As demonstrated by Patrick D. Miller's *They Cried to the Lord*, William P. Brown's *Seeing the Psalms*, Susan Gillingham's *Psalms through the Centuries*, and Alan Lenzi's (ed.) *Reading Akkadian Prayers and Hymns*, there are points of international convergence in all these areas, which should be further developed in the future.

Unlike the fourth edition of the German original, which includes an extensive appendix, the American edition has incorporated the contents of this appendix in their respective places within the text, which is therefore more unified. The readers will appreciate the fruits of this laborious task, and I would like to thank the copyeditor, S. David Garber, for his excellent work as well as the proofreader, Tina E. Noll, for her patience and care. Last but not least my heartfelt thanks go to Dr. Armin Siedlecki, Head of Cataloging at the Pitts Theology Library at Emory University in Atlanta, for his excellent translation, which makes my ideas accessible to my new readers in America.

Bernd Janowski
Tübingen, July 2013

Preface

> I spent the night in solitude and finally . . . read the Psalms, one of the few books in which one can bring every bit of oneself under shelter, however distraught and disordered and bothered one may be.
>
> Rainer Maria Rilke, *Letters*, 126

Answers to the question "What is a human being?" are more difficult to give today than in earlier times. "What is man?" asks one of the best-known texts of the Old Testament, and immediately continues, "that you are mindful of him?" (Ps. 8:4/5). This continuation is surprising to our secular contemporaries, because it indicates that it is only through God or through God's thoughts that one can say what human beings are. Only through God do human beings attain the ability to assume their position in the world—with regard to nonhuman creatures (8:6–9) and by contemplating the heavens, the "works of your fingers" (8:3). There is nothing in Psalm 8 that prompts human beings to engage in self-glorification, but in everything to praise God the Creator.

Today we have moved far from this understanding of humanity, which focuses on the experience of createdness. On the one hand, the authority of traditional and especially religious views of humanity has decreased as a result of Christianity's loss of plausibility. On the other hand, the increasing economization of our social conditions has caused a dissolution of traditional ways of life without which a coexistence based on trust and empathy is not possible. "The language of the market enters today in all pores and presses interpersonal relationships into a schema of self-centered orientation on individual preferences."[1] This is particularly true of the complexity of a highly fragmented society, in light of which no plausible answers to the most elementary question of life are readily found.

What view of humanity will eventually establish itself in response to the controversies that have erupted around genetic and biotechnology remains to be seen. The silent but momentous revolution that is taking place in this field calls for a regulatory structure for the moral guidance of the potentials offered by genetic and biotechnology in ever shorter intervals. Scientists in this country increasingly side with the view of American geneticists that society stands in its own way if it tries to prevent progress in biomedicine on the basis of religious or metaphysical arguments. Such progress not only expands known possibilities of action; it also enables new types of procedures resulting in a technological transformation of human life: the production of artifacts to be

1. Habermas, *Glauben und Wissen*, 23.

incorporated within the individual. The impact of this *self-transformation of the species* on human self-understanding cannot be foreseen: "Whether we consider ourselves as responsible authors of our own life story and respect each other as 'equal' persons depends in some ways on how we understand ourselves anthropologically as a species. Can we view the genetic self-transformation of the species as a way to increase the autonomy of the individual? Or do we in this way undermine the normative self-understanding of persons, who live their own lives and encounter each other with equal respect?"[2]

Remembering biblical images of humanity and their message in light of these infractions and reorientations is more than an academic affair. To inquire of them, as we shall do in this book, means to imagine "what it is like to be human in situations very different from our own."[3] According to P. Brown,

> it is essential to take that risk. For a history course to be content to turn out well-trained minds when it could also encourage widened hearts and deeper sympathies would be a mutilation of the intellectual inheritance of our own discipline. It would lead to the inhibition, in our own culture, of an element of imaginative curiosity about others whose removal may be more deleterious than we would like to think to the subtle and ever precarious ecology on which a liberal western tradition of respect for others is based.[4]

The Psalms of Israel are particularly well suited for this task because they are both strange and familiar to us. They belong to the world of the first millennium before Christ yet are incorporated in our two-part Christian Bible. Mostly, however, they combine a *small degree of historical contextualization* with a *highest degree of situational contextualization*, which is what has made it possible for them to be recited even today. The idea that the Psalter is a "mirror of the soul" in which a human being can recognize oneself,[5] or as Martin Luther writes in his second preface to the Psalter, in which "you will find . . . also yourself and the true *Gnōthi seauton* [Know yourself], as well as God himself and all creatures"[6]—this mirror-of-the-soul idea runs like a common thread throughout the history of Christianity. The reason for this high esteem of the Psalms is not least of all their language, with its harsh and unsettling contrasts of light and darkness. These texts are not accounts by an uninvolved bystander, but expressions of a troubled or passionate, helpless or grateful human being, whose *nepeš* (life, vitality) complains, to confront God with his suffering, and who praises God, to thank him for his salvation. The language of the Psalms, like the language of prayer, is therefore perhaps "the only language in which a human being gesticulates as a human being and . . . does not appear as a subsequently harmonized, imaginary subject of a system of signs and codes or finally a mere number."[7] Whenever the linguistic, spiritual, and moral competence of Christianity is addressed, the Psalter—the "book of pure spirituality"[8]—cannot be left out.

2. Habermas, *Zukunft der menschlichen Natur*, 54; cf. 41.
3. P. Brown, *Society and the Holy*, 4.
4. Ibid.
5. Cf. Athanasius, "Letter of St. Athanasius to Marcellinus," 116.
6. Luther, "Preface to the Psalter: 1545 (1528)," 28.
7. Metz, "Gotteskrise," 81–82.
8. Lévinas, *Outside the Subject*, 131.

The anthropology of the Psalms presented here begins with the basic questions posed to God in the songs of lament and thanksgiving: "My God, my God, why have you forsaken me?" (Ps. 22:1/2) or "How long will my enemy rise above me?" (13:2/3). What constitutes the affliction of the Old Testament supplicant is not being pitiful and complaining about this or that—to put it in modern terms, "about bad times, the weather, taxes and low wages, neighbors, coworkers, or society as a whole"[9]—but that "God has abandoned him, and he is left to face a world full of injustice and derision." Despite these never-ending questions, the Psalms know of a way that does not lead to death but into life: "You show me the path of life, filled with joy before your face, pleasures in your right hand forevermore" (Ps. 16:11). The metaphor of the "way" signifies both the way from life to death, and the way that leads past the powers of death into life.

According to this twofold structure of the human path of life, this book gives a general introduction to Old Testament anthropology in "Part 1: From Life to Death," with the basic anthropological themes of "being forsaken by God," "enmity," "legal difficulties," and "sickness." After an "Interlude" on twentieth-century images of death, in "Part 2: From Death to Life" it proceeds to the themes "transience," "praising God," "salvation from death" and—with a New Testament perspective—"trust in God." Each chapter follows the same pattern: After a definition of the problem, with consideration of corresponding anthropological insights of related fields of study, a thematically relevant example from the Psalms is exegeted, and a central aspect of this Psalm is explored in other texts from the Old Testament or the ancient Near East. Each discussion concludes with a section titled "Anthropological Keyword," in which the problem sketched in the introduction is placed in the larger context of Old Testament anthropology. Finally, placed throughout the book and inserted in appropriate places are ten "Excursuses," on themes of biblical anthropology.

On the cover of the German edition is a reproduction of Alexej von Jawlensky's (1864–1941) painting "Crown of Thorns." This painting is from the year 1918 and stands at the beginning of an early twentieth-century artistic genre, which connects to the tradition of Christian meditative images. Avoiding any form of narrative description, it focuses on the abstracted depiction of a face—that of Jesus of Nazareth as the Man of Sorrows—which occupies the entire area of the picture. In this image of Christ "a human being is shown; the man/woman distinction becomes irrelevant; Jesus Christ is the universal human being who truly 'destroys all schemas' (Schweizer). The human face reveals itself as a window to the soul. Jawlensky constructs it as a window to the divine."[10]

In the Synoptic Gospels this suffering is expressed with the help of the Psalms of Lament and Thanksgiving, thereby situating the Son of God in the tradition of Israel's Psalms. The significance of this line of tradition and reception has been expressed with regard to the Psalms as the "great school of prayer" in unequaled way by Dietrich Bonhoeffer in his short tract from 1939 *Life Together*. "Second, we learn from the prayer of the psalms what we should pray. Certain as it is that the scope of the prayer of the psalms ranges far beyond

9. Anderegg, "Zum Ort der Klage," 193.
10. Lange, *Bilder zum Glauben*, 92.

the experience of the individual, nevertheless the individual prays in faith the whole prayer of Christ, the prayer of him who was true Man and who alone possesses the full range of experiences expressed in this prayer."[11] These connections are explored at the end of part 2 with the example of the reception of Psalm 22 in the Markan Passion story (Mark 14:1–16:8).

Several times throughout the book, we shall consider twentieth-century poetry that makes use of the Psalms. Since these complain to God about the loss of closeness between God and suppliant, it is possible "to overcome once more the threat of silence, to direct words from a position of feeling abandoned to what was thought to be lost and to restore it anew with these words. In this way, psalms of the present uphold the enigmatic, incomprehensibly dark side of God, which is so significant for the ambivalence of the Old Testament understanding of God and has been lost to the church's spiritual consciousness with the disappearance of the biblical Psalms of Lament, but which should be spiritually restored in the light of today's much-invoked 'crisis of God.'"[12] Modern psalms teach us that a relevant discourse about God must always also reflect the limits of what can be said or known.

No other work in world literature has been translated more often into German than the book of Psalms. Corresponding to this is the variety of translations.[13] Best known among German translations of the Psalms, because of its literary beauty and emotional quality, that of Martin Luther in his German Bible of 1545 has become normative. Luther's language is therefore "so foundational, because he himself understands the language of lament. . . . Luther . . . suffers and laments himself and writes down what he himself expresses in the midst of challenges. It is for this reason that the Psalms in his translation remain an instruction in the language of prayer, especially of lament."[14] In addition, there are other translations, like that of Martin Buber in his *Buch der Preisungen* (1958) or the translation of the Psalms in the New Zurich Bible (1996). I have made occasional use of these classics, but for the most part, the translations in this book are my own. They are not primarily concerned with literary aesthetics, but with closeness to the Hebrew original. The true task of a translation consists of "creating a new text in a different language without making it appear alien in this language"[15] and without losing the unique character of the original language.[16] I hope to have done justice to this challenge by orienting myself after the principle of "understood otherness."[17]

Every translation of the Psalms has to confront the problem of everyday language, which in most cases is not fundamental enough but too worn-out or too stilted in order to do justice to the language of the Psalms.[18] The author Arnold Stadler has recently tried to find a way out of this dilemma by recom-

11. Bonhoeffer, *Life Together*, 47.
12. Gellner, "Moderne Psalmgedichte," 48–49.
13. For an informative survey, see Baldermann, *Ich werde nicht sterben*, 79ff.
14. Ibid., 86; cf. Stolt, *Rhetorik des Herzens*.
15. Dohmen, *Vom Umgang*, 17.
16. On the various problems involved in this challenge, see the contributions in Gross, *Bibelübersetzung heute*.
17. Berger, *Historische Psychologie*, 20–21; cf. Stolt, *Rhetorik des Herzens*, 96–97.
18. See the examples in Baldermann, *Ich werde nicht sterben*, 82ff.

posing the Psalms.[19] This problem of translation is particularly marked in rendering basic anthropological terms. For example, how should one translate נֶפֶשׁ? With "soul," with "life," with "need," or if expanded with the first-person pronominal suffix "[my life>] I"? The "Anthropological Keyword 4: Vitality" shows why this question is so difficult to answer. In order to describe the basic meaning "life, vitality," I have often left the Hebrew text untranslated and have merely transliterated it as *nepeš*. I am aware, of course, that this is only a makeshift solution.

Since I first taught a seminar on the Songs of Lament and Thanksgiving almost twenty years ago, I have not been able to let go of these texts. I have since had meaningful conversations with my wife as well as my colleagues Jan Assmann, Michaela Bauks, Oswald Bayer, Angelika Berlejung, Beate Ego, Ottmar Fuchs, Hartmut Gese, Walter Gross, Christof Hardmeier, Friedhelm Hartenstein, Eilert Herms, Frank-Lothar Hossfeld, Jörg Jeremias, Othmar Keel, Klaus Koch, Hermann Lichtenberger, Arndt Meinhold, Thomas Podella, Hermann Spieckermann, Michael Welker, and Erich Zenger. In this way, prepared by lectures and essays on individual aspects of the subject, the foundation of the current book has grown and has been presented in different forms at Heidelberg (1994), Tübingen (1995), and Jerusalem (Dormition Abbey / Hagia Sion, 2000). The Heidelberg lectures of 1994 were dedicated to the memory of Hans Walter Wolff, whose *Anthropology of the Old Testament* has been a constant conversation partner, and with whom I maintained contact until his death on October 22, 1993. On a piece of paper added to his last will and testament, he had written verse 13 of Psalm 27, which reads like his spiritual bequest: "And yet I believe that I shall see the goodness of God in the land of the living." This book is dedicated to the memory of this unforgotten teacher of theology.

A book that has grown over such a long period of time has had many companions along the way. Not all of them can be named here, but of my former colleagues I would like to thank D. Erbele-Küster, A. Grund, W. Hüllstrung, A. Krüger, U. Neumann-Gorsolke, and P. Riede. I owe a special thank-you to my assistants G. D. Eberhard and K. Liess as well as my doctoral students D. Bester-Twele and M. Lichtenstein. They have all read this *Anthropology of the Psalms* in its final phase, have discussed numerous ideas with me, and have also in part produced the indexes (K. Liess). I cordially thank Dr. V. Hampel of the Neukirchener Verlag for the electronic editing of the manuscript.

Bernd Janowski
Tübingen, December 2002

19. Stadler, *"Die Menschen lügen. Alle."*

Abbreviations

ABD	*Anchor Bible Dictionary*. Edited by David Noel Freedman. New York: Doubleday, 1992.
AfO	*Archiv für Orientforschung*
ÄHG	*Ägyptische Hymnen und Gebete: Übersetzt, kommentiert und eingeleitet*. Translated by Jan Assmann. 2nd ed. Göttingen: Vandenhoeck & Ruprecht, 1999.
ANET	*Ancient Near Eastern Texts Relating to the Old Testament*. Edited by James P. Pritchard. 3rd ed. Princeton: Princeton University Press, 1969.
Bab	*Babyloniaca*
BE	*Biblische Enzyklopädie*. Edited by Walter Dietrich and Wolfgang Stegemann. Stuttgart: W. Kohlhammer, 1996–.
BHS	*Biblia Hebraica Stuttgartensia*. Edited by Karl Elliger and Wilhelm Rudolph. 5th ed. Stuttgart: Deutsche Bibelgesellschaft, 1997.
BibInt	*Biblical Interpretation*. Edited by J. Cheryl Exum. Leiden: E. J. Brill, 1992–.
BWL	*Babylonian Wisdom Literature*. By William George Lambert. Oxford: Clarendon Press, 1960; corrected reprint, 1967. Winona Lake, IN: Eisenbrauns, 1996.
CBL	*Calwer Bibellexikon*. Edited by Otto Betz, Beate Ego, and Werner Grimm. 2 vols. Stuttgart: Calwer Verlag, 2003.
CT	*Cuneiform Texts from Babylonian Tablets in the British Museum*. London: Trustees of the British Museum, 1959–.
EBR	*Encyclopedia of the Bible and Its Reception*. Edited by Hans-Josef Klauck and Dale C. Allison. Berlin and New York: Walter de Gruyter, 2009–.
ET	English translation
FS Janowski	*Was ist der Mensch, daß du seiner gedenkst? (Psalm 8, 5): Aspekte einer theologischen Anthropologie; Festschrift für Bernd Janowski zum 65. Geburtstag*. Edited by Michaela Bauks, K. Liess, and P. Riede. Neukirchen-Vluyn: Neukirchener Verlag, 2008.
GB^{18}	Gesenius, Wilhelm, Frants Buhl, et al. *Hebräisches und aramäisches Handwörterbuch über das Alte Testament*. Edited by R. Meyer, U. Rüterswörden, and H. Donner. 18th ed. Berlin: Springer Verlag, 1987–2012.

GKC — *Gesenius' Hebrew Grammar*. Edited by Emil Kautzsch. Translated by Arthur Ernest Cowley. 2nd ed. Oxford: Oxford University Press, 1910. ET of Wilhelm Gesenius and Emil Kautzsch. *Hebräische Grammatik*. 28th ed. Leipzig: Vogel, 1909.

HALOT — *The Hebrew and Aramaic Lexicon of the Old Testament*. Edited by Ludwig Köhler and Walter Baumgartner. Leiden: E. J. Brill, 1994–2000.

HGANT[2] — *Handbuch theologischer Grundbegriffe zum Alten und Neuen Testament*. Edited by Angelika Berlejung and Christian Frevel. 2nd ed. Darmstadt: Wissenschaftliche Buchgesellschaft, 2009.

HWP — *Historisches Wörterbuch der Philosophie*. Edited by Joachim Ritter, Karlfried Gründer, Gottfried Gabriel, and Rudolf Eisler. 12 vols. Basel: Schwabe, 1971–2001.

KAI — *Kanaanäische und aramäische Inschriften*. Herbert Donner and Wolfgang Röllig. 2nd ed. 3 vols. Wiesbaden: O. Harrassowitz, 1966–69.

KJV — King James Version

KTU — *Die keilalphabetischen Texte aus Ugarit*. Edited by Manfried Dietrich, Oswald Loretz, and Joaquin Sanmartín. Neukirchen-Vluyn: Kevelaer, Butzon & Bercker, 1976.

LCL — Loeb Classical Library

LXX — Septuagint (the Greek Old Testament)

MT — Masoretic Text, presented in *BHS*

NBL — *Neues Bibel-Lexikon*. Edited by Manfred Görg and Bernhard Lang. 14 vols. Zurich: Benzinger, 1991–2001.

olim — formerly

RGG[4] — *Religion in Geschichte und Gegenwart: Handwörterbuch für Theologie und Religionswissenschaft*. 4th ed. Edited by Hans Dieter Betz et al. Tübingen: Mohr Siebeck, 1998–.

SWB — *Sozialgeschichtliches Wörterbuch zur Bibel*. Edited by Frank Crüsemann et al. Gütersloh: Gütersloher Verlagshaus, 2009.

THAT — *Theologisches Handwörterbuch zum Alten Testament*. Edited by Ernst Jenni and Claus Westermann. Munich: Christian Kaiser, 1971–.

ThWAT — *Theologisches Wörterbuch zum Alten Testament*. Edited by G. Johannes Botterweck, George W. Anderson, and Helmer Ringgren. Stuttgart: W. Kohlhammer, 1970–. ET, *Theological Dictionary of the Old Testament*. Translated by John T. Willis. rev. ed. 15 vols. Grand Rapids: Wm. B. Eerdmans Publishing Co., 1977–2006.

TRE — *Theologische Realenzyklopädie*. Edited by Gerhard Krause, Gerhard Müller, Siegfried Schwertner, et al. Berlin: Walter de Gruyter, 1976–.

TUAT — *Texte aus der umwelt des Alten Testaments*. Edited by Otto Kaiser et al. Gütersloh: Gütersloher Verlagshaus G. Mohn, 1982–.

Urk. — *Urkunden des ägyptischen Altertums*. Edited by Georg Steindorff. Leipzig: J. C. Hinrich, 1903–.

WA	Weimarer Ausgabe. *D. Martin Luthers Werke: Kritische Gesammtausgabe*. Weimar edition. Weimar: Böhlau, 1883–2009.
WA.DB	*Die deutsche Bibel*. Translated by Martin Luther. 1522–45. In the Weimarer Ausgabe.
ZNT	*Zeitschrift für Neues Testament*. Edited by Stefan Alkier et al. Tübingen, 1998–.

Introduction
What Is a Human Being?

1. Fundamental Questions of Old Testament Anthropology

> True and substantial wisdom principally consists of two parts, the knowledge of God and the knowledge of ourselves.
>
> John Calvin, *Institutes of the Christian Religion* 1.1.1

Thinking about human beings of the past, considering their needs, hopes, and passions, one imagines what human beings desire and what their needs are. The natural sciences as well as the humanities have for a long time been trying to answer the question what or who a human being is; they have always developed new images of humanity according to the condition of their times.[1] Theological anthropology and biblical anthropology in particular also confront this challenge, contributing their own specific perspective, without losing or dismissing the connection to neighboring disciplines. But what do we mean when we speak of an Old Testament human being, with needs, hopes, and passions? Is it even possible to develop an image of such a being?

a. The Image of the Human Being

Already the singular form "the human being" proves to be problematic, because it suggests the existence of a basic, anthropological constant that has remained the same across times and spaces.[2] But is it possible to discover the same type of human being in Jerusalem, in Samaria, in the Negev, in Galilee, in Elephantine, and by the "rivers of Babylon" (Ps. 137:1)? Moreover, is this Old Testament human being the premonarchic hero of the book of Judges, or rather the radically different type of human being envisioned by the prophets of the eighth and seventh centuries, or by priests of the sixth and fifth centuries? The image of the human being, like all manifestations in nature and society, is also subject to historical change. An Old Testament anthropology that incorporates this insight can rely on the research of historical anthropology.

1. See overview in Hampe, "Anthropologie"; see also the following anthologies: Gadamer and Vogler, *Neue Anthropologie*; Rössner, *Der ganze Mensch*; Kamper and Wulf, *Anthropologie nach dem Tode*; Gebauer, *Historische Anthropologie*.

2. One might argue that it is part of any anthropology to reflect what is unchangeable in human beings, such as their mortality or their distinction from animals. Though this is undoubtedly the case, the problem is that even the unchangeable within humanity is subject to historical change, and that other periods and cultures have expressed different views on, e.g., human mortality than those prevalent in Western culture during the late 20th and early 21st centuries. The relationship between consistency and change is a fundamental theme in historical anthropology; cf. 4ff.

α. *Historical Anthropology*

To avoid the danger of an ahistorical perception of human beings in ancient Israel,[3] while keeping open the question of their nature, this study will examine a limited body of literature—individual psalms of lament and of thanksgiving—and consider the life situations in which a human being in ancient Israel is portrayed as harassed, persecuted, ill, or dying, but also as saved, praising, or giving thanks. It is therefore not a matter of general characteristics of human nature or of "basic anthropological constants," but rather of the unique experiences and behavior patterns that show the speakers of these psalms in existential conflict situations, which they seek to overcome through lament and prayer.

The problem associated with the term "basic anthropological constants" has been of concern to the humanities and social sciences for some time now. Thus the question of human nature, which moved to the center of natural and human sciences with the "anthropological revolution"[4] of the eighteenth century, has been categorically relativized by twentieth-century philosophical anthropology,[5] and especially through a growing familiarity with human biology, psychology, and sociology. If we are both nature and history, as Wilhelm Dilthey thought,[6] is it reasonable to expect a definitive answer to the question of human nature? Is it possible, asks Helmuth Plessner in following Dilthey,

> to define definitively a being whose evolution from prehuman life-forms can be doubted as little as the open-endedness of its future possibilities and whose origin and destiny are equally obscure to us? Can the different ways in which human beings have understood themselves in the course of history and in many cultures which are not part of one history be passed over through a generalizing process and fit into a formulaic nature?[7]

On the other hand, the evolutionary derivation of the human species from prehuman life-forms not only had repercussions for traditional anthropology, but also gave rise to an exploration of a dimension encompassing the "entire" nature of humanity. Here we find, beginning in the 1920s (Max Scheler, Arnold Gehlen, Adolf Portmann), the discoveries and insights of medicine, biology, psychology, sociology, linguistics, and history, as well as religious and cultural studies.[8]

In the past few decades, cultural studies have turned increasingly toward the reciprocal relationships between body and soul, society and individual, person and world, as well as self and others; through the incorporation of these aspects,

3. What is needed in modern research is a "historical anthropology of the Old Testament." Such an approach would consider and describe material conditions of life, demographic and social characteristics of individual periods and regions, historically variable cognitive and behavioral patterns—in short, the varieties of human beings' concrete forms of existence in Old Testament times; cf. the methodological and thematic suggestions of H. Weippert, "Altisraelitische Welterfahrung"; Janowski, "Das biblische Weltbild." For New Testament anthropology, cf. Berger, *Historische Psychologie*, 17ff.; Schnelle, *The Human Condition*, 1ff.; Lichtenberger, "Mensch V."

4. Cf. Bödeker, "Anthropologie"; idem, "Mensch"; and the respective bibliographies.

5. See the excellent overview by Arlt, *Philosophische Anthropologie*; and the annotated anthology by Schüssler, *Philosophische Anthropologie*.

6. Cf. Marquard, "Anthropologie," 368–69.

7. Plessner, "Anthropologie II," 411; cf. also Marquard, "Anthropologie," 372ff.

8. Cf., e.g., Engels, "Natur- und Menschenbilder," 15ff.

such studies have learned to ask the basic anthropological question "What is a human being?" both more comprehensively and with more specific detail.[9] A philosophical anthropology that excludes medical, psychological, sociological, and cultural experiences, and therefore does not acknowledge human openness toward the world, will not be able to answer the question of human nature and destiny. In other words, "an answer to the question of humanity without reference to the human sciences is now no longer realistically possible."[10] The same is true for theological anthropology, as Wolfhart Pannenberg has rightly emphasized.[11] In the twentieth century, philosophical anthropology learned to express its insights with new terminological tools gained by the cognitive sciences and to apply them to their own question of human nature; thus it became increasingly evident that human nature is itself historical. Human self-perceptions and self-expressions seen throughout the course of history can therefore not be subsumed by a single formula but need to account for historical change.

This also applies to biblical views of humanity. Here too we must note differences in our ways of thinking, feeling, and acting, which may still be so familiar that they appear completely natural to us. "The dictum of every assessment of the past," argues legal historian Wolfgang Schild, "must be: everything was different than it is today, different even from the way it can be understood."[12] Whoever ignores this dictum runs the risk of assuming too readily a consistent context and experience for the ancient world, or a "more or less uniform anthropology (and by implication psychology) applicable to all times."[13] It is essential to understand the conceptual autonomy and dissimilarity of biblical texts and ideas in comparison to our own thought. "For it is the dissimilarity of the text, rather than our affirmation of it, that constitutes the basis of a critical function to correct our view of God and the world."[14]

To attempt to do justice to the distinctiveness of Old Testament anthropology, it is therefore essential to combine "objective analysis and empathetic considerations"[15] and to look at the texts and their view of the human being, sometimes up close and other times from a distance. What is called for is the historical work of understanding,[16] which in itself—in the spirit of the historian

9. Good overviews of methods and themes on the basis of selected 20th-century source texts are found in Keupp, *Lust an der Erkenntnis;* H. Böhme, Matussek, and L. Müller, *Orientierung Kulturwissenschaft;* Daniel, *Kompendium Kulturgeschichte.*

10. Lachmann, *Susanne K. Langer*, 10.

11. Cf. Pannenberg, *Was ist der Mensch?* (2nd ed.); idem, *Anthropologie in theologischer Perspektive.* In the case of theological anthropology, "openness toward the world" is joined by human "openness toward God." Indeed, "human openness toward the world presupposes openness toward God. Wherever this is not clearly understood, the concept of 'openness toward the world' will remain unfocused, as if human beings were placed in opposition to the world, while it is rather the case that they need to inquire further into everything they encounter as their world. This unique characteristic of human existence, its infinite dependence, can only be understood as a question about God. Unlimited openness toward the world results only from human orientation beyond the world." Pannenberg, *Was ist der Mensch?* (2nd ed.), 12–13; cf. 8ff., "Theological Anthropology."

12. Schild, *Alte Gerichtsbarkeit*, 8.

13. Berger, *Historische Psychologie*, 19.

14. Ibid., 20. The expression "conceptual autonomy" (*Eigenbegrifflichkeit*) was coined by the Assyriologist Benno Landsberger, who introduced it in his 1926 inaugural lectures in Leipzig. Cf. Landsberger, "Eigenbegrifflichkeit."

15. Vernant, *Der Mensch*, 11.

16. Cf. Gese, "Der Tod," 31–32; for the same reason, Berger speaks of "assumed dissimilarity" (*verstandene Fremdheit*) as a necessary presupposition for the reconstruction of past contexts and meanings; see his *Historische Psychologie*, 19–20.

Peter Brown[17]—cannot and must not dispense with either an "expanded sensitivity" nor a "deeper sense of empathy." Anyone who is only concerned with the similarities between our own views and those of the Old (and New) Testament, or who even judges ancient texts on the basis of our own moral understanding, as frequently happens with the so-called Enemy Psalms—such a person forfeits the opportunity to bring the Bible's dissimilar and at times strange view of reality into conversation with our own, and thus *to understand that which is different*. Yet precisely that must be the goal of any task that seeks to make past constructions of meaning,[18] formulations of problems, and perceptual horizons relevant for the present.

The implications of these methodological considerations and paradigmatic questions for an anthropology of the Old Testament can be seen more clearly from the perspective of related disciplines. For example, historical anthropology, which came to Germany at the end of the 1970s, researched "the fundamental sense in which human beings are historical."[19] It situates human beings concretely with their thoughts and actions, emotions and suffering, at the center of analysis and focuses on the historical and cultural limitations and diversity of human life:

> The well-known but vague observations that human beings are the "not yet determined animal" (Nietzsche), or that they have no nature, are only substantiated if, on the basis of one's own culture, one recognizes that, even in its most fundamental structures, human beings have not remained the same. Historical mutability is not only a matter of occupational means, family structures, or administrative systems, but of anthropological organization itself. The astonishment over this dissimilarity of our ancestors is almost surpassed by another astonishment: the fact that we can understand them despite their dissimilarity. Not immediately, to be sure, and not without effort, . . . but in this encounter we recognize that we have this Other also within ourselves. We sense that we could—in theory—experience and perceive the same as human beings before us.[20]
>
> What distinguishes human beings from other forms of life is the orientation of their physical and intellectual activities toward the establishment of a world of communication and connections, a world of achievements that are objects worthy of preservation and transmission, but which also show themselves in significant ways to be languages that express intellectual content. All human behavior patterns show themselves to be part of large

17. In his essay "Learning and Imagination," P. Brown writes: "In the middle of an exacting history course, it takes a high degree of moral courage to resist one's own conscience: to take time off; to let the imagination run; to give serious attention to reading books that widen our sympathies, that train us to imagine with greater precision what it is like to be human in situations very different from our own. It is essential to take that risk. For a history course to be content to turn out well-trained minds when it could also encourage widened hearts and deeper sympathies would be a mutilation of the intellectual inheritance of our own discipline. It would lead to the inhibition, in our own culture, of an element of imaginative curiosity about others whose removal may be more deleterious than we would like to think to the subtle and ever-precarious ecology on which a liberal Western tradition of respect for others is based" (P. Brown, *Society and the Holy*, 4).

18. I use this term "constructions of meaning" (*Sinnbildungen*) in the sense intended by Rüsen and Klaus Müller, "Sinn der Geschichte?," 17ff.; cf. also J. Assmann, *Ägypten*, 15ff.

19. H. Böhme, Matussek, and L. Müller, *Orientierung Kulturwissenschaft*, 264.

20. Ibid. For an introduction to the questions and tasks of historical anthropology, see ibid., 131ff.; Dülmen, *Historische Anthropologie*; Klaus Müller, "Perspectives in Historical Anthropology," 33ff.

> organizational structures, which—as recorded by historians—form different types of evidences of civilization. Because they are variable, these evidences are always associated with a place and date. It is therefore impossible for us to assume that there is an immutable spirit behind the changes in behavior and in human actions or that there is a static inner subject hidden behind consistently present psychological impulses. We must therefore recognize that in their essence human beings themselves are the setting for a developing story.[21]

The task of historical anthropology to describe the historical variability of seemingly constant human behavior patterns—such as acting, thinking, feeling, and suffering—is characteristically different from traditional philosophical anthropology and the quest for the nature of humanity and the conditions of existence. As the command of an abstract norm has come to an end, the time has come to "consider the conclusions offered by the humanities, together with a critique of anthropology based on historical philosophy, and to develop new grounds for innovative, paradigmatic questions."[22] This is an opportunity for Old Testament studies,[23] which also are interested in contributing their perspectives and conclusions to the resolution of problems posed by violence. Anthropological approaches are a suitable starting point for this purpose.

In my essay "Hans Walter Wolff und die alttestamentliche Anthropologie," I have further delineated the question of human nature ("What is the human being?") in conversation with historical and philosophical anthropology: I have advanced the theses that an Old Testament anthropology has to define carefully the three essential elements of *concrete circumstances*, *literary contexts*, and *anthropological constants* and to relate them to each other in the sense of an integrative approach. "Integrative approach" on the one hand means that anthropological totalizations of a metaphysical-speculative nature are to be avoided as much as the one-sidedness of a too-narrowly conceived historical anthropology. On the other hand it means that one should hold on to the *multidimensionality of the Old Testament view of the human being*, leaving room for particularities (*concrete circumstances, literary contexts*) as well as universal characteristics (*anthropological constants*). The precise definition of the relationship of Old Testament anthropology to philosophical and historical anthropology is a problem that remains to be solved. In the meantime, we can outline the following commonalities and differences:

- It shares with *philosophical anthropology* the persistent relevance of the question of anthropological constants. The difference is that this question is answered by Old Testament anthropology with the assumption of a theological anthropology of "God's orienting presence in this world"[24] and that

21. Vernant, "Mythos und Geist," 359.
22. Wulf, *Vom Menschen*, 13.
23. For a summary of (older) research, see Lang, *Anthropological Approaches*; for New Testament studies, see Malina, *The New Testament World*; also Berger, *Historische Psychologie*, 17ff. An important consideration for our purposes is the question of methodologically reliable approaches to emotions of earlier periods. For the state of research, see Benthien, Fleig, and Kasten, *Emotionalität*. This question will be discussed in more detail in connection with the themes of "enemy" and "happiness"; see chaps 4 (97ff.) and 9 (285ff.) below.
24. Klein, "Inhumanität," 444.

it sees the human being principally as "God's human being,"[25] as a created being.

- Old Testament anthropology shares with *historical anthropology* the idea that the question of human nature cannot be answered by way of essences. The difference between them is that although Old Testament anthropology shares with historical anthropology the axiom of human coexistence and its ambivalences, it assumes that a life-affirming approach to these ambivalences is only possible *sub specie Dei.*

Old Testament anthropology can incorporate the contribution of historical anthropology, thereby sharpening the cognizance of the *historical nature of the human being*. At the same time, it can go beyond it by including the axiom of createdness, the principle of justice, and the experience of finality, thereby asserting the constants of a genuine *theological anthropology*. It does so on the basis of *biblical texts* and their unique literary, social, traditional, and religiohistorical profiles. It does not ignore the *concrete physical environment* as uncovered by the archaeology and iconography of Israel/Palestine. The beginning and end of an Old Testament anthropology is therefore the *correlation of textual world and physical environment*[26] and the idea that "anthropological problems . . . cannot be solved by screening off theology, but only in complete openness to the divine witness of the Bible."[27]

Resources

On the subject of *historical anthropology*, see Wulf, *Anthropologie*, 105ff.; Tanner, *Historische Anthropologie*; Ricken, "Menschen," 152ff.; Burke, *Kulturgeschichte*, 47ff.; A. Assmann, *Kulturwissenschaft*, 105ff.; Jaeger and Straub, *Mensch*; and Winterling, *Anthropologie*. On the subject of *philosophical anthropology*, see the contributions in H.-P. Krüger and Lindemann, *Philosophische Anthropologie*; as well as J. Fischer, *Philosophische Anthropologie*; and Thies, "Mensch," 1515ff. (with their respective bibliographies).

β. Theological Anthropology

H. W. Wolff, whose *Anthropology of the Old Testament* will be our regular conversation partner throughout the following pages, did not yet have the approach of historical anthropology in view. Nevertheless, he too asked the questions of "how the problem of a reliable doctrine of man can be surmounted at all."[28] For here, Wolff observes:

> The scholar is faced with the extreme borderline case in which the impossibility of objectification presents an insoluble problem. Just as it is impossible for a man to confront himself and to see himself from all sides or for a person who is still developing to know of himself whose child he is, just so certainly does man fundamentally need the meeting with another, who investigates

25. Cf. Härle, "Mensch Gottes," 529ff.
26. Cf. the complaint in this regard by Schüle, "Anthropologie," 409.
27. H. W. Wolff, *Anthropology*, 3.
28. Ibid., 1.

and explains him. But where is the other to whom the creature man could just put the question: Who am I?[29]

In contrast to earlier endeavors by F. Delitzsch, J. Koeberle, or J. Pedersen,[30] as well as more recent ones by K. Galling, W. Eichrodt, or W. Zimmerli,[31] Wolff posed the question of a biblical anthropology comprehensively and proceeded to develop a language primer under the three categories of anthropology, biography, and sociology.

Following an analysis of human existence on the basis of an anthropological language primer, which examines the terms נֶפֶשׁ (life [force], vitality, soul),[32] בָּשָׂר (flesh), רוּחַ (breath, wind, spirit), לֵבָב/לֵב (heart),[33] and so forth, the second part consists of a description of human life situated in time as "biographical anthropology," in which fundamental rhythms like life and death, illness and healing, hope and anticipation are depicted in light of different conceptions of time and creation. In the third part, called "sociological anthropology," Wolff addresses—while carefully correcting the traditional ontology of time/space—the world of human beings, in which the positions of the individual within society (and before God: "The human as the image of God") are designated: husband and wife, parents and children, friends and enemies, masters and slaves, the wise and the foolish. The last part consists of an examination of the "destiny of man" in relation to God, fellow humans, and creation. These are the conclusions of Wolff's anthropology: (1) "The human being is destined to live and not to fall victim to death."[34] (2) "The human being is destined to love and to overcome hate."[35] (3) "The human's destiny in the world of extrahuman creation is just as unequivocal: the destiny is to rule."[36] (4) "The human is destined to praise God."[37] "In praise such as this, the destiny of human beings—their destiny in the world, their destiny to love fellow humans, and their destiny to rule over all nonhuman creation—finds its truly human fulfillment. Otherwise humans, becoming their own idol, turn into tyrants—either that or falling dumb, they lose their freedom."[38]

Despite critical inquiries,[39] the intention of Wolff's anthropology to suggest a comprehensive "destiny of the human"[40] is conceptually convincing. This is already evident in the title to his second chapter, which is "*nepeš*—Needy Man" and not "*nepeš*—Soul." This demonstrates the effort to overcome the dichotomy

29. Ibid., 1–2.
30. Koch, "Gibt es ein Hebräisches Denken?"
31. H. W. Wolff, *Anthropologie*, 15–16. An introduction to an anthropology from a Jewish perspective is provided by Adler, *Der Mensch*.
32. See "Anthropological Keyword 4: Vitality," 188ff.
33. See "Anthropological Keyword 3: Heart and Kidneys," 155ff.
34. Wolff, *Anthropology*, 223.
35. Ibid., 225.
36. Ibid., 226.
37. Ibid., 228.
38. Ibid., 229.
39. Cf. Kegler, "Körpererfahrung"; Ogushi, "Nur das Herz?"; H.-P. Müller, Review of *Anthropologie*, by H. W. Wolff; Zenger, Review of *Anthropologie*, by H. W. Wolff; and the reply by Wolff, *Anthropologie* (8th ed.), 365ff. Adding a further point of critique: a future anthropology of the Old Testament must engage precisely what Wolff calls "sociological anthropology" in a more comprehensive and substantial manner. Lacking are, e.g., explanations of the social-anthropological terms like כָּבוֹד, "honor, prestige"; שֵׁם, "name, person"; or תֹּם, "integrity, uprightness"; cf. 264ff below.
40. So the title of the final chapter, Wolff, *Anthropology*, 223.

of "body and soul," or rather the trichotomy of "body, soul and spirit,"[41] which took root under the influence of Greek thought during the Hellenistic era, and to replace it with a more appropriate interpretation. The criteria for what is appropriate are supplied by the Old Testament texts themselves. Thus Wolff develops the semantic dimension of the anthropologically foundational term נֶפֶשׁ (life-force, vitality), not as does J. Pedersen in his well-known study of 1926/1940[42] on the basis of a dynamic theory of the soul,[43] but on the basis of an analysis of linguistic contexts, which indicate the *correlation between body organs and bodily functions and emotional and cognitive processes*.[44] If, for example, body organs like the "heart" (לֵבָב/לֵב) or the "kidneys" (כְּלָיוֹת) are associated with emotional or cognitive processes like "joy" or "rejoicing" (cf. Ps. 16:7–9; Prov. 23:16), or conversely, if social or psychological tensions like "hostility" or "embitterment" affect specific body organs like the "heart" or the "kidneys" (cf. Ps. 73:21), then the concern is with the human being as a whole, including somatic and psychological/cognitive aspects and processes.

Resources

On the "integrated" anthropology of the Old Testament and on the Old Testament concept of the person (see above 5ff., and cf. chap 2 below (36ff.)), see the Hedwig-Jahnow-Forschungsprojekt, *Körperkonzepte*; S. Schroer and Staubli, *Körpersymbolik der Bibel*; S. Schroer and Zimmermann, "Mensch/Menschsein"; also Bester, *Psalm* 22; Frevel, "Altes Testament"; idem, "Anthropologie"; cf. idem, "Fleisch und Geist I"; idem, "Herz"; idem, "Körper"; Gillmayr-Bucher, "Body Images"; idem, "Meine Zunge"; Gruber and Michel, "Individualität"; Janowski, "Mensch im alten Israel"; idem, "Anerkennung"; Klaus Neumann, "Person"; A. Wagner, "Körperbegriffe"; idem, "Reduktion des Lebendigen."

Here are three Old Testament texts that speak of the inner life of human beings:

> I bless YHWH, who has [always] given me counsel,
> even at night, **my kidneys** *have instructed me.*
> (Ps. 16:7)
>
> I have put YHWH always before me,
> indeed, he is at my right hand; I shall not stagger. (v. 8)
> Therefore **my heart** *is glad* and **my honor** *rejoices,*
> even **my flesh** *dwells securely.* (v. 9)
>
> My son, if your heart is wise,
> **my heart** *is also glad;*

41. On this complex problem, see Hastedt, *Das Leib-Seele-Problem*, 146ff.; for the perspective of comparative religion, see Hasenfratz, *Die Seele*, 68ff. Dualistic anthropologies first appear in early Judaism in the 2nd century BCE; cf. Gzella, *Lebenszeit und Ewigkeit*, 104ff. Surprisingly, or perhaps characteristically, the Septuagint Psalter, like its Hebrew *Vorlage*, does not distinguish between body and spirit; cf. ibid., 96ff.

42. Pedersen, *Israel*, vols. 1/2 and 3/4.

43. "Soul" is viewed as a kind of fuel within human beings, elevating them above the appearance of only external bodies. For the construction of the concept and the history of research, cf. Hasenfratz, *Die Seele*, 33ff.

44. Cf. W. Schmidt, "Anthropologische Begriffe," 90; and below, n. 81 on p. 17.

> **my kidneys** *rejoice*
> when your lips speaks what is just.
> (Prov. 23:15–16)
>
> When **my heart** *was embittered,*
> and **my kidneys** *felt a sharp sting,*
> then I was a fool and did not understand;
> I stood before you [entirely] a beast.
> (Ps. 73:21–22)

According to these texts, "heart," "kidneys," and "flesh" are complementary aspects of a psychosomatic unity.[45] "Thus the 'essence' of human beings manifests itself in their 'actions'; what a human being is, 'expresses' itself in what that human does."[46] This connection is so central for our purposes that it should, even at this point, be duly noted. We can find an initial connecting point in Luther's conceptual rhetoric,[47] as it is evident in his understanding of the fundamental anthropological concept of the "heart." The heart is, for Luther,

> the spiritual organ of human cognition, . . . the innermost center of personality, removed from external manipulation, visible only to God. It is in the heart that God is encountered. Heart and mind are inextricably linked to each other. Thinking does not occur in the head, but in the heart.[48]

This connection is again carefully noted in more recent scholarship. M. S. Smith[49] has devoted a short but substantial study to it, focusing on the concepts "liver" (כָּבֵד), "heart" (לֵב/לֵבָב), and "innards, intestines" in reference to findings in human biology and psychology. At the end of his analyses, Smith addresses the role played by emotions in the process of private and public communication, in particular in regard to prayer. Contrary to popular opinion ("people often believe that they feel their emotions first and then communicate emotions before they recognize them cognitively"[50]), psychology has observed, according to Smith,

> that people communicate emotions as or before they recognize them cognitively. Accordingly, emotions are part of the larger process of human communication. . . . Emotion "is said to be a form of readiness for adaptive action. In other words, emotions change an ongoing situation and help the individual prepare for appropriate action." Following this approach, the emotions expressed in the Psalms may be viewed as serving to address an ongoing situation and to help people move toward action. This emotional communication is a religious and ritualized reaction to situations of disaster or relief.[51]

Human emotions are therefore an expression of the internal world of the soul, but also the medium through which human beings communicate with the

45. Other examples include Pss. 63:1/2; 73:26; 84:2/3; 119:120; etc.; cf. also Gzella, *Lebenszeit und Ewigkeit*, 99ff.; Di Vito, "Old Testament Anthropology," 226–27.
46. W. Schmidt, "Anthropologische Begriffe," 90; cf. Di Vito,"Old Testament Anthropology,"227–28.
47. See Stolt, *Rhetorik des Herzens*, 46ff.
48. Ibid., 50.
49. Smith, "Heart and Innards."
50. Ibid., 434.
51. Ibid., 434–35.

world outside.[52] This relationship between the internal and the external can be illustrated by the example of the concept of enemies.[53]

Even though the fundamental anthropological concepts of the Old Testament characterize the human being as a whole under different aspects with regard to somatic, emotional, cognitive, and volitional functions and capabilities,[54] and there is no "devaluation of the physical, no dualism of body and spirit/soul,"[55] there is no single, unified doctrine of the human being that underlies the Old Testament. This does not have to be a disadvantage since the absence of a unified human image is compensated for by the *dialogic quality*, the individual variability of which characterizes the anthropological texts of the Old Testament in general. This quality refers to the dialogue of the human being with God and of God with the human being, or "Israel's answer" in praise and lament (songs of praise and lament),[56] and to "YHWH's answer to Job" (Job 38–41), to name only two prominent examples. The task of biblical anthropology, which emphasizes the "theological understanding of anthropological phenomena,"[57] is described by H. W. Wolff as follows:

> Biblical anthropology as a scholarly task will seek its point of departure where there is a recognizable question about the human within the texts themselves. The whole breadth of the context must be drawn upon in order to work out the specific answers. It will become evident that the essential contributions bear the character of dialogue and that the consensus in their testimony about the human is, in spite of all mutations in its linguistic form, astonishing from the point of view of the history of thought. Above all, in dialogue with God, the human sees oneself as called in question, searched out, and thus not so much established for what the human is as called to new things. As is, the human is anything but the measure of all things.[58]

According to the Old Testament witness, it is "before God, in God's presence" (*coram Deo*), that human beings become human.[59] This idea is well expressed in Psalm 8, when the question of the nature of human beings—"What are human beings?" (v. 4/5a)—is answered in reference to "remembering" (זָכַר) by YHWH and thus becomes "the poetic compendium of classical anthropology in the theology of the Psalms:[60]

52. Cf. ibid., 436; Di Vito, "Old Testament Anthropology," 225ff.

53. See 97ff. On the significance of emotion(s) for Old Testament anthropology, see Gillmayr-Bucher, "Rauchende Nase"; P. A. Kruger, "On Emotions"; idem, "Depression in the Hebrew Bible," citing wider literature; Wagner, *Emotionen, Gefühle*; van Wolde, "Culturally Constructed Emotions." For a comparison with emotions in ancient Greece, see Konstan et al., *Émotions*.

54. Cf. Johnson, *Vitality of the Individual*, 87; W. Schmidt, "Anthropologische Begriffe"; idem, "Alttestamentliche Anthropologie," 156–57; Albertz, "Mensch," 465–67; Kaiser, *Gott des Alten Testaments*, 2:290ff.; Smith, "Heart and Innards"; Frevel, "Fleisch und Geist I."

55. Albertz, "Mensch,"466; regarding the concept of "human being as a whole," see "Excursus 2: The Whole Human Being," 36ff below.

56. G. von Rad used the expression "Israel's answer" to describe the form of theological anthropology in which Israel responds with thanks and praise to the saving acts of its God; see 248ff below.

57. H. W. Wolff, *Anthropology*, 3.

58. Ibid., 3.

59. Kraus, *Psalmen*, 3:179.

60. Spieckermann, *Heilsgegenwart*, 237; see also Waschke, "'Was ist der Mensch?'"; Lux, "Die Bibel"; Irsigler, "Frage nach dem Menschen," 6ff., 10ff.; Kaiser, *Gott des Alten Testaments*, 2:279ff.; Neumann-Gorsolke, "'Mit Ehre und Hoheit,'" 44ff.; idem, *Herrschen in den Grenzen*, 71ff.; Meinhold, "Menschsein in der Welt."

When I look at the heavens, the work of your fingers,
  moon and stars, that you have established,
what are human beings that you remember them,
  or a single person that you care for that one?
(Ps. 8:3–4 [4–5])

Human beings live and are human because God remembers them and cares for them (cf. Ps. 144:3)[61] or because they examine their "heart" and direct it toward God, characteristically adapting the idea of God's remembering, as in Job 7:17–18.[62] In considering God's creation, human beings become aware of their humanity, which manifests itself in their relation to other creatures or their dominion over the animals,[63] as the continuation of Psalm 8:5–8 (6–9) shows.

You have made them [only] a little lower than God,
  and have crowned them with honor and majesty. (v. 5/6)
You have made them rulers over the works of your hands;
  you have put everything under their feet, (v. 6/7)
sheep and cattle—all of them,
  as well as the [wild] animals of the fields, (v. 7/8)
the birds of the sky and the fish of the sea,
  whatever crosses the paths of the sea. (v. 8/9)

"None but the small, negligible human beings have been so gloriously equipped by Yahweh. Nothing in the psalm encourages human beings to praise themselves: instead, everything encourages them to give praise to God."[64] Genesis 2:7, the foundational anthropological statement of the nonpriestly creation story, also emphasizes the orientation of human beings toward God.

> Then YHWH formed the human being [אָדָם] from the soil of the earth and breathed the breath [נִשְׁמַת] of life into his nostril, so the human being became a living thing/creature [נֶפֶשׁ חַיָּה].[65]

On the basis of our considerations so far, we can conclude that the biblical discourse about human beings is characterized by the *impossibility of objectification*.[66] Even in places where the nature of humanity is the object of consideration, such observant reflections occur in astonished consternation rather than neutral description.[67] The third-person speech—"What are human beings?"—flows immediately into an address of God: "that you remember them, or a single person that you care for that one?" According to the Old Testament understanding, it is only from the perspective of God that one can ask who or what human

61. See Fabry, "'Gedenken,'" 185; idem, "לֵבָב/לֵב," 449; Kaiser, *Gott des Alten Testaments*, 2:280; Neumann-Gorsolke, *Herrschen in den Grenzen*, 74–75.

62. For Job 7:17–18, see Waschke, "'Was ist der Mensch?,'" 806–7; Spieckermann, *Heilsgegenwart*, 237–38; Ebach, *Streiten mit Gott*, 1:83–84; Köhlmoos, *Das Auge Gottes*, 170ff.

63. See Janowski, "Herrschaft über die Tiere"; idem, "Gottebenbildlichkeit"; Kaiser, *Gott des Alten Testaments*, 2:301ff.; Neumann-Gorsolke, "'Mit Ehre und Hoheit,'" 59ff.; idem, *Herrschen in den Grenzen*, 78ff. Also see Frevel, "Theologie der Menschwürde"; and Sedlmeier, "'Vom Mutterschoß her.'"

64. Irsigler, "Frage nach dem Menschen," 25; cf. Spieckermann, *Heilsgegenwart*, 231.

65. On this text see 163ff.

66. "Impossibility of objectification," *Nichtobjektivierbarkeit*; cf. H. W. Wolff, *Anthropology*, 1.

67. Cf. W. Schmidt, "'Was ist der Mensch?,'" 2.

beings are.[68] For this reason the anthropological concepts of the Old Testament are *open toward God*: Human beings of the Old Testament are not characterized by openness toward the world, but by "openness toward God," which designates their dependence on an "infinite, not finite, transcendent opposite."[69] The programmatically intended opening sentence from Calvin's *Institutes*—"True and substantial wisdom principally consists of two parts, the knowledge of God and the knowledge of ourselves"[70]—thus indicates the foundation of any theological anthropology that is aware of its limitations.

According to the biblical understanding, where the relationship to God is obscured, and thus human self-knowledge is prevented, the destiny and future of human beings is jeopardized: this is the central theme of the individual's Psalms of Lament and Thanksgiving. Their basic motif, the *antithesis of life and death*, makes them "Disputes with God," as we shall see.

b. The Language of Human Beings

The question of how to approach biblical anthropology is further problematized by the question of the language of human beings. This problem is illustrated by looking at the fundamental anthropological terms, which are the elements of anthropological language.[71] Using earlier insights, H. W. Wolff pointed to a unique quality of Semitic languages, which B. Landsberger had called "stereometric expression of thought."[72] What is meant by this?

α. Stereometry

To answer this, let us first turn to the parallelism of members, or "thought-rhyme," which is so typical for Hebrew poetry. The *parallelismus membrorum* is based on the idea of "symmetrical completeness,"[73] the idea that the whole always consists of a plurality of parts and is linguistically expressed by placing complementary or contrasting elements in relation to one another. The "world" consists of "heavens and earth" (Gen. 1:1; etc.), the all-encompassing knowledge is the knowledge of "good and evil (or bad)" (Gen. 2:17; 3:5), and the "human race" is "male and female" (Gen. 1:27):

68. Cf. von Rad, "Die Wirklichkeit Gottes," 142; Link, "Menschenbild"; etc.

69. Pannenberg, *Was ist der Mensch?*, 11; cf. idem, *Anthropologie in theologischer Perspektive*, 25ff.; idem, *Systematische Theologie*, 2:203ff.; Link, "Menschenbild," 67ff.

70. Cf. above, p. 3. The idea that human beings cannot obtain self-knowledge from themselves, but only *before God, in God's presence* (*coram Deo*), and *from God*—this is a characteristic element of Reformation theology. This connection between knowledge of God and knowledge of self (*cognitio dei et hominis*) was inimitably described by Luther in his second preface to the Psalter of 1528; on this, see chap. 10 below. On the modern influence and history of interpretation of the Delphic inscription (in the forecourt of the temple of Apollo) γνῶθι σεαυτόν, "Know thyself," see Hager, Huhn, and Speer, "Selbsterkenntnis," 420ff.

71. Cf. Wolff, *Anthropology*, 7ff.

72. Landsberger, "Eigenbegrifflichkeit," 17–18; on the following discussion, see also Janowski, "Die 'Kleine Biblia,'" 132ff.

73. Gese, "Dekalog als Ganzheit," 79–80; idem, "Johannesprolog," 160–61; detailed discussions in Kugel, *Biblical Poetry*; Watson, *Hebrew Poetry*, 114ff.; Koch, *Was ist Formgeschichte?*, 114ff.; Berlin, *Biblical Parallelism*, 62–63; Seybold, "Poesie, biblische," 745; Ebach, "Poesie der Bibel," 15ff. On the discovery of this principle by Robert Lowth (1710–87), see Smend, "Entdecker des Parallelismus."

> The defining structure of Hebrew poetry, the *parallelismus membrorum* or so-called thought-rhyme, is not only an external characteristic. The double, intensifying formulation brings the apprehension and comprehension of a thing in a dynamic process. Only the double represents completeness, according to early, ancient views (cf. Isa. 40:2; the word for double designates wholeness), and every thesis has an antithesis, as right has left, and so forth. Order is displayed by showing symmetry. The antithetical parallelism expresses the whole on the basis of contrasting aspects. The synonymous does not repeat the same with different words, but rather completes the statement, intensifying it to fullness and wholeness, while the explicative-synthetic constructs the entire statement from its individual parts.[74]

This principle of arrangement in pairs is a basic characteristic of Hebrew poetry and not based on mechanical repetition and lack of expressivity, as Alciphron charges in discussion with his dialogue partner Eutyphron in J. G. Herder's "Vom Geist der ebräischen Poesie" (1782).

> You are describing, I suppose, the celebrated parallelisms, in regard to which I shall hardly agree with you. Whoever has anything to say, let that person say it at once, or carry the discourse regularly forward, but not repeat forever. Whoever is under the necessity of saying everything twice shows that one has but half or imperfectly expressed it the first time.[75]

After some back and forth, the two begin to speak about the beautiful aspects of Hebrew parallelism, which Alciphron does not want to acknowledge, but which Eutyphron readily defends.

> The two divisions of their chorus confirm, elevate, and strengthen each other in their convictions or their rejoicings. In the song of Jubilee, this is obvious; and in those of lamentation, it results from the very nature of the feelings that occasion them. The drawing of the breath confirms, as it were, and comforts the soul, while the other division of the chorus takes part in our afflictions, and its response is the echo, or as the Hebrews would say, "the daughter of the voice" of our sorrow. In didactic poetry one precept confirms the other, as if the father were giving instruction to his son and the mother were repeating it. By this means the discourse acquires the semblance of truth, cordiality, and confidence. In alternate songs of love the subject itself determines the form. Love demands endearing intercourse, the interchange of feelings and thoughts. The connection between these different expressions of feeling is so unaffected and sisterly, in short, that I might apply to it the beautiful and delicate Hebrew ode:
>
> Behold how lovely and pleasant
>   for brethren to dwell together. (Ps. 133:1)
> It is like soothing oil upon the head,
>   which runs down upon the beard,
> even upon the beard of Aaron,
>   and descends to the hem of his garment. (v. 2)

74. Gese, "Johannesprolog," 160–61.

75. Herder, *Hebrew Poetry*, 1:39. On the poetics of the Psalms (*parallelismus membrorum*, etc.) see Weber, *Caractère poétique*, 481ff.; idem, "Poetologische Überlegungen"; idem, "Poetologie der Psalmen"; Seybold, *Poetik*, 83ff.; van der Lugt, *Cantos and Strophes*; A. Wagner, "Parallelismus"; and the contributions in idem, *Parallelismus membrorum*. For specific studies on R. Lowth and J. G. Herder, see Smend, "Lowth in Deutschland"; and Witte, "'Vom Geist der Ebräischen Poesie.'"

It is like the dew of Hermon,
  descending upon the mountains of Zion,
when the Lord commanded a blessing,
  even life eternal.[76] (v. 3)

The principle of arrangement in pairs states, as we can learn from Herder's discussion, that the two parallel lines (*membra*) of a poetic verse (A–B) reflect on a situation from two (or more) different perspectives, but are arranged in such a way that it is expressed as a single situation. Let us take the example of Proverbs 10:16: "The wage of the righteous [leads] to life, the gain of the wicked [leads] to sin." These parallel members express the contrast between the righteous and the wicked (shown with Hebrew following the English word order):

	a	b	c
A	The wage פְּעֻלַּת	of the righteous צַדִּיק	to life, לְחַיִּים
	a'	**b'**	**c'**
B	the gain תְּבוּאַת	of the wicked רָשָׁע	to sin לְחַטָּאת

To us, the doubling of the thought inhibits the development of the statement and makes it tedious. It also diminishes its clarity and obviousness, since no two words ever fully overlap in meaning. But precisely the fact that no two words ever fully overlap in meaning is crucial, because the whole sense can never be captured by a single word or a single thought, but only by several complementary aspects, as in the case at hand. In Proverbs 10:16, the two words for "wage, earning" and "gain, yield" are synonymous except for a small nuance: "wage" (פְּעֻלַּת) contains the verbal root פָּעַל, "to make, do," so that this noun gives expression to the relationship between action and consequence. Whatever a person does, that person shall also "earn."[77] Likewise the second part of the verse uses the word "gain" (תְּבוּאַת), which is based on the verbal root בּוֹא, "to come." Here we have the image of something that "comes" to the person. In each of its halves the couplet thus formulates the action-consequence relationship according to both its *active* ("wage" < "make, do") and its *consequential* side ("gain" < "come [to]").[78] The two statements are therefore not identical.

The principle of symmetrical complementarity, or arrangement in pairs, is also found in the fact that anthropological terms in poetic texts are frequently exchangeable or appear to be parallel to each other,[79] as in Psalm 63:1/2 and in Psalm 84:2/3:

God, you are my God, I seek you,
  my life [*nepeš*] thirsts for you,
my body yearns for you
  in a dry land without water.
(Ps. 63:1/2)

76. Herder, *Hebrew Poetry*, 1:40–41.
77. See Koch and Roloff, "Tat-Ergehen-Zusammenhang"; Janowski, "Die Tat"; and 128ff below.
78. Meinhold, *Die Sprüche*, 176.
79. See 5 n.9 above with references cited in 10, n. 41.

> **My life** [*nepeš*] longed and even fainted for the courts of YHWH,
> **my heart** and **my flesh** rejoice over the living God.
> (Ps. 84:2/3)

Such complementarity also appears in the lament over transitoriness in Psalm 102:3–5 (4–6) as well as in Proverbs 23:16:

> For my days have vanished in smoke;
> **my bones** [עַצְמוֹתַי], they burn like a furnace. (Ps. 102:3/4)
> Withered like grass and dried up is **my heart** [לִבִּי].
> Indeed, I forgot to eat my bread. (v. 4/5)
> Because of my loud groaning
> my bones cling to **my flesh** [בְשָׂרִי]. (v. 5/6])

> My son, if your heart [לִבְּ] is wise,
> my heart [לִבִּ] is also glad,
> My kidneys [כִלְיוֹת] rejoice,
> if your lips [שְׂפָתֶים] speak what is just.
> (Prov. 23:15–16)[80]

With "life, vitality," "heart," and "flesh," Psalm 84:2/3 identifies different aspects—*needfulness*, *reason*, and *frailty*—of the supplicant's person, which can be described on the basis of individual components, but which only ever appears in its totality.[81] Terms for body organs (e.g., "heart" in Ps. 84:2/3) also designate noetic abilities ("reason"), and on the other hand psychological experiences affect body organs (e.g., the "kidneys" in Prov. 23:16). On the basis of this correlation between somatic and emotional/cognitive aspects, the human being is viewed in its psychosomatic wholeness.[82] The anthropological concepts of the Old Testament can therefore describe the "human being as a whole or with regard to different components"[83] and can consequently also substitute it with personal pronouns, as in Psalm 6:1–3 (2–4):

> YHWH, in your anger do not rebuke me,
> and in your wrath do not discipline me! (v. 1/2)
> Be gracious, YHWH, for **I** [אָנִי] am withering;
> heal me, YHWH, for numb with terror are **my limbs** [עֲצָמָי]. (v. 2/3)

80. See n. 9 above. For the word pair "heart and kidneys," see "Anthropological Keyword 3: Heart and Kidneys," in chap. 5 below.

81. Cf. Albertz, "Mensch," 465; also Johnson, *Vitality of the Individual*, 87; W. Schmidt, "Anthropologische Begriffe," 90; Fabry, "לֵבָב/לֵב," 425–26; Kegler, "Körpererfahrung," 28–29, 35; S. Schroer and Staubli, *Körpersymbolik der Bibel*, 24ff.; Di Vito, "Old Testament Anthropology," 225ff.; Gzella, *Lebenszeit und Ewigkeit*, 99ff.; Janowski, "Mensch IV"; et al. Perhaps one should speak of a *complex and differentiated wholeness*, i.e., of the human body not as an organism, but as a composition of *limbs and organs and their respective functions*. This view finds a parallel in the Egyptian understanding of the human body, which Brunner-Traut (*Frühformen des Erkennens*, 72) has explained by using the term "aspective": "The body . . . is understood, as the terminology attests, not as an organism, even if the heart is often seen as a kind of center, from which thoughts, emotions, as well as the blood vessels proceed. The body is composed of a number of parts, tied up and knit together; it is perhaps what we can call a 'group of members.'" See also the discussion in ibid., 71ff. For the term "aspective," see idem, "Aspektive." The concept of aspective, which does not perceive a unity as such, but rather divides it into its constitutive components, is analogous to the concept of connectivity, which is concerned with connecting elements between individual components. J. Assmann, like Brunner-Traut, sees this connection as located in the "heart" as the central organ of the perceiving and comprehending human being.

82. Gunild Brunert, *Psalm 102*, 114ff.; Gzella, *Lebenszeit und Ewigkeit*, 99ff., 118ff.

83. Albertz, "Mensch," 465; also see n. 10 above.

My life [נַפְשִׁי] is very numb with terror,
but you, YHWH—how long? (v. 3/4)

Verse 3–4 has the lexemes "I"—"my limbs"—"my life" in parallel positions (cf. Prov. 2:10–11; etc). Of course, these words are in the strictest sense not synonymous, but "the teachers believe that there is no better way of presenting their subject-matter in appropriate fashion, not by the use of terms which are clearly differentiated one from the other, but by the opposite means, namely by the juxtaposition of words related in meaning."[84] It is not the exactness of the *concept* that is sought, but as von Rad explains,

> precision in the reproduction of the *subject matter*, if possible over its whole range. As far as that is concerned, the book of Proverbs is full of incomparably vivid and also very precise statements. Ancient Israel, too, was aware of a duty to make a given statement precise, but she demanded this precision not in the coining of terms but in reproducing of facts.[85]

This "reproduction of facts" follows its own laws. Since the *parallelismus membrorum* is based on the fact that *one* situation is described in *two* or *three* different aspects,[86] the statement results in a *productive vagueness* and *plasticity*.[87] The superimposition of images and motifs, which is what characterizes the poetic effect of stereometry, does not only intensify the concreteness of the individual statement, but also prompts a bursting open [*Aufsprengung*], or a multiperspectiveness. The words and texts become transparent through their significance with regard to each other and thus expose each other's meaning. This multidimensionality of meaning is comparable to a space within which one's understanding can move about.[88] Applied to Old Testament anthropology, stereometric thinking "pegs out the sphere of man's existence by enumerating his characteristic organs, thus circumscribing man as a whole."[89]

The phenomenon of multiperspectiveness or stereometry can also be observed, as we shall see in detail below, in more complex concepts like "justice," "life," "sickness," or "death." A good example for this *perspective-dependent* and *spatial thinking* is the opening predication of majesty in Psalm 104:1b–4, which also imitates, or rather linguistically models, the movement constituted by the actions of the royal God YHWH, which encompass heaven and earth.

YHWH my God, you are very great.
You are clothed in majesty and splendor, (v. 1)
wrapped in light as in a mantle.
You stretch out the heavens like a tent. (v. 2)
You secure the beams of his chambers in the waters [of the heavens].
You choose the clouds as your chariot,
you ride about on the wings of the storm. (v. 3)

84. Von Rad, *Wisdom in Israel*, 53.
85. Ibid., 27, emphasis added.
86. See above, 14ff..
87. In the strictest sense, Krieg, *Todesbilder.*
88. Cf. Lohfink, "Psalmengebet," 12; also idem, "Der Psalter," 199; Janowski, "Die 'Kleine Biblia,'" 132ff.
89. H. W. Wolff, *Anthropology*, 8.

You make the wind your messenger,
and fire and flame your servants. (v. 4)

Hence K. Seybold comments regarding this passage:

> The art of parallelism is found in the fact that a movement of thought develops from one line to the next, which infuses each verse, despite the static-stereometric structure. This movement is achieved so that the different segments of the verse do not talk about the same event, but rather about different ones. Thus the focus is directed to the light, then to the heavens, from the heavens to the firmament, on to the clouds, from the clouds to the wind, then to the storms, from the storms to lightning and on to the earth, and so forth. The parallelism is theologically reduced, so to speak, to the uniformity of the different acts of creation.[90]

The technique of adding or placing phenomena next to each other is found especially in ancient Near Eastern art. As H. Schäfer and E. Brunner-Traut have shown, human beings are shown aspectively in Egyptian paintings and reliefs (fig. 1): face in profile, eye in front view, shoulders also in front view, and the torso and legs again in profile. Since the human body is understood "not as an organism, but as a composition of parts,"[91] it is not depicted as it would look from a particular perspective, but in a manner that is typical for a particular situation. "Egyptian and ancient Near Eastern viewers are more interested in the body—simply in the body as a vehicle of signification, or rather its socially constructed aspects."[92]

After the impossibility of objectifying the biblical image of human beings,[93] a second characteristic feature can be noted: the semantic expansiveness of key anthropological terms. The third feature is metaphoric language, which characterizes the songs of lament and thanksgiving of the individual as well as the books of Proverbs and Job. Before I discuss it, the aspect of semantic expansiveness of anthropological terms should be treated in more detail because it touches on the function of figurative language.

As we have seen, human body organs, according to the ancient Near Eastern understanding, designate at the same time emotional, cognitive, and volitional functions and capabilities of human beings.[94] This relationship between body organs and life functions plays a role in numerous Old Testament texts that seem to be primarily concerned with the description of external, physical characteristics. The depiction of the messenger of joy of Isaiah 52:7–8 coming to Jerusalem is a pertinent example:

90. Seybold, *Die Psalmen*, 63.

91. Brunner-Traut, *Frühformen des Erkennens*, 71; cf. S. Schroer and Staubli, *Körpersymbolik der Bibel*, 27ff.; on the term "aspective," see 17, n. 81 above.

92. S. Schroer and Staubli, *Körpersymbolik der Bibel*, 25. On the Egyptian view of the human being, see Meyer-Dietrich, *Senebi und Selbst*, 4ff.; and Fischer-Elfert, "Herkunft, Wesen"; on the the understanding of the human being in Mesopotamia, see M. Streck, "Person"; Wilcke, "Wesen des Menschen," 235ff.; Pongratz-Leisten, "Anthropology I"; Zgoll, "Betende Mensch"; Steinert, *Aspekte des Menschseins*. There are older (classical) and contemporary essays on this subject in Janowski, *Der ganze Mensch*, in which also see the introduction, "Der 'ganze Mensch,'" 9–21.

93. Cf. H. W. Wolff, *Anthropology*, 1; see 13 above.

94. Cf. above, 9ff.

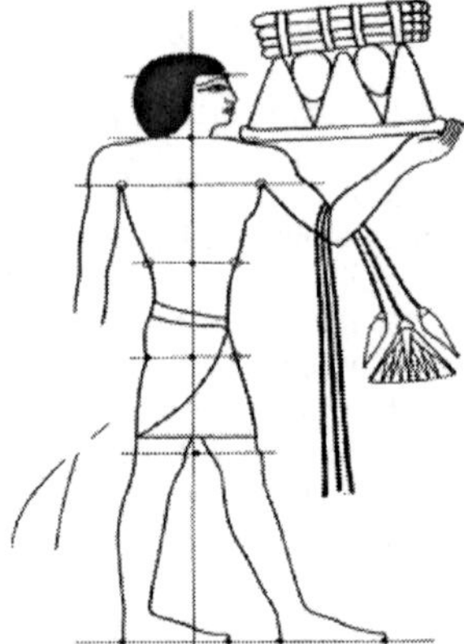

Figure 1. Composition of a male figure (Egypt, Old Kingdom)

How lovely upon the mountains are the feet of the messenger,
who lets peace be heard, who proclaims peace, who lets help be heard,
who says to Zion, "Your God rules as king!"
The voice of your sentinels:
They raise their voice,
they rejoice together,
for with their own eyes they see
the return of YHWH to Zion.

In the history of theology, this text belongs to the exilic/postexilic promises of the "return of YHWH to Zion."[95] It describes the arrival of the messenger of good news with his message, the "gospel" of the coming royal God. What is unusual is *how* this event is depicted. It does not say, "The messenger comes beaming with joy to proclaim peace . . . ," but rather, "How lovely upon the mountains are the feet of the messenger who lets peace be heard . . ." (cf. Nah. 2:1). To look in this description for something representational misses the point. In that case one would need to conclude, with C. R. North, that the feet are not "lovely" but rather "small" or "comely."[96] However, such a judgment misunderstands that we are not dealing with a "beauty pageant" here,[97] because the beautiful is different in Hebrew thought than it is for us:

> The beautiful is something that comes about; and 52.7 is a particularly clear example of this idea of it. The messenger's feet are not objectively beautiful. Their beauty consists in their intimation of the beauty of the coming of the tidings; and this is beautiful because it awakens jubilation (cf. in English, "How charming of you to come"). "Upon the mountains" is practically the only factual touch in the description, but it is quite enough to make the scene

95. W. Schmidt, *Alttestamentlicher Glaube*, 300–301.
96. C. North, *The Second Isaiah*, 221.
97. Baltzer, *Deutero-Jesaja*, 477, 482–83. Baltzer does not, however, associate Isa. 52:7 with a human messenger. On the the understanding of the term "beautiful" in the Old Testament, see A. Grund, "'Aus der Schönheit.'"

of the messenger's arrival come to life for the people in Babylon; cf. Ps. 125.2, "as the mountains are round about Jerusalem."[98]

Isaiah 52:7 says "feet" but means a swift approach; the Old Testament says "hand" but means a forceful grasp. With the naming of a body part, its function is also signified. O. Keel has successfully applied this observation by H. W. Wolff[99] to the figurative language of the Song of Songs.[100] Aside from a few exceptions,[101] body parts are never seen in biblical Hebrew with regard to their form, but with regard to their *function and dynamic quality*. To put it more broadly, "in biblical anthropology dynamic quality rather than form is foremost."[102] Thus the ancient Israelite person thinks of יָד, "arm, hand," as "power, might," and of עַיִן, "eye," not as something round or almond shaped, but as "gleaming, shining," and of צַוָּאר, "neck," as "pride, sovereignty, inviolability"—so that the tower-like neck of the beloved in Song 4:4 does not evoke its massive form, but her "pride" and "remoteness":

> Your neck is like the tower of David,
> built in layers / with merlons [?];
> a thousand shields hang on it,
> all round shields of heroes.[103]

Or Song 7:7–8, where the beloved's beauty is compared to a tall date palm:

> How beautiful you are and pleasant, beloved,
> daughter of all joys.
> Your stature is like that of a palm tree,
> and your breasts are like clusters [of dates].[104]

These texts are not concerned with describing the *form* but rather the *function* of a body part. This correlation of body organs and life function is, according to Wolff, also one of the reasons for the *semantic expansiveness of anthropological terms*. This quality is characteristic of the figurative language of the Old Testament in general and in particular of the songs of lament and thanksgiving of the individual.

98. Westermann, *Isaiah 40–66*, 250–51; cf. idem, "Das Schöne."

99. Cf. H. W. Wolff, *Anthropology*, 8.

100. Keel, *Deine Blicke*, 27ff.; cf. idem, *Das Hohelied*, 35ff.; and the reception of this idea by S. Schroer, *In Israel gab es Bilder*, 329, with n. 117; S. Schroer and Staubli, *Körpersymbolik der Bibel*, 27ff.

101. Keel, *Deine Blicke*, 27 n. 70.

102. Ibid., 27.

103. Cf. the translation by Keel, *Das Hohelied*, 129; and H.-P. Müller, *Das Hohelied, Klagelieder, Das Buch Ester*, Das Alte Testament Deutsch 16/2 (Göttingen: Vandenhoeck & Ruprecht, 1992), 42–43. Seidl speculates whether the image is not drawn from the realm of architecture (with the meaning of "pride, sovereignty, inviolability") but is rather a "reference to a specific edifice, which has its own tradition and must be interpreted in the framework of royal travesty of the Song of Songs or . . . whether the practice of wearing amulets conveys this meaning; in this case we are dealing with jewelry on the woman's neck." Theodor Seidl, "'Schön bist du meine Freundin': Wahrnehmung des Körpers im Hohen Lied," in *Der Körper und die Religion: das Problem der Konstruktion von Geschlechterrollen*, ed. Elmar Klinger, Stefanie Böhm, and Theodor Seidl (Würzburg: Echter Verlag, 2000), 137. The example shows how cautiously one must proceed with the concrete interpretation of figurative language. See also Christoph Uehlinger,"Achabs "Elfenbeinhaus" und der "Elfenbeinturm" in Hld 7, 5: Archäologie und Poetik," *Biblische Notizen*, no. 102 (2000): 95ff.

104. Translation by Keel, *Deine Blicke*, 221; cf. H.-P. Müller, *Das Hohelied*, 72, 75. On the language of the Song of Songs, see H.-P. Müller, "Menschen, Landschaften"; Seybold, "Zur Sprache."

β. Metaphors

In his essay "The Rise of Literal-Mindedness," the cultural critic Peter Burke describes the rejection or devaluation of the symbolic, which has affected the analysis of texts, rituals, and other forms of human interpretation and behavior. This process did not develop in a linear fashion but came about as a gradual but clearly noticeable paradigm shift since the Reformation. In its course, literal-mindedness replaced traditional symbolic thinking step by step. While the latter created a "system of correspondences"[105] that was thought of as inscribed by the hand of God, literal-mindedness is characterized by "a sophisticated . . . incapacity to understand symbolism,"[106] or an inability to perceive correspondences such as between microcosm and macrocosm, between the natural and a "supernatural" or "political" body.[107] Burke describes this paradigm shift on the basis of biblical interpretation, the veneration of images, and the understanding of the Eucharist in the sixteenth and seventeenth centuries. Despite the fact that there were repeated countercurrents, the development of Western history shifted in the direction of literal-mindedness.[108] Today, early in the twenty-first century, we are faced by other, new challenges.[109]

One must keep this complex development in mind in order to appreciate that with premodern religious symbol systems,[110] we are entering a world of meaning that is opposed to literal-mindedness. This world of meaning is not unlike that of the Psalms. Over thirty years ago, O. Keel sought to find access to it through the iconography of the ancient Near East; in this context he has pointed to the relationship between the "concrete" and the "abstract."[111] While we are used to separating strictly the concrete and the abstract, or to working with concrete objects like *tree*, *throne*, or *mountain* or with abstract concepts like *life*, *kingdom*, or *place of the Deity*, ancient Near Eastern cultures prefer to use "concepts that by themselves are concrete yet often indicate something extending far beyond their concrete meaning."[112] Ancient Near Eastern cultures did not distinguish

105. Burke, "Rise of Literal-Mindedness," 109.

106. Ibid., 110.

107. A famous example of the correspondence between the natural and "supernatural/political" body is the political theology of the "two bodies" of a king, described in detail by Kantorowicz, *Zwei Körper des Königs*.

108. On the transition from a body-focused *Gedächtniskultur* prevailing in the Middle Ages to a *Memorialkultur* supported by texts and images, see esp. Wenzel, *Hören und Sehen*; cf. Stolz, *Religionswissenschaft*, 134ff.

109. J. Assmann, *Das kulturelle Gedächtnis*, 11ff.

110. I am using the expression "religious symbol system" in the sense defined by Geertz, "Cultural System"; cf. Stolz, *Religionswissenschaft*, 101ff.; Keel and Uehlinger, *Göttinnen, Götter* (2001), 7ff.; Janowski, "Das biblische Weltbild," 13ff.; idem, "Die heilige Wohnung," 26ff.

111. See Keel, *Die Welt*, 8–9; Keel and S. Schroer, *Schöpfung* (2002), 101–2; on the relationship between the abstract and the concrete, see Claessens, *Das Konkrete*, 288ff. The metaphoric language of the Psalms (metaphors for God, enemies, body, war, death, etc.) has been more closely examined in recent years. On the subject, see W. Brown, *Seeing the Psalms*; Janowski, "*De profundis*" (2003), 244ff.; Zenger, "Funktion der Todesbilder"; Seybold, *Poetik*, 193ff.; van Hecke, *Metaphor in the Hebrew Bible*; van Hecke and Labahn, *Metaphors in the Psalms*; Basson, *Divine Metaphors*; and A. Wagner, *Gottes Körper*; esp. for the lion metaphor, see Strawn, *Leonine Image*, 46ff. For the semantics and motif of the Pit's nearness to the realm of the dead (cf. 32ff. below), see Lanckau, *Der Herr der Träume*, 213–14. Of importance is also the metaphoric language of the ancient Near East and Egypt. On Egypt, see Grapow, *Die bildlichen Ausdrücke*; on Mesopotamia, see M. Streck, *Bildersprache*; W. Mayer, "*Gebetsbeschwörungen*"; on Ugarit, see Parker, "Use of Similes."

112. Keel, *Die Welt*, 8.

between the concrete and the abstract, but upheld the interrelation between them by representing the "unity of reality" with the help of symbols. The act of symbolization achieves, as the following sketch may illustrate, the connection between the abstract and the concrete by bringing about a transformation of substantial into insubstantial meaning (idea), while supporting each side by means of the authority of the other:[113]

Concrete	Tree	Throne	Mountain	
	|	|	|	← *Symbolization*
Abstract	Life	Kingdom	Place of the Deity	

Since a consensus about the definition of the term "symbol" cannot be easily achieved, it is all the more necessary to explicate each of its uses. Symbolization is used here in the sense defined by S. K. Langer as a preconceptual but not a prerational act. As a function of the human spirit (*Geist*), symbolization is

> the starting point of all understanding in a specifically human sense, which encompasses more than thoughts, ideas, or actions. For the brain is not a mere connecting station, a superswitchboard, but rather a great transformer. The current of experience that runs through it changes its nature, not through the intervention of the sense that perceives it, but by means of the primary use, which is immediately applied: it is pulled into the stream of symbols that constitutes the human spirit.[114]

If one understands "symbols" as material objects and/or linguistic signs that point beyond their concrete meaning and through this type of reference establish semiotic relationships to that which is signified,[115] different levels can be distinguished, levels in which symbols are perceived in their referential or iconic quality. Two of these levels, the *level of images* and the *level of language*, are outlined below.

The Visual Dimension

In the cultures of the ancient Near East, visual symbolism is generally based on aspective (dividing) and connective (joining) principles.[116] By combining several elements of the perceivable reality, thus making them accessible to recognition, different experiential interrelations are synthesized. Let us take the example of the morning sunrise, a fundamental image for the religious worldview of ancient Near Eastern cultures.[117] The sky-goddess Nut, who "gives birth" to the solar disc in the morning, was as real for the Egyptians as the Eastern mountains on the horizon, over which the sun-god Re appeared every morning above the desert mountains (fig. 2) and which make up the word for

113. On the process of symbolic transformation, see S. K. Langer, *Philosophie*, 34ff.; Keel, *Recht der Bilder*, 267ff.; Keel and Uehlinger, *Göttinnen, Götter*, 13–4; Janowski, "Das biblische Weltbild," 13ff., 18–19.

114. S. K. Langer, *Philosophie*, 50; for an introduction to her philosophy, see Lachmann, *Susanne K. Langer*.

115. Stolz, *Religionswissenschaft*, 101ff.; Peil, "Symbol."

116. For examples of Egyptian art and thinking, see Brunner-Traut, *Frühformen des Erkennens*, 7ff.; J. Assmann, *Tod und Jenseits*, 34ff.; cf. also 17, n. 81 above.

117. See Janowski, *Rettungsgewissheit*.

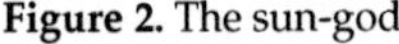

Figure 2. The sun-god

Figure 3. The world edifice

"horizon" (ʿḫt) together with the hieroglyph for sun (fig. 3).[118] The problem that posed itself for the ancient Egyptian was that of imaginability. An Egyptian saw the sun, or sun-god, rise from behind the Eastern horizon, but knew at the same time that this event did not take place ten or twenty miles away, but much further in the distance, on the edge of the inhabited world. The observer, having no concept of these remote and obscure fringe regions, was compelled to make sense of them with the help of analogies from the biological or technical realm. Thus the sunrise becomes the *birth of the sun-disc* from the body of Nut and is understood and pictorially represented by the *entry through the gate of heaven* (fig. 4).[119] One was as real to him as the other.

While we "always [run] the risk of seeing these pictures too concretely and, once we have moved away from this, again too abstractly,"[120] the few imprecise pieces of information available to the ancient Egyptian about the distant and inaccessible peripheries of the universe provided room for numerous speculations of a symbolic and technical kind. In this, the interest in the relationship of the abstract with the concrete and conversely of the concrete with the abstract always stood in the foreground. The view described here is characteristic of the nature of the ancient Near Eastern and the biblical worldview, the basic coordinates of which have been rendered into a sketch by O. Keel and I. Cornelius,[121] which combines relevant statements from Old Testament texts with iconographic elements from Palestine/Israel and the ancient Near Eastern context (fig. 5). However, the problem with such a reconstruction is evident since quite disparate elements, belonging to dissimilar contexts, are summed up into a *single* image to stand for "the ancient Near Eastern worldview." In the

118. This depiction of the world edifice contains the sky (*pt*), the Earth (double lion), and the horizon (ʿḫt); see ibid., 150ff.; as well as the seminal work of H. Schäfer, "Weltgebäude der alten Ägypter," 100–101.

119. Keel, *Die Welt*, 18ff., 25ff.

120. Ibid.

121. Keel, "Sogenannte altorientalische Weltbild," 161; cf. Cornelius, "Sun Epiphany," 217.

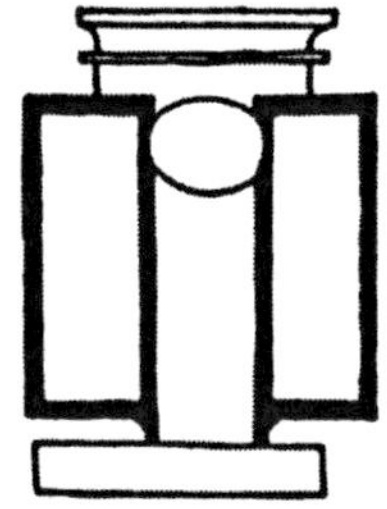

Figure 4. Cosmic gate with sun-god (left), sun disc (center), and in closed position (right)

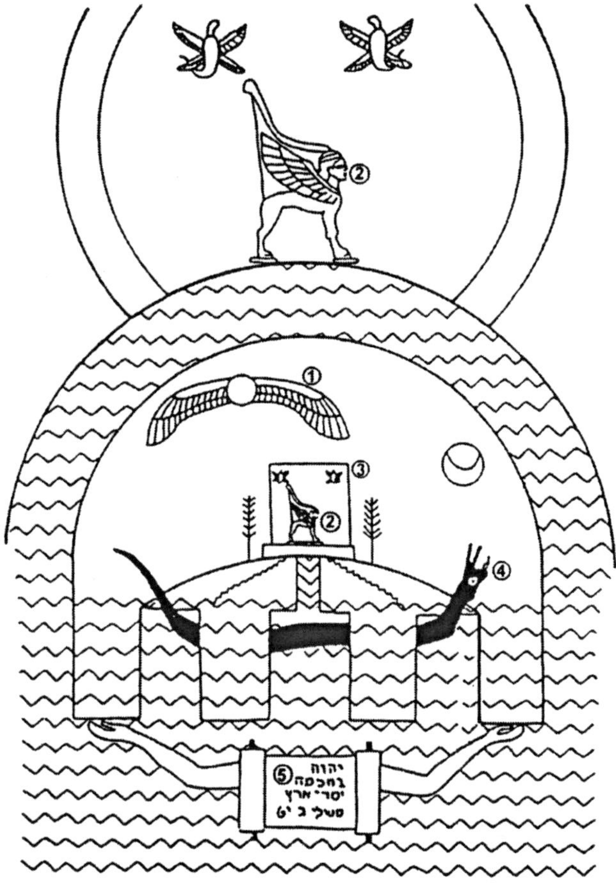

Figure 5. Reconstruction of the biblical worldview
(1) Winged sun. (2) Cherub throne. (3) Seraphs. (4) Chaos monster.
(5) Divine wisdom as the foundation of creation (cf. Prov. 3:19).

interest of a historical cosmology of the Old Testament, however, diachronic aspects must be considered and included in the representation. On the basis of Isaiah 6:1–5, for instance, and its vision of the enthroned royal Deity, one could construct *the vertical worldview of a Jerusalem temple theology*, sketching its structure[122] as follows (fig. 6):

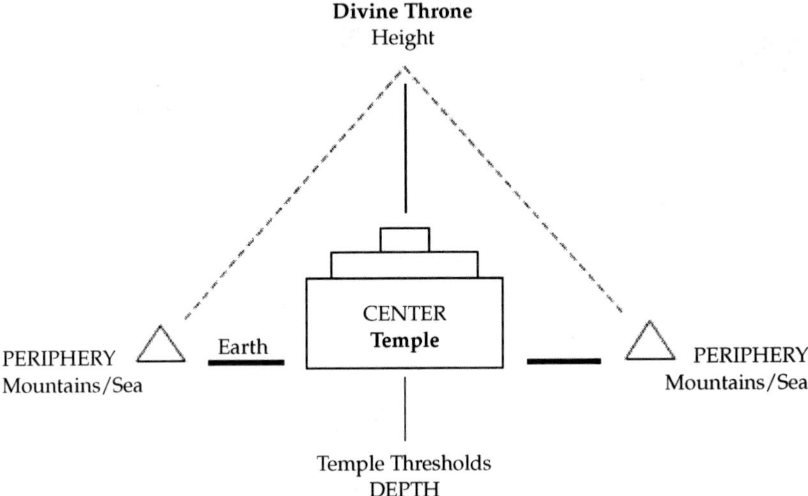

Figure 6. Symbol system for Jerusalem of the Middle Monarchy (8th c. BCE)

In addition to the vertical axis (divine throne [v. 1] and temple thresholds [v. 4]), Isaiah 6:1–5 also contains an horizontal axis as the glory of YHWH fills the entire earth (v. 3b).

Excursus 1: The Biblical Worldview

In contrast to the "domed cheese cover model," common in textbooks and popular treatments, in which the biblical worldview appears as a closed and profane system (see the illustrations in Keel, *Die Welt*, 47–48), O. Keel and I. Cornelius have rendered the basic coordinates of the ancient Near Eastern and biblical worldview in a sketch, which combines relevant statements from Old Testament texts with iconographic elements from Palestine/Israel and the ancient Near Eastern context: On the open Torah scroll (**5** in fig. 5) is the text of Proverbs 3:19a ("YHWH has founded the earth on wisdom"; cf. Ps. 104:24; etc.), a statement that is depicted in reference to an Egyptian image as two open and angled arms (cf. the hieroglyph for *Ka*, "Life-force"). These arms support the "pillars," or rather the foundations of the mountains/

122. This refers to the worldview of the Jerusalem temple theology during the Middle Monarchy; see Janowski, "Heilige Wohnung," 32ff.

earth, on which YHWH has established the world (1 Sam. 2:8; cf. Pss. 18:7, 15 [8, 16]; 75:3/4; Job 9:6; Isa. 24:18; etc.). The horned serpent dragon *mušḫuššu* (**4**), which is taken from Mesopotamian images (Kudurru from Susa, 12th c. BCE), symbolizes the constant threat by the powers of chaos, which are embodied in the Old Testament view by the "sea" (יָם; cf. Ugaritic *Yammu*, the sea-god) and its representatives Leviathan (Ps. 74:14; etc.), Rahab (Isa. 51:9) and Tannin (Pss. 74:13; 148:7; etc.). The temple and Zion, with the cherub throne (**2**; cf. Pss. 80:1/2; 99:1; Isa. 37:16; etc.) and the winged seraphs (**3**) that flank the enthroned royal Deity (Isa. 6:2–3), are the unshakable stronghold against the advancing and flooding chaos. YHWH's presence transforms the threatening waters into fertile canals and life-giving streams (cf. Pss. 46:4/5; 65:9/10; 104:10ff.), while the stylized trees flanking the temple characterize the sanctuary as a "divine garden" (cf. Ezek. 31:8–9, 16, 18; Ps. 104:16; etc.). The light of heaven (**1**), symbolized by the winged sun (Mal. 4:2 [3:20]; cf. Ps. 139:9), proclaims the glory of God, whose splendor is shared by all creation. For a person living in this world, it was an incomprehensible wonder that the earth, held up by YHWH above the abyss (cf. Job 26:7), did not sink into the chaos of floods.

The guiding principle for understanding the biblical worldview was described by Keel as follows: "There is a continual osmosis between the real and the symbolic. This openness of the mundane, earthly world to the spheres of divine-intensive life and bottomless, devastating isolation is probably the main difference to our understanding of the world as a functionally closed, mechanical system. . . . According to the biblical and ancient Near Eastern understanding, the world is transparent and open toward the supernatural and infernal" (ibid., 47).

Resources

Cornelius, "Sun Epiphany"; Dux, *Logik der Weltbilder*; Frankfort and Dülberg, *Alter Orient*, 9ff.; Gese, "Frage des Weltbildes"; Hartenstein, *Unzugänglichkeit Gottes*, 11ff.; Houtman, *Himmel*, 283ff.; Janowski, *Rettungsgewissheit*, 19ff.; Keel, *Die Welt*, 13ff., 333ff.; idem, "Altorientalische Weltbild"; idem, "Altägyptische und biblische Weltbilder"; Keel and S. Schroer, *Schöpfung*, 102ff.; Koch, "Weltbild"; Lang, "Weltbild"; Metzger, *Wohnstatt Jahwes*; Pongratz-Leisten, *Programmatik*, 13ff.; Rogerson, "Enemy"; Seybold, *Die Psalmen*, 143ff.; Stadelmann, *Hebrew Conception*; Stolz, *Weltbilder der Religionen*; H. Weippert, "Altisraelitische Welterfahrung."

On the subject of worldview or conceptions of the world, see Markschies et al., *Atlas der Weltbilder*; Oeming, "Welt/Weltanschauung/Weltbild IV/2"; P. Neumann, "Weltbild"; Janowski, "Weltbild III"; Berlejung, "Weltbild/Kosmologie"; Ebach, "Weltbild." On specific aspects, see Ego, "Wasser, Fels"; Janowski, "Gott, Mensch und Raum"; Janowski and Grund, "Raum und Zeit" (and further references there); Hartenstein, "Weltbild und Bilderverbot."

A Worldview Centered on the Temple

In the year of the death of King Uzziah
  I saw the Lord,
sitting on a high and exalted throne,
  and the fringes of his garment filled the temple.
(Isa. 6:1)
Seraphs stood above him,
  each one with six wings:
with two he covered his face,
  and with two he covered his feet,
  and with two he was flying [continuously]. (v. 2)
And one called to the other and said:
  "Holy, holy, holy is YHWH Sabaoth;
    the fullness of his whole earth is his glory!" (v. 3)
Then the posts of the thresholds shook from the voice of the caller,
  and the temple filled with smoke. (v. 4)
Then I said:
  "Woe is me,
    for I have been silenced [=destroyed]!
  Because I am a man of unclean lips,
    and I live in the midst of a people with unclean lips!
  For my eyes have seen the King YHWH Sabaoth!" (v. 5)

To be sure, this is only one of many examples. Another example is the *horizontal worldview* of Psalm 46:1–7 (2–8), and also the examples of others: Amos 9:1–4; Genesis 1:1–2:4a; 2:4b–25; Isaiah 66:1–2; Job 38:1–38. In this sense, the variations and transformations of the preexilic, exilic, and postexilic worldview are to be described text by text, in order to assess the entire development. This task has only recently been recognized.[123] For this reason, the reconstruction presented by O. Keel and I. Cornelius still possesses heuristic value, even if it offers only an idealized compilation of central elements within the Jerusalem symbol system. It illustrates the fundamental view that the world, according to ancient Near Eastern and biblical understandings, was not a closed and profane system, but represented a magnitude that was "transparent and open toward the supernatural and infernal."[124]

The "openness of the world toward the supernatural and infernal" is only one side. The other side consists in the challenges that this openness posed to the cognitive and behavioral abilities of human beings. Since a world that is open toward the supernatural and infernal is principally ambivalent, it is the task of human beings to disambiguate this inherent ambiguous world, to classify a reality that is infused in multiple ways by antagonistic forces (cosmos/chaos, light/darkness, life/death, purity/impurity, health/sickness, fertility/bareness, etc.) as a stable world in which meaningful life is possible.[125] The question is whether the experience of ordered and meaningful interconnections is consistently possible in a world that is open to the supernatural and infernal, or

123. See the contributions in Janowski, "Das biblische Weltbild."

124. Keel, *Die Welt*, 47; see also "Excursus 1: The Biblical Worldview," 26 above.

125. In ancient Near Eastern cultures, stability is primarily the responsibility of the king; see Otto, *Krieg und Frieden*, 25–26, 28ff., 34ff., 51ff., etc.

whether they are only occasionally granted the experience of a salutary ordered setting. The problem that arose for the individual as well as the community was significant. It consisted of "overcoming the tension between the necessary order of the world and the factual conditions, within which elements of order and disorder are continuously interchanged."[126] To do so calls for constantly executing this process of "disambiguation" with the help of cultic-ritual, magic, divinatory, medical, (sacred-)legal, or even mathematical-astronomic operations. Elementary orientations are suggested by the visible symbols of the religious symbol system, as those in the above reconstructions of the biblical worldview (fig. 5), the seraphs, cherubs, heavenly/earthly throne, mountain, (divine) trees, fertile streams/chaotic floods, Leviathan, and so forth, which do not only refer to "that for which they stand,"[127] but which are also always integrated into fundamental constellations.[128] One had to be as familiar with these images and constellations as with any language:

> Any culture—including any of its components, such as religion—consists of a limited number of visible and audible signs, which form a specific pattern, a fabric. . . . Just as a language cannot be reconstructed only on the basis of its vocabulary, a culture's religious worldview cannot be reconstructed on the basis of isolated images. Anyone who wishes to understand a language must know its syntax and sentences; anyone who wishes to understand images must focus the attention on complex constellations, wherever they may be found.[129]

One must therefore know the rules of a religious symbol system, its order and coherence, its "grammar" and "syntax," in order to "read" corresponding images and texts and to understand their "language." This is also true for the modern interpreter. In addition to the iconography of Palestine/Israel, metaphors, a fundamental characteristic of the Psalms, also offer access to this particular language of the religious symbol system.

The Linguistic Dimension

Metaphoric language is of fundamental significance for an anthropology of the Psalms.[130] In comparison to the information-oriented language of daily life and the concept-oriented language of commerce, the image-oriented language of the Psalms is characteristically vague (blurred) and enigmatic (dark). One should not, however, misjudge it as lacking in focus and clarity, which are to be found on a different level. Poetic language, as it manifests itself in similes and metaphors, is an event that invades the ordinary and is founded, in the words of the literary critic J. Anderegg, on the *transformation of the mundane.*

> As poetic language interrupts the ordinary, it breaks open the firm, the closed. Liberating in this fashion, it posits that which is alive opposite the stable and

126. H. Schmid, *Gerechtigkeit als Weltordnung*, 152.
127. Stolz, *Religionswissenschaft*, 101.
128. See Keel and Uehlinger, *Göttinnen, Götter*, 13–14; and Janowski, "Die heilige Wohnung," 26ff.
129. Keel and Uehlinger, *Göttinnen, Götter*, 14.
130. See again Keel, *Die Welt*, 8ff., 13ff.; also Görg, "Bildsprache"; Wehrle, "Metapher"; Berlin, "Role of Metaphor"; Seifert, *Metaphorisches Reden*; Zimmermann, "Metapherntheorie"; Schwienhorst-Schönberger, "Gottesbilder," 364ff.; Zenger, "'Du thronst," 18ff. On metaphor in Mesopotamian texts, see Westenholz, "Symbolic Language"; M. Streck, *Bildersprache*, 21ff.

ordered. This explains the fascination of poetic language: it enables a liberating experience of the self even and especially when we no longer or not yet understand what it means.[131]

The concept of metaphor designates the unusual word-and-image combinations that are not backed by convention, that cannot be traced back to a particular vocabulary, and that are not founded on their own grammar.[132] Metaphoric language arises rather through a *process of transformation*: from familiar language material, metaphoric language builds "medial signs that, no longer intelligible through convention, permit us now to transcend familiar worlds."[133] The Psalter is full of such metaphoric language usage, which transcends the mundane.[134] Let us take the word "depth" as an example. In our everyday language, depth is primarily a type of measure that indicates how far a given point is located below a baseline. We speak of the "depth of the sea" or the "depth of a mine." Of course, our language also knows the figurative meaning of depth, as in idioms like the "depth of one's heart" or the "depth of character" or the "depth of an emotion or thought."[135] The problem is that the gap between the *technical* and the *figurative* meanings is greater for us than it is in the Psalms. For this reason we tend to resort to metaphorical language in order to express feelings, moods, or values, to speak of "fields of meaning that are at any rate difficult to put into words."[136] Thus the word "depth" of Psalm 130:1 appears in Luther's familiar adaptation of 1524 as "deep distress":

> Aus tiefer Not schrei' ich zu dir,
> Herr Gott, erhör' mein Rüfen.
>
> In deep distress I cry to thee,
> Lord God, hear thou my calling.[137]

Instead of "deep distress," the Hebrew text speaks of "depths" (מַעֲמַקִּים), from which the supplicant calls out to God:

> Out of the depths I have called out to you, YHWH!
> Lord, hear my voice!
> May your ears be attentive
> to my loud cry for mercy.
>
> (Ps. 130:1–2)

131. Anderegg, *Sprache und Verwandlung*, 33; cf. Schweizer, "Metaphorik," 791: "A metaphor breaks through the usual understanding, challenges the imagination to new possibilities of sensation, creates—even if only poetically fictitious at first—a new worldview and as such is . . . in the broader sense (= parable) a particularly appropriate form of language." This corresponds to H. Blumenberg's designation and analysis of metaphors as a "special case of incomprehensibility" (*Schiffbruch mit Zuschauer*, 75ff.). On the subject from a systematic perspective, see Dalferth, "In Bildern denken"; Werbick, "Metapher," 189–90; idem, "Spur der Bilder," 8–9; Werbick and Vanstiphout, *Den Glauben verantworten*, 405ff. Literature on metaphor is boundless; see, e.g., the reader and extensive bibliography by Blumenberg, "Licht als Metapher"; also Peil, "Metapherntheorien"; Zimmermann, "Metapherntheorie."

132. Cf. Anderegg, *Sprache und Verwandlung*, 60–61. For definitions, see also M. Streck, *Bildersprache*, 30ff.

133. Anderegg, *Sprache und Verwandlung*, 61.

134. On the discussion below, see also Janowski, "Die 'Kleine Biblia,'" 137.

135. Cf. Wahrig, *DTV-Wörterbuch*, 774, e.g., "Tiefe des Herzens [depth of heart]," "Höhen und Tiefen des Lebens [height and depth of life]," "Tiefe eines Gefühls oder Gedankens [depth of feeling or thought]."

136. Schweizer, "Metaphorik," 792.

137. See below, 199. ET by Z. Philip Ambrose, cited in Burns, *Bach's Modal Chorales*, 233.

The context of Psalm 130 makes it clear that the word "depths" (מַעֲמַקִּים) circumscribes the *situation of being lost*, which is depicted in the related passages of Psalm 69:2, 14 (3, 15) (inverted by Isa. 51:10) and Ezekiel 27:34 as sinking into the *depths of the waters* or *depths of seas*:

Save me, O God,
  for the waters have come up to my neck!
          (Ps. 69:1/2)
I have sunk into the deep mud,
  and [there is] no foothold.
I have come into the **depths of the waters**,
  and the current has swept me away. (v. 2/3)
I am exhausted from my cries,
  my throat is parched,
my eyes have become dim,
  as I wait for my God. (v. 3/4)
. . . .
YHWH, in your kindness
  hear me through the faithfulness of your salvation!
Rescue me from the mud, that I may not sink,
  that I may be saved from those who hate me
  and from the depths of the waters.
Let the flood of the waters not sweep over me,
  and let the depth not swallow me,
  and let not the well close its mouth over me.
          (vv. 13b–15 [14b–16])

Is it not you, who has dried up the sea,
  the waters of the great flood,
who has made the **depths of the sea** into a path
  for the liberated to pass through?
          (Isa. 51:10)

Now you are broken on the seas
  in the depth of the waters;
your trading goods and all your crew,
  have fallen in your midst.
          (Ezek. 27:34)

The images of water and mud are particularly evocative for the condition of being lost. The Hebrew word בְּאֵר (Ps. 69:15/16b) that is used here means technically "a well." Its similarity to a cistern (בּוֹר; see fig. 7) and its semantic proximity to the "realm of the dead" (שְׁאוֹל; cf. Pss. 30:3/4; 88:3/4) or "death" (מוֹת/מָוֶת; cf. Isa. 38:18) explains why dying can be depicted as sinking into a cistern, or "the Pit."[138] Strikingly, this imagery has not lost any of its relevance even today (see fig. 8).

138. Cf. Pss. 28:1; 30:3/4; 88:4/5; etc.; see Keel, *Die Welt*, 53ff., 60ff.; Tillmann, "*Das Wasser bis zum Hals!*," 178ff.; Hossfeld and Zenger, *Die Psalmen*, 2:269ff.; Schorch, *Euphemismen*, 97–98; Rudman, "Water Imagery." On images of death as "water" (sea, wadi, mud) and "depth" (pit, city, darkness), see Krieg, *Todesbilder*, 601ff., 603ff. The most famous examples of people held captive in a cistern are Joseph (Gen. 37:18ff.; cf. 40:15; 41:14) and Jeremiah (Jer. 37:16; 38:6). On Joseph, see Lux, *Josef*, 86–87.

Figure 7. Cross-section of a typical cistern

Figure 8. Drawing by a person suffering from depression (2001)

The supplicant of Psalm 130 is conscious of being literally trapped in an "abysmal place"—as in a cistern (בּוֹר) or a well (בְּאֵר)—where the antiworld of chaos begins. In the noun "depths" (מַעֲמַקִּים), which is based on the verb "to be deep" (עָמַק), two semantic spheres intersect: a concrete understanding of space and an existential description of a situation, whereby the tension between the meaning of the lexeme מַעֲמַקִּים (space below) and the contextual significance of מַעֲמַקִּים (situation of abysmal despair) remains. The ordinary plurale tantum (plural only) "depths" thus becomes a reference point for the Old Testament understanding of chaos ("devouring depths") in the context of Psalm 130.[139]

The use of metaphor has to do with the "transformation of the ordinary" by means of sublation or delimitation of concreteness. However, "sublation of concreteness" does not mean negation of the concrete, but *transformation* of concreteness *without* negation of the concrete.[140] In this sense, Psalm 91:1 speaks of "shadow" (צֵל) and means "protection":

> You who dwell in the shelter of Elyon
> abide in the shadow [צֵל] of Shadday.
> I say to YHWH:
> My refuge [מַחְסֶה] and my fortress [מְצוּדָה],
> my God, in whom I trust!
> (Ps. 91:1–2)

The fact that linguistic signifiers, in this case "shadow," can evoke the intended situation, in this case "protection," is based on the mental association that exists between the two and is now established anew. The intended situation of "protection" is in some way comparable to the object of reference that is usually represented by the linguistic signifier "shadow," making the translation possible in the first place.[141] Likewise the petitioner of Psalm 102:1–7 (2–8) is compared to a "bird in the desert," indicating approaching death:

> YHWH, hear my prayer,
> let my cry reach you. (v. 1/2)
> Do not hide your face from me
> on the day of my distress.
> Incline your ear toward me;
> when I call, hear me soon. (v. 2/3)
> For my days have vanished in smoke;
> my bones, they burn like a furnace. (v. 3/4)
> Withered like grass and dried up is my heart.
> Indeed, I forgot to eat my bread. (v. 4/5)
> Because of my loud groaning
> my bones cling to my flesh. (v. 5/6)
> I *am like* a bird in the desert,
> *like* an owl among ruins. (v. 6/7)
> I wake up and am/cry
> *like* a bird, lonely on the rooftop. (v. 7/8)

139. See also Rudman, "Water Imagery."
140. Cf. Hossfeld, "Metaphorisierung," 22–23.
141. Kedar-Kopfstein, *Biblische Semantik*, 165ff.

The "bird in the desert" and the "owl among ruins" are symbols for the transience/mortality of the supplicant. The meaning of symbol or symbolic quality in this context is defined by the literary critic H. White as follows:

> The hackneyed phrase "My love, a rose" is not, obviously, intended to be understood as suggesting that the loved one is *actually* a rose. It is not even meant to suggest that the loved one has the specific attributes of a rose—that is to say, that the loved one is red, yellow, orange, or black, is a plant, has thorns, needs sunlight, should be sprayed regularly with insecticides, and so on. It is meant to be understood as indicating that the beloved shares the *qualities* which the rose has come to *symbolize* in the customary linguistic usages of Western culture. That is to say, considering the message, the metaphor gives directions for finding an entity that will evoke the images associated *with loved ones and roses alike* in our culture. The metaphor does not *image* the thing it seeks to characterize, *it gives directions* for finding the set of images that are intended to be associated with that thing. It functions as a symbol, rather than as a sign: which is to say that it does not give us either a *description* or an *icon* of the thing it represents, but *tells us* what images to look for in our culturally encoded experience in order to determine how we *should feel* about the thing represented.[142]

In this sense the comparisons and metaphors discussed here are not aesthetic ornamentations of reality, but expressions of an understanding of reality that can be termed, following H.-P. Müller, *religious appropriation of being*.[143] "Appropriation of being" means that through comparison the situation of the petitioner is so closely tied to the lived-in external reality that some of the *nature* of the subject being compared ("bird in the desert" // "owl among ruins") is attributed to the object of the comparison (the supplicant).[144] This is how the supplicant of Psalm 102:1–7 (4–8) perceives self in creatureliness—"like a *furnace*" // "like *grass*" (vv. 3–4 [4–5]); "like a *bird*" // "like an *owl*" (vv. 5–6 [6–7])—and experiences this creatureliness under the aspect of despair ("like a bird, *lonely on the rooftop*"). These comparisons also break open the traditional understanding of transience as figurative language brings boundary situations of human experience into view, situations inaccessible to conceptual thinking.

Let us briefly summarize our observations about the stereometric and metaphoric quality of the language of the Psalms:

Stereometry

The *superimposition of motifs and images* (stereometry) causes not only an intensification of the concreteness of an individual statement, but also a bursting open (*Aufsprengung*), or multiperspectiveness. The texts become transparent through their significance alongside each other and thus expose each other's meaning.

142. White, *Tropics of Discourse*, 91, emphasis original; cf. Berlin, "Role of Metaphor," 30: "Metaphor involves more than simple comparison or equation of one object with another. By placing the two objects in juxtaposition, a relationship between them is established such that their qualities may become interchanged."

143. "Religiöse Daseinsaneignung": H.-P. Müller, *Vergleich und Metapher*, 49ff.

144. Westermann, *Vergleiche und Gleichnisse*, 80ff.

This multidimensionality of meaning is comparable to a space within which one's understanding can move about.[145]

Metaphors

The concreteness of individual situations is sublated by means of *figurative language* (metaphors). The objective of poetic language, to transcend the conventionally familiar, characterizes the language of the Psalms. This "transformation of the mundane"[146] takes place without negation of the concrete and thus preserves the open-endedness ("productive vagueness") and liveliness ("plasticity") that is characteristic of poetic language.

The characteristics that are outlined here, and to which more will be added in the course of this study, make the Psalms indeed into a text in which "one can bring every bit of oneself under shelter."[147]

145. Cf. Lohfink, "Psalmengebet," 12.
146. Anderegg, *Sprache und Verwandlung*, 59ff.
147. Rilke, *Letters*, 126; cf. xv above.

2. The Psalms as Fundamental Anthropological Texts

> For I think that in the words of this book all human life is covered, with all its states and thoughts, and that nothing further can be found in man. For no matter what you seek, whether it be repentance and confession, or help in trouble and temptation or under persecution, whether you have been set free from plots and snares or, on the contrary, are sad for any reason, or whether, seeing yourself progressing and your enemy cast down, you want to praise and thank and bless the Lord, each of these things the divine Psalms show you how to do, and in every case the words you want are written down for you, and you can say them as your own.
>
> Athanasius, *Letter to Marcellinus*[1]

So far we have explored preliminary aspects of our subject and have discussed several relevant methodological facets. Now we want to go one step further and describe the individual's Psalms of Thanksgiving and Lament as fundamental anthropological texts. However, right at the outset we encounter an obstacle, which has always made access to these texts more difficult. This obstacle has to do with the lack of laments or lamenting in our own ecclesiastical practice and theological reflection. The question that always poses itself is this: is the lament even an appropriate form of speaking with God?

The lament has hardly been considered by systematic theological reflections, and even though it is not completely absent from our religious practice within the church, it appears only within a "restrained context."[2] Although it has been noted in Old Testament scholarship for over twenty years, nothing has significantly changed.[3] This is true despite the fact that almost one-third of the psalms are prayers of lament.[4] The reasons for this are evidently connected to our concepts of God, humanity, and the world. Two of these reasons, which are joined by

1. Athanasius, "Letter of St. Athanasius to Marcellinus," 116. On this text and its importance for understanding the Psalter, see Günter Bader, *Psalterium affectuum palaestra*, 112ff.; Zenger, "'Du thronst,'" 16ff.

2. O. Fuchs, "Klage: Eine vergessene Gebetsform," 941; cf. Limbeck, "Die Klage," 3ff.; Bayer, "Klage III," 1391: "Since the earliest history of the church, the liturgical lament has almost vanished in the daily life of Christians, has been repressed—under the influence of Stoicism—and is without form whenever it surfaces in elementary ways; systematic theological reflections have almost completely neglected it."

3. See the survey by O. Fuchs, "Klage: Eine vergessene Gebetsform"; and the two collections on the subject of lament, one by Steins, *Schweigen wäre gotteslästerlich*; another by O. Fuchs and Janowski, *Klage*. The situation is beginning to change somewhat in the field of practical theology; see Baldermann, "Klage IV."

4. Cf. the classification by Gunkel and Begrich, *Introduction to Psalms*, 121–22; Westermann, "Struktur und Geschichte der Klage," 139ff.

others, such as the widespread reservation that Jewish prayer practices "could not possibly be relevant" to Christian spirituality,[5] shall be briefly outlined.[6]

The *first* reason is based on the modern use of the term "lament." The expression "lament" is on the one hand too broad and on the other too narrow. It is too broad, because based on its origin it includes lamenting the dead and lamenting distress or suffering. While a lament over the dead mourns the death of another and *looks back* on that life (with the family), a lament over suffering presents one's own suffering before God and desires its cessation, therefore *looking ahead*:[7] "The *Sitz im Leben* of the lament over the dead is the funeral and its various parts; the *Sitz im Leben* of the lament over suffering is the worship service."[8]

The term "lament" is also too narrow because it always refers to something specific: the lament addressed to an authority (*accusation*), the relationship of the lament to the lamenter (*complaint*), or the lament directed toward a legal opponent (*lawsuit*). These variations, the result of linguistic development, always refer to a single dimension in the Old Testament, which is an integral component of the lament.

The God-Lament

YHWH, in your anger do not rebuke me
  and in your wrath do not discipline me!
(Ps. 6:1/2)
Be gracious, YHWH, for I am withering;
  heal me, YHWH, for numb with terror are my limbs. (v. 2/3)
My life is very numb with terror,
  but you, YHWH—how long? (v. 3/4)

My God, my God, why have you forsaken me,
  [you who are] far from my deliverance,
  [far from] the words of my crying?
(Ps. 22:1/2)

Wake up! Why do you sleep, Lord?
  Wake up, do not banish [us] forever!
Why do you hide your face?
  Do you forget our affliction and oppression?
(Ps. 44:23–24 [24–25])

The Self-Lament

Like water I am poured out,
  my limbs are out of joint;
my heart has become like wax,
  melted within my bowels.

5. Usually, the Enemy and Curse Psalms have had to serve as examples; on this type of Christian "nagging" with regard to the "Jewish Psalms," see Zenger, *Das Erste Testament*, 38ff. On the expression Enemy and Curse Psalms, see below, 98ff.

6. Cf. Westermann, "Struktur und Geschichte der Klage," 129 n. 15; idem, *Die Klagelieder*, 84ff.; for the perspective of literary criticism, see Anderegg, "Zum Ort der Klage."

7. Cf. Westermann, "Die Rolle der Klage," 251–52.

8. Westermann, *Die Klagelieder*, 88.

Dried up like a potsherd is my (life-)force,
and my tongue cleaves to the roof of my mouth,
you have laid me down in the dust of death.
(Ps. 22:14–15 [15–16])

But I thought in my fear:
I have been banished from your presence.
(Ps. 31:22/23a)

Save me, O God,
for the waters have come up to my neck!
I have sunk into the deep mud
and [there is] no foothold.
I have come into the depths of the waters,
and the current has swept me away.
(Ps. 69:1–2 [2–3])

The Enemy-Lament

For see, the wicked bend their bows,
they have set their arrow against the string,
to shoot in the darkness at those
who have an upright heart.
(Ps. 11:2–3)

They lie in wait for me—now they have encircled me;
their eyes are set to throw me to the ground.
(Ps. 17:11)

They return in the evening;
they growl like dogs and encircle the city.
See, they slobber at the mouth,
swords are on their lips;
because [they say]: "Who should hear it?"
(Ps. 59:6–7 [7–8])

Perhaps the modern disappearance of the concept of lament[9] has resulted in the lament's taking on a connotation that is virtually an inversion of its original meaning. Not only has the self-lament been understood as an expression of sentimentality, but the God-lament too has become suspect and has been understood to be blasphemous, according to a common view: "One must not argue with God!" No Christian, but only Christ on the cross (Mark 15:34),[10] is allowed what the Old Testament supplicant presumes to do with personal lament before YHWH. That, at least, was Luther's judgment in his interpretation of Psalm 22:1/2: "If one were to transfer to us that which occurred in Christ, in all its elements and in the same way, it would be a blasphemy and murmuring, whereas in him it was nothing but, in a certain sense, a shattering

9. This disappearance of the concept of lament is of course connected with the modern approach to prayer; see below, 339.

10. On this text, see below, 334ff.

of weak nature, which, however, was similar in all things to our blasphemy and murmuring."[11]

For the most part, shift in language use points to conceptual shift. This is the *second reason* for the absence of the lament today. It is the "inability to mourn,"[12] or theologically speaking, the inability "to enter with trust and courage into an encounter with God."[13] The deeper root for this failure is, according to O. Fuchs, "the disappearing ability to seek shelter not in safe and secure concepts [*Denkfiguren*], but in God."[14] In other words:

> If the lament should stray . . . from association with God, from the space and time "before God," it changes and loses itself in a general sentimentality, thus shifting toward self-pity, looking at others as evil, as "enemies," as addressees of the accusation, and manifesting its lament in certain forms of social protests and causing tension in public life, even in the church. As a result, an unenlightened blend of religion and politics leads to a bitter and destructive reshaping of religion into morality and politics.[15]

In looking for a way out of this dilemma, a new consideration of the biblical spirituality of lament presents itself. From it we can learn that the lament before God is "not only a legitimate but also an indispensible element of faith."[16] In both the Old and the New Testaments, the lament is, as we shall see, a natural part of the existence of human beings before God. In its basic theme, the *life/death alternative* is linguistically developed in such way that literally no anguish or suffering the supplicant might encounter in life is dropped from the association with God. On the contrary, "all recognition of disastrous realities that does not go through the lament is lethal and irresponsible. An association with God in which no conflictual dialogues are possible is shallow and far from real life: Abstinence from lament means loss of relationships and of life."[17]

This thesis will be developed below in view of the structure of the Psalms of Lament and Thanksgiving.

a. Structure of the Psalms of Lament and Thanksgiving

In the Psalter, we not only find an individual psalm of lament next to a psalm of thanksgiving (e.g., Pss. 17 and 18), we also find the succession of lament and thanksgiving within a single psalm (e.g., Ps. 22:22–31 [23–32] after Ps. 22:1–21 [2–22]).[18] The common theme of both genres can be defined as the conceptual pair of "life and death," in the two-way direction of meaning, each of which articulates a different experience, *"from life to death"* (lament) and *"from death to life"* (praise/thanksgiving). The song of thanksgiving or praise gives thanks

11. Luther, *Von wahrer und falscher Frömmigkeit*, 150.
12. Cf. A. Mitscherlich and M. Mitscherlich, *Die Unfähigkeit zu Trauern*.
13. O. Fuchs, *Klage als Gebet*, 356.
14. Ibid.
15. Bayer, "Erhörte Klage," 341; see also Anderegg, "Zum Ort der Klage," 185ff.
16. Fuhs, *Sehen und Schauen*, 221; cf. O. Fuchs, *Klage als Gebet*, 359 n. 12; Bayer, "Klage III."
17. O. Fuchs, *Klage als Gebet*, 359; cf. Janowski, "Klage II"; Bayer, "Klage III."
18. See 323ff. below.

to God for *rescue that has already happened*, assuming a retrospective view;[19] the lament expresses the distress that affects the supplicant *at the moment*. In both cases, the prayer is a "direct reaction to an extreme boundary experience of human existence."[20]

For anthropological and theological reasons, however, it is not best to begin with praise, since only the lament lends the necessary force and dramatic energy to praise.[21] "A human being," writes O. Fuchs, "cannot, because of his psychological structures and historical nature, in short because of his *conditio humana*, praise God spontaneously in a moment of distress; to demand this would be inhumane and would eventually lead to a break in the communication between the human person, who lives through and endures time, and God."[22]

We shall therefore begin with the lament, describing its function on the basis of its construction. For the sake of completeness, it should be remembered that in addition to the laments of the individual (LI), other *genres of lament*[23] existed in ancient Israel:

- Laments for the dead: 2 Samuel 1:19–27; 3:33–34; and others.
- Laments for the city and over its destruction: Jeremiah 4–10;[24] Lamentations 2 and 4;[25] 4Q179; and others.
- Communal laments: Psalms 44; 60; 74; 79; 80; 83; 89; 137; also Isaiah 63:7–64:11; and lament liturgies like Micah 7:8–20 and Jeremiah 14:1–15:4.[26]
- Confessions of Jeremiah: 11:18–23; 12:1–6; 15:10–21; 17:(12) 14–18; 18:18–23; 20:7–13; 20:14–18.[27]
- Wisdom laments: Job 7:11ff.; 10; others in Job; Psalms 37; 49; 73.
- Laments of God: Jeremiah 2:10–32; 3:20; 8:7; 12:7–13; 15:5–9; 18:13–15a.

Regarding the *history of lament*, C. Westermann[28] distinguishes three phases, which should, however, be understood less as historical and more typically as ideal:

- The short "early lament" addressed to God (so-called personal prayer) such as the lament of Rebecca (Gen. 25:22; cf. 27:36; Tob. 3:15; 1 Macc. 2:7, 13; 2 Esd. 5:35; etc.),[29] the lament of the mediator (Exod. 5:22; Judg. 6:13;

19. See Hossfeld, "Lob I"; and 257ff. below.
20. Albertz, "Gebet," 35.
21. Cf. O. Fuchs, *Klage als Gebet*, 359.
22. Ibid.
23. For more specific information, see Westermann, "Struktur und Geschichte der Klage," 125ff.; Westermann, "Die Rolle der Klage"; Gerstenberger, "Der klagende Mensch," 64–65; O. Fuchs, *Klage als Gebet*, 302ff.; Albertz, "Gebet," 36, 38–41; Reventlow, "Gebet II"; Janowski, "Klage II."
24. See Wischnowsky, *Tochter Zion*.
25. See Levin, "Klagelieder Jeremias."
26. See Emmendörffer, *Der ferne Gott*; Hieke, *Psalm 80*, 225ff. On laments in exilic prose prayers (cf. 1 Sam. 23:10–11a; Judg. 6:13; Josh. 7:6–9), see Veijola, "Das Klagegebet in Literatur und Leben."
27. See Hermisson, "Jahwehs und Jeremias Rechtstreit," 5ff. (with notes on references to the Psalms in the confessions, 15ff.); G. Fuchs, "Die Klage des Propheten"; idem, "Verwandte Motive"; et al.
28. Westermann, "Struktur und Geschichte der Klage"; cf. idem, "Die Rolle der Klage," 253; Albertz, "Gebet," 39–40.
29. On laments in intertestamental literature, see Ehrmann, *Klagephänomene*.

Deuteronomistically: Exod. 32:11ff., 31ff.; Num. 14:13ff.; Josh. 7:6ff.; etc.), the lament of a childless woman (Gen. 15:2–3; 30:2; 1 Sam. 1:10; etc.).[30]

- The ritualized lament of the individual (LI) and of the book of Job.
- The lament in later prose prayers (Ezra 9; Neh. 9; Dan. 9; etc.).

In contrast to the short "early lament" (personal prayer) and the late, postexilic prose prayers with their divergence of lament and praise and the increase in confessions of sin, the Psalter's laments of the individual have a formal structure, which generally consists of the following basic elements (exemplified by Ps. 13):[31]

I	Invocation	*YHWH*
L	Lament	How long . . . ?
P	Petition	Look on me . . .
T	Expression of trust	I have trusted in your goodness . . .
G/I	Confession of guilt/ Assertion of innocence	(lacking in Ps. 13)
P	Pledge of praise	I shall sing . . .

While the order and number of these elements may vary, the laments of the individual are essentially "petitions in which the element of petition plays the central role within the larger framework. Their situation in life can be generally described as follows: An afflicted person turns for help and deliverance to the mighty one, to God, who is close to him. The prayers or lament mirror a classic situation of petition."[32]

Beyond this, what is characteristic of the structure of lament—aside from the general movement from lament to praise[33]—is the *threefold lament section*: The lament is oriented toward YHWH (*God lament / Accusation of God*), toward the supplicant himself (*self-lament*), and toward his enemies (*enemy lament*). All three components are found in Psalm 13:1–2 (2–3):[34]

How long, YHWH? Will you forget me forever? **God**
How long will you hide your face from me?

30. In these short laments, "the petition is implicitly contained; they are at the same time a protest against adversity and a plea for deliverance from distress" (Albertz, "Gebet," 36). Other examples are given by Westermann, "Struktur und Geschichte der Klage," 150ff. A collection of texts organized on the basis of form-critical and historical aspects is provided by Miller, *They Cried to the Lord*. Even if the element of thanksgiving dominates, the names of the saving responses by God (replacement of a dead child, granting of a request, assistance, protection, deliverance, etc.) point implicitly to a situation of adversity; at times the context or an aetiology (cf. 1 Sam. 1:20) sheds light on the situation in question; see Albertz, *Persönliche Frömmigkeit*, 49ff.; idem, "Gebet," 38; Rechenmacher, *Personennamen als theologische Aussagen*, 84ff.

31. On form-historical aspects, see Westermann, "Struktur und Geschichte der Klage"; Gerstenberger, *Der bittende Mensch*, 118ff.; idem, *Psalms, Part 1*, 11ff; Krieg, *Todesbilder*, 333ff.; Bail, *Gegen das Schweigen klagen*, 56ff.; Janowski and Schwemer, *Hymnen, Klagelieder*. On the form and fuction of the lament in ancient religions, see Jaques, *Klagetraditionen*. On the genre of laments and Psalms of Lament aside from the individual laments, see Berges, *Klagelieder*, 36ff.; and Keel, "Profil der Klagelieder." On Ps. 13, see 57ff. below. On the lament of Job 3, see Bauks, *Die Feinde des Psalmisten*, 55ff.; and Ha, *Frage und Antwort*.

32. Gerstenberger, *Der bittende Mensch*, 126.

33. See discussion 45ff. below.

34. On the interpretation of Ps. 13, see 57ff. below.

How long shall I bear sorrows in my *nepeš*, have grief in my heart day after day?	**Supplicant**
How long will my enemy tower above me?	**Enemy**

The same is true mutatis mutandis for the communal lament of the people,[35] as Psalm 80:4–6 (5–7) can show:

YHWH, God of hosts, how long will your wrath smolder against the prayers of your people? (v. 4/5)	**God**
You feed them with bread of tears, and give tears to drink in three measures. (v. 5/6)	**Supplicant**
You make us the source of strife for our neighbors, so that our enemies mock us. (v. 6/7)	**Enemies**

Because of this structure of the lament, which is expressed as the interweaving of the *reference to God* (YHWH/you), *self-reference* (supplicant/I), and *reference to the world* (enemy, enemies / he, they), one can speak of an *anthropological depth dimension of lament*[36] because it addresses the human situation comprehensively. The basic relationships in which the supplicant is involved—relating to God, to the world, to other human beings—are afflicted and put into question. The web of relations can represented as follows for Psalm 13:1–2 (2–3):

Reference to God (you)	How long, **YHWH**, will you forget me?
Reference to self (I)	How long shall **I** bear my sorrows?
Reference to the world (he/they)	How long shall **my enemy** tower over me?

Since a human being, in accordance with the communal orientation of Hebrew thought,[37] does not exist as an isolated "I" but is involved in constitutive constellations within the society in which one lives and acts (*constellatory understanding of the human person*),[38] the lament—and retrospectively the individual's psalm of thanksgiving—refers to the experience of a crisis situation in which different levels of experience (God, self, world) are closely connected. The human concept of the Psalms of Lament and Thanksgiving must therefore be called holistic. Holism in this sense refers to the relation of the lamenting/praising speaker to God and world:

> The lament of the individual refers to the holistic experience of a crisis situation in which the different realms of experience (God, self, environment) are closely connected to each other. The actual situation (illness, accusation,

35. See Hieke, *Psalm 80*, 296ff.

36. See again Westermann, "Die Rolle der Klage," 255ff.; cf. Albertz, "Gebet," 35–36; etc.

37. See esp. Joachim von Soosten, "Die 'Erfindung' der Sünde," 89ff., and cited literature; also Gerstenberger, *Der bittende Mensch*, 147ff.; Di Vito, "Old Testament Anthropology," 221ff.

38. On the constellatory understanding of the human person, see Janowski, "Das biblische Weltbild," 4ff.; following J. Assmann, *Tod und Jenseits*, 13ff., 34ff., 54ff., et al.; cf. also H. Weippert, "Altisraelitische Welterfahrung," 18; Di Vito, "Old Testament Anthropology," 221ff.

suffering) that is the occasion for the lament loses its contours in the representation of the experience in the prayer of lament. The supplicant does not lament a specific illness but calls on God, because one's *whole* world, relation to God, personal existence, and interpersonal relationships have turned negative.[39]

The question Why has the supplicant's whole world turned negative? when or if only a *part* of this world—such as enemies—have turned against the supplicant, will receive more attention in relation to our discussion of the role of enemies.

It is expedient to make an interjection at this point. I have been speaking of the "supplicant" [masculine form, *Beter*] here, but not of the "female supplicant" [feminine form, *Beterin*]. This not out of disregard for the role of women in ancient cultures but for reasons of linguistic simplification. The issue reaches deeper, however, beyond such simplifications and has, within the larger context of our topic, received a contentious note by H. Gunkel. In his *Einleitung in die Psalmen*, he provides detailed explanations of the cultic *Sitz im Leben* for the Psalms of Lament[40] and also addresses the role of women: "One should also add that the singers of the complaint songs were only men. Women do not sing these songs. This also leads one to conclude that in the ancient Israelite view, the complaint song belonged in the worship service, where women had no place."[41] With this observation, Gunkel could hardly have meant that such prayers were not offered by women in ancient Israel because they had no experience of hardship and suffering, but rather because they did not have access to the cult. It is true that, according to the priestly view, menstruation rendered a woman unclean (Lev. 15:19–30; cf. Lev. 12, woman in childbirth), which restricted her from activity in the cult. Nevertheless, women participated in sacrificial meals (cf. 1 Sam. 1:4–5) and could of course also pray for themselves or make their own vows within the context of a local cult,[42] as in the temple at Shiloh (1 Sam 1:10–11). The (late) Song of Hannah of 1 Samuel 2:1–10 comes to mind (a "hymn of the individual"),[43] which she offered, as the context specifies, after the unexpected birth of her son Samuel. In it are found verses that praise YHWH's power (to save from death) and greatness in polar metaphors.

Excursus 2: The Whole Human Being

"It is not the senses that sense, it is not the brain that thinks; with the help of senses and organs given to a person, it is the entire human being that senses, thinks, acts" (Wiesenhütter and Stokvis, *Mensch in der Entspannung*, 43). The formula "whole human being [*ganzer Mensch*]" seeks to generalize what this

39. Seidel, *Auf den Spuren der Beter*, 21, emphasis original; cf. also Gerstenberger, *Der bittende Mensch*, 153ff., 156ff.

40. Gunkel and Begrich, *Introduction to Psalms*, 123–30.

41. Ibid., 126.

42. This subject has been researched more extensively in recent years; see Bird, "Place of Women"; Bechmann, "Frau I," 695; Gerstenberger, "Weibliche Spiritualität"; Miller, *They Cried to the Lord*, 233ff.; Bail, *Gegen das Schweigen klagen*, 78ff.; Braulik, "Durften auch Frauen in Israel opfern?" See also I. Fischer, "Zwischen Kahlschlag, Durchforstung"; idem, "Egalitär entworfen"; Hossfeld, "Die Aufwertung Hannas"; Eder and I. Fischer, *Zur Brisanz der Geschlechterfrage*.

43. See, e.g., Bartelmus, "Tempus als Strukturprinzip"; Tita, *Gelübde als Bekenntnis*, 71ff.; et al.

sentence expresses with regard to a physician and the interaction with the patients. It objects to the partition of the human person that is the result of dichotomous or trichotomous views of humanity and thereby takes up the protest, already noted in the anthropology of the Enlightenment, against the separation of body and spirit (see Hastedt, *Leib-Seele-Problem*; A. Hahn and Jacob, "Der Körper als soziales Bedeutungssystem"; H. Böhme, Matussek, and Müller, *Orientierung Kulturwissenschaft*, 133ff.).

The Old Testament also knows of the "whole human being" without having a corresponding expression for it. M. Krieg ("Leiblichkeit im Alten Testament," 14ff.) has therefore defined four relational dimensions and their interconnected links: the *vital* dimension: the relation of the human being to oneself (bodily sphere); the *personal* dimension: the relation of the human being to one's own actions (action-result relationship); the *social* dimension: the relation of the human being to the environment (social sphere); and the *transcendental* dimension: the relation of the human being to one's own intellect (figurative language). The human person is always in a holistic relation to these four dimensions. "Wholeness or increase of one relational dimension means life. Full life then would be (eschatologically) greatest closeness and relationality. On the other hand, injury or decrease of one relational dimension means death. Accordingly, complete death would be (hamartologically) the greatest distance and lack of relationality" (ibid., 21).

The integrating purpose of the formula "whole human being" (see Rössler, "Mensch, ganzer") can also be explained on the basis of the fundamental anthropological concepts of the Old Testament (see Albertz, "Mensch"; also Jürgen Kegler, "Beobachtungen zur Körpererfahrung"; S. Schroer and Staubli, *Körpersymbolik der Bibel*, 77ff.). The crucial element in the concept of the "whole human being," however, is the *correlation of the view of the body and the structure of society*. As wholeness and health belong to the bodily sphere, integrity and vitality belong to the social sphere (on the "constellary concept of the person," see Di Vito, "Old Testament Anthropology," 221ff.; Janowski, "Mensch IV"). "The wholeness and vitality of the social self is as essential for life as wholeness and health of the bodily self. With the birth of the body, life is given only as a possibility, which is only actualized through the development of a social self in the process of socialization" (Jan Assmann, *Tod und Jenseits*, 16; cf. 34ff., 54ff.). As the Psalms of Lament of the individual show, whenever enmity, illness, or legal adversity dominate, the process of socialization also breaks down. Forces take effect that dissolve the integration of the human being in the social sphere. As we shall see in more detail later, the Psalms of Lament and Thanksgiving localize these forces in the figure of the enemy (see below, 97ff.).

A notable example for the significance of the social sphere is provided by Ecclesiastes 4:9–12. The critique of individualism in Ecclesiastes 1:12–2:26 calls into the question the orientation of actions on the basis of one's own desires and emphasizes instead the importance of human work within "the framework of a fundamental solidarity with fellow human beings" (T. Krüger, *Kohelet*, 192). Already Genesis 2:18 says, "It is not good that the human being should be alone" (see Keel and S. Schroer, *Schöpfung: Biblische Theologien*, 147–48, 53–54. See also the references in section 22ff.

From Lament to Praise

YHWH kills and gives life;
he brings down to the realm of the dead
and brings up [again].
(1 Sam. 2:6)
YHWH makes poor and makes rich;
he brings low and raises up again. (v. 7)
He lifts the lowly from the dust,
raises the poor from the ashes,
makes [them] sit among nobles,
lets them inherit a seat of honor.
For his are the pillars of the world,
and on them he has founded the earth. (v. 8)

The God before whom Hannah laments her childlessness and who hears her prayer (1 Sam. 1:19ff.) is the same God who had previously closed her womb (1:5). The lament does not resolve the tension, which 1 Samuel 2:6–7 builds up, but puts voice to it—in two antithetical lines about YHWH, coming from a woman's lips. The way in which YHWH deals with Hannah is therefore a characteristic example of how YHWH can intercede in human lives and change the harshest adversity.[44]

In the preceding discussion, we have examined the structure of the lament on the basis of its constitutive elements: invocation, lament, petition, expression of trust, assertion of innocence / confession of guilt, pledge of praise. This construction varies in individual cases, but it is consistent insofar as it exhibits a *movement from lament to petition or praise*. There is no Psalm of Lament that stays at the level of lament.[45] Even Psalm 88, the "death Psalm" in the Old Testament, which is dominated by the description of adversity and an accusation against God, is characterized in its middle portion (vv. 10–12 [11–13]) by a final appeal to YHWH.[46] In this *appeal function of the lament*, it becomes clear that the purpose of the lament is not the lament itself: "The point of the lament is not a self-depiction of suffering or self-pity, but [to bring] the end of suffering. The lament is an appeal to the one who can end suffering."[47]

Because of this dynamic of prayer, the Psalms of Lament and Thanksgiving of the individual[48] are fundamental texts of a theological anthropology.

44. Cf. Farmer, "Psalms," 139–40; Kessler, "Der antwortende Gott," 53; Millard, *Komposition des Psalters*, 84ff. With regard to the Psalms of Lament and Thanksgiving of the Individual, Gerstenberger notes that descriptions of hardship do not exhibit language specific to women: "Women, . . . according to the example of Hannah, Miriam, and Deborah, participate fully in the masculine language of prayer and conversely men participate in the female (Ps. 131?)": Gerstenberger, "Weibliche Spiritualität," 361; cf. 354ff.; cf. Miller, *They Cried to the Lord*, 237ff. The fact that "a woman's pregnancy and the event of birth itself . . . [can become] a threatening image for the situation of the supplicant and of the suffering righteous" shows in the lament 1QH 11 (*olim* 3). 1–8 from Qumran: Berger, *Psalmen aus Qumran*, 140. Bail, on the other hand, recognizes a female voice in the background to these Psalms and seeks to support this claim through an intertextual reading of Pss. 6 and 55 and 2 Sam. 13:1–22: Bail, *Gegen das Schweigen klagen*, 76ff. On this reading, see also Kselman and Barré, "Psalm 55."

45. Cf. Westermann, "Die Rolle der Klage," 255; also Hossfeld, "Lob I."

46. See 229ff. below.

47. Westermann, "Die Rolle der Klage," 255; cf. also Markschies, "Vertrauensäusserungen," 391; Hossfeld, "Lob I."

48. Due to their retrospective orientation (looking back on past suffering), the songs of thanksgiving of the individual have a more complex temporal structure than the songs of lament. See 254ff. below.

b. The Anthropology of Lament and Thanksgiving

Based on the structure described here, the supplicant moves along a path leading *from the lament*—with its components of God-lament, self-lament, and enemy-lament—to *the praise of God*. This implies that the crisis situation is *transcended* in the process of prayer. By bringing one's suffering before God, the afflicted person reaches for an end to the suffering. In this sense, the Psalms of Lament testify to a fundamental trust in God: they are spoken within a situation of [seeming] abandonment by God, but nevertheless with the hope that God is near, especially in this affliction. Westermann notes: "If it is understood in this way, the Psalm of Lament, indicating direction toward the end of suffering, is one of the strongest testimonies to the experience of God's actions in the Old Testament."[49]

In addition to *reference to God*, the lament of the individual incorporates a second component, *reference to the world*. The supplicant appeals to God because this lamenter's entire world has changed as a result of enmity, illness, legal adversity, being ostracized, and loneliness.[50] Central to the experience of these adversities is always the *experience of disintegration* or exclusion from the social space of family, friends, or specific communities. The supplicant, whose life has been embedded in the community, moves "to the edge" in this situation, or "into the realm" of death.[51] Here we encounter a specific *understanding of life and death* that is significant for the Psalms of Lament and Thanksgiving.[52] To be sure, there is also a view in the Old Testament that a person can die "in old age after a full life"[53] and then is united with the ancestors at burial. It was also known that death can come too soon or unexpectedly, even in the royal house (2 Sam. 12:15–25).[54] Both experiences—death at the end of a full life as well as of a life that has barely begun—fit the insight regarding the inevitability of death, as formulated by the wise woman of Tekoa before David: "We all must die, and we are like water that cannot be gathered up again once it is spilled on the ground; yet God does not take away life, but he devises plans so that an outcast is not banished forever" (2 Sam. 14:14).[55]

In addition to these views of death, there are others that include more than the biological death, such as all forms of "social death," like enmity, disrespect, or loneliness.[56] "Death" and "dying" thus represent the broken world of alien-

49. Westermann, "Die Rolle der Klage," 256.

50. On the main types of the supplicant's adversity, see Krieg, *Todesbilder*, 341ff.; Dietrich, "Unheil"; Fabry, "Leiden II."

51. On the embeddedness of the individual in the social, economic, and legal community, see von Soosten, "Die 'Erfindung' der Sünde," 89–90; Di Vito, "Old Testament Anthropology," 221ff. This social orientation plays an eminent role in the Psalms of the Individual and is a central theme, esp. if it is called into question by social disregard or exclusion. See 229ff. below.

52. For a more detailed discussion, see 254ff. below.

53. Gen. 25:8 (Abraham); 35:29 (Isaac); Job 42:17 (Job); 1 Chr. 29:28 (David); 2 Chr. 24:15 (the priest Jehoiada). See Wächter, *Der Tod*, 64ff.; Warmuth, "שָׂבַע"; Meinhold, "Bewertung," 104; cf. also the idea of dying "at a good age" (Gen. 15:15; Judg. 8:32; etc.); see Stähli, "Tod und Leben," 176; also Liess, "Sättigung"; Neumann-Gorsolke, "Tod zur rechten Zeit."

54. On a "bad death," see Stähli, "Tod und Leben," 176–77.

55. German translation by Stoebe, *Das zweite Buch Samuelis*, 337; on this text and its understanding of death, see Kaiser, "Tod, Auferstehung," 23ff.

56. See C. Barth, *Errettung vom Tode*, 42ff.; also Krieg, *Todesbilder*, 351ff.; Bail, *Gegen das Schweigen klagen*, 57ff.; for the perspectives of comparative religion and cultural criticism, see Hasenfratz, *Die toten Lebenden*; idem, "Zum sozialen Tod"; Macho, *Todesmetaphern*.

ation from God and human beings, which ultimately leads, or can lead, to biological death. In this experiential perspective, "being near death" is something quite different from a temporal category, which merely shortens the remaining life-span.

This experience of "death in the midst of life" (*media vita in morte sumus*)[57] is ubiquitous in the Psalms of Lament. Gunkel notes, "The extreme anger that blows from these poems, or the fierce, agonizing tone that the psalmist takes here, is the place *where the religion of the Psalms confronts death.*"[58]

For this reason, the desired deliverance is a *deliverance from death*—characteristically in richly figurative language, which makes use of the metaphors of "depth" and "height," of "bringing down" (into the Pit/Sheol, etc.) and "pulling up" (from great waters, deep mud, etc.):

> He [YHWH] will stretch out [his hand] from **on high**, take me,
> he will pull me up [מָשָׁה] from **deep waters**.
> He will rescue [נצל Hiphil] me from my powerful enemies,
> and from those who hate me,
> for they were stronger than I.
> (Ps. 18:16–17 [17–18])

> Save [ישׁע Hiphil] me, YHWH,
> for **the water** has come up to my neck!
> (Ps. 69:1/2)
> I have sunk into the **deep mud,**
> and [there is] no foothold,
> I have come into the **depths of the waters**,
> and the current has swept me away. (v. 2/3)

> Rescue [נצל Hiphil] me from the **mud**, that I may not sink,
> that I may be saved from those who hate me
> and from the depths of the waters. (v. 14/15)
> Let the **flood of the waters** not sweep over me,
> and let the **depth** not swallow me,
> and let not the **well** close its mouth over me. (v. 15/16)

> Stretch out your hands from **on high**;
> save me [פָּצָה] and rescue me [נצל Hiphil]
> from mighty waters,
> from the power of strangers,
> whose mouth speaks falsehoods
> and whose right hands [i.e., oaths] are deceitful.
> (Ps. 144:7–8)

These statements of rescue reflect the *direction of the experience* as proceeding *from the bottom upward*: the supplicant understands oneself as being "pulled

57. The phrase *media vita in morte sumus* is based on the church hymn "Mitten wir im Leben sind" (*Das Evangelisches Gesangbuch* [EG], # 518), the first verse of which (Salzburg 1457) follows the identical-sounding 11th c. Latin antiphon; see Franz and Becker, "Mitten wir im Leben sind." The border between life and death, on which the experience of "death in the midst of life" is based, was defined differently in ancient cultures than it is in ours; see "Excursus 7: Life and Death," 239-40 below.
58. Gunkel and Begrich, *Introduction to Psalms*, 131.

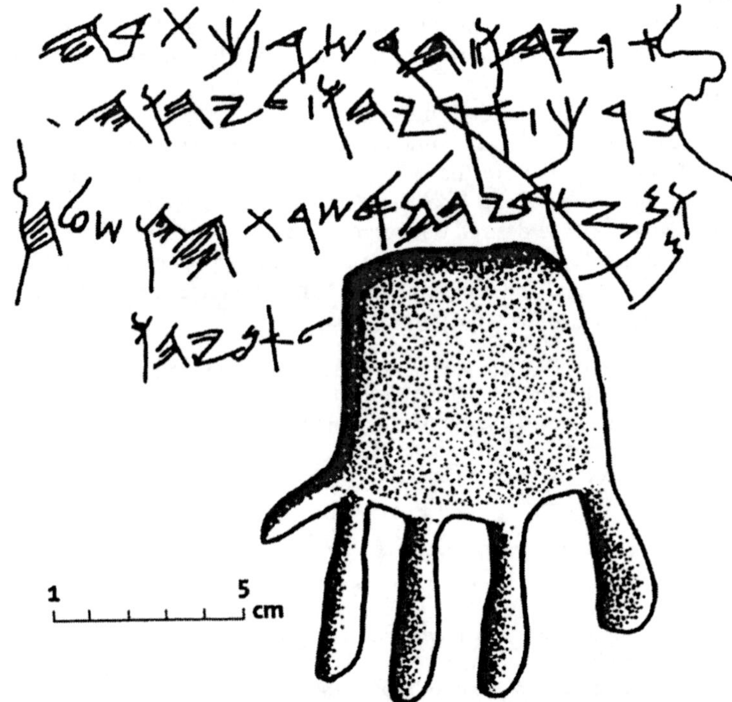

Figure 9. Hand symbol from Ḫirbet el-Qôm (SE of Lachish, 8th c. BCE)

up" or "led upward" by the hand of YHWH from a situation of existence that is situated lower.[59] A graphic example for this idea is the hand symbol (fig. 9) found next to funerary inscription 3 at Ḫirbet el-Qôm (or Khirbet el-Qôm; late 8th c. BCE):[60]

1. ʾŪrīyahû, the rich has [let it be] written.
2. Blessed was ʾŪrīyahû before YHWH.
3. And from his enemies he has saved [*yšʿ* Hiphil] him
   because of his Ashera / his Ashera's will

59. On verbs expressing rescue, see C. Barth, *Errettung vom Tode*, 98ff.

60. On the text, see Renz and Röllig, *Althebräischen Epigraphik*, 207ff.; also Jeremias and Hartenstein, "'JHWH und seine Aschera,'" 115ff.; Janowski, "Die Toten loben JHWH nicht," 14–15. See also Leuenberger, "'Deine Gnade,'" 354–55: "Keeping in mind . . . that like life, blessing was understood temporally, a blessing at the boundary of life—or even clearly beyond it: in the tomb of Uriyahu, i.e., within the realm of death—is most remarkable. For it clearly shows that YHWH was ascribed a (continuing) influence in the realm of death—regardless of whether we are dealing with a blessing or a request for a blessing. Thus YHWH's jurisdiction—at least with regard to the individual—has expanded beyond this life to include the realm of death, which is no longer unrelated to YHWH, but is subject at least to YHWH's influence." I agree with this position. For a different interpretation, see Köckert ("Wandlungen Gottes," esp. 11ff., 28), who bases his skepticism on the arguably controversial interpretation of the symbolism of the hand ("right hand of God" as apotropaic), but not on the inscription itself. In addition, Köckert speaks of YHWH as the "patron god of the deceased" (ibid., 29). Regardless of the interpretation, however, the point is that we are dealing with a tomb and death, i.e., with YHWH's active—in this case protective—relationship to the deceased. See also Eberhardt, *JHWH und die Unterwelt*, 366ff., 388ff.; and the discussion with Janowski, "Der Gott Israels," 283ff., and literature cited there.

4. By ʾŌnīyahû
5. and by his Ashera.
6. [. . . ?] and by his A[sh]era.

The hand symbol probably signifies the [back of the] right hand of God[61] and thus the "representation of divine protection and divine salvation, not of an unknown numen, but of YHWH, as experienced by the owner of the grave while he was alive."[62] At the same time, the hand symbol is an iconographic commentary on the corresponding statements of rescue in the individual psalms cited above (Pss. 18:16–17 [17–18]; 69:1–2, 14–15 [2–3, 15–16]; 144:7–8).

Let us summarize: The tripartite structure of the lament reveals a view of the human person "in which the existence of the individual human being without the community of which one is part (social orientation), and without relation to God (theological orientation), is not conceivable."[63] All three aspects—*reference to God*, *self-reference*, and *reference to the world*—belong together in the sense of mutuality, which I had called relationality above.[64] The human person is, according to the Old Testament view, a *constellary being*: involved in the fundamental constellations of the society in which the individual lives and acts.[65] This social orientation is also the key for the understanding of "life" and "death" in the Psalms of the Individual.[66]

Life

"Life" is the principle of strength that ties everything together. The Psalms call such a life "righteous" (צַדִּיק), expressing this righteousness by means of very specific semantics, which focus on the involvement of the individual in a social community (*social sphere of the human person*). A text that exemplifies this is Psalm 15, which responds to the question of the right to hospitality in God's "tent" and on the "mountain of his sanctuary" (v. 1b) with a catalog of basic rules of conduct.

A Psalm of David

YHWH, who dwells as guest in your tent,
who lives lies on the mountain of your sanctuary?
(Ps. 15:1)

The person who walks blamelessly and who does justice,
who speaks in one's heart what is trustworthy, (v. 2)

61. See the interpretation in Mittmann, "Symbol der Hand."

62. Jeremias and Hartenstein, "'JHWH und seine Aschera,'" 116–17.

63. Westermann, "Die Rolle der Klage," 257. On the theological anthropology of the individual's Psalms of Lament and Thanksgiving, see Berges, *Klagelieder*, 38–39; Achenbach, "Klagegebete II"; Ballhorn, "Gefährliche Doxologie," 12ff.; R. G. Kratz, "Klage"; idem, "Lob/Dank"; for a systematic theological position, see Harasta, *Lob und Bitte*; and Dirscherl, *Grundriß theologischer Anthropologie*, 65ff.

64. Cf. 42–44 above.

65. On the term "constellary person," see 44 above.

66. Cf. Matthias Krieg, "Leiblichkeit," 20–21; idem, *Todesbilder*, 351ff., 612ff.; Di Vito, "Old Testament Anthropology," 225ff. On the comparable Egyptian view of life and death, see J. Assmann, *Tod und Jenseits*, 34ff., esp. 39. See also Weber, "Lob und Klage"; Liess, *Der Weg des Lebens*; idem, "Tod II"; idem, "Von der Gottesferne"; Pola, "Was ist 'Leben'?"; Leuenberger, "'Deine Gnade'"; Zenger, "Funktion der Todesbilder"; Janowski, "Gott, Mensch und Raum," 18ff.; Frevel, "Leben"; Riede, "Was ist 'Leben'?"; cf. also the references in chap. 6, section b (188ff.)

who has not borne slander on the tongue,
  who has not done evil to the neighbor,
  who has not brought shame on the neighbor, (v. 3)

in whose eyes the wicked person is despised,
  but who honors those who fear YHWH,
who has sworn to [one's own] hurt
  and does not change it [even then], (v. 4)
who has not lent his money for usury,
  who has not taken a bribe against the innocent. (v. 5ab)

The person who does these things shall never falter [מוט]. (v. 5c)[67]

The psalm concludes that the person who acts in this way "shall never falter" (v. 5c). "Faltering" (מוט) is no ordinary word here, as we shall see in the example of Psalm 13:4/5:

Death

"Death," on the other hand, is the principle of disintegration that dissolves and isolates. The Psalms call such a life as "marked by death"[68] and express this mark of death with similarly specific semantics, which focuses in particular on the body of the afflicted person and the variety of its limbs and organs (*bodily sphere of the human person*). A text that exemplifies this is Psalm 13:3–4 (4–5), which makes the promise of 15:5c, that such a person "shall never falter," the object of a petition:

Look here and answer me, YHWH my God!
  Let my eyes shine, that I do not sleep in death,
that my enemy may not claim: "I have prevailed!"
  and my opponent not rejoice that I am faltering [מוט]!
(Ps. 13:3–4 [4–5])

Again, the verb "falter/stagger" (מוט) indicates a motif with a "evocative reference to the chaotic."[69]

As the life/death dichotomy shows paradigmatically, in the Old Testament understanding "personal identity" is based on the relationship of *bodily sphere* and *social sphere*. The complexity and internal differentiation of these two spheres can be illustrated with the following outline:

Bodily Sphere of the Human Person

Positive	*Negative*
health	illness
vitality	"paralysis due to terror"
light	darkness
satisfaction	hunger, thirst
joy	mourning
"old and full of life"	early death

67. On this text (as well as Ps. 24), see Beyerlin, *Weisheitlich-Kultische Heilsordnung*; Otto, *Theologische Ethik*, 94ff.; Podella, "Transformationen," 108ff.; Zenger, "'Ich liebe den Ort,'" 195ff.
68. On the expression "marked by death" (*Todesbefallenheit*), see J. Assmann, "Todesbefallenheit im alten Ägypten."
69. Steck, *Friedensvorstellungen*, 37 n. 85; see 72–73 below.

Social Sphere of the Human Person

Positive	*Negative*
justice	legal adversity
honor	shame
communication	silence
community	loneliness
freedom	captivity
integrity	sin

"Life" means connectivity:[70] the integration of the individual into the social fabric, which is the basis for communal life. "Death," on the other hand, means dissolution and destruction of these connections, which provide support for the individual within the community and before God. Life can therefore end even before death if the social bonds loosen and the forces take effect, which the Psalter associates again and again with the person of the enemy[71] (*social death*).[72] Bodily sphere and social sphere, body and social structure, therefore correspond to each other. The analysis of Psalm 13 (in chap. 3 below), which Gunkel has rightly called the "model of a lament of the individual,"[73] will show how fundamental this correspondence is.

But first let us return to the point of departure for our discussion, to the question of human nature: "What is a human being?" This is the basic question of every anthropology, theological as well as philosophical. The Old Testament text that poses it then develops it further by a reference to the providential "remembering" of God, which, as we saw, is among the honorific designations of human beings: A human being is a human being, because God "remembers" and "cares for" the person (Ps. 8:4/5).[74] The Psalms also know of God's "forgetting," which is more than an incidental refusal to think of someone. It is the "dark counterpart" of God's "remembering," the cancellation of every relationship of the Creator to his creature. "In the state of true forgetting, there is no before and after, no earlier or later, no yesterday or tomorrow, not even a Now, that could connect the times."[75] Psalm 13 illustrates the drama of this loss or abandonment: in a prayer the supplicant fearfully inquires of the duration of forgetting—and directs this inquiry to no one other than "YHWH my God."

The fundamental question of anthropology is Who or what is a human being? The Old Testament asks this question several times (Pss. 8:4/5; 144:3; Job 7:17–18) yet offers a different answer in each case. Even if there is no such thing as *the* Old Testament view of the human being, "but only complementary and at times contrasting aspects" (Frevel, "Anthropologie," 1), it is nevertheless necessary to inquire about its constituents. In my essay "Mensch im alten

70. Following J. Assmann, *Tod und Jenseits*, 13ff., 34ff., 54ff., etc., who uses the term "connectivity" also in reference to the Egyptian view of the body. The relationship between *bodily sphere and social sphere* also plays a central role in current cultural studies; on this see Wulf, *Anthropologie*, 137ff.; Tanner, *Historische Anthropologie*, 123ff.; Burke, *Was ist Kulturgeschichte?*, 105ff; M. Schroer, *Soziologie des Körpers*; A. Assmann, *Kulturwissenschaft*, 89ff.; G. Böhme, *Ethik leiblicher Existenz*, 119ff., 165ff.; and from the perspective of Old Testament anthropology, Gruber and Michel, "Körper"; Janowski and Bester, "Anthropologie."

71. On the subject of enemies, see 97ff. below.

72. See above, 46, n. 56.

73. Gunkel, *Die Psalmen*, 46; cf. 60 below.

74. See 12–13 above.

75. Sofsky, *Zeiten des Schreckens*, 203.

Israel," I have suggested developing an Old Testament anthropology on the basis of the components "unity of the person," "social sphere," and "perception of the world" and to define it as "constellative anthropology" (J. Assmann). The term "constellation" points to the complex relationships and contexts that give meaning and direction to human life (cf. J. Assmann, "Maʿat—Gemeinschaftskunst"; K. Neumann, "Kultur und Mentalität," 38f.; and Janowski, "Anerkennung und Gegenseitigkeit"). The individual components can be further described as follows:

The Unity of the Person

Characteristic of Old Testament anthropology is the correlation of bodily organs and vital functions. In contrast to dichotomous or trichotomous views of the human being and their conception of body/soul or body/soul/spirit, the Old Testament—as seen on the basis of its fundamental anthropological concepts—assumes an integrative understanding of the "whole human being." Since the body anchors the human being in the world, another constitutive element besides the bodily sphere is the social sphere.

The Social Sphere

Another feature of Old Testament anthropology is the concept of community orientation in Hebrew thought, as a result of which the behavior of the individual is consistently seen in relation to the social context in which it takes place. The human being is therefore a "constellative" being, integrated into a social community. The term "constellation" gives expression to complex, mutually oriented relations of human existence (man/woman, individual/community, God/human being).

The Perception of the World

Every religion, including that of ancient Israel, possesses a system of symbols or a worldview on the basis of which it claims the authority to structure reality as a whole and to provide interpretations for the conduct of life of the individual. Familiarity with religious symbol systems has provided the chance to resolve the tensions between the imagined world order and its factual ambivalences in favor of cosmos-preserving forces and thus to answer affirmatively the question of the coherence of reality.

According to the Old Testament, the human being in ancient Israel moved in all three contexts at the same time—the *individual*, the *social*, and the *religious contexts*—whereby the emphasis of each textual example differs depending on its literary profile and place in history. Added to this is the decidedly *theological character* of Old Testament anthropology: in an elementary sense, the human being in the Old Testament is characterized not only by the person's openness to the world, but also—and especially—by one's relation to God. This relation to God is addressed already in the first chapter of the Bible, which speaks in Genesis 1:26–28 of the creation of the human being in the "image of God" and of its designation to rule over the animals and to make use of the earth (see Janowski, "Die lebendige Statue Gottes"; for a systematic position, see Dirscherl, *Grundriß theologischer Anthropologie*, 109ff.). As "image of God" the human being has a twofold orientation toward *God* and toward the *world*, being designated by God to "rule" and exercise this rule over nonhuman creatures. Relation to God and to the world together characterize the nature of the human being, which does justice to the relation to the world only by acting *responsibly in reference to the Creator* (cf. Keel and S. Schroer, *Schöpfung*, 173ff.).

The basic question of all anthropology, "What is a human being?," receives in Genesis 1:26–28 an answer comparable with that of Psalm 8. The human being is human, according to Psalm 8:4/5, because YHWH is mindful of the person and benevolently looks after each one (cf. Ps. 144:3). The *intentionality* inherent in the verb פָּקַד ("be mindful < think of") and the action resulting from it—these are also characteristic for the parallel זָכַר, which gives expression to YHWH's providence in the sense of a benevolent interest in human affairs ("look after, take into view"): YHWH does not abandon the human being in situations of acute need, but "in such situations is always compassionately and benevolently concerned with the person, so that YHWH attentively cares for each and inquires of any needs" (Schnieringer, *Psalm 8*, 231; also see Janowski, "Schöpferische Erinnerung"). This attentiveness of God is focused on *all human beings* and, as the protasis of Psalm 8:3/4 demonstrates, with its reference to the majestic height and breadth of the heavens and its constellations (moon and stars), is directed at human beings in their *smallness and frailness*. Thus it serves the exposition of the Creator's greatness (Ps. 8:1b + 9 [2b + 10]!) and with it "the grace, that consists of the great God's inclination to the small/frail human being" (Schnieringer, *Psalm 8*, 233; cf. Irsigler, "Frage nach dem Menschen," 12f., 21f., 25, 39ff., 42ff.; Janowski, "Anerkennung und Gegenseitigkeit").

In Psalm 8:5, פָּקַד continues the intended meaning of זָכַר and even intensifies it by adding to the *mental* aspect ("be mindful < think of") a *sensory* aspect ("look after, take into view"), exhibiting the *decision to intervene with action* (cf. Schnieringer, *Psalm 8*, 231; on the parallelism of the two verbs, see Jer. 14:10; 15:15; Hos. 8:13; 9:9; and Ps. 106:4). YHWH does not merely remember from afar, from the heavens, but also comes to the aid of the human being (פָּקַד) who is in need of such saving help. Thus the statement that YHWH "is mindful" does not mean that God remembers a specific matter while forgetting another, but rather that YHWH "institutes a reality in the coherencies of a creature's life that is not realized in such dual abstractions themselves" (Schüle, "Gottes Handeln," 269). Through God's attentiveness the human being attains a dignity founded in being included by the creativity of God, in YHWH's providential "mindfulness" and "looking after" each one (see also Ringleben, "Was ist der Mensch?"; Frevel, "Würde").

Part 1
From Life to Death

3. "How long will you hide your face?" (Ps. 13:1/2)
The Complaining Human Being

a. The Hiddenness of God

David

But at the age of manhood
he, the father of poets, measured
in desperation
the distance to God,
and built the shelters of the Psalms
for those worn down by the journey.
Nelly Sachs, *Fahrt ins Staublose*, 104

α. God Near and Distant

"I call you from afar; hear me from nearby!" With this formula,[1] found in numerous Babylonian invocations, the Mesopotamian supplicant turns to the deity in the hope of care, well-being, and protection against all hardships of life.[2] The correlation of "calling" and "hearing" is a fundamental form of encountering the divine, which was developed in rich forms in Mesopotamia, as in this prayer:

> I call on you, O mistress, come and hear what I am saying!
> I call on you, O lord, hear me from nearby, save the breath of my life!
> Most glorious of goddesses, great and mighty mistress, I call on you,
> hasten to my help![3]

The cited formula of prayer (above) receives its incisiveness from the juxtaposition of the adverbs of location "from afar" (*ruqiš*) and "from nearby" (*qerbiš*). The supplicant calls the deity "from afar, from a remote position," in order to overcome the distance that lies between self and god: "'Remoteness' and 'distance' are two conceptually spatial terms that serve to put into words the

1. See Mayer, "'Ich rufe dich'"; also the collection of texts in W. Mayer, *"Gebetsbeschwörungen,"* 130ff. In its simplest form the formula is this: "Hereby I call on you, O god [name of the god]: hear me!" Cf. Mayer, "'Ich rufe dich,'" 305. The invocation of god to hear or be close, or the report of a petition that was received—these are also reflected in the conventions of naming; see W. Mayer, *"Gebetsbeschwörungen,"* 130 n. 23; Mayer, "'Ich rufe dich,'" 307 n. 28; Braulik, "Weisheit, Gottesnähe," 81.
2. On the Mesopotamian motif of a god's turning away, see Perlitt, "Die Verborgenheit Gottes."
3. Texts provided in Mayer, "'Ich rufe dich,'" 305.

difference in nature of the deity and his realm."[4] The supplicant, aware of being distant from the inscrutable gods, turns to them from the place of praying, "from afar," humble and pleading, asking to hear them "from nearby." What is asked for is the attention that turns toward the supplicant and responds accordingly:

> As a further specification of this attention, one first might expect a statement about the ways and means in which this calling from afar should be perceived or rather received—in other words, a *modal* specification. A "nearby" hearing would be one in which remoteness and distance have been removed and are no longer there. If "remoteness" is understood spatially here, it would mean, "Hear me loud and clear"; however, if remoteness and distance are understood figuratively, comparable to the way we speak of "distant behavior" in our language, it would mean, "Listen to me attentively, with interest, willingly, promptly" (in contrast to listening "unapproachably, uncaringly, distantly, indifferently," as in the semantic field of *rūqu*, the antonym of *qerbu*).[5]

The Old Testament also shares this experience of the distance and concealment of God, but always counters this experience with the certainty of the Deity's closeness.[6] This is true not only for the great Deuteronomistic prayer at the dedication of the temple in 1 Kgs. 8:14–66,[7] with its inner tension of the closeness and distance of God (cf. Jer. 23:23), but also for the late-Deuteronomistic text of Deuteronomy 4:5–8, which praises YHWH as a God who is "close" to all the calls of his people:

See,
  I [hereby] teach you laws and statutes,
    as YHWH my God has commanded me,
  so that you may act accordingly in the land,
    which you will enter in order to take possession of it.
                                        (Deut. 4:5)
  You shall heed [them] and act [accordingly]!
    For this is your wisdom and your insight in the eyes of the peoples,
  who will hear all these laws and say:
    "Indeed, a wise and insightful people
    [is] this great nation." (v. 6)
  For what great nation [is there],
    that has a God [as] close to it[8]
    as YHWH our God,
    whenever we call on him? (v. 7)
  And what great nation [is there],
    that [has] laws and statutes [as] just,
    as all this teaching
    that I put before you today? (v. 8)[9]

4. Ibid., 312.

5. Ibid., 315.

6. See the outline in Kaiser, *Gott des Alten Testaments*, 2:128ff.

7. See Braulik, "Weisheit, Gottesnähe," 75ff.; Nentel, *Trägerschaft und Intentionen*, 187ff.; Janowski, "'Ich will,'" 127ff.

8. The Hebrew text is אֱלֹהִים קְרֹבִים אֵלָיו. On other relevant examples for the closeness of YHWH, see Janowski, "'Ich will,'" 134 n. 64.

9. On the translation and text arrangement, see Braulik, "Weisheit, Gottesnähe," 54–55. On this text see also Braulik, "'Weisheit' im Buch Deuteronomium"; and Miller, "Deuteronomy and Psalms," 8; on 5, Miller also uses the example of "God's closeness" to document a structural analogy between Deuteronomistic language and the language of the Psalms.

Spatial categories like YHWH, or rather his name, dwelling on the earth / in the heavens, on which 1 Kgs. 8:46ff. still reflects,[10] are absent here. There is also no mention of the temple. Instead, Israel is characterized by *wisdom* and *closeness to God*.

> They had wisdom in their king Solomon and closeness to God in the temple that was built by him. It is here that the reinterpreting correction of the exilic period takes effect. Israel always possesses wisdom, even if it no longer has Solomon, and God is close to YHWH's people whenever and wherever they call on YHWH, even if the temple does not exist anymore.[11] The closeness of YHWH is a direct "call-hear-answer contact."[12]

The affirmation of YHWH's closeness, as promised by the exilic text of Deuteronomy 4:5–8,[13] does not preclude the experience of adversity in the present, but on the contrary makes it all the more severe. This is also specifically attested by those Psalms of Lament in which the lexemes קרב, "(to be) near," and קרא, "to call," occur more frequently with reference to each other,[14] or those in which expressions of *pleas, appeals, calling out to God*, or *seeking refuge with God* are found.[15] Here the complaint over God's remoteness or concealment of God can be articulated in different ways. What is central is the complaint over YHWH's *hidden face*, over the *silence*, the *forgetting*, the *not hearing*, and YHWH's *not seeing*. This context includes Psalm 13, with its theme of the concealment of God.

β. Psalm 13 as a Case Study

For the choirmaster. A Psalm of David.

How long, YHWH? Will you forget me forever?
  How long will you hide your face from me?
        (Ps. 13:1/2)
How long shall I bear sorrows in my *nepeš*,
  grief in my heart day after day?
How long will my enemy rise above me? (v. 2/3)

Look here and hear me, YHWH my God!
  Let my eyes shine, so that I will not sleep the sleep of death, (v. 3/4)
that my enemy cannot claim: "I have prevailed over him,"
  and my opponents rejoice that I am stumbling! (v. 4/5)

But I—I have trusted in your goodness,
  my heart rejoices over your salvation: (v. 5/6ab)
"I shall sing to YHWH for what he has done for me!" (v. 6/6cd)

10. See Janowski, "'Ich will,'" 129ff.
11. Braulik, "Spuren einer Neubearbeitung," 32–33.
12. Braulik, "Weisheit, Gottesnähe," 253.
13. The motif of the averting/hiding of God is esp. characteristic of the exilic period; see Perlitt, "Anklage und Freispruch Gottes"; cf. Perlitt, "Die Verborgenheit Gottes," 14ff.; Lindström, *Suffering and Sin*, 65ff.; Gross, "Das verborgene Gesicht Gottes," 185ff.; Brueggemann, *Theology of the Old Testament*, 318ff., 333ff.; Emmendörffer, *Der ferne Gott*; Hermisson, "Der verborgene Gott."
14. Pss. 34:17–18 (18–19); 69:3/4, 18/19; 119:145–52; 145:18; cf. Isa. 55:6; Lam. 3:57.
15. Pss. 17:6; 88:1/2; 119:58, 145; 130:1; 140:6/7; 141:1; 142:5/6; 143:6; etc.; see also Perlitt, "Die Verborgenheit Gottes," 13; Mayer, "'Ich rufe dich,'" 306–7.

Textual Notes

1/2. The interrogative adverb עַד־אָנָה, "how long," asks about the duration and stands therefore in semantic tension to נֶצַח, which functions adverbially here, meaning "forever, completely," as in Pss. 74:10; 79:5; and 89:46/47, in each case with לָנֶצַח (cf. Irsigler, "Psalm-Rede," 77).

2/3. עֵצוֹת as the plural of עֵצָה, "plan, contemplation," may be kept (cf. LXX, Vulgate); a proposed emendation to עַצֶּבֶת, "pain, infliction, grief," or to its plural, עַצְּבוֹת (cf. Seybold, *Psalmen: Eine Einführung*, 64) is unnecessary since the "plans, contemplations" refer to the plight of the supplicant and are therefore "sorrowful thoughts, sorrows," which torment the complainant daily; compare Prov. 27:9; Sir. 30:21: "Do not give yourself over to sorrow, // and let not your contemplations [עֵצָה] cause you to fall." (See Kraus, *Psalmen*, 1:239; Hossfeld and Zenger, *Die Psalmen*, 1:97; etc.).

2/3. Here יוֹמָם, "by day," is not in contradistinction to night ("at night"; cf. the addition by LXX$^{A, al.}$, Syr^{h}), but climactically ("even by day," i.e., always at night; cf. Hossfeld and Zenger, *Die Psalmen*, 1:97–98) or in the sense of "daily, day by day"; the addition of καὶ νυκτός, "and by night" (LXX$^{A, al.}$, Syr^{h}) is unnecessary. According to ibid., 96, there are several indications that v. 2/3 is a later addition, which "might have been done through an exilic redaction by the poor who are responsible for the composition of [Pss.] 11–14."

3/4. Here אִישַׁן הַמָּוֶת is a shorter form of אִישַׁן שְׁנַת הַמָּוֶת, "I sleep the sleep of death > I succumb to the sleep of death" (see GKC §117r, note 1; and Jer. 51:39).

4/5. According to O. Steck ("Klage und Bitte," 61–62), the second colon does not relate to the conjunction פֶּן, "lest," in the first colon but is rather the introduction to v. 5/6a: "My opponents rejoice that I am stumbling, But I—I have trusted in your goodness" (against this, see Irsigler, "Psalm-Rede," 73 n. 30).

6/6cd. This is to be understood as the quotation of the shout of joy or the content of the praise indicated in 5/6ab (cf. Hossfeld and Zenger, *Die Psalmen*, 1:97; and esp. Irsligler, "Psalm-Rede," 71–72, 73 n. 31, 81; see also below, 75–76, 83–84).

Psalm 13 is, according to Gunkel, "the model of an 'individual lament' in which the individual elements of the genre are particularly well demarcated."[16] It consists of three parts: a *complaint* with invocation, introduced by the interrogative adverb "how long?"; a *plea* with imperative forms (vv. 3–4 [4–5]) characteristic of the genre; and an *affirmation of trust* with the quotation of a promise of praise (vv. 5–6 [6]).[17]

Complaint

1/2a	God complaint	How long . . . ?	(5 accents)
1/2b	God complaint	How long . . . ?	(5 accents)
2/3a	Self-complaint	How long . . . ?	(5 accents)
2/3b	Self-complaint	[How long] . . . ?	(5 accents)
2/3c	Enemy complaint	How long . . . ?	(5 accents)

16. Gunkel, *Die Psalmen*, 46; see also Janowski, "Das verborgene Angesicht Gottes."

17. On the metrical structure of the text ("layered pyramid structure"), see Seybold, *Psalmen: Eine Einführung*, 61; cf. idem, *Die Psalmen*, 64; Irsigler, "Psalm-Rede," 73–74.

Plea

3/4a	God	Look here . . .	(4 accents)
3/4b	Supplicant	Let my eyes shine . . .	(4 accents)
4/5a	Enemy	that my enemy cannot . . .	(4 accents)
4/5b	Enemy	my opponents [not] . . .	(4 accents)

Trust and Praise

5/6ab	Affirms trusting/rejoicing	But I . . .	(3 + 3 accents)
6/6cd	Promise of praise	I shall sing . . .	(2 + 2 accents)

The individual components of the genre are clearly recognizable and reference each other in the organization of the psalm. The *Complaint* (vv. 1–2 [2–3]) is stylistically ordered by four "How long?" questions, in which three different aspects of the supplicant's affliction are shown:

Reference to YHWH
the withdrawal of YHWH's presence ("forget" // "hide your face") presented in the form of two parallel "How long?" sentences (v. 1/2)

Reference to the supplicant
bearing "sorrows" in the *nepeš* // "grief" in the heart (v. 2/3a)

Reference to the enemy
overpowering and destruction of the supplicant (v. 2/3b)

In contrast, the petition (vv. 3–4 [4–5]) is introduced by three jussives or imperatives (v. 3/4a) characteristic of the genre, with a jussive and an imperative asyndetically ("see" // "hear" + subject YHWH), while the second jussive sentence (3/4b) has two dependent "lest" phrases (פֶּן).[18] Its keyword, "rejoice" (גִּיל), represents a sharp contrast to the affirmation of trust in verse 5/6ab, having two parallel cola with three accents each: "But I—I have trusted in your goodness // my heart rejoices over your salvation"). In the parallelism "I" // "my heart," we encounter the phenomenon of stereometry.[19]

All three aspects of the complaints reappear in the petition section in the same order:

- Reference to *God* (v. 3/4a), who is asked to take notice ("see") and to hear ("answer"). Corresponding to verse 1/2, we also find two verbs in asyndetic parallelism, whereby the statements concerning YHWH constitute a chiasm:

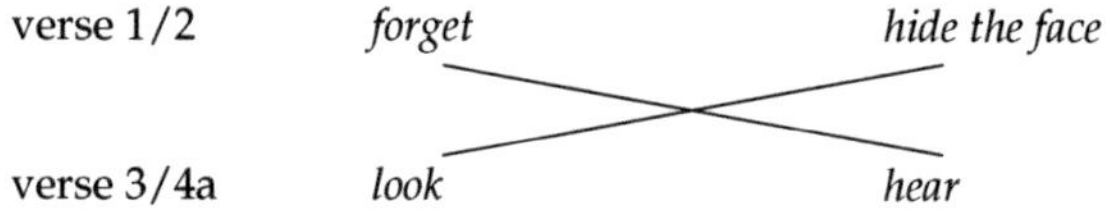

- Reference to the *supplicant* (v. 3/4b), who formulates the antithesis of life and death by means of the metaphor of light ("let shine").

18. See 59 above.
19. See 14ff. above.

- Reference to the *enemy* (v. 4/5), whereby the neutral verb רום, in the "rise"-of-the-enemy complaint of verse 2/3c is further detailed by the two verbs "prevail," יָכֹל (enemy's reaction), and מוט, "stumble" (supplicant's reaction).

There is, however, one stylistic difference that stands out between complaint and petition and points to a concrete problem: while the enemy in the complaint receives a personal "How long?" sentence (v. 2/3b), the enemy is not subject of a plea in the petition section: the supplicant does not ask for the enemy's destruction.[20] This stylistic difference prompts the question of how and by what means the enemy is to be overcome or the end of enmity to be achieved. This is a basic problem in the Psalms of the Individual, which will be treated in greater detail in the context of Psalms 7 and 41.

Thematic Aspects

The typical structure of the individual's complaints is characterized by the subjects of YHWH, supplicant, and enemy, which are placed in relation to each other as communicative units. This corresponds to the tripartite division of the element "complaint" into God-complaint, self-complaint, and enemy-complaint.[21] In certain Psalms (Pss. 4; 11–12; 14; 52; etc.) the communicative units of God, supplicant, and enemy are joined by the group of the "poor," which usually also includes the supplicant.[22] Among the six possible combinations—YHWH-supplicant, supplicant-YHWH, supplicant-enemy, enemy-supplicant, enemy-YHWH, and YHWH-enemy[23]—the following relationships dominate:

- Supplicant-YHWH / YHWH-Supplicant. The most common combination is the relationship supplicant-YHWH or YHWH-supplicant. The relational structure in this case is twofold, as in the following:

> My voice—I call upon YHWH,
> so he answers me from his holy mountain. *Selah.*
> (Ps. 3:4/5)
>
> Justify me, YHWH, according to my righteousness
> and my integrity, which is upon me!
> (Ps. 7:8bc/9bc)[24]
>
> YHWH my God,
> I pleaded before you, and you have healed me.
> (Ps. 30:2/3)

- Supplicant-YHWH-Enemy. The second combination, which also underlies Psalm 13, is the supplicant-YHWH or YHWH-supplicant relationship, in

20. See Odil Hannes Steck, "Klage und Bitte," 59, 61; cf. also Irsigler, "Psalm-Rede," 75 n. 33.
21. See 42 above.
22. See Hossfeld and Zenger, *Die Psalmen*, 2:62ff.
23. Cf. Kleinknecht, *Der leidende Gerechtfertigte*, 25 n.11.
24. On this translation, see 134ff. below.

combination with the YHWH-enemy relationship. The relational structure in now threefold,[25] as here:

> YHWH has heard my pleading,
> YHWH will receive my prayer.
> Let all my enemies be ashamed and deeply dismayed,
> let them turn back in shame at once.
> (Ps. 6:9–10 [10–11])[26]
>
> Let the malice of the wicked come to an end,
> but lift up the just!
> (Ps. 7:9ab/10ab)
>
> See, God is my helper,
> my Lord among those who uphold my life [*nepeš*].
> Let evil be turned back on my adversaries;
> in your faithfulness destroy them!
> (Ps. 54:4–5 [6–7])

- Supplicant-YHWH-Enemy-Poor. Finally, a fourfold relational structure appears, consisting of the supplicant/speaker, YHWH, the enemy/enemies, and the "poor/devout" or a group of "poor/devout" that also includes the supplicant, as found in Psalms 4; 11–12; 14; and 52:[27]

> Help, YHWH, for the devout are no more,
> the faithful among human beings are vanquished.
> (Ps. 12:1/2)
> They speak deceptively, one to another,
> with smooth lips and a double heart they speak. (v. 2/3)
> May YHWH cut off all smooth lips,
> and the tongue that speaks proudly, (v. 3/4)
> and who say: "With our tongues we are powerful,
> our lips are our own—who can be master over us?" (v. 4/5)
> "Because of the oppression of the weak and the groaning of the poor,
> I shall now arise," says YHWH;
> "I shall bring salvation to the one
> against whom they are puffed up." (v. 5/6)[28]

While the twofold relationships of supplicant-YHWH or YHWH-supplicant are readily apparent in their directness, the threefold and fourfold relationships of YHWH-supplicant-enemy or YHWH-supplicant-enemy-poor are more difficult to define. We ask, How is YHWH's negative attention toward the enemy connected to YHWH's positive attention toward the supplicant? This question sounds simple, but it is not. It touches on the central problem of the laments of the individual: When and how shall the affliction of the supplicant come to an end? Through the destruction of the enemy? Or through YHWH, who turns

25. This can be observed paradigmatically in the first five Psalms (Pss. 3–7) of the composition Pss. 3–14, as shown by Hossfeld and Zenger, "'Selig.'"

26. On the translation, cf. Lohfink, "Was wird anders?," 31.

27. See Hossfeld and Zenger, "'Selig.'" On the so-called Psalms of the Poor, see Albertz, *Religionsgeschichte Israels*, 569ff.; Ro, *"Armenfrömmigkeit,"* 113ff.; Sticher, *Die Rettung der Guten*, 303ff.

28. On the text of Ps. 12:5/6, see also Hossfeld and Zenger, *Die Psalmen*, 1:94.

divine attention toward the supplicant and thus puts an end to the works of the enemy? Psalm 13 can help us to delineate this problem in more detail.

1. The Hidden God

In the complaint (vv. 1–2 [2–3]) as well as the petition (vv. 3–4 [4–5]) of Psalm 13, "YHWH" stands at the beginning and is therefore specifically emphasized. The two "How long?" questions of verse 1/2 have a twofold implication: the accusation of God and the hope of an end to affliction.[29] In contrast to Psalm 22:1/2 ("My God, my God, *why* have you forsaken me?"),[30] the question is not of the purpose of God's absence but rather of the duration of God's absence. Neither is a reason for the existence of the affliction given—such as the sin of the supplicant, as in Psalm 51, or YHWH's anger[31]—but it is only stated *that* the affliction persists and what it is in its essence: being forgotten by YHWH, "which threatens to annihilate the person."[32]

The dark and mysterious actions of God, which Psalm 13:1/2 expresses through the parallel expressions "forgetting" (שָׁכַח) // "hiding the face" (הִסְתִּיר פָּנִים),[33] lead to the center of the complaint. However, this way of speaking is not limited to the Psalms of the Individual, but is also found in the "Why?" questions and the "How long?" questions[34] of Lamentations (5:20–22; etc.), the exilic laments of the community (Ps. 44:23–26 [24–27]), and in Second Isaiah (Isa. 40:27–31; etc.). In all cases the problem is the turning away and the hiddenness of God,[35] as in these examples:

> Why would you forget us forever,
>   and abandon us for all times?
>   (Lam. 5:20)
> Turn us toward you, YHWH, so that we shall return!
>   Renew our days as of old! (v. 21)
> For you have indeed rejected us completely
>   and are very angry with us. (v. 22)[36]

> Why, YHWH, have you rejected [us] forever,
>   and does your wrath smolder against the sheep in your pasture?
> Remember your congregation, which you once acquired,
>   which you have redeemed as the tribe of your inheritance,
>   Mount Zion, where you have made your dwelling.
>   (Ps. 74:1–2)[37]

> Wake up! Why do you sleep, Lord?
>   Wake up, do not banish [us] forever!
>   (Ps. 44:23/24)

29. Cf. ibid., 99.
30. For an explanation of the "Why?" question, see below, 334, n. 56.
31. On this topic, see also Gross, "Das verborgene Gesicht Gottes," 187.
32. Ibid., 189.
33. On this parallelism, see also Pss. 10:11; 44:24/25; and references in Irsigler, "Psalm-Rede," 77 n. 37.
34. See Michel, "'Warum' und 'wozu'?," 21ff.
35. See Perlitt, "Anklage und Freispruch Gottes"; cf. Lindström, *Suffering and Sin*, 65ff.; Gross, "Das verborgene Gesicht Gottes"; Emmendörffer, *Der ferne Gott*, 64ff.; Hermisson, "Der verborgene Gott."
36. Emmendörffer, *Der ferne Gott*, 64ff., esp. 74ff.; and Hartenstein, *Unzugänglichkeit Gottes*, 244ff.
37. See Emmendörffer, *Der ferne Gott*, 77ff., esp. 83ff.; Hartenstein, *Unzugänglichkeit Gottes*, 229ff.

Why do you hide your face?
  Do you forget our affliction and oppression? (v. 24/25)
For our life [*nepeš*] dissolves into dust,
  our bodies cling to the earth. (v. 25/26)
Rise up to help us,
  and save us for your mercy's sake. (v. 26/27)

As in Lamentations 5:20; Psalms 44:24/25; and 74:1, so also Psalm 13:1/2 does not understand the "forgetting" (שָׁכַח) as an incidental failure, but as an eminently grievous act of God. To say that God "forgets" is actually an inadequate claim, which according to Psalm 10:11 comes from the mouth of the godless (cf. Ps. 50:22). But it belongs to the anthropomorphic discourse about God[38] and describes a "no-longer-knowing and no-longer-wanting-to-know, a distancing and disregarding."[39] The extent of this formidable act of God is made clear in Psalms 44:24/25 and 13:1/2 by the parallel expression הִסְתִּיר פָּנִים, "hide the face" (with YHWH as subject).[40] While the presence of God's face bestows life, prosperity, and health,[41] the turning away of YHWH's face evokes fear and alarm, even death.[42] This contrast between life and death is especially drastically formulated in Psalm 30's hymn of thanksgiving:

But I, in my carelessness I thought:
  "I shall never stumble [מוֹט]."
YHWH, by your favor you have set [me] "upon strong mountains";
  then you hid your face—I was alarmed [בהל Niphal].
(Ps. 30:6–7 [7–8])[43]

The motif of "terror of death" is also found in the creation psalm, in 104. In the summarizing conclusion (vv. 27–30), YHWH is praised as the Giver of life: it expresses the experience that the provision of food (vv. 27–28) and the possibility of life ("spirit of life," vv. 29–30) are gifts of the Creator God.

These all [animals and human beings] look to you,
  that you give them their food at the proper time:
When you give it to them, they gather it up;
  when you open your hand, they eat their fill of good things.
(Ps. 104:27–28)

When you hide [סתר Hiphil] your face, they are alarmed [בהל Niphal],
  when you take away your spirit of life, they die and return to their dust.
When you send out your spirit of life, they are created,
  and you renew the face of the earth. (vv. 29–30)

38. See Preuss, "שָׁכַח," 1322–23.
39. Ibid., 1323.
40. See S. Wagner, "סָתַר," 972–73; Gross, "Das verborgene Gesicht Gottes"; and esp. Hartenstein, *Das Angesicht JHWHs*, 61ff., 192–93; Hartenstein proposes YHWH's "refusal of an audience" (with the warrior god YHWH) as a contextual explanation for most occurrences of this expression.
41. Cf. Pss. 31:16/17; 67:1/2; 80:3, 7, 19 (4, 8, 20); 119:135; also Num. 6:24–26; see discussion 66ff. below.
42. Cf. Pss. 10:11; 13:1/2; 22:24/25; 27:9; 30:7/8; 44:24/25; 69:17/18; 88:14/15; 102:2/3; 143:7. Ps. 88 speaks of the realm of the dead as the "land of oblivion" (v. 12/13) and of the dead, whom YHWH no longer remembers (88:5/6, זָכַר); see 223ff. below.
43. On this text, see 251ff. below.

The theme of God's act of sustaining life is echoed in 104:13–15 (grass for the cattle, plants for the labor of human beings) and in verse 21 (young lions "demand/call for" their food from God).[44] In verses 27–30, the dependence of human beings and animals on the Creator God is further depicted by the image of their longing for the life-giving God, who cares for the creatures with all that is essential for life (food and the breath of life). The element of the "spirit of life" (רוּחַ)—Genesis 2:7 also speaks in a basically similar context of "breath [נְשָׁמָה] of life"[45]—is directly tied to the divine face, whose turning away brings death (Ps. 104:29)[46] and whose presence brings life for all creatures (v. 30).[47]

Another element can further underscore the connections discussed here: the motif of "terror of death" or "paralyzing alarm," which Psalms 30:7/8 and 104:29 express through the verb בהל Niphal, and which is associated with the turning away of the divine face or the violence of divine wrath.[48] The idea that the turning away of the divine face gives rise to the beginning of chaos ("silence" in the text below, cf. line 75) as well as the dissolution of all social ties ("roof" in the text below, cf. line 78) is also a theme in Mesopotamian prayers. As an example, one can cite a passage from the neo-Babylonian prayer of lamentation to Ishtar, in which the complaints (lines 56–78) are governed by the motif of the turning away of the deity's face:[49]

56 How long, O my Lady, shall my adversaries be looking upon me,
57 in lying and untruth shall they plan evil against me?
58 Shall my pursuers and those who exult over me rage against me?
59 How long, O my Lady, shall the crippled and weak seek me out?
60 One has made for me long sackcloth; thus I have appeared before you.
61 The weak have become strong; but I am weak.
62 I toss about like floodwater, which an evil wind makes violent.
63 My heart is flying; it keeps fluttering like a bird of heaven.
64 I mourn like a dove night and day.
65 I am beaten down, and so I weep bitterly.
66 With "Oh" and "Alas" my spirit is distressed.
67 I—what have I done, O my god and my goddess?
68 Like one who does not fear my god and my goddess, I am treated;
69 While sickness, headache, loss, and destruction are provided for me;
70 so are fixed upon me terror, disdain, and fullness of wrath,
71 anger, fury, and indignation of gods and men.
72 I have to expect, O my Lady, dark days, gloomy months, and years of trouble.
73 I have to expect, O my Lady, judgment and confusion and violence.
74 Death and trouble are bringing me to an end.
75 Silent is my chapel, silent is my holy place;
76 over my house, my gate, and my fields, silence [*šaqummatu*] is poured out.

44. Kratz, "Gnade des täglichen Brots," 2ff.

45. See 190 below.

46. For Ps. 104:29, see Ps. 13:1/2 and also Pss. 10:1; 30:8; 44:24/25; 69:17/18; 88:14/15; 143:7; etc. For Ps. 104:29b–30; cf. Ps. 146:4; Job 10:12; 12:10; 34:14–15.

47. On the relationship between "breath of life" and "being alive," see H. W. Wolff, *Anthropology*, 59ff.

48. See Otzen, "בָּהַל"; and Sticher, *Die Rettung der Guten*, 80–81 n. 233.

49. King, *Seven Tablets*, vol. 2, plate 81; trans. Ferris J. Stephens, in *ANET* 384–55.

77 As for my god, his face is turned to the sanctuary of another.
78 My family is scattered; my roof is broken up.[50]

The invocation hymn (lines 1–41) closes with praise of Ishtar, attributing life-saving power to the gaze of the goddess:

40 Where you do look, one who is dead lives; one who is sick rises up;
41 the erring one who sees your face goes aright.[51]

As this text shows, the turning away of the divine face invokes the "evil world," a world of darkness and death.[52] The chaotic counterworld is manifested in the physical and emotional symptoms of illness (lines 62ff.), in the silence that encompasses everything (lines 72ff.), and in the dissolution of all social ties (lines 77–78).

The corresponding associations and oppositions can be schematized as follows:

Divine closeness: Light and life			**Divine distance: Darkness and death**		
Aspects					
cosmological	*social*	*anthropological*	*anthropological*	*social*	*cosmological*
Light	Life	Purity	Impurity	Death	Darkness
Day	Blessing	Health	Illness	Curse	Night
Vitality	Protection	Salvation	Doom	Vulnerability	"Silence"
City	Family	Joy	Mourning	Enemies	Desert
Temple	Celebration	Laughter	Crying	Disintegration	Wilderness
House	Community	Praise	Lament	Loneliness	Underworld

The experience of divine distance and "being marked by death"[53] is also expressed in Psalm 13: As YHWH "forgets" the suffering supplicant (v. 1/2a) and "hides" YHWH's face from the petitioner (v. 1/2b), the "evil world" comes over the complainant in the form of the enemy or of enemies and afflicts the physical and social spheres of the supplicant.[54] The speaker of Psalm 13, who is accustomed to the presence of the divine face (as expressed, e.g., by Ps. 104:27–30),[55] holds on to this experience against the fact of the suffering, doing so by appealing to YHWH implicitly as the *Creator* (complaint, Ps. 13:1/2) and explicitly as "*my* [*personal*] *God*" (petition, v. 3/4a).[56] In this sense, the complaint to God already establishes something that transcends the current situation of the

50. Rendered with some minor adjustments. For textual notes and interpretation, see Falkenstein and von Soden, *Sumerische und akkadische Hymnen*, 331–32, on lines 70ff.; see also Cassin, *La spendeur divine*, 39–40; Perlitt, "Die Verborgenheit Gottes"; Janowski, *Rettungsgewissheit*, 58 n. 207. For a comparison of this text with Ps. 13, see also Irsigler, "Psalm-Rede," 90 n. 55.

51. Trans. Ferris J. Stephens, in *ANET* 384.

52. On the binary opposites of cosmos/chaos, light/darkness, life/death, which are characteristic of the Mesopotamian way of thinking, and their function in myths and epics, see esp. Cassin, *La spendeur divine*, 27ff. (with table 52).

53. On the expression "being marked by death," see 50 above.

54. On the relation between the physical and social spheres, see 50-51 above.

55. See 65 above.

56. On the "ascending line" of trust connected to the two names of God (Ps. 13:1/2, 3/4), see 83–84 below.

supplicant's affliction: faith in *YHWH, the God of life and salvation*, who does not abandon YHWH's creatures (cf. Ps. 36:9/10).[57] Everything now depends on this faith again becoming a reality that can be experienced by the supplicant.

2. The Complaining Supplicant

Psalm 13:2/3a and likewise verse 3/4b focus more closely on the supplicant, the former in the self-complaint, the latter in the petition to YHWH to turn aside the petitioner's affliction through direct intervention. Yet this affliction is not further specified. According to verse 2/3a, however, it is located in the center of the supplicant's life—"in my vitality/liveliness [נֶפֶשׁ]" // "in my heart [לֵבָב]"—threatening to bring about death, according to Psalm 13:3/4b:

> Look here and hear me, YHWH my God!
> Let my eyes shine, so that I will not sleep the sleep of death.

Some interpreters may think of an (eye-)disease here.[58] This is, however, not intended by the expression. Since the more detailed references "in my vitality" // "in my heart" (v. 2/3a) concern the entire human being[59]—in its vital-emotional and cognitive-intentional dimensions—C. Westermann has looked for a different interpretation: "When God will again look this way and listens, all can be well again. This is what is expressed here: 'Let my eyes shine again!' i.e. let me be happy again!"[60]

It is a common theme in the individual laments that sorrow and grief can make the eyes downcast and can bring death through their burden.[61] The wording of Psalm 13:3/4b, however, points more precisely to the correspondence between "light" and "life" and between "darkness" and "death." The biblical understanding of life does not mean mere existence, but that which is "living," the salutary, fulfilled life; that concept is likewise used comprehensively, as in Psalm 18:28/29:

> Yes, you light [אור Hiphil] my lamp [נֵר];
> YHWH my God brightens [נָגַהּ] my darkness [חֹשֶׁךְ].

Or in Psalm 80:3/4:

> Restore us [שׁוב Hiphil], O God,
> and let your face shine [אור Hiphil]),
> that we may be saved [ישׁע Niphal].

On the other hand, the phrases "gates of darkness" (Job 38:17, 22), "grave" (Pss. 16:10; 49:9/10) or "to see death" (Ps. 89:48/49) are direct expressions for death and dying,[62] as in the following:

57. For this text, see 310ff. below.
58. See notes in Irsigler, "Psalm-Rede," 85, with n. 47.
59. See H. W. Wolff, *Anthropology*, 10ff., 40ff.
60. Westermann, *Ausgewählte Psalmen*, 58.
61. Pss. 6:7/8; 31:10/11; 116:3; cf. Lam. 5:17; etc.; also Irsigler, "Psalm-Rede," 85, with n. 49, who also refers to Gen. 42:38; 44:31.
62. Fuhs, "רָאָה," 242.

Yes, you do not abandon my life [נֶפֶשׁ] to the underworld;
you do not allow your holy one to see the Pit.
You show me the way of life:
fullness of joy before your face;
in your right hand are pleasures forever.
(Ps. 16:10–11)

In order to be "alive," a human being must be able to *see* the light of the sun or of life (cf. Ps. 56:13/14). Yet the person must also be *visible* to the eyes of others, in particular to the eyes of God.[63] Both ways of seeing, the active (seeing) and the passive (being seen), are named in Psalm 13. Verse 3/4b ("Let my eyes shine, so that I will not sleep the sleep of death") asks for the restoration of the life-force.[64] Yet the structural corollary to verse 3/4a ("Look here . . .") and to verse 1/2b ("How long will you hide your face from me?") makes it clear that this can only be brought about by the divine face's turning toward the supplicant—"through the meeting of YHWH's eyes and the supplicant's eyes!"[65]

Excursus 3: Light and Darkness

In Egypt, many prayers of personal piety are characterized by the metaphoric symbolism of light and darkness. This symbolism serves a religious phenomenology, which explicates the nature of the deity as characteristics and actions of the sun. Thus the plea for "illumination" in the prayer of Hui signifies salvation from the *darkness of divine distance*:

14 Come with mercy, [my] lord Neb-Kheperu-Ra!
15 Every day I see the darkness you have made.
16 Bring me light, so that I can see you;
17 then I will tell of your might to the fish in the river.[66]

This wording is based on the understanding of the deity as light and therefore on the conviction that "the light-like nature of the gods corresponds to the human eye's sensitivity to light" (Brunner, "Blindheit," 830–31). The idiom "to let see the light" is therefore an expression for "to be merciful." Likewise it can be said that God rises as sun for human beings (see J. Assmann, *Weisheit, Loyalismus*, 66; Janowski, *Rettungsgewissheit und Epiphanie*, 173–74). This understanding is suggested in a unique way in the Amarna period's theology of light, with its world-centeredness of Aton, god of light, who shines only for his creation (cf. J. Assmann, "Aton," 532). The metaphoric symbolism of light and darkness is also characteristic of the language of prayer in Mesopotamia (see Janowski, *Rettungsgewissheit und Epiphanie*, 56ff.; B. Langer, *Gott als "Licht,"* 156ff.; more generally, Cassin, *La spendeur divine*, 27ff.; also

63. On (God's) light as a symbol of life, see C. Barth, *Errettung vom Tode*, 28–29; on Pss. 56:13/14 and 80:3/4, see Hossfeld and Zenger, *Psalmen 51–100*, 116, 461.
64. Cf. Ps. 19:8/9; Prov. 29:13; Ezra 9:8–9; on this topic see C. Barth, *Errettung vom Tode*, 29; Kraus, *Psalmen*, 1:243.
65. Hossfeld and Zenger, *Die Psalmen*, 1:98; cf. Simian-Yofre, "פָּנִים," 641: "The glow of YHWH's face is the all-encompassing sign that God attends to human beings. The 'glowing' face of a human being . . . is a reflection of this gracious presence of God among human beings (cf. Ex. 34, 29–30)."
66. *Urk.* IV.2075.14–17; cf. Brunner, *Grundzüge der altägyptischen Religion*, 115.

A. Berlejung, "Licht/Finsternis"; Janowski, "Licht des Lebens" (with references); and Ebach, "Licht").

Based on the light-darkness contrast is the Old Testament understanding of *cosmos/creation and chaos* (cf. Gese, "Johannesprolog," 190ff.; Janowski, "Licht und Finsternis II"). Thus, the precreation world is confined by the light that is created first (Gen. 1:2), while the stars are created as luminous entities, whose light causes the differentiation of day and night (Gen. 1:14–18; cf. Isa. 58:8; Jer. 4:23; Ps. 74:16; Job 38:19–20; etc.). The elementary relationship between *light and life* (Pss. 18:28/29; 56:13/14; etc.) has its counterpart in the relationship between *darkness and death* (Job. 3:4ff.; 33:28ff.; etc.). The light-life relationship is frequently connected to the "face of God," since the divine face is seen as the source of blessings (Pss. 4:6/7; 31:16/17; 67:1/2; 80:3, 7, 19 [4, 8, 20]; 118:27; 119:135; cf. Num. 6:24–26; etc.), so that God's closeness is experienced as the light of God's face (Pss. 36:6, 9 [7, 10]; 42:5, 11 [6, 12]; 43:5; 89:15/16; etc.). Just as the expression "to see the light (of the sun)" is a metaphor for "life," its negation is a metaphor for "death" and "dying" (see Fuhs, "רָאָה," 242; Krawczack, *"Es gibt einen Gott,"* 265ff.; Egger-Wenzel, *Von der Freiheit Gottes*, 120ff.).

"Light" can also be an epithet of God (Ps. 27:1; cf. 2 Sam. 22:29; etc.) and a metaphor for truth (Ps. 43:3). In Ps. 27:1 (cf. 44:3/4; etc.), the light metaphor is further associated with the YHWH epithet "my salvation," in order to express the close connection between *light* and *salvation*. Solar images are probably secondary in this case (Hos. 6:3, 5; Zeph. 3:5; Ps. 37:6; Isa. 51:4; etc.; cf. Janowski, "JHWH und der Sonnengott," 205ff.; Hartenstein, *Das Angesicht JHWHs*, 173ff.). Morning is an auspicious time of God's saving justice (Isa. 17:14; 29:7; Ps. 46:5/6; cf. Isa. 26:9; 33:2; Pss. 5:3/4; 90:14; 143:8; etc.): with the rising of the morning star, the destructive judgment over Sodom begins (Gen. 19:15), the divine being that attacked Jacob at night at the Jabbok releases him (Gen. 32:26/27), and the wicked are shaken off the earth (Job. 38:12–15; cf. 24:13–17).

The Light of God

The world-focus of the Creator, who gives light to his creation, corresponds to the light-focus of human beings, who live by the light of God. The text that captures in words this fundamental correlation of Old Testament anthropology is the Aaronite priestly blessing of Numbers 6:24–26:

And YHWH spoke to Moses: (Num. 6:22)
Speak to Aaron and his sons, saying:
This is how you shall bless the Israelites, saying to them: (v. 23)
May YHWH bless you,
and keep you! (v. 24)
May YHWH let his face shine on you,
and be gracious to you! (v. 25)
May YHWH lift up his face toward you,
and give you peace! (v. 26)
And if they put my name on the Israelites in this way,
I shall bless them. (v. 27)

If one compares Numbers 6:24–26 and Psalm 13:1b–3b (2b–4b),[67] the following correspondences result:

Numbers 6:25–26	**Psalm 13:1b, 3b (2b, 4b)**
May YHWH let his face *shine* [אור Hiphil] on you . . .	How long will you *hide* [סתר Hiphil] your face from me? . . .
May YHWH lift up [נָשָׂא] his face toward you . . .	Let my eyes *shine* [אור Hiphil] . . .

Numbers 6:25–26 is a *contrasting formulation* to Psalm 13:1/2b and a *parallel formulation* to Psalm 13:3/4b. The "illuminated" face of the supplicant is a reflection of the presence of God, who has turned YHWH's face toward the supplicant and let it "shine" graciously and benevolently over or toward the petitioner:[68] "For the suffering, death would be a finalization of an irreversible separation from Yahweh. It would be triumph of the enemy, whose efforts were all aimed at overpowering the suffering with definitive judgments."[69]

Equally important as the petition for one to be seen by God is, according to Psalm 13:3/4a, the plea to receive an answer from him. The Psalms repeatedly issue the reminder that YHWH not only hears the cry of the afflicted in their suffering and leaves it at that, but that YHWH may "answer," as in these examples:

Hear my voice, YHWH, when I call to you;
  have mercy on me and answer me!
(Ps. 27:7)

From the depths I have called to you, YHWH!
  Lord, listen to my voice!
May your ears take notice
  of my loud cry for mercy!
(Ps. 130:1b–2)[70]

In Egypt, the plea for God's audience was brought before the deity not only in words but also in images. A notable example of these so-called ear stelae,[71] which were set up in Egyptian temples, is the limestone stela from Thebes (fig. 10). It shows the worshiper Bai in supplication before the ram-headed God Amun; his ability to hear is symbolized by three pairs of ears (principle of intensification). "The all-hearing and all-knowing god could possess not only the quality of protection and of receiving prayers, but also that of a knowing and supervising judge"[72]—not in the sense of total control, but in the sense of

67. On comparing the Aaronite blessing with the Psalms, see Seybold, *Aaronitische Segen*, 56ff. For Num. 6:25, cf. also Pss. 4:6/7; 31:16/17; 67:1/2; 80:3/4, 19/20; 119:135.

68. On the "letting shine" of the divine face, see Reindl, *Angesicht Gottes*, 143ff.; Gruber, *Nonverbal Communication*, 557ff.; Simian-Yofre, "פָּנִים," 640–41; and esp. Hartenstein, „Das 'Angesicht JHWHs," 167ff., 170ff., etc.

69. Kraus, *Psalmen*, 1:243.

70. Cf. Pss. 4:1/2; 34:15/16; 116:1–2; etc. On the subject of God answering, see Kessler, "Der antwortende Gott."

71. See Guglielmi, "Bedeutung"; Guglielmi and Dittmar, "Anrufungen," 128ff.

72. Guglielmi, "Bedeutung," 120.

Figure 10. Limestone stela from Thebes (ca. 1200 BCE)

a "social authority," watching over the maintenance of a legal and social order and therefore also over the fate of his worshiper. YHWH too is called upon as a "social authority" in the laments of the individual, to bring about the "justification of the righteous" over against all challenges by his enemies.[73]

The Triumphant Enemy

"God has forgotten, he has hidden his face, he has never even seen it": according to Psalm 10:11, this is how the wicked jeer after committing their unscrupulous acts. The imminent danger of destruction by the enemy is also invoked by the supplicant of Psalm 13 and placed urgently before YHWH: ". . . that my enemy cannot claim: 'I have prevailed over him'" (v. 4/5a).

The presence of the enemy is mentioned in the complaint (v. 2/3c) as well as in the petition (v. 4/5) of our psalm. We have noticed a stylistic difference between these two genre elements: a petition for the destruction of the enemy is lacking. Instead, the actions of the enemy or enemies in the negative final sentences of verse 4/5 are linked back to the imperatives of cohortatives of verse 3/4. This means that the actions of the enemy will cease when YHWH once again turns YHWH's face toward the supplicant and makes the petitioner's eyes "shine." What role does the enemy play then?

73. See 140ff. below.

In the laments of the individual, there is a characteristic distinction between the correlations of distress / sin of the supplicant, and distress / oppression by the enemy:[74]

- Group 1. The first group includes psalms in which the supplicant's affliction is caused by a life-threatening illness. This illness is understood—according to the logic of the act-consequence relationship—as a result ordained by YHWH for a "sin"; thus the illness calls the enemies unjustifiably into the plan, although the supplicant is innocent in regard to them. Accordingly, petitions for the destruction of the enemies are lacking since their actions lose their basis as a result of YHWH's healing/salvation of the supplicant and therefore cease by themselves. Examples are the laments of Psalms 38 and 88 and the thanksgiving hymns of Psalms 30; 32; and 41.
- Group 2. The second group defines the relationship differently: The supplicant's affliction is not the result of sin: the supplicant is presented as innocent and just before YHWH. Instead, the affliction is rather caused by the enemies. Accordingly, we now find petitions for the destruction of the enemies, which are lacking in the first group. Examples are the laments of Psalms 3; 5; 7; 17; 35; 42–43; 54–57; 71; 109; 140; and 142.

Which of these positions applies to Psalm 13? I have already pointed out that no reason is given for the presence of the affliction. It is only stated that the affliction persists ("How long?" questions) and that it is based in God's mysterious forgetting of the supplicant. Neither is the enemy the cause of the affliction, as in the texts of the second group; rather, the enemy is a *bitter concomitant phenomenon* in light of this affliction, by means of "performative speech"[75] finalizing the terminal fate of the supplicant: "I have prevailed over him" (v. 4/5a). This prospect, to be prevailed over by the enemy, is most likely the existential *Sitz im Leben* of the psalm and the motivation for the supplicant's appeal to YHWH.

The primary way in which Psalm 13 speaks of the enemy is evident in two details, which are essential for a basic understanding of the Psalms of the Individual. One detail is connected to the term מוט, "stumble, falter" (v. 4/5b). This is no everyday word: מוט has "within the framework of the YHWH's universal activity a significant relation to the chaotic."[76] In texts associated with the Jerusalem temple theology and with wisdom, the *experiences of the chaotic* in the form of harassment by enemies, illness, or legal problems are expressed through the verb מוט, "stumble, falter."[77] The *opposite experience of assistance by God* is expressed through the negation of this verb[78] or through the verb סָעַד, "support," as in Psalm 46:4–6 (5–7):

74. See also Steck, *Friedensvorstellungen*, 38 n. 92.
75. In the classic formulation by J. L. Austin (*Do Things with Words*, 5), "the uttering of the sentence is, or is a part of, the doing of an action, which would not *normally* be described as, or as 'just,' saying something"; see A. Wagner, *Sprechakte und Sprechaktanalyse*, 7ff. The speech-act of Ps. 13:4/5a belongs, according to speech-act theory and the terminology of J. R. Searle, to the "assertive" class. Typical examples of this genre are observations, assertions, predictions, explications, classifications, diagnoses, and descriptions. See also Irsigler, "Psalm-Rede," 64ff., 91ff.; Wagner, *Sprechakte und Sprechaktanalyse*, 20ff.
76. Steck, *Friedensvorstellungen*, 37 n. 85; see also Jeremias, "Die Erde 'wankt.'"
77. Pss. 46:2/3, 5/6, 6/7; 82:5; 96:10; and 104:5.
78. Pss. 10:6; 15:5; 30:6/7; 112:6; and Prov. 10:30.

A river—its streams make glad the city of God,
the holiest of the dwellings of the most high.
(Ps. 46:4/5)
God is in her midst, so that she may not stumble [מוט],
God helps her at the break of day. (v. 5/6)
Nations roared, kingdoms stumbled / fell—
he has raised his voice [of thunder], so that the earth is shaking.[79] (v. 6/7)

Or in the pilgrimage song Psalm 125:1:

Those who trust in YHWH are like Mount Zion,
which will not shake [מוט] in all eternity.

Psalm 125:1 assures the supplicant, when close to YHWH, of being "like Mount Zion," which does not shake.[80] Since the protective presence of God is not given for the supplicant of Psalm 13, and the enemy is actively seeking to finalize the deadly fate of the supplicant, "stumbling" (v. 4/5b) signifies the *manifestation of the chaotic in the life of the supplicant*,[81] corresponding to the lamented withdrawal of life by YHWH.

The affirmation of trust in Psalm 125:1, like the enemy petition of 13:5, is based on the "explicit connection of the universal realm with the individual realm,"[82] relating *macrocosm* (mythic-divine dimension) and *microcosm* (historical-social dimension). This is a basic feature not only of the individual's Psalms of Lament and Thanksgiving in the Old Testament.[83] One could consider this feature a *mutual modeling of the mythic and historical dimension*.[84] "Mutual modeling" means that events in the historical-social realm (world of human beings) are seen and portrayed as if they occur in the mythic-divine realms (world of the gods/God) and vice versa. The divine mountain Zion, in the Jerusalem temple theology, is for anthropology the "vitality" (נֶפֶשׁ) or the heart (לֵבָב/לֵב) and the central human organ. If it is full of sorrow and grief, as in Psalm 13:2/3a, the shaken supplicant shakes like the city of God that is attacked by enemies in Psalm 46. The supplicant is therefore a reflection of the divine city or—pars pro toto—an "Israel in nuce."

The *second detail* in the depiction of the enemies of Psalm 13 concerns the change in number from "my enemy" (vv. 2b, 4a [3b, 5a]) to "my enemies" (v. 4/5b), which can also be observed elsewhere.[85] Psalm 140, for example, speaks of an enemy in the singular in verses 4a, 8, 11 (5a, 9, 12) and in the (collective) plural in verses 1–3, 4a, 5, 9–10 (2–4, 5a, 6, 10–11), and just like 13:4ab/5ab in immediate succession. Thus we read Psalm 140:8–11 (9–12):

Do not grant, YHWH, the desires of the wicked, (v. 8/9, sg.)
do not let their plans succeed.

79. On this text and its cosmological implications, see Janowski, "Die heilige Wohnung," 42ff.
80. See Beyerlin, *Weisheitliche Vergewisserung*, 51–52.
81. Cf. Steck, "Klage und Bitte," 62.
82. Steck, *Friedensvorstellungen*, 37 n. 85.
83. Cf. Janowski, *Rettungsgewissheit*, 16–17; idem, "'Dem Löwen gleich,'" 63–64.
84. On this feature in Ps. 125, see Riede, "Psalm 125."
85. Cf. Pss. 5; 7; 10; 11; 14; 17; 22; 55; etc. See also Hossfeld and Zenger, *Die Psalmen*, 1:72, 81; 2:97; Janowski, "'Dem Löwen gleich,'" 55–56.

"Let those who surround me not raise their head!" (v. 9/10, pl.)
  Let the mischief they speak about me come on themselves,
Let him "rain" coals over them, cast them into the fire, (v. 10/11, pl.)
  into pits, so that will not rise again!
Let the slanderer not be established in the land, (v. 11/12, sg.)
  the violent man—may disaster hunt him down![86]

A common explanation for the change in number is that among the many enemies of the supplicant, *one* stands out in particular. However, the actions of the alleged ringleader (sg.) are not distinguished in any way from those of his allies (pl.). It is therefore more plausible to assume that the singular form serves to establish the *type* ("the enemy"), while the plural emphasizes the *enemy force* ("that which is hostile") in the form of its representatives.[87] The subject, the individual bearer of this hostile power, remains curiously undefined. The singular thus signifies the referent as a *unit*, while the plural represents a *multiplicity*.[88] The change from singular (type) to plural (individuals) therefore implies that the supplicant sees in this personal enemy the personification of that which is hostile or evil, in other words, the enemy force. The concrete enemy thus always bears traits that transcend the individual.

Here we encounter a phenomenon that characterizes the Psalms of the Individual in general: their *generalizing* or *typological* language. The individual is viewed neither as an unmistakable subject nor as possessing an individual biography. The songs of lament and thanksgiving of the individual are no biographical testimonies at all.[89] They rather attempt to advance into the realm of the general and typical—as their repeatability shows even today—without leaving the level of concretization; they do this by elevating individual suffering to paradigmatic suffering, to the "original suffering of being abandoned by God,"[90] and characterizing the appearance of the personal enemy as *manifestation of the chaotic in the life of the supplicant*. The "extent but not the individual type of suffering"[91] as well as the oppression by the enemy is the focus for depicting the enemy and is distinctly emphasized.

With the affirmation of trust in Psalm 13:5a/6a, "But I—I have trusted in your goodness," the supplicant suddenly[92] steps out of the complaints and the petition connected to it. This turn is linguistically prompted by the so-called *wāw-adversative*,[93] which marks the transition from—or the contrast between—complaint and petition to trust (with a concluding pledge of praise):

86. For textual notes, see Kraus, *Psalmen*, 2:1103.

87. Cf. Keel, *Feinde und Gottesleugner*, 68–69.

88. See Brockelmann, *Hebräische Syntax*, 84ff.

89. On this essential quality, see Steck, *Friedensvorstellungen*, 36 n. 84; Krieg, *Todesbilder*, 351ff.; Bail, *Gegen das Schweigen klagen*, 56ff.

90. Von Rad, *Theologie*, 1:413; cf. idem, "'Gerechtigkeit' und 'Leben,'" 236; Hermisson, "Glauben," 39; Gerstenberger, *Der bittende Mensch*, 139 n. 04; Füglister, "Verwendung des Psalters," 207; Irsigler, "Psalm 22," 210 n. 23; Markschies, "Vertrauensäusserungen," 387; Bornkamm, "Das überlebensgrosse Ich," 103; Janowski, "Die 'Kleine Biblia,'" 153–54.

91. Cf. Steck, *Friedensvorstellungen*, 36 n. 84; already Gunkel and Begrich, *Introduction to Psalms*, 130–34.

92. Regarding this "suddenness," 77ff.

93. The contrast introduced by וַאֲנִי ("but I," Ps. 13:5/6a) is not the result of the *wāw*, which is only a copula or a syntactic conjunction meaning "and," but of the word order in the sentence. The so-called *wāw-adversative* always stands, together with its subject (I/God), at the beginning of a sentence: "The juxtaposition is therefore more deeply anchored in the structure of the sentence than merely through a conjunction" (Westermann, *Lob und Klage*, 53).

. . . that my enemy cannot claim: "I have prevailed over him,"
  and my opponents rejoice that I am stumbling!
(Ps. 13:4/5)

But I [וַאֲנִי]—I have trusted[94] in your goodness,
  my heart rejoices over your salvation: (v. 5/6ab)
"I shall sing to YHWH
  for what he has done for me!" (v. 6/6cd)

The psalm reaches its climax in the verb "trust" (בָּטַח), which functions as the antithesis to the verb "stumble" (מוֹט), here as well as in Psalm 125:1.[95] For trust is the *basic motif* in the laments of the individual, which are to be understood as "purposeful paradigms of trust,"[96] according to C. Markschies. The pledge of praise in verse 6 ("I will sing") identifies "the help that has come, Yahweh's intervention, as the object of the petition."[97] The supplicant *anticipates* reintegration into the cultic and social community. But not only that: when the petitioner has once again "gained the ability to sing Yahweh's praises without any fear in his heart (6b),"[98] the goal of the prayer, to overcome being forgotten by God and the enemy's triumph that results from this forgetting, is anticipatorily[99] achieved.

But how is it possible that the move to trust occurs so suddenly, even though the supplicant's affliction persists and the enemies have not yet been overcome? Perhaps this move does not occur so suddenly after all. In Old Testament scholarship, this question has been given an answer under the name of "change of mood."[100]

94. Or "I have [hereby] placed my trust," since the intransitive verb בָּטַח ("trust") in the first-person singular "allows . . . also for a syntactic *Koinzidenzfall*, i.e., a semantic interpretation as direct and explicit performative speech-act. It places [בָּטַח] dynamically at the beginning: 'Hereby I place my trust in Yahweh's goodness.' It is a declarative speech-act, in which the speaker explains the proposition as actually brought about. . . . The speaker validates his trust in Yahweh anew" (Irsigler, "Psalm-Rede," 79–80).

95. See 73–74 above.

96. Markschies, "Vertrauensäusserungen"; see also 77ff. below.

97. Irsigler, "Psalm-Rede," 74. From a lexical point of view, גָּמַל ("act") in Ps. 13:6b/6d does not necessarily imply an action by God, but because of the context (v. 5/6ab, חסדך // ישׁועתך), only the *saving intervention of YHWH* can be intended; cf. ibid., 81 n. 45.

98. Ibid., 82.

99. This anticipation is also connected to the assurance of being heard, expressed in Ps. 22:21/22 as an anticipated fact; see 77ff. below.

100. On Ps. 13 and the subject of "change of mood," see Loretz, *Psalmstudien*, 81–82, 134ff., 158ff., 160ff.; Bauks, *Die Feinde des Psalmisten*, 36ff.; Weber, "Zum sogenannten 'Stimmungsumschwung'"; Villanueva, *The "Uncertainty of a Hearing"*; and Weber's review thereof; Weber, *Werkbuch*, 3:69ff.; Hardmeier, "Lobpreis des verborgenen Gottes"; Hieke, "Orientierung," 267ff.; K. Schmid, "Was heißt Vertrauen?" According to Weber ("Zum sogenannten 'Stimmungsumschwung,'" esp. 135–36), the traditional view as advocated by J. Begrich, "Das priesterliche Heilsorakel," is to be modified in view of the literary form of the individual lament. Siding on the other hand with the traditional explanation—i.e., the change of mood as the result of external impact of an oracular formula conveyed to the supplicant or an assurance regarding God's judicial intervention ("legal case pattern")—is Loretz (*Psalmstudien*, 134ff., 158ff., 160ff.), with reference to the evidence of an oracular formula in Ps. 5:3/4 (cf. 146) and Mesopotamian divination parallels (cf. ibid., 159); cf. idem, *Götter*, 155ff. But in my opinion Ps. 5:3/4 is to be interpreted differently (see Janowski, *Rettungsgewissheit*, 188): the reference to the "juridical assumptions . . . characteristic of a complaint before a divine forum and for a divine judgment" (Loretz, *Psalmstudien*, 146; cf. 147ff., 159, etc.) has, in my estimation, a particular veri[ty]; cf. 146ff. below. Furthermore, the motif of assurance of being heard occurs several times in Mesopotamian prayers; see Zgoll, "Für Sinne, Geist und Seele," esp. 39 with n. 52. For these and other reasons, the objections formulated by Loretz (*Psalmstudien*, 160ff.) do not match the literary (!) observations by Irsigler, Weber, and myself regarding the change of mood in individual laments.

γ. *Change of Mood*

At their conclusions, as a rule, many laments of the individual contain a thanksgiving section or praise portion, which appears to give expression to already having been heard by God. The problem is, however, that a supplicant cannot make a lamenting petition *and* offer praising thanks at the same time. As can be easily demonstrated with the example of Psalm 13:6, the problem described by the expression "change of mood" is not to be solved at the level of an individual sentence, but is likely connected to the expressive orientation of the text as a whole.

The idea of the so-called change of mood[101] is based on the assumption that the lament of the individual suddenly moves or "switches" from complaint into thanksgiving or praise. The element suggesting thanksgiving or praise is then an answer or reaction to a process that, according to consensus opinion, takes place *outside* or external to the text. Since J. Begrich, this external factor has been associated with the "priestly salvation oracle,"[102] given to the supplicant by a cultic official between complaint and thanksgiving.

J. Begrich has proposed the thesis that the "change of mood" in the lament of the individual is based on a "priestly salvation oracle," which "assures the supplicant on behalf of . . . God that one's petition is heard, and which has its place after the complaint and petition and before the affirmation of being heard and the pledge."[103] According to Begrich, an echo of such a salvation oracle is heard in Lamentations 3:57:

> You were near on the day I called to you,
> and you said: "Do not be afraid!"[104]

Following this passage, Begrich continues: The genre of the "salvation oracle" including the consolation formula "Do not be afraid!" which is typical of the genre, was taken up by Deutero-Isaiah (Isa. 41:8–13; etc.). This was made possible by the presentation of Israel as an individual person.

To the seven texts in Deutero-Isaiah that were initially defined as "salvation oracles" (Isa. 41:8–13; 41:14–16; 43:1–3a; [44:2–5]; 48:17–19; 49:7–15; 51:7–8; 54:4–8), Begrich added several others (totaling 24), but in doing so he defined the characteristics of the genre only vaguely. Regarding the problem of the "change of mood," he observed that in certain parts Deutero-Isaiah's language was infused by the language of the Psalms, especially in places where the form of a "salvation oracle" could be recognized. In the laments of the individual, the sudden change from complaint to certainty of being heard suggested that a third party (priest or cultic prophet) assured the supplicant of acceptance. Begrich called this assurance a "priestly salvation oracle" and saw it as the model for the "prophetic salvation oracle" in Deutero-Isaiah. Its position was,

101. See J. Becker, *Psalmenexegese*, 59ff.; Kaiser, *Einleitung*, 337ff.; Boecker, "Psalmen," 195–96; Oeming, *Psalm 1–41*, 147ff.

102. Begrich, "Das priesterliche Heilsorakel"; on the history of scholarship, see O. Fuchs, *Klage als Gebet*, 314ff.

103. Begrich, "Das priesterliche Heilsorakel," 217.

104. On this text and its relation to Begrich's thesis (ibid., 219), see Kessler, "Der antwortende Gott," 50ff.

as Psalm 22 shows, between complaint and praise, enabling the transition from challenge to assurance:

Complaint: My God, why have you forsaken me? (Ps. 22:1/2)

↓ **Salvation oracle**: Do not be afraid, for I am with you! (cf. Isa. 41:10)

Praise: . . . You have answered me.

(Ps. 22:21/22b)

This thesis has achieved almost normative recognition in Old Testament scholarship.[105] For the present discussion, if we leave aside the question of the salvation oracle in Deutero-Isaiah[106] and limit ourselves to the laments of the individual in Psalms, we notice that the "priestly salvation oracle" is, strictly speaking, an entirely hypothetical genre.[107] The sudden change from complaint to praise can certainly be found in the laments of the individual (as with the transitions in Pss. 3:7/8; 6:7–8 [8–9]; 31:18–19 [19–20]; 36:11–12 [12–13]; or in 57:6–7 [7–8]), but Begrich has not been able to supply confirmation that it has been brought about by the word of God from the lips of a priest. There is no evidence in the laments of the individual for the assumption that a word of God has come from the lips of a priest or cultic prophet. Even psalms that allude to words of God, like 35:1–3, cannot support Begrich's thesis:

Contend, YHWH, with those who contend with me,
  fight those who fight me!
(Ps. 35:1)
Take up shield and buckler,
  and set out to help me! (v. 2)
Draw out spear and javelin against my pursuers,
  Say to me [my *nepeš*]: "Your salvation am *I*!" (v. 3)[108]

Even in places like Psalms 12:5/6 or 60:6–8 (8–10) = 108:7–9 (8–10), where a divine assurance of salvation is given in the context of a psalm of lament, the change from complaint to praise is absent.[109] The conclusion to

105. See the survey in Boecker, "Psalmen," 195–96.

106. See the critique by M. Weippert, "Aspekte israelitischer Prophetie," 310; idem, "Assyrische Prophetien," 99ff.

107. See the critique by Kilian, "Ps 22"; O. Fuchs, *Klage als Gebet*, 314ff.; A. Müller, "Stimmungsumschwung"; Kessler, "Der antwortende Gott," 50ff.; Millard, *Komposition des Psalters*, 53ff., 84ff.; Bail, *Gegen das Schweigen klagen*, 53–54; Oeming, *Psalm 1–41*, 147ff.; Schroeder, "Psalm 3"; Erbele-Küster, *Lesen als Akt des Betens*, 161ff.

108. See Kilian, "Ps 22," 180; Kessler, "Der antwortende Gott," 50ff.; Koenen, *Gottesworte in den Psalmen*, 5–6; Doeker, *Funktion der Gottesrede*, 27–28, 152ff., 305–6. Kraus (*Psalmen*, 1:428) sees here a "prime example of a priestly salvation oracle"; but Hossfeld and Zenger (*Psalmen*, 1:220) leave the type of transmission of the word of God open. In contrast, Doeker's thesis (*Funktion der Gottesrede*, 305) that "the Psalms with speech by God . . . do not reflect an 'actual' dialog" might be on target. Nevertheless, these psalms contain "as their basic principle a dialogic structure. . . . There is a movement from the speaker of the psalm (upward) to God, which is called anabasis. . . . The direct speech of God contains—contrary to the usual orientation of a prayer—also a movement from God (downward) to the supplicant, the catabasis. In this way, the Psalms subsist on the mutual infusion of human and divine speech" (ibid., 180–81). See also the references in 322ff. under "Paradigmatic Experiences of Suffering."

109. Cf. M. Weippert, "Aspekte israelitischer Prophetie," 312 n. 53; on Ps. 12:5/6, see Koenen, *Gottesworte in den Psalmen*, 5–6, 11–12, 26; on Ps. 60:6/8ff. (= 108:7/8ff.), see Kilian, "Ps 22," 180–81.

these consideration can only be that the change of mood, which does in fact exist, must be explained differently. Let us take a short detour by way of Psalm 22.

The example of Psalm 22:1–21 (2–22) shows that the Psalms of Lament, precisely by being spoken, already contain an element of trust in God and represent a "purposeful paradigm of trust."[110] They may be spoken in a situation of abandonment by God or distance from God, but nevertheless with the hope that God is near especially in these afflictions. This tension between *experienced abandonment by God* and *anticipated closeness to God* is constitutive for the Psalms of Lament in general and for the question of "change of mood" in particular. The expression "change of mood" suggests, however, that the change from complaint to praise of God occurs *suddenly* and is prompted by something *on the outside*, and that the "change of mood" is a deliberate and *institutionalized* occurrence. The reference to the tension "between the experienced (abandonment) by God and the believed (closeness) of God,"[111] on the other hand, assumes that there is a process, or more precisely a *prayer-process*, behind the change from complaint to praise, which commences with the beginning of the prayer and permeates the entire text.

In view of Psalm 22:1–21 (2–22), this process can be divided into three speech-acts,[112] which the supplicant performs successively in the course of the text: *speech-act 1: verses 1–11 (2–12)* (complaint: vv. 1–2, 6–8 [2–3, 7–9] → trust: vv. 3–5, 9–11 [4–6, 10–12] → petition: v. 11/12); *speech-act 2: verses 12–21 (13–22)* (complaint: vv. 12–18 [13–19] → petition: vv. 19–21 [20–22]); and *speech-act 3: verses 22–31 (23–32)* (praise). The lament Psalm 22:1–21 (2–22) reads as follows in translation:

Speech-Act 1: Psalm 22:1–11 (2–12)

Complaint I + Invocation — *God-complaint, 1–2 (2–3)*

My God, my God, why have you forsaken me,
[you who are] far from my salvation, from the words of my groaning?
I call by day: "My God!" but you do not answer,
and by night, but I find no rest.

Expression of Trust — *Trust, 3–5 (4–6)*

But you are holy,
enthroned on the praises of Israel! (v. 3/4)
In you our ancestors placed their trust;
they trusted and you saved them. (v. 4/5)
To you they called and were saved;
in you they trusted, and they were not put to shame. (v. 5/6)

Complaint II — *Enemy-complaint, 6–7 (7–8)*

But I am a worm and no [longer a] human,
the reproach of others, despised by the people!
All who see me laugh about me;
they curl their lips and shake their heads.
"Place [it] on YHWH!" "Let [YHWH] save him [/her],
let [YHWH] deliver him, for [YHWH] delights in him!"

110. Markschies, "Vertrauensäusserungen."
111. O. Fuchs, *Klage als Gebet*, 98.
112. Cf. Irsigler, "Psalm 22," 213–14.

Expression of Trust
Yes, it is you who pulled me *Trust, 9–10 (10–11)*
from my mother's womb,
who fed me with hope at my mother's breasts!
On you I was cast ever since my mother's womb;
since my mother's womb, you have been my God.
Do not be far from me, *Petition*, 11/12
for affliction is near,
indeed, there is no helper!

Speech-Act 2: Psalm 22:12–21 (13–22)

Complaint III
Many bulls surround me, *Enemy-complaint*, 12–13 (13–14)
the "strong of Bashan" encircle me.
They have [already] opened their mouths wide against me:
a lion, ravening and roaring.
Like water I am poured out, *Self-complaint*, 14–15 (15–16)
my limbs are out of joint,
my heart has become like wax,
melted within my bowels.
Dried up like a potsherd is my [life-]force,
and my tongue cleaves to the roof of my mouth;
you have laid me down in the dust of death.
Indeed, dogs have surrounded me, *Enemy-complaint*, 16ab/17ab
a pack of evildoers has encircled me!
[Too short are] my hands and feet, *Self-complaint*, 16c–17a (17c–18a)
I can count all of my bones.
But they keep looking at me, *Enemy-complaint*, 17b–19 (18b–20)
staring at me,
they divide my clothes among themselves,
and for my coat they cast lots.
Petition + Invocation *19–21 (20–22)*
But you, YHWH, do not be distant;
my strength, hasten to my help! (v. 19/20)
Wrest from the dagger my life [*nepeš*],
"my only one" from the power of the dogs. (v. 20/21)
Save me from the lion's mouth,
from the horns of wild animals—you have answered me. (v. 21/22)[113]

Speech-Act 3: Psalm 22:22–31 (23–32)

Thanksgiving
I will tell my brothers [and sisters] of your name;
in the midst of my congregation I will praise you. . . . (v. 22/23)

In the first two complaint segments (vv. 1–5 + 6–11 [2–6 + 7–12]) the *speech-act of complaint* is dominant, whereby elements of complaint and trust alternate. This implies that the complaint contains something uncompleted, anticipatory, and open with regard to God. The third complaint segment (vv. 12–21 [13–22]) culminates in the petition (vv. 19–21 [20–22]), the urgency of which

113. On the translation and for textual notes, see 322ff. below.

is emphasized by the description of the affliction—enemy-complaint/self-complaint (vv. 12–18 [13–19]). One complaint is not simply followed by another complaint: instead, the moments of trust continue to grow and result in the *speech-act of petition* (speech-act 2: vv. 12–21 [13–22]).[114] In the following hymn of praise by the individual (vv. 22–31 [23–32]), the communication between supplicant and God then changes, being governed by the most intensive form of trust in God, the *speech-act of praise* (speech-act 3). Here no further linguistic or imaginative symbolic element from the realm of the supplicant's abandonment by God is to be found.

The transition from complaints to the thanksgiving segment thus happens in verse 21/22, notably in the middle of the sentence, if one takes the Masoretic Text's עֲנִיתָנִי as original:[115]

> Save me from the lion's mouth,
> from the horns of wild bulls—*you have answered me* [עֲנִיתָנִי]!

This also establishes a correlation to the introductory complaint and invocation of verses 1–2 (2–3), according to which the supplicant calls to YHWH day and night without receiving an answer:

> I call by day: "My God!" but you do not answer,
> and by night, but I find no rest. (Ps. 22:2/3)[116]

The force of verse 21/22 is based on the fact that the reversal does not *follow the complaint* as in other laments of the individual, but that both parts are connected to each other, because while עֲנִיתָנִי still belongs *in form* to the complaint and petition section, it has *in content* already crossed into the realm of regained trust.[117]

This transition is not effected by a "priestly salvation oracle"—for which there is no evidence in Psalm 22—in other words, not by an element *external to the text*, but it takes place *inside the text*, as it is carried out by the speaker in the process of praying. The so-called change of mood is the result of the certainty of being heard by God, coinciding with the affirmation of this certainty through the words "You have answered me" (v. 21/22b). Thereby the new situation—the change from complaint to praise—is anticipatorily executed by the verbalization of this situation.

Following O. Fuchs, we can call this grammatical phenomenon, which effects a *proleptic horizon of meaning*, an "anticipated fact." In other words, at

114. Cf. Kilian, "Ps 22," 183–84.

115. Cf. O. Fuchs, *Klage als Gebet*, 178ff.; Kraus, *Psalmen*, 1:323, 329–30 (albeit in reference to Begrich's thesis); Hossfeld and Zenger, *Die Psalmen*, 1:145, 150; Seybold, *Die Psalmen*, 95, 99; etc.; in contrast, see Gese, "Psalm 22," 181, with n. 1: "my affliction" (= my wretched life), i.e., "to read v. 20/21 *yĕḥîdātî* [my only one / precious life] most likely as *ʿănîyyatî* [my wretched life]; cf. LXX, Syr (Wellhausen et al.)"; cf. Irsigler, "Psalm 22," 195–96.

116. Because of the inclusio with v. 2/3a, which frames the three complaint segments in vv. 1–21 (2–22) and their motifs of trust vv. 3/4ff, 9/10ff. (!), then v. 21/22b does not appear as "overly emphasized contextually free-floating filler" (Irsigler, "Psalm 22," 199); on trust as a basic motif in the Psalms of Lament, see 81ff. below.

117. On the following discussion, see O. Fuchs, *Klage als Gebet*, 178ff.; A. Müller, "Stimmungsumschwung," 423ff.

the moment in which the certainty of being saved by God[118] is again achieved, it is irrelevant for the situation, whether it is formulated through a *past tense* in terms of an completed action ("You have answered me") or whether it is emphasized as God's simultaneously occurring response in the *present* ("Now I know that you have answered me"). The Hebrew perfect permits both possibilities of interpretation.[119] Regarding Psalm 22:1–21 (2–22), the climax therefore consists of the two speech-acts of verses 1–11 (2–12) and 12–21 (13–22) being enriched by elements of trust (vv. 3–5 + 9–11 [4–6 +10–12]) and intensified by petitions (19–21 [20–22]) such that verse 21/22b assumes the quality of an *anticipated fact*:

> Salvation becomes an already-decided and completed action of God drawn from the future into the present. "The word of Yahweh has already been given, and now the enemies must vanish as a result." Yahweh's answer is therefore already spoken; everything else is merely the result of this decision that has yet to be experienced. From the supplicant's perspective, this is a *perfectum confidentiae* or *propheticum*; from the perspective of the acting God, it is the perfect on a definitive future tense. The *determined certainty* of future salvation corresponds to the trustful confidence of the hope to be heard.[120]

This understanding is supported by C. Markschies's thesis that trust is the basic motif of the lament of the individual, which is thereby made into a "purposeful paradigm of trust."[121] It appears not only at the end, but in all parts of the lament: in the introduction through the invocation, after the complaint, after the petition, and in the conclusion.[122] The trust motif is

118. The "answer" in v. 21/22b therefore does not consist of a verbal expression, but of YHWH's savaing action, which is experienced by the supplicant as the "being heard" of his complaints and petitions; cf. Kessler, "Der antwortende Gott," 53ff.; and Hossfeld and Zenger, *Die Psalmen*, 1:150: The supplicant achieves the sudden certainty of being heard probably "through gaining confidence himself. The [expression] 'you have answered me' has cancelled God's nonresponse, which had prompted the complaints."

119. See Gross, "Otto Rössler," 62ff.; cf. GKC §106g/n; as well as Kilian, "Ps 22," 182–83; Vanoni, "Psalm 22," 176–77, etc.

120. O. Fuchs, *Klage als Gebet*, 184; also Kilian, "Ps 22," 176–77.

121. Markschies, "Vertrauensäusserungen," 386ff. Recently, Albertz, "Warum 'Wozu'?," 318ff., has argued against the idea that the trust motif was the basic motif of the individual lament, which functions as the "purposeful paradigm of trust" (cf. Markschies [earlier], O. Fuchs, Janowski) in the individual lament. Such a strong emphasis of the trust motif virtually lessens the radicalness of the lament, according to Albertz, and softens "its hardness in part by philological means" (320). Albertz even speaks of an attempted "theological domestication" of the Old Testament laments, which are for him testimonies of "despair."

The main point of the argument is the idea that the Psalms of Lament are "spoken in a context of being abandoned by God or being distant from God, but still in the hope that God is near especially in this affliction" (see 79 above). I generally affirm this idea, but would further add that the Psalms of Lament were spoken in the hope (!) that God is near in this affliction, even if everything seems to contradict such nearness and the relation to God is deeply disturbed. This counterfactual, or perhaps desperate, hope appears at the beginning of many Psalms of the Individual (a fact overlooked by Albertz), first quite unremarkable in the invocation of the supplicant, who then enters through the lament with increasing intensity into an argument with God. We are therefore not dealing with naked, hopeless despair. Likewise, I cannot agree that the supplicant has lost all hope: why and to whom would the petitioner otherwise be praying? I would rather say that the Psalms of Lament keep the question of God open and do not answer it prematurely, but they never fully leave the foundation of trust, fragile as it may be. This is in my opinion also true for Mark 15:20ff.; see 322ff. in chap. 9, under "Disputes with God." Following Albertz is Wöhrle, "Gott"; for a more comprehensive discussion of the problem, see Rechberger, *Von der Klage zum Lob*, passim.

122. See the arrangement in Markschies, "Vertrauensäusserungen," 392ff.

> nothing other than the appeal to YHWH, which underlies all prayer in the laments of the individual, to take the life of the supplicant, who places personal trust in God's hand, under YHWH's protection. The petition is formulated as an expression of trust because, *even before any specific prayer*, the supplicant can confidently hope that YHWH will indeed intervene on one's own behalf. It is this confidence that characterizes the faith, which prompts the supplicant to pray to YHWH.[123]

The observation that the complaints are framed by the motif of trust and that the entire process of prayer is oriented toward the concluding confession of confidence and certainty of being heard also applies to the example of Psalm 13. Already the invocation "YHWH" (v. 1/2a) in the opening complaint of verses 1–2 (2–3) shows that the supplicant trusts YHWH—counterfactually—and expects to be saved only by YHWH. It is intensified in the petition of verses 3–4 [4–5] through an appositional vocative "YHWH my God" (v. 3/4a), which "adds to the name of the national Deity the characterization of a personal God."[124] Finally, the appositive "my God" (v. 3/4a) points ahead to the speech-act of the expression of trust in verse 5ab/6ab, which further intensifies the discourse in contrast to the complaint of verse 3/4. This expression of trust is

> a warning of Yahweh's loss of sovereignty as Lord over life and death, if the enemy—understood as mortal enemy—should be able to claim: "I have prevailed over him," if the supplicant's oppressor could rejoice, because the supplicant has been caused to fall. In a positive sense, this warning points in a perlocutionary way to a motivating appeal to Yahweh's honor.[125]

This warning points specifically to an appeal to YHWH's honor, not to consent to the enemy's triumph and therefore the fatality of the supplicant. If one also considers the series of four questions and two petitions and their high potential of expectation with regard to YHWH's answer or reaction, an ascending line emerges in Psalm 13, which begins with the articulation of YHWH's name in verse 1/2, builds up in the invocation "YHWH, my [!] God" of verse 3/4, and culminates in the expression of trust "your [!] goodness // your [!] salvation" of verse 5/6:

How long, **YHWH**? Will you forget me forever?
How long will you hide your face from me? (Ps. 13:1/2)

Look here, answer me, **YHWH my God**!
Let my eyes shine, so that I will not sleep the sleep of death. (v. 3/4)

But I—I have trusted in **your goodness**,
my heart rejoices over **your salvation.** (v. 5/6ab)

This ascending line of trust corresponds inversely to a descending line of complaints:

123. Ibid., 386–87, emphasis added.
124. Irsigler, "Psalm-Rede," 78.
125. Ibid., 78.

Increasing trust	(vv.)	Decreasing complaint	(vv.)
↓ YHWH 1/2		↓ Complaint	1–2 (2–3)
↓ YHWH my God	3/4	↓ Petition	3–4 (4–5)
↓ Your goodness//salvation	5/6ab	↓ Trust/pledge of praise	6/6cd

The expression of trust in verse 5/6a, which is formulated with the perfect of בָּטַח—"I have trusted in your goodness > I place my trust"—indicates that it is the same basic trust that has carried the prayer from the beginning, although it had not been experienced as such by the supplicant amid the feeling of abandonment by God (v. 1/2). It is only posited "as a new fact"[126] by the declarative language of the praise in verse 5/6ab.

The full reality of being heard and the salvation that comes with it is, according to Psalm 13 as well as 22:1–21 (2–22), only demonstrated in the future biography of the supplicant. Now, at the transition from complaint and petition to praise (Ps. 13:4→6 [5→6]; cf. 22:21→22 [22→23]), the supplicant is situated in an intermediate state, which has the quality of an "anticipated fact," into the active realm of which he *has* presently entered.[127] The exact extent of the *petitionary* (petition) and the *factual* (certainty of being heard) dimensions cannot be determined with certainty. Even if the perfect form of Psalm 22:21/22b ("You have answered me") suggests a greater component of the certainty of being heard,[128] the element of petition has not completely disappeared: it moves along within the process of prayer—until the supplicant is back on solid ground in trusting in God.

A premature explanation of this situation between complaint and praise through the hypothesis of a "priestly oracle of salvation" should also be avoided on the basis of pastoral theology. This would imply the insertion of an institutional unambiguousness, which does not do justice to the dynamic character of the laments of the individual. The complaint of the individual is a temporally compressed representation of a *process*: a passage through the states of distress → petition → certainty, which requires time in the life of the supplicant.[129] It can take days and nights, weeks and months, or even years, and it cannot be cut short by external formulas. An obligatory cultic institution like the "priestly oracle of salvation" from the time of ancient Israel would signify a precarious step—aside from the fact that there is no evidence for it. Rather, the laments have a particular kind of existence in mind, which is also constitutive of the human condition: a *situation between complaint and praise*, which can only be overcome through trust in God, and which may not be bypassed under any circumstances.[130] The obstacles that accompany the journeying supplicant

126. Irsigler, "Psalm-Rede," 86.
127. Cf. O. Fuchs, *Klage als Gebet*, 184 n. 25.
128. This is also true for Ps. 13:6/6cd: "I shall sing to YHWH for what he has done for me!" (כִּי גָמַל עָלָי); cf. 74–75 above.
129. Cf. Bayer, "Klage III," 1392.
130. Cf. A. Müller, "Stimmungsumschwung," 426. In this regard, Irsigler ("Psalm-Rede," 88ff.) rightly identifies the "speaker's 'experiential process' as the Psalm's effective potential." "Ps. 13 as a whole, including the anticipated praise at the end, presupposes the situation of a petition that has not yet been heard. In this situation, the psalm does not exhibit a bilateral effect that has already occurred. Nevertheless, Ps. 13:6b/6d, 'for he has done to me,' expresses precisely such an effect as an observation or report" (ibid., 87).

are too severe for this. We shall examine them in greater detail in the following chapters.

Hermann Gunkel has rightly called Psalm 13 a "model of a 'complaint of the individual.'"[131] This is true not only because it unsparingly expresses the hiddenness of God and the resulting distress of the supplicant, but also because it suggests a path to overcome it. This path is the psalm itself—to be prayed and to be read—with its elements of complaint plus invocation (vv. 1–2 [2–3]), petition (3–4 [4–5]), affirmation of trust and promise of praise (5–6 [6]). It contains all that, expressing in words the distress of the afflicted, as well as that which allows the psalm to transcend the distress in order to open up new realms of experience.[132] The Psalms of Lament do not only instruct the supplicant to give expression to fears through words and images, but also to bring them before God in prayer. They can therefore be called, as my thesis suggests, conflict-resolution dialogues with God. Lohfink has characterized the therapeutic quality of the Psalms of Lament through the identification of the threat of the enemy as follows: "They are associated with an appeal to God. The sick person, who complains about enemies and thereby gives public expression to fear, places oneself at the same time in the hand of his [/her] God, knowing that God stands above the power of every possible enemy."[133]

Between the first and the last verses of Psalm 13, the path covered by the supplicant leads the petitioner to an observation of this certainty, the effect of which is already being experienced anticipatorily in the situation of being abandoned by "my God."

b. Anthropological Keyword 1: Seeing and Hearing

A hearing ear and a seeing eye—
YHWH has indeed made them both.
Proverbs 20:12

With the ear, I had heard of you,
But now, my eye has seen you.
Job 42:5

Resources

Arambarri, *Der Wortstamm "hören"*; J. Assmann, "Auge und Ohr"; Berlejung, *Theologie der Bilder*; Blumenberg, "Licht als Metapher"; Boman, *Hebräische Denken*; Brunner, "Das hörende Herz"; Dohmen, "'Nicht sieht mich'"; Fuhs, "רָאָה"; idem, *Sehen und Schauen*; Gross, "Das verborgene Gesicht Gottes"; Hartenstein, *Das Angesicht JHWHs*; idem, "Unvergleichliche Gestalt JHWHs"; Janowski, "JHWH und der Sonnengott"; Konersmann, "Augen der

131. Cf. 60 above.

132. As Erbele-Küster's reading (*Lesen als Akt des Betens*, 1) with regard to reader-response theories has shown, the praying and reading of the Psalms is an anthropological "act that opens to us a transformed relationship to the self, the world, and to God."

133. Lohfink, "Über die Feinde," 155.

Philosophen"; idem, "Sehen"; Kraus, "Hören und Sehen"; Lang, "Ein Kranker"; idem, "Sehen und Schauen"; Podella, *Lichtkleid JHWHs;* Rüterswörden, "שָׁמַע"; Schult, "שָׁמַע"; S. Schroer and Staubli, *Körpersymbolik der Bibel;* Seeligmann, "Erkenntnis Gottes"; Smith, "'Seeing God'"; idem, "Solar Language"; Tournay, *Seeing and Hearing God;* Vincent, *Das Auge hört;* Vernant, *Der Mensch;* Wenzel, *Hören und Sehen;* H. W. Wolff, *Anthropology;* Zenger, "'Gib deinem Knecht.'"

On the topic in general, see also T. Krüger, "Ohr/Hören"; Savran, "Seeing Is Believing"; Schwienhorst-Schönberger, "Sehen im Nicht-Sehen"; Dyma, "'Gottes Angesicht schauen'?"; Hartenstein, "Vom Sehen und Schauen Gottes." Theological reflections on the relationship of seeing and hearing and the thesis that (for Christians) seeing follows hearing are found in Bayer, "Schöpfungslehre" (esp. 30ff.).

Seeing and hearing are the dominant senses of human beings. We respond to the body language of other people, we react to their facial expressions and gestures, and we consider the rhythms and intonations of their speech. To be sure, there are cultural differences. Western culture is, according to the philosopher R. Konersmann, "a culture of seeing. A look pierces and surveys, inquires and examines, connects and divides, and continues even if there is nothing left to see. . . . The history of seeing is long and multifaceted. Far from following a single, clearly outlined path, this history includes countless and not infrequently rival opinions and positions."[134]

These opinions generally take pre-Socratic theories as their point of departure and continue across historical watersheds into modernity.[135] Hearing constitutes a particularly effective competitor but never achieves primacy in the unfolding of history. This appears to be different in the Hebrew tradition, which at the most accords the realm of empirical verification to seeing, but which otherwise follows the paradigm of the word that is heard and heeded. Matters are, however, not as simple as the established contrast of "seeing and hearing" would suggest.

α. *Primacy of Hearing?*

The critique brought against the pre-Socratics and their heirs is that true recognition is reserved for the mind's eyes. One must therefore avert or close the physical eye at the right time:

> M. Luther carries this reservation over the threshold of modernity when he teaches that the kingdom of Christ "is a hearing kingdom, not a seeing kingdom. For the eyes do not guide and lead us to the place where we find Christ and learn to know him, but the ears must do so." The *competition of the senses,* which is thereby intensified and in the long run replaces the coordinating efforts of the Aristotelian sensus communis, thus enables the development

134. Konersmann, "Augen der Philosophen," 9.

135. See Konersmann, "Sehen." On the cultural history of eye and ear, see esp. A. Assmann, "Auge und Ohr: Bemerkungen."

> of a dualistic pattern. The invisible could, on the one hand, be radicalized into the absent, for which no positive information can be found in the visible realm, or it could be resolved into the potentially visible, which will reveal itself in due time.[136]

Going back from here to the biblical roots, the primacy of hearing before seeing does not appear to be in question.[137] Thus H. W. Wolff speaks of the nature of the human at the end of the first part of his *Anthropology of the Old Testament*[138] and sees it as defined by human capacity for speech.[139] It is the hearing and responding human being, according to Wolff, that is the truly existing human being. The fact that the human also sees is evident but is secondary to hearing and responding. "It is the hearing, the hearing above all . . . [Ps. 38:13a, 14a (14a, 15a)], that makes man—that, and the corresponding opening of the mouth, the being able to answer [38:13b, 14b (14b, 15b)],"[140] writes Wolff:

> But I am like one who is deaf, I do not hear;
> like one who is dumb, who does not open the mouth.
> I became like a person who does not hear,
> who has no reply in the mouth.
> (Ps. 38:13–14 [14–15])

According to H. W. Wolff, these verses constitute the climax of the complaint of Psalm 38:9–14 (10–15): "The man who is threatened with becoming deaf and dumb must fear for his humanity." Accordingly, "the hearing ear and the properly directed tongue are the essential organs for man."[141]

The thesis of "the importance of hearing and of speech for true human understanding"[142] has long been a fundamental rule of Old Testament studies, and has led T. Boman, for example, to the idea that "the Greeks experienced their existence by seeing and the Hebrews by hearing."[143] This assumption was based on the idea that the creative word of God in Genesis 1:1–2:4a calls the world into being and is continually active in history. However, one should be cautious not only with regard to the image of God—noting only the formula of approval in Genesis 1, which begins with the verb "to see" (רָאָה), "and God *saw* . . ." (vv. 4, 10, 12; etc.)—but also with regard to the image of humanity.[144] One must ask if "human privilege," according to Genesis 2:18–23, lies simply in the fact "that [the human] is allowed to speak."[145] To be sure, that speech begins with naming the animals and thus responding to the Creator's gift (vv. 18–20). However, it is precisely the perception of the eye, to which the praise of

136. Konersmann,"Sehen," 123. The Luther quote is taken from a sermon given in Merseburg on August 6, 1545 (WA 51:11).

137. This primacy is the legacy of Aristotle's Logos theory (Aristotle, *De sensu* 473a; *Metaphysics*, 980b.23–25), which scrutinizes the phenomenal world in order to find the Logos. See Gadamer, *Wahrheit und Methode*, 466–67; cf. also Fuhs, "רָאָה," 234; Vincent, *Das Auge hört*, 30–31.

138. H. W. Wolff, *Anthropology*, 74ff.

139. Ibid., 79.

140. Ibid., 74.

141. Ibid., 74–75.

142. Ibid., 75.

143. Boman, *Das hebräische Denken*, 6; cf. 60ff., 180ff.; for the significance of seeing in ancient Greece, see Vernant, *Der Mensch*, 7ff.

144. See Kraus, "Hören und Sehen," 89ff.; and esp. Fuhs, "רָאָה," 232ff.

145. H. W. Wolff, *Anthropology*, 77.

Genesis 2:23 responds: "This [the woman] is finally bone of my bone and flesh of my flesh!"[146]

Human vision also has a fundamental significance in other ways in the Old Testament.[147] It can *verify* or *correct* what has been heard. There are numerous examples for both instances. The Zion Psalms praise the beauty of God's city and the majesty of the royal God YHWH, who resides there (Ps. 48:1–3 [2–4]). On the occasion of a pilgrimage to Zion, the pilgrims could verify through observation that the reports of the beauty of Zion correspond to the reality of what has been seen:

> As we have heard [שָׁמַע], so we have seen [רָאָה]
> in the city of YHWH Sabaoth, in the city of our God:
> God establishes her forever! *Selah.*
> (Ps. 48:8/9)

That which has been heard remains lifeless knowledge if it does not come alive through the act of seeing and become an experience that enriches life.[148] The second example, concerning the correction of what has been heard by what has been seen, is found in the book of Job, specifically in 42:1–6, which ascribes Job's repentance to a visionary encounter with God:

> I had heard of you with my ears [שָׁמַע],
> but now my eye has seen you [רָאָה];
> therefore I retract and repent,
> with/as dust and ashes.
> (Job 42:5–6)[149]

This text shows that "seeing God" is a personal experience of God, which goes beyond hearing and overthrows everything one has heard about God thus far, because it is a direct encounter with the living God. The force of this statement becomes clear only if one compares it with other statements about the possibility—or rather impossibility—for human beings to see God's face.[150]

In addition, there is another strand of tradition in the Old Testament that bases the true form of Israelite cultic worship on the transcendence of YHWH. According to this tradition, the prohibitions of having images and worshiping other gods constitute the main commandments of the YHWH religion.[151] It is in this sense that in the late Deuteronomistic text of Deuteronomy 4:9–31,

146. Even earlier one can speak of "successful human speech . . . that recognizes what it encounters in its own nature and 'assimilates' it to human existence before returning it" (H.-P. Müller, "Mythische Elemente," 29), esp. at the naming of the animals (Gen. 2:19–20). The human speech-act finds its first climax in the relation-formula of Gen. 2:23.

147. See Kraus, "Hören und Sehen," 94ff. Furthermore, "vision" is the most common sense in the Old Testament; cf. S. Schroer and Staubli, *Körpersymbolik der Bibel*, 123ff. Also the parallel of "seeing" and "recognizing" (יָדַע) is much more common than that of "recognizing" and "hearing"; cf. Seeligmann, "Erkenntnis Gottes," 427ff.

148. Cf. Fuhs, "רָאָה," 234.

149. For textual notes and the interpretation of v. 6, see Ebach, *Streiten mit Gott*, 2:155; Strauss, *Hiob*, 336, 348, 388–89, etc. See also Savran, "Seeing Is Believing," 335ff., 350ff; Rohde, *Der Knecht Hiob*, 67ff.; and Janowski, "Gerechtigkeit Gottes," esp. 10–11.

150. Cf. Lang, "Ein Kranker," 143ff.; Gese, "Frage nach dem Lebenssinn," 180–81. Job 42:5 refers to 19:27, i.e., a text that is thematically related to Ps. 73:23–26; see 318ff. below.

151. Exod. 20:4; Deut. 5:8; cf. Deut. 4:12, 15, 16, 23, 25. On the prohibition of images, see the survey in Uehlinger, "Bilderverbot."

the Horeb theophany points to Israel's hearing YHWH,[152] but not to its seeing YHWH's likeness:

YHWH's Divine Transcendence at Horeb (Deut. 4:9–14)

> You came closer and stood at the foot of the mountain,
> while the mountain was blazing with fire up to the midst [= heart]
> of the heavens
> in darkness, clouds and dark clouds, (v. 11)
> and YHWH spoke to you from the midst of the fire.
> You heard the sound of words,
> but a likeness [תְּמוּנָה] you did not see! Only a voice . . . (v. 12)

The Prohibition of Images as Specification of the Main Commandment (Deut. 4:15–22)

> So take good care of your lives—
> for you have not seen any likeness [כָּל תְּמוּנָה]
> on the day YHWH spoke to you at Horeb
> from the midst of the fire— (v. 15)
> that you do not become corrupt and make a cultic image [פֶּסֶל]
> [in] the shape [תְּמוּנָה] of anything at all. . . . (v. 16)

As described in Deuteronomy 4:15–22, the impossibility of a symbolic representation of YHWH[153] is not without precedent within the literature of the Old Testament. Older traditions, such as Exodus 3:6 (Moses and the burning bush) or 1 Kgs. 19:13 (Elijah at Horeb), speak of Moses or Elijah as covering his face in fear of "looking at" God (Exod. 3:6, נבט Hiphil). The act of covering one's face is an expression of reverence before God and at the same time of protecting the person from the vision of God's consuming majesty. The unspoken premise here is formulated in Exodus 33:20 as a general precept:

> You cannot see my face,
> for no human being can see me and live![154]

The difference between God and humanity is "too great for humans' seeing God—in the sense of an unmediated encounter—to even be possible."[155] The basis for this difference is in the biblical understanding of revelation:

> God's care for his people is linguistically expressed in the idea of God's seeing, as looking out for them. Consequently the human endeavor to seek God, to turn toward God, can also be expressed through the idea of seeing. Insofar as *seeing God* is largely determined by the understanding of revelation in the Old Testament, theophanies and experiences of the closeness/grace of God

152. On the "auditory experience at Sinai," see Zenger, "'Gib deinem Knecht,'" 33ff., esp. 39–40.
153. On the interpretation of this text, see Hartenstein, "Unvergleichliche Gestalt JHWHs"; cf. Braulik, *Deuteronomium*, 4ff., Podella, *Lichtkleid JHWHs*, 180ff.; Keel, "Warum im Jerusalemer Tempel," 252ff.
154. Cf. Exod. 19:21; etc.; on the topic, see W. Schmidt, *Exodus*, 55–56, 159; Dohmen, "'Nicht sieht mich,'" 36, 46; Hartenstein, „Das Angesicht JHWHs," 171ff., esp. 178ff.
155. Dohmen, "'Nicht sieht mich,'" 46.

are more significant for this understanding than specific traditions regarding cultic images.[156]

β. Seeing God

It is, however, precisely that human beings *do* see God and nevertheless remain alive, or even have a heightened experience in their encounter with God, that the Old Testament relates in various places, not only in the patriarchal traditions,[157] but also within the Sinai pericope in Exodus 24:9–11.[158] It is told here that Moses, Aaron, Nadab, and Abihu together with seventy elders went up Mount Sinai and "saw the God of Israel" there (v. 10):

> Moses, Aaron, Nadab, and Abihu and seventy of the elders of Israel went up, (Exod. 24:9)
> and they saw [רָאָה] the God of Israel,
> and below his feet was something like a pavement of lapis lazuli,
> and [it was] just like the heavens in clearness/purity. (v. 10)
> But against the nobles of Israel he [God] did not stretch out his hand,
> and they beheld [חָזָה] God, and they ate and drank. (v. 11)

How unusual this vision of God is becomes clear in comparison to the volcano and thunderstorm visions of 19:16–19 and their "hearing-focused imagery."[159] The God, whom the representatives of Israel saw, is a God whose throne is in the heavens and under whose feet is something "like a pavement of lapis lazuli, and [it was] just like the heavens in clearness/purity." If one adds to this depiction of God—God as "King of the world, enthroned above the mountain that reaches into the heavens"[160]—the parallel texts of Ezekiel 1:22, 26 and 10:1, one can only conclude that we have in Exodus 24:1, 9–11 not a genuine Sinai tradition, but rather a Jerusalem temple theology, which was later associated with Sinai.[161] Although the text is aware of the danger of seeing God—it is implicitly assumed in verse 11—it states explicitly that such danger was not present here: "Those who saw were astonished; their meal gives expression to their joy. They do not celebrate with God, but in honor of God, in his presence, before him."[162]

The Old Testament's vision reports,[163] which include Exodus 24:9–11, are so significant that their content cannot be disregarded, perhaps from the assumption that faith is based only on hearing (cf. Rom. 10:17; in contrast, Job 42:5). This is also true, as we have seen, for the laments of the individual and their theme of "seeing God." Thus Psalm 13:1/2 complains of YHWH's forgetting

156. Ibid., 50, emphasis original.
157. Thus notice ראה Niphal (appear) + subject YHWH: Gen. 12:7; 17:1; 18:1; 26:2; etc.
158. On this text, see esp. Jeremias, *Theophanie*, 204ff.; W. Schmidt, *Alttestamentlicher Glaube*, 51ff.; Willi-Plein, *Opfer und Kult*, 64ff.; Vincent, *Das Auge hört*, 81ff.; Hartenstein, "Wolkendunkel," 136ff.
159. See Zenger, *Am Fuss des Sinai*, 101ff.; idem, "'Gib deinem Knecht,'" 33–34. On the compositional structure of Exod. 19, see esp. Blum, *Komposition des Pentateuch*, 45ff.
160. Jeremias, *Theophanie*, 205.
161. See ibid., 205–6; and esp. Hartenstein, "Wolkendunkel," 138ff.
162. Perlitt, *Bundestheologie*, 187.
163. See the survey in Willi-Plein, "Vision."

(in parallelism to "hiding your face") and therefore pleads for YHWH to "look" (v. 3/4a) and to "hear" (v. 3/4a), so that the supplicant may not die (v. 3/4b).[164] The courtly and cultic temple-theological context of this expression can be explained on the basis of Numbers 6:24–26.[165] It has, however, also other connecting points in the Psalms, as the following examples show.

The Shining "Face of YHWH"

The expression "to behold [חָזָה] or see [רָאָה] God/YHWH or the face of God/YHWH" describes a particularly intensive, concretely "physical" form of contact with God:

> Seeing includes comprehensive effects of blessing and grace. Illness, isolation, and the threat of death are overcome "before the face" of YHWH, just as being present in the sphere of his throne promises the individual protection and salvation from persecution and oppression by the enemy. To "see God" therefore signifies *life and fullness of life* in the most intensive form that one can imagine *in the context of a court-centered spatial symbolism.*[166]

Some texts have as their backdrop the idea of YHWH's *connection to the sun,* such as the postexilic Zion Psalm 84:10–12 (11–13):

> Yes, better is one day in your courts
> than a thousand of my own choosing;
> it is better to stand at the threshold to the house of my God,
> than to dwell in the tents of wickedness. (v. 10/11)
> Yes, YHWH God is sun [שֶׁמֶשׁ] and shield [מָגֵן],
> YHWH bestows grace and glory;
> [YHWH] denies nothing that is good
> to those who walk in completeness/integrity. (v. 11/12)
> YHWH Sabaoth,
> blessed is the one who trusts in you. (v. 12/13)[167]

The metaphors of verse 11/12a contain a depiction of God that appears to presuppose a *solar presence of YHWH in the temple*[168] and points to the saving (sun) and protective (shield) aspects of YHWH. That this implies a visual act is indicated by verse 7/8, in which the supplicant hopes "to see" (רָאָה) YHWH as the goal of his deprivations:

164. Cf. Ps. 38:10/11; etc.; see also chap. 3, 64ff., 68ff. On the contrast of light/darkness, see also "Excursus 3: Light and Darkness," 69–70 above.

165. See 69-70 above.

166. Hartenstein, *Das 'Angesicht JHWHs,* 124, emphasis original.

167. It is therefore "better to stand at the threshold to the house of my God, than to dwell in the tents of wickedness" (Ps. 84:10/11d), because the flame of the fire is extinguished in the tent of the wicked, and the lamp is put out inside the tent; cf. Job 18:5–7 and 307 below.

168. On "solar symbolism with regard to YHWH," which has shaped the understanding of God and the royal ideology since the Middle Monarchy (8th c. BCE), see Smith, "'Seeing God'"; idem, "Solar Language"; Keel, "Fern von Jerusalem," 484ff.; Keel and S. Schroer, *Schöpfung,* 77ff.; Janowski, "JHWH und der Sonnengott," 199ff.; Martin Arneth, *"Sonne der Gerechtigkeit,"* 1ff., 109ff., 201ff.; Hartenstein, *Das Angesicht JHWHs,* 173ff.

> They [the pilgrims] go from strength to strength,
> [until they] see the God of gods in Zion.
> (Ps. 84:7/8)[169]

A similar vision of God in the temple is also found in Psalm 42:1–2 (2–3):

> As the deer cries over [dried up] riverbeds,
> so my *nepeš*[170] cries for you, O God.
> My life thirsts[171] for God, the living God:
> when shall I come and "behold"[172] the face of God?

As the context of the two verses clearly shows, seeing the divine face in the sanctuary on Zion[173] is for the supplicant as vital as water for a panting deer, dying of thirst. This image appears on numerous Judahite seals and bulla of the eighth and seventh centuries (fig. 11). This predilection of Judahite seal-makers for deer

> is hardly based on the traditio-historical connection of these animals to the goddess, but can be explained indirectly through Psalm 42:1/2, where the deer seeking water is used as a metaphor of craving for life by the *nepeš* of the praying subject. . . . The deer represents the owner of the seal as supplicant and worshiper.[174]

God cannot be touched but can be heard and even seen. In the cultures of the Ancient Near East are striking examples of texts regarding the significance of seeing the deity or rather the deity's cultic image.[175] No less impressive are the figures of supplicants set up in Sumerian temples in the third millennium BCE (fig. 12), which represent the supplicant before the deity in order to direct the eyes on the deity and experience closeness through the senses. Even in the late Old Testament period we find personal names like Eliehoenai "my eyes [are fixed] on YHWH" (1 Chr. 26:3; Ezra 8:4) and Elioenai (1 Chr. 3:23–24; 4:36; 7:8; Ezra 10:22, 27; Neh. 12:41), that belong to the category of theophoric names and which effectively summarize the understanding of prayer as based on seeing the Deity.

169. The MT has the Niphal of ראה in 84:7/8b with the preposition אֶל־, "with/before": "he appears with/before God." However, the "appearance before God" is usually expressed through אל־פני or לפני; cf. Hossfeld and Zenger, *Psalmen 51–100*, 509. The MT is probably based on a dogmatic correction to avoid implying the corporeality of YHWH; cf. Kraus, *Psalmen*, 2:747; Hossfeld and Zenger, *Psalmen 51–100*, 509. A similar situation is found in Deut. 16:16; Ps. 42:2/3; etc.; and is also characteristic of the Septuagint-Psalter; see Fuhs, *Sehen und Schauen*, 251–52; Willi-Plein, *Opfer und Kult*, 131 (re Deut. 16:16); Vincent, *Das Auge Hört*, 244ff. On Ps. 84:7/8, 10–12 (11–13), see Jerome, *Desire for God's House*, 154ff., 178ff., 187ff., 202ff.; Janowski, "Ort des Lebens."

170. This is one of the (many) cases in which the lexeme נֶפֶשׁ cannot be translated any more precisely: although the context suggests the symbolic usage "life," the concrete meaning "throat" still resonates in it (esp. in connection with the verb עָרַג, "cry"); see Dockner, *Psalm 42 und 43*, 177.

171. On "thirsting for God" (Pss. 42:2/3; 63:1/2; 143:6), see Ruppert, "Dürsten nach Gott," 213ff.

172. MT: "I shall appear" (ראה Niphal); see n. 169.

173. The connection to the sanctuary is based on the combination of פָּנִים, "face" [of God], and the verb רָאָה, "see"; see Dockner, *Psalm 42 und 43*, 177–78; cf. Hartenstein, *Das Angesicht JHWHs*, 157 n.2.

174. Keel and Uehlinger, *Göttinnen, Götter*, 210; see also Keel, *Die Welt*, 347, fig. 498.

175. For Mesopotamia, see the reference in Lang, "Ein Kranker," 145ff.; and Gzella, *Lebenszeit und Ewigkeit*, 239; for Egypt, see J. Assmann, "Der schöne Tag," 209ff.; J. Assmann, "Ocular Desire"; for a textual example, see *ÄHG* 369ff.

Figure 11. Deer seeking water (7th c. BCE)

Figure 12. Sumerian supplicant from Tell Asmar (3rd millennium BCE)

The Saving "Likeness of YHWH"

Besides Psalm 42:1–2 (2–3) and 84:10–12 (11–13), the theme of seeing God or God's face is also found in Psalms 11:7; 17:15; 27:4, 13; and 63:2/3.[176] Psalm 27, which introduces YHWH in verse 1a as "light" and "salvation"—"YHWH, my light and my salvation, who should I fear?"—virtually describes the perception of divine closeness as a process of seeing:

> One thing I have asked of YHWH,
> therefore I ask it again:
> to dwell in the house of YHWH
> all the days of my life,
> to see the kindness [נֹעַם] of YHWH
> and to look upon his temple.
> (Ps. 27:4)
>
> If I was not confident,
> that I would see the goodness [טוֹב] of YHWH
> in the land of the living . . . (v. 13)[177]

Later I will discuss what "looking upon" or "seeing" YHWH or YHWH's "face," "kindness," or "goodness" means, in contrast to the texts prohibiting images,[178] using the example of Psalm 17:15.[179] According to this text, the supplicant has an experience that is in no way inferior to the vision described in Exodus 24:10. Yet the context is different, as already suggested by the term תְּמוּנָה ("visible likeness"), the polemical key term in the texts prohibiting images.[180]

> As for me, I shall behold [חָזָה] your face;
> I shall be satisfied [שָׂבַע] by your likeness [תְּמוּנָה] when I awake.
> (Ps. 17:15)

The singular occurrence of the expression "be satisfied by the likeness of YHWH" (v. 15b) has always been the subject of debate.[181] It can perhaps be explained on the basis of the parallelism of verse 15a ("behold the face of YHWH"). The expression "to be satisfied, sated" (שָׂבַע) with regard to the supplicant is not unusual and has a corresponding contrast in the motif of "thirsting

176. See Fuhs, *Sehen und Schauen*, 273ff., 6ff.; Smith, "'Seeing God,'" 171ff., 180ff.; Janowski, "JHWH und der Sonnengott," 206; idem, "Der barmherzige Richter," 69–70; Vincent, *Das Auge hört*, 27ff.; Podella, *Lichtkleid JHWHs*, 187ff.; Gzella, *Lebenszeit und Ewigkeit*, 237ff., 244ff.

177. According to Zenger, 22:4 and 13 are to be seen as reflecting a morning motif: "The supplicant wishes to look upon YHWH as upon the rising morning sun, which becomes for him a sign of victory over chaotic opponents" (Hossfeld and Zenger, *Die Psalmen*, 1:174). Cf. ibid., 175 on v. 13: "The morning epiphany of the sun is for the vulnerable supplicant a sign of divine power and decisiveness to overcome the mortal enemies through legal action." On the morning motif, see 95 below.

178. See 88–89 above.

179. See Kwakkel, *My Righteousness*, 96ff.; Sigurvinsson, "Ps 17, 14c–e," esp. 66–67; Basson, *Divine Metaphors*, 94–95; Janowski, "Angesicht/Schauen Gottes"; and comprehensively, Hartenstein, *Das Angesicht JHWHs*.

180. See תְּמוּנָה, "form, likeness," Exod. 20:4 // Deut. 5:8; cf. Deut. 4:12, 15, 16, 23, 25; also Num. 12:8; Job 4:16. See Dohmen, *Das Bilderverbot*, 216ff.; S. Schroer and Staubli, *Körpersymbolik der Bibel*, 335–36; Ernst-Joachim Waschke, "תְּמוּנָה"; Hartenstein, *Das Angesicht JHWHs*, 112ff.

181. See Fuhs, *Sehen und Schauen*, 272–73; Warmuth, "שָׂבַע," 697; also see the commentaries.

for God."[182] However, the question is whether the image in its context is to be understood literally or metaphorically.

The Quality of Satisfaction

As in Psalm 104:27–28,[183] שָׂבַע, "to be satisfied," indicates something concrete. In contrast to that text, however, the means of satisfaction is not physical food (אֹכֶל, "food" // טוֹב, "goodness") from the hand of God, but the "visible likeness" (תְּמוּנָה) of YHWH (17:15). According to Dohmen, this likeness could indicate an "ambiguous, shadowy seeing,"[184] or the shape or outline of an apparition.

The Timing of Satisfaction

The moment of "satisfaction" is said to be the "waking" (בְהָקִיץ) in the morning (17:15).[185] (Cf. the reference to "night" in v. 3 and generally the pattern of time in Pss. 3–7: (evening / morning, 3:5/6; evening, 4:8/9; morning, 5:3/4; night, 6:6/7; day, 7:11/12).[186] This could be, but does not have to be, a reference to the daily morning epiphany of the "sun-god" YHWH,[187] who saves the supplicant from his enemies (17:13–14) as God of justice (vv. 1–2).[188]

Regardless of how the singular expression of Psalm 17:15 is understood—literally or metaphorically—the "seeing" of the royal likeness of YHWH describes a vision in which YHWH's saving justice (cf. vv. 2–3) is manifested to the senses of the supplicant, becomes "visible" and experienceable to the petitioner, without necessarily pointing to a solar theophany. The experience of the divine vision, according to Gzella's interpretation of the text in question, relates to

> the specific end of the night of the lamenting cry for help and therefore . . . the sudden salvation from a momentary and very concrete affliction, here with the acquittal in a divine court case. . . . This experience is consolidated in the explicit vision of the One who alone can bring salvation, as indisputable proof of [God's] presence. When it occurs, the supplicant "sees" clearly that God is at work: it can be no one else. In the same way, "justice" at waking is to be understood: The innocence of the supplicant in this specific case becomes manifest.[189]

182. Cf. צָמְאָה, "[it] thirsts," Pss. 42:2/3; 63:1/2; cf. 84:2/3; 143:6. See n. 171 above.

183. See 65 above.

184. Dohmen, "'Nicht sieht mich,'" 39 n. 23.

185. In the Septuagint, this expression and the verse in general are reinterpreted eschatologically. See Gzella, *Lebenszeit und Ewigkeit*, 240ff.

186. See Janowski, "Der barmherzige Richter," 69ff.

187. Cf. Hossfeld and Zenger, *Die Psalmen*, 1:118: "Overcoming the dangers of the night at sunrise, survival in spite of enemies is, for the supplicant, a sign of YHWH's assistance and at the same time a vindication of one's status as 'righteous.'" Cf. also Podella, *Lichtkleid JHWHs*, 199, who relates the divine vision described in Ps. 17:15 to the rising of the "sun-god" YHWH in the morning. On the idea that תְּמוּנָה is to understood as a cultic statue of YHWH (Loretz, Niehr, et al.), see Keel, "Warum im Jerusalemer Tempel."

188. The scrutinizing eyes that "see what is right" (v. 2b) are, according to Hossfeld and Zenger, *Die Psalmen*, 1:116, those of the judging and saving "sun-god" YHWH. Cf. also Pss. 11:4–6; 14:2; and "Anthropological Keywords 3: Heart and Kidneys," 155ff. below.

189. Gzella, *Lebenszeit und Ewigkeit*, 238. Whether an "acquittal in a divine court case" constitutes the background to this text, however, is in my opinion purely hypothetical. See Janowski, *Rettungsgewissheit*, 6ff.; Oeming, *Psalm 1–41*, 64ff.

The "satisfaction," which the supplicant experiences upon seeing the "likeness" of YHWH, describes therefore a *manifestation of YHWH's salvation*: the justification of the supplicant with regard to the enemies.[190] "To see God in this way means to inhabit [God's] 'realm' of justice, of protection and fullness of life."[191] That this form of "satisfaction of life" was not at all self-evident to the supplicant will be discussed in greater detail in the analysis of Psalm 88:3/4,[192] the countertext of 17:15, so to speak.

Summary: Seeing and Hearing

Neither of these two human senses has priority over the other. Both make the "mouth which expresses what ear and eye had perceived . . . the organ that distinguishes [the hu]man from all other creatures,"[193] or as Proverbs 20:12 emphasizes: "The hearing ear and the seeing eye—YHWH has indeed made the both!" For human beings,

> God has created two sense organs, with which they can perceive different things, for one teaching through hearing, for the other experience through seeing. It is now the responsibility of human beings to make use of both. YHWH has established the conditions for a good, not a failed existence, but human beings have to make their own use of them.[194]

The ability of human beings to use these conditions and to live accordingly is one of the central motifs of the individual's Psalms of Lament and Thanksgiving. It recurs especially when human beings who are called enemies in the Psalter deny the supplicant the "good, not failed existence." The following chapter will provide an introduction to the offensive world of the enemy.

190. On the theme of "justification of the righteous," see 128ff. below.

191. Hartenstein, *Das Angesicht JHWHs*, 115; see also the considerations of Erbele-Küster, *Lesen als Akt des Betens*, 168ff.

192. See 223–24 below.

193. H. W. Wolff, *Anthropology*, 76.

194. Meinhold, *Die Sprüche*, 273.

4. "Swords are on their lips" (Ps. 59:7/8)
The Hostile Human Being

a. The Incomprehensibility of Evil

In the Enemy's Hand

You are in the enemy's hand
already they are grinding your
bones, they crush
your gaze,
they extinguish your gaze
with trampling feet,
trill into your ear
with alarm whistles
alarm.

Ingeborg Bachmann,
Gedichte, 20

α. The Enemies of the Supplicant

The scene is well known, but still as shocking as ever: "And when they were in the field, Cain rose up against his brother Abel and killed him" (Gen. 4:8b). This verse concludes the narrative of the gruesome act that entered the annals of human history as the "first fratricide" (Gen. 4:3–8). Prior to this it was reported that Cain had been angry with his brother because YHWH had not looked with favor at his own offering, but favored Abel's (vv. 3–5). Nothing is said about God's reasons, only about the reaction of the spurned: Cain became very angry, so that his face [facial features] fell (v. 5b). Before he was completely overcome by bitterness, YHWH issued a warning to him, which is important for the view of God in this narrative.

Then YHWH said to Cain:
  Why did [your anger] flare up,
  and why did your face [facial features] fall? (4:6)
Is it not true:
  If you let it be well, [it yields] a friendly reception,
  and if you do not let it be well,
  it settles as an [opening>] occasion to slip,
  and yet, its desire is [directed] toward you,
  and you are the one who may rule/control it.[1] (4:7)

1. On the translation, see Janowski, "Jenseits von Eden."

This warning reveals that God's rejection is not caused by hatred, for "God loves Cain, therefore he warns him."[2] YHWH sees the terrible possibility of murder and worries that his creature may make use of this possibility.

But Cain does not heed God's warning. He waits for an opportunity "in the open field" (בַּשָּׂדֶה)—"because screaming has no effect there"[3]—then rises up against Abel and kills him. No more is said about it. In the end we even learn that the one who murdered his brother received neither the death penalty[4] nor any other kind of sanction. On the contrary: Cain receives a sign from YHWH, which protects him from attempts by others to kill him—from "anyone who finds him" (v. 14b; cf. 15b). Between this end and the beginning of the narrative, Cain's act is described without any emotional appeal or moralizing overtones as a naked fact, which therefore appears all the more shocking. One human being kills another, who is even his brother. The murder of one's brother, the antihumane act per se, is the original pattern of interpersonal conflicts. "We are all Cainites,"[5] comments Manfred Görg.

One can, however, also kill with words. In any case, such is the dubious reputation of the Enemy Psalms in the Old Testament.[6] Their wishes for destruction and vengeance have prompted Christians again and again to designate the Old Testament as a "pre-Christian book"—not in the historical sense but with a pejorative meaning. Erich Zenger speaks of a "Christian nagging over the 'Jewish' Psalms,"[7] which gives categorically bad ratings to these texts or even imposes significant amputations on them. One either ignores the unpopular psalms or "sanitizes" incriminating passages. Especially the so-called Curse or Vengeance Psalms (Pss. 58; 59; 69; 70; 109; 137; etc.)[8] were often used in this context. They are indeed difficult to digest, as Psalms 58:3–9 (4–10) and 137:8–9 demonstrate:

> The wicked are rebellious from the womb;
>   the liars go astray from the mother's womb.
> (Ps. 58:3/4)
> Their venom is like a serpent's venom,
>   like [that of] a deaf adder, stopping its ears, (v. 4/5)
> [so that] it does not hear the voice of the [snake]-charmer
>   or the spellcaster of spells. (v. 5/6)

2. Zimmerli, *1. Mose 1–11*, 213.

3. Willis, *Genesis*, 104 n. 16. Not until the blood shed by Abel "cries" (צָעַק) from the soil to YHWH is the Deity prompted to curse the murderer (Gen. 4:11–12) and cause him to be estranged from the soil he has stained with his bloody act (4:11).

4. In this case, human history would have ended almost immediately after it began; cf. Dietrich and Link, *Die dunklen Seiten Gottes*, 1:153 n. 407. A decision similar to YHWH's in Gen. 4:1–6 had to be made by David after 2 Sam. 14:6, 11, and "he like YHWH decided *in favor* of the murderer's life (v. 11)" (ibid., 153 n. 411).

5. Görg, *Der un-heile Gott*, 103; cf. Lohfink, "Das vorpersonale Böse," 192ff.

6. On the subject of enemies in the Psalms, see Bauer, *Rachgier*, 80ff.; and esp. Frevel, "'Mögen sie fluchen'"; Dietrich and Mayordomo, *Gewaltüberwindung*, 144ff.; Brüning, "Zu den Feindaussagen"; Eidevall, "Images of God, Self, and the Enemy"; Berlejung and Merz, "Feind"; Hossfeld, "Das göttliche Strafgericht"; Weber, *Werkbuch*, 3:116ff.; and Hartenstein, "Funktion der Feindbilder."

7. Zenger, *Das Erste Testament*, 38ff. (including relevant examples); cf. idem, *Ein Gott der Rache*; Baldermann, *Einführung in die Bibel*, 89ff.; O. Fuchs, "Die Herausforderung Israels," 89ff., 93ff., etc. A particularly crass example of such "nagging" is a pamphlet by Buggle, *Denn sie wissen nicht*, 78ff.; see Janowski, "'Hingabe' oder 'Opfer'?," 19ff.; Krawczack, *Psalm 58*, 3–4.

8. See Ruppert, "Fluch- und Rachepsalmen"; Zenger, "Fluchpsalmen"; Lang, "Rachepsalmen"; Krawczack, *Psalm 58*, 1ff., 6ff.; and references in Janowski, "Dem Löwen gleich," 51 n. 10.

O God, break the teeth in their mouths;
smash the teeth of the young lions, O YHWH! (v. 6/7)
Let them vanish like water that flows away;
when they shoot their arrows, let them fall down. (v. 7/8)
Let [them] perish like a miscarriage that you allow to perish,
[like] a woman's stillbirth that does not see the sun. (v. 8/9)
Before your pots can feel the bramble [burning],
He [YHWH] will blow them away alive and also [in] fury. (v. 9/10)[9]

Daughter Babel, you who ordained destruction,
blessed be he who repays you for your actions
that you have done to us.
Blessed is he who grabs and smashes
your children on a rock. (137:8–9)

Such verses make every halfway decent person shudder. This is especially true since Psalm 137 begins with the image of a nostalgic memory:

By the rivers/canals of Babylon, there we sat,
and we wept, when we remembered Zion.
On the poplars [of the Euphrates] there,
we hung our lyres. (137:1–2)

Can we still be understanding of such texts as Psalm 58 or 137 and still pray them, in particular in view of Jesus' commandment to love one's enemies?[10] As one knows, the sixth antithesis of the Sermon on the Mount, which deals with loving one's enemies (Matt. 5:43–48), begins as follows:

"You have heard it said:
'You shall love your neighbor
And hate your enemy.' (v. 43)
But I say to you:
Love your enemies
and pray for your persecutors, (v. 44)
that you may be children of your Father in heaven,
because he lets his sun rise on the wicked and the good,
and lets it rain over the just and the unjust." (v. 45)

9. Based on the German translation of Hossfeld and Zenger, *Psalmen 51–100*, 131; cf. also the translation by Uehlinger, "Antiker Tell," 176. On the carnage described in Ps. 58:10/11, see esp. Krawczack, *Psalm 58*, 292ff., 299ff.; Hossfeld and Zenger, *Psalmen 51–100*, 138–39.

10. See Krawczack, *Psalm 58*, 420ff., 445ff. We must be prepared, however, to familiarize ourselves with the way of thinking found in the Bible, which assumes a close connection between the concrete and the abstract levels of expression; see 22–23 above; and Keel, *Die Welt*, 8–9: "Every Old Testament scholar will understand the 'horn of the wicked' (Ps. 75:5, 11) figuratively as 'power of the wicked.' However, as soon as an idiom can be visualized more concretely, any consideration of the ANE [ancient Near Eastern] way of seeing and expression are quickly forgotten. Thus, the (blessing) wish 'Blessed is he who grabs and smashes your children on a rock!' (Ps. 137:9), spoken with regard to Babylon, causes usually nothing but shock. One may wonder, however, whether these 'children' are not to be understood as symbolic as their 'mother Babylon.' The inhabitants of the oppressing city or the children of the ruling dynasty signify the continuation of the unjust regime. The meaning of the verse could be rendered as: 'Blessed is the one who makes an end of your ever-regenerating rule!' That way, the verse would likely not offend anyone, although it also invokes a brutal act. Its brutality is, however, cloaked by the large mantle of abstract formulation." On Pss. 58 and 137, see also Zenger, *Ein Gott der Rache*, 88ff., 108ff.; and Krawczack, *Psalm 58*. On Ps. 137:8–9, see Risse, "Zur Auslegungsgeschichte von Ps 137, 9."

This is one of the most central Christian texts, which continues to exert a lasting influence on social norms of behavior. It is based, according to Ingo Baldermann, "on the simple insight that in places where vengeance is not restrained, there is no possibility of living in a larger community with others. Thus the vengeance prayers of the Psalms do not only contradict the ethics of the Sermon on the Mount, but also the commonly accepted ethical norms of our society."[11]

One might be glad over such an impact of Jesus' words—yet in reality we do not live accordingly. What we do in regard to our enemies is usually the opposite of that which the commandment to love one's enemies calls for: the commonplaceness of a "pattern of vengeance" gives expression to an elementary psychological law:

> Sustained injuries do not heal by themselves, but remain open wounds if there is no reconciliation. Vengeance is the possibility to bring about this reconciliation and this restoration of emotional integrity by oneself. . . . If the path to a direct retaliation is blocked, there are possibilities of transference or deflection onto weaker parties; these patterns are well known, and it is only a matter of determining the threshold of the compulsion it generates.[12]

We therefore need to take the challenge posed by enemies more seriously than a superficial reading of the commandment in Matthew 5:43–48 to love one's enemies would suggest.[13] Let us approach this problem through a reading of Psalm 59 and then return to the question of loving ones enemies and neighbors.[14]

β. Psalm 59 as an Example

To the choirmaster. To the tune "Do not destroy!" By David. A Miktam song. When Saul sent and they watched the house in order to kill him.

Deliver me from my enemies, my God,
  from those who rise up against me, protect me!
(Ps. 59:1/2)
Deliver me from the evildoers,
  from the men of blood, save me. (v. 2/3)
For see: they have lain in wait for me,
  strong men attack me.
No wickedness and no sin is in me, YHWH; (v. 3/4)
  for no fault [of mine] they attack and take up position.
Wake up, toward me, and see. (v. 4/5)
But you, YHWH, God Sabaoth, God of Israel,
  wake up to visit all the peoples;
have no mercy on any who commit faithless evil! *Selah*. (v. 5/6)

11. Baldermann, *Einführung in die Bibel*, 90. On the antitheses of the Sermon on the Mount, see Luz, *Nach Matthäus*, 244ff.; and Grünwaldt, *Auge um Auge*, 150ff.

12. Baldermann, *Einführung in die Bibel*, 90.

13. Far away from such superficiality was, e.g., D. Bonhoeffer, *Widerstand und Ergebung*, 226 (letter on the second Sunday of Advent, 1943, to E. Bethge). The task, in view of the church's treatment of the so-called Cursing Psalms, which cannot be further pursued here, consists among other thing in a reevaluation of the "difference between a 'scriptural' and 'liturgical' use of the Psalter" (Krawczack, *Psalm 58*, 443); see the discussions by O. Fuchs, "Die Herausforderung Israels"; Zenger, *Ein Gott der Rache*, 165ff.; Jauss, "Fluchpsalmen beten?"; van der Velden, *Psalm 109*, 176ff.; Krawczack, *Psalm 58*, 443ff.

14. See "Anthropological Keyword 2: Revenge," below, 120ff.

They return in the evening;
they growl like dogs and encircle the city. (v. 6/7)
See, they slobber at the mouth;
swords are on their lips
because [they say]: "Who should hear it?" (v. 7/8)

But you, YHWH, you laugh at them;
you mock all the peoples. (v. 8/9)
[My strength], I will side with you,
for God is my fortress. (v. 9/10)

May the God of [my] goodness/grace march ahead of me;
may God let me look [down] upon my opponents. (v. 10/11)
Do not kill them, lest my people forget;
disperse them with your army and throw them down;
our shield is the Lord. (v. 11/12)
The sin of their mouth is the word of their lips;
let them be trapped by their pride,
and by the curse and the lie they utter. (v. 12/13)
Destroy them in wrath;
destroy, so that they be no more!
So that it be known that God rules in Jacob
until the ends of the earth. Selah. (v. 13/14)

They return in the evening;
they growl like dogs and encircle the city. (v. 14/15)
They [wander about] in order to eat;
if they do not get their fill, they stay all night. (v. 15/16)

But I, I will sing of your strength;
I will rejoice over your goodness/grace in the morning.
For you are my fortress,
my refuge on the day of my distress. (v. 16/17)
My strength, I will make music for you,
for God is my fortress,
the God of my goodness/grace. (v. 17/18)

Textual Notes

4/5. Following the *BHS* apparatus, עָוֹן should be read with a first-person-singular suffix (of mine), which likely dropped out as a result of haplography (cf. Riede, *Im Netz des Jägers*, 199; etc.).

5/6. Following Kraus (*Psalmen I*, 580), "5/6a is . . . metrically overstretched due to supplemental additions. אלהים is to be deleted in favor of the ancient designation of God יהוה צבאות. . . . אלהי ישראל should be disregarded as a later addition." The solution to the problem is more likely to be found on a redaction-historical level, in assuming a collective redaction ("perspective of the people") in vv. 5a, 8, 11, 13cd (6a, 9, 12, 14cd—italicized above; cf. Hossfeld and Zenger, *Die Psalmen*, 2:142–43; Weber, *Werkbuch*, 1:164; and Krawczack, *Psalm 58*, 391–92). The following interpretation is based on the final text with its intended crossover of individual and collective expression (individual lament / perspective of the people).

7/8. The MT's "swords [are] on their lips" is emended by Kraus (*Psalmen*, 1:580) to "their lips are swords" by removing the ב from שׂפתות. The image is, however, self-explanatory (cf. Riede, *Im Netz des Jägers*, 200; Hossfeld and Zenger, *Die Psalmen*, 2:141–42; etc.). The phrase כי־מי שׁמע does not represent a rhetorical question (so Riede, *Im Netz des Jägers*, 200; etc.), but—as a quotation of speech by the enemy—an actual question: "because [they think]: 'Who should hear it?'" Compare Keel, *Feinde und Gottesleugner*, 171; Hossfeld and Zenger, *Die Psalmen*, 2:149; as well as Pss. 10:4, 11, 13; 14:1; 64:5/6; and Ps. 58:11/12 as a contrasting expression. Kraus (*Psalmen*, 1:580) deletes the half verse *metri causa*.

9/10. Read עֻזִּי, "my strength," with several manuscripts and LXX (cf. v. 17/18a).[15]

Psalm 59 is the climax of the group of individual Enemy Psalms: 52–59.[16] The analysis of its composition has always been problematic because verse 14/15 refers to verses 6–7 (7–8) and verse 17/18 to 9/10.[17] Kraus does not consider verse 14/15 to be a refrain, but rather a textual variant: "14/15 has (introduced by ו) the same text as 6/7, but introduces an expansion with 15/16."[18] Gerstenberger, Riede, Hossfeld and Zenger, and Weber[19] see verse 14/15 as a refrain of 6/7, while verses 7/8 and 15/16 differ textually and effect a significant intensification of the expression.

They return in the evening;
  they growl like dogs and encircle the city.
    (Ps. 59:6/7)
See, they slobber at the mouth,
  swords are on their lips,
  because [they say]: "Who should hear it?" (v. 7/8)

They return in the evening;
  they growl like dogs and encircle the city. (v. 14/15)
They [wander about] in order to eat;
  if they do not get their fill, they stay all night. (v. 15/16)

Psalm 59:7/8 and 15/16, which have similar beginnings in the Hebrew text (alliteration of the first two words), describe the danger and insatiability

15. Since we are focusing on the first stanza, Ps. 59:1–9 (2–10), textual remarks are limited to this passage. For the remainder, see Riede, *Im Netz des Jägers*, 199ff.; Hossfeld and Zenger, *Psalmen 51–100*, 141; Beat Weber, *Werkbuch*, 1:262ff.; and Krawczack, *Psalm 58*, 391ff. For reasons of clarity, the refrains on vv. 6/7, 9/10, 14/15, and 17/18ab are emphasized through boldface. The italics in vv. 5/6ab, 8/9, 11/12, 13/14cd designate a collectivizing redactional layer.

16. Cf. Hossfeld and Zenger, *Psalmen 51–100*, 143. See also Basson, *Divine Metaphors*; Riede, "Die Sprache der Bilder"; Doyle, "God as a Dog"; Kselman, "Double Entendre in Psalm 59"; and Wälchli, *Gottes Zorn*, 53–54.

17. For a summary of positions, see Hossfeld and Zenger, *Psalmen 51–100*, 144–45.

18. Kraus, *Psalmen*, 1:580; see also already Gunkel, *Die Psalmen*, 253.

19. Gerstenberger, *Psalms, Part 1*, 236–37; Riede, *Im Netz des Jägers*, 203; Hossfeld and Zenger, *Psalmen 51–100*, 145; Weber, *Werkbuch*, 1:264–65.

of the enemies; they are therefore corresponding expressions. Furthermore, verses 14–15 (15–16) represent a progression of thought with regard to verses 6–7 (7–8), insofar as 15/16 describes the permanent voracity of the enemies // dogs:[20] They return in the *evening*, or evening after evening and stay all *night* if their greed is not satisfied (לָעֶרֶב, "in the evening," v. 14/15; לִין, "spend the night," v. 15/16). As a result, the expression of trust, Psalm 59:16/17 and its *morning motif* is especially significant:

> But I, I will sing of your strength;
> I will rejoice over your goodness/grace *in the morning* [לַבֹּקֶר].
> For you are my fortress,
> my refuge *on the day of my distress* [בְּיוֹם צַר־לִי].

The psalm appears to use the temporal designations "in the evening" (vv. 6, 14 [7, 15]), "night" ("spend the night," v. 15/16),[21] and "morning" (v. 16/17b) deliberately, in order with their help to present the *"day of distress"* in the right light. The twofold refrains in verses 6/7 and 14/15 on the one hand (each following a concluding "Selah" in vv. 5/6 and 13/14), and in verses 9/10 and 17/18ab on the other hand, divide the psalm into two stanzas, each of which is analogously structured and contains the elements of *petition* (**P**: vv. 1–5 [2–6] + 10–13 [11–14]), *complaint* (**C**: vv. 6–7 [7–8] + 14–15 [15–16]), *trust in God* (**T**: vv. 8–9 [9–10]), and *vow of praise* (**V**: vv. 16–17 [17–18]). The individual sections are connected not only by textual signals like references to time, but are also framed by constellations of keywords, which are established through the motifs of "protection" ("protect," "fortress," in vv. 1/2b and 9/10b; cf. 16–17 [17–18]) and the "goodness of God" (vv. 10/11a and 17/18bc; cf. vv. 16–17 [17–18]):

Stanza I. Psalm 59:1–9 [2–10]	
Petition for deliverance from enemies (vv. 1–5 [2–6])	
Complaint over actions of the enemies (6–7 [7–8])	Evening (6/7)
Trust in God (8–9 [9–10])	
Stanza II. Psalm 59:10–17 [11–18]	
Petition for deliverance from enemies (10–13 [11–14])	
Complaint over enemies' actions (14–15 [15–16])	Evening (14/15) / Night (15/16)
Vow of praise (16–17 [17–18])	Morning (16/17)

The twofold movement from petition over complaint to an affirmation of trust is an expression of a "heightened dynamic of prayer."[22] It provides a space for the supplicant's experience of being at the mercy of an unappeasable will to overwhelm[23] and contrasts these horrific images with the motif of YHWH as "fortress,"[24] in which the psalm joyfully culminates (vv. 16–17 [17–18]).

20. This voracity is not only suggested by v. 7/8 ("swords" as instruments of death), but also vv. 6/7 and 14/15.

21. The evening and the night/morning motif is already suggested by the heading's reference to 1 Sam. 19:11; cf. Hossfeld and Zenger, *Psalmen 51–100*, 164; Krawczack, *Psalm 58*, 391. On the interpretation of v. 15/16b, see also Riede, *Im Netz des Jägers*, 203; Hossfeld and Zenger, *Psalmen 51–100*, 150–51.

22. Hossfeld and Zenger, *Psalmen 51–100*, 145.

23. Cf. the graphic description by Riede, *Im Netz des Jägers*, 212–13.

24. Cf. מָנוֹס, "refuge," v. 16/17; מִשְׂגָּב, "fortress," vv. 9/10, 16–17 (17–18); cf. שָׂגַב, "protect," v. 1/2; see ibid., 89ff., 201–2, 213, etc.; cf. 373ff.

Thematic Considerations

But who are the enemies, who visit the supplicant like stray pariah dogs evening after evening (Ps. 59:6, 14 [7, 15]) and who even stay all night if they "do not get their fill" (v. 15/16)? How are their actions described, and what are the conditions under which the image of the enemy developed in ancient Israel? To answer these questions, let us look at the designation of enemies and how their actions are depicted.

The Terminology for Enemies

Following Ruppert[25] and Keel,[26] the terminology for enemies in the Psalms of Lament and Thanksgiving of the individual can be divided into four groups: (1) *enemies as such*, with a distinction between (a) the אֹיֵב "enemy" group (general opposition) and (b) the רָשָׁע "wicked" group (religious connotation); (2) *disloyal friends/relatives*; (3) *neutral enemy designations*; and (4) *comparison with wild animals*. Based on this catalog, a simple picture emerges for Psalm 13: The designation אֹיְבִי, "my enemy" (vv. 2b, 4b [3b, 5b]), falls into the category of 1a, as does the designation צָרַי, "my oppressor" (v. 4/5b).[27] As for all the Psalms 52–59, the situation is more complex. Here are the enemy terms for Psalm 59:

Term		*Verse*	*Group*
אֹיְבַי	my enemies	1/2a	1a
מִתְקוֹמְמַי	those who rise up against me	1/2b	1a
פֹּעֲלֵי אָוֶן	those who do what is sinister[28]	2/3a	1b
אַנְשֵׁי דָמִים	men of blood	2/3b	1b
עַזִּים	strong men	3/4a	3
כָּל־הַגּוֹיִם	all the peoples	5/6c, b/9b	3
כָּל־בֹּגְדֵי אָוֶן	all who commit faithless evil	5/6b	1b
כָּלֶב	dog	6/7, 14/15	4
שֹׁרְרָי	my opponents	10/11b	1a

There are nine different terms for enemies in Psalm 59: eight plural forms and one singular form (כָּלֶב, "dog"), belonging to category 4 (comparison with wild animals). We shall see below why precisely this category prefers the singular form. Relevant for our question is also that category 1b (designation of enemies with religious connotations) is presented in construct forms: men of blood (אַנְשֵׁי דָמִים), those who do what is sinister (פֹּעֲלֵי אָוֶן), and others.

Of equal importance as the terminology for enemies is the description of the *enemies' actions*.[29] The following types of actions can be identified:

25. Ruppert, *Eine Wortfelduntersuchung*, 6ff.

26. Keel, *Feinde und Gottesleugner*, 93ff.; cf. idem, "Der bedrängte Beter"; idem, "Die 'Feinde' in den Psalmen."

27. For Ps. 13, see 59ff. above.

28. On this term, see 110ff. below.

29. See Ruppert, *Eine Wortfelduntersuchung*, 110ff.; Keel, *Feinde und Gottesleugner*, 155ff.; Riede, *Im Netz des Jägers*, 19ff.; Janowski, "'Dem Löwen gleich'"; van der Velden, *Psalm 109*.

Concrete expressions

Schadenfreude, mockery, derision, hatred
overpowering, use of violence, attempt to destroy
abuse of the law, oppression
conspiracy, intrigue, slander, false accusation
inquisitive behavior
presumption, pride, triumph
loss of friends or relatives

Figurative expressions
hunting
war
animals

According to this, the laments of the individual contain literally everything that is possible in the realm of oppression by enemies: it always involves the actions of violent men.[30] If this catalog is applied to Psalm 59:1–9 (2–10), we find eight verbs that describe the actions of the enemies:

ארב	lie in wait, ambush	v. 3/4
גור II	attack, assault	v. 3/4
רוץ	run up, attack	v. 4/5
כון Hitpolel	take position	v. 4/5
שׁוב (לָעֶרֶב)	return (in the evening)	v. 6/7
המה	make noise, uproar	v. 6/7
סבב Polel	surround, encircle	v. 6/7
נבע Hiphil	slobber, bubble forth	v. 7/8

In classifying these terms, a more detailed image emerges: in addition to *concrete expressions* like "slobber," there are *figurative expressions* relating to *"war"* ("attack," "run up," "surround," "encircle," "swords [on their lips]") and *"animals"* ("lie in wait," "surround," "encircle," "make noise," "uproar," "dog").

Some of the verbs used here—like ארב, "lie in wait, ambush," and סבב Polel, "surround, encircle"—can be assigned either to the motif field "war" or the motif field "animals."[31] This *overlap of imagery,* to which we shall return later, is also maintained in the enemy complaint verses 6–7 (7–8): the enemies "growl like dogs" (v. 6/7)[32] and "slobber at the mouth," indeed, "swords are on their lips" (v. 7/8). The *tertium comparationis* for the imagery in verse 7/8 is "the lust for fighting and feeding of these dogs, that maul and devour everything they come across: likewise the mouth and teeth of the enemies—from their mouth come words that are similarly hurtful and deadly."[33]

The enemies in Psalm 59, who use their words like "swords" (v. 7/8) to slaughter and devour the supplicant (v. 14/15),[34] are fought with the help of figurative language, as the fears they cause in the supplicant are bluntly named.

30. The appearance of the "violent man" is also a theme in Prov. 1–9; see Meinhold, "Der Gewaltmensch."
31. See Riede, *Im Netz des Jägers*, 43ff., 66–67, 176–77, 383–84, etc.
32. On the comparison with dogs, see ibid., 195ff.
33. Hossfeld and Zenger, *Psalmen 51–100*, 149.
34. Cf. ibid., 144.

How do such drastic images come about, which obviously stand in the way of repeated liturgical use?[35]

The Actions of the Enemies

In my analysis of Psalm 13, I have already pointed out the change in number in reference to the enemies: אֹיְבִי, "my enemy" (vv. 2/3b, 4/5a), and צָרַי, "my opponents" (v. 4/5b).[36] Since the singular form is often used in Hebrew to describe a type ("*the* enemy") and the plural expresses multitude and also intensification ("the *power* of the enemy"), the change in number indicates that no single person is intended to stand out in the description of the enemy, but rather the power of the enemy, "that which is hostile." Although present, the subject, the specific carrier of this power, is strangely unspecified. Nevertheless, the supplicant sees in that adversary "my" enemy or "my" enemies.

The same phenomenon appears also in the descriptions of the enemy and the interchange of figurative and concrete expressions. One can call this phenomenon the *generalizing* and *typifying language of complaint*. We are generally inclined to see an overstated tendency toward self-recognition behind it, and to view the supplicants in the Psalms of Complaint as people of unrestrained exaggeration.[37] Doing so, we underestimate or even fail to notice the particular form of experience one can see in this form of expression. In this regard, Keel has argued that the ranking of a phenomenon in ancient Israel was determined by the "degree of its efficacy" as accorded by the experiencing self:

> The decisive element in the ranking of a phenomenon was the level of its efficacy. That which is efficacious is, and that which is not efficacious is not. Whether this reality is assigned to something objectively or subjectively, if its effect comes from the inside or the outside, from a sleeping or waking state, is of little significance for the *projective self*, which easily combines reality and fantasy.[38]

On the basis of this efficacy of things, we can speak with Keel of a "confluence of the interior and the exterior world," or even of a "homogeneity of reality."[39] This has far-reaching consequences for the supplicant's dealings with malice and grief.[40]

The Homogeneity of Reality

For the supplicant in the Psalms of Lament and Thanksgiving, the threat of the enemy entails apparently something fundamental: it calls into question one's fundamental relationships, so that petitioner begins to stumble (cf. Ps.

35. See the references in n. 13 above.
36. Cf. 74–75 above.
37. In this context one often sees a reference to the "vivid imagination of the Semites" and the "burning passion of the Orientals"; see C. Barth, *Errettung vom Tode*, 13–14; and Keel, *Feinde und Gottesleugner*, 51–52. We shall encounter these representations also in the metaphors of death: see 250ff. below.
38. Keel, *Feinde und Gottesleugner*, 63–64, emphasis added.
39. Ibid., 64.
40. On the discussion below, see Janowski, "'Dem Löwen gleich,'" 57ff.

13:4/5), like the divine city attacked by its enemies (cf. Pss. 125:1; 46:4–6 [5–7]).[41] Under the threat of the enemy, as in all types of distress, of which the Psalms of Laments are full, the supplicant experiences the *power of death* if not the spatial closeness of the realm of death (cf. Ps. 88:3/4).[42] Constitutive for the form of experience is the process of projective thinking. Keel speaks of a "projective-participatory self" of the supplicant, which the petitioner projects onto the environment, thus participating in its expressions of life. The external reality, as this form of experience can be called, is not "objectively" experienced by the supplicant: not as reality itself, but rather experienced participatorily, with regard to what effect it has within the supplicant. Already Gunkel made a significant observation in his introduction to the Psalms about the unification of the interior and the exterior world:

> It is often impossible to coordinate the individual references of the complaint in the graphic depictions created by the images. From this recognition, one can see how unbelievably difficult it often is to communicate the specific distress standing behind the complaint. One can see how little tangible material the psalmist provides about the external situation. Conversely, these observations about the discontinuity of the images make it completely clear that whatever unites these images has to be sought outside the images themselves. This unity may lie in the spiritual condition of the poet. The poet does not place as much weight on a completely faithful rendition of the external circumstances as on *communicating the internal circumstances*, by expressing the impressions that the external events release within oneself.[43]

The supplicant interprets the appearance of the enemies or of "my enemy" in terms of the effect it has within the self: the fear of being exposed to an impalpable but nevertheless real overwhelming force. The supplicant's complaints are not to be ascribed, as has always been presumed, to an inferiority complex, paranoia, or unrestrained exaggeration,[44] but are the result of a particular form of experience and its unique interior-exterior relationship. According to H. Weippert's description of this intensive integration of the individual in space and time, human beings in ancient Israel could not

> position [themselves] at a distance . . . from spatial and temporal influences, but experienced both intimately. We are therefore barely able to retrace the boundary [they] perceived between the interior and the exterior world, since space and time are only rarely experienced concretely in our world. . . . The world was larger and time less fragmented. . . . In this more expansive world and more calmly flowing time, human beings had to develop a different relationship to the environment that surrounded them and had to encounter their own kind, animals, plants, and objects differently than we are accustomed [to do].[45]

41. See 73–74 above.
42. See 192 and 196 below.
43. Gunkel and Begrich, *Introduction to Psalms*, 134, emphasis added; von Rad, *Theologie*, 1:41ff.; and Janowski, "Die 'Kleine Biblia,'" 135ff.
44. See references in n. 37 above.
45. H. Weippert, "Altisraelitische Welterfahrung," 15–17; see also Janowski, "Das biblische Weltbild," 4ff.

Connected to the integration of the individual in nature and society is also a particular understanding of the person, which I have termed "constellatory":[46] the individual is integrated with every fiber of one's being, *with body and soul,* into the lived-in society and the surrounding natural world. Since the individual is therefore vulnerable and exposed to the actions of one's "enemies," the complaint is often the only weapon in dealing with the incomprehensibility of evil.

The Incomprehensibility of Evil

In their book *Das Böse* [Evil], the two editors C. Colpe and W. Schmidt-Biggemann[47] have collected contributions to a "historical phenomenology of the inexplicable" (so the subtitle) and have introduced this collection with an insightful foreword. According to the two authors, the inexplicability of evil consists in the fact that "evil . . . has no logic, it cannot be explained and defined. Evil cannot be exorcized with the logic of the good, its opposite; if this were possible, evil would have been abolished long ago."[48] It is, however, very much present, also in the Enemy Psalms, and arrests the imagination in different ways. The question how it can be exorcized always becomes acute when evil appears, when it becomes visible. It is here that the Enemy Psalms have their *Sitz im Leben.* They make the incomprehensible phenomenon of evil evident by presenting it from the perspective of the experiencing self.[49]

One of the forms of presentation is intended to characterize the supplicant's enemies as "those who do what is sinister" (פֹּעֲלֵי אָוֶן) or as "men of blood" (אַנְשֵׁי דָמִים), who embody the *uncanny world of evil.*[50] Indicative of this are, in addition to the change in number,[51] the participial forms and the construct forms. The enemy terms that are formed with participles, which express the efficacy of that which is hostile, are among the most common designations for enemy,[52] such as these examples (among many such) in the Psalms:

מִתְקוֹמְמַי	(those who rise up against me) my opponents	59:1/2
פֹּעֲלֵי אָוֶן	those who do what is sinister[53]	5:5/6
רֹדְפַי	(those who pursue me) my pursuers	7:1/2
שֹׂנְאַי	(those who hate me) my haters	86:17
שֹׂטְנַי	(those who accuse me) my accusers	109:20

The subject that threatens and opposes the supplicant "often remains obscure in the background. In the foreground is the functional *description of the event.*"[54]

That the menacing power of evil is emphasized in the description of the enemy and not specific individuals is also suggested by the frequent use of construct forms, in which the particular is further defined by means of the general, as in these examples in the Psalms:

46. See 42 above.
47. Colpe and Schmidt-Biggemann, *Das Böse.*
48. Ibid., 7.
49. See also "Excursus 4: The Enigma of Evil," below, 109–10.
50. Keel, *Feinde und Gottesleugner,* 91.
51. See 74–75 above.
52. See Keel, *Feinde und Gottesleugner,* 69, 98–99; Ruppert, *Eine Wortfelduntersuchung,* 6ff.
53. On this term, see the discussion at 108ff. below.
54. Keel, *Feinde und Gottesleugner,* 98, emphasis added.

אַנְשֵׁי דָמִים	men of blood	5:6/7
אִישׁ חָמָס	men of violence	18:48/49
כִּסֵּא הַוּוֹת	throne of destruction	94:20
לְשׁוֹן מִרְמָה	tongue of deception	52:4/6
רֶגֶל גַּאֲוָה	foot of haughtiness	36:11/12

This grammatical form also shows that the descriptions of the enemy "do not primarily aim at a single human being as an individual personality, but at the *power of corruption*."[55]

In the classification of terms for the enemy in Psalm 59, I pointed out that the category with moral or religious connotations (1b) is particularly interesting because the enemy terms included in it are usually formed with a construct form. In Psalm 59, these expressions include "evildoers" (פֹּעֲלֵי אָוֶן, v. 2/3a), "men of blood" (אַנְשֵׁי דָמִים, v. 2/3b), and "all who commit faithless evil" (כָּל־בֹּגְדֵי אָוֶן, v. 5/6b). All three designations appear in the petition and complaint section of verses 1–9 (2–10). Verses 1–2 (2–3) alone contain four enemy designations.

> Deliver me from my enemies [אֹיְבַי], my God;
> from those who rise up against me [מִתְקוֹמְמַי], protect me! (v. 1/2)
> Deliver me from the evildoers [פֹּעֲלֵי אָוֶן],
> from the men of blood [אַנְשֵׁי דָמִים], save me. (v. 2/3)

Excursus 4: The Enigma of Evil

"One does not have to trouble the devil to understand evil. Evil is part of the drama of human freedom. It is the price of freedom" (Safranski, *Das Böse*, 13). The questions What is evil? and Where does it come from? have occupied every era and culture in different ways. Consequently there are different answers (see Dietrich and Link, *Allmacht und Ohnmacht*, 56ff., 118ff., 301ff.). The problem is and always has been that

> evil . . . [is] not just a concept, but also a name for the menacing that confronts free will and can be performed by free will. Evil confronts free will in nature, where free will denies the desires of its own senses, in chaos, in contingency, in entropy, in eating, and in being eaten—in the void of outer space as well as in one's own self, in the black hole of existence. And the will can choose cruelty and destruction for its own sake. The reason for this is the abyss that opens within the human being. (Safranski, *Das Böse*, 14; cf. Colpe and Schmidt-Biggemann, *Das Böse*, 7ff.; see also Dalferth, *Leiden und Böses*; idem, *Das Böse*; Ricoeur, *Das Böse*; and Ebner et al., *Das Böse*)

It speaks for the Old Testament songs of complaint and thanksgiving that they confront evil and do not simply repress it. "In contrast to the religion of Mesopotamia, Israel is denied the possibility of seeing evil subsistent in the world. Heaven and earth were created as good by Yahweh; there is no room for demons that cause arbitrary harm. The only carrier for malicious enmity

55. Ibid., 99, emphasis added.

is the human being. Just as the Israelite cannot see the soul as independent from the concrete human being, so the Israelite is unable to see evil independently from those who are evil" (Keel, "Der Bedrängte Beter," 106). Since the Psalms instruct us to resist evil, we can often identify with them (Limbeck, "Der Beter," 70). Such a protest always remains fragmentary and therefore an expression of hope in the saving justice of God (see 128ff. below): this fact constitutes the dignity of these texts.

But what about the good? Good is the opposite of evil. It is, however, as the discussion on "Happiness and Closeness to God" shows (see 285ff. below), more than the absence of evil. Happiness is not the object of human effort, but the by-product of success: the quality of a meaningful or *good* life. The difficulty of achieving this is shown paradigmatically in the nonpriestly creation and paradise story (Gen. 2:4b–3:24) and its reference to the dilemma of the "knowledge of good and evil" (Gen. 2:17; 3:5). This knowledge implies a compulsion "to make evaluations and decisions: for one another or against one another, open or hidden, together or every person for oneself—and often enough only between two evils" (Hardmeier, "Mensch und sein Tod," 219).

Yet the question is not only about the end of evil (cf. Bayer, "Wann hat das Böse endlich ein Ende?") but also about the justification of its existence. In the end there is no answer for this (cf. Körtner, *Wie lange noch?*, 7ff.). What is left besides the plea for deliverance from evil (cf. the final petition in the Lord's Prayer: "Lead us not into temptation, but deliver us from evil" [Matt. 6:13]; see Philonenko, *Das Vaterunser*, 93ff.) is the power derived from prayer to preempt evil with good (Rom. 12:21; cf. Jüngel, "Böse, das, V"). Prayer lets "evil be God's affair in the end and entrusts its resolution to God alone; it urges and beseeches God to deliver us from evil" (Bayer, "Wann hat das Böse endlich ein Ende?," 202).

The expression פֹּעֲלֵי אָוֶן ("those who do what is sinister") is particularly significant here because as both participial construction and construct form, it unites two elements: "description of event" (participial construction) and "power of corruption" (construct form). Its meaning has been intensely debated in Old Testament scholarship. Thus Mowinckel[56] assumed that the enemies of the supplicant were always magicians or demons. This hypothesis was affirmed by Vorländer,[57] specifically with reference to evidence in Mesopotamian "prayers to a personal god." Like Mowinckel, Vorländer understands the פֹּעֲלֵי אָוֶן as magicians; images of an attacking or besieging army, of the hunt, of aggressive wild animals—these he connects to magicians or demons; and he sees references to tongue, lips, and the enemy's evil words as allusions to magic practices of assumed magicians.

56. Sigmund Mowinckel, *Psalmenstudien*, 1:76ff.
57. Vorländer, *Mein Gott*, 265.

This theory of a *magic understanding of the enemy* has since been proved wrong.[58] Nevertheless, the enemies of the supplicant in the Psalter are surrounded by a "demonic aura," as can be demonstrated on the basis of Psalm 59:1–9 (2–10).[59]

The Uncanny

The פֹּעֲלֵי אָוֶן (found 16 times in the Psalter, 7 times outside the Psalter)[60] are no regular evildoers, but "doers of that which is sinister": "אָוֶן is (*abysmal*) *wickedness*, the dark counterpart to צֶדֶק (cf. פֹּעֵל צֶדֶק in Ps. 15:2)"[61] The strength of this contrast gives the enemies a "dark-demonic quality."[62] In Psalm 59, they are paralleled with the "men of blood" (v. 2/3). They harass the supplicant with lies (כַּחַשׁ) and curses (אָלָה, v. 12/13): they effectively desire his destruction (v. 3/4). Their domain is the night.[63]

Collectivity

The פֹּעֲלֵי אָוֶן are characterized by collectivity. The word combination exists exclusively in the plural: they are a community sworn to evil. This can also be seen in the fact that they do not call to YHWH, who hates them (cf. Ps. 5:5/6), but they "devour, consume" (אָכַל, Ps. 14:4 = 53:4/5; cf. Ps. 59:15/16)[64] the supplicant's people (= the righteous). Such cannibalism is also a theme in prophetic social criticism (cf. Mic. 3:2–3).[65] The enemies of the supplicant therefore also deny God,[66] and their actions are a form of "practical atheism."

Treachery

The פֹּעֲלֵי אָוֶן do not confront the supplicant openly; instead, they act treacherously from a concealed position (Ps. 59:3/4; cf. Ps. 141:9: "Save me from the trap that was prepared for me, from the snares of the evildoers"). Apparently the supplicant does not even know them personally. This distinguishes them from the "men/sons of Belial," who are usually very specific, well-known persons.[67]

58. See Ruppert, "Klagelieder in Israel und Babylonien—verschiedene Deutungen der Gewalt" in Lohfink (ed.), *Gewalt und Gewaltlosigkeit im Alten Testament* (Freiburg im Breisgau: Herder Verlag, 1983, pp. 111–58), 133ff. Cf. Keel, "Der bedrängte Beter"; Karl-Heinz Bernhardt, "אָוֶן," 156ff.

59. On the text, see 100ff. above.

60. See discussion in Ruppert, *Eine Wortfelduntersuchung*, 59ff.; Kraus, *Psalmen*, 3:161ff.; also Riede, *Im Netz des Jägers*, 201, 205, 209–10.

61. Kraus, *Psalmen*, 1:163, emphasis original. On Ps. 15:2, "Those who walk blamelessly and do justice [וּפֹעֵל צֶדֶק] and speak in the heart what is trustworthy," see 49 above.

62. Ibid., 164.

63. On the night motif, see 103 with n. 21.

64. According to Ps. 59, the enemies use "their speeches as 'swords' (v. 7/8) in order to slaughter the supplicant and then to devour him (v. 14/15)" (Hossfeld and Zenger, *Psalmen 51–100*, 144).

65. See Hossfeld and Zenger, *Die Psalmen*, 1:102; and Kessler, *Micha*, 149–50.

66. The פֹּעֲלֵי אָוֶן references are found largely in exilic and postexilic texts, which are likely connected to an increasing demonization—not without its problems—of the enemy in later texts of the Old Testament. See Ruppert, "Klagelieder in Israel und Babylonien"; cf. Keel, *Feinde und Gottesleugner*, 109.

67. See 180–81 below.

Psalm 10:3–11 describes the actions of the enemies in graphic terms. Their mouths are full of cursing, deception, and violence, and under their tongues are corruption and mischief:

> The wicked boasts in his impudent avarice,
> the greedy mocks, despises YHWH. (v. 3)
> The wicked thinks haughtily:
> He will not care, he is no God.
> Such is his thinking. (v. 4)
> His ways always persist.
> Far from him, your judgments are high above;
> he scoffs at all his opponents. (v. 5)
> He says in his heart: I shall not stumble;
> From generation to generation I have been spared adversity. (v. 6)
> His mouth is full of curses, full of cursing, full of deception and violence;
> under his tongue are corruption and mischief. (v. 7)
> He lies concealed in ambush;
> in a hidden place he murders the innocent.
> His eyes look out for the helpless. (v. 8)
> He waits in hiding like a lion in the thicket.
> He lies in ambush to catch the wretched;
> he catches the wretched, drags him off in his net. (v. 9)
> Shattered, the helpless sink down
> and fall to his violence. (v. 10)
> He says in his heart: God has forgotten,
> he has hidden his face, he will never see it. (v. 11)[68]

In the depiction of the enemy, the wicked person is compared to a hunting predator (cf. terminology in vv. 8–10) that has singled out a specific victim—the wretched—and has its mind set on murder (הָרַג, "kill," v. 8).[69] In verse 11 this depiction of the enemy uses the same terminology as the God-complaint in Psalm 13:1/2 ("forget" // "hide the face") and the corresponding petition to YHWH in Psalm 13:3/4 ("see").[70] Furthermore, the wording of verse 11b ("He [God] will never see [it]") also shows clearly that the enemies in Psalm 59:1–9 (2–10) assume that there is no God (Ps. 10:4),[71] who would see and hear the distress of the supplicant:

> See, they slobber at the mouth,
> swords are on their lips,
> because [they say]: "Who should hear it?"
> (Ps. 59:7/8)

68. Translation based on the *Die Züricher Bibel* (1996). Ps. 10:3–11 is one of the most elaborate descriptions in the Psalter of the godless actions of the wicked; cf. also Pss. 52: 2–6 (3–7); 73:4–12; Job 21:7–34.

69. In a total of 42 psalms of the 150 in the book, the supplicant is referred to as "poor" or "lowly" (אֶבְיוֹן, עָנִי, דַּל); see the list in Lohfink, "Von der 'Anawim-Partei,'" 153; for a comprehensive treatment, see Ro, *"Armenfrömmigkeit,"* 1ff. On the so-called Psalms of the Poor, see the references in 63 n. 27 above.

70. See 63ff. above.

71. Cf. Pss. 14:1; 53:1/2; and Zeph. 1:12.

If we look ahead a little and ask why Psalms 10 and 59 describe the uncanny actions of the enemies so elaborately, it is probably not to present the complaint in the most colorful and gory way, but to provide motivation for the petition for salvation. Psalm 10:16–18 and also Psalm 59:13/14 verbalize explicitly what is at stake in the petition for divine intervention against the denial of the (poor) supplicant's rights: on the one hand it is *justice for the poor*,[72] and on the other hand it is the *royal dominion of God*. One cannot exist without the other, for the royal God YHWH is on the side of the poor, as Psalm 10:16–18 declares:

> **YHWH is king** forever and ever;
> the nations have vanished from YHWH's land. (v. 16)
> You have heard the desire of the meek, O YHWH;
> you strengthen their heart, you incline your ear (v. 17)
> **to do justice** for the orphaned and oppressed.
> No one on earth shall be violent anymore. (v. 18)[73]

Now let us return, following these remarks, to the observation that the enemies of the supplicant represent the *uncanny world of evil*. To substantiate this, I have pointed to the change in number, the participial forms, and the construct forms with which the enemy is depicted. We saw in these syntactic forms a tendency toward a basic delineation of the supplicant's *concrete* hardship. The change in number indicates that it is not an individual enemy, but the enemy's power: "that which is hostile" emphasized. The participial forms underline the efficacy of this hostile force by describing the character of the enemy's hostility. Likewise the construct forms do not primarily focus on an individual carrier of hostility, but rather on the malicious dynamics of the enemy or enemies.

This type of representation is also expressed in the attempt to delineate the dimension of evil likewise categorically, as in these examples:

> You have crushed the **chin** of all my enemies;
> you have broken the **teeth** of the wicked.
> (Ps. 3:7/8)

> Let the **malice** of the wicked come to an end,
> but raise up the righteous.
> (Ps. 7:9/10)

> Break the **arm** of the wicked and of the one who is evil;
> avenge his **wickedness**, so that one finds no [more of him].
> (Ps. 10:15)

> O God, break the **teeth** in their mouths;
> smash the **teeth** of the young lions, O YHWH!
> (Ps. 58:6/7)

72. See also Ro, *"Armenfrömmigkeit,"* 187: "The teachers and supplicants who express themselves in these Psalms are concerned that they, unlike their enemies, are exclusively dependent on the assistance and help of Yahweh. For the members of this type of religiosity, terms indicating the poor are a kind of honorific designation or 'trademark,' with which they intend to signal their special status to God and the world. Unlike the opposing party, groups in the political leadership of Jerusalem and the temple administration, they stand truly and exclusively by Yahweh. As these 'poor' they are the truly 'righteous,' the 'servants' of Yahweh. Only a posture of humility that is practiced in this way can stand before Yahweh and find recognition." Cf. ibid., 186ff., 203ff.

73. On the justice of the royal god YHWH, see 127ff. below.

That which shall be taken from the wicked and violent are "their weapons, which cause deadly injury, and their ability to attack. It is no longer the wish for revenge that is being expressed here, but the hope for deliverance."[74]

There is a crucial difference! The effort to capture the uncanny or the inexplicable in words and perhaps thereby to overcome it is seen again and again. This effort can also be credited with the rich imagery that characterizes the enemy-complaint—and mutatis mutandis also the self-complaint—in the Psalms of the Individual.[75]

γ. *Animal Similes in the Enemy-Complaint*

Similes and metaphors are typical for images of the enemy in the songs of lament and thanksgiving of the individual.[76] However, only recent interpretations have tried to unlock this figurative language and to understand its peculiar significance. Westermann,[77] who was the first to engage this topic more systematically, distinguished three groups of meaning in the similes of the enemy-complaint: danger from *wild animals* (lion, bull, dog, snake), from *hidden dangers* (pit, net, snare, trap), and from the *aggressive word* (word as weapon). In the following discussion, I shall limit myself to the animal similes in the enemy-complaint,[78] among which we find five animals in the Psalms:

- Lion: 7:2/3; 10:9–10; 17:11–12; 22:13/14, 21/22; 57:4/5; 58:6/7; cf. 91:13
- Bull: 22:12/13, 21/22
- (Pariah) dog: 22:16/17, 20/21; 59:6/7, 14–15 (15–16)
- Snake: 58:4/5; 140:3/4; cf. 91:13
- Bee: 118:12[79]

What is noteworthy in this lineup is that enemies are never compared to domestic animals, but only with predatory and wild animals. How these animal similes are to be understood is at first quite unambiguous: "The animal similes underscore a trait of the wicked and godless that is also otherwise conspicuous: They do not want the supplicant's possessions; they do not want to deprive the petitioner of an office or anything else; they are exclusively after the supplicant's life."[80] Unlike the pariah dog, whose behavior is described with negative connotations also in other parts of the Old Testament,[81] the lion and the wild bull also possess the ambivalence of the royal-commanding *and* the demonic-horrific.

74. Baldermann, *Ich werde nicht sterben*, 30. On the subject of revenge, see "Anthropological Keyword 2: Revenge," below, 120ff.

75. On animal imagery in the self-complaint, see Riede, *Im Netz des Jägers*, 279ff.

76. On metaphors, see the general discussion at 22ff. above.

77. Westermann, *Vergleiche und Gleichnisse*, 80ff.; cf. idem, *Ausgewählte Psalmen*, 32ff.; Keel, *Die Welt*, 75ff.; and for a comprehensive treatment, Riede, *Im Netz des Jägers*, 279ff.

78. See Keel, *Die Welt*, 75ff.; Keel, "Der bedrängte Beter"; Ruppert, *Eine Wortfelduntersuchung*, 96ff.; Jenni, "Zur Semantik," 157ff.; and Riede, *Im Netz des Jägers*, 150ff.

79. The bear appears in Lam. 3:10; see Riede, *Im Netz des Jägers*, 271ff.

80. Keel, *Die Welt*, 77–78.

81. See Riede, *Im Netz des Jägers*, 195ff.

By being compared to predatory and wild animals,[82] the enemies of the supplicant are ascribed part of the named animal's nature. At the center of this is the idea that the supplicant is at the mercy of an *unpredictable will to overpower*. Let us take the example of the enemy complaint of Psalm 22:12–13 (13–14), within the third complaint, verses 12–18 (13–19), and the subsequent petition verses 19–21 (20–22).

Many bulls surround me, *Enemy-complaint*, 12–13 (13–14)
  the "strong of Bashan" encircle me.
They have [already] opened their mouths wide against me:
  a lion, raving and roaring.

Like water I am poured out, *Self-complaint*, 14–15 (15–16)
  my limbs are out of joint,
  my heart has become like wax,
  melted within my bowels.
Dried up like a potsherd is my (life-)force,
  and my tongue cleaves to the roof of my mouth;
  you have laid me down in the dust of death.

Indeed, dogs have surrounded me, *Enemy-complaint*, 16ab/17ab
  a pack of evildoers has encircled me!

[Too short are] my hands and feet. *Self-complaint*, 16c–17a (17c–18a)
  I can count all of my bones.

But they keep looking at me, *Enemy complaint*, 17b–18 (18b–19)
  staring at me.
They divide my clothes among themselves,
  and for my coat they cast lots.

But you, YHWH, do not be distant, *Petition*, 18–20 (19–21)
  my strength, hasten to my help!
Wrest from the dagger my life [*nepeš*],
  "my only one" from the power of the dogs.
Save me from the lion's mouth,
  from the horns of wild bulls—you have answered me![83]

For the moment, let us set aside the self-complaint in verses 14–15 (15–16) and its imagery of water and dust[84] and focus on the enemy complaints of verses 12–13 (13–14), with the lion and bull imagery. Alluding to representatives of animals that can be domesticated as well as wild animals, the supplicant's enemies are characterized as the "strongest representative pair of

82. Because of the affinity of lion, wild bull, pariah dog, and snake to the realm of the demonic/chaotic, it has been repeatedly argued that the animal similes in the enemy complaint try to represent the enemies as *animal-shaped* demons. However, this assumption is as erroneous as Mowinckel's magician hypothesis (see 110 above). Rather, "the danger facing the supplicant is compared to the danger posed by wild animals" (Westermann, *Vergleiche und Gleichnisse*, 84); see also Riede, *Im Netz des Jägers*, 277–78.

83. For textual notes and notes on the translation, see 323ff. below.

84. See 201–202 below.

the nonhuman *nepeš*-world."[85] For the supplicant, both kinds of animals are "not primarily representatives of a zoological species, but carriers of specific forces and powers."[86] Their threat is depicted as encircling and surrounding (v. 12/13; cf. 59:6/7, 14/15), as opening the mouth (22:13/14a), and as raving and roaring (v. 13/14b).[87] The supplicant thus verbalizes the experience of being at the mercy of an unpredictable will to overwhelm. This is also achieved by the figurative language of verses 12–13 (13–14; cf. 16/17, "dogs" // "pack of evildoers"), whereby the enemies have assumed the might and aggressiveness represented by bull and lion. In this context especially expressive are the lion similes and metaphors of the Psalms of the Individual,[88] such as these examples:

> [The enemy] is like a lion, eager for prey,
> like a young lion, lying in ambush. (Ps. 17:12)
>
> My life [*nepeš*] is / I am in the midst of lions;
> I must lie down among those who eat human prey;
> their teeth are spears and arrows,
> and their tongue is a sharp sword.
> (Ps. 57:4/5)

When we take a look from here at the self-complaint of Psalm 102:3–7 (4–8),[89] another image of the supplicant's distress emerges:

> For my days have vanished in smoke,
> my bones, they burn like a furnace. (v. 3/4)
> Withered like grass and dried up is my heart;
> indeed, I forgot to eat my bread. (v. 4/5)
> Because of my loud groaning,
> my bones cling to my flesh. (v. 5/6)
> I *am like* a bird in the desert,
> *like* an owl among ruins. (v. 6/7)
> I wake up and am/cry
> *like* a bird, lonely on the rooftop. (v. 7/8)

Here too, the enemies are indicated, as the subsequent enemy-complaint in Psalm 102:8/9 shows:

> All day long, my enemies mock me;
> those who ridicule me use my name as a curse.[90]

In Psalm 102, the effects of the enemies on the supplicant read like a catalog of abused creatures. They are conveyed by *images of fragility*, physical frailty, and social isolation. However, unlike the animal similes of Psalm 22:12–13, 16

85. Gese, "Psalm 22," 188; cf. Keel, *Die Welt*, 75ff.; Janowski and Neumann-Gorsolke, "Das Tier als Exponent."
86. Keel, *Feinde und Gottesleugner*, 73.
87. For individual interpretations, see Riede, *Im Netz des Jägers*, 183, 213, 221ff.
88. Pss. 7:2/3; 10:9; 17:12; 22:13/14, 21/22; 35:17; 57:4/5; 58:6/7; etc.; see also G. Johannes Botterweck, "אֲרִי"; Riede, *Im Netz des Jägers*, 150ff., 193–94.
89. See 34–35 above; cf. also Riede, *Im Netz des Jägers*, 292ff.
90. On the subject of the "curse," cf. Pss. 10:7; 59:12/13; etc.

(13–14, 17), Psalm 102:3–7 (4–8) names small and weak animals:[91] a bird in the desert, an owl among ruins. and a lonely bird on the rooftop.

But why use similes and metaphors in the first place? Why does the supplicant not state directly what the situation is? The petitioner speaks without circumlocution, albeit in images! These images are not illustrations of emotional content, which could just as well be absent, but they are an expression of an understanding of reality that can be termed *religious appropriation of being*.[92] Through comparison, the supplicant's situation is so closely tied to the lived-in external reality that the object of the comparison (the supplicant) is accorded some *nature* of the subject of the comparison (bird in the desert, etc.). In the image of the bird in Psalm 102:7/8, the suffering experienced by the supplicant is depicted "as a movement toward death, as an increase of death's power in the midst of life."[93] Unlike the enemies of 22:12/13 and their *aggressiveness*, like bulls and lions, the supplicant of 102:6–7 (7–8) shares the *loneliness* of birds and owls, unclean animals in the realms of death—"desert" and "ruins"—in which the supplicant sees self as a result of the hostility.

What is true for the animal similes of 22:12–13 (13–14) applies analogously also to the two corresponding enemy complaints of Psalm 59:1–9 (2–10):

> Deliver me from my enemies, my God;
>   from those who rise up against me, protect me! (v. 1/2)
> Deliver me from the evildoers,
>   from the men of blood, save me. (v. 2/3)
> For see: they have lain in wait for me;
>   strong men attack me.
> No wickedness and no sin is in me, YHWH; (v. 3/4)
>   for no fault [of mine] they attack and take up position.
> Wake up, toward me, and see. (v. 4/5)
> But you, YHWH, God Sabaoth, God of Israel,
>   wake up to visit all the peoples;
> have no mercy on any who commit faithless evil! *Selah*. (v. 5/6)
>
> They return in the evening;
>   they growl like dogs and encircle the city. (v. 6/7)
> See, they slobber at the mouth,
>   swords are on their lips,
>   because [they say]: "Who should hear it?" (v. 7/8)
>
> But you, YHWH, you laugh at them;
>   you mock all the peoples. (v. 8/9)
> [My strength], I will side with you,
>   for God is my fortress. (v. 9/10)

91. Other animals in the self-complaint are the dove, the worm, the grasshopper, the deer, and the sheep; see Riede, *Im Netz des Jägers*, 279ff.

92. *Religiöse Daseinsaneignung* = "religious appropriation of being"; see H.-P. Müller, *Vergleich und Metapher*, 49ff.

93. Westermann, *Vergleiche und Gleichnisse*, 81. On the boundary between life and death, see "Excursus 7: Life and Death," 239–40 below.

The images chosen for the enemies in these texts are virtual war metaphors. The enemies *lie in wait* for the supplicant; they *attack* him and *take up position* (v. 4–5a).[94]

In the second depiction of the enemies, in verses 6–7 (7–8), the representational level changes, and *human beings become animals*: the enemies are first compared to pariah dogs, which circle the home of the supplicant evening after evening (v. 6/7).[95] Then this animal image is decoded by means of expressions like "slobber (at the mouth)" and "swords on their lips," so that *animals become human beings*—but in the image of aggressive and demonic animals.

What is central here is the combination or rather the "superimposition" of the two imageries of "war" and "animals," to which imagery of the "hunt" is added, if one considers the enemy metaphors in the Psalms of the Individual as a whole.[96] The figurative language provides the supplicant with access to the *boundaries of human experience*, which often are difficult to verbalize since they concern emotions, moods, and values and thus are usually closed off from conceptual thinking.[97] Their strength consists in their capacity to explain the inexplicable, making the inconceivable conceivable through reference to images of war, animals, and hunting. The following diagram can be constructed:

Actions of the enemy
Planning what is evil and attempting to set the plan in motion

↓

Figurative language of the Psalms
Metaphorization of "evil" through figurative language:
War metaphors
Animal metaphors
Hunting metaphors

↑

Experience of the supplicant
Fear of "evil" and attempting to overcome it

This technique of superimposing different image and representation levels is also found among Israel's neighbors. To illustrate this, I have chosen a scene from Egypt (fig. 13) depicting Horus and Pharaoh in a fight with a *mythical* and a *historical* enemy. The war-god Horus (on the right) uses his long lance to stab a hippopotamus (wild boar?), which represents his opponent Seth, the "god of confusion." Analogous to this action, Pharaoh (on the left), stabs a human enemy who is tied up. How is this scene to be understood? It is not two different enemies that are stabbed, but the *enemy of Egypt* depicted in two different forms. "As the one power of Horus is manifest in the king and in both lances, which are topped by falcon heads, so the same life-*opposing* power resides in both *opponents*."[98] Overcoming historical-political enemies (left) is

94. On war metaphors in the Psalms of the Individual, see Riede, *Im Netz des Jägers*, 20ff.
95. On the night motif, see 103, n. 21 above.
96. On the significance of these three constitutive imageries, see the summary in Riede, *Im Netz des Jägers*, 21ff.
97. See above 22ff. above.
98. Keel, *Die Welt*, 97, emphasis original.

Figure 13. Horus and Pharaoh conquer their opponents

on the same level of significance as the mythic struggle between Horus and Seth, or an animal representing the latter (right). Both struggles are aimed at restoring order by overcoming the chaotic, by defeating mythic and historical enemies.

Similar examples from Mesopotamia can be cited, especially from prayer and ritual texts. Maul[99] called attention to a late Babylonian *eršemma*-prayer that contains the motif of a god (Ninurta) setting out for battle, to save the world, which is threatened by chaos. In the account, the defeat of the mythic enemy ("chaotic force") is linked to the contemporary situation in the second stich: the actual enemy of the land figures in the role of a mythic enemy:

1. *Sumerian version*: The hero sets out as a flood that surges across the enemy land.
   Akkadian version: The hero sets out to [the house of the enemy land] as an overwhelming flood.
2. When he sets out, [indeed] when the hero sets out, he is a flood that surges across the enemy land.
3. When the word of [the Great An] goes out, [it is a flood that surges across the enemy land]. . . .[100]

The principle of *mutual modeling* of mythic and historical spheres, which was already mentioned in regard to Psalm 13,[101] can be examined particularly well in the example of this text. While Ninurta and his manifestations in the *eršemma*-prayer oppose the (real) enemy, the king sets out in reality—as reflected in Assyrian royal inscriptions—against this enemy with his army. Correspond-

99. Maul, "'Wenn der Held.'"
100. Ibid., 316.
101. See 74 above.

ingly, the political rhetoric of the Assyrian royal inscriptions receive mythic connotations. They show that "the king understood his fight against the enemy as a realization of the mythic struggle of the hero Ninurta and also himself as the god's earthly and contemporary representative, who has been charged by An and Enlil to save the land (on behalf of Ninurta)."[102]

Such images and texts can help us gather a better understanding of the enemy image in the Psalms. The enemy of the individual is more than the supplicant's personal opponent: that enemy represents a *chaotic power*, which is intent on breaking into the supplicant's world and separating the supplicant from God and fellow human beings. In order to achieve this, the texts on the one hand use a *generalizing way of speaking* and on the other hand a *figurative way of speaking*. Since the enemies also already deny God, there is more at stake in their attacks than "only" the fate of the individual supplicant—as grave as that may be in itself. Rather, the image of the enemy affects the image of God, which is the disconcerting other side of that image. For this reason, the petitions directed to YHWH to put an end to the malice of the wicked (cf. Ps. 7:9/10; etc.)[103] are not primarily wishes for revenge, but a *cry for justice in a world full of injustice*.[104] This cry is the only thing left to the supplicant in a hopeless situation.

But what about today? Unfortunately, the world is "not yet at a point where we can eliminate from our prayer books these witnesses of protest against all forms of social oppression and replace them with innocent phrases, unless we are ill informed, stupid, or insensitive."[105]

Even if we agree with this view, as I believe we must, there are difficulties that cannot be overlooked. Since they are fundamentally connected to the subject of "revenge," it is necessary to take a closer look.

b. Anthropological Keyword 2: Revenge

Cain shall be avenged sevenfold,
but Lamech seven times sevenfold.
Lamech, in Genesis 4:24

Do not say: "I shall repay evil!"
Place your hope in YHWH, for YHWH will save you.
Proverbs 20:22

Resources

Baldermann, *Einführung in die Bibel*, 89–93; idem, *Ich werde nicht sterben*, 25–33; Berger, *Historische Psychologie*, 294–96; Dietrich, "Rache"; Dietrich and Link, *Willkür und Gewalt*, 128–48; Ebach, "Gott des Alten Testaments"; Flaig, *Ödipus*, 104–11; Görg, *Der un-heile Gott*, 114–17; Grünwaldt, *Auge um*

102. Maul, "'Wenn der Held,'" 329. On victory over the forces of evil in the ancient Orient, see idem, "Der Sieg"; and Röllig, "Begegnungen mit Göttern."

103. See 143ff. below.

104. On the subject of justice, see 128ff. below

105. Keel, "Die 'Feinde' in den Psalmen," 60.

Auge?, 123–43; Höffe, "Ehre"; Janowski, "JHWH der Richter"; idem, "Die Tat"; Koch and Roloff, "Tat-Ergehen-Zusammenhang"; Krawczack, *Psalm 58*, 282–92; Lang, "Rachepsalmen"; Edward Lipiński, "נָקַם"; Mathys, *Liebe deinen Nächsten*; Meinhold, "Umgang mit dem Feind"; Otto, *Theologische Ethik*, 243–48, 57; M. Rösel, "Tun-Ergehen-Zusammenhang"; Ruppert, "Fluch- und Rachepsalmen"; Schüle, "Verständnis des alttestamentlichen Liebesgebots"; Schwienhorst-Schönberger, "Vergeltung"; Singer, "Rache"; Sofsky, *Zeiten des Schreckens*, 187–201; Stolz et al., "Rache"; van der Velden, *Psalm 109*, 162–65; Vogt and Zingerle, *Ehre*, 9–34; H. W. Wolff, *Anthropology*, 185–91; Zenger, *Ein Gott der Rache*; idem, "Fluchpsalmen."

On cultural anthropological aspects of revenge, see Paul, "Die Rache"; and the essays in Sünker and Berner, *Vergeltung ohne Ende?* On the semantics and anthropology/theology of revenge in the Old Testament, see Brünenberg, "Wenn Jahwes Widerstand sich regt"; E. Hahn, "Vergeltung"; Zenger, "Rache II"; Dietrich, "Im Zeichen Kains"; Janowski, "Vergeltung II"; and Grund, "'Auge für Auge.'"

The sociologist W. Sofsky opens the chapter on retribution ["Vergeltung"] in the book *Zeiten des Schreckens* with the observation that revenge "knows no forgiveness and no forgetting. Time may pass, but revenge holds on to its goal. It has a long memory and knows of no statute of limitations. It patiently waits for the moment of fulfillment. The memory of the act does not fade away. Burnt into consciousness, it generates ever-new obsessions of retribution."[106]

The Song of Lamech in Genesis 4:23–24, with its principle of "augmented retribution,"[107] is an especially relevant example. In light of this diagnosis, a biblical "God of revenge"[108] would be a particularly incriminating problem.

The Old Testament speaks of "revenge" in more than fifty passages, without condemning it one single time in principle. To exact vengeance appears if not as a positive, at least as a possible behavior by God and by human beings. The vocabulary of revenge includes above all the verb נָקַם and the nouns נָקָם and נְקָמָה, which are usually rendered as "take vengeance" and "vengeance" in lexicons, but also terms and words that are not usually translated with "(take) vengeance," like פָּקַד, "attend to, inspect, visit"; רִיב, "conduct a lawsuit"; or שָׁפַט, "judge, bring about justice"; as well as verbs that are often translated as "repay, return," such as שׁוב Hiphil; or שׁלם Piel.[109]

If one takes these associated terms into consideration, there are about 130 references on the subject of "revenge" in the Old Testament. This is a considerable number and generally an embarrassing situation. It is so embarrassing that one is either ashamed and silent about it or points to it gloatingly, as in the example set by Marcion of Sinope in his hateful tirades against the Old Testament, which has since been followed unrelentingly by some. For Marcion,

106. Wolfgang Sofsky, *Zeiten des Schreckens*, 187.

107. On the principle of "augmented retribution," according to which a strike is answered with a double strike, etc., see Flaig, *Ödipus*, 104ff. Gen. 4:24 escalates this principle to excess (77-fold retribution).

108. See esp. Zenger, *Ein Gott der Rache*; also Dietrich and Link, *Die dunklen Seiten Gottes*, 1:128ff.

109. See Dietrich, "Rache," 453ff.

the Old Testament was the book of a despotic creator god, "who is above all concerned about his honor, who . . . values submission in his subjects, and who . . . destroys his opponents."[110] This proscription of the Old Testament God of vengeance has been etched deeply into the consciousness of Marcion's contemporaries and is periodically revitalized as a foil to the New Testament God of love.[111]

But are God's love and love for one's neighbor categories that belong exclusively to the New Testament or even to Christian ethics, on the basis of which the normative quality of the Old Testament for Christianity and for the church can be questioned? Here too, a more detailed analysis is necessary in the interest of informed understanding of the Enemy Psalms.

α. Love for Enemy and Neighbor

"How does brother behave to brother (*'āḥ*) and sister (*'āḥôt*)?" asks H. W. Wolff in part 3 of his *Anthropology*. "How does a man behave to his neighbor and companion (*rēa'*), to his friend (*'ōhēb*), and to his enemy (*'ōyēb*)? How, in fact, does the Old Testament view [the hu]man as fellow [humans]?"[112] There are unambiguous statements about love for enemy and neighbor in the Old Testament. Let us begin with love for one's neighbor. The commandment to love in Leviticus 19:17–18 is unique and has no parallel in the ancient Near East. It attains a central significance in the New Testament:[113]

> You shall not hate your brother in your heart.
> You shall carefully reprimand your fellow countryman,
> but you shall not hold a fault against him!
> Do not take revenge [נָקַם]
> and do not be angry with the members of your people,
> but love your neighbor; he is like you [כָּמוֹךָ]!
> I am YHWH.

In verse 34 of the same chapter, this commandment is expanded to include strangers, resident aliens. In both cases, the key sentence is "You shall love your neighbor" (v. 18) / "love the stranger" (v. 34)—who "is like you [כָּמוֹךָ]!"[114] In this formula, the love for one's neighbor is not compared to the love for oneself;[115] in other words, it does not refer to the *type of love*, but to the *neighbor* (Israelite or alien), who is to be loved. Grammatically, as Schüle has shown, the expression in question—כָּמוֹךָ, "[who is] like you"—is to be linked attributively

110. Harnack, *Marcion*, 100; on this subject, see Reventlow, *Epochen der Bibelauslegung*, 1:144ff.

111. To give an example, let me only point to Hanna Wolff, *Neuer Wein—alte Schläuche*, 65ff. She contrasts "Jesus' religion of grace" with the "Jewish religion of sacrifice and law," and Jesus' God of love with the Jewish God of vengeance. See Zenger, *Das Erste Testament*, 28ff.; and Janowski, "'Hingabe' oder 'Opfer'?," 19ff. In this context Zenger (*Am Fuss des Sinai*, 20ff.) rightly speaks of a virtual "psycho-Marcionism."

112. H. W. Wolff, *Anthropology*, 185.

113. Cf. Matt. 22:39; Luke 10:27; Rom. 13:9; Gal. 5:14; and Jas. 2:8.

114. On the expression כָּמוֹךָ, see Mathys, *Liebe deinen Nächsten*, 6ff., who confirms the traditional translation; also Schüle, "Verständnis des alttestamentlichen Liebesgebots," 524ff.

115. As argued, e.g., by H. W. Wolff, *Anthropology*, 189. On this tradition of interpretation, see Schüle, "Verständnis des alttestamentlichen Liebesgebots," whose translation I am following here.

to the "neighbor" and not adverbially to "love."[116] An important perspective then emerges with regard to the image of humanity in Leviticus 19:18 and 34:

> Whoever loves another only on the basis of one's own self-understanding, one's own status and prestige, can only begin with *oneself* and in an empty self-referential loop end with *oneself*. In doing so, the person will lose sight of what Leviticus 19 is trying to show: that even among equals, some are more equal than others. . . . The human being is not only an organically constituted [creature] but also a "dependent" social creature: each person depends on environments that have to meet one's different needs, but in which one is already present, and whose form can only be partially influenced by one or not at all. This recognition, that a human being is dependent on environments that are welcoming and conducive of life, and that *all* human beings are equal in this regard, regardless of which part of the social hierarchy one is situated on, can, in view of the question "What shall I do?," only be this: Behave toward your fellow human being in such a way that the Other finds in you an environment accommodating that person in ways that are welcoming and conducive of life: in the words of the Old Testament, וְאָהַבְתָּ אֵת רֵעֲךָ, "Love your neighbor!"[117]

But if it is not speaking of just the love for one's neighbor, what is the situation but the love for the stranger or even the enemy? The characteristics of loving acts toward another who is not one's neighbor are set out in legal regulations and wisdom sayings, which deal thematically with help for the domestic animals of an "enemy" (Exod. 23:4–5) or "brother/neighbor" (Deut. 22:1–4) or even with the love of an enemy (Prov. 25:21–22; cf. 24:17). The two regulations of the covenant code demand, for example, that one assist an enemy whose livestock is threatened and even lend a helping hand to prevent further injury to an animal:

> When you come upon your enemy's [אֹיֵב] lost ox or donkey,
> you shall surely return the animal to the owner.
> If you see the donkey of one who hates you [שֹׂנֵא], lying under its burden,
> you shall refrain from keeping your distance from [the one who hates].
> Together with him, you shall raise [the donkey] up again.
> (Exod. 23:4–5)[118]

The ethical principle here is "Solidarity before law!" The laws of Exodus 23:4–5 transform the personal enmity into an "ethics of generosity and assistance" within the community, ethics that usually occurs only within the realm of the family. The animal's suffering, which must be alleviated, is more important than the hostility of its owner—which must come to an end. The end of enmity is brought about when someone—in this case the Israelite addressed as "you"—takes the first step.

Such an "ethics of the first step" is also the basis of Proverbs 25:21–22 (alt.):

116. Cf. the summary in Schüle, "Verständnis des alttestamentlichen Liebesgebots," 526–27.

117. Ibid., 529–30, emphasis original. On the subject, see also Grünwaldt, *Auge um Auge*, 133ff.

118. On the translation, see Boecker, "'Feindesliebe,'" 20–21. On the interpretation, see Schwienhorst-Schönberger, *Das Bundesbuch*, 384; F. Crüsemann, *Die Tora*, 220ff.; and Boecker, "'Feindesliebe,'" 19ff. Thus Deut. 22:1–4 does not speak of an "enemy" but specifically of a "brother." On the Deuteronomic ethics of kinship, see Braulik, *Deuteronomium*, 160–61; and Boecker, "'Feindesliebe,'" 23–24.

If some who hate you [שֹׂנֵא] are hungry, give them bread to eat;
if they are thirsty, give them water to drink!
You are surely heaping fiery coals upon their heads,
and YHWH shall reward you [שׁלם Piel] [for it].

The command is to provide the "hater" with bread and water, in other words, the essentials of life, and therefore to forgo enacting revenge for an evil deed (enacted "hate") through a commensurate act. This mandate demonstrates how little the sage, who is addressed here, regards or should regard the actions of the enemy. By loving the enemy, a change is caused in his disposition, which Proverbs 25:22 expresses in the image of heaping fiery coals on the head of the one who is now reformed.[119] YHWH responds to the sage's act by rewarding him (cf. Prov. 16:7).[120] Important for the subject of "revenge" is that the sage's consideration of one's own desires—the provision of bread and water—becomes "the spur toward loving action toward the other."[121] In this way, love overcomes hate and prevents revenge from (re)emerging.

However, the road to overcoming hate is stony. In H. W. Wolff's conclusion of the section cited here, the Old Testament sees "that men lose sight of one another and destroy themselves if they do not progress along the road that leads to the overcoming of hate; after all, Israel's God has begun the process and has promised it consummation. . . . For man is the being who is called to brotherhood."[122]

How are the "wishes for revenge" in the Psalms of Lament to be regarded in light of this background? Do they not follow the principle of kinship—or are they to be understood differently?

β. Revenge and Renunciation of Revenge

I have often pointed to the so-called curse-and-revenge Psalms,[123] which have been seen in theology and by the church as countertexts to the New Testament's commandment to love one's enemies.[124] For one thing, the designation "curse-and-revenge Psalms" is misleading, because actual curse formulas are not found in the Psalter, with the exception of 119:21. According to Ruppert, the jussive expressions are considered form-critically rather as "curse expositions, which—integrated in prayers—only lend emphatic stress to the petition."[125]

The relevant question, however, is whether the wish for or the imploring petition for YHWH's "revenge" or "retribution" [נְקָמָה/נָקָם] is based on mere vindictiveness or has different motives. Psalm 58:3–10 (4–11)[126] states:

The wicked are rebellious from the womb;
the liars go astray from the mother's womb. (v. 3/4)

119. On the interpretation, see Meinhold, *Die Sprüche*, 429ff.
120. On the term "reward" and an analysis of Prov. 25:21ff., see Janowski, "Die Tat," 186ff.
121. H. W. Wolff, *Anthropology*, 188.
122. Ibid., 191.
123. Pss. 58; 59; 69; 70; 109; 137; etc.; see the references on 98–99 above.
124. Matt. 5:43–48 // Luke 6:27–28, 32–35; cf. Rom. 12:19–21; see 99–100 above.
125. Ruppert, "Fluch- und Rachepsalmen," 685; on the subject, see also Zenger, "Fluchpsalmen."
126. See 98–99 above.

Their venom is like a serpent's venom,
  Like [that of] a deaf adder, stopping its ears, (v. 4/5)
[so that] it does not hear the voice of the [snake]-charmer
  or the spellcaster of spells. (v. 5/6)

O God, break the teeth in their mouths;
  smash the teeth of the young lions, O YHWH! (v. 6/7)

Let them vanish like water that flows away.
  When they shoot their arrows, let them fall down. (v. 7/8)
Let [them] perish like a miscarriage that you allow to perish,
  [like] a woman's stillbirth that does not see the sun. (v. 8/9)[127]
Before your pots can feel the bramble [burning],
  He [YHWH] will blow them away alive and also [in] fury. (v. 9/10)

The righteous will rejoice when [they] see vengeance [נָקָם];
  [they] shall bathe [their] feet in the blood of the wicked. (v. 10/11)

As we have seen, the wording of verse 6/7—"O God, break the *teeth* in their mouths; smash the *teeth* of the young lions, O YHWH"—shifts attention from the aggressors to their aggressiveness: what is to be taken away from the wicked are their deadly weapons and therefore their ability to attack.[128] Furthermore, it is noteworthy that the psalm does not conclude with the supplicant imagining a bloody triumph over the godless (v. 10/11)[129] but with asserting God's justice:

And a humanity shall say:
  indeed, the just shall receive a reward;
  indeed, there is a God, who is judge on earth.[130]

As the context for many of the "wishes for vengeance" or "pleas for revenge" shows, the point is not a *realization of fantasies of vengeance*, but a *restoration of justice* through God's saving righteousness. The complaint is therefore a cry for justice in a world full of injustice.[131] In God's presence, it insists that the cruelty and ruthlessness the enemies heap on their victims cannot be allowed. "When people have to endure unbearable circumstances without the prospect of change, no one should throw psychological stones at them if they call for vengeance."[132]

It is, after all, typical for the Enemy Psalms that the supplicant transfers one's own "revenge" or "vengeance" to God; as a rule it is not described how

127. As "seeing the sun" is a metaphor for "living," "not seeing the sun" signifies its opposite and is therefore equivalent to "being dead"; see Krawczack, *Psalm 58*, 165ff.

128. See 113–14 above.

129. On the interpretation of v. 10/11b, see esp. Krawczack, *Psalm 58*, 292ff., 299ff.; cf. Hossfeld and Zenger, *Psalmen 51–100*, 138–39.

130. The "reward of justice" that is accorded to the plagued supplicant with regard to the enemies through the just action of YHWH is the "flourishing," "abundant," and therefore "justified" life of the supplicant in the presence of God; see Janowski, "Frucht der Gerechtigkeit," 125ff.; also Krawczack, *Psalm 58*, 303ff.

131. Cf. Dietrich, "Rache," 463ff.; Dietrich and Link, *Die dunklen Seiten Gottes*, 1:130ff.

132. Dietrich, "Rache," 467; cf. Zenger, "Fluchpsalmen."

the supplicant takes revenge or plans to take revenge on the enemies.[133] There appears to be a clear line. The delegation of vengeance to God in the so-called revenge-and-curse Psalms is, according to Ruppert, "virtually equivalent to the renunciation of one's own vengeance"[134] and at the same time reflects a belief in God's care for the world. The measures taken by YHWH to execute the requested revenge on the supplicant's enemies are left open by the texts. The supplicant hopes, however, that God's justice, which puts an end to the enemy's hostility, will prevail in the end.[135] Likewise the petitioner hopes that God's attention will lead to one's own justification, in other words, will bring about justice. In the context of prayer, the so-called wishes for revenge are "extreme self-defense, a passionate appeal to Yahweh's justice to save the one who is falsely accused by punishing one's slanderers."[136]

The portrayal of the enemy in the Psalms of Lament has thus led us to the question of God. What remains is the unease that occurs when we read these texts in light of the commandment to love one's enemies. Jesus says, after all: "Love your enemies and pray for those who persecute you!" (Matt. 5:44). What then is to be done with the enemies? Do we have to evoke the same old images again and again? Could we not speak of enemies in a more understanding and sympathetic way? In view of such vague recommendations, the Psalms help us to understand the nature of the enemy's hostility and after that—and only after that—what is meant by loving one's enemy.

It is my thesis that the Enemy Psalms, with their harsh and direct imagery, put the supplicant in a position in which the petitioner can address the enemy problem: they make that which is incomprehensible in the enigma of hostility to become comprehensible and addressable. At the same time, they presuppose that God identifies with the *cause of the one who suffers*, whom God has created, and becomes the sufferer's advocate despite all denials by the enemy. "The word of Jesus concerning the love for one's enemies is certainly always misunderstood where this identification with the suffering is set aside or even reversed, so that the norm of peacefulness should suddenly serve to admonish the suffering and compassionate to be silent and to wait."[137]

In this case, the admonition to be silent and to wait would not only be unbiblical but also unchristian.[138] At the same time, we notice that the cry for justice does not itself change into a *mechanism for revenge*: this cry does not tangibly approach the possibility of the sufferer's bringing about the reestablishment of one's own integrity. In his interpretation of Romans 12:19–21, Karl Barth confronted precisely this problem by asking, "Who is my enemy?" He has pleaded for the difficult *path of renouncing revenge*:

133. "As a rule" means in the majority of all cases. There are, however, a few references in the Psalter to an independent execution of vengeance (Ps. 18:47/48 by the king) or participation in God's "revenge" or "vengeance" (Pss. 58:10/11b; 149:7); see van der Velden, *Psalm 109*, 162ff.; and Krawczack, *Psalm 58*, 282ff.

134. Ruppert, "Fluch- und Rachepsalmen," 685.

135. On the topic of justice and the end of malice or of the wicked, see 140ff., 143ff. below.

136. Ruppert, "Fluch- und Rachepsalmen," 685.

137. Baldermann, *Einführung in die Bibel*, 92.

138. D. Bonhoeffer, *Widerstand und Ergebung*, 225ff.: "Only if God's wrath and vengeance on his enemies can stand as a valid reality, [only then] can our hearts be touched by forgiveness and love of one's enemies" (226: letter on the second Sunday of Advent, 1943, to E. Bethge).

> The "enemy" is the one who opens my eyes to that which aggravates me in other human beings. He reveals it to me as evil. He shows me that evil is the ultimate and most genuine in well-known human beings. . . . He prompts a passionate cry in me for a (nonexistent) higher, equalizing, retributive justice, for an (absent) judge over him and me. Who should present a crisis to me but the "enemy"? . . . What should I do when it becomes clear to me, in light of the "enemy," that that which is to be "done" against him could only be evil, evil as the work of that higher justice, whose appearance against the enemy I miss so bitterly? Here the last temptation of titanism is uncannily close, the temptation to bring about my own justice, to take up the fight for what is right, to put myself in the place of the invisible God, and to become an enemy to the enemy, a titan to the titan.[139]

The Enemy Psalms, which remind Christians of the power of evil and which are therefore part of Christian prayer,[140] move on a fine line between *presumption of revenge* and *renunciation of revenge*. Their point of departure lies in the experience that the suffering, who had until now lived in a beneficial relationship to God and to fellow human beings, now finds oneself in discord with both. This experience of discord and fragmentation is addressed by the Psalms of Lament, which create an awareness of this experience by including it in prayer, thereby making the *incomprehensible comprehensible*, in the true sense of the word. In Israel, the sufferer was taught to express one's fears in prayer and not to exclude conflicts with the enemy from one's own relationship with God. In this way the "God of justice" was confronted with the suffering of his creatures. Now God was compelled to intervene on their behalf, as is exemplified by Psalm 7.

139. K. Barth, *Der Römerbrief*, 456.

140. Yet one should—and this does not happen often enough—think more intensively about the place of these prayers within the Christian community and in the Christian liturgy; see references in 100, n. 13 above.

5. "Establish justice for me according to my righteousness, YHWH!" (Ps. 7:8/9)
The Persecuted Human Being

a. The Justification of the Righteous

> And if God is not possessed of them [the attributes of his judicial office: anger, love, and mercy], the life of man will be thrown into confusion, and the condition of things will come to such disturbance that the laws will be despised and overpowered, and audacity alone reign, so that no one can at length be in safety unless he who excels in strength. Thus all the earth will be laid waste, as it were, by a common robbery. But now the wicked can expect punishment, the good can hope for favor, and the afflicted can look for aid.
>
> Lactantius, *The Anger of God*, 273 (alt.)

α. The God of Justice

"Justice" as an ethical term has two basic interrelated meanings: one *political*, in which justice is a moral principle for law, state, and politics; and a *personal*, according to which justice has been counted since Plato and Aristotle among the cardinal virtues. For the second meaning, justice is

> the moral stance in relation to the human being which—unlike friendship, love, or benevolence—is neither based on sincere affection nor does it exceed in its actions whatever is owed to another. Justice as a personal characteristic does not simply refer to doing what is just, but also to doing it on the basis of a specific conviction: because it is just and not because one would otherwise be punished or socially ostracized. Justice as a virtue is shown if one does not try to take advantage of others, despite greater power or intelligence, or if one's actions—as lawmaker, judge, teacher, parent, citizen—are focused on the idea of objective justice when there are gaps or room for interpretation in law and morality or their enforcement is highly unlikely.[1]

As a civic virtue, justice is an important barrier against a society's decline into conditions of flagrant lawlessness. In Western art, its idea has always been represented by the symbol of the scales (fig. 14), by which conditions of injustice are balanced. But what happens when justice will not or cannot prevail and—as the Old Testament Wisdom literature notes—when the act-consequence

1. Höffe, "Gerechtigkeit," 91–92.

Figure 14. Justice, in the Bamberg Cathedral

correlation breaks down?[2] From where should saving help come? Who should guarantee that "the one faithful to the community," "the just" (צַדִּיק), will be saved and the wicked (רָשָׁע) be put within bounds? Is there even such a basis for just living and acting that transcends all social reality and that serves as a final appeal? For the Old as well as the New Testament, the answer is unambiguous: The God of justice is "the morally authoritative foundation of all reality and the positive force of all processes that constitute reality."[3]

Anyone who inquires about the subject of "God's justice" will, in explorations of its impact on Western history, come upon a problematic legacy that is formative to this day, claiming

> that God presides over the world as the highest being, constantly registering all human behavior and from time to time responding accordingly by rewarding the good person and ordaining temporal or eternal punishment to the wicked. This understanding of God, as judge of the world, passing judgment on all human beings, found its way already into the ancient Greek and even more the Latin Bible translations, through a plethora of words describing judgment, punishment, and revenge. It assumes a worldview in which—in addition to the realm of nature, which is ethically neutral with regard to cause

2. On the act-consequence correlation, see Koch and Roloff, "Tat-Ergehen-Zusammenhang"; Janowski, "Die Tat"; Krawczack, *Psalm 58*, 317ff.; also the summaries in M. Rösel, "Tun-Ergehen-Zusammenhang"; Schwienhorst-Schönberger, "Vergeltung"; Sticher, *Die Rettung der Guten*, 18ff. There are different ways in which the act-consequence correlation can break down, such as described in the book of Job or in the Wisdom Psalms (Ps. 73; etc.); see 321–22 below. See also Freuling, *Der Tun-Ergehen-Zusammenhang*; Grund, "Tun-Ergehens-Zusammenhang"; and M. Saur, *Einführung*, 54–55f.

3. Koch and Roloff, "Tat-Ergehen-Zusammenhang," 493.

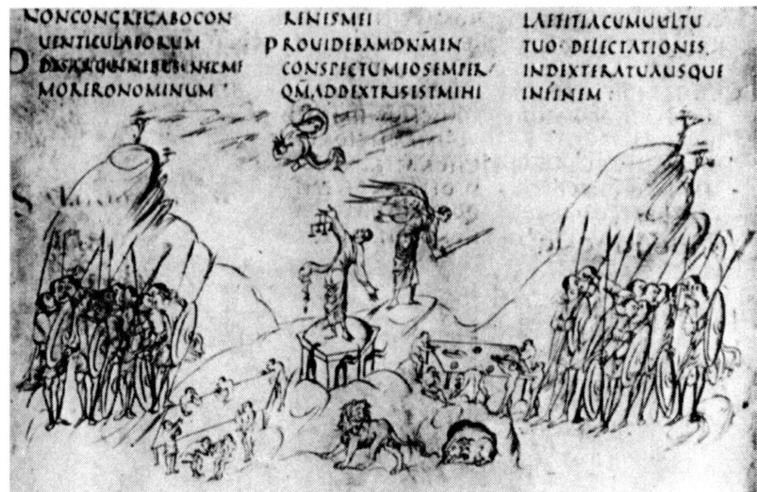

Figure 15. Illustration of Psalm 17 from the Utrecht Psalter (9th c.)

and effect—there is a separate realm of morality and values; only the latter realm is relevant for religion.[4]

The understanding of God or Christ as judge of the world, passing judgment on all human beings and assigning reward and punishment to each individual according to divine estimation (*iustitia distributiva*),[5] has not only found its way into the ancient Bible translations (Septuagint, Vulgate) through a variety of expressions for judgment, punishment, and revenge, but has also shaped the visual memory of Western culture through images of the judgment day or the judgment of the world.[6] However, the inner-worldly "examination of the righteous" has also been depicted in Western art, especially through the motif of the scales of judgment. This can be seen e.g. in an illustration of Psalm 17 in the late-Carolingian Utrecht Psalter (fig. 15). The psalmist, who turns to God with a "just cause," stands atop a fiery furnace and with his left hand raises a pair of scales up to Christ. He addresses the following words to YHWH:

> From your presence shall come what is my due;
> your eyes shall see my righteousness!
> (Ps. 17:2)

4. Ibid., 493.

5. "Justice," according to Ulpian's famous definition, is "the constant and perpetual will to render everyone what is their due" (*iustitia est constans et perpetua voluntas ius suum cuique tribuens/tribuendi*), *Digesta* 1.1.10. see Janowski, "Die Tat," 170 n. 11. On the subject of distributive justice, see also Werbick, *Bilder sind Wege*, 169ff.

6. See Schild, "Gott als Richter"; as well as the insightful thematic issue (of *ZNT*) edited by Riniker, *Gericht und Zorn Gottes*. Images of a punishing, judging, and vengeful God are particularly frightful to children; see Biesinger and Hänle, "Zwischen Horror und Erlösung." See also Kruck and Sticher, *Zorn und Erbarmen Gottes*; Barta, Rollinger, and Lang, *Recht und Religion*; Greiner et al., *Recht und Literatur*; Witte, *Gerechtigkeit*; Loretz, *Götter*, 9ff.; Spieckermann, "Der Retter ist nah," here esp. 34ff; K. Bieberstein and Bormann, "Gerechtigkeit/Recht"; Janowski, "Rettende Gerechtigkeit"; Krebernik, "Sonnengott." On systematic and practical theological aspects, see I. Schoberth, "Die Verharmlosung der Gottesrede"; Zeindler, *Gott der Richter*; and Moltmann, "Sonne der Gerechtigkeit."

You have examined my heart,
you have visited [me] by night.
You have reformed me—you shall find nothing;
I have considered—nothing shall escape my mouth! (v. 3)

"One could therefore," W. Pleister comments with regard to this illustration, "interpret the one scale as the justice/justification that proceeds from God, and the other scale as the justice/justification that the human being brings before God, who examines the heart of the faithful and finds it to be pure."[7]

This iconic tradition leads us to the motif of the "justification of the righteous" (*iustificatio iusti*), which is attested throughout the Psalms.[8] The God of justice, these texts emphasize, does not abandon the righteous in their distress, but intervenes as "social authority" against the unjust and the wicked and has mercy on those who are persecuted and oppressed. The premise for this connection of ideas is the *correlation of God and justice*, as expressed paradigmatically by Psalm 82:

A Psalm of Asaph.

God [YHWH] stands in the divine assembly,
in the midst of the gods he holds judgment:
(Ps. 82:1)

"How long will you judge/rule unjustly
and favor the wicked? (v. 2)
Plead for the weak and the orphan;
to the afflicted and needy give justice; (v. 3)
deliver the lowly and poor;
from the power of the wicked save [them]!" (v. 4)

They have neither comprehension nor insight;
they walk about in darkness;
all the foundations of the earth are shaking. (v. 5)
I say: "You are gods
and sons of the Most High, all of you! (v. 6)
But truly, you shall die like human beings
and fall like one of the princes!" (v. 7)
Arise, O God [YHWH], judge the earth,
for you have inherited all the peoples![9] (v. 8)

Since this text defines the concept of God on the basis of the concept of justice, it represents an important development in the biblical understanding of God and justice. This process, which can be termed "theologization of justice," indicates that "God's reign . . . becomes the confining limit of human reign over other human beings."[10]

7. Pleister, "Mythos des Rechts," 37.

8. Pss. 3:4–5 (5–6); 4:8/9; 5:3/4, 8–10 (9–11); 6:4/5; 7:6–11 (7–12); 9:4/5, 8/9; etc.; see Janowski, "Der barmherzige Richter," 55ff.

9. For the interpretation of this text, see ibid., 58ff.; also Hossfeld and Zenger, *Psalmen 51–100*, 479ff.; Loretz, *Psalmstudien*, 251ff.; idem, "Mythische Götterrebellion und königliche Sozialpflichten" (with problematic hypotheses about the history of religion and theology); and D. Human, "Psalm 82: God Presides." An appealing sermon on Ps. 82 is found in Moltmann, *Gotteslehre*, 110–17.

10. Otto, *Theologische Ethik*, 83. On the "theologization of justice," see also Albertz, "Theologisierung des Rechts"; and J. Assmann, "Theologisierung der Gerechtigkeit."

Excursus 5: Connective Justice

As a central concept of legal, economic, and political-social life in ancient Near Eastern cultures, justice is the force that holds the world together at its core by linking cause to effect. This understanding posits a connection between act and consequence, according to which all consequences can be related back to a preceding act and the presence of an all-connecting justice constitutes the "connective" aspect of justice (*iustitia connectiva*). As J. Assmann has demonstrated for the example of Egypt, all actions are linked to each other in such a way and therefore "just": anyone who remains passive ("idle") interrupts the continuity of reality that rests on the "interconnectedness" of all actions (J. Assmann, "Vergeltung und Erinnerung"; idem, *Maʿat: Gerechtigkeit*, 58ff., 178–79, 283ff.; etc.; idem, "Der Eine lebt'"; idem, *Tod und Jenseits*, 16, 73ff., 78ff.; etc.). In the Instruction for Merikare (9th/10th dynasty), this theory is explained on the basis of a "wicked act" (on this text see Janowski, "Die Tat," 179; cf. J. Assmann, "Maʿat—Gemeinschaftskunst"; idem, "Konstellative Anthropologie"; Kügler, "Gerechtigkeit"; and Janowski, "Anerkennung"):

> There is no benefit if one is rebuilding what he has ruined,
> restoring what he has demolished.
> Beware of it!
> A blow is repaid by its kind;
> this is the interconnectedness of all actions!

Connective actions presuppose a social memory, which reaches into the past as a time-transcending horizon and links today to yesterday. This dimension of the "grateful remembrance" is used as a central motif in the Tale of the Eloquent Peasant (on this text see Janowski, "Die Tat," 180):

> Do not hide your face from the one whom you have known;
> do not be blind to the one on whom you have looked.
> Do not reject the one who turns to you with pleas,
> but refrain from this hesitation, to let your statement be heard;
> act on behalf of the one who acts on your behalf!

The concept of justice also has a connective meaning in the Old Testament. It describes not only the positive relation of the king to YHWH, but also the relationship of the individual to the community as well as that of the perpetrator to the evil act (Otto, "Gerechtigkeit und Erbarmen"; Janowski, "Die Tat," 175ff.; Schwienhorst-Schönberger, "Vergeltung," 655; Krawczack, *Psalm 58*, 317ff.). This principle was theologized during the social and political crises in the middle of the monarchic period (see Otto, *Theologische Ethik*, 81ff.). As the sun-god symbolism was transferred to YHWH, justice (צְדָקָה/צֶדֶק) became a hypostatization of YHWH, which brings about "peace and well-being" (שָׁלוֹם) in nature and society, with the attention of the king as the mediator of justice toward the *personae miserae* (Ps. 72:1–4, 12–14; see Janowski, "Frucht der Gerechtigkeit"). As Psalm 72:5–7 shows, justice is the "fruit" of the king's just actions (v. 7!). Such a "flourishing" life, characterized by connectivity, is also the subject of Psalms 1:1–3; 52:9/10; 92:12–15 (13–16); Jeremiah 17:7–8; and Proverbs 11:28, 30, which compare the righteous to a tree planted by streams of water (Ps. 1:3; see ibid., 125ff.)

The legal system is transformed wherever the principle of God's reign prevails, and legislations are expanded by the *ethos of compassion*. This transformative process, which appears to have its historical beginning in the social and political crisis in the middle of the monarchic period (second half of the 8th c. BCE),[11] is reflected in the Covenant Code's regulations concerning social protection, as found in Exodus 22:21–27 (20–26; alt.):

> You shall not oppress a stranger [resident alien]. . . . (v. 21/20)
> If you indeed oppress them and they cry out to me,
> I shall hear their lament. . . . (v. 22/21)
> If, among my people, you lend money to the poor among you,
> you shall . . . exact no interest from them. (v. 25/24)
> If you take your neighbor's cloak as a pledge,
> you shall return it before sunset; (v. 26/25)
> for it is the neighbor's only cover, a covering for the skin.
> In what else shall the neighbor sleep?
> If your neighbor cries out to me, I shall listen,
> for I am compassionate. (v. 27/26)[12]

Because of the divergence of law and justice, and in reaction to the changes in society and in values of their time, the eighth-century prophets called for unity of law and justice. On the other hand, the authors of the older Covenant Code found the solution by combining law and ethos into *one* legal code, and thereby "to integrate both aspects, for which quite different human representatives were in fact responsible (priests, elders, judges), into one and the same legal will of Yahweh."[13] Thus the paraenesis of Exodus 22:21–27 (20–26) has its focus in the explanation of verse 27/26 and its motif of compassion: "For I am compassionate" (כִּי־חַנּוּן אָנִי; cf. Exod. 34:6; etc.). It depicts YHWH in the role of a divine king, who hears the cry of the socially disenfranchised and enables them to be justified—just as the ancient Near Eastern sun-god or his representative king saves the oppressed and punishes wrongdoing.[14]

In summary, the theologization of law gains significance in Judah in the eighth and seventh centuries BCE, which allows God's justice to become a determining force for social norms.[15] But not only that. The enforcement of laws, the source and subject of which was now God and not—in contrast to Egypt and Mesopotamia—the king,[16] also became a *critical institution*, which protected the law from being absorbed by the state or even being turned into its opposite.[17] It was not the authority of the state but "divine revelation that legitimized law in Judah."[18]

11. See references in Janowski, "Der barmherzige Richter," 56 n. 115.

12. On this text see F. Crüsemann, *Die Tora*, 217ff.; Otto, "Bedeutung der altorientalischen Rechtsgeschichte," 165ff.; idem, *Theologische Ethik*, 83ff., 88ff. For textual and redaction-critical points, see Schwienhorst-Schönberger, *Das Bundesbuch*, 331ff.

13. Albertz, "Theologisierung des Rechts," 122.

14. See 146ff. below.

15. On the subsequent history of the theologization of law after the Covenant Code (Deut. 12–26; Lev. 17–26; et al.), see Albertz, "Theologisierung des Rechts," 124ff.; Otto, "Recht/Rechtstheologie/Rechtsphilosophie," 204ff.

16. On the role of the king, who did not create the law but only instituted it, and who was charged to study the Torah daily (Deut. 17:14–20), see Albertz, "Theologisierung des Rechts,"125ff.

17. Cf. Otto, "Bedeutung der altorientalischen Rechtsgeschichte," 167; Otto, "Recht/Rechtstheologie/Rechtsphilosophie," 202–4.

18. Otto, "Recht/Rechtstheologie/Rechtsphilosophie," 203.

This association of God and justice, implicit in the motif of the compassionate royal God, is "a central event in the history of biblical theology and its understanding of God."[19] It is found in the late preexilic and the exilic–postexilic era primarily in those psalms that acclaim God as Judge and Savior in heaven or in the temple,[20] such as the following:

- In the *songs of complaint and thanksgiving in the first David-Psalter, Psalms 3–41.* See 3:4–5 (5–6); 4:8/9; 5:4, 9–11; 6:4/5; 7:6–11 (7–12); 9:5, 9; 10:5, 18; 11:4–6; 12:7–8 (8–9); 13:3–4 (4–5); 14:2. Compare 17:1–2; 26:1; 35:24; 54:3 (etc.).
- In the *historical-theological Asaph Psalms, 50; 73–83.* See 50:4, 6; 74:22; 75:3–4; 76:8–9 (9–10); 81:4–5 (5–6); 82:1, 3–4, 8 (etc.). Compare 79:9; 80:3/4, 7/8, 19/20 (etc.).
- In the late *YHWH-King-Psalms, 96–99.* See 96:10, 13; 97:6, 8; 98:1–3, 9; 99:4. Compare 48:10–11 (11–12) (etc.).
- In *Psalm 145* and in the final *Hallel Psalms, 146–150.* See 145:14, 17–20; 146:5–9; 147:6; 149:4. Compare 138:4–7 (etc.).

These texts always deal with the justification requested from and brought about by God. However, in everyday language the term "justification" has different aspects of meaning. They emphasize the *object* (a specific thing, oneself), the *authority* (law, conscience, God), or the *process* (recognition, trust).[21] There are limits to justification, especially in cases where a person cannot justify oneself even though being in the right. This case of "justification of the righteous" (*iustificatio iusti*)[22] is presented by Psalm 7 and related texts that closely associate human and divine justice, while making divine justice the standard for human justice.

β. Psalm 7 as an Example[23]

A šiggāyôn of David, which he sang to YHWH
because of the words of Cush, the Benjaminite.

YHWH my God, in you I take refuge;
  save me from all my pursuers and deliver me, (v. 1/2)
so that they may not tear my life/throat [*nepeš*] like a lion,
  as one who tears off [pieces], and there is no one to rescue! (v. 2/3)

19. F. Crüsemann, *Die Tora*, 224.

20. More than half of all occurrences of צֶדֶק and צְדָקָה with reference to YHWH occur in the Psalter; see Crüsemann, "Jahwehs Gerechtigkeit," 437ff. (with statistical data); Preuss, *Theologie*, 1:200–201; and esp. Spieckermann, "Gerechtigkeit Gottes II"; Janowski, "Der barmherzige Richter," 58ff.

21. See Jüngel, *Evangelium von der Rechtfertigung*, 4ff.

22. This form of justification is theologically surpassed by the justification of the sinner (*iustificatio impii*), i.e., by the faith that "one who is rightly accused, the human being who is entirely in the wrong before God and therefore deserves to be called *sinner* or *godless*, will be *justified* by God" (ibid., 6, emphasis original); see also Moltmann, "Die Rechtfertigung Gottes." On the question of whether this type of justification is found already in the Old Testament, see Spieckermann, "Rechtfertigung I"; and Hossfeld, "Rechtfertigung."

23. On the interpretation of Ps. 7, see Kwakkel, *My Righteousness*, 17ff.; Bons, "Le Psaume 7"; Hieke, "Psalm 7"; Grohmann, "Images of Birth"; idem, *Fruchtbarkeit*, 186ff.; Basson, *Divine Metaphors*, 63ff.; Backhaus, "Psalm 7"; and Wälchli, *Gottes Zorn*, 41ff. On the expression "Arise!" in Ps. 7:6/7, see W. Herrmann, "Von göttlichem Schlafen," here esp. 188. W. Herrmann understands the thematic parallel in Ps. 44:23/24 literally (see 141 above) and interprets it as an element of "old-fashioned piety." In contrast, see Kwakkel, *My Righteousness*, 212ff.; Basson, *Divine Metaphors*, 182–83; and Schönemann, *Der untreue Gott*, 138ff.

YHWH my God, if I had done this,
  if there is guilt in my hands, (v. 3/4)
if I have done something to the one who [now] repays me with evil,
  or have robbed the one who [now] troubles me without cause, (v. 4/5)
then let the enemy pursue and overtake my life / me [*nepeš*],
  and trample my life to the ground,
  and lay my honor into the dust. *Selah.* (v. 5/6)

Arise, YHWH, in your anger;
  rise up against the raging of my enemies
  and awake toward me, you who have offered a judgment! (v. 6/7)

Let the assembly of the nations gather around you,
  and return above it on high! (v. 7/8)
(YHWH, judge the peoples!)
Establish justice for me according to my righteousness,
  and according to my innocence, [that is] in me! (v. 8/9)
Let the malice of the wicked come to an end,
  but raise up the righteous,
you who test the heart and kidneys,
  righteous God! (v. 9/10)
My shield [protection] is with God,
  a savior of those who are upright in heart. (v. 10/11)
God is a righteous judge,
  and a God who is wrathful every day. (v. 11/12)

Truly, he [the enemy] sharpens his sword again;
  he has drawn his bow and is ready [to shoot]. (v. 12/13)
Against himself he has prepared deadly weapons;
  he has lit his arrows. (v. 13/14)
See: he is in labor with injustice,
  pregnant with malice, and gives birth to lies. (v. 14/15)
He has dug a pit and scooped it out,
  and fell into the trap he had made. (v. 15/16)
He has caused his malice to return on his own head;
  violence descends on his own skull. (v. 16/17)

I shall praise YHWH according to his righteousness,
  and sing to the name of YHWH, the most high. (v. 17/18)

Textual Notes

1/2. Against the proposal to read רדפי as a singular (Kraus, *Psalmen*, 3:190; cf. *BHS* apparatus; et al.), the MT is to be retained, in my estimation (cf. Weber, *Werkbuch*, 1:68; et al.). A change in number (second-person plural / third-person singular) is not uncommon in the laments of the individual; see above 74–75.

2/3. The MT is to be retained, *pace* Kraus (*Psalmen*, 1:190–91), who changes the MT's פֹּרֵק into אֵין פֹּרֵק with LXX and Syriac and associates it syntactically with the second stich. On the translation of פֹּרֵק, see Riede, *Im Netz des Jägers*, 163, 166–67.

3/4. Here זאת ("this") relates to what follows, not what precedes it (cf. Baethgen, *Die Psalmen*, 16). For a different position, see Beyerlin (*Die Rettung*, 96–97) on the interpretation of this verse.

6/7b. Here is an asyndetic attributive clause; see Michel, *Tempora und Satzstellung*, 195; for a different position, see Kraus, *Psalmen*, 1:191 (et al.).

7/8. Usually שׁוּבָה ("return") is changed to שֵׁבָה ("Take your seat, preside on your throne"); so Beyerlin, *Die Rettung* (98, with n. 91); Kraus, *Psalmen* (1:191; et al.); in my opinion, the MT is to be preferred (cf. Baethgen, *Die Psalmen*, 17–18, and his interpretation of this verse).

8/9. The first colon is probably a later addition, connected to the redaction of the YHWH-King Psalms, as in 96:10b, 13; 98:9 (cf. Hossfeld and Zenger, *Die Psalmen*, 1:71).

10/11. Perhaps the עַל in מָגִנִּי עַל־אֱלֹהִים ("My shield is with God") can be retained if it is understood analogously to 62:7/8a ("My salvation and my honor are with God") (cf. Baethgen, *Die Psalmen*, 33; Craigie, *Psalms 1–50*, 98–99; et al.). Relevant is also the expression "My violence [the violence done to me] is on you [is your responsibility]" in Gen. 16:5 (cf. Boecker, *Redeformen des Rechtslebens*, 59–60.

12–13 (13–14). In my opinion, these verses describe the actions of the wicked (cf. Baethgen, *Die Psalmen*, 18–19; Michel, *Tempora und Satzstellung*, 246–47; Kraus, *Psalmen*, 1:199; Gerstenberger, *Psalms, Part 1*, 63, 65; et al.); for a different position, see Hossfeld and Zenger, *Die Psalmen*, 1:74; and the interpretation of the verse below. At the beginning of v. 13, אם־לא is probably to be understood as an emphatic particle ("truly, indeed"), as in Isa. 5:9; Job 31:31; etc. (cf. GKC §149e; Michel, *Tempora und Satzstellung*, 246–47; Kraus, *Psalmen*, 1:191; et al.). Krammer offers a literal translation: "if he does not return [again], sharpening his sword, drawing his bow, and taking aim" ("'Wer anderen eine Grube gräbt,'" 244). Compare also Weber, *Werkbuch*, 1:68: "Truly! Now he sharpens his sword (or: When he does not return), . . ."

13/14. The meaning is "as flaming arrows" (cf. *HALOT*, 214, s.v. דלק Qal 1). On the change in form, see Michel, *Tempora und Satzstellung*, 247.

14/15. For the translation, see also Michel, *Tempora und Satzstellung*, 247 (cf. *HALOT*, 274 s.v. IV חבל.)[24]

The structure of Psalm 7 is transparent. Aside from the superscription, the Psalm is divided into five sections: the *introductory petitions* (vv. 1–2 [2–3]), *the assertion of innocence* (purifying oath, in vv. 3–5 [4–6]), the central *appeal for judgment* with the *judgment doxology* (vv. 6–11 [7–12]), the sapiential *description of the wicked* (vv. 12–16 [13–17]), and the *promise of praise* (v. 17/18).

Introductory petitions and invocation

1/2	Petition to be saved (+ invocation)
2/3	Motivation for petition (lion metaphor)

24. For a more detailed analysis, see Janowski, "JHWH der Richter," 98–99.

Assertion of innocence	
3–4 (4–5)	Protasis (+ invocation): Condition
5/6	Apodosis: Self-curse
Appeal for judgment and judgment doxology	
6–7 (7–8)	YHWH's arrival for judgment
8–9 (9–10)	YHWH's ruling in favor of the supplicant
10–11 (11–12)	Hymnic praise of judging and saving God
Description of the wicked	
12–13 (13–14)	Actions of the wicked
14/15	Nature of the wicked (metaphors of pregnancy/birth)
15/16	Consequences for the wicked
Promise of praise	
17/18a	Praise of YHWH's justice
17/18b	Praise of YHWH's name

A significant development in the theological interpretation of the psalm—as in contrast to Duhm's commentary[25]—was the recognition that the motif of the "justification of the righteous" (*iustificatio iusti*) does not signify "self-righteousness," but, as Kraus has rightly emphasized, the idea "that God will bring the righteousness of the just to light against all questions as challenges."[26] This theme is found in all parts of the psalm, beginning with the dramatic image of a tearing lion.

Thematic Aspects

1. *Like a Tearing Lion*

Like most of the laments of the individual, Psalm 7 also begins with an invocation (v. 1/2). Noteworthy is the form of the double invocation ("YHWH my God"), which emphasizes the *personal* relationship of the supplicant to God and appears again at the beginning of the assertion of innocence (v. 3/4a). The effect is a close correspondence of verses 1–2 (2–3) and 3–5 (4–6). The *introductory petitions* and the *assertion of innocence* are also interconnected in other ways. Thus the image of the lion of verse 2/3 resonates in 5/6a and is "always heard in the background."[27] The enemy's aggression is modeled after the movement of an attacking, biting, and mauling lion (cf. fig. 16)[28] and

25. Ps. 7:9b–11 (10b–12) is seen as an alien component ("the debris of various sentences"), and as a result its statements about justification are limited (Duhm, *Die Psalmen*, 31ff.). Characteristic are also statements like the following: "Whoever lives a moral life will not encounter misfortune; whoever is just in this higher sense is sure of his reward. We encounter this reward-obsession, which is elevated by the mechanical doctrine of reward and punishment, in the Psalms as well as among the New Testament Pharisees" (ibid., xxxi). The basis for such judgments is the "nature of Christian humility" (ibid., xxxi), which the "pre-Christian" Psalter did not have yet. The implications of such exegeses have been extensively explained by Zenger, *Das Erste Testament*, 38ff., 42ff., 48ff.; idem, *Ein Gott der Rache*, 26ff., 39ff.

26. Kraus, *Psalmen*, 1:198; cf. 202.

27. Hossfeld and Zenger, *Die Psalmen*, 1:75.

28. Cf. Ps. 17:11–12 (see 116 above); on the lion metaphor in particular, see Keel, *Die Welt*, 75–76; Lohfink, "Ps 7, 2–6," 63ff.; Riede, *Im Netz des Jägers*, 150ff.

Figure 16. Attacking lion, Nimrud
(Assyria, 8th/7th c. BCE)

finds its conclusion in the hopelessness of verse 2/3c ("and there is no one to rescue") and the corresponding hopelessness of 5/6c ("and lay my honor into the dust").[29]

Compared to the last line of Psalm 7:2/3, which describes the threatening situation of the supplicant ("and there is no one to rescue"), the repeated double invocation of verse 3/4 represents the greatest possible contrast. The supplicant now undertakes a second attempt, to demonstrate not only the hopeless situation faced, but also individual innocence, and thereby to prompt YHWH to intervene. The petitioner does so in the form of a "purification oath," which consists of a *protasis* (vv. 3–4 [4–5]) and an *apodosis* (5/6), in which a succession of three *conditional clauses* formulated with אִם ("if"; in vv. 3/4a, 3/4b, 4/5) mirrors a sequence of three *successive curses* (in vv. 5/6a, 5/6b, 5/6b).

Conditional clauses
YHWH my God, *if* I had done this: (Ps. 7:3/4a)
  if there is guilt in my hands, (v. 3/4b)
if I have done something to the one who [now] repays me with evil, (v. 4/5a)
  or have robbed the one who [now] troubles me without cause— (v. 4/5b)

Successive curses
then let the enemy pursue and overtake my life / me [*nepeš*] (v. 5/6a)
  and trample my life to the ground, (v. 5/6b)
  and lay my honor into the dust. (v. 5/6c)

29. Cf. Lohfink, "Ps 7, 2–6," 65–66.

As in the protasis, the last element is also the most concrete in the apodosis: the "honor" (כָּבוֹד),[30] the *legal and social integrity of the supplicant*, is destroyed if the petitioner has committed the crime as accused. This may indicate the physical death, but certainly the "social death"[31] of the supplicant.

The protasis-apodosis construction of verses 3–5 (4–6) represents a *conditional self-curse*: a self-curse in case of the alleged act of verses 3–4 (4–5). It is difficult to say what this act was, but it seems to involve an accusation of theft (חלץ Piel, in v. 4/5b; cf. Exod. 22:11/10).[32] In light of this, the supplicant asserts self-innocence and makes use of a legal argumentation for this purpose: a so-called purification oath.

In ancient Israelite legal proceedings, the *purification oath* and the *ordeal* (as in Num. 5:12–18; cf. Deut. 17:8–13) belong to the "nonrational" forms of evidence, in contrast to witnesses and corroborating evidence.[33] In legal disputes, the charge is usually brought forward by the victim or by a witness. If the accused who does not confess denies the charge and demands proof, it has to be presented by witnesses or through the presentation of documents. If such evidence is lacking or is insufficient, a purification oath (assertive oath) or a divine judgment (ordeal) can be imposed on the accused. Generally speaking, the oath confirms the stated claims by lending them a reliable validity.

In a court case, the *purification oath* is part of the process of establishing the evidence. An example of a purification oath that decides a court case is found within the deposition law of Exodus 22:7–15 (6–14).[34] The first case, in verses 7–8 (6–7), describes the theft of goods entrusted for safekeeping and the thief is found or remains unknown. Consequently a primary scenario (v. 7/6a) and two secondary scenarios (perpetrator is known/unknown: vv. 7/6b, 8/7) are constructed:

> If someone [**A**] gives the neighbor [**B**] money or goods for safekeeping,
> and it is stolen from that person's house [**B**], (v. 7/6a)
>
> the thief [**C**], if found, shall make double restitution; (v. 7/6b)
>
> if the thief [**C**] is not found,
> the owner of the house [**B**] shall be brought before God
> [so that it may be established by divine judgment]
> if he has laid hands on the neighbor's [**A**] property.

If the perpetrator is not known, the owner of the house shall be taken "before God," to the sanctuary, apparently to wait there for a divine judgment.

The purification oath, which is based on the rule *aut iuret aut componat* ("either the accused makes an oath or pays restitution"), is essentially the oath of an

30. Cf. Pss. 3:3/4; 4:3/4; etc.; see Hossfeld and Zenger, "'Selig,'" 40–41 on the term "honor." It is noteworthy that we encounter in Ps. 3:3/4—as in Ps. 7:10/11—a shield metaphor: "But you, YHWH, are a shield around me; you are my honor and the one who lifts up my head." In terms of *content* (מָגֵן, "shield," as metaphor for "protection"), Ps. 3:3/4 is comparable to Ps. 7:10/11, but the *formulation* is different.

31. On "social death," see the references on 46–47 above.

32. On the meaning of חלץ Piel in Ps. 7:4/5, see Macholz, "Ps 7, 4–6."

33. See Boecker, *Recht und Gesetz*, 20ff.; Seybold, "Gericht Gottes," 464–65; Niehr, *Rechtsprechung in Israel*, 87ff.; and finally van der Toorn, "Ordeal Procedures"; idem, "Ordeal."

34. Schwienhorst-Schönberger, *Das Bundesbuch*, 193ff.

accused and has a decisive quality with regard to the court case. By the power of the conditional self-curse expressed by the oath, the punishment defined by the oath will befall the accused if that person is guilty. In Psalm 7:3–5 (4–6) the supplicant defines the punishment by means of the consequences in verse 5/6.

> . . . *then* let the enemy pursue and overtake my life / me [*nepeš*],
> and trample my life to the ground,
> and lay my honor into the dust

Despite the similarity in form, the purification oath of Psalm 7:3–5 (4–6) does not have a decisive quality, because the decisive act (YHWH's verdict in favor of the supplicant) is expected beyond the situation described in verse 5/6.[35] This act is YHWH's judicial intervention desired by the one in distress against enemies (vv. 6–11 [7–12]). Nevertheless, the purification oath functions to prepare for the encounter with God brought about by this judgment.[36] This preparation is done with the awareness that in case of a negative outcome, the disastrous reality invoked by the self-curse of verse 5/6 would occur and would have to be accepted with all of its consequences. The gravity of the accusation (vv. 3–4 [4–5]) mirrors the gravity of the consequences to be born (v. 5/6). In this situation, the distressed supplicant appeals to the "heavenly judge."

2. *Saving Justice*

The assertion of innocence is the precondition for the *appeal for judgment* in Psalm 7:6–11 (7–12) (with its concluding hymn to the judging and saving God in vv. 10–11 [11–12]).[37] Already the first request for YHWH's intervention ("Arise!," v. 6/7a // "Rise up," v. 6/7a) constitutes a linguistic contrast to the last element of the definition of legal consequences of verse 5/6 ("He shall lay my honor into the dust," v. 5/6b) and at the same time takes up the introductory petition against the pursuers. The triad of imperatives or cohortatives in verse 6/7, which call for the arrival and intervention of YHWH, corresponds to the sequence of two stichs in verse 7/8, which describe the judicial office of God:

> Arise, YHWH, in your anger;
> rise up against the raging of my enemies
> and awake toward me, you who have offered a judgment!
> (Ps. 7:6/7)

35. Beyerlin and Kraus have tried to explain this situation on the basis of a cultic-sacral divine court case: Beyerlin, *Die Rettung*, 196ff.; Kraus, *Psalmen*, 1:193. See the criticism in Janowski, *Rettungsgewissheit*, 9–10, 180–81; also Gerstenberger, *Psalms. Part 1*, 66; Hossfeld and Zenger, *Die Psalmen*, 1:72; Millard, *Komposition des Psalters*, 55 n. 300, etc.

36. Gerstenberger, *Der bittende Mensch*, 155–56.

37. According to van der Toorn, the connection between the assertion of innocence and the appeal for judgment is also emphasized by the corresponding content between the *self-assessment* of vv. 3–5 (4–6) as innocent, and the *depiction of God* in v. 9c/10c as one "who tests heart and kidneys." Van der Toorn ("Ordeal," 40) declares: "The conceptual basis for this judicial practice was the belief that God possessed knowledge surpassing that of humans. A crime might have been committed without a soul in sight, but the LORD had been a witness. 'The eyes of the LORD are in every place, keeping watch on the evil and the good,' says Prov. 15:3 (cf. Zech. 4:10; 2 Chr. 16:9). The LORD 'tries the kidneys and the heart' of men (Jer. 11:20; 17:10; 20:12; Pss. 7:9/10; 26:2), and from his investigation there is no escaping (Ps. 139:1–12). In this respect, the LORD had assumed functions attributed elsewhere in the ANE (= Ancient Near East) to solar deities, like the Mesopotamian Shamash."

Let the assembly of the nations gather around you,
and return above it on high! (v. 7/8)

How is YHWH portrayed here, and how does the supplicant imagine YHWH's intervention? Contrary to earlier research, the cohortatives in 7:6–7 (7–8) are to be understood as appeals to YHWH *to take action* against the supplicant's enemies ("Arise!"), or *to put an end to their actions* ("Return!").[38] The meaning of the expression "return above it on high," which deviates from the simple שׁוּבָה (cf. Num. 10:36), will be discussed below.

Connected to this is the sense of the cohortative "awake" (Ps. 7:6/7b). I assume, with M. Weippert,[39] that the cohortatives in 7:6/7 are to be understood in light of Psalm 44:23–26 (24–27) (and other texts).

Awake, why are you sleeping, O Lord?
Awake, do not banish us forever!
(Ps. 44:23/24)
Why are you hiding your face,
forgetting our affliction and oppression? (v. 24/25)
For our life [*nepeš*] dissolves into dust,
our bodies cling to the earth. (v. 25/26)
Arise to help us,
and save us for the sake of your mercy. (v. 26/27)

The meaning of the terms "sleep" (יָשֵׁן) and "awake" (עוּר) // "wake up" (קיץ Hiphil) can be derived from verbs that are used in comparable ways: the verb "sleep" correlates to the verbs "banish" (זָנַח) // "hide (the face)" (סתר Hiphil + פָּנִים) // "forget" (שָׁכַח), while "awake" and "arise" (קוּם) stand in semantic parallelism to "save" (פָּדָה). "One could therefore," concludes M. Weippert, "interpret 'sleeping' in this context with 'being passive, inactive,' and 'awaking' with 'proceeding to act, becoming active, intervening.'"[40] In any case, the hypothesis of a "cultic call to wake up"[41] here or in Psalm 7:6/7 is not convincing.

If one applies the semantic field "proceeding to act, becoming active, intervening" also to Psalm 7:6/7,[42] a clear sense for the construction of verses 6–7 (7–8) emerges. While the supplicant calls on YHWH to *proceed to act as judge* against the petitioner's enemies,[43] the cohortatives of verse 7/8 infuse the theme of judgment with a universal note by positing the image of a *heavenly court*: YHWH shall "return" above, to the heavens,[44] in order to assume the function of a royal judge.[45] The image of YHWH's "return to the heavens" is

38. See the references in Janowski, "JHWH der Richter," 105–6.
39. M. Weippert, "Psalm 121, 4."
40. Ibid., 79; cf. Mettinger, *In Search of God*, 88ff.; Willis, "*Qûmāh* YHWH," 213ff.
41. So Kraus, *Psalmen*, 1:196; see Janowski, "JHWH der Richter," 106.
42. The analogy is even closer if one considers that Ps. 44:25/26 (as Ps. 7:5/6) speaks of life (Israel) as lying on the ground (אֶרֶץ // עָפָר).
43. Cf. Pss. 76:8–9 (9–10); 82:8.
44. Here in Ps. 7:7/8, מָרוֹם designates "height [of the heavens]", cf. Firmage, Milgrom, and Dahmen, "רוּם," 430–31 (with other examples); on the parallelism, שָׁמַיִם // מָרוֹם, see Bartelmus, "שָׁמַיִם," 208–9; for a different interpretation, see Houtman (*Himmel*, 342ff.), who assumes a symbolic sense for Ps. 7:7/8 ("high [social] position"). In terms of figurative content, Ps. 7:7/8 can be compared with Ps. 68:18/19, "You have ascended on high [לַמָּרוֹם + עָלָה]"; see Janowski, "Das Königtum Gottes," 193ff.
45. Cf. Gerstenberger, *Der bittende Mensch*, 155–56; idem, *Psalms, Part 1*, 66. On "cosmic acts of judgment" in Mesopotamian invocations of the 2nd/1st millennium BCE, see 149ff. below.

> not to be understood as the return to the heavens *after* judgment has been executed on earth; for this execution is only mentioned in the following verse; the word (i.e., שׁוּבָה) rather describes . . . the *reassuming of the (heavenly) throne of judgment*, which God seemed to have left, since God did not punish the enemies. Thus the word (i.e., שׁובה) corresponds to "arise" (i.e., הִנָּשֵׂא) and "awake" (i.e., ועורה).[46]

—or it corresponds to the act of "setting up" the throne (כון Polel, Ps. 9:7/8b) from which YHWH executes judgment, according to Psalm 9:7–9 (8–10):

> But YHWH is enthroned [יֵשֵׁב] forever,
> he establishes / who establishes [כון Polel] his throne for judgment. (v. 7/8)
> He judges the world in righteousness,
> and passes judgment on the peoples in fairness. (v. 8/9)
> YHWH is a refuge for the oppressed,
> a refuge in times of trouble.[47] (v. 9/10)

Between the appeal for judgment in Psalm 7:6–7 (7–8) (+ 8/9a) and the judgment doxology verses 10–11 (11–12), this psalm has the central *petition for YHWH's judgment in favor of the supplicant*, verses 8–9 (9–10):

> Establish justice for me according to my righteousness,
> and according to my innocence, [that is] in me!
> (Ps. 7:8/9)
> Let the malice of the wicked come to an end,
> but raise up the righteous.
> you who test the heart and kidneys,
> righteous God! (v. 9/10)

Both formulations with *kĕ-* (-כְּ, "according to") in verse 8/9, which are the basis of the petition for judgment "establish justice for me," are concrete declarations of loyalty by the supplicant, which have their basis on the purification oath of verses 3–5 (4–6). The supplicant considers self subjectively to be "just" and submits to YHWH's declarative judgment. The point is to bring to light the supplicant's "righteousness" (צֶדֶק) and "integrity" (תֹּם) against all misgivings of the enemies, by putting an end to the "malice of the wicked,"[48] while "firmly establishing" the just.[49] In verse 8/9 the expression שָׁפְטֵנִי יהוה thus clearly contains the aspect of helping justice and is therefore best translated as "establish justice for me / help me obtain justice, YHWH!"[50] The supplicant continues

46. Friedrich Baethgen, *Die Psalmen*, 17–18, emphasis partly in original; on the formulations, cf. also Pss. 44:23/24; 59:4/5; 94:2; etc.

47. Cf. Ps. 11:4; see 143, n. 51 below. Pss. 9:4/5, 7/8ff.; 11:4; etc. provide evidence that the court imagery of Ps. 7:6–11 (7–12) represents a particular variant of the image of YHWH's kingship and that both images are integral components of the Jerusalem (temple) theology.

48. This formulation suggests emphasis on the dimension of what is hostile/evil, and at the same time the evil is categorically described; cf. Ps. 3:7/8; on this subject, see 114–15 above.

49. The "raising up, establishing" (כון Polel) of the supplicant is a contrasting statement with regard to the actions of the enemy in vv. 12–13 (13–14), who "makes [his bow] ready [for shooting]" (כון Polel, v. 12b/13b) and "prepares" (כון Hiphil, v. 13a/14a) his deadly weapons.

50. Cf. Pss. 26:1 (// בָּחַן, 26:2); 35:24; 43:1; also Pss. 17:13; 82:8; 119:84; Lam. 3:59; etc.; on the subject, see Janowski, "JHWH der Richter," 109 n. 65.

with the YHWH-epithet "who tests the heart and kidneys" (v. 9/10b)[51] and on to the hymnic description of the divine judge, thereby not only giving the reason on which this petition is based,[52] but also invoking on self, in case of a negative result, the judgment of the unerring and all-perceiving God.

The petition for judgment in Psalm 7:8–9 (9–10) is therefore not an expression of excessive "self-righteousness,"[53] but trust in the divine "Judge," who is a savior. The hymnic praise of verses 10–11 (11–12), following 8–9 (9–10), emphasizes this connection between *judging* and *saving* in stylistically impressive ways:

> My shield [protection] is with God,
> a savior of those who are upright in heart.
> (Ps. 7:10/11)
> God is a righteous judge,
> and a God who is wrathful every day. (v. 11/12)

The idea of *saving justice*, which stands at the center of verses 8–9 (9–10) (+ 9/10a) is repeated or rather modified in verse 11/12 through the correlation of "judgment" and "wrath": God is a "righteous judge" (שׁוֹפֵט צַדִּיק, v. 11/12a), who helps the righteous to obtain justice (cf. v. 8ab/9ab) and "scorns" (זֹעֵם, v. 11/12b)[54] the wicked. YHWH's "wrath" aimed at the *wicked* is seen as the antithesis of the salvation of those who are *upright in heart* (v. 10/11b). Likewise the protection statement of verse 10/11a looks ahead to the description of the enemy in verses 12–16 (13–17), from whose continued attack (with sword, bow/arrow, and deadly weapons, vv. 12–13 [13–14]) only YHWH's "(protective) shield" can save.

3. *The Enemy's Self-Destruction*

The sapiential description of the wicked and of their fate (Ps. 7:12–16 [13–17]) provides a specification of that which verse 9/10a calls in antithetical formulation the "end of malice of the wicked" and the "raising up of the righteous." How, we must ask, does the end of the wicked come about? Is it through self-destruction or through divine retribution?[55]

First we must ask, however, who the subject of verses 12–13 (13–14) is: YHWH or the wicked? Hossfeld, for example, holds the opinion that the syntax of verse 12/13a suggests YHWH, "because YHWH is the next subject to which the verb (i.e., שׁוּב, "return") can be connected. The verb describes the same action of God as [does v.] 7/8b."[56]

51. Cf. Ps. 26:2; Jer. 11:20; 17:10; 20:12; also Pss. 11:4–5; 17:3; Prov. 17:3; etc.; see 159ff. below. The hymnic confession of Ps. 11:4 in particular shows that the "testing" of the just and the wicked is an act of the royal God present in the temple/heavens: "YHWH is in his holy temple, / YHWH—his throne is in the heavens; his eyes see, / his gaze examines human beings." See Hossfeld and Zenger, *Die Psalmen*, 1:91.

52. Cf. Baethgen, *Die Psalmen*, 18.

53. Cf. Kraus, *Psalmen*, 1:196ff.

54. On זָעַם, "scorn, be wrathful," see Wiklander, "זָעַם," 623–24; also Miller, *They Cried to the Lord*, 100. On the "wrath of God," see Gross, "Zorn Gottes"; Sticher, *Die Rettung der Guten*, 71–72, etc.

55. This question concerns not only Ps. 7, but also other Psalms of the Individual; see Sticher, *Die Rettung der Guten*, 71–72, etc.

56. Hossfeld and Zenger, *Die Psalmen*, 1:74. Hossfeld's translation (and paraphrase) is as follows: "[7:12/13] If he [God] does not return [from his punishing office of judgment], then he will sharpen

In my opinion, however, the context as well as several parallels in content suggest that the *enemy* is the subject of verses 12–13 [13–14].[57] In chiastic arrangement of their components (*sharpen* the sword, string the bow, and *prepare [to shoot]* [כון Polel] // *prepare* [כון Hiphil] deadly weapons, make the arrows *flaming*), the two verses describe how the wicked prepares repeated attacks on the supplicant and makes use of the deadly weapons. The danger invoked by the lion imagery of verses 2/3 and 5/6 is not over. On the contrary, the enemy—like the dogs of Psalm 59:6/7, 14/15[58]—resumes the pursuit and sets out after the supplicant. This time the terminology and expressions used here (cf. Ps. 37:14–15) are taken from the realm of war:[59]

> Truly he [the enemy] sharpens his sword again;
> he has drawn his bow and is ready [to shoot].
> (Ps. 7:12/13)
> Against himself he has prepared deadly weapons;
> he has lit his arrows. (v. 13/14)

That the supplicant's enemy is the subject of v. 13–14 is also shown by the parallels in content with Psalms 11:2 and 57:4/5.

> In YHWH I have found refuge.
> How can you say to me:
> "Flee to the mountains like a bird"?
> (Ps. 11:1)
> See: the wicked string the bow,
> they have fitted their arrow to the string,
> in order to shoot in the dark
> at those who are upright in heart. (v. 2)
> If the foundations are torn down,
> what can the righteous do? (v. 3)
>
> My life [*nepeš*] is / I am in the midst of lions;
> I must lie down among those who eat human prey;
> their teeth are spears and arrows,
> and their tongue is a sharp sword.
> (Ps. 57:4/5)

Especially Psalm 57:4/5 suggests for Psalm 7 a connection of 7:12–13 (13–14) with verses 2/3 and 5/6:[60] to describe the actions of the enemy, the supplicant first uses an *animal image* (lion metaphor, v. 2/3; cf. the continuation in v. 5/6), and then employs a *war image* (vv. 12–13 [13–14]; cf. the hunting image in v. 15/16). Their symbolism governs the view of the enemy in Psalm 7:

---

his [the enemy's] sword; his [the enemy's] bow is strung and aimed. [13/14] And he [the enemy] has set up his deadly weapons and his [the enemy's] arrows; flaming he will prepare [them]." See also Weber, *Werkbuch*, 1:70–71.

57. For a grammatical explanation, see 135–36 above.

58. See 105–106 above.

59. See Ruppert, *Eine Wortfelduntersuchung*, 156ff.; cf. Kraus, *Psalmen*, 1:199.

60. On the relationship of v. 2/3 and v. 5/6, see 137ff. above.

Introductory petitions
. . . that they [my pursuers] may not tear my life/throat like a lion,
as one who tears off [pieces], and there is no one to rescue.
(Ps. 7:2/3)

Purification oath (apodosis)
. . . then let the enemy pursue and overtake my life/me
and trample my life to the ground,
and lay my honor into the dust. (v. 5/6)

Description of the wicked
Truly, he [the enemy] sharpens his sword again,
he has drawn his bow and is ready [to shoot] . . . (v. 12/13)

Since Gunkel, it has been a basic assumption in Psalms research that the descriptions of affliction in the individual's songs or lament and praise overlap in various "imageries"[61] so that the "teeth" and the "tongue" of lions are named, but that at the same time the "weapons" (spear, arrows, sword) of the hostile enemies are intended. An example of this is Psalm 57:4/5, but also 59:6–7 (7–8) or 64:3–4 (4–5). In my opinion, the same phenomenon of *overlapping enemy images* is also found in Psalm 7:2/3 (animal imagery) and 7:12–13 (13–14, war imagery). Through the description of the enemy with the help of war terminology ("Truly, he sharpens his sword again . . ."), the supplicant again invokes the affliction being suffered, in order to point to the aggressive presence of the enemy and the desired help from YHWH. In doing so, the supplicant comes to a general insight, expresses it through the image of "pregnancy and birth of malice" (v. 14/15), and describes it with the help of a sapiential *mashal* (Ps. 7:15–16 [16–17]):

He has dug a pit and scooped it out,
and fell into the trap he had made.
He has caused his malice to return on his own head,
violence descends on his own skull.

What is the function of these two verses? By themselves, they correspond to familiar statements about the action-consequence-relationship in Wisdom literature.[62] The supplicant wants to say that the digging of a pit stands in connection with the evil nature of the wicked/enemy (v. 14/15)[63]—but that it will turn back on the enemy in the end. However, in the context of the whole book of Psalms, it has a slightly different significance: it is concerned with YHWH's bringing the righteousness of the just to light against their enemies, so that the (acts of) violence of the wicked/enemy will "descend" on the evildoer's own head (7:16/17; cf. 11:5–6). For this reason, the supplicant praises YHWH in the concluding *promise of praise* (7:17/18) "according to his [YHWH's] righteous-

61. Gunkel and Begrich, *Introduction to Psalms*, 134–35; cf. 114ff. above.
62. Cf. Prov. 26:27: "One who digs a pit falls into it; one moves a stone—it rolls back on that one." See also Pss. 9:15/16; 35:7–8; 57:6/7; 141:10; Eccl. 10:8–9; Sir. 27:26; Wis. 11:16. For a detailed discussion, see Krammer, "'Wer anderen eine Grube gräbt.'"
63. Cf. Michel, *Tempora und Satzstellung*, 247.

ness"—just as the petitioner had asked in verse 8/9b that YHWH establish justice for self "according to my [the supplicant's] righteousness // integrity":

> Establish justice for me according to my righteousness,
> and according to my innocence, [that is] in me!
> (Ps. 7:8bc/9bc)

> I shall praise YHWH according to his righteousness
> and sing to the name of YHWH, the most high. (v. 17/18)

In the context of the psalm, the section about the action-consequence-relationship in 7:14–16 (15–17), with its concluding promise of praise (v. 17/18), should have the same function as the affirmation of trust in Psalm 13:5/6a, with its subsequent promise of praise 13:5b–6 (6bcd):[64] to assure the supplicant of YHWH's help (cf. 7:9/10a) in the form of an "anticipated fact." In this respect, the sapiential image of the enemy's falling into a pit dug for someone else (v. 15/16), which is didactically explained by verse 16/17, is an expression of a "bold certainty"[65] regarding the end of the wicked—that he will invariably bring about his own self-destruction.[66] This certainty is grounded in the doxology of verse 11/12,[67] which explains the salvation of the supplicant on the basis of YHWH's judicial action:

> God is a righteous judge,
> and a God who is wrathful every day.
> (Ps. 7:11/12)

The temporal designation "every day" (v. 11/12b) points out that the judicial action of YHWH, the *universal judge* (vv. 6–7 [7–8], 17/18b),[68] is explained and concretized through "the daily governance of the world in the full sense."[69] In this way the supplicant conveys the *knowledge based on faith* (doxology), as formulated by the hymn of verses 10–11 (11–12), and the *knowledge based on experience* (empiricism), as described by the teaching of verses 12–13 (13–14) and 14–16 (15–17). This situation makes the promise of praise of verse 17/18 possible, which anticipatorily gives "bold expression to the fact that the enemy has already been judged."[70]

γ. *God as Judge among Israel's Neighbors*

Our analysis has shown that the supplicant invokes YHWH as "righteous judge," so that the petitioner may know justice in the face of the aggressive

64. See 82ff. above.
65. Kraus, *Psalmen*, 1:200.
66. On this subject cf. Sticher, *Die Rettung der Guten*, 333ff., esp. 41ff. The process of self-destruction of the wicked is described particularly drastically in Ps. 109:16–19: "[18] Because he has clothed himself with a curse like a garment, and it has soaked into his body like water, like an oily salve into his bones—[19] therefore let it be for him like a garment, in which he wraps himself, like a belt that surrounds him forever."
67. Ibid., 341ff.
68. On the meaning of עֶלְיוֹן in Ps. 7:17/18b, see Hossfeld and Zenger, *Die Psalmen*, 1:76; also Hossfeld and Zenger, "'Selig,'" 39.
69. Hossfeld and Zenger, *Die Psalmen*, 1:76.
70. Kraus, *Psalmen*, 1:201.

pursuers. Since YHWH's judicial action takes place from the heavens, according to Psalm 7:6–7 (7–8) and other texts,[71] "the image of YHWH as 'Judge' is connected to the heavenly council, which passes judgment on human beings."[72] An important parallel for this motif of a *cosmic trial* is Psalm 82.[73] Its implications take on more detailed contours against the background of ancient Near Eastern views of a solar deity.[74]

1. Egypt

In Egypt, the idea that the sun-god Ra was the guarantor of justice (Maʿat, "law, justice, order, truth") was developed and passed on especially in the sun-theology of the New Kingdom (18th–20th dynasties, 1567–1085 BCE).[75] Its main motif consists of the establishment of the "world-order," which signifies not so much a well-ordered space, but rather a successful process of continued governance.[76] The exercise of this rule, consisting in overcoming the enemy, is depicted as a *cosmic court trial* (fig. 17). The enemy, explains J. Assmann,

> confronts the sun-barge in the form of a giant water-serpent, which threatens to hypnotize the barge deities with its "evil eye" and to drink the heavenly ocean dry. Under the sign of Maʿat, the conquest of the enemy does not take the form of a battle but of a trial. The enemy is "punished" (*szwn*), the sun-god is "vindicated." For the Egyptians, this court case is the prototype of every confrontation of antagonistic powers.[77]

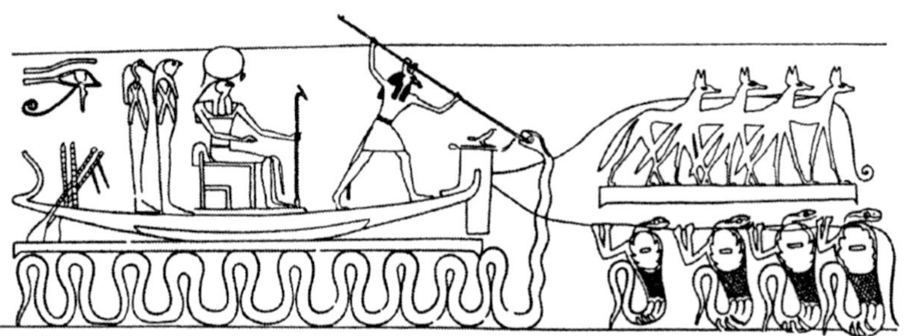

Figure 17. The triumph over the Apep-serpent (Egypt, New Kingdom)

71. Cf. Pss. 9:4/5, 7/8; 11:4; 17:2; etc.
72. Gerstenberger, *Der bittende Mensch*, 156 n. 71.
73. See 131 above.
74. On the following discussion, see already Janowski, "Der barmherzige Richter," 43ff.
75. See Janowski, *Rettungsgewissheit*, 112ff.; and J. Assmann, *Maʿat: Gerechtigkeit*, 160ff.; also Otto, *Theologische Ethik*, 123ff. On the expression Maʿat, see the concise summary in J. Assmann, "Maʿat," 633: "It [the term Maʿat] relates to the principle of a solidarity that brings about harmony among human beings and, applied to the cosmos, secures the success of the 'sun's course' and therefore the continued existence of the world. Maʿat is something one speaks (truth), and does (justice). An Egyptian definition of Maʿat is 'the reward of one who acts lies in being acted on his behalf. This, God considers Maʿat." See also excursus 5, 132.
76. Cf. J. Assmann, *Maʿat: Gerechtigkeit*, 174.
77. Ibid., 10; cf. 196–97. On the subject, see also Keel, *Die Welt*, 187ff.; Keel and S. Schroer, *Schöpfung*, 123ff.; Janowski, *Rettungsgewissheit*, 135ff., etc.

As the Egyptian prototypically experiences the overcoming of evil and of death in this justification event,[78] the righteousness of the sun-god, who embodies the success of the cosmic process in his judicial action, is linked to the action of human beings in complex ways.[79]

In the context of this understanding of justice, the king represents the creator-god and brings earthly and cosmic order into a visual relationship as he—as it says in a cultic theological tractate from the New Kingdom—establishes Maʿat and banishes Isfet, malice.[80] The establishment of Maʿat takes place on three interconnected levels, which represent the central aspects of the concept of Maʿat: providence and abundance, truth and justice, as well as continuation and immortality.[81] Thus Ramses III praises the salutary nature of his own rule through the establishment of the three aspects of Maʿat:

> I have sustained life in the entire land,
> strangers, subjects,
> *pʿt*-people and *ḥnmmt*-people,
> men and women.
> I have saved everyone from their demise;
> I gave him air;
> I saved him from the strong, who oppressed him.
> I put everyone in his place in their regions;
> I revived the others in the hall of the underworld.[82]

From the Ramesside period onward (19th–20th c. BCE), this correlation of cosmos and society became a central theme in the hymns to Amun-Ra.[83] The view of god conveyed by these texts marks the end of a theological development, in the course of which different themes influenced each other and were integrated into a sustainable overall concept within the context of personal piety in the New Kingdom. Its distinguishing feature lies in the experience that the activity of Amun-Ra manifests itself as the activity of a god, who intervenes as *judge and savior* in the collective and individual life, and who—as a "good shepherd"—is close to the afflicted in their prayers.[84] This view of god is expressed in almost classic fashion in the final section of the Amun-Ra hymn (Papyrus Chester Beatty IV.11.8–12, 14 = *ÄHG* nos. 195.274–334), especially in stanzas II and IV.

Stanza II

> 282 [How beautiful are you,] when you rise,
> 283 Ra, my lord.
> 284 You, creator, who created [also] me, who cares [for me],
> 285 who responds to my call!

78. J. Assmann, *Maʿat: Gerechtigkeit*, 196.

79. On this homology of cosmos and society, see ibid., 196ff.; and J. Assmann, *Herrschaft und Heil*, 53ff.

80. See J. Assmann, *Herrschaft und Heil*, 48ff., 53ff.; and Janowski, "Frucht der Gerechtigkeit," 117ff.—both with their respective references.

81. See J. Assmann, *Maʿat: Gerechtigkeit*, 222ff.

82. Cited in ibid., 231.

83. See Janowski, *Rettungsgewissheit*, 154ff.

84. On the shepherd metaphor in ancient Near Eastern cultures, see Kügler, *Der andere König*, 109ff.; and Hunziker-Rodewald, *Hirt und Herde*, 16ff.; cf. also Janowski and Neumann-Gorsolke, "Der 'gute Hirte' und seine Herde."

286 May you save [me] from the [. . .],
287 who turns his heart to the one who says "Why?"[85]
288 The shepherd, before whom one is placed,[86]
289 until one reaches the residence.

Stanza IV
297 How beautiful are you, when you rise,
298 Ra, you great shepherd!
299 Come all, all you herds!
300 See, you have spent the day grazing with him.
301 He has banished evil,
302 when he is in peace in his realm of light;
303 your lands [. . .][87]

Amun-Ra is a god who turns against evil in all its manifestations—mythical and historical—and who contends with it in his "wrath" (*bʿw*).[88] The personal piety of the Ramesside period[89] moved this belief in the judging and saving power of the sun-god into the center and strengthened its normativity through sapiential verses.[90]

2. Mesopotamia

Also in Mesopotamia, where the development of sun-theology developed differently, the primary responsibility of the king was establishing justice.[91] Already in the prologues of the Šulgi Codex (end of 3rd millennium BCE) and the Lipit-Ištar Codex (early 2nd millennium BCE) the establishment of justice is understood as the protection of the poor from the strong; the principle of saving justice is formulated accordingly.[92] More elaborate and significant in this respect is the framing of the Code of Hammurapi (Hammurabi), which begins after the introductory verse of the prologue (I.1–49)[93] with the primordial deities Anu and Enlil and continues with the city's deity Marduk and up to the kingship of Hammurapi in Babylon. The Epilogue (KH XLVII.2-LI.91) reads as follows:

> So I became the beneficent shepherd, whose scepter is righteous; my benign shadow is spread over my city. In my bosom I carried the peoples of the land of Sumer and Akkad; they prospered under my protection; I always governed them in peace; I sheltered them in my wisdom. In order that the strong might not oppress the weak, that justice might be dealt the orphan [and]

85. I.e., the ignorant.
86. I.e., to whom one is assigned.
87. Translation [into German] by J. Assmann, *ÄHG* 437–38 (nos. 195, 282–289, 297–303); cf. Janowski, *Rettungsgewissheit*, 163, 165.
88. On the Egyptian idea of the just "wrath of God," see J. Assmann, *Herrschaft und Heil*, 53ff.
89. See J. Assmann, *Ägypten: Theologie*, 258ff.; idem, *Ägypten: Eine Sinngeschichte*, 259ff.
90. See the text in *ÄHG* 420–21 (nos. 190.20–25), cited in Janowski, *Rettungsgewissheit*, 174.
91. See Otto, "Bedeutung der altorientalischen Rechtsgeschichte," 146ff.; idem, *Theologische Ethik*, 81ff.; idem, "'Um Gerechtigkeit,'" 109ff.; Albertz, "Theologisierung des Rechts"; Maul, "Der assyrische König"; and references in Janowski, "Frucht der Gerechtigkeit," 114ff.
92. See Otto, *Theologische Ethik*, 86; idem, "'Um Gerechtigkeit,'" 115ff.; Janowski, "Frucht der Gerechtigkeit," 114ff.
93. *ANET* 164.

> the widow, in Babylon, the city whose head Amun and Enlil raised aloft, in Esagila, the temple whose foundations stand firm like heaven and earth, I wrote my precious words on my stela, and in the presence of the statue of me, the king of justice, I set [it] up in order to administer the law of the land, to prescribe the ordinances of the land, to give justice to the oppressed. (KH XLVII.42–78)[94]

The reason for Hammurapi's presenting himself as the protege of the sun-god, is based on the function of Šamaš as guarantor of legal order: Šamaš is "the great judge of heaven and earth" who secures justice for humanity (*dŠamaš* [= Sumerian *Utu*] *dayyānum rabium ša šamê u erṣetim muš[tē]šer šaknat napištim*; KH L.14–18; cf. XLVII.84–86)[95] and who has given "steadfastness" (*kī nātum*) to Hammurapi, the "king of justice" (*šar mī šarim*; KH LVIII, 95–98). In his reign, the king thus represents the sun-god. For just as Šamaš upholds the cosmic order through his judgment, the royal shepherd, through acts of *kī nātum/kittum*- and *šarum*, preserves the political-social cosmos from the powers of chaos.[96] Thus there is a correspondence between "the earthly law and the divine order of creation . . . , which was just."[97]

That the establishment of justice by the king, who thereby assumes the functions of Šamaš, includes the protection of the weak from the strong and thus possesses soteriological qualities, is found in Mesopotamia in the Old Babylonian *mī-šarum*-edicts[98] and especially in ritual and prayer texts from the second and first millennia BCE.[99] For example, the extensive collections of omens of the Neo-Assyrian period, which were arranged by subject and compiled on clay tablets,[100] had the function of explaining all abnormal phenomena of the natural and spiritual world, in order to determine the intentions of the gods.

In this context, the Namburbi rituals[101] were performed to avert an impending misfortune and contained the following elements: *sacrifice* to the offended deities, *court trial* before Šamaš, *purification* of the affected person/s and of their house, ritual *reintegration*, preventative measures.[102] The person who sought to achieve a revision of the fate ordained for oneself by the gods would then turn to the divine triad Enki/Ea, Šamaš, and Asalluḫi/Marduk. As the most striking phenomenon in the cosmic order, the central addressee of the ritual event was the sun-god, "whose pronouncement is irrevocable"[103] and who, as "judge of heaven and earth" (*bēl šamê u erṣeti*),[104] was able to rescind the unfavorable judg-

94. Ibid., 178; cf. Janowski, *Rettungsgewissheit*, 87; Otto, "'Um Gerechtigkeit," 116ff.

95. *ANET* 178; on this motif, see also the middle section (lines 95–129) of the great hymn to (the sun-god) Šamaš, probably composed toward the end of the 2nd millennium BCE (*BWL* 126–38; *ANET* 388); see Janowski, *Rettungsgewissheit*, 37ff.; on the epithets of Šamaš, see Maul, "Der assyrische König," 201–2.

96. Cf. Janowski, *Rettungsgewissheit*, 87–88; Otto, *Theologische Ethik*, 87–88.

97. Wolfgang Röllig, "Gleich und ungleich," 46. On the subject of "establishing justice" in Neo-Assyrian royal inscriptions, see Janowski, "Der barmherzige Richter," 48ff.

98. See Otto, *Theologische Ethik*, 87–88; idem, "'Um Gerechtigkeit," 116ff., 120ff.

99. See Janowski, *Rettungsgewissheit*, 68ff.

100. See Maul, *Zukunftsbewältigung*, 3ff.

101. Namburbi: "[Ritual for] averting thereof [a misfortune that has been announced but has not yet been realized]"; see ibid., 11–12.

102. On the performance of the ritual, see ibid., 39ff.

103. Text in ibid., 310.

104. See Janowski, *Rettungsgewissheit*, 31.

ment and to set the human being who was threatened by an unfavorable future on the right path (*muštēširu*) once again.[105]

To understand these rituals, it is crucial that the divine judgment over the unfavorable omen is styled as a *court trial,* in which the defendant and his enemy, the so-called omen-prosecutor, stand before the judging god. In this scenario, the gods Enki/Ea and Asalluḫi/Marduk served as assessors. Usually the defendant did not appear alone before Šamaš, but rather in the company of a conjurer, who followed the model of the introductory scenes, held the defendant's hand,[106] and could represent that person also in the recitation of the petition section of the invocation.

> In this court trial, the unfavorable decree about the future of the defendant, which was in effect brought about *legitimately* by the omen-prosecutor to bring harm to the person, is judged anew to be revised in favor of the person, before it was realized in the form of physical damage. The omen-prosecutor, on the other hand, was to be judged and destroyed.[107]

The desired verdict was therefore the act of a compassionate judging god.

As an example of the forensic nature of these rituals, let us consider an invocation (*Journal of Cuneiform Studies* 21.2–7, lines 1–9; and 21.9–10, lines 86–101)[108] from the first millennium BCE, which is part of the *bīt rimki*-ritual and consists of two prayers, one prayer by the priest pronouncing the invocation (lines 1–59) and a corresponding prayer by the king (lines 86–101). In both prayers, the petition sections are introduced by formulations that use the language of law and invoke the sun-god in his capacity as judge and savior:

> 44 For the king, the son of his god, establish justice,
> decide in his favor!
>
> 92 Come near on this day of my trial.

Noteworthy in this context is the characterization of the language of prayer by terms and idioms from the realm of law and justice. A compilation of terminology relating to law, light/darkness, and life/death (lines 44ff. and 92ff.) then yields the following picture:

- Law and justice

dīna danû	pronounce judgment
ešēru Št	establish/maintain order
išaru(m)	straight, in order, normal, just
mīšaru(m)	straightness, justice
purussâ parāsu	decide the legal case

105. Cf. Maul, *Zukunftsbewältigung*, 9, 60, 67, etc. On the Šamaš epithet *muštēširu* ("he who guides correctly"), see Janowski, "Der barmherzige Richter," 48 n. 80.

106. In the rituals, the conjurer played the role held on seal images by the personal god, who leads the threatened person before the enthroned god. See Maul, *Zukunftsbewältigung*, 68.

107. Ibid., 60.

108. For textual notes, see Janowski, *Rettungsgewissheit*, 41, 68–69, 81ff. On the ritual tablet of the series *bīt rimki*, see *TUAT* 2/2:246ff. (ed. W. Farber).

- Light and darkness

namāru D + *ekletu*	to illuminate the darkness
zakû D + *dalḫātu*	to clear up the "murky" (= darkness)

- Life and death

balāṭu D + *mītu*	to revive the dead
qâšu + *napištu*	to grant life

An answer to the question how the language of prayer acquired this juridical quality can be found in the parallel petitions in the conjurer's prayer lines 44ff.:

44 For the king, the son of his god, establish justice,
decide in his favor!
45 Dispel the malignant illness from his body!
46 Pour out clean, pure, and clear water over him!
47 When he washes himself with water over his surrogate image,
48 when the water flows down his body,
49 so may the evil *utukku*, the evil *alû*, the evil spirit of death,
the evil *gallû*, the evil god, the evil lurker,
50 the *lamaštu*, the *labaṣu*, the snatcher,
51 the *lilû*, the *lilītu*, the *lilû*-girl,
52 the evil *namtaru*, the troublesome *asakku*, the malignant illness
53 of the king's body, the son of his god,
[be] like water flowing down and leaving his body.
54 Šamaš, whose authoritative word is not changed,
55 may loosen his tongue on this day.
56 May the evil tongue move aside.

Here the requested *healing* of the king (lines 45, 52–53) is understood as a *judicial process* (line 44), as a court trial of the sun-god against the demonic powers (lines 49–52). Other prayers demonstrate that the ill supplicant presents the personal *affliction as a legal matter* and turns to Šamaš for judgment (= healing; cf. *Keilschrifttexte aus Assur religiösen Inhalts,* 184 verso 31–32; etc.).[109] The petition in the royal prayer (lines 92–97) further shows clearly that the sun-god's judicial action aimed at healing and removal of sin takes place in the *area of tension between light and darkness*, and the sun-god's judiciary "illumination of darkness" brings about the salvation from death (line 97):

92 Come this day to my judgment!
93 Illuminate my darkness, clear up my obfuscation,
94 remove my confusion! From the evil of signs and omens,
95 from the signs of magic circles, from human scheming of any kind
96 that I encounter, save me,
97 loosen my bond, grant me life!

The invocations of the two prayers—lines 1–9 (in the conjurer's prayer), lines 86–87 (in the king's prayer)—contain another aspect. After lines 86–90 the king's prayer is addressed to the god who, as "judge of heaven and earth" (line 86), dispels the darkness and brings light. This *light-darkness contrast* is

109. See the texts in Janowski, *Rettungsgewissheit*, 89ff.

Figure 18. Šamaš appears on the eastern horizon (Akkadian period)

even more explicit in the conjurer's prayer because reference is made, in the language of mythology, to the epiphany of the sun-god, who appears in the morning as the heavenly judge on the eastern horizon, while human beings and animals are waiting for that god:

1 Conjuration: Šamaš, when you step out of the great mountain,
2 when you step out of the great mountain, the mountain of the deep well,
3 when you step out of the Duku,[110] where the fates are ordained,
4 when you step out from the heavens' foundations to the place
where heaven and earth meet,
5 then the great gods come to you for judgment,
6 the Anunnaki[111] come to you for a decision.
7 Human beings, all people await you,
8 the beasts that move, the four-legged creatures,
9 direct their gaze to your great light.[112]

This passage contains in lines 5 (*dīnu*) and 6 (*purussû*) two terms used to express the judicial actions of the sun-god also in other Šamaš texts.[113] This cosmic event has been depicted on Mesopotamian seals in always new variations since the Akkadian period (2370–2190 BCE). The famous seal of Adda (fig. 18)[114] shows the sun-god rising from the mountains on the eastern horizon, marching through the guarded gates of heaven, and thus bringing about the new day.

The place where the sun rises, which marks the border between this world and the world beyond, is the place from which Šamaš sets out on the daily course across the heavens and to the heavenly court. The connection between *epiphany* and *judgment* indicates that the sun-god—as the prayer of the conjuring priest

110. The *duku* / du_6-ku_3 ("pure, holy hill/mound" in Sumerian cuneiform) is a cosmic place, the abode of the gods, according to the mythic geography of Mesopotamia, located in the eastern border mountains of Babylon—the place where the sun rises. See Janowski, *Rettungsgewissheit*, 42 n. 115; and references in idem, "Der barmherzige Richter," 53 n. 99.

111. I.e., the gods below (the earth) in contrast to gods above (the earth).

112. For textual notes, see Janowski, *Rettungsgewissheit*, 41–42; cf. 83–84.

113. On these terms, see also W. Mayer, *"Gebetsbeschwörungen,"* 221ff.

114. See Janowski, *Rettungsgewissheit*, 48ff.; cf. also Cornelius, "Sun Epiphany," 27–28.

Figure 19. Sentencing of a lion-headed demon (Akkadian period)

(*JCS* 21.2–7, lines 1–59) specifies—on emerging as judge from the eastern horizon (lines 11, 14–5), "revives" (*balāṭu* D, line 39)[115] all those who are close to death as the result of evil plots or demonic threats and "brings about justice" for them (*dīna dânu, purussâ parāsu*, line 44; cf. *ešēru Št*, line 40). This event—the triumph over chaotic darkness and its demonic exponents through the light of the sun-god—is also represented in Akkadian glyptography, as the battle of the god of rays with another deity and as the procedural presentation of a captured lion-headed demon before Šamaš (fig. 19), who sits as heavenly judge on his mountain throne and passes judgment. In this iconic tradition, the sun-god is the universal judge, who—according to the prayer—judges the representatives of chaos and saves the sick supplicant, who is returned safe and sound into the hands of the petitioner's personal god.

We encounter a consistent symbolism in these texts and iconic traditions: The heavenly judge, who as sovereign sun-god sees and perceives everything, enters the world of human beings and animals to save the afflicted and sever the "thread of evil."[116] In distress the supplicant turns to the sun-god because Šamaš is "compassionate"; the petitioner has reason for hoping to be freed from the affliction. Despite profound differences between YHWH and the sun-deities of the ancient Near East, significant elements of this understanding of justice were adapted by Israel and in the course of solarization were gradually integrated into its understanding of God.[117] In this process, YHWH assumed the roles of the judging and saving sun-god, especially in cases where YHWH—or the king as YHWH's representative on earth (cf. Pss. 45:6–7 [7–8]; 72:2, 4, 12–13)[118]—was the "social authority" against injustice and the wicked.

With its theme of "justification of the righteous," Psalm 7 is, as we have seen,[119] part of this conceptual context. It praises YHWH as "righteous judge" (v. 11/12a), thus as a god who is heir to the ancient Near Eastern sun-deities

115. On the expression "to revive the dead," see Janowski, *Rettungsgewissheit*, 64ff.

116. On the image associated with the epithet "he who severs the thread of evil," see Maul, *Zukunftsbewältigung*, 5, 119, 225; cf. Maul, "Der assyrische König," 201.

117. See references in 91, n. 168 above.

118. On Ps. 72, see Janowski, "Frucht der Gerechtigkeit," 101ff.

119. See 134ff. above.

and reveals YHWH's saving justice anew "every day" (v. 11/b12b).[120] When the divine "sun of justice" (cf. Mal. 4:2 [3:20]) rises in the morning, the darkness of night is over and the power of evil is broken. The "theologization of justice"[121] seen in this *correlation of justice and light* is not original to Israel, but is unmistakably characteristic of Israel's faith. Likewise the association of judging and saving in the *motif of saving justice*, which is attested in numerous psalms, is a central element of the Old Testament concept of justice. It is central because it imparts a decidedly theological interpretation of the experience of reality: it is about *salvation* and *mercy*, which only the God as the Judge—or the king as mediator of divine justice—can bring to the oppressed and wretched of God's people.[122]

This hope for the God of justice is known also to the individual's songs of laments and thanksgiving, as seen when those songs emphasize the *universality of God* and the *fate of the individual*, or insist on the connection of the universal to the individual.[123] This connection is also based on the concept of the heavenly judge (Pss. 7:6–11 [7–12]; 9:4/5, 7–8 [8–9]; 17:2), who looks down from heaven and whose eye "examines" human beings:

> YHWH is in his holy temple;
> YHWH—his throne is in heaven;
> his eyes look,
> his gaze examines [בָּחַן] humankind.
> YHWH examines the righteous and the wicked,
> and the lover of violence, his *nepeš* hates.
> (Ps. 11:4–5)

What are we to make of the gaze of the judging God, who sees inside the human person and "examines" heart and kidneys?

b. Anthropological Keywords 3: Heart and Kidneys

> For a human sees with the eyes,
> but YHWH looks at the heart.
> 1 Samuel 16:7

> I, YHWH, examine the heart and test the kidneys,
> to give each according to their ways,
> according to the fruit of their deeds.
> Jeremiah 17:10

120. Pss. 3–7, sharing the certainty that YHWH hears the complaints and petitions and will intervene to save, are characterized by a noteworthy temporal structure: 3:5/6, evening/morning; 4:8/9, evening; 5:3/4, morning; 6:6/7, night; 7:11/12, day. See Hossfeld and Zenger, "'Selig,'" 37ff.; and Janowski, "Der barmherzige Richter," 96–97.

121. See 131ff. above.

122. In addition, relating to the concept of justice is another theme: YHWH's wrath of judgment is contained and overcome through his love. The key passage for this is Hos. 11:8–11; see Jeremias, *Der Prophet Hosea*, 143ff.; also Janowski, "Der barmherzige Richter," 40ff.

123. Cf. Steck, *Friedensvorstellungen*, 37 n. 85.

Resources

Albertz, "Mensch," 465–66; J. Assmann, "Geschichte des Herzens"; idem, *Tod und Jenseits*, 36–38, 68–71, 116–18, 39–43; Frevel, "Herz"; Johnson, *Vitality of the Individual*; Brunner, "Das hörende Herz"; idem, *Altägyptische Weisheit*, 23–24; Fabry, "לֵבָב/לֵב"; Janowski, "Anerkennung"; Kegler, "Körpererfahrung"; Kellermann, "כִּלְיוֹת"; idem, "Niere"; T. Krüger, "Menschliche Herz"; idem, "Das 'Herz'"; Lauha, *Psychophysischer Sprachgebrauch*; Lüpke, "Herz"; R. North, "Medicine and Healing," 16–19; idem, "Heart?"; Ogushi, "Nur das Herz?"; Schenker, "Tafel des Herzens"; C. Rösel, "Menschliche Herz"; M. Rösel, "Hebräische Mensch," 237ff., 245–46; W. Schmidt, "Anthropologische Begriffe"; S. Schroer and Staubli, *Körpersymbolik der Bibel*, 45–60, 75–91; Smith, "Heart and Innards"; idem, "Herz"; Watson, "Word Pair"; Wehrle and Kampling, "Herz"; H. W. Wolff, *Anthropology*, 40–44, 65–66; Zenger, "'Gib deinem Knecht,'" 40–42; Zimmer, *Zwischen Tod und Lebensglück*, 15–17.

An anatomical view inside the human body is a relatively recent development and has been employed only since the early sixteenth century.[124] Since then, medical science has progressed rapidly and has also included the study and treatment of the heart. Even though the significance of the heart to confirm death has been relativized in recent times by the possibility of heart transplants and the introduction of brain death as a criterion, "the psychosomatic experience of the beating heart is still associated with the awareness of finality."[125] Likewise it is true that the "basic act of symbolic representation to materialize the spiritual and to spiritualize the material"[126] finds its anchor and substance in the heart—with regard to emotional as well as physical experience.

In the view of the Old Testament, since the inner organs of the human body—the heart, liver, gallbladder, kidneys, bowels, uterus, and abdomen[127]—are the seat of strong emotions, like fear, despair, longing, and love,[128] "the inside of the body . . . is of less interest anatomically and physiologically than psychologically, in the broadest sense of the word."[129] These organs are of anthropological interest because they represent different aspects of the "inner person." Since they are not visible, there was intense speculation also in ancient Israel about their function and their significance. How could a human being understand anything if not with the "listening heart"?

α. *The Listening Heart*

In the Old Testament, the two terms for heart (לֵב and לֵבָב) occur a total of 861 times, most often in the Psalms (ca. 137 times) and in Proverbs (ca. 98 times).

124. See, e.g., Budde, "Der sezierte Tote," 11ff.
125. Lüpke, "Herz," 1696.
126. Ibid.
127. On inner organs, see R. North, "Medicine and Healing," 16ff.; Erbele-Küster, "Gender Trouble," 75ff. Absent are terms for the intestines, the lung, the stomach, and the muscles. Digestion takes place in the abdomen (בֶּטֶן).
128. With the exception of the heart, these organs are also less frequently the place of reason; see, e.g., 1 Kgs. 3:28; etc.
129. H. W. Wolff, *Anthropology*, 63–64.

Both terms are almost exclusively associated with human beings.[130] In these cases, the heart takes on functions that concern the vegetative, the emotional, the noetic, and the voluntative nature of humanity.

Vegetative Function

The *somatic-vegetative function* of the heart is indicated by the concentration of the living, physical nature of humanity in it. In order to stay alive, one has to feed or "support" one's heart, usually with bread (Judg. 19:5, 8, 21–22), but also with wine (Ps. 104:15). It is, however, not only eating and drinking, but also the certainty of being heard that lends new vitality to the human heart (Ps. 69:33). "Most of the images and ideas in the topology of the lament are drawn from this vegetative layer of the structure of the person."[131] A human being complains on feeling touched in the innermost realm of experience: the heart is throbbing fiercely (Ps. 38:10/11), is bitter and trembles (Jer. 4:19), is dried up (Pss. 61:2/3; 102:4/5), is soft as wax and melts (Ps. 22:14/15); it shakes (1 Sam. 28:5) and burns inside like fire (Ps. 39:3/4).

Emotional Function

The view of the heart as the *seat of emotions* only gradually replaced the vegetative function. This is again seen, according to Fabry, in the topology of the lament, which "describes the emotional experiences of the human person on the basis of vegetative processes: palpitations, tremors, heart spasms, and so forth as images for agitation, fear and anxiety . . . ; [cf.] the heart's skipping a beat for joy."[132] Thus the heart becomes the starting point for the lament: it cries out (Isa. 15:5) and complains (Jer. 48:36) and weeps before YHWH (Lam. 2:18); pain (Pss. 13:2/3; 34:18/19), fear and distress (25:17), poverty (109:16, 22), disgrace (69:20/21), and despair (Isa. 65:14; Lam. 1:20) are reasons to lose heart. Characteristic is the plea of the afflicted in Psalm 25:17: "Widen the narrowness of my heart!"

Noetic Function

The intellectual functions of the heart include the entire realm of *noetic capabilities*, or what we ascribe to the head or the brain. The Old Testament person thinks with the heart, because recognition and remembering take place there, thinking and comprehending as well as attentiveness. Since this is at the semantic center of לֵב and לֵבָב,[133] I will elaborate on this now.

Voluntative Function

Finally, the heart is the *seat of the will and of planning*, whereby the transition between the rational-noetic and the noetic functions is fluid, since the Old Testament also does not linguistically distinguish between "hearing" (as an act of

130. On the "heart of YHWH" (26x), see Fabry, "לֵב/לֵבָב," 448–49.
131. Ibid., 426.
132. Ibid., 427.
133. Cf. also H. W. Wolff, *Anthropology*, 51.

insight) and "obeying (as an act of the will), or between theory and practice.[134] The heart is "the driving force of human voluntative efforts, as the subject of reflection and planning in numerous attestations, as well as the seat of courage and thirst for action."[135]

By far most occurrences of לֵבָב/לֵב refer to the rational-noetic function of the human heart. Of the numerous nuances of meaning, only a few are pointed out here. First, we must guard against the false impression that "biblical man is determined more by feeling than by reason. This mistaken anthropological direction is all too easily derived from an undifferentiated rendering of [*lēb*]. The Bible sets before [humans] . . . clear alternatives, which have to be *recognized*."[136]

That לֵבָב/לֵב is often better rendered as "mind, reason" than as "heart" is shown almost definitively by (e.g.) Deuteronomy 29:4/3, where it is assumed that eyes are intended for seeing, ears for hearing, and the heart for understanding (לָדַעַת; cf. Deut. 8:5):

> But a mind [לֵב] that truly understands,
> eyes that truly see, and ears that truly hear,
> YHWH has not given you to this day.
> (Deut. 29:4/3)

Consequently many texts in the Psalms and Proverbs see the real task of the heart as the search for prudence and wisdom. The "wise heart" enables a realistic worldview that also affirms the reality of death:

> Teach us to number our days,
> that we may obtain a wise heart!
> (Ps. 90:12)

> The heart of one who has knowledge seeks insight,
> but the mouth of the self-satisfied feeds on foolishness.
> (Prov. 15:14)

Where does the heart's fullness of insight come from? It comes from understanding listening, which Solomon asks of YHWH:

> May you therefore give your servant a listening heart (לֵב שֹׁמֵעַ)
> to judge your people,
> to understand the difference between good and evil;
> for who is able to judge this your great people?
> (1 Kgs. 3:9)

The "listening heart"[137] possesses "breadth," a comprehensive understanding, to grasp and process the fullness of impressions from the senses:

> And God gave Solomon wisdom and insight in great measure,
> and breadth of heart (רֹחַב לֵב)
> like the sand at the edge of the sea.
> (1 Kgs. 4:29 [5:9])

134. Cf. Fabry, "לֵבָב/לֵב," 437.
135. Ibid., 437.
136. H. W. Wolff, *Anthropology*, 47, emphasis added.
137. The same idiom is already found in Egyptian; see Brunner, "Das hörende Herz."

"The Solomon of 1 Kgs. 3," writes von Rad, "could—regarded objectively—have said that he would yield to Yahweh so that the world not remain dumb for him, but that it might be understood by him."[138] It became audible to him, as 1 Kings 4:29–34 (5:9–14) impressively relates,[139] for he possessed international education, comprehensive erudition, sharp decisiveness, and poetic articulation. All these were seated in his "listening heart."

However, the insight found in the heart also seeks lasting awareness; the heart thus becomes a treasury of knowledge, of recollection, and of memory.[140] Associated with this aspect of meaning of לֵב/לֵבָב as "lasting insight, awareness" are incisive metaphors, like the "tablet of the heart," on which are inscribed words of wisdom (Prov. 7:3) and "the sin of Judah" (Jer. 17:1).[141] According to the new covenant in Jeremiah 31:31–34,[142] YHWH will inscribe his Torah not on the stone tablets of the covenant but inside the people (קֶרֶב) and write it on their heart (לֵב; v. 33).[143]

This constitutes a new anthropological concept for Israel: as the place of emotion, recognition, and desire, Israel's heart will henceforth be occupied by the Torah, so that the person living under the new covenant cannot do else but live according to one's own good, that is, according to the Torah.

We can then summarize that the expression לֵב/לֵבָב, "heart," functions as a designation for all layers of the human person: the vegetative, the emotional, the noetic, and the voluntative layer. The word captures the *multiple layers of the biblical structure of the human person*[144] like no other anthropological term. This is also seen in many lists in which the term "heart" dominates,[145] but also in merisms like "heart and kidneys"[146] (= the innermost being of the human person, to which only God has access) or "heart and lips"[147] (= inside versus outside, which should correspond in a righteous person).

β. "Who Tests Heart and Kidneys"

The Old Testament associates inner organs of the human being,[148] especially the kidneys, with various sentiments. The kidneys are viewed as the *seat of emotions*, ranging from joy to deepest grief:

> My son, if your heart is wise,
> **my heart** will indeed be glad;
> **my kidneys** *rejoice*,
> if your lips speak what is right.
> (Prov. 23:15–16)

138. Von Rad, *Wisdom in Israel*, 297; cf. Zenger, "'Gib deinem Knecht,'" 40–41.
139. On Solomon's wisdom in 1 Kgs. 4:29–34 (5:9–14), see Wälchli, *König Salomo*, 67ff.
140. Cf. Fabry, "לֵב/לֵבָב," 434–35.
141. See Schenker, "Tafel des Herzens."
142. See esp. Gross, *Zukunft für Israel*, 134ff.
143. Regarding this text, T. Krüger ("Menschliche Herz," 82) rightly speaks of an "implantation-perspective."
144. Cf. Fabry, "לֵב/לֵבָב," 425–26; on the concept of the human person, see also 43 above.
145. Cf. ibid., 426.
146. See 159ff. below.
147. Prov. 23:16–17; cf. 26:25.
148. See also 155–56 above.

When my heart became bitter,
  and I could feel a sharp stabbing in my kidneys.
I was a fool and did not understand,
  [indeed] I was like a beast before you.
(Ps. 73:21–22)

Deepest emotional pain is located in the kidneys. The God who causes grief appears as a hostile archer, who aims his arrows at the afflicted and fatally wounds them in the kidneys:

I lived in peace, then he [God] shook me;
  he grabbed me by the neck and cut me to pieces.
He set me up as a target for him;
(Job 16:12)
  his arrows surround me.
He splits my kidneys and does not spare;
  he pours out my gall on the ground. (v. 13)
He tears me up, piece by piece;
  he runs up against me like a warrior hero. (v. 14)[149]

He brought over my kidneys
  the sons of his quiver [his arrows].
(Lam. 3:13)

According to Psalm 139, the kidneys were *created by God* in special way. "To make clear his certainty that man cannot flee before God into any obscurity (v. 11), since God can even penetrate the night (v. 12), he draws on his personal history of creation as proof (*kî*, v. 13)":[150]

Yes, you have made my kidneys;
  you have knit me together in my mother's womb.
(Ps. 139:13)
I thank you that I am so wonderfully made.
  Wonderful are your works,
  my life [-force] is well aware of it. (v. 14)
My bones were not hidden from you,
  when I was made in secret,
  when I was shaped in the depths of the earth. (v. 15)

Finally, there is the image in Psalm 16:7 of the kidneys as the *nocturnal schoolmaster*, which has no parallel elsewhere in the Old Testament:

I praise YHWH, who has [always] counseled me,
  even at night my kidneys have instructed me.[151]

In Jewish exegetical tradition, this verse was interpreted as a reference to Abraham, who had neither a father nor a teacher who could have taught him the

149. For notes on the translation, see Jürgen Ebach, *Streiten mit Gott*, 1:136.
150. H. W. Wolff, *Anthropology*, 96. On the correlation of the womb and the depths of the earth, which is characteristic of this text, see Keel and S. Schroer, *Schöpfung*, 109ff.
151. See 301–302 below.

Figure 20. Weighing of the heart in an Egyptian judgment scene (New Kingdom)

Torah. "Therefore God gave him two kidneys, which supplied him at night with wisdom and knowledge (cf. *Midrash Tehillim* to Ps. 16:7 and to 1:1–3 [*sic*])."[152]

As the seat of the inmost emotions of the human person, the kidneys are, just as the heart, the *place of God's intervention*. The expression of "testing heart and kidneys"—found in Jeremiah 11:20; 12:3; 20:12; and in Psalms 7:9/10[153] and 26:2—represents the innermost nature of the human person, to which only God has access and which he "tests" (בָּחַן):

YHWH Sabaoth is one who tests the righteous,
  who sees into kidneys and heart.
I shall see your vengeance on them,
  for I have placed my case before you.
(Jer. 20:12)

Although the process in its entirety is different, one is reminded of the "weighing of the heart" in the judgment of the afterlife (fig. 20).[154] In this scenario, the deceased is taken to the judgment hall of Osiris and his forty-two associates and is questioned. While the black-headed god of the dead Anubis (on the left, guiding the deceased) is watching, the deceased's heart is being weighed against the Maʿat, or rather the symbol that represents it (a feather), and the deceased is reciting the negative confession of sins (cf. Book of the Dead, chap. 125). Misconduct on earth causes the scale to move, and Thoth, the god of arithmetic (on the right), unerringly records the sins. A person who is convicted as an "enemy" or a "reprobate" is delivered up to the mouth of hell, or rather the "devourer," a creature with the head of a crocodile, the body of

152. Kellermann, "כִּלְיוֹת," 190.

153. See 142–43 above.

154. On the justification event of the Egyptian afterlife-judgment or judgment of the dead, see esp. J. Assmann, *Tod und Jenseits*, 106ff., 200ff., 380ff., 531ff., etc. The main difference between the judgment of Osiris in the Egyptian afterlife-judgment and that of YHWH according to the Psalms of the Individual relates to the place of the divine judgment: in these psalms (traditional songs of lament and thanksgiving), it is *this world*; in the Egyptian Book of the Dead (liturgies for the dead), it is the netherworld; see Kunz, "Vorstellung vom Gerichtshandeln Gottes"; Krawczack, *Psalm 58*, 325ff., 445ff. However, even in Israel, as Ps. 73 shows, the reckoning of justice did not always take place in this world; see 318ff. below.

a lion, and the backside of a hippopotamus (to the left of the scale bearing the Ma'at-feather). The postmortem existence of a human being therefore depended on one's ethical conduct on earth, which is tested in the "weighing of the heart." An excerpt from chapter 125 of the Book of the Dead reads as follows:

13 I [the deceased] have committed no wrong against human beings.
14 I have abused no animals.
15 I have not placed the "crooked" in place of the right.
16 I do not know that which does not exist.
17 I have looked at no evil.
18 I have not raised the required work quota at the beginning of each day.
19 My name was not brought before the "leader of the barge" [sun-god?].
20 I have offended no god.
21 I have harmed no orphan with regard to his property.
22 I have not done what the gods abhor.
23 I have maligned no servant to the master.[155]

The fact that the Old Testament identifies "heart and kidneys" as objects of divine examination is probably based on an attempt to characterize the whole human being, by specifying a particularly important organ for each of the two parts of the human body: The heart as the organ of the upper body (chest), above the diaphragm, and the kidneys as representatives of the lower body, which extends below the diaphragm.[156] In this way, the innermost emotional sentiments, which are said to be located in the kidneys, and the rational senses, which are ascribed to the heart, are understood together as the "whole human being,"[157] who is subjected to an examination by YHWH. There are numerous examples that express the same theme—divine knowledge of a human being—on the basis of the heart alone, such as Psalm 33:15:

He [YHWH] who has formed everyone's heart,
who knows of all their deeds.

The creator of hearts is at the same time the universal judge, and the human heart is "in a unique way the place where YHWH encounters human existence."[158] This is also the point of departure for the complaint if a person is afflicted by a severe illness. The following chapter deals with this dark side of life.

155. Based on the translation of Hornung, *Totenbuch der Ägypter*, 234. For chap. 125 of the Book of the Dead compared with the assertions of innocence in Job 31, see Kunz, "Vorstellung vom Gerichtshandeln Gottes," 236ff.

156. Cf. Kellermann, "כִּלְיוֹת," 191. On the medical aspect of this view, see esp. Smith, "Heart and Innards"; and R. North, "Medicine and Healing," 16ff.

157. On the concept of the "whole human being," see "Excursus 2: The Whole Human Being," 43–44 above.

158. Fabry, "לֵב/לֵבָב," 439; cf. 438–39.

6. "When will he die and his name perish?" (Ps. 41:5/6)
The Human Being in Sickness

a. The Affliction of the Sick

> Finally, there is the experience, which the individual has to process, the impulse behind many psychosomatic or emotional-physical illnesses. Processing an experience: this means that a human being within the limits of his abilities has to come to terms with the realities of his environment, with the moral laws of his society—or not.
>
> Alexander Mitscherlich, *Krankheit als Konflikt*, 9

α. Sickness as Conflict

What sickness is and especially what its origin is, has always been a difficult question to answer. Sickness can be seen as the result of a defective structure in the morphology, tissue, or cells or as the result of an interruption of vital processes. This is the scientific understanding of sickness, which developed in the mid-nineteenth century in the pathology of cells and is based on specific premises: Every illness has a specific cause, it is characterized by an initial damage, and it produces clinical symptoms, which lead among illnesses of same origin to run a similar course.[1]

In contrast to the scientific understanding of sickness, psychosomatic medicine assumes that the impulses for the origin of sickness include not only the physiology of human beings, but also the processing of experiences.[2] Rich examples for this social and environmental interpretation of sickness and health are also the Old Testament texts that deal with sickness. Thus Job 19:13–20 describes Job's illness not only as physical suffering (cf. vv. 17 and 20),[3] but also as psychological and social anguish, which is even intensified by the behavior of the so-called in-group, the familiar circle of family and friends:[4]

1. See Siegrist, *Lehrbuch der Medizinischen Soziologie*; and Labisch, *Homo hygienicus*. On the understanding of sickness in ancient Israel and the ancient Near East, see Briend, "Krankheit und Heilung"; Achenbach, "Klagegebete I," 367ff.; Maul, "Die 'Lösung vom Bann'"; Otto, "Magie—Dämonen—göttliche Kräfte"; Beyerle, "'Medizin'"; Ruwe and Starnitzke, "Krankheit/Heilung"; Janowski, "'Heile mich'"; and in the same volume (Thomas and Karle, *Krankheitsdeutung*), see the contributions of D. Bester, D. Erbele-Küster, T. Staubli, J. Ebach, and K. Bieberstein. On ethical and medical aspects of sickness and health, see Körtner, "Mit Krankheit leben"; Etzelmüller, "Der kranke Mensch"; and Schramme, *Krankheitstheorien*.

2. Schöpf, "Krankheit"; and comprehensively in Beck, *Seele und Krankheit*.

3. See Lang, "Ein Kranker," 138–39.

4. Cf. Pss. 27:10; 31:11/12; 35:13–14; 38:9–14 (10–15); 41:5–6 (6–7), 9/10; 55:13–14 (14–15); 69:8/9; 88:18/19; etc.

neighbors become strangers, and friends become enemies. Even the people in Job's closest circle—his wife, his children, his servants and maidservants—keep their distance and avoid contact with the afflicted:

> He [God] has removed my brothers from me,
> and my acquaintances have become estranged from me.
> (Job 19:13)
> Those close to me stay away,
> and my friends forget me. (v. 14)
> Those entrusted to me in my house
> and my maidservants think me a stranger,
> and I have become a foreigner in their eyes. (v. 15)
> I call my servant, but he does not answer,
> with my mouth I plead with him. (v. 16)
> My breath has become abhorrent to my wife,
> and the sons of my mother's womb are disgusted with me. (v. 17)
> Even little boys reject me;
> I stand up and they talk about me. (v. 18)
> The men in my circle of confidants despise me;
> those whom I loved have turned away from me. (v. 19)
> My bones cling to my skin and my flesh,
> and I have escaped by the skin of my teeth. (v. 20)[5]

Psychosomatic medicine sees experiences as the impulse behind many illnesses, which a human being processes in tension with the determinants of one's personal life—abilities, socialization, and the social conventions. Within this tension, according to Mitscherlich, "between the perceiving self and the internal world, and between the self and the external world, a traceable line to the origin of an illness becomes visible."[6] The texts that are cited below will demonstrate for us this tension between the ill self and its environment.

Here we immediately encounter a basic problem: the question of the *criteria for the definition of the illness- and healing-Psalms* in the Old Testament.[7] In response to this question, Seybold[8] has identified four factors that convey a complex image of illness and healing in ancient Israel. They are as follows:

- *Linguistic factors*
  Terms for illness are חָלָה, "become/be weak, ill"; כָּאַב, "experience pain, suffer"; צָלַע, "limp, walk lamely"; and the like. Terms for healing are חָיָה Qal/Piel/Hiphil, "revive, (let) recover"; חָלַם, "become strong, gain strength"; רָפָא, "heal"; and the like.
- *Conceptual forms*
  Specific views about life and death, the Sheol-motif, remnant of beliefs in magic, the sin-punishment correlation,; and so forth.
- *Social implications*
  Isolation, expulsion, ostracism, enmity, cultic impurity; and so forth.

5. Based on the German translation by Ebach, *Streiten mit Gott*, 1:151–52; on this text see also Seybold, *Gebet des Kranken*, 51ff.

6. A. Mitscherlich, *Krankheit als Konflikt*, 9.

7. Seybold (*Gebet des Kranken*, 98ff., 123ff., 153ff., 169–70ff.) specifies psalms with a certain reference to illness and healing (Pss. 38; 41; 88; Syriac Ps. III [= 11QPs^a 24 = Ps. 155]), those with a probable reference (Pss. 30; 39; 69; 102; 103; Isa. 38:9–20), and others with an uncertain reference (Pss. 6; 13; 32; 51; 91). See also H. W. Wolff, *Anthropology*, 143ff.; Oeming, "'Mein Herz'"; idem, *Psalm 1–41*, 75–76.

8. Seybold, *Gebet des Kranken*, 17ff., 165–66.

- *Religious practices*
  Conjuring, consultation of oracles, prayers for illness, penitential rites, cultic healing practices; and so forth.

Yet a relatively clear image of the ill person's situation emerges because, according to Seybold,

> the specific physical, psychological, social, religious situation of the ill person has produced and developed specific linguistic expressions, concrete ideas, and behavior patterns *in praxi*, which have assumed an almost stereotypical quality and have gained normative influence (including institutionalization). The conventional typology thus constitutes a substitute for lack of conceptual clarity and is almost appropriate for the Psalms, insofar as it corresponds to the unique character of these texts.[9]

There is therefore something like a *basic pattern of the course of illness and healing*, which is based on a combination of the individual factors listed here and which can be shown ideal-typically on the basis of texts like Psalms 6 (lament), 30 (thanksgiving), 38 (lament), 41 (thanksgiving with citation of a lament), 69 (thanksgiving), 88 (lament), 102 (lament), and 116 (thanksgiving). The following diagram (fig. 21) shows the main line of thought of the Old Testament interpretation of illness: The correlation of *guilt/sin* or *punishment/illness* and the correlation of *reprieve/healing*.[10] Within this framework are several particularities, which appear in various combinations in many psalms: the *depiction of affliction* (A–C: divine strike as a result of "sin," fall, diminishing of life), the *Sheol-motif* (D: separation from God, social disintegration, closeness of the underworld), and the *procedure of healing* (C'–A': recovery, return to life, cultic restitution).

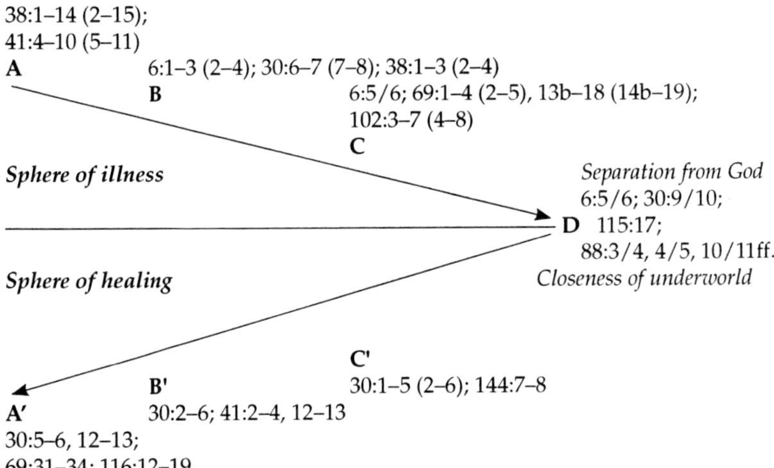

Figure 21. Ideal-typical course of illness and healing

9. Ibid., 167–68; cf. Seybold, *Die Psalmen*, 133; Gerstenberger, "Krankheit," 542–43.
10. Seybold, *Gebet des Kranken*, 170.

Since the experience of illness and healing is incorporated in the larger context of coming to terms with human existence [*Daseinsbewältigung*], one can speak with Seybold of an "adapted typology" [*konventionierten Typik*].[11] This typology constitutes a "substitute because of lack of conceptual clarity"[12] and shows itself to be particularly appropriate insofar as it corresponds to the linguistic and thematic characteristics of the illness and healing psalms. Telling examples for this are the depictions of affliction in Psalms 38:2–8 (3–9) and 102:1–7 (2–8) in which emotional suffering and physical affliction are in close correspondence to each other:

Yes, your arrows have descended into me,
  and your hand has come down on me.
(Ps. 38:2/3)
There is nothing healthy in my flesh because of your anger;
  nothing sound is in my bones because of my sin. (v. 3/4)
Truly my iniquities have grown over my head;
  like a heavy burden, they are too heavy for me. (v. 4/5)
My wounds have begun to stink;
  they have begun to fester because of my foolishness. (v. 5/6)
I have bowed down, crouched very low;
  all day I have walked about in a mourner's garment. (v. 6/7)
Truly my loins are filled with burning,
  and there is nothing healthy in my flesh. (v. 7/8)
I have become feeble and crushed;
  I roared [louder] than a [lion's] growl. (v. 8/9)[13]

YHWH, hear my prayer;
  let my cry reach you.
(Ps. 102:1/2)
Do not hide your face from me
  on the day of my distress.
Incline your ear toward me;
  when I call, hear me soon. (v. 2/3)
For my days have vanished in smoke;
  my bones, they burn like a furnace. (v. 3/4)
Withered like grass and dried up is my heart;
  indeed, I forgot to eat my bread. (v. 4/5)
Because of my loud groaning
  my bones cling to my flesh. (v. 5/6)
I *am like* a bird in the desert,
  like an owl among ruins. (v. 6/7)
I wake up and am/cry
  like a bird, lonely on the rooftop. (v. 7/8)[14]

The complaint over transience in Psalm 102:3–4 (4–5) shows particularly vividly how different body images combine to form a general impression: "The terms עצם (bones as frame and center of strength), לב (heart as the center of

11. Ibid., 168.
12. Ibid.
13. Cf. also the translation by Weber, *Werkbuch*, 1:182. On the interpretation of Ps. 38, see Kuckhoff, *Psalm 6*, 173ff., etc.; Zernecke, *Gott und Mensch*, 194ff.
14. On this text, see Brunert, *Psalm 102*, 113ff.

emotions and reason), [and] בשׂר (skin as the visible sign of human frailty) function here as components of a linguistically and conceptually differentiated image of the *person as a whole*."[15]

Trying to derive an exact medical diagnosis from this seems inappropriate. The point is rather "the subjective experience of a disturbed life,"[16] or the theme of imminent death, which is not expressed through the semantic content of the basic anthropological terms "bones," "heart," and "skin," but through their deliberate combination into a whole image. According to this understanding of illness, the experience of healing is also not expressed through medical terminology, but as a spatial return to life by "being led up from the underworld" by YHWH (Ps. 30:3/4).[17]

The second problem besides the criteria for defining the illness- and healing-Psalms concerns the question of the *actual affliction* of the supplicant.[18] Here too one encounters, as Psalms 38 and 102 demonstrate, a lack of conceptual clarity. Instead, what dominates, as was first noted by Gunkel, is a great vagueness, even contradictoriness in the depiction of the supplicant's illness and threat of death:

> No *specific situation* for the one praying is clear from the portrayals of mortal distress. They are too generally maintained. Seldom is it clearly expressed whether sickness, misfortune, or persecution from enemies has created the problem. More commonly, the images of the complaint contradict one another and do not allow themselves to be coordinated into one self-contained situation. For example, *within a single context*, the singer of Ps. 22 asks for liberation from wild animals and deliverance from the sword that persecutes him. He believes himself to be already in the underworld, then he sees that wild animals have been turned loose on him that want to rob him of his life. Then he speaks of himself as one who is deathly ill, whose belongings are divided by those who survive him.[19]

In many Psalms of Complaint the actions of the enemy appear indeed next to references to illness,[20] accusations,[21] guilt,[22] poverty,[23] or social disintegration,[24] so that one can often not be sure "if the afflicted is ill, depressed, captured, persecuted, or threatened."[25] The "discontinuity of the images"[26] often makes it impossible to identify the actual affliction of the ill person.

15. Ibid., 115. For further examples of such basic anthropological terms, see Karl-Martin Beyse, "עֶצֶם," 331. On the concept of the "whole person," see "Excursus 2: The Whole Human Being," 43–44 above.
16. Brunert, *Psalm 102*, 116.
17. See 257ff. below.
18. On the following discussion, see F. Crüsemann, "Im Netz"; and Janowski, "Die 'Kleine Biblia,'" 134ff.
19. Gunkel and Begrich, *Introduction to Psalms*, 134. On Ps. 22, see 323ff. below.
20. Cf. Pss. 6; 13; 22; 42–43; 69; 102; 109; et al.
21. Cf. Pss. 3; 4; 5; 7; 17; 26; 27; 57; 63; 69; et al.
22. Cf. Pss. 6; 38; 51; 69; 88; 143; et al.
23. Cf. Pss. 22; 31; 38; 69; 88; et al.
24. Cf. Pss. 22; 35; 69; 88; 102; 109; et al.; on the subject, see also F. Crüsemann, "Im Netz," 139, with nn. 2–6.
25. Seybold, *Die Psalmen*, 133.
26. Gunkel and Begrich, *Introduction to Psalms*, 134.

Nevertheless, the various impressions of the experiencing self are, as we have already seen with the subject of the enemy, brought together into a coherent whole.[27] Gunkel has described this process as follows:

> The poet does not place as much weight on a completely faithful reflection of the external circumstances as he does on communicating the internal circumstances, by expressing the impressions which the external events release in him. He wants to "pour out his sorrow before YHWH" [Ps. 102:1–2 (2–3); cf. also 42:5/6]. He reaches for images that powerfully and poignantly reflect his pain and distress, his abandonment, and his betrayal. He appropriates an image as an expression of his feeling to the extent that it appropriately suggests the mood of his spiritual condition. If one image does not suffice, then he multiplies images, unconcerned about whether their appearances agree as long as they shock and provoke with their burning colors. In other words, they provide a dynamic impression of what is occurring in his soul.[28]

Several years ago F. Crüsemann has explored this subject again and has asked Gunkel's virulent question of the "actual affliction" of the complaining supplicant once more. In doing so, he came across two explanatory patterns in Psalms research—the assumption of an initial cause[29] and the differentiation in genre of specific groups of texts[30]—both of which overlook the unique character of these texts. In contrast, F. Crüsemann has made the thesis of a "nonmonocausal view of suffering" plausible:

> Perhaps the way in which the complaints describe the affliction is more realistic than the assumption of a single cause. Those texts, which exhibit only one factor, whether illness or accusation, are according to their frequency exceptional cases, while a multiplicity of factors, which are confusing to us, constitute the norm by which this genre is measured. Perhaps it is precisely this nonmonocausal view of suffering that is connected to the effect and usability of these texts up to our current time.[31]

Illness therefore consists not only of physical but also of social suffering: disregard,[32] disintegration, loneliness—in short, the destruction of the supplicant's social world. Conversely, *health* mirrors the balance that the individual must restore in engagement with the environment and the challenges implicit in such an engagement—if one is able to do so! However, the Old Testament concepts of health and illness not only have the interaction between subject and environment in common, but also the integration of this interaction in the theological conceptualizations of the YHWH-religion. This correlation can be studied particularly effectively with the example of Psalm 41.

27. See 106ff. above.
28. Gunkel and Begrich, *Introduction to Psalms*, 134.
29. So, e.g., Gunkel suggests that "sickness would have originally been the *characteristic* distress" (ibid., 137). In the subsequent discussion, objections against this include the observation that there are Complaint Psalms that do not mention enemies, as well as those that contain no reference to illness or physical ailments.
30. E.g., they differentiate between a group of "prayers by an accused" (H. Schmidt, W. Beyerlin), a group of "songs by a sinner" (H.-J. Kraus), or a group of "illness-psalms" (K. Seybold). Yet this is problematic because the variety within these groups of texts is so large that all precise identifications of a *Sitz im Leben* are bound to be artificial; cf. F. Crüsemann, "Im Netz," 140–41.
31. Crüsemann, "Im Netz," 141.
32. On social disregard in ancient Israel, see 183ff. below.

β. Psalm 41 as a Case Study

For the choirmaster. A Psalm of David.

Blessed are those who consider the lowly: (quote alt.)
on the day of disaster, YHWH will deliver them.
(Ps. 41:1/2)
YHWH will guard them and keep them alive;
they will be praised as happy in the land—
yes, you will not give them up to the greed [*nepeš*] of their enemies. (v. 2/3)
YHWH will sustain them on their sickbed—
their entire bed you have changed in their illness. (v. 3/4)

I myself said: YHWH, be gracious to me!
heal my life/me [*nepeš*], for I have sinned against you! (v. 4/5)
My enemies speak evil of me:
"When will he die and his name perish?" (v. 5/6)
And if one comes to see [me], his heart speaks falsely;
he gathers trouble, he goes out, he talks. (v. 6/7)
Together they whisper about me, those who hate me,
against me they devise my harm: (v. 7/8)
"A matter of ruin is poured out over him,
and once he lies down, he will not rise again!" (v. 8/9)
Even the friend of my well-being, whom I trusted,
who has eaten my bread, has acted big [bragged] against me. (v. 9/10)
But you, YHWH, be gracious to me and raise me up,
that I may repay them. (v. 10/11)

By this I have known that you are pleased with me:
that my enemy cannot triumph over me. (v. 11/12)
As for me—you have upheld me in my integrity,
and have placed me before your face/you forever. (v. 12/13)

Praised be YHWH, the God of Israel,
from eternity to eternity!
Amen and Amen. (v. 13/14)

Textual Notes

1/2. Two interpretations are grammatically possible with regard to the relationship of the blessing (v. 1/2a) and the subsequent explication (1b–3 [2b–4]); see exegesis below.

2/3. The Tetragrammaton is not to be deleted for metrical reasons since it connects vv. 2/3 and 1/2b (cf. Hossfeld and Zenger, *Die Psalmen*, 1:261). The petition אַל־תִּתְּנֵהוּ, "You will not give him up," interrupts the third-person speech about YHWH in vv. 1b–3 (2b–4), according to Hossfeld and Zenger (ibid., 261) and Kraus (*Psalmen*, 1:465). Some ancient versions (LXX, Symmachus, Syriac, Vulgate) therefore render this colon in the indicative. All proposals for editing notwithstanding, the address style is to be kept in vv. 2/3b // 3/4b.

3/4. For the meaning of מִשְׁכָּב, "bed" (< שָׁכַב, "lie down"), the parallelism with עֶרֶשׂ דְּוָי, "sickbed," is of particular interest; see Seybold, *Gebet des Kranken*, 68, 106; and Schorch, *Euphemismen*, 157–58.

6/7. For metrical reasons, לִבּוֹ, "his heart," is to be seen as part of v. 6/7a (cf. Baethgen, *Die Psalmen*, 118). For the meaning of the expression "He gathers trouble," see also Baethgen, *Die Psalmen*, 118: "The visitor feigns participation; in reality he only wants to observe the symptoms that point to an imminent end."

7/8. While Seybold (*Psalmen*, 171) considers the first עָלַי questionable, Kraus (*Psalmen*, 1:465) deletes the second עָלַי and moves the *athnach* (*'athnāḥ*, chief pause within the verse) before "those who hate me." In my opinion, both moves are unnecessary (cf. also Craigie, *Psalms 1–50*, 318: "against me, they are plotting my misery"; *HALOT* 346 under חשׁב 5a).

9/10. Deleting עָקֵב, "heel," as a marginal gloss (< עֵקֶב, "reward," Ps. 40:15–16 [16–17]) are Kraus, *Psalmen*, 1:465; and Hossfeld and Zenger, *Die Psalmen*, 1:261. On the expression הִגְדִּיל עַל, "brag, talk big against someone," see Pss. 35:26; 38:16/17; 55:12/13; Lam. 1:9 (and GB[18] 201 under גדל Hiphil 4; *HALOT* 172 under גדל Hiphil 2); see also exegesis below.

11/12. On the meaning of the expression בְּזֹאת יָדַעְתִּי, "by this I have known," see exegesis below.

There are three basic forms of the Individual Thanksgiving Psalms (ITP), which also includes Psalm 41:[33] (1) The ITP does not exist independently, but as a continuation of the Lament of the Individual at the occasion of a *tôdâ*-celebration (Pss. 22:22/23ff.; 31:7–8, 19–24 [8–9, 20–25]; 69:30/31ff.).[34] (2) The ITP exists independently and contains sufficient references to the content of the complaint: a review of the affliction, a report about the petition, and a reference to the deliverance (Ps. 116). Finally, (3) the ITP can exist independently yet can cite the lament in a closed section. In addition to Psalm 18 (review of affliction vv. 4–5 [5–6]) or Psalm 30 (review of affliction, vv. 6–7 [7–8]),[35] this is also the case in Psalm 41.

At its core Psalm 41 is a lament of the individual in the style of a prayer to YHWH (vv. 4–10 [5–11]),[36] which is framed on one side by a sapiential-paraenetic section (vv. 1–3 [2–4]) and on the other side by a profession of thanks (vv. 11–12 [12–13]). Verses 1–3 (2–4) speak of YHWH predominantly in the third

33. See Westermann, *Lob und Klage*, 77; also Gese, "Psalm 22," 190 n. 17. See also Bauks, *Die Feinde des Psalmisten*, 84ff.; Janowski, "'Heile mich,'" 55ff ; Kuckhoff, *Psalm 6*, 176ff., 184ff., 192ff., etc.

34. See 278ff. below.

35. See 254ff. below.

36. There are different placements for the caesura, after either Ps. 41:9/10 or v. 10/11; see Hossfeld and Zenger, *Die Psalmen*, 1:258–59; Weber, *Werkbuch*, 1:195; et al. The division used here (vv. 4–10 [5–11] / 11–12 [12–13]) is supported by the framework of v. 4/5a to v. 10/11a, and by the retrospective semantic references of v. 10/11 to vv. 4–9 (5–10): "rise" in v. 8/9b, "raise up" in v. 10/11a, desire for revenge on the enemies in vv. 11–12 (12–13). At the same time v. 10/11 functions as a transition to vv. 11–12 (12–13). Here I shall not address Hossfeld and Zenger's conclusions about the history of redaction (*Die Psalmen*, 1:259–60: double redaction of a preexilic lament vv. 4–10 (5–11) now appearing in vv. 11–12 (12–13) and vv. 1–3 (2–4). The assumption of a single redaction (base text vv. 4–12 [5–13] and an expansion along the lines of a theology of the poor) is in my opinion more plausible.

person; then verse 2/3b // 3/4b take the form of address, the style of prayer; and verses 11–12 (12–13) look ahead to the healing and cultic restitution of the supplicant and thereby assume elements of other Thanksgiving Psalms of the Individual. The retrospective description of the affliction, introduced by a citation formula (v. 4/5a) and closed by petition (vv. 4–10 [5–11]), contains not only two direct speeches by the enemy (vv. 5/6b, 8/9), but is also framed by identical invocations "YHWH, be gracious to me!" (vv. 4/5a, 10/11a). Schematically, the following outline emerges.

For the choirmaster. A Psalm of David.

Sapiential-paraenetic section
General benediction (v. 1/2)
Explication in view of (2–3 [3–4])
  Oppression by enemies (2/3) (b: petition for salvation)
  Illness (3/4) (b: petition for healing)

Complaint with concluding petition
Citation formula (4/5a)
Petition and confession of sins (4/5bc) (a: "YHWH, be gracious to me")
Description of affliction (= enemy complaint) (5–9 [6–10])
Petition and desire for revenge (10/11) (a: "YHWH, be gracious to me")

Profession of thanksgiving
Certainty of being heard (11/12)
Cultic reintegration (12/13)

Final doxology to Book I of the Psalter of David
Praised be YHWH, the God of Israel,
  from eternity to eternity!
  Amen and Amen. (13/14)

Thematic Aspects

The background to Psalm 41 is constituted by the situation of illness. Yet this whole psalm was hardly composed on a sickbed—only its middle section, the complaint prayer of verses 4–10 (5–11). The context for the psalm as a whole therefore points to the framework surrounding this complaint, verses 1–3 (2–4) and 11–12 (12–13), whereby the psalm was presented (in the temple?) *after* the supplicant's successful recovery (vv. 3/4b, 12/13). The healing of the sick person thus occurred in the period between the complaint prayer on the sickbed (vv. 4–10 [5–11])[37] and the public presentation of the entire psalm (vv. 1–12 [2–13]) before the cultic community. The supplicant's situation in reciting this psalm is indicated by verses 11–12 (12–13) and especially by 12/13b ("before your face"). The supplicant is "in a *cultic situation* . . . in which the Deity believed to be present *and* at the same time the listening community can be spoken to without formal address and prayer formula."[38]

37. Cf. the reference to the sickbed in v. 3/4a.
38. Seybold, *Gebet des Kranken*, 109, emphasis original.

Two basic issues have to be clarified regarding the interpretation of the whole psalm: the meaning of verses 1–3 (2–4) (including the association of this passage with the complaint portion vv. 4–10 [5–11]) and the question of the time(s) for verses 11–12 (12–13): is this profession of thanksgiving a retrospective narrative? or a present or future expression of trust?

1. *The Healing of the Sick*

Two explanations about the relationship of the blessing in verse 1/2a and the subsequent explication in verses 1b–3 (2b–4) are grammatically possible:

- The blessing of verse 1/2a is connected to verses 1b–3 (2b–4) in such a way that all suffixes refer to *the one who is blessed*: "Blessed is the one who considers the lowly; on the day of disaster YHWH will deliver [the one who is blessed] . . ." (v. 1/2).
- The blessing of verse 1/2a functions as a caption-like call to attention: it addresses the reader and reciter of the psalm with a call to consider the "*lowly*" (דַּל), who is the protagonist of the psalm as a whole: "Blessed is the one who considers the lowly; on the day of disaster, YHWH will deliver [the lowly] . . ." (v. 1/2)

The style of verses 1–3 (2–4) lends more support to the second possibility, although both interpretations are syntactically possible.[39] As the verb שׂכל Hiphil ("be cognizant, regard, perceive")[40] shows, the blessing is intended to inspire compassion for the lowly. In older Wisdom literature, this concern for the poor is expressed through the word חָנַן, "to be gracious, have mercy," as in Proverbs 14:31:

> Those who despise the lowly scorn their Maker,
> but those who have mercy on the poor—blessed are they!
> (Prov. 14:31)[41]

The blessing of Psalm 41:1/2 thus suggests a sapiential regard for the lowly, so as to learn from their fate. The backdrop for the blessing of verse 1/2a is probably a *sapiential ethos of poverty*, which instills just action with regard to the weak.[42]

Psalm 41:2–3 (3–4) develops the general assurance of salvation: "On the day of disaster, YHWH will deliver [the lowly]" (v. 1/2b)—in view of the *enemies* (v. 2/3) and in view of the *illness* (v. 3/4). The connection of illness and oppression by enemies, as described in verses 4–10 (5–11), is therefore already invoked. The two petitions to YHWH in verses 2/3b // 3/4b underscore once again that

39. Cf. Hossfeld and Zenger, *Die Psalmen*, 1:258–60.
40. See Koenen, "שָׂכַל."
41. Cf. Prov. 19:17; 22:9; on the ethos of poverty in older Wisdom literature, besides Prov. 14:31 see also 22:22–23; 29:7; 30:14; as well as the "better than . . ." sayings: 15:16; 16:8; 19:1; 28:6. On this subject see Delkurt, *Ethische Einsichten*, 124ff.
42. See Hossfeld and Zenger, *Die Psalmen*, 1:258, 262, referring to a redaction to fit a theology of the poor, which shaped Ps. 40 and may have given rise to the blessing of Ps. 41:1/2a "to place both Psalms 40 and 41 next to each other as prayers of a poor person and to illustrate the poor one's ambivalent existence between lament and thanksgiving" (ibid., 258).

the oppressed and ill person is the protagonist, who is to be the beneficiary of YHWH's saving and healing intervention:

Blessed are those who consider the lowly:
  On the day of disaster, YHWH will deliver them. (v. 1/2)
YHWH will guard them and keep them alive;
  they will be praised as happy in the land—
  yes, you will not give them up to the greed [*nepeš*] of their enemies. (v. 2/3)
YHWH will sustain them on their sickbed—
  their entire bed you have changed in their illness. (v. 3/4)

The second problem concerns the meaning of the profession of thanksgiving in verses 11–12 (12–13), especially the function of the introductory demonstrative pronoun בְּזֹאת, "by this," with the subsequent יָדַעְתִּי, "I have known" (v. 12a). Here also two interpretations appear to be possible:

- The expression is to be understood *anaphorically* ("By this *I have known* that . . .") and refers back to *what has already happened*, yet which is *not further specified* in the psalm. This gap has often been filled by the assumption of a priestly salvation oracle. I have already commented on the difficulties of such an assumption in the interpretation of Psalm 13.[43]
- The expression is to be understood *cataphorically* ("By this *I shall know* that . . .") and refers to a *future experience* of deliverance, the fulfillment of which is described in verses 11b–12 (12b–13).[44] The confirmation for this experience would then be the second clause (v. 11/12b, "that my enemy cannot triumph over me"), while the first clause is to be closed by a colon.

By this I have known that you are pleased with me:
  that my enemy cannot triumph over me.
  (Ps. 41:11/12)
As for me—you have upheld me in my integrity,
  and have placed me before your face forever.[45] (v. 12/13)

The question of the temporal status of verses 11–12 (12–13) can therefore be answered as follows: The supplicant recognizes that YHWH has acted upon "me" (v. 11/12a), because "my enemy cannot [any longer] triumph over me" (v. 11/12b).

The supplicant attains such insight on the basis of this experience, which seems to be connected to a concrete observation.[46] YHWH has not abandoned

43. See 77ff. above.

44. Cf. Gerstenberger, *Psalms*, 1:176. According to Hossfeld and Zenger (*Die Psalmen*, 1:259), the tenses in 41:11–12 (12–13) do not permit this interpretation "since they clearly describe what has already happened." Correspondingly, v. 3/4b ("you have turned . . .") also interprets the subsequent events of vv. 11–12 (12–13) proleptically, assuming that the healing has already occurred; i.e., the perfect tenses of vv. 11–12 (12–13) "suggest that the intervention has happened and that the healing has taken place in the past" (259).

45. Cf. also the translation by Weber, *Werkbuch*, 1:194. For a different reading, see Seybold, *Gebet des Kranken*, 110–11 with n. 16: the demonstrative pronoun בְּזֹאת, "by this," in v. 11/12 refers to the first כִּי ("that") sentence in the verse, which is the basis for recognition of YHWH's benevolence.

46. On the fact that "the attaining of insight" (יָדַע) is expressed as the *result* of an experience, see Seeligmann, "Erkenntnis Gottes," 416ff. For the realization of insight, the perfect tense is consistently used, which often has a present meaning, analogous to the Greek οἶδα, "I have realized (and now know)"; see ibid., 419–20. The perfect expresses the achieved state of realization, i.e., a result.

the supplicant or "left me lying" (cf. v. 8/9b), but "raised me up" (v. 10/11a; cf. 8/9b) and "upheld me" (v. 12/13a). On the basis of this *experienced truth*, the recognition of which is expressed through a perfect verb functioning as a present, the supplicant infers that YHWH has "placed me"—a formerly sinful but now upright human being (v. 12/13a)[47]—before YHWH's face forever.[48]

From this experience, already expressed in the wisdom statement of verse 3/4b, the supplicant thus infers a general situation, according to which verse 12/13b indicates an effect[49] that concerns the supplicant's *future* but has *already* occurred in reality—through the recognition expressed by verse 11/12a. The temporal sequences of verses 11–12 (12–13) can therefore be described as follows:

Recognition sequence (v. 11/12)
YHWH's delight in the supplicant and defeat of the enemy
a By this I have known that you *are pleased* [perfect tense][50] with me:
b that my enemy *cannot triumph* [modal imperfect][51] over me.

Basis of recognition (v. 12/13)
Integrity of the supplicant and being placed before YHWH
a As for me—you *have upheld* [perfect tense] me in my integrity,
b and *have placed* [consecutive imperfect as successive tense] me
before your face/you forever.

2. *The Friend Who Becomes an Enemy*

At the center of Psalm 41 is the detailed complaint-prayer (vv. 4–10 [5–11]), which contains, after an introduction to direct speech (v. 4/5a), two petitions: one for mercy (v. 4/5a // v. 10/11a) and the other for healing (v. 4/5b):

I myself said: YHWH, be gracious to me!
heal my life/me [*nepeš*], for I have sinned against you!

A petition for healing is found also in other laments,[52] whereby Psalm 6:1–3 (2–4) is of particular interest since this petition shows that "healing" (רָפָא) is not only the treatment of wounds, but also the "animation" of body and soul:

YHWH, do not rebuke me in your anger,
and do not discipline me in your wrath!
(Ps. 6:1/2)
Have mercy [חנן], YHWH, for I am withering;
heal me [רָפָא], YHWH,
for my bones are struck with terror [בהל Niphal)! (v. 2/3)

47. On the meaning of תֹּם as "wholeness, integrity," see Seybold, *Gebet des Kranken*, 110; Hossfeld and Zenger, *Die Psalmen*, 1:259–60. The image of "upholding" (v. 12/13a) suggests YHWH's saving, rescuing, supporting hand; see 48 above. Seybold's reference to a "ritual act of a royal ceremony (Isa. 45:1) or legal procedure (Ps. 63:8/9; Job 8:20)" is in my opinion erroneous.

48. The supplicant's "being placed" before the face of YHWH probably suggests the context of an audience in the throne room of the living God; cf. Hartenstein, *Das Angesicht JHWHs*, 198.

49. Cf. ibid., 23.

50. The perfect חָפַצְתָּ in v. 11/12a describes an action in the present: "you have found [me] pleasing and are now pleased [with me]"; cf. Michel, *Tempora und Satzstellung*, 148.

51. On the modal use of the imperfect, see ibid., 148.

52. Cf. Pss. 6:2/3; 30:2/3; 60:3/4; 107:20; 147:3, et al.

My life [נֶפֶשׁ] is struck with terror [בהל Niphal],
but you, YHWH—how long? (v. 3/4)

As we have seen, the hiding of the divine face also causes all creatures, according to Psalm 104:29, to be terror struck (בהל Niphal)[53] and leads to the departure of life-giving breath. "Being terror struck" as a result of the hiding of the divine face is *experiencing death*. This experience of death can be overcome only through a act of "healing," through a "resuscitation" or a *return to life* (cf. חיה Piel, "revive, keep alive," Ps. 41:2/3a!). "Since the illness was seen as being seized by death, healing is a return to life"[54]—a return that can be brought about only by "YHWH the physician" (Exod. 15:26).[55]

With the confession of sin in Psalm 41:4/5b, the supplicant suggests knowing about sin as the cause of illness. Perhaps the petitioner knows the rule:

Those who conceal their transgressions shall not prosper,
but whoever confesses and renounces them shall find mercy.
(Prov. 28:13)[56]

More important is the observation that the description of the enemy in Psalm 41:5–9 (6–10) is in many ways reminiscent of Job 19:13–20: because of the supplicant's illness (in Ps. 41), the people closest to the petitioner become enemies and thus bring about the "progressive dissolution of social ties."[57] The enemies appearing here belong to different groups:

General opposition. First we encounter the אוֹיְבִים enemies.[58] The opposition to the supplicant escalates to mortal enmity, expressed especially though the *destructive word*. The speech by the enemy in verse 5/6b ("When will he die and his name perish?") communicates a twofold death wish: the *damnatio vitae* and the *damnatio memoriae*. The supplicant's physical death is to be further amplified and sealed by the disappearance of his name (שֵׁם) from the social memory of the community. In Egypt, the view of death as social isolation is also contrasted with the view of life as social connectivity. This view, according to J. Assmann,

> can be best explained on the basis of two proverbs. . . . The first is "the one lives when the other accompanies him," referring primarily to life *before* death. The other is "the one lives when his name is mentioned," referring primarily to life *after* death. Both, however, refer to an understanding of life that is based on the principle of social "connectivity." A single person alone is not able to live, or not alive in the full sense. There must be another who takes his hand and accompanies him. But he by no means is dead as long as there are people who mention his name, as long as the bond of connectivity is not severed.[59]

53. See 65 above.
54. Lohfink, "'Ich bin Jahweh, dein Arzt,'" 126 n. 102.
55. Cf. Deut. 32:39–40; 1 Sam. 2:6; and Hos. 6:1.
56. Cf. Hossfeld and Zenger, *Die Psalmen*, 1:263.
57. Ibid., 263. On Job, see 163–64 above.
58. See 104ff. above.
59. J. Assmann, *Tod und Jenseits*, 54, emphasis original; cf. 73 et al. On the concept of conectivity, see 132 above. Just as naming is a creative appropiating or acknowledging act (cf. Keel and S. Schroer, *Schöpfung*, 135), the passing away of the name is equivalent to the annihilation of every memory of the bearer; cf. Hossfeld and Zenger, *Die Psalmen*, 1:263.

Neighbors and relatives. According to Psalm 41:6/7 ("And if one comes to see [me] . . ."), neighbors and/or relatives (?) apparently visit the sick person. These enemies do three things: (1) their heart, the central organ of the human being,[60] speaks "falsely" (שָׁוְא);[61] (2) they gather "trouble" (אָוֶן), incriminating evidence, and go outside with it,[62] (3) in order to spread gossip in the streets or alleyways. The section of verses 7–8 (8–9), which completes the description of the enemy, is formulated with great sensitivity to (social-)psychological dynamics: the "matter of ruin," which the enemies want to pin on the sick person, is shown to come from themselves. One can consult Proverbs 6:12–15 to see how such a dynamic operates:

> A scoundrel [*bĕlîya'al*], a wicked person [is that]
> who walks with a deceitful mouth, (v. 12)
> winks with the eye, shuffles the feet,
> points with the finger. (v. 13)
> With treachery in the heart, that one commits evil,
> constantly stirring up conflict. (v. 14)
> Therefore ruin will come suddenly on such a person,
> who will be abruptly broken, and there is no healing.[63] (v. 15)

False friend. In Psalm 41:9/10, with the appearance of the "person of my well-being" (אִישׁ שְׁלוֹמִי) and the one "who has eaten my bread" (אוֹכֵל לַחְמִי), the description of the enemy reaches its climax, introduced by "even" (גַּם). The "person of my well-being," that is, the person with whom the supplicant has lived in *shalom* until now,[64] was one whom the supplicant trusted (בָּטַח) and with whom meal fellowship was enjoyed. This one now "brags" against the supplicant. The magnitude of this betrayal of trust is illustrated by Job 19:19 and especially in the "friend complaints" of Psalm 55:12–14 (13–15) and Sirach 37:2:

> Those in my circle of confidants despise me;
> those whom I loved have turned away from me.
> (Job 19:19)[65]

> Indeed, if an enemy despised me,
> I would endure it.
> If one who hates me exalted self over me,
> I would hide from that one.
> (Ps. 55:12/13)

60. See 155ff. above.
61. See Reiterer, "שָׁוְא," esp. 1108.
62. Noteworthy is the contrast in 41:6/7 between the "heart" (inside) and "outside."
63. See translation by R. Schäfer, *Die Poesie der Weisen*, 162–63. Despite differences between the book of Job and the Psalms of the Sick, it can be seen on the basis of Job 2:11–13 how those who visit the sick in Ps. 41:5–8 (6–9) should have acted: Job's three friends "[v. 11] arranged a visit, in order to lament and to console him. [12] Already from a distance they raised their eyes and did not recognize him. Then they raised their voices and wept. They tore their garments and put ashes on their heads toward heaven. [12] Then they sat with him on the ground for seven days and seven nights. No one said a word, for they saw that his pain was very great." See the excellent interpretion by Lohfink, "Phase des Schweigens?," 263ff.; also Strauss, "Die 'Freunde' Hiobs," 73.
64. Cf. Jer. 20:10; 38:22; and Obad. 7
65. On this text see 163–64 above.

But [it is] you, a person like me,
  my confidant, my companion; (v. 13/14)
we took sweet counsel together;
  in the house of the Lord we walked in the noise of the multitude. (v. 14/15)[66]

Is it not a grief that reaches unto death,
  if a friend, who stands very close to you, turns into an enemy?
(Sir. 37:2)[67]

The description of the enemy in Psalm 41:4–10 (5–11), which represents a small *phenomenology of social death*,[68] is particularly dramatic: It begins with the outside enemies' devastating wish for the supplicant's death (v. 5/6). It has a single visitor of the sick appear (neighbor or family member?), who takes advantage of the supplicant's helplessness (v. 6/7) and accompanies him outside in the street. There one is ready to finish off the victim through conspiracy and downright death threats (vv. 7–8 [8–9]). As if this were not enough, a familiar friend appears, who stands out from the multitude of enemies because of belonging to the immediate environment of the abused (meal fellowship),[69] but who has now become a great danger to the supplicant. This *contrast of intimate closeness and great danger* is introduced in verse 9/10 with the intensive particle "even."

Enemies, neighbors, relatives (vv. 5–8 [6–9])

5/6a	"My enemies speak evil of me . . ."
5/6b	Wish for the supplicant's death: "When will he die ...?"
6/7	Visiting the sick: speaking falsely // gathering
7/8	Conspiracy: whispering // devising harm
8/9	Pronouncement of death: "A matter of ruin ..."

False friend (v. 9/10)

9/10a	"Even the man of my well-being, whom I trusted ..."
9/10b	Who has eaten my bread . . .

The hostility against the sick is articulated in Psalm 41:7/8 as "hatred," which is at the same time expressed as conspiracy: "all" who hate the ill person whisper against that one and devise harm against the sick supplicant. The nature of this harm is identified in 41:8/9 with reference to the rare expression "a matter of ruin" (דְּבַר־בְּלִיַּעַל),[70] which is "poured out" (יָצַק) over the sick like a liquid. As in Psalm 18:4–5 (5–6), this description evokes the image of a human being who has already entered the underworld and has experienced its life-destroying powers:

66. See translation by Hossfeld and Zenger, *Psalmen 51–100*, 94. On the expression "friend complaint," see ibid., 97, 100; and Keel, *Feinde und Gottesleugner*, 132ff.
67. Sir. 37:1–6 also speaks of the meal fellowship with the friend that breaks apart in times of suffering: "How bad is a friend, who sits at your table, but rises against you in times of suffering!" (v. 4).
68. On the concept of "social death," see 46–47 above.
69. In addition to the texts named here, the element of social closeness and its abuse is also expressed in Ps. 35:13–14; cf. Jer. 20:7–18; see Bail, *Gegen das Schweigen klagen*, 171ff.; and Hossfeld and Zenger, *Psalmen 51–100*, 100.
70. Cf. Pss. 18:4/5 and 101:3.

Ropes of death [חֶבְלֵי־מָוֶת] surrounded me;
the torrents of destruction [נַחֲלֵי בְלִיַּעַל] frightened me. (v. 4/5)
Ropes of the underworld [חֶבְלֵי שְׁאוֹל] encompassed me;
Snares of death [מוֹקְשֵׁי מָוֶת] confronted me.[71] (v. 5/6)

Excursus 6: The World of the Sick

An authentic view into the psychological world of the sick as conveyed by Psalm 41 and other Psalms of the Sick (Pss. 38; 88; etc.) is given by an Assyrian bronze tablet from the early first millennium BCE (fig. 22). In the **middle panel** the sick—an adult male—is seen lying on his bed with his hands raised to the great gods represented in the **upper panel**: *Anu* (horned cap), *Ea* (ram's head), *Adad* (bundle of lightning), *Marduk* (digging stick), *Nabu* (writing utensils), *Ištar* (Venus star), *Šamaš* (winged sun), *Sîn* (moon sickle), and *Sebettu* (seven-star constellation). At the head and foot of the bed two invocation priests (*āšipu*) with fish masks are working with purification vessels, into which they apparently dip bundles of plants in order to sprinkle the sick. All this seems to be taking place at night, as the burning oil lamp on the left suggests. The meaning of the scene is provided by the **lower panel**: the fever demon *Lamaštu*—with a lion's head and double-headed serpents in each hand and the unclean animals pig and dog on her breasts—is threatened by the demon *Pazuzu* and is sent away from the vicinity of the sick in a boat, on a journey across the river Ulaja and the sea (so-called journey scene). Lamaštu is kneeling on an onager (wild donkey), which is standing inside a boat with raised animal protomes. The gesture of expulsion (raised right hand) is also performed and thus intensified by the animal-mask-wearing cultic agents in the second and third panel. The apotropaic head of the demon *Pazuzu* ("packer"), who also appears in the lower panel, driving out the fever demon, looks over the upper edge of the amulet.

As one can see, *animal symbolism* plays a central role in the healing procedure: "Pure animals (suitable for eating) appear to represent the positive powers, impure animals (not suitable for eating) the negative. . . . Every culture has developed its own criteria for purity. Some animals, however, have an ambivalent character like the demons themselves and represent both powers (lion, serpent)" (Keel and Staubli, *Tiere in der Bible*, 52; see also Janowski and Neumann-Gorsolke, "Reine und unreine Tiere"). Furthermore, invocation priests in fish costumes and lion masks appear while other figures with animal masks mediate between the world of the gods above (upper panel) and the world of humans (middle panel). Even the illness itself is represented as an animal-like chimera (fever demon Lamaštu). On the Lamaštu amulet, see Kaelin, "Pazuzu" (esp. 369–70, fig. 4); and Pezzoli-Olgiati, "Gegenwelt" (with a nice tracing of the image by U. Zurkinden-Kolberg).

Important for our case is finally the *cosmic quality of representation*. The situation of the sick person forms "wide circles on earth, in two lower and one upper realms (earlier one spoke of a "Hades-Relief"); sets events in motion

71. On the theme of chaos, see Adam, *Der königliche Held*, 55ff.; and Köckert, "Die Theophanie," 212–13.

that begin in the social and cultic-ritual sphere and touch upon the entire occupied world, gods, and demons; prompting battles in the intermediate realm, where spirits fight over the sick person; and only the intervention of the upper powers through the priest of Ea is able to save him" (Seybold, "Krankheit als Problem," 24).

Resources

Keel, *Die Welt*; Keel and Staubli, *Tiere in der Bible*; Röllig, "Begegnungen mit Göttern"; Seybold, "Krankheit als Problem"; Wiggermann, "Magie, Magier I."

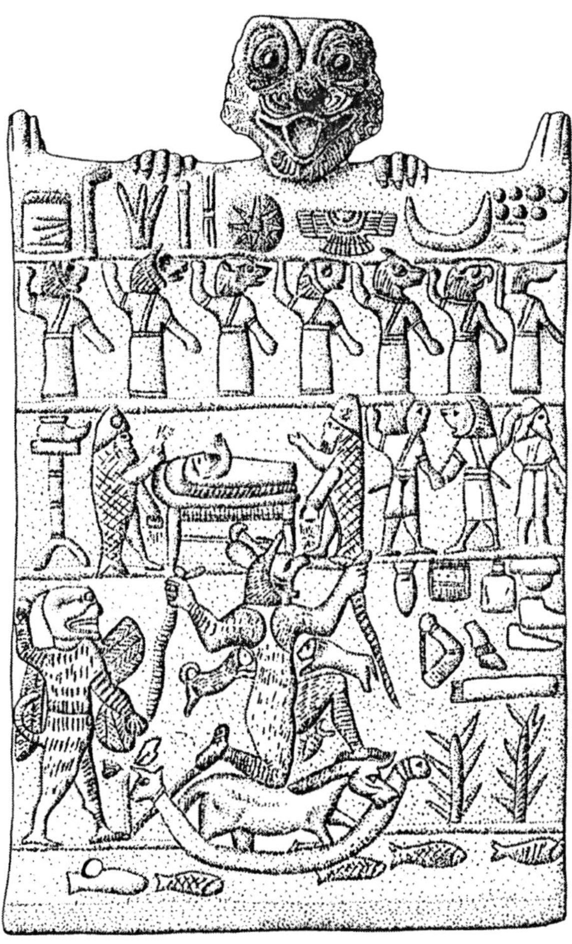

Figure 22. Assyrian Lamaštu-Amulet
(early first millennium BCE)

In light of this lament, the pronouncement of death in Psalm 41:8/9 suggests that in the eyes of the enemies, the supplicant has already been seized by the "torrents of destruction" (Ps. 18:4/5b) and is surrounded by them on all sides.[72] Since the word בְּלִיַּעַל *relates to the chaotic,* as the semantic context of Psalm 18:4–5 (5–6) also suggests,[73] it is primarily used for that which is opposed to God and the community.[74] A parallel to this *cosmic dimension* is found in the famous bronze tablet of Assyria (fig. 22), according to which the sick person saw self as exposed to the works of demonic powers and hoped for triumph in the battle of good over evil.

The petition of Psalm 41:10/11 begins after a double invocation: "But you, YHWH" with a plea for mercy (חָנַן; cf. v. 4/5a)[75] and restoration (קוּם Hiphil, "let rise).[76] Strange and unique, however, is the final plea for a settling of scores by the supplicant with the enemies (v. 10/11b). In connection with the theme of revenge, I had spoken of the thin line between *presumption of revenge* and *renunciation of revenge,* on which the Psalms of Lament are located.[77] This line is crossed here by the supplicant in the direction of self-sanctioned vengeance. In doing so, the supplicant also contradicts the otherwise heeded warning of Proverbs 20:22:

> Do not say: "I shall repay evil [אֲשַׁלְּמָה־רָע]!"
> Place your hope in YHWH, who will save you![78]

But as if the wish for revenge had become lodged in the throat, the supplicant in verse 11/12—"By this I have known that you are pleased with me: that my enemy cannot triumph over me"[79]—admits the possibility that the end of the enemy may be for entirely different reasons than self could imagine in the suffering.[80]

3. Development in Judaism and Christianity

There is a twofold development of Psalm 41 in ancient Judaism and early Christianity, which should be addressed in our conclusion.

As Lohfink[81] has shown, there is the development of an extensive theology of the poor in the *Hodayot* (*Thanksgiving Hymns*) from Qumran, especially in 1QH 13 (*olim* 5). 20–39, that makes use of Psalm 41:9/10 as a proof text. According to

72. Cf. Benedikt Otzen, "בְּלִיַּעַל," 656. The sense of being surrounded by enemies, encircled and caught as in a net, or bound up—this a typical experience of suffering in the laments of the individual; see Lamp and Tilly, "Öffentlichkeit als Bedrohung," 51–52.

73. Noteworthy is the chiasm of death—destruction (v. 4/5): underworld—death (v. 6).

74. On the meaning of בְּלִיַּעַל, see Otzen, "בְּלִיַּעַל," 654ff.; R. Schäfer, *Die Poesie der Weisen*, 162 n. 648; and Adam, *Der königliche Held*, 55 nn. 37–39.

75. See 172–73 above.

76. See the contrasting expression from the lips of the "hater" (41:7/8a): "and once he lies down, he will not rise again!" (קוּם Qal, v. 8/9b).

77. See 124ff. above.

78. Cf. also Pss. 31:23/24; 62:12/13; 94:23; and 109:15, 20.

79. On the interpretation of this verse, see 85ff. above.

80. We touch again on the question of how the end of the wicked/enemy is depicted in the laments of the individual. The answer is usually this: the wicked/enemy perish as a result of the self-destructiveness of their actions, while YHWH saves the righteous from their suffering/death. See now Sticher, *Die Rettung der Guten*, 151ff.

81. Lohfink, *Lobgesänge der Armen*, 78ff.

Lohfink, the text is structured as a great hymn with introduction, stanza A (lines 10–18), stanza B (19–27), stanza C (28–36), stanza D (37–43), stanza E (44–?), and possibly a concluding coda.

Let us focus on the double stanza A, because it addresses concrete conflicts that are known from Psalm 41. They are "conflicts with an inner circle with which the supplicant is connected in special ways and which has betrayed him."[82] These enemies are described in this Qumran hymn's lines 10–16 in seven different ways:

10/19 my opponents
11/20 my friends
12/21 who had entered into a covenant with me
13/22 all who are gathered around me
14/23 all who have eaten my bread (cf. Ps. 41:9/10b)
15/24 all who are tied to my (secret) circle
16/25 all men of my counsel

This depiction of hardship is grouped around a single Psalm verse that stands at the center of the double stanza (line 14/23) and cites Psalm 41:9/10. The introduction too could consist of two parts: lines 2–5, which speak in the *singular* of an individual person's salvation (orphan // lowly), while lines 6–9 speak in the *plural* of the salvation of the poor (afflicted by misery, despondent, poor). The poor person is joined here by the poor in general, meaning the entire Qumran community: the supplicant refers to self as an "orphan" and as "lowly," while the Qumran community is called the "misery-afflicted" people, those "despondent about justice," and "all the poor of compassion."

Such terminology indicates the theological nuance of this hymn: God, with his righteousness and grace, turns toward the poor, because they are poor. The terminology of poverty thus falls into the "realm of justification."[83] In other words: poverty is defined in relation to the *sphere of death*, in which people may find themselves as a result of enmity, illness, or legal emergency, and at the same time in relation to *care of God*, which is accorded to them in the form of vindication or justification. This connection of *deadly poverty* and *life-giving justification* is also characteristic of Psalm 41.

Blessed are those who consider the *lowly*:	*Poverty*
On the *day of disaster*, YHWH will deliver them.	*Closeness to death* (v. 1/2)
As for me—you have upheld me in my *integrity*,	*Righteousness*
and have placed me *before your face* forever.[84]	*Closeness of God* (v. 12/13)

The other branch of the development of Psalm 41 is the *Markan passion account*. The passage relating the prediction of Jesus (Mark 14:17–21) cites

82. Ibid., 81–82. Line numbers before a slash are based on Lohfink's numbering; those after a slash are according to García Martínez, 330.

83. Lohfink, *Lobgesänge der Armen*, 86.

84. In the older wisdom tradition, the *innocent* can be equated with the *poor*, as in Prov. 19:1: "Better one poor person who lives beyond reproach [הוֹלֵךְ בְּתֻמּוֹ] than one who turn the lips and is a fool"; cf. Prov. 28:6, on which the later redaction of Ps. 41:1–3 (2–4) may be based, influenced by a theology of the poor; cf. Hossfeld and Zenger, *Die Psalmen*, 1:258, 264.

Psalm 41:9/10 in a context that presupposes the setting of the Passover meal (Mark 14:22–25):

> [17] And when it was evening, he came with the twelve. [18] And while they were reclining at table and eating, Jesus said: "Amen, I say to you: One of you eating with me will betray me" [cf. Ps. 41:9/10]. [19] They became distraught and said to him one after another: "Surely not I?" [20] But he said to them: "One of the twelve, who is dipping into the bowl with me. [21] Indeed, the Son of Man passes on, as has been written about him; but woe to the one through whom the Son of Man is betrayed. It would be better for him, if that man had not been born!"

Both the "Amen" statement of Jesus (v. 18b) and his answer to the outcry of the disciples, which identifies the betrayer as one of them (vv. 20–21), are situational, presupposing the setting of the Passover meal. In this way the violation of the social relationship implicit in the Passover meal is specifically emphasized: Jesus comes *with* the twelve (v. 17), and one "who is eating *with* me" "will betray me" (v. 18; cf. v. 20). With the subsequent and therefore especially emphasized reference to Psalm 41:9/10, "a *passio iusti* motif is introduced, which fits the context of the meal and marks the sacrilegious violation of the community."[85]

Psalm 41:9/10 is particularly well suited for such a reference, because this psalm is a thanksgiving hymn into which has been woven a description of affliction characteristic for a lament (vv. 4–10 [5–11]). This development also exhibits the Psalms-centered Christology characteristic for the Markan passion account.[86]

Summing Up the Effect of Psalm 41

A text like Psalm 41 is another testimony for the *remarkable sensitivity of the Old Testament for social concerns*. This sensitivity can be explained on the basis of its communally oriented thought, according to which the actions of the individual are consistently seen in reference to the social context in which they take place.[87] As a result, no one can claim self-integrity (תֹּם, Ps. 41:12/13)[88] entirely for oneself, since integrity required then, as it does today, "the stabilization of a web of symmetrical relations of recognition, in which unacceptable individuals can only *mutually* secure their fragile identity as members of a community."[89]

The Psalms teach us that the religion of YHWH aims at the preservation or strengthening of the integrity of the person, which is repeatedly called into question by *hostility* (vs. love, friendship), *degradation* (vs. respect, honor),[90] or *disenfranchisement* (vs. recognition, justice). It does this, because it does not close its eyes before the reality of social contempt. In closing, let us take a look at this particularly disheartening chapter of biblical anthropology.

85. Pesch, *Das Markusevangelium*, 349; cf. Gnilka, *Markus (Mk 8, 27–16, 20)*, 236–38, etc. Since Ps. 41:9/10 (אֹכֵל לַחְמִי = LXX ὁ ἐσθίων ἄρτους μου) is not cited directly, one should speak more precisely of an allusion; cf. also John 13:38; Matt. 26:21 has avoided the reference to Ps. 41:9/10 "because the Psalter has no value as theological evidence for him" (ibid., 236 n. 10); see also Luz, *Nach Matthäus*, 88.

86. See the more detailed discussion 329ff. below.

87. See von Soosten, "Die 'Erfindung' der Sünde," 89ff. On the concept of "social sphere," see 51–52 above.

88. See 174 n. 47 above.

89. Habermas and Krebs, "Ethik," 96, emphasis original.

90. On the "honor" of the supplicant, see 264–65 below.

γ. *Social Contempt in Ancient Israel*

In his book *Kampf um Anerkennung* [*Struggle for Recognition*], the social philosopher A. Honneth has examined the elements of a *Moral Grammar of Social Conflicts* (the book's subtitle); on their basis he develops a normative, sophisticated theory of society. According to him, social conflicts are motivated by specific types of contempt, which can be defined as *abuse and rape*,[91] as *disenfranchisement and exclusion*, and as *dishonor and insult* of the other.[92] These are contrasted by three forms of interpersonal recognition, which enable an undisturbed relationship to self and society as *love/friendship*, as *legal recognition*, and as *social respect*.[93] The three forms of contempt—abuse, disenfranchisement, dishonor—represent attacks on a person's physical, social, and moral integrity and on their ability to interact.

In this complex structure involving relations of social recognition or contempt, the phenomenon of sickness—in the sense of Mitscherlich's idea of "sickness as conflict"[94]—attains a central significance, insofar as the individual consequences of the experience of contempt are always described with metaphors that refer to states of deterioration of the human body. Social contempt is said to be hurtful or even to cause injury:

> In psychological tests that examine the effects of an individual's experience of torture and rape, a frequent theme is "psychological death"; in research focusing on the example of slavery and the collective processing of disenfranchisement and social exclusion, the concept of "social death" has become commonplace; with regard to the type of contempt found in cultural dishonor, the category of "hurting" is preferred.[95]

Such metaphorical allusions to physical suffering and death express a structural similarity between social contempt and physical injury. This structural similarity is significant also because it permits certain conclusions with regard to the integrity of persons: "anticipatory avoidance of sickness corresponds . . . to the social guarantee of conditions of recognition, which are largely to protect the subjects from the experience of contempt."[96]

The questions What can guarantee the conditions for interpersonal recognition? and What can make such a guarantee reliable? are currently again the subject of debate in sociology and social philosophy.[97] In light of the Psalms, which are the subject of our discussion, it should be the *principle of justice*. In the Old Testament "justice" is the common frame for the relation to society and to God.[98] The integrity of the human person is defined by the connection of these

91. Ps. 55:12–14 (13–15) could be cited as an example (on this text, see 176–77 above), which Bail (*Gegen das Schweigen klagen*, 160ff., esp. 170ff.) reads against the backdrop of raped women.

92. See Honneth, *Kampf um Anerkennung*, 212ff. On social contempt through "harmful speech," see Häusl, "Zuraten" (with material from Proverbs); Grund, "Ehre und Scham." On the issue in general, see the contributions in S. Herrmann, Krämer, and Kuch, *Verletzende Worte*.

93. See Honneth, *Kampf um Anerkennung*, 148ff.

94. Cf. 163–64 above.

95. Honneth, *Kampf um Anerkennung*, 218.

96. Ibid., 219.

97. In addition to Honneth, *Kampf um Anerkennung*, see also Popitz, "Gewalt"; Sofsky, *Traktat über die Gewalt*; Sofsky, *Zeiten des Schreckens*; and Paris, *Stachel und Speer*.

98. See 128–29 above.

two types of relation: ethics and religion. When one of these relations is distorted or prevented through forms of contempt, a person's integrity is injured.

This injury of the other is associated in the laments of the individual with the appearance of the enemy[99] and the enemy's "power to inflict injury," with the intention to "do harm" to the other.[100] The particular kinds of injury that can be inflicted on the other are thereby unsparingly identified. In our analysis of the enemy's depiction in the Psalms, we have repeatedly come across the *indescribability and anonymity* of the enemy/enemies, which are also reflected in open-ended terms like "many" (רַבּוֹ/רַבִּים)[101] or "all < totality of" (כֹּל).[102] The aspect of anonymity includes an element of *superiority,* which prompts the supplicant to exaggerate the number and power of the enemies, like these examples:

I do not fear a host of ten thousand
who have set themselves up around me.
(Ps. 3:6/7)

More numerous than the hairs on my head
are those who hate me without cause.
(Ps. 69:4/5a)[103]

As numerous as the enemies are also the forms and actions of social contempt that come from them. A sequence of forms of contempt, as can be found in the laments of the individual, could look as follows:

- mocking winks with the eye as the sign of agreement to exclude another (Ps. 35:19; cf. Prov. 6:13; 10:10; etc.)
- shaking the head as a sign of incredulous astonishment (Pss. 22:7/8; 109:25; cf. Ps. 44:14/15; Job 16:4; Lam. 2:15; etc.)
- sneering (Ps. 22:7/8) and baring/grinding of teeth (Pss. 35:16; 37:12; 112:10; cf. Job 16:9; Lam. 2:16) as a sign of humiliation
- verbal insults (Ps. 69:7/8), derision (Pss. 22:6/7; 31:18/19), and shame (69:20/21)
- boastful speech (Pss. 35:26; 38:16/17; 41:9/10; 55:12/13; cf. Jer. 48:26, 42; etc.)[104]

A locus classicus of social contempt is Jesus' being mocked in the Synoptic Gospels (Mark 15:25–32 par.; Matt. 27:39–44; cf. Luke 23:35ff.). In Mark 15 the bypassers, the high priests, and the scribes cannot refrain from mocking the crucified; even those crucified with him revile him:

99. On the subject of enemies, see the more detailed discussion on 97ff. above.

100. Popitz, "Gewalt," 43: "The most immediate form of power is the sheer power to act: the power to inflict damage on others through actions directed against them—to 'do harm' to others."

101. See Blum and Fabry, "רַב."

102. Cf. Pss. 3:1–2 (2–3); 6:7/8; 22:7/8; 31:13/14; 38:19/20; 52:4/6; 53:3/4; 7/:7; etc.

103. Cf. Pss. 25:19; 62:3/4; etc.

104. Cf. Lamp and Tilly, "Öffentlichkeit als Bedrohung." On the subject, see also Bail, *Gegen das Schweigen klagen*, 31ff. These behaviors are largely gestures of body language, expressed though *verba gesticulationis*; see also Jenni, "Verba gesticulationis im Hebräischen," with an insightful table on 159ff.

Figure 23. Paul Klee, *Versuch einer Verspottung* (1940)

> [25] And it was the third hour, and they crucified him. [26] And the inscription of his charge was written: THE KING OF THE JEWS. [27] And with him they crucified two robbers, one to his right and one to his left. [29] And those who passed derided him by shaking their heads [cf. Ps. 22:7/8][105] and said: "O you who would destroy the temple and rebuild it in three days, [30] save yourself by climbing down from the cross!" [31] Likewise the high priests were mocking among themselves with the scribes and said: "Others he saved, but he cannot save himself! [32] Let the Messiah, the King of Israel, come down from the cross, so that we may see and believe!" Even those who were crucified with him reviled him.[106]

In the year of his death, Paul Klee produced a picture of the Man of Sorrows crowned with thorns (fig. 23) and gave it the title *Versuch einer Verspottung* [Attempt at Mocking]." The contrast between Christ, who remains in the background in silent dignity, and his mockers could hardly be greater. The idea that is graphically represented here is clear: those surrounding Christ try to mock him, but in doing so they mock themselves, or rather for the viewer, they become the real object of derision:

105. Regarding the allusion to Ps. 22:7/8, see 329ff. below.
106. Cf. translation by Lührmann, *Das Markusevangelium*, 257–58.

> Their attempt at mocking falls back on them, because their hatred distorts their humanity. Christ in contrast, on whom the eye focuses only gradually, despite the labyrinthine entanglements in the forms that jump out at him aggressively, is withdrawn into himself with his eyes closed. Their combined derision does not reach him, he does not allow himself to be drawn into it, let alone to return it. Rather, in his silent suffering he is like a catalyst that exposes them.[107]

Let us return to ancient Israel: the common place for social contempt was apparently the gate (שַׁעַר) of the town or city. Here was not only the place to hold court, to buy, and to sell:

> approval and disapproval were traded as well. . . . Here people lingered to converse, to spread rumors, and to form judgments, where opinions intensified, where everything could be observed by everyone, and the human person became most concretely aware of one's outward-oriented nature. Whoever could command attention here or become the subject of conversation was spoken of by everyone; thus whatever was gossiped "in the gate" about the supplicant and the news that was exchanged, perhaps in mocking verses over wine (or vice versa), that would have been called out after the supplicant in the street as soon as that one was sighted.[108]

Such mocking is also attested in the Psalms:

> All who see me laugh about me;
> they curl their lips and shake their heads.
> (Ps. 22:7/8)

> For my enemies talk about me,
> and those who lie in wait for my life conspire against me.
> (Ps. 71:10)

> I have become the object of derision;
> they see me and shake their head.
> (Ps. 109:25)

How does the supplicant react to these expressions of contempt? With an abundance of complaints, in which he gives expression to the pain of his affliction.

> I am exhausted from groaning;
> I flood my bed all/every night;
> with tears I dissolve my couch.
> My eye is blurred by grief;
> it has become dull because of all my oppressors.
> (Ps. 6:6–7 [7–8])[109]

107. Ringleben, *Dornenkrone und Purpurmantel*, 69.

108. Lamp and Tilly, "Öffentlichkeit als Bedrohung," 51; on the gate as "place of judgment and the public sphere for men," see I. Fischer, *Rut*, 231ff.

109. On the interpretation of this text, see Bail, *Gegen das Schweigen klagen*, 118ff., 121ff. See also Kuckhoff, *Psalm 6*, passim; Rechberger, *Von der Klage zum Lob*, 249ff.; Wälchli, *Gottes Zorn*, 39ff.

Hear my prayer, O God,
  and do not hide from my pleas.
      (Ps. 55:1/2)
Consider me and hear me.
  I wander about in desperation,[110] and I am distraught (v. 2/3)
because of the shouts of the enemy,
  because of the oppression by the wicked.
Indeed, they bring down trouble on me,
  and in anger they accuse me. (v. 3/4)
My heart trembles inside me,
  and fear of death has fallen on me. (v. 4/5)
Fear and trembling come to me,
  and terror has overwhelmed me. (v. 5/6)
And I said: Would that I had wings like a dove!
  I would fly and rest. (v. 6/7)
See, I would flee far away,
  spending the night in the desert.[111] *Selah.* (v. 7/8)
I would hasten to my shelter,
  away from the raging wind and the storm.[112] (v. 8/9)

Calling to mind that isolation and exclusion from the community (village or city)—which provided food, shelter, and justice—were life threatening for the supplicant,[113] one realizes the extent of such suffering, which Psalm 55:6–7 (7–8) portrays with escape imagery like "far away" and "desert." "In normal times, the city is seen as a place of refuge, in which one can live securely, while the desert is a place of death, hopelessness, and uninhabitable surroundings. These conditions have been reversed: The city has become uninhabitable, while the desert has become the only chance for survival."[114]

What remains is not quiet submission to fate, but the course of complaint/accusation, directed at YHWH as the God of justice.[115] This course—usually not without hardship, since "faithfulness among people has disappeared" (Ps. 12:1/2[116])—is taken by the laments of the individual, which do not tire in raising their voice against injustice and to appeal to the God of justice:

For the choirmaster. According to the Eighth. A Psalm of David.

Help, O YHWH, for the devout are disappearing;[117]
  vanished indeed are the faithful among human beings.
      (Ps. 12:1/2)

110. The expression שִׂיחַ + רוּד indicates the actions of a depressed person; see Barré, "'Wandering About,'" 184.

111. Cf. Ps. 102:6–7 (7–8); see 34–35 above.

112. Cf. Pss. 22:6–7 (7–8), 14–15 (15–16); 69:20/21; 102:6/7; etc.; also Jer. 9:1; etc. On the interpretation of Ps. 55:1–5 (2–6), 6–8 (7–9), see Bail, *Gegen das Schweigen klagen*, 160ff.; Riede, *Im Netz des Jägers*, 279ff.; Hossfeld and Zenger, *Psalmen 51–100*, 93ff.

113. Cf. Lamp and Tilly, "Öffentlichkeit als Bedrohung," 54–55.

114. Hossfeld and Zenger, *Psalmen 51–100*, 98–99. On the cosmos/chaos dichotomy, see 236ff. below.

115. See 34ff. above.

116. Cf. Ps. 14:1–3.

117. In Ps. 7:9/10, the same verb גָּמַר, "to be finished, cease," is used to ask that the malice of the wicked come to an end and the righteous "prevail." The context there is the question of the justification of the righteous; see 140ff. above.

They speak idly to one another;
they speak with smooth lip and twofold heart. (v. 2/3)
Let YHWH destroy all smooth lips,
the tongue that speaks great things, (v. 3/4)
those who say, "With our tongue we are powerful;
our lips are with us—who is master over us?" (v. 4/5)

"For the rape of the weak, for the groaning of the poor,
I shall rise up," says YHWH;
"I offer safety to the one at whom they snort." (v. 5/6)
The words of YHWH are pure words,
silver refined in the earthen [clay] furnace,
purified seven times. (v. 6/7)
You, O YHWH, will guard them;
you will save each from this generation forever, (v. 7/8)
even if the wicked roam about freely,
and vileness rises up among people.[118] (v. 8/9)

The fact that the supplicant does not remain silent in the face this injustice—as the prophets had not remained silent about it—is testimony to the petitioner's dignity in the midst of all the suffering. The price for it may have been high. However, also in this case silence would be blasphemous because it only contributes to the "dissolution of the YHWH ethos passed down from ancient times, for which love for God and love for neighbor were the foundational pillars."[119]

Let us now take another look at Psalm 41 from this perspective. We saw that this text conveys a view of death as social contempt and a *via negationis*, and it projects a view of life as social connectivity.[120] According to this, an isolated person is not able to survive and therefore not alive in the full sense. There must be one—a family member, a neighbor, a friend—who accompanies the supplicant *in personal life*, who cares for that one and sees to it that the petitioner's "name" does not disappear *after that person's death*.[121] "Vigor, vitality," which Hebrew expresses with the term נֶפֶשׁ, is therefore not a matter of autonomous life-force, but a matter of constellatory integration and social recognition.[122] Let us explore the significance of the term נֶפֶשׁ for the anthropology of the Psalms in greater depth.

b. Anthropological Keyword 4: Vitality

Why do you melt away, my life,
and what do you desire against me?
(Psalm 42:5/6, 11/12; 43:5)

118. On this text see Bail, *Gegen das Schweigen klagen*, 45ff., 72–73.

119. Hossfeld and Zenger, *Psalmen 51–100*, 94; cf. also Lamp and Tilly, "Öffentlichkeit als Bedrohung," 55ff.

120. On the concept of "connectivity," see "Excursus 5: Connective Justice," 132 above.

121. On the significance of the "name," see 175 above.

122. On the concept of the human person as constellatory, see 42–43 above.

God, you are my God, I seek you,
my life has thirsted for you;
my flesh longs for you,
in a dry land without water.
(Psalm 63:1/2)

Resources

Albertz, "Mensch"; Baldermann, "Psalmen"; Barr, *Garden of Eden*, 36–47; T. Bonhoeffer, *Ursprung und Wesen*, 7–21; Bratsiotis, "בָּשָׂר," 859–60; Dockner, *Psalm 42 und 43*, 176–77, 179–82; Ebach, *Streiten mit Gott*, 1:34–35, 80–81; Gzella, *Lebenszeit und Ewigkeit*, 96–111; Haag, "Seele und Unsterblichkeit"; Haag, "Seele IV"; Hennig, "Wie . . . Seelsorge?" 182–85; Johnson, *Vitality of the Individual*, 3–22; von Rad, *Theologie*, 2:291–94; Kraus, *Psalmen*, 3:181; Krieg, "*Leiblichkeit*," 12–13; Lauha, *Psychophysischer Sprachgebrauch*, 50–57; Liess, *Der Weg des Lebens*, 135–36; Michel, "*Næpæš* [*Nepeš*] als Leichnam"; Rendtorff, "Die sündige *Næfæš* [*Nepeš*]"; W. Schmidt, "Anthropologische Begriffe," 80–84; Schöpflin, "Seele II"; S. Schroer and Staubli, *Körpersymbolik der Bibel*, 61–73; Seebass, "נֶפֶשׁ"; Talmon, "Wertung von 'Leben'"; Di Vito, "Old Testament Anthropology," 225–30; Werner, "Leben I," 595–96; Westermann, "נֶפֶשׁ"; H. W. Wolff, *Anthropology*, 10–25; Ziemer, *Seelsorgelehre*, 41–49; Zimmer, *Zwischen Tod und Lebensglück*, 9–13.

In most discussions about Old Testament anthropology, the term נֶפֶשׁ occupies a significant amount of space. This is true also for H. W. Wolff, who attempts to find a more appropriate interpretation to replace the dichotomy of body and soul, or rather the trichotomy of body, soul, and spirit, familiar to us due to the influence of Greek thought. This is already evident in the heading of the relevant chapter "*nepeš*—Needy Man."[123] Wolff does not develop the meaning of נֶפֶשׁ on the basis of a dynamistic theory of the soul as (e.g.) Pedersen does,[124] in the sense of a psychological monism, but rather on the basis of a semantic analysis of the linguistic contexts that constitute the web of signification between vegetative, emotional, and cognitive functions. The meaning of the term, according to H. W. Wolff, can be divided into seven different aspects:[125] (1) throat, (2) neck, (3) desire, (4) soul, (5) life, (6) person, (7) pronouns.

123. H. W. Wolff, *Anthropology*, 10ff.

124. Cf. 9 above.

125. Westermann, "נֶפֶשׁ," proposes a similar structure, albeit with an interesting nuance: (1) basic meaning of breath, breathing; throat, gullet; (2) craving, desire; (3) soul; (4) life; (5) living being, human being; and (6) corpse. On the term "נֶפֶשׁ," see also Strola, *Il desiderio di Dio*, 89ff.; M. Rösel, "Hebräische Mensch," 237ff., 245ff.; Kühn, *Totengedenken*, 128ff.; T. Krüger, "Der Verlust der Seele"; and Wagner, "Körperbegriffe." The polemic of Loretz, "'Seele, Totenseele' in ugaritisch-biblischer Sicht," is not congruent with the content of Gen. 2:7; 35:18; etc.; see Janowski, "Anerkennung"; and for a more detailed discussion, idem, "Die lebendige *næpæš* [*nepeš*]." Furthermore, Loretz fails to consider the semantic development of ψυχή from Homer to Plotinus; see Vernant, "Individuum, Tod, Liebe"; Burkert, "Mikroskopie der Geistesgeschichte"; Meyer, "Der Wandel des Psyche-Begriffs"; Szlezák, "Psyche: Ihr Ort im Menschen"; Halfwassen, "Die Seele und ihr Verhältnis"; Bremmer, "Die Karriere der Seele"; M. Rösel, "Geburt der Seele"; idem, "Kehle zur Seele"; Jüttemann, Sonntag, and Wulf, *Die Seele*.

As the discussion responding to H. W. Wolff[126] has shown, the term has initially had an *organic focal point*, which is constitutive for each individual facet of meaning:

Initially נֶפֶשׁ signified the "throat" or "gullet" (Isa. 5:14; Ps. 107:5, 9; Prov. 25:25; etc.) and their function: breathing (aspect 1), but not the "neck" (צַוָּר).[127] The meaning "breath" (Job 41:21/13) is based on the fact that the movements of the throat are connected to breathing (cf. the triple appearance of the verb נפשׁ Niphal, "breathe, be refreshed," in Exod. 23:12; 31:17; and 2 Sam. 16:14)[128] and that human beings stop breathing at the moment of death. This function of the body is related to the semantic aspect "desire" (aspect 2), which is expressed through hunger (Hos. 9:4), desire (Exod. 15:9), wish/longing (Ps. 35:25) and which is characteristic of a certain intentionality. In place of the traditional but misleading translation of נֶפֶשׁ as "soul,"[129] Seebass has rightly argued that the term refers to "vitality, effervescent life energy, passion" (aspect 3).[130]

Often נֶפֶשׁ and "animation, vitality" are synonymous: the term נֶפֶשׁ describes the "vital self" and can therefore also assume the function of a reflexive pronoun. In the sense of "individual life-force" or "individual life" (aspect 4), נֶפֶשׁ does not mean life in general, but rather the life residing in individual creatures (animal or human; Gen. 9:10; 19:17; Exod. 21:23; Lev. 24:18; Deut. 19:21; etc.). This sense gives rise to the meaning "living individual, individual creature, person" (aspect 5), which is found in casuistic laws or sacrificial regulations as a general designation of the offender or participant (Lev. 2:1; 4:2; 5:1; etc.), as well as in person narratives (Josh. 10:28, 30, 32; etc.) and finally in the identification of family members (Gen. 36:6) or dependents (Gen. 12:5). Finally, נֶפֶשׁ is also applied to (**6**) God (Isa. 42:1; Jer. 51:14; Amos 6:8; etc.)

From the broad semantic field of the term, two aspects that are particularly relevant for our purposes shall be highlighted below: the aspect of "animation, vitality" and the unique view of the "*nepeš* of the dead."

α. *The Living Nepeš*

According to the nonpriestly creation account in Genesis 2:4b–25, the first created human being did not receive a "living soul" through the breath of life blown into the human by God but *became* a נֶפֶשׁ חַיָּה, a creature characterized by "animation, vitality:

Then God formed [יָצַר] the human being [אָדָם]
from a clump of soil [עָפָר] of the earth [אֲדָמָה]
and blew in the [human's] nose [= in both the nostrils] breath of life [נִשְׁמַת חַיִּים];
and the human became a living being [נֶפֶשׁ חַיָּה].

(Gen. 2:7)[131]

126. See esp. Westermann, "נֶפֶשׁ"; Seebass, "נֶפֶשׁ"; Albertz, "Mensch," 466; Kaiser, *Gott des Alten Testaments*, 2:291ff.

127. Cf. Seebass, "נֶפֶשׁ," 538–39.

128. See ibid., "נֶפֶשׁ," 538; Westermann, "נֶפֶשׁ," 73–74.

129. See Seebass, 543ff.; also H. W. Wolff, *Anthropology*, 17; Westermann, "נֶפֶשׁ," 79ff., 84; Di Vito, "Old Testament Anthropology," 229; Schöpflin, "Seele II," 737–38.

130. Seebass, "נֶפֶשׁ," 545.

131. On this text, see Kaiser, *Gott des Alten Testaments*, 2:291–92; Seebass, *Genesis*, 1:106–7; Witte, *Die biblische Urgeschichte*, 158; Di Vito, "Old Testament Anthropology," 225–26; Schöpflin, "Seele II," 738.

This anthropological key verse of the nonpriestly creation account consists of two clauses, both of which describe an action by YHWH: YHWH "formed" the human being from a clump of soil of the earth (human being's tie to the earth) and "blew" breath of life into the human's nose (human being's dependence on the Creator); a following description states that the human creature does not *have* a vital self but rather *is* this vital self.[132] According to the perspective of Genesis 2:7—as well as 2:19, saying that the animals of the field are also "living beings"[133]—נֶפֶשׁ in the sense of "life, vitality" signifies an intentionality that is expressed in the dependence of all creatures on God through their createdness:

> They all [animals and human beings] look to you [God],
> for you give them their food in due season:
> (Ps. 104:27)
> When you give it to them, they gather;
> when you open your hand, they are filled with good things. (v. 28)
>
> If you hide [סתר Hiphil] your face, they are frightened [בהל Niphal];
> if you take away their life-force, they die and return to the dust; (v. 29)
> if you send out your life-force, they are created,
> and you renew the face of the earth. (v. 30)[134]

There also are numerous other attestations in other contexts within the Old Testament for the meaning of נֶפֶשׁ as "vitality, vital self," as in Abram's instruction to Sarai in Genesis 12:13:

> Say that you are my sister,
> so that I will fare well because of you,
> and my *nepeš* remains alive because of you.

In Genesis 19:19–20 Lot says to YHWH:

> Your servant has indeed found favor in your eyes,
> for the kindness you have shown me to keep my *nepeš* alive [חיה Hiphil] was great.
> As for me, I am not able to escape to the hills,
> lest misfortune would cling to me and I would die. (v. 19)
> See, this city [over there] is near enough to flee to,
> and it is only a small matter.
> Let me escape there. Is it not only a small matter?
> But my *nepeš* would remain alive [חיה]! (v. 20)

Constitutive for the term נֶפֶשׁ in both passages is the meaning "life" in the sense of life-force or preservation of life. Conversely, the terms "death" (מָוֶת)[135] and "underworld" (שְׁאוֹל) can be antonyms of נֶפֶשׁ, as in Psalm 16:9–10:

132. Cf. H. W. Wolff, *Anthropology*, 10–11. On the concept of "life" in the Old Testament, see Leuenberger, "Deine Gnade"; Utzschneider, "Verständnis des Lebens"; K. Schmid, "Fülle des Lebens?" See further the notes in chap. 2, under "The Anthropology of Lament and Thanksgiving."

133. Cf. Gen. 1:20, 24, 30; 9:10, 12, 15–16; etc.

134. On this text see 65–66 above.

135. Num. 23:10; Judg. 16:30; et al.; see H. W. Wolff, *Anthropology*, 23–24.

Therefore my heart [לֵב] is glad and my honor [כָּבוֹד] rejoices;
even my flesh [בָּשָׂר] dwells securely.
Indeed, you will not abandon me/my life [נֶפֶשׁ[to the underworld;
you do not allow your faithful one to see the Pit.[136]

According to H. W. Wolff's analysis, the *nepeš* is precisely the subject of the Psalms of Lament.[137] As "vital self," it is not only the organ of empathy (Job 30:25), passion (Ps. 103:1–2; Prov. 19:2), and joy (Isa. 61:10; Sir. 51:29), but also the subject of grief, sorrow, despondency, and tribulation:

- The *nepeš* is paralyzed by terror (Ps. 6:3/4).
- It melts away and is in turmoil (Pss. 42:11/12; 43:5).
- It feels weak and despondent (Jonah 2:7/8).
- It is exhausted and defenseless (Jer. 4:31).
- It suffers from oppression (Ps. 31:13/14; cf. Gen. 42:21) and tribulation (Isa. 53:11).
- It is bitter (Judg. 18:25; 1 Sam. 1:10; 22:2; 2 Sam. 17:8; Isa. 38:15; Job 3:20; 7:11; etc.).[138]

According to Psalm 88:3/4, the *nepeš* is so "full" of troubles that the supplicant's life "touches" the underworld:

For my *nepeš* is full of troubles,
and my life [חַיִּים] has touched the underworld.[139]

The supplicant is not "full" as the result of a fulfilled life[140] or a special communion with God,[141] but from the troubles that have come upon oneself from YHWH.[142] This usage also provides the background to understand the idiom of "pouring out" (שָׁפַךְ) of the *nepeš*.[143]

Particularly instructive is Psalm 42–43, where *nepeš* assumes the position of a key anthropological concept[144] and the supplicant faces self as one's own *nepeš*. The first stanza of this lament begins with an animal simile, which emphasizes the existential torment with a double reference to "thirst of life" // the supplicant's longing for God (42:1–2 [2–3]):

136. On this text see 301ff. below.

137. H. W. Wolff, *Anthropology*, 17–18.

138. See Westermann, "נֶפֶשׁ," 79–81; and Di Vito, "Old Testament Anthropology," 228–29.

139. On this text see 223ff. below.

140. Cf. Gen. 25:8; 35:29; 1 Chr. 23:1; etc.; see 46 above.

141. Cf. Pss. 16:11; 17:15; 63:5/6; etc.

142. Cf. Ps. 123:3–4, which describes the people of God—or rather their *nepeš*—as full from the derision and contempt of the haughty.

143. Ps. 42:4/5; cf. 1 Sam. 1:15 and Job 30:16; see also Pss. 102:title/1 ("Prayer of one afflicted, who pours out his grief [שִׂיחַ] before YHWH") and 142:2/3 ("Before him I pour out my grief [שִׂיחַ]; my affliction [צָרָה] I make known before him"). "Poured out" before God is also the heart (as an expression of lament: Lam. 2:19; Ps. 62:8/9) and the liver (as an expression of pain: Lam. 2:11); see Liwak, "שָׁפַךְ," 434–35.

144. In Pss. 42–43 נֶפֶשׁ is the second most common lexeme after the references to God (YHWH, 1x; El, 4x; Elohim, 17x = 22, or the total number of letters in the Hebrew alphabet); cf. Dockner, *Psalm 42 und 43*, 145.

As the deer cries over [dried-up] riverbeds,
so **my life** cries for you, O God.
(Ps. 42:1/2)
My life thirsts for God, the living God:
when shall I come and behold the face of God? (v. 2/3)
My tears have become my bread by day and by night,
while they say to me all day long:
"Where is your God?" (v. 3/4)
These things[145] I remember
and pour out **my life** within me,
that I would go to the house of the Lord [in the company of nobles],
with the voice of praise and thanksgiving of a celebrating crowd. (v. 4/5)
Why do you melt [pass] away, **my life**,
and who do you desire against me?
Wait for God,
for I will yet thank [God]
for the salvation of my face. (v. 5/6)[146]

The supplicant, YHWH, and the supplicant's *nepeš* are the main characters of this text. Even the deer (v. 1/2a) is connected to the supplicant's *nepeš* through a simile and thus reinforces the introductory function of this character. The supplicant's affliction, expressed in the question regarding God's presence, is constituted by YHWH's absence. It is God, the living God, whose face the *nepeš* desires to "see" again,[147] for whom the dried-up *nepeš* thirsts. This question regarding God's presence is posed by the supplicant's social surroundings (v. 3/4b) and represents a sharp contrast to the memory of very different times, when the supplicant experienced the nearness of God in the company of temple pilgrims (v. 4/5). This contrast calls attention to the current distress and causes the supplicant to "pour out" personal life,[148] to express grief to self over the current situation:

These things I remember
and pour out **my life** within me,
that I would go to the house of the Lord [in the company of nobles],
with the voice of praise and thanksgiving of a celebrating crowd. (v. 4/5)

With a most extreme emotional outburst, the lamenting *nepeš* then launches into the supplicant and assails that person (v. 5/6a), who then points to the living God (v. 5/6b):

Why do you melt [pass] away, **my life**,
and who do you desire against me?

145. "These [things]," אֵלֶּה, is a cataphoric reference here, directing the attention to the consecutive clause introduced by כִּי.

146. On the textual problems of this text, see Hossfeld and Zenger, *Die Psalmen*, 1:268; and esp. Dockner, *Psalm 42 und 43*, 159ff.

147. On the expression of "seeing" the face of YHWH, see 90ff. above.

148. The idiom can also be compared to Hannah's reply to Eli in 1 Sam. 1:15: "No, my lord, for I am only a troubled woman. I have drunk neither wine nor strong drink, but I have poured out my heart before YHWH." See also the remark in Lam. 2:12, "Children cried out their *nepeš* in their mother's bosom," and the interpretation by Seebass ("נֶפֶשׁ," 544) that "the life-force could turn over its burden of grief and affliction to YHWH."

Wait for God,
  for I will yet thank [God],
  for the salvation of his face.

Two interpretative trajectories of this text shall be briefly noted—its use in Christian iconography and in Christian pastoral theology.

Christian Iconography

In medieval Christian art, the *motif of the lamenting soul* is frequently expressed. A prominent example is an illustration from the Stuttgart Psalter (Saint-Germain des Près, first half of the 9th c.; see fig. 24), which provides an iconigraphic commentary to the refrain of Psalms 42:5/6, 11/12; 43:5 ("quare tristis es anima mea et quare conturbas me spera in Deum quoniam adhuc confitebor illi salutare vultus mei et Deus meus" [Vulgate]):

> The singer, playing a psaltery, is situated in the left margin. The painter has expressed his inner turmoil perceptively and powerfully by depicting him as looking away to the side. This is all the more striking since it implies that the "soul," which the psalmist addresses, is located outside the field of vision: its personification—identified through inscription as ANIMA—sits on a hill that rises up steeply over lush flowers and in front of a tree.[149]

Figure 24. Stuttgart Psalter (early 9th c. CE)

149. Zenger and Wetzel, *Die Psalmen: Mit Meisterwerken*, 60.

Christian Pastoral Theology

On the basis of the refrain Psalms 42:5/6, 11/12; 43:5, the difference between biblical and Greek *conceptions of pastoral theology* becomes evident. Thus Socrates in Plato's *Apology* turns to his fellow citizens, who are concerned about property, glory, and honor, but not about their own souls:

> "Most excellent man, are you who are a citizen of Athens, the greatest of cities and the most famous for wisdom and power, not ashamed to care for the acquisition of wealth and for reputation and honor, when you neither care nor take thought for wisdom and truth and the perfection of your soul?" (*Apology* 29DE, trans. H. N. Fowler, in LCL)

And a few lines further down:

> "For I go about doing nothing else than urging you, young and old, not to care for your persons or your property more than for the perfection of your souls, or even so much; and I tell you that virtue does not come from money, but from virtue comes money and all other good things to [humans], both to the individual and to the state."

Here we see the contrast between "care for the body" and "care for the soul," which has always been connected to dichotomous anthropology in the philosophical tradition, with its understanding of "pastoral care" [German *Seelsorge* = care for the soul] as care for one's own self.[150]

In contrast, the *nepeš* in Psalms 42:5/6, 11/12; 43:5 is asked to wait for (יחל Hiphil) God, who will take it under divine saving care. This human groundedness in trust in God, which has nothing to do with consoling through deferment, but rather with a "serene waiting,"[151] is a basic characteristic of Old Testament anthropology as well as an appropriate starting point for Christian pastoral theology. For "God's loving nature and benevolent acts—this is the care of the soul before all pastoral care."[152] It is grounded in the relationship to God, who is benevolently inclined toward the human being[153] and to whom the *nepeš* cries out, complains, and appeals, but whom the *nepeš* also praises and thanks.[154] This is a connecting point for Christian poimenics (shepherding), to let itself be guided by the *honesty* but also the *confidence* of the Psalms of Lament and Thanksgiving.

For the term נֶפֶשׁ, it is characteristic that the memory of the body part "throat, gullet"[155] and its specific function of "desire" is preserved in the psalms cited here. The supplicant of Psalm 88 is "full" of troubles (v. 3/4), and since troubles deplete rather than satisfy a person, therefore the supplicant desires God, the

150. See T. Bonhoeffer, *Ursprung und Wesen*, 8–9.
151. Cf. Hossfeld and Zenger, *Die Psalmen*, 1:269.
152. Ziemer, *Seelsorgelehre*, 42; cf. idem, "Schreie aus der Not"; Baldermann, "Psalmen," 28ff.; Bukowski, *Die Bibel ins Gespräch bringen*; Karle, "Chancen der Seelsorge"; and Gerhard Hennig, "Wie . . . Seelsorge?"
153. Cf. Hennig, "Wie . . . Seelsorge?," 184.
154. Cf. Pss. 103:2, 22; 104:1, 35; etc.
155. Cf. Ps. 107:5, 9; etc.

source of life. Psalm 84[156] speaks of this source of life in its admiring praise of the temple[157] and the God who is present there:

How lovely are your dwellings,
YHWH Sabaoth!
(Ps. 84:1/2)
My life [*nepeš*] has longed, indeed, has been consumed
by longing for the courts of YHWH;
my heart and my flesh sing for joy,
to the living God. (v. 2/3)
Even the sparrow has found a home,
and the swallow has its own nest,
where she has laid her young,
[near] your altars, YHWH Sabaoth,
my king and my God. (v. 3/4)
Blessed are those who dwell in your house,
praising you always. *Selah.* (v. 4/5)[158]

The supplicant's goal in life is the experience of God's presence in the sanctuary, while longing with "body and soul" (cf. v. 2/3!) for the courts of YHWH and the living God. Psalm 63:1/2 expresses this longing for God through images of the *nepeš* as "thirsting" (צָמֵא)[159] for God, a thirst that can only be quenched by God himself:

God, you are my God, I seek you,
my life has thirsted for you;
my flesh longs for you
in a dry land without water.
(Ps. 63:1/2)
So I have looked for you in your sanctuary,
to see your power and your glory. (v. 2/3)
Your goodness is better than life,
(therefore) my lips shall praise you. (v. 3/4)
So I praise all my life;
in your name I lift up my hands. (v. 4/5)

The theology of the temple is of direct anthropological relevance, as this text shows. The fact that it is the temple, for whose God the supplicant's *nepeš* longs, is based on the cosmological function of this place, together with the efficacy of the God of life and salvation present there.[160] With God originates the "goodness" that is better than "life," as the text paradoxically states (v. 3/4a).

156. Within the context of the Psalms of Korah (Pss. 84–85; 87–88), Pss. 84 and 88 form "a contrasting correlation in which Ps. 84 depicts a 'soul' as wandering 'from strength to strength' [v. 7/8], while Ps. 88 depicts a 'soul' that says of itself that it has become a [person] in whom no strength is left [v. 4/5]" (Zenger, "Das Mythische," 247–48); cf. Jerome, *Desire for God's House*, 91ff.; and see 221 below.

157. In its form, Ps. 84:1/2 can be compared to the admiring praise of Ps. 104:24: "How numerous are your works, YHWH; in wisdom you have made them all; the earth is full of your creatures!"

158. Space does not permit us to address the text-critical and philological problems of this text. I consider v. 3/4abc as part of the original text, *pace* Hossfeld and Zenger, *Psalmen 51–100*, 5–7ff., 512ff.

159. See Ruppert, "Dürsten nach Gott."

160. See Zenger, "'Ich liebe den Ort,'" 180ff., 185ff.; on 186–87 Zenger rightly points to the textual-structuring function of the term *nepeš*.

Through meditation and recitation of this text, the distressed supplicant "lives" in the presence of the life-giving God of the temple.[161]

β. The Nepeš of the Dead

On the basis of the meaning "person, individual," H. W. Wolff[162] and C. Westermann[163] have suggested that נֶפֶשׁ can also mean "corpse." This would, however, be strange if the element of vitality is constitutive for the term נֶפֶשׁ. Recently D. Michel[164] has explored this problem again and has proposed a different solution. Like H. W. Wolff, Michel begins with Numbers 6:6,[165] where the expression נֶפֶשׁ מֵת (*nepeš* of a dead person) is used in the context of laws pertaining to Nazirites:

> For the whole time of his [the Nazirite's] devotion to YHWH,
> he shall not go near the *nepeš* of a dead person.

In contrast to H. W. Wolff, D. Michel does not interpret this expression as "dead life = corpse," but—because נֶפֶשׁ is feminine—as "*nepeš* of a dead person."

This conclusion is supported by the other occurrences of נֶפֶשׁ with the assumed meaning of "corpse."[166] All these occurrences pertain to cultic legislation, with the exception of Leviticus 19:28:

> You shall not cut yourselves in your skin for a spirit of the dead [לָנֶפֶשׁ].

The circumstances are always defilement through the *nepeš* of a dead person. How did this idea come about? Within the context of directions for the preparation and use of a purifying water, Numbers 19:14–15 states:

> This is the law: When someone dies in a tent,
> everyone who enters the tent and everyone who is in the tent
> shall be unclean for seven days;
> (Num. 19:14)
> And every open vessel, which is not covered by a tied-down lid,
> shall be unclean. (v. 15)

Instructive for understanding the expression "life (force) of a dead person" is the regulation regarding the impurity of every vessel that is not covered by a tied-down lid. According to D. Michel's interpretation of the passage, "it could result from the idea of something movable detaching itself from the corpse and attempting to slip into a vessel. . . . One could imagine that after the death the *næpæš* [*nepeš*] is looking for a new body and is trying to slip into it—even if it is 'only' an open vessel."[167]

161. Cf. ibid., 203. On Old Testament metaphor for life, see 305ff. below.
162. H. W. Wolff, *Anthropology*, 22.
163. Westermann, "נֶפֶשׁ," 90–91.
164. Michel, "*Næpæš* [*Nepeš*] als Leichnam," 81ff.
165. Cf. also Lev. 21:11: "[The exalted priest] shall not go near a corpse[כָּל־נַפְשֹׁת מֵת]; even for father or mother he shall not incur impurity."
166. Lev. 19:28; 21:1; 22:4; Num. 5:2; 6:11; 9:6, 7, 10; 19:11, 13; Hag. 2:13.
167. Michel, "*Næpæš* [*Nepeš*] als Leichnam," 83.

This demonstrates that the assumption of the meaning "corpse" for the term נֶפֶשׁ is unnecessary. All passages in question are better explained by the assumption that we are dealing with the life-force that escapes at the moment of death and "aspires to find a new dwelling place before descending into Sheol."[168] This is also the reason why the *nepeš* of a dead person is defiling.

If a human being dies, the *nepeš* leaves the body according to the Old Testament understanding. Yet it does not return to God, but "having become powerless without the breath of life, it sinks back into the earth, and that means into the underworld."[169] For a religion that assumes—like the YHWH religion—the primacy of life and the God of life, this closeness of death to the underworld and distance from God is an enormous theological challenge. How could it be overcome? As we shall see in the case of Psalm 88,[170] the individual Psalms of Lament and Thanksgiving have faced this challenge and have thereby gained new impulses for the biblical understanding of life and death.

168. Ibid., 84.
169. Kaiser, *Gott des Alten Testaments*, 2:294.
170. See 218ff. below.

Interlude
The Gate to the Abyss

I am prepared,
I am not here,
I am in the abyss,
am far away . . .
I am so far away . . .
I glow among the dead.
Paul Klee, *Gedichte,* 86

In Martin Luther's sermons after January 10, 1524, we find repeated allusions to Psalm 130, which, in his famous arrangement "Out of the Depths I Cry to Thee," became a creedal hymn of the Reformation.[1] The hymn *De profundis* unites, however, not only the basic tenets of Reformation theology like no other hymn, but also gives expression to the human situation before God with an openness and immediacy, which Luther viewed as a basic characteristic of the Psalms:[2]

Out of the depths I cry to you:
O Father, hear me calling.
Incline your ear to my distress,
In spite of my rebelling.
Do not regard my sinful deeds;
send me the grace my spirit needs;
without it I am nothing.

This text brings us to a crucial point in our discussion: the "abyss,"[3] from which no salvation and no way "up" seems to exist. This low point of human existence shall be interpreted by means of three excursive reflections about two pictures by Paul Klee and a poem by Paul Celan, which shed light on the theme of the "depths" of Psalm 130:1. Without attempting to be illustrations of Old Testament texts, all three artistic expressions, which can be thematically con-

1. Cf. *Evangelisches Gesangbuch* (Stuttgart: Gesangbuchverlag, 1996), 299, #1: "Aus tiefer Not schrei ich zu dir, Herr Gott, erhör mein Rufen"; see Jeremias, "Psalm 130"; Nitsche, "Die Psalmenrezeption," 141ff.; Weber, "'Wenn du Vergehen aufbewahrtest.'" On the history of reception in German literature from Luther to the present, see Kurzke, "Säkularisation oder Realisation?"; and H. Becker, "Aus tiefer Not." On Luther's translation of Ps. 130 in WA.DB 10/1:541, see Kurzke, "Säkularisation oder Realisation?," 70–71.
2. See 341ff. below.
3. The Hebrew text of Ps. 130:1 speaks of "depths" out of which the supplicant is calling out to YHWH; see 30 and 32 above.

nected to the Psalms of Lament and Thanksgiving, demonstrate in their own way how relevant their imagery is.

1. Paul Klee, *Outbreak of Fear*

Among the late works of Paul Klee we find a pen-and-ink drawing from the time of his illness in 1939 titled *Angstausbruch II* (*Outbreak of Fear II*, fig. 25), which offers a new artistic representation of the image of deformity through illness. "Fear," according to Ringleben's description of this image,

> takes the form of loss of cohesion here, of designed decay. The idea that cohesion—lost as a result of disintegration through fear—is still present in some way, precisely as the formal framework of the fearful experience of its loss, is evoked in three ways:

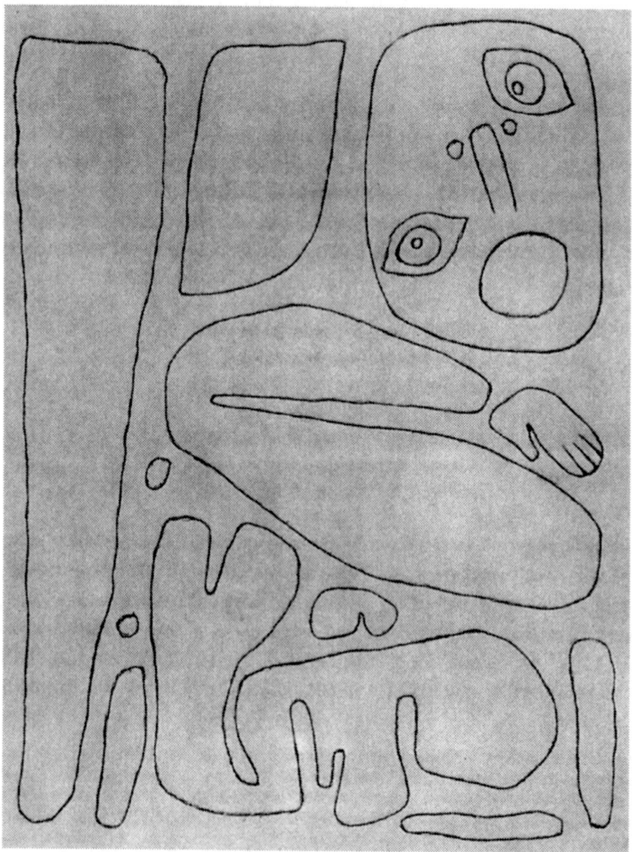

Figure 25. Paul Klee, *Outbreak of Fear II* (1939)

1. The implied border surrounding the partial fragments, which are ordered in such a way as to imitate visually the external border of the paper: they constitute an approximate rectangle.
2. Through the formal correlation of lines outlining the individual fragments.
3. Finally, through the representational traces of a fearfully distorted face in the upper right corner and below it a hand, which can be connected to an arm. Klee represents *linear* fear as the precipitous slope toward disintegration into insular fragments and as the desperate struggle against the dissolution of unity, even amid the breakdown. With its wide-open eyes and mouth, the face, in an eccentric position, seems to stare despairingly as the disconnected body parts slip away. In all its fragmentation, the self is bound up in the confinement of an invisible cohesion, and it is precisely this contrast between chaos and confinement that paralyzes in this outbreak of fear.[4]

Fear is a phenomenon that takes possession of the body and is itself physical. This is attested by a wide array of imagery; for example, when we speak of

> fear as causing our heart to beat faster or even to skip a beat. Knees become wobbly, and we are unable to walk. The pulse begins to race, hair stands on edge, a chill comes over us and runs down our back while we break out in sweat at the same time, stop breathing, or begin to pant. We fight a choking feeling in our throat, which threatens to separate head and body. The eyes are wide open, and the pupils are dilated in terror; our limbs tremble and tense up spasmodically.[5]

The fears we experience have an immediate physical presence but at the same time are culturally mediated.

In the Psalms of the Individual, the supplicant's fear is also described as physical deformity, which escalates to a dissolution of the person. The *semantics of dissolving, melting away, breaking apart* on the one hand, and of *drying up, wilting, and withering* on the other,[6] is typical for fear imagery in biblical and postbiblical Psalms of the Individual. The metaphors used here are semantic signs, which establish a correlation between the human body and natural elements—like water ("being poured out") or dust ("dried up").[7] The biblical locus classicus for this is the self-complaint of Psalm 22:14–15 (15–16), which expresses the supplicant's despair in imagery of a "melting heart" and of "loosening of limbs":

> Like water I am poured out,
> and my limbs are out of joint;
> my heart has become like wax,
> melted within my bowels.
> (Ps. 22:14/15)

4. Ringleben, *Dornenkrone und Purpurmantel*, 56, emphasis original.
5. H. Böhme, "Codierungen der Angst," 218.
6. See Gerleman, "Der Sinnbereich," 405ff.; Fabry, "מַיִם," 857; Ringgren, "מָסַס," 1016–17; Bail, *Gegen das Schweigen klagen*, 118ff., 121ff.; and Gillmayr-Bucher, *Die Psalmen im Spiegel*, 228ff. A particularly characteristic image of fear is the "melting of the heart" (מָסַס + לֵב); Ps. 22:14/15; cf. Deut. 1:28; Josh. 2:11; 5:1; 7:5; 2 Sam. 17:10; Isa. 13:7; 19:1; Ezek. 21:7/12, 15/20; Nah. 2:10/11), which is not so much expressive of fear as of being disheartened.
7. These appear to be culturally universal; see G. Böhme, "Kulturgeschichte des Wassers," 20ff.

Dried up like a potsherd is my [life-]force,
  and my tongue cleaves to the roof of my mouth;
  you have laid me down in the dust of death. (v. 15/16)

But I—trembling and shaking have taken hold of me;
  all my bones are breaking apart.
My heart is melting like wax before fire,
  and my knees give way like water spilled on a slope.
(*Hodayot*, 1QH 12 [*olim* 4]. 33)[8]

The language of "drying up," which is dominant in Psalm 22:15/16, and its imagery of "dried-up [life-]force" and the "parched tongue"—these are also found in several other places:

As the deer cries over [dried-up] riverbeds,
  so my life cries out for you, O God.
My life thirsts for God, the living God:
  when shall I come and behold the face of God?
(Ps. 42:1–2 [2–3])[9]

God, you are my God, I seek you,
  my life has thirsted for you,
my flesh longs for you
  in a dry land without water.
(Ps. 63:1/2)[10]

I am weary of crying out;
  my throat is parched,
my eyes have grown dim,
  as I wait for my God.
(Ps. 69:3/4)

The effect of the Klee drawing, as of the Psalm texts cited here, is the emergence of a particular view of the human being through the use of body imagery. Both the artist Paul Klee and the composer of the Psalms make use of images as soon as they begin talking about the human body, its pains and fears. One may see this as outdated and obsolete—not "obsolete" in the sense that we no longer need such imagery, but rather in the sense that it may have no future. Already "the temptation arises," as the art historian Belting speculates, "to breed a new type of human being, which means not only to raise a new human being, but also to invent a different body. This temptation is in itself expressive of the fact that we have disconnected the body from the traditional image of the human being."[11] The loss resulting from this "disconnection" is immeasurable.

8. Cf. the related passages 1QH 10 (*olim* 2). 28; 16 (*olim* 8). 31ff.; etc.; for an interpretation of these texts, see Gerleman, "Der Sinnbereich," 406–7; and Lichtenberger, *Menschenbild*, 59ff., 65ff.
9. On the text of Ps. 42:2/3, see 92 above.
10. Cf. Ps. 143:6: "I stretch out my hands to you; my life [thirsts] for you like parched land."
11. Belting, "Körperbild als Menschenbild," 87.

2. Paul Celan, "Psalm"

The second example for our interlude reflections comes from twentieth-century poetry. In extreme situations modern poetry asks about God precisely in places where such questions are deliberately omitted. Such inquiry bordering on the ineffable is naturally related to silence. It operates within the paradox of applying words to something that defies linguistic specification—as Paul Celan's poem "Psalm" with its "disturbing imagery."[12]

"Psalm"

No one kneads us again out of earth and clay,
no one incants our dust.
  No One.
Blessed art thou, No One.
In thy sight would
we bloom.
In thy
spite.

A Nothing
we were, are now, and ever
shall be, blooming:
the Nothing—the
No-One's-Rose.

With
our pistil soul-bright,
our stamen heaven-waste,
our corona red
from the purple word we sang
over, O over
the thorn.[13]

It is the dead who speak here, the collective "we" of the murdered Jewish people, who are written into the biblical history of suffering of the King of the Jews—for the "corona red over the thorn" points to Jesus' crown of thorns. They plead for their life, in other words, a new creation: No one will create them again. Is this "blasphemy" or "devout song"? From the nothing we were grows—blessed be *No One—the Nothing, the No-One's-Rose,* which Celan used as the title for his collection of poems. By lamenting Israel's collective fate (stanza 1), he follows

> the tradition of the Psalter, but he does so not without a shift in emphasis: the countenance of the one to whom his hymnic invocation is addressed (stanza 2) is radically removed. Whether the unexpressed name refers to the inexpressibility of that One's nature, or whether this "name" *No one* is a deliberative expression of doubts concerning his existence remains open. . . . Celan's

12. Emmerich, *Paul Celan*, 42. On Celan's poem "Psalm," see also Hörisch, "Die Poesie der Medien"; H.-P. Müller, "Rückzug Gottes ins Namenlose"; Tück, *Gelobt seist Du, Niemand*, 69ff.; Lescow, *Das hadernde Wort*, 61ff.

13. Felstiner, *Paul Celan: Poet, Survivor, Jew*, 167–69.

> *Psalm* is testimony to a struggle that does not seem to push beyond the paradoxical coexistence of belief and doubt. Nevertheless, he holds on to the act of appeal, as if a new encounter with the wholly Other can occur through the night of uncertainty.[14]

Celan's *Psalm* is a paradoxical text, an impossible Psalm, so to speak, because it lets the dead speak and praise—"Blessed art thou, No One"—the dead, who are specifically unable to praise, according to the Old Testament understanding of God:

> For in death there is no remembrance of you;
> who shall praise you in Sheol?
> (Ps. 6:5/6)
>
> What gain is there in my blood,
> if I should go down to the Pit?
> Does the dust praise you?
> Does it proclaim your faithfulness?
> (Ps. 30:9/10)
>
> Should you work wonders for the dead,
> or shall the spirits of the dead rise up to praise you?
> (Ps. 88:10/11)
>
> It is not the dead who praise Yah,
> not those who descend into silence.
> We, we praise Yah,
> from now to eternity: Hallelujah!
> (Ps. 115:17–18)[15]

Celan's "Psalm" is a paradoxical text also because by playing discretely with the vowel "o," it expresses precisely what cannot be said anymore, according to Celan: "God." Furthermore, he speaks the language of the biblical Psalms: based in suffering and to be read with the memory of the unnamed places where millions of the chosen people were murdered and turned to dust, to nothingness.

It is no coincidence that it was poets of Jewish provenance like Nelly Sachs and Paul Celan who resorted to the Psalms' invocations of God to give voice to the silence defying outrage over the horror of the Shoah. "The loss of biblical-religious hope and promise, like the impossibility of dialogue with God constitutive for the biblical Psalms—since God can now only be invoked through negation—is expressed in this [Celan's] psalm-poem as the attempt to invoke and preserve both [hope and promise] in the remembrance of biblical language."[16]

In his collection of "essays by a survivor" published in German under the title *Macht Gebete aus meinen Geschichten* (Turn my stories into prayers), Elie Wiesel reports that there were Jews in the concentration camps for whom

14. Tück, *Gelobt seist Du, Niemand*, 94.
15. Cf. also Isa. 38:18–19 and Sir. 17:27–28; see 246–47 below.
16. Gellner, "Moderne Psalmgedichte," 47.

prayer was a way to "sanctify" the name of God "in spite of the mass graves and to shout out our blessings in spite of the blood-red shadows darkening the horizon. 'Out of the depths we cry to you,' it says in the Psalms. Even though we are in the deepest abyss, we cry to you, yearn for you. Despite everything you have done or have allowed to be done to your people, we sing your praise. The more difficult it is, the more fervent is our song."[17]

3. Paul Klee, *The Gate to the Abyss*

Our third example, Paul Klee's picture *The Gate to the Abyss* from 1936 (fig. 26), is related in its form to the compositions of irregular, puzzle-like interlinked, angular color patches already developed in the early 1930s. In contrast to earlier works, the aspect of spatiality is however given a position of emphasis in this work, as Inge Herold explains:

> The apparent expansiveness of fields in predominantly warm, muted colors, which have received a lively structure through the varnish, is offset by the strong undertow of the black form. What results is a spatiality based on the contrast of color and black. In the nonrepresentational formation of geometric color fields, a symbolism emerges with regard to content, which also has as its central element the black area. When Klee's mother died in 1921, he created works with titles like *Gate to Hades* and *Gate to the Night*. There the gate evidently symbolizes for Klee, as it does in the work produced in 1936, a field of transition from life to death.[18]

The understanding of spatiality connected to this lament, according to which the supplicant passes through the *gate to the abyss* on his way to the underworld, is addressed more fully in the second part of this book.

Already in April of 1914, Klee made a connection in his diary between the abysmal depth and the sphere of death:

> I am prepared,
> I am not here,
> I am in the abyss,
> am far away . . .
> I am so far away . . .
> I glow among the dead.[19]

The black area in the picture from the year 1936, suggesting nontransparent depth, thus becomes a sign for endlessness and otherworldliness. "Did Klee," one may ask, "give expression to his own experience of sickness and impending closeness of death?"[20] Klee's picture *The Gate to the Abyss* also illustrates the basic theme of the Old Testament laments, as poignantly put into words by Psalm 88:3/4:

17. Wiesel, *Macht Gebete*, 41–42.
18. Inge Herold, cited in Fath, *Paul Klee—die Zeit der Reife*, 94.
19. Klee, *Tagebücher von Paul Klee*, 318; cf. idem, *Gedichte*, 86.
20. Inge Herold, cited in Fath, *Paul Klee—die Zeit der Reife*, 94.

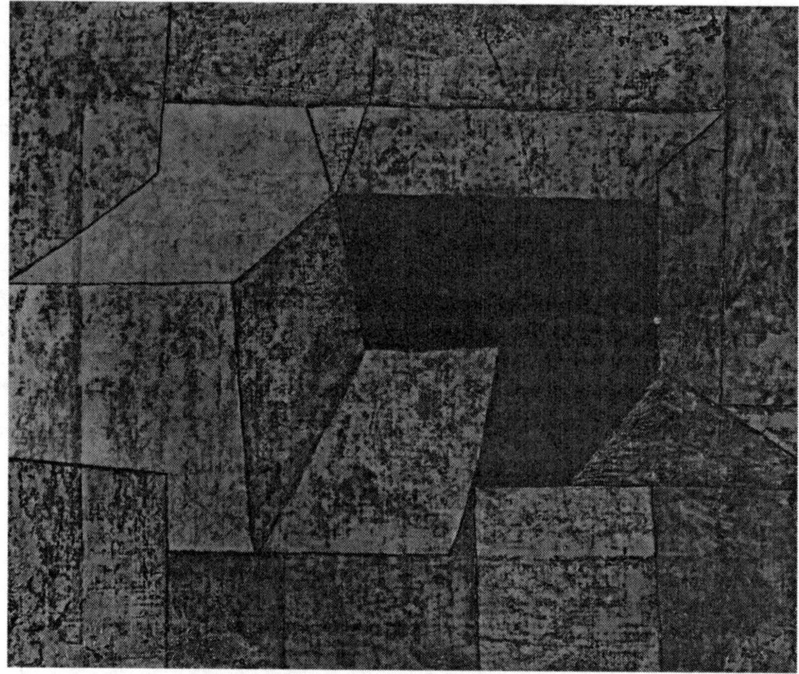

Figure 26. Paul Klee, *Gate to the Abyss* (1936)[21]

For my *nepeš* is full of troubles,
  and my life has touched the underworld.

This darkest of all Old Testament Psalms, to which we shall turn our attention next,[22] has its modern counterpart in Ingeborg Bachmann's "Psalm-Prayer" of 1956, in which, however, in contrast to Psalm 88, "God is neither counted on nor called to account. The context of prayer nevertheless remains, since it a quest for that which can no longer be experienced."[23]

But I lie alone
in the icy shack covered with wounds.
The snow has not yet
bandaged my eyes.
The dead, pressed close to me,
are silent in every tongue.
No one loves me and has
swung a lamp for me.[24]

21. For a color reproduction of this image, go to http://de.wikipedia.org/wiki/Paul_Klee and http://de.wikipedia.org/w/index.php?title=Datei:Das_Tor_zur_Tiefe,_1936.jpg&filetimestamp=20110106165447.
22. As we shall see, however, Ps. 88 is not only a "dark" text; see 218ff. below.
23. Gellner, "Moderne Psalmgedichte," 48.
24. Bachmann, *Werke*, 1:139.

Perhaps this text can, "especially in its cautious reticence, keep the lack, the absence, and the longing for God relevant, not least as a critique of overly loquacious, mollifying-defusing God-talk."[25] This is certainly true for Psalm 88.

4. Franz Schubert, "With My Hot Tears"

In addition to literature and art, music is another context in which images of death are found. One could therefore add this fourth example: "Franz Schubert, 'With My Hot Tears.'" The music of Franz Schubert (1797–1828), to which Theodor Adorno devoted a haunting essay, is full of images of death.[26] In this essay on "landscapes" in Schubert's music, Adorno speaks of its "chthonic depths," its "abysses and shafts." A good example is the discussion on the hermeneutics of death:[27]

> The hermeneutics of death, which insinuate so many of the images into Schubert's music and inflect its objective character, nevertheless do not tell us the whole story. Death—because it is the effect of sorrow about the human condition, not in our inner pain, that is modeled in Schubert's landscape—is the gateway to the underworld, into which Schubert is escorting us. . . . The wanderer follows nothing but empty words into the deep, rather than their bright illuminated intention, and even his human passion becomes a means of open-eyed descent leading not to the seat of the soul, but into the tangled web of fate.
>
> Ich will den Boden küssen
> durchdringen Eis und Schnee
> mit meinen heißen Tränen
> bis ich die Erde seh.
>
> I will kiss the ground,
> my hot tears piercing
> ice and snow,
> until I see the earth.[28]
>
> It is down there that the harmony takes us, the true measure of music's profound nature: nature is not, though, what makes sense of the profound human instinct for it, but the images of nature are allegories of the chthonic deep—allegories as useless as any words of poetry.

25. Gellner, "Moderne Psalmgedichte," 48; see also I. Mieth and D. Mieth, "'Im Eisverhau.'"
26. Adorno, "Schubert (1928)."
27. Ibid., 12. On the biographic context, see M. Korff, *Franz Schubert*, 145ff.
28. From *Winterreise*, Song no. 4, "Erstarrung," v. 2: text and translation from Youens, *Retracing a Winter's Journey*, 145.

Part 2
From Death to Life

7. "My life has touched the underworld" (Ps. 88:3/4)
The Transitory Human Being

a. The Experience of Death

What are we human beings then?
  A home for burning sorrow,
Will-o'-the-wisp of our age,
  a ball of false delight,
A theatre of bitter fear,
  its cast relentless fright,
A candle that is soon burned down,
  and snow that melts tomorrow.
    Andreas Gryphius, Sonnet 6,
      in *Gedichte*

α. The End of Life

In the history of attitudes toward death in the West,[1] there are several approaches to human mortality and the finitude of human existence. In his late essay "Über die Einsamkeit der Sterbenden in unseren Tages" (On the loneliness of dying in our age), the cultural historian N. Elias has identified these approaches as mythologization, as repression, and as realism.

> One can mythologize the end of human life, which we call death, by positing a continuation of life in Hades, in Valhalla, in hell, or in paradise. This is the oldest and most common form of human efforts to come to terms with the finitude of life. One can try to avoid the idea of death by distancing oneself as far as possible from the undesirable—concealing or repressing it, or perhaps through the firm belief in one's own personal immortality—"Others may die, but not I"—there is a strong trend toward this in today's developed societies. Finally, one can face death as a condition of one's own existence and can arrange one's life, in particular one's actions toward other human beings, according to this limited time span.[2]

1. See Ariès, *Western Attitudes toward Death*; and the literature cited in Niehr, "Aspekte des Totengedenkens," 2–3. On the sociology of death, see Feldmann and Fuchs-Heinritz, *Der Tod ist ein Problem*; on the philosophical problem of death, see Gadamer, "Die Erfahrung des Todes," 84ff.; Schulz, "Wandlungen der Einstellungen zum Tode."
2. Elias, *Uber die Einsamkeit der Sterbenden*, 7–8.

The fact that a premature isolation of the dying is especially frequent in developed societies is "one of the flaws of these societies"[3]—a flaw that apparently has its roots in the modern understanding of death.[4]

Other societies frame this question differently and as a result have developed different views of death.[5] The example we shall examine is the understanding of death in ancient Israel. Research on this subject has grown remarkably in the past two decades due to religiohistorical, epigraphic, and archaeological work on the subjects of "graves and burial," "ancestral cults and cults of the dead," and "concepts of the underworld and the afterlife" in Iron-Age Israel and Judah.[6]

The general development was thereby governed by the single fact that it took a relatively long time for ancient Israel to begin to understand death and dying as encounter with their God YHWH and as the beginning of a more intensive form of communion with God with respect to life. It seems that this change only came about in late Wisdom texts and sapiential psalms (Pss. 16; 73; etc.),[7] even if a guiding hand had long been preparing it. YHWH's distance to the realm of death was apparently connected to the fact that in ancient Syria-Palestine as well as in Israel and Judah—at least up to the Josianic era and its extension of YHWH's claim to exclusiveness for familial piety[8]—this realm was religiously organized through rites like ancestral veneration and the cult of the dead, which served to establish a relationship between the living and the dead on the social (family, clan) as well as the local (tomb, local sanctuary) level.[9] According to the official religion, there is, besides YHWH, the God of life, no second authority that possessed or could claim religious autonomy or responsibility like the ancestors.[10] In view of the first phase in the development of the Old Testament understanding of death, we have to assume this sacred dimension of death. It is preserved, for example, in the tradition of the necromancer of Endor in 1 Samuel 28:3–25,[11] albeit along with later annotations.

In most societies the death of a family member is an incisive experience for those left behind, which is overcome/negotiated with the help of mourning rites. These rites turn the *biological* event into a *social* occurrence, by responding

3. Ibid., 9.

4. On the denial of death in modernity, see Fuchs-Heinritz, *Todesbilder in der modernen Gesellschaft*; Gadamer, "Die Erfahrung des Todes," 84ff.; etc.

5. See Stephenson, *Leben und Tod*; and von Barloewen, *Der Tod in den Weltkulturen*.

6. For recent surveys, see Kaiser, "Tod, Auferstehung"; Gese, "Der Tod"; Tropper, *Nekromantie*, 340ff.; Zenger, "Israel und seine Toten"; Loretz, *Ugarit und die Bibel*, 125ff.; Blenkinsopp, "Post-mortem Existence"; Podella, "Nekromantie"; idem, "Ahnen/Ahnenverehrung III"; S. Bieberstein, "Auferstehung der Toten"; Niehr, "Aspekte des Totengedenkens"; Dietrich and Link, *Die dunklen Seiten Gottes*, 2:160ff.; Dietrich and Vollenweider, "Tod II"; Janowski, "Die Toten loben JHWH nicht," 28ff.; Veijola, "'Fluch des Totengeistes'"; etc.

7. See 313ff. below.

8. See the survey in Albertz, *Religionsgeschichte Israels*, 327ff.

9. Esp. with regard to funeral rites, see Wenning, "Grab"; idem, "Bestattungen"; Wenning and Kuhnen, "Bestattung II–III"; Dietrich and Vollenweider, "Tod II."

10. Ancestral sculptures (תְּרָפִים, as in Judg. 17:5; 1 Sam. 19:13; sometimes also אֱלֹהִים, as in Judg. 17:5; 1 Sam. 28:13; Isa. 8:19) and some of the most important instruments for the commemoration of the dead in the domestic cult; see van der Toorn and Niehr, "Totenkult im frühen Israel," 114ff.; Niehr, "Aspekte des Totengedenkens," 3–4, with cited literature. According to Niehr, "Mourning took place in the sleeping area . . . near the ancestral sculptures" (ibid., 3); cf. van der Toorn and Niehr, "Totenkult im frühen Israel," 115. However, the Individual Psalms of Lament and Thanksgiving no longer reflect (clearly enough) this situation from the history of religion.

11. See Tropper, *Nekromantie*, 205ff., 340ff.

typically to the loss of the dead person with ancestral cults and other forms of communication with the world beyond. In ancient Israel, these mourning rites occupied an important place in the rituals surrounding death. The canon of these rites included manipulations of clothing and body, such as these:

- tearing one's own clothes (Gen. 37:34; 2 Sam. 1:11; 3:31; etc.)
- removing turban and sandals (Ezek. 24:17, 23)
- putting on a coarse *śaq*-garment (sackcloth: Gen. 37:34; 2 Sam. 3:31; 1 Kgs. 20:31–32; Amos 8:10; etc.)
- shaving the head (Job 1:20; Jer. 16:6; Amos 8:10)
- trimming the hair on one's temples and beard (Lev. 19:27; Isa. 15:2; etc.)
- covering mustache and head (Ezek. 24:17; 2 Sam. 19:5)
- beating one's chest (Isa. 32:12) and thigh (Jer. 31:19)
- cutting the skin (Lev. 19:28; Deut. 14:1)
- sprinkling ashes or dirt on one's head (Josh. 7:6; Ezek. 27:30; Lam. 2:10; etc.)
- rolling in ashes (Jer. 6:26)
- fasting (1 Sam. 31:13; 2 Sam. 1:12)
- lamenting (Gen. 23:2; 1 Sam. 3:13; 2 Sam. 1:19ff.; etc.)
- crying by wailing women (Jer. 9:17–20 [16–19]; Ezek. 32:16; 2 Chr. 35:25)[12]
- the embalming of Jacob and Joseph (Gen. 50:2–3, 26; unique for the Hebrew Bible)

The practice associated with putting on a coarse *śaq*-garment made from goat or camel hair is illustrated by Genesis 37:32–35 or 2 Samuel 3:31. Thus Joseph's brothers brought his multicolored coat, dipped in the blood of a slaughtered goat, to their father Jacob and said:

> "This is what we found. Examine if it is your son's coat or not!"
> (Gen. 37:32)
> He examined it and said: "My son's coat! An evil beast has devoured him.
> Torn to pieces, torn to pieces is Joseph!" (v. 33)
> And Jacob tore his garment, put on sackcloth on his loins,
> and mourned for his son a long time. (v. 34)
> Then his sons and daughters got up to comfort him,
> but he refused to be consoled and said:
> "I shall go down mourning to my son in Sheol!"
> So he wept for him. (v. 35)

The practice of crying by wailing women, which is also attested in the Old Testament,[13] can be well illustrated—various cultural and religious differences notwithstanding—by an Egyptian drawing from the time of the New Kingdom (fig. 27), which depicts a burial in a shaft tomb: At the opening of the shaft tomb stands a priest, offering incense and libations; the wife of the deceased; and three wailing women, throwing up their arms. Inside the shaft, at the bottom of which are two side chambers and one lower chamber, a man is climbing up or

12. See the summary by Emmendörffer, *Der ferne Gott*, 8–9; Thiel, "שַׂק," 851ff.; Dietrich and Vollenweider, "Tod II," 583ff. On the basis of Job 2:11ff.; Ezra 9:3ff.; Ezek. 26:15ff.; etc., Lohfink ("Phase des Schweigens?") has convincingly argued that Old Testament rituals surrounding death also included a period of silence and motionlessness,

13. Jer. 9:17–20 (16–19); Ezek. 32:16; 2 Chr. 35:25; cf. Matt. 9:23 and Luke 23:27–28.

Figure 27. Burial in a shaft tomb
(Egypt, New Kingdom)

down. In the left chamber and in the shaft corridor, two priests, one of whom is wearing a jackal mask, are working on a mummy.

The "rites of self-deprecation," as Kutsch has called the mourning rites,[14] seem to have a sympathetic core: they express the bereaved's vicarious suffering with the deceased. It is noteworthy, however, that dying was not understood "as a moment of encounter with YHWH, let alone as the beginning of a closer communion with YWHW with respect to life."[15] This separation of the YHWH religion from the realm of death or the dead is also documented by the polemic against necromancy and funeral banquets that first appear in the eighth/seventh century BCE.[16]

The fact that the official YHWH religion found it difficult to understand YHWH as a God who is also close to the dead and even saves people from the underworld is related to the specific characterization of YHWH as a God of life, or living God,[17] from whom the dead in Sheol were kept strictly separate.

14. Kutsch, "'Trauerbräuche.'"
15. Zenger, "Israel und seine Toten," 142.
16. See Tropper, *Nekromantie*, 161ff., 340ff.
17. Cf. 2 Kgs. 19:4; Ps. 42:2/3; etc.

Anyone who died "old and full of days"[18]—as did Abraham, Isaac, David, or the priest Jehoiada—could look back on a full and godly life.[19] Even Job 42:16–17, the conclusion to the book of Job, assumes that Job could live further after lengthy suffering, before dying "old and full of days" at 140 years of age. But whoever was threatened by sickness and hardship "did not encounter YHWH therein (this idea is relatively late), but the destructive power of death as a mysterious possibility."[20] YHWH and the power of death were mutually exclusive.

Nevertheless, since the fate of death was common to all and it was precisely here that the question of God's presence had to come up, a position registered in the individual Psalms of Lament and Thanksgiving pays the closest attention to the problem of death and associates YHWH directly with the realm of death. How could it be that death and dying came to be connected to the God of life after all? Because, some have speculated, the realm of death was "systematically dedivinized" and death "had been freed from powers that could limit YHWH's might."[21]

From the perspective of the history of religion, matters are, however, significantly more complex, because they are, following Fernand Braudel, part of the "long term" (*longue durée*) or the "medium term" (*moyenne durée*). Ancestor worship and funerary cults could not be eliminated quite so easily from the lives of the people, as the corresponding prohibition texts extensively attest.[22] After all, ancestral worship and funerary cults are, like all ritual behavior, *repetitive structures*, which people "deliberately accept, ritualize, culturally enrich, and adjust to maintain a continuity that helps stabilize their respective societies."[23]

Instead of speaking of a "systematic dedivinization," one should more appropriately refer to an *expansion of divine responsibility*, which took place in Judah between the end of the eighth century (?) and the beginning of the sixth century BCE and thereafter. Two extrabiblical documents from Iron-Age Judah attest this slow process of expansion of YHWH's responsibility: One document, the funerary inscription from Ḫirbet el-Qôm (late 8th c. BCE) will also be discussed in connection with Psalm 88:5/6b.[24] The other documents, the two silver amulets from Ketef Hinnom (southwest of Jerusalem, overlooking the Hinnom valley; late 7th/early 6th c. BCE [?]), contain not only a variant of the priestly blessing of Numbers 6:24–26 (amulet I, lines 14–18; amulet II, lines 5–12); they also seem to assume—if one accepts the reading by Uehlinger (et al.)[25] of amulet I, lines 11–14—the authority of YHWH in the underworld:

11	*ky bw g'l*	For with him [YHWH] is salva-
12	*h ky yhwh*	tion, for YHWH

18. Cf. Gen. 25:8; 35:29; etc.; and 46 above. On life expectancy (an average of ca. 40 years) in ancient Israel, see Gerstenberger, "Lebenslauf"; and Meinhold, "Bewertung."

19. Cf. Ps. 91:16; etc.; and H. W. Wolff, *Anthropology*, 112.

20. Zenger, "Israel und seine Toten," 144.

21. Ibid., 145; cf. Gese, "Der Tod," 38ff.

22. Cf. Lev. 19:31; 20:6, 27; Deut. 18:9–14; etc.; see also Niehr, "Aspekte des Totengedenkens," 10–11.

23. Koselleck, *Zeitschichten*, 12–13.

24. See 224–25 below.

25. See Keel and Uehlinger, *Göttinnen, Götter*, 447ff.; also Uehlinger, "Gab es eine joschijanische Kultreform?," 68–69; Jaroš, *Zu den Silberamuletten*, 5, 9; Berlejung, "Tod und Leben," 489–90; etc.

13	[y]*šybnw* [x?]	[r]eturns us
14	*'wr*	light.[26]

The tomb belonged to a wealthy Jerusalem family in the late Iron Age (IA IIC), whose piety was oriented toward Jerusalem, according to grave goods (seal with lotus decoration, etc.).[27] According to Uehlinger, "If salvation through Yahweh was connected to the idea that Yahweh returned light, it is reminiscent of a broader Near Eastern idea, best known from Egypt, that the sun-god, who rides through the underworld at night, returns the light in the morning."[28] For the religious imagination of the Jerusalem elite of the late seventh or early sixth century BCE, as documented by the silver amulets, the expansion of divine responsibility seems to be characteristic—if one is permitted to generalize—according to which YHWH is praised as a God who also works among the dead: for them YHWH shall keep faithfulness and let the "light" of YHWH shine also in the grave (darkness).[29]

The complex history of the understanding of death in ancient Israel can be outlined as follows (cf. Janowski, "Gott Israels," 271f.):

	Life / This World ***YHWH as God of the Living***	Death / Otherworld ***YHWH and the Dead***
	Early Wisdom (Prov. 10ff.) *"Living God"* (Josh. 3:10; etc.) *Prophetic literature* (Amos 5:4ff., 14f.; Hos. 6:1ff.; etc.)	***Mourning rituals?*** ***Royal cult of the dead*** Kings as recipients of sacrifices (tombs in Jerusalem? in Samaria)
8th/7th c. BCE	*Creation texts* (Gen. 2:7; 7:15, 22; etc.)	***Hebrew inscriptions*** Divine protection also in death/ beyond death (Ḫirbet el-Qôm, Ketef Hinnom)
7th/6th c. BCE	Oath formula חַי־יְהוָה (Judg. 8:19; etc.) *"God of life"* (Deut. 5:26; etc.) *Iconography of Palestine/Israel* (tree of life, symbols of life) Names: *yḥw'ly*, "God preserves alive" (2 Chr. 29:14); בְּאֵר לַחַי רֹאִי (Gen. 16:14); and *other examples* in the later history	 ***Psalms of the Individual*** Salvation from "death in life" (Hos. 13:14? Ps. 68:19–20 [20–21]? Individual Laments and Thanksgiving) YHWH's "access to the underworld" (Prov. 15:11? Individual Laments and Thanksgiving)

(*continued on next page*)

26. A different reading is suggested by Renz and Röllig, *Althebräischen Epigraphik* 447ff.: [line 10] [.] and (?) from evil [11] [. . .] he has delivered. [12] Is YHWH then [13] (?) a [hu]man being that slumbers or [14] [. . .]?

27. Cf. Jaroš, *Zu den Silberamuletten*, 29–30.

28. Uehlinger, "Gab es eine joschijanische Kultreform?," 69. The problem is also connected to the question of integration of solar elements into the preexlic YHWH religion; see Janowski, "JHWH und der Sonnengott."

29. Cf. Keel and Uehlinger, *Göttinnen, Götter*, 421–22; Uehlinger, "Gab es eine joschijanische Kultreform?," 69; Jaroš, *Zu den Silberamuletten*, 30. This interpretation should be valid, esp. in light of the priestly blessing of Num. 6:24–26 found in one grave, and also if the reading of amulet I, lines 11–14, is disputed; cf. Puech, "Funerary Inscriptions," 127: "The amulets worn by the living accompanied the dead in the tomb in order to continue a protective and apotropaic role in their favor. In this sense, these inscriptions also interest the world of the dead."

(continued from previous page)

Expansion of YHWH's authority
YHWH as God of the Living and the Dead

After 587 BCE	*Psalms of the Individual* Salvation from "death in life" (Individual Laments and Thanksgiving) YHWH's "access to the underworld" (Prov. 15:11? Individual Laments and Thanksgiving; Job 26:5–6?)
539–333 BCE	*Wisdom literature* "Eternal life" / Immortality (of relationship with God) (Job 19:25ff.; Pss. 49:14–15 [15–16?]; 63:3/4; 73:23ff.) Skepticism: Eccl. 3:19ff.; 9:4ff. (3rd c. BCE)
4th/3rd c. BCE	*Apocalyptic literature* Resurrection from death (Ezek. 37:1ff.; Isa. 25:8; 26:19; Ps. 22:27/28ff.; etc.)
2nd c. BCE	Dan. 12:2–3, 13

Resources

On the history of the concept of death in the Old Testament, see Albani, "Die postmortale Hoffnungsperspektive"; Berlejung, "Geschichte und Religionsgeschichte," esp. 81ff; Berlejung and Janowski, eds., *Tod und Jenseits*; Ego, "Vergänglichkeitsmotivik"; Frevel, "Tod"; Hasenfratz, "Tod und Leben"; Hieke, "Sichtweisen des Todes"; Schnocks, *Rettung*, 20ff.; Utzschneider, "Tod und Sterben"; Zenger, "Funktion der Todesbilder."

On funerary rituals in Israel/Judah, see Kamlah, "Grab und Begräbnis." On mourning rites and mourning in the Old Testament and the ancient Near East, see Bail, "Hautritzen"; Berges, *Klagelieder*, 39ff.; Janssen and Kessler, "Trauer"; Kratz, "Trauer"; P. A. Kruger, "World of Mourning"; Maul, "Altorientalische Trauerriten"; Noort, "Der Tod und die Gerechtigkeit"; Podella, "Trauerbräuche II"; S. Schroer, "Kompetenzen israelitischer Frauen"; idem, "Trauerriten und Totenklage."

On the so-called expansion of YHWH's authority, see the references at 39ff. Relevant for this context are the silver amulets from Ketef Hinnom (Barkay et al., "Amulets from Ketef Hinnom"), which appear to go a step further than the inscription from Ḫirbet el-Qôm (see references at 39ff.): according to amulet I, lines 11–14, 17–18, YHWH is praised as a God who "returns light to us [?] / is our restorer and rock [?]" (lines 13–14), and who "makes his face shine" (lines 17–18; cf. Num. 6:24–26) over/toward the dead. Important for the interpretation is the context of tomb and death/dead (see Eberhardt, *JHWH und die Unterwelt*, 375ff.). Whether it is plausible that this expansion of YHWH's authority occurred as a result of his solarization (so C. Uehlinger; et al.) is questionable. Nevertheless, the silver amulets allow for "certain conclusions with regard to approximation of YHWH toward Sheol, in similar ways as tomb inscription 3 from Ḫirbet el-Qôm: the uniting element between the two discoveries is the divine patronage of YHWH" (Eberhardt, *JHWH und die Unterwelt*, 387; cf. 384ff.); see also Leuenberger, "Deine Gnade," 355ff.; Köckert, "Wandlungen Gottes," 29–30 (late dating based on J. Renz); S. Schroer, "Beobachtungen," 294ff.; Berlejung, "Programm fürs Leben" (Persian period); Janowski, "Gott Israels," 284ff.

The precise time of origin for the connection between YHWH and the dead is difficult to establish. While a first possible link exists in the royal funerary cult of the (late) preexilic era,[30] a second link may be found in the funerary inscriptions of Ḫirbet el-Qôm (late 8th c. BCE)[31] and of Ketef Hinnom (late 7th/early 6th c. BCE), which mark the transition to the nonroyal dead and therefore belong to the "realm of family piety on the local or household level."[32] This point probably also marks the origin of the reflections found in the (preexilic) Psalms of the Individual, which present new perspectives on the problem of death. One of these perspectives is the experience that the supplicant, besieged by enemies, facing legal adversity, and afflicted by illness, "[comes] in contact with the reality of death; but precisely this is sufficient for that one to experience the entire reality of death."[33] This corresponds to the opposite experience of YHWH's intervention for the supplicant to be saved "not only from mortal danger, but also from death itself, from inside the realm of death, and from the power of death."[34] This relation of YHWH to death and to the dead introduces a new development in the Old Testament understanding of death, as Psalm 88 demonstrates very clearly.

β. Psalm 88 as a Case Study

A song. A Psalm. By the Korahites. For the choirmaster.
According to the tune Māhălat Lĕʿannôt. A maśkîl. By Heman, the Ezrahite.

YHWH, God of my salvation,
  by day I have cried and [every] night before you.
      (Ps. 88:1/2)
Let my prayer come before you;
  incline your ear to my cry. (v. 2/3)
For my life [*nepeš*] is full of troubles,
  and my life has touched the underworld. (v. 3/4)
I have been counted among those who go down to the Pit;
  I have become like a man without strength. (v. 4/5)
[I am] one set free among the dead,
  like the slain who lie in the grave,
  whom you no longer remember;
  they are cut off from your hand. (v. 5/6)

30. Cf. Niehr, "Aspekte des Totengedenkens," 10–11.
31. See 48 above.
32. Niehr, "Aspekte des Totengedenkens," 11.
33. C. Barth, *Errettung vom Tode*, 92.
34. Ibid., 93.

You have placed me in the deepest pit,
  in dark places, in the depths [of the sea]. (v. 6/7)
Your wrath has laid upon me;
  with all your waves you have overwhelmed [me]. (v. 7/8)
You have removed from me all my close friends;
  you have made me an abomination to them. (v. 8/9)
My eye has wasted away because of affliction. (v. 9/10a)

I have called to you every day, YHWH;
  I have spread out my hands to you. (v. 9bc/10bc)
Should you work miracles among the dead,
  or shall the spirits of the dead rise to praise you? *Selah.* (v. 10/11)
Is your goodness spoken of in the grave,
  your faithfulness in the place of doom? (v. 11/12)
Are your miracles proclaimed in the darkness,
  and your righteousness in the land of forgetfulness? (v. 12/13)

But I, I have called for help to you, YHWH,
  and let my prayer come before you [every] morning! (v. 13/14)

Why have you banished my *nepeš*, YHWH,
  and have hidden your face from me? (v. 14/15)
Afflicted am I and sick unto death since my youth;
  I have borne your terrors, I am arrested by fear (?). (v. 15/16)
Your burning anger has passed over me;
  your terrors have silenced me. (v. 16/17)
They have surrounded me like water every day / all the time;
  they have encircled me completely. (v. 17/18)
You have removed from me friend and companion,
  my close friends—[there is a place of] darkness. (v. 18/19)

Textual Notes

1/2. Here יוֹם, "by day" (in contrast to night), is used adverbially; see Jenni, "יוֹם," 708–9; בַלַּיְלָה, like בַבֹּקֶר in v. 14, means "at all times"; see Jenni, *Präposition Beth*, 298–99; the Targum presupposes the more common יוֹמָם; see also Tate, *Psalms 51–100*, 395–96.

5/**6.** The Masoretic חָפְשִׁי, "one who is set free," should be retained, understood as referring to the dead as having no ties to God and to the living; cf. GB[18] 383, s.v. חָפְשִׁי, 3; Janowski, "Die Toten loben JHWH nicht," 6; Schorch, *Euphemismen*, 119–20 with n. 260; for verses below, see 237–38.

7/8. Kraus (*Psalmen*, 2:772) considers עִנִּיתָ ("you have overwhelmed") as "out of place" and follows LXX in reading אִנִּיתָ, "you have allowed to strike" (cf. Baethgen, *Die Psalmen*, 272; *HALOT* 807, s.v. II ענה Piel; Lindström, *Suffering and Sin*, 199, etc.), which is incorrect in my opinion; cf. Dahood, *Psalms II*, 301, 305; Tate, *Psalms 51–100*, 397; and others.

8/9. Here תּוֹעֵבוֹת is a plural of intensification ("epitome of abomination"); see GKC §124e; and Brockelmann, *Hebräische Syntax*, §19b. Kraus (*Psalmen*, 2:772) sees כָּלֻא, Qal passive participle of כלא, "hold back, enclose," as an apposition to the personal suffix in שַׁתַּנִי, which is syntactically difficult to justify; cf. LXX and the *BHS* apparatus to this verse; the word can perhaps be seen as a second object dependent on שִׁתַנִי; cf. Michel, *Tempora und Satzstellung*, 130; Gross, "Gott als Feind?," 160.

13/14. Gross ("Gott als Feind?," 160) also suggests the translation "Ich aber, zu dir, YHWH, rufe ich hiermit" and its interpretation of an immediate expression of the complaint; see 220, n. 36 below.

14/15. On the translation of לָמָה as "Why?," see Michel, "'Warum' und 'wozu'?"

15/16. Instead of אָפוּנָה (derived from the hapax legomenon פּוּן, "become rigid" [?]; cf. Kraus, *Psalmen*, 2:773), *HALOT* 866 (s.v. פוג Qal 2) proposes the form אָפוּגָה, "I grow weary"; cf. the *BHS* apparatus; and Tate, *Psalms 51–100*, 398, "I despair of life."

16/17. The MT's צִמְּתוּתֻנִי should be emended to צִמְּתָתְנִי; cf. Ps. 119:139; Kraus, *Psalmen*, 2:773; and Lindström, *Suffering and Sin*, 199.

18/19. The term מַחְשָׁךְ, "[place of] darkness," was already frequently emended in ancient versions. Nevertheless, the MT is to be followed here; cf. Gross, "Gott als Feind?," 160; Seybold, *Psalmen: Eine Einführung*, 343–44, 346; Zenger, *Dein Angesicht suche ich*, 71; Tate, *Psalms 51–100*, 398.[35]

Structural Aspects

Significant with regard to the structure of Psalm 88 is the triple *introductory complaint with invocation* in verses 1–2 (2–3), 9/10bc, and 13/14,[36] each of which introduces a particular section: the *first account of affliction* in verses 3–9a (4–10a),[37] the *appeal to YHWH* in verses 10–12 (11–13), and the *second account of affliction* in verses 14–18 (15–19). The introductory complaints of verses 1–2 (2–3) and 9bc/10bc that structure the psalm are connected by common elements:

- *by the divine name*: "YHWH, God of my salvation" (v. 1/2a); "YHWH" (v. 9/10b, 13/14a)
- *by verbs of complaining, "shouting/crying"*: צָעַק, "clamoring" (v. 1/2); קָרָא, "call" (v. 9/10b); שׁוע Piel, "call for help" (v. 13/14); compare תְּפִלָּה, "prayer" (vv. 2/3, 13/14)

35. For a detailed discussion, see Janowski, "Die Toten loben JHWH nicht," 5–6; and Hossfeld and Zenger, *Psalmen 51–100*, 565–66. See also Loretz, *Psalmstudien*, 285ff.; idem, *Götter*, 273ff.; F. Crüsemann, "Rhetorische Fragen!?"; F. Crüsemann and M. Crüsemann, "Tod"; Berges, *Schweigen ist Silber;* Bauks, *Die Feinde des Psalmisten*, 90–91; Schlegel, *Psalm 88;* de Vos, *Klage als Gotteslob*, 21ff.; Lescow, "Psalm 22, 2–22 und Psalm 88"; Weber, "'JHWH, Gott meiner Rettung!'"; Schnocks, *Rettung*, 56ff.; idem, "Metaphern für Leben und Tod"; Wälchli, *Gottes Zorn*, 67ff.

36. In the three complaint sections, the *different times* are to be noted: Ps. 88:1–2 (2–3) is a *current* petition (v. 2/3), or rather a quotation of a previous crying out (v. 1/2); then v. 9/10bc contains *past* complaints; and v. 13/14 marks a *current* expression of the complaint: "In v. 13/14 we have reached the complaint of his current prayer; it appropriately occurs in the morning, the typical time for YHWH's helpful intervention" (Gross, "Ein Schwerkranker betet," 103). Then vv. 3–9a (4–10a) and 14–18 (15–19) supply the content of the lament.

37. On this division, see also Zenger, "Zur redaktionsgeschichtlichen Bedeutung," 181; idem, *Dein Angesicht suche ich*, 70, 72; Gross, "Ein Schwerkranker betet," 102; idem, "Gott als Feind?," 164 n.2.

- *by a climactic time frame:* "by day" / "[every] night" (v. 1/2); "every day" (v. 9/10b; cf. v. 17/18a); "[every] morning" (= time of divine intervention, v. 13/14b)[38]
- *by the contrast of light and darkness:* "night" (v. 1/2b) versus "morning" (v. 13/14v); compare the juxtaposition of "morning" (v. 13/14b) and "[place of] darkness" (v. 12/13a)
- *by the coram-Deo relation: "before you"* (נֶגֶד + suffix, v. 1/2b); "before you" (לִפְנֵי + suffix, v. 2/3a); "to you" (אֶל + suffix, v. 9/10c, 13/14a); "come before" (קָדַם Piel, v. 13/14b)

The tripartite structure of the psalm is highlighted by several features:

- the *syntactically emphasized beginning* of the three sections, verses 3–9a (4–10a; see "For" in v. 3/4), 10–12 (11–13; with interrogative ה starting 10/11, 11/12, 12/13), 14–18 (15–19; with "Why?" in 14/15)
- the *lexical relation* of the two outside sections verses 3–9a (4–10a) and 14–18 (15–19) through the key terms נַפְשִׁי, "my life" (3/4a / 14/15a), and רחק Hiphil, "remove" + subject YHWH (8/9a and 18/19a)
- the *motif of darkness*, which appears at the end of each section ("eye has wasted": 9/10a; "darkness": 12/13a, 18/19b)

Moreover, if Psalm 88 is read in the context of the Psalms of Korah (Pss. 84–85; 87–88), additional structural and semantic elements emerge. Thus the two outside Psalms 84 and 88 are related contrastingly to each other as they present themselves as

> "petitions" (cf. the key term תפלה [prayer] in Pss. 84:9; 88:3, 14) of a "soul" (נפשׁ: 84:3; 88:4, 15) that longs for and cries out (84:3c; 88:2b, 10b, 14a) to see the saving face of YHWH (84:8b; 88:3a, 15b), to encounter him "as the sun" (84:12) that brings light "in the morning" and puts an end to darkness (88:14 in the context of 88:2, 7, 13, 19). The two psalms thus constitute a contrasting interconnection in which Ps. 84 presents a "soul" that wanders "from strength to strength" (84:8), while Ps. 88 presents a "soul" that speaks of itself as a man in whom there is no more strength (88:5).[39]

The core of Psalm 88 is thereby constituted by verses 10–12 (11–13), since the supplicant does not speak of self here as in verses 3/4ff. and 14/15ff., but speaks of the dead in general. As we shall see, this segment, which is stylistically held together by the triple interrogative ה, is also theologically the central part. Arranged around it are two longer sections, verses 3–9a (4–10a) and 14–18 (15–19), in which the supplicant speaks *complaints* and *accusations*—complaints

38. Cf. Pss. 5:3/4; 30:5/6; 59:16/17; 90:14; 143:8; etc.; see Tournay, *Seeing and Hearing God*, 155–56; Janowski, "Der barmherzige Richter," 65ff., etc.; a different interpretation is offered by Lindström, *Suffering and Sin*, 205.

39. Zenger, "Das Mythische," 247–48; cf. idem, "Zur redaktionsgeschichtlichen Bedeutung," 186ff.; idem, *Dein Angesicht suche ich*, 76ff.; Gross, "Ein Schwerkranker betet," 113–14.

with regard to the self's own situation ("I"), and accusations with regard to God ("You"), in whom the supplicant sees the cause of the self's suffering.[40]

Both accounts of the affliction begin with the key term נֶפֶשׁ (life-force, vitality) in 88:3/4a and 14/15a, and then end in verses 8/9a and 18/19a with a reference to the supplicant's friends and confidants, who have been removed from self by YHWH (רחק Hiphil, "keep away").[41] YHWH thus appears as the cause of the supplicant's affliction—the only cause, as we shall see.

The threefold repetition of the introductory complaint with invocation and account of the affliction (88:1–2 [2–3] + 3–9a [4–10a]; 9/10b + 10–12 [11–13]; 13/14 + 14–18 [15–19]) call to mind the form of an individual psalm of lament. It is, however, a unique lament, for compared to the usual form, as presented in Psalm 13,[42] important elements are lacking, such as an affirmation of trust,[43] a petition, and a promise of praise. Furthermore, the element of "complaint" is not, as is typical for the genre, divided into the three parts of God-complaint, self-complaint, and enemy-complaint, but the enemy-complaint is shifted entirely to the God-complaint and has therefore been recast as an accusation of God. One must ask, Can this psalm still be called a prayer?

Thematic Aspects

Psalm 88 is a unique and central text for the theology of the Old Testament—but why? The answers given to this question are usually of an emotional nature like "the breath of imminent death blows through every line,"[44] or "the most gloomy and melancholy of all Old Testament Psalms."[45] This assessment of Psalm 88 is, of course, not without reason, common to virtually all commentaries. But are such judgments sufficient to understand the problem addressed in this text? This problem consists of the experience and depiction of God as "enemy of the individual," even though this person does not cease to "cry out" to this God (vv. 1–2 [2–3]). In this sense, a supplicant dares to say *to* YHWH that which probably would have been difficult to bear if it had been said in a different genre *about* God: "The relationship of the individual to God is, from the perspective of the Old Testament, not decided by what is said about God, but rather by what is said to God, not monologically but dialogically. However, since the individual person is not only fighting for one's own life here, but at the same time for the divinity of one's God, the speech has virtually no limits."[46] Psalm 88 thus deals with the *life of the supplicant* and the *divinity of God*—the former not without the latter! On the basis of an exegesis of verses 3–9a (4–10a) and 14–18 (15–19), we will see how the text develops this idea.

40. The "I" and "you" passages alternate irregularly; see Janowski, "Die Toten loben JHWH nicht," 8–9.

41. Cf. Pss. 22:1/2, 11/12, 19/20; Job. 19:13; etc.

42. See 59ff. above.

43. Lacking unless the invocation "YHWH, God of my salvation" (88:1/2a) contains an expression of trust: see 228 below.

44. Kraus, *Psalmen*, 2:773.

45. Haag, "Psalm 88," 149.

46. Gross, "Gott als Feind?," 159–60; see also Janowski, "Die 'Kleine Biblia,'" 143ff.

1. The Terrors of Sheol

What do we learn in the two outside sections verses 3–9a (4–10a) and 14–18 (15–19) about the supplicant and about YHWH? Important with regard to the supplicant[47] are the I-statements in verses 3–5 (4–6), 8–9a (9–10a), and 15/16, which depict the petitioner's suffering in extreme terms:

- The supplicant is already counted among the dead by the local social network, has lost all strength, and has been cut off from the hand of God (vv. 4–5 [5–6]).
- The supplicant has become an abomination (תּוֹעֵבוֹת)[48] // a prisoner, whose eye has wasted away because of affliction (vv. 8/9b, 9/10a).[49]
- The supplicant is afflicted and sick unto death since youth and is arrested by fear (v. 15/16).

The supplicant's deathlike situation is described already in the first line of the account of the affliction, verses 3–9a (4–10a):

> For my life is full of troubles,
> and my life has touched the underworld. (v. 3/4)

This supplicant is not "full" (שָׂבַע/שְׂבַע) because of a fulfilled life[50] or because of a special association with God,[51] but because of the "troubles" (רָעוֹת) that have come upon self from God. For the supplicant, there will be no "waking up"—unless YHWH intervenes after all—because the petitioner's life has "touched" (נגע) the underworld, and "darkness" is self's only companion (v. 18/19). The terrors of Sheol are thereby described in bleak images. Thus the place references "Pit" (בּוֹר, v. 4/5), "grave" (קֶבֶר, v. 5/6; cf. 11/12), "deepest depths" (תַּחְתִּיּוֹת, v. 6/7), "dark places" (מַחֲשַׁכִּים, v. 6/7; cf. 12/13) and "depths [of the sea]" (מְצֹלוֹת, v. 6/7; cf. 17/18) indicate that the supplicant—in contrast to the intended "no" of the rhetorical questions of Job 38:16–18![52]—is situated in spatial proximity to the underworld (cf. v. 3/4) and accordingly in insurmountable distance from YHWH and the world of the living. Appropriate therefore are comparisons to the dead: the supplicant is counted among those who go down to the Pit (v. 4/5a), is like a man without strength (v. 4/5b), like one set free among the dead (v. 5/6a), and like the slain who lie in the grave (v. 5/6b):

47. Cf. Gross, "Gott als Feind?," 165–66; and Gross, "Ein Schwerkranker betet," 105ff.

48. Cf. Job. 19:19: "The men in my circle of confidants despise [תעב Piel] me; those whom I loved have turned away from me"; see Strauss, *Hiob*, 14.

49. On the wordplay of עֵינִי, "my eye," and עֳנִי, "affliction," in Ps. 88:9/10a, see Tate, *Psalms 51–100*, 402: "The 'eye' of the speaker is a synecdoche for the whole person, an indicator of the vitality and health of a person (cf. 1 Sam. 14:27; Deut. 34:7; Ps. 19:8/9; Ezra 9:8) or of the lack of vitality and of depleted strength (Gen. 27:1; Job 17:7; Pss. 6:7/8; 38:10/11; Lam. 5:17)." On the correlation of "light [eyesight]" and "life," see Stendebach, "עַיִן," 35; "Excursus 3: Light and Darkness," 69–70 above; also 305ff. below.

50. Cf. Gen. 25:8; 35:29, etc.; see 46 above.

51. Cf. Pss. 16:11; 17:15; 63:5/6; on this kind of "fullness," see Warmuth, "שָׂבַע," 696ff.; and Liess, *Der Weg des Lebens*, 240ff.

52. See Strauss, "Tod (Todeswunsch; "Jenseits"?) im Buch Hiob," 246–47; and Köhlmoos, *Das Auge Gottes*, 152ff., 331ff.

For my *nepeš* is full of troubles,
  and my life has touched the underworld.
    (Ps. 88:3/4)
I have been counted among those who go down to the Pit;
  I have become like a man without strength. (v. 4/5)
[I am] one set free among the dead,
  like the slain who lie in the grave,
  whom you no longer remember;
  they are cut off from your hand. (v. 5/6)
You have placed me in the deepest depths,
  in dark places, in the depths [of the sea]. (v. 6/7)

The underworld vocabulary can be more precisely defined in terms of the history of religion as well as semantically. Two references shall be sufficient here:

One set free among the dead (v. 5/6a). This expression, which has been explained by Willi as referring to the release of a legally responsible subject from an obligation,[53] has a parallel in the Ugaritic expression *bt ḫpṯt* "house of the *ḫupšu*-position" or "house of the order of the *ḫupšu*-mercenaries,"[54] which possesses an unmistakable *underworld connotation*. This is evident in a passage from the Baal cycle, in which Baal sends a scout to Mot in the underworld with the following message:

And descend to the house of the order of the *ḫupšu*-mercenaries
  in the underworld [*arṣ*];
 be counted among those who go down into the underworld [*arṣ*].
    (*KTU* 1.4.VIII.7–9)[55]

The "house of the *ḫupšu*-position" describes an institution of low reputation,[56] which served in Ugarit as a metaphor for the underworld.[57] A similar process of association probably lies behind Psalm 88: Just as a "person set free" could be released into a socially most difficult situation, the supplicant, according to Psalm 88:5/6, exists among the dead as "one set free"—in other words, as someone who can offer no further service to YHWH and is therefore no longer subject to God's power. The supplicant of Psalm 88:5/6 "complains before God that self has already reached a state that is the lowest and worst even in the underworld."[58]

Cut off from the hand of God. The expression "to be cut off" is associated with an aspect of the verb גָּזַר, "cut off," that deals with "being cut off/excluded"

53. Willi, "Die Freiheit Israels," 536–37: Initially the expression has a positive core meaning, which appears, however, in a negative light in Ps. 88. Accordingly, the bitterness of death "consists precisely . . . of being released from numerous obligations and the possibility to fulfill them before God. God will forget the supplicant . . . because the supplicant can offer YHWH no further service and therefore no longer stands under the burdensome as well as protective hand [*yād*] or power of God."

54. See Loretz, "Akkadisch-ugaritisch *ḫalbu/ḫlb*—hebräisch *ḥlb*," 232 with n. 52.

55. Based on the translation found in ibid., 232; cf. Loretz and Dietrich, in *TUAT* 3/6:1171 (ed. M. Dietrich).

56. Cf. the mention in 2 Kgs. 15:5 = 2 Chr. 26:21 of a house separated from the Jerusalem palace (בֵּית הַחָפְשִׁית), in which the leprous king Uzziah of Judah had to live until his death. See GB[18] 383, s.v. חָפְשִׁית; and Loretz, "Akkadisch-ugaritisch *ḫalbu/ḫlb*—hebräisch *ḥlb*," 233.

57. See Healey and Niehr, "Land ohne Wiederkehr," 97ff.

58. Loretz, "Akkadisch-ugaritisch *ḫalbu/ḫlb*—hebräisch *ḥlb*," 232.

from the land of the living (Isa. 53:8) or the house of YHWH (2 Chr. 26:21), or with "being separated" from God (Ps. 31:22/23).[59] The scapegoat sent into the "cut-off land" (// "wilderness"), according to Leviticus 16:22, carries there Israel's transgressions. The expression may signify a "barren land" but perhaps also an area that is strictly separated from any cultically relevant region.[60]

The expression of Psalm 88:5/6d also receives its incisive meaning from the reference to the *"hand of God,"* which provides protection, strength, and safety,[61] from which the supplicant of Psalm 88 sees self as cut off like the dead // slain. Especially the "right hand" (יַד יָמִין) or "right" (יָמִין) of YHWH protects and supports the supplicant,[62] who knows self to be held up by it (Ps. 63:8/9), so that he is not shaken (Ps. 16:8).[63] The fact that the supplicant hopes to be rescued from "deep distress" is attested by Psalms 18:16–17 (17–18) and 144:7–8.

> He [YHWH] reached down from on high, took me,
> drew me out [מָשָׁה] of mighty waters.
> (Ps. 18:16/17)
> He rescued [נצל Hiphil] me from my strong enemy,
> those who hate me, who were too powerful for me. (v. 17/18)
>
> Stretch out your hands from on high,
> save me [פָּצָה] and rescue me [נצל Hiphil]
> from mighty waters,
> from the power of strangers,
> (Ps. 144:7)
> whose mouth speaks lies
> and whose right hand is a right hand of deception.[64] (v. 8)

The supplicant's location in Psalm 88, which the nouns "Pit" (v. 4/5a; cf. 6/7a); "grave" (v. 5/6a); "deepest depths," "dark places," and "depths [of the sea]" (v. 6/7) have already *characterized as the underworld,*[65] is also reached by the supplicant through a *continuous downward movement*:

- The supplicant's life reaches[66] or touches the underworld (v. 3/4b)
- The petitioner is counted among those who go down to the Pit (v. 4/5a) // who lie in the grave like the slain (v. 5/6b).
- The supplicant sees self as placed in the deepest depths, in dark places, in depths [of the sea] by YHWH.

59. Cf. Ezek. 37:11; Lam. 3:54; and Görg, "גָּזַר," 1003–4. On Isa. 53:8, see Janowski, *Stellvertretung*, 85 n. 67; on 2 Chr. 26:21, see 224 n. 57 above.

60. Görg, "גָּזַר," 1003. On the negative connotations of מִדְבָּר, "wilderness," see Talmon, "מִדְבָּר," 690–91.

61. Cf. Pss. 31:5/6, 15/16; 37:24; 80:17/18; 95:7; 139:5; etc.; Ackroyd, "יָד," 447ff.; idem, "Hand," 27; Korpel, *A Rift in the Clouds*, 108ff.; Norin, "Die Hand Gottes," 54ff. On the symbolic use of hand in general, see S. Schroer and Staubli, *Körpersymbolik der Bibel*, 171ff.

62. Cf. Pss. 18:35/36; 109:31; 110:5; 121:5; etc.

63. Cf. Ps. 73:23; see Soggin, "יָמִין," 662–63. On Ps. 73:23, see 319 below.

64. These two texts, as well as funerary inscription 3 from Ḫirbet el-Qôm, inform this context—on which see 48 above.

65. See Keel, *Die Welt*, 223–24; also Särkiö, "Hilferuf zu Jahwe aus dem Versteck," 48ff.

66. Cf. Schwienhorst-Schönberger, "נָגַע," 223–24. Grimm translates Ps. 88:3/4b as "Vitaler in der *šĕʾôl* eintreffen [arriving in Sheol as a living being]" and argues that the expression "touches on the semantic field of movement and . . . apparently [signifies] much the same as *bôʾ* [enter]." Grimm, *Vergänglichkeit in den Reden Ijobs*, 197.

The idea of "touching the underworld" (v. 3/4b) may even signify something similar to the idea of "touching a corpse": just as contact with a corpse defiles,[67] so the supplicant of Psalm 88, whose life (חַיִּים) touches the realm of death and defilement of Sheol, is to the local social environment unclean, becoming the "epitome of revulsion" (תּוֹעֵבוֹת, v. 8/9;[68] cf. Job 19:19; etc.). The supplicant of Psalm 88, whose life touches the underworld (v. 3/4), experiences personal suffering therefore as "humiliating, completely isolated, and forgotten deathlike existence."[69] Equally strong is the aversion by the close friends, whom YHWH has removed from the supplicant (v. 8/9; cf. 18/19). This aversion is a reflection of the aversion against the power of death, which has already reached for the life of the supplicant and has surrounded that sufferer with "darkness"[70] (v. 18/19). This closes the cycle of death images, which illustrate the two descriptions of affliction of verses 4ff. and 15ff. so vividly.

2. *God as the Supplicant's Enemy*

What does Psalm 88 tell us about God?[71] The second-person statements in verses 6–8 (7–9) and 14/15, 16–18 (17–19) make it unmistakably clear that the supplicant's afflictions (v. 3/4) are caused by YHWH. The supplicant admits to no sin but persistently maintains the self's innocence; in other words, the petitioner "does not let self be talked into believing one's own guilt."[72] There is not even an enemy who confirms the supplicant's fate through a declaration "I have prevailed over him," as was the case in Psalm 13:4/5.[73] The cause of the affliction through YHWH is invoked with an increasing number of new metaphors:

- YHWH has placed the supplicant in the underworld (v. 6/7).
- YHWH's wrath and waves have overwhelmed the supplicant (v. 7/8).
- YHWH has brought about the supplicant's "social death" (v. 8/9).
- YHWH has expelled the supplicant and has hidden YHWH's face from the petitioner (v. 14/15).
- YHWH's burning anger and terrors have seized and silenced the supplicant (vv. 15–16 [16–17]).
- Those terrors surround the supplicant all the time (v. 17/18).
- YHWH has socially isolated the supplicant (v. 19).

67. Cf. Lev. 11:39; Num. 19:11, 13, 16, 18; and Schwienhorst-Schönberger, "נָגַע," 222: "in these passages *nāgaʿ* signifies the immediate . . . contact between two mutually exclusive spheres: the sphere of life and death, pure and impure, sacred and profane. These two spheres may not come in contact with each other." See also Illman, *Formulas about Death*, 143–44.

68. On the plural form, see 219 above.

69. Gross, "Ein Schwerkranker betet," 107.

70. Or "a place of darkness"; cf. 88:6/7 (pl.); מַחְשָׁךְ means "a place of darkness": cf. the singular in Isa. 29:15; 42:16; and the plural in Pss. 74:20; 88:6/7; 143:3; Lam. 3:6; see Helmer Ringgren, "חָשַׁךְ," 268–69; Tate, *Psalms 51–100*, 404; Lindström, *Suffering and Sin*, 207ff. As the comparison with Ps. 143:3 shows ("the enemy . . . consigns me to darkness / to dark places like those forever dead"), the "removal" of friends, companions, and confidants by YHWH, the supplicant's enemy, causes the supplicant to be placed "in the darkness of death / the place of darkness" (88:18/19).

71. Cf. Gross, "Gott als Feind?,"166–67, cf. idem, "Ein Schwerkranker betet," 107–8.

72. Gross, "Gott als Feind?," 166.

73. See 72 above.

This perspective on the supplicant's affliction as caused by God can be further underscored by a comparison of verses 3/4 and 14/15: each of the two lines introduces the respective subsequent description of affliction:

> *Supplicant*
> For my *nepeš* is full of troubles,
> and my life has touched the underworld. (v. 3/4)
>
> *YHWH*
> Why have you banished my *nepeš*, YHWH,
> and have hidden your face from me? (v. 14/15)

Psalm 88:14/15 has the only "Why?" question[74] of the psalm. Otherwise the supplicant only makes declarative statements and persistently claims that YHWH is the cause of the suffering. The supplicant avoids any kind of self-accusation, thus changing the traditional enemy-complaint into an accusation against God, and not committing self to a declaration of trust nor to a direct petition for healing—although the supplicant repeatedly asks that the call for help be heard (vv. 1–2, 9a, 13 [2–3, 10a, 14]); hence the result is radical beyond compare both in regard to content and language. The constellation of "God—supplicant—enemy,"[75] typical for the Psalms of Lament, has become a direct confrontation: supplicant → YHWH, or YHWH → supplicant. Everything suffered by the supplicant is only the work of YHWH, who now is the supplicant's enemy; thus the psalm detours around human enemies.

A certain similarity with the portrayal of God in Psalm 88 is found in Job's speech in Job 16:7–14.[76] There God gnashes his teeth against Job (v. 9), as enemies do against the supplicant in the Enemy Psalms; God turns Job over to mockery by hostile people (vv. 10–11), has shaken and cut Job to pieces in the midst of a quiet life (v. 12), and charges Job like an enemy warrior (v. 14):

> But now he has exhausted me:
> you have made desolate everything around me.
> (Job 16:7)
> You have seized me; my wasting away has become
> a witness against me and has risen up against me;
> it testifies against me. (v. 8)
> His snorting anger has torn me; he has made me an enemy.
> He gnashes his teeth against me;
> my oppressor focuses his eyes on me. (v. 9)
> They open the mouth against me,
> they hit me on the cheek with derision,
> they gather together against me. (v. 10)
> God has delivered me over to a boy;
> he has thrown me into the hands of wicked men. (v. 11)
> I lived in peace, then he shook me;
> he grabbed me by the neck and cut me to pieces.
> He set me up as a target for him; (v. 12)
> his arrows surround me.

74. See 220 above.
75. See 42 above.
76. Cf. Job 19:8–12 and 30:12–14.

He splits my kidneys and does not spare;
he pours out my gall on the ground. (v. 13)
He tears me up, piece by piece;
he runs up against me like a warrior hero. (v. 14)[77]

Why does the supplicant of Psalm 88 nevertheless call YHWH the "God of my salvation" (אֱלֹהֵי יְשׁוּעָתִי, v. 1/2a) at the beginning of the prayer? In this context W. Gross speaks of two mutually conflicting views of God: the one God in whom the supplicant has faith on the basis of personal religious tradition and whom the petitioner calls "God of my salvation"—and the other God whom the supplicant has experienced as the cause of personal suffering.

The unity of that *God of the supplicant's faith* and this *God of personal suffering* can no longer be maintained "positively by other content-related statements."[78] The supplicant can neither resort to a sin committed by the petitioner, nor can the supplicant commit to an expression of faith in God that goes beyond death. There is nothing here that leads beyond, not even hope in the resurrection. What remains is the *gulf between faith and experience*. Nevertheless, this supplicant is not (yet) giving up on God, even if the psalm's final word is no longer "YHWH" (v. 1/2) but "darkness."[79]

Let us insert a brief consideration into the discussion here. One could follow Gross, who is of the opinion that the unity between the God of the supplicant's faith and the God of the supplicant's experience is broken. There is much that speaks for this explanation.

However, the question poses itself if the psalm, or rather the supplicant, is not undertaking a—last—attempt somehow to bring about this unity. The classical attempts at bridging the gap—a *confession of sin* with an articulation of personal responsibility for the affliction, or the affirmation of *faith in God* with an expression of certitude beyond death—are not found in Psalm 88. Instead, what is articulated is the experience of God as the sole cause of the affliction.

Nevertheless, the Psalm is not yet exhausted if one does not go beyond the observation that the supplicant is "the passive object of YHWH's injurious actions."[80] Something else is said about YHWH and YHWH's actions. This brings us to the middle section, verses 10–12 (11–13) and its theme of "YHWH and the dead."

77. Based on the translation by Ebach, *Streiten mit Gott*, 1:136; see his brief exegesis on 1:140–41; see also Köhlmoos, *Das Auge Gottes*, 235ff.; and Riede, *Im Netz des Jägers*, 66ff. After Job 16, Job no longer describes a "mysterious, but a demonic God, to whom Job has lost every possible connection and who—conversely—has no further connection to the world. Job's entire image of God has been reduced to that of the merciless warrior" (Köhlmoos, *Das Auge Gottes*, 238); on this "Satanization of God," see esp. Spieckermann, "Die Satanisierung Gottes"; and Jürgen van Oorschot, "Menschenbild, Gottesbild," 326ff. Job's accusation of God as enemy of human beings is not the expression of a factual godlessness, i.e., a practical atheism as found in Pss. 10:11; 64:5/6; 73:11; or 94:7. Rather, it "has the function of an appeal. [The supplicant wants] God to be moved to intervene in the sense of Job 16:18–22 and 19:25–27" (ibid., 328 n. 49). More specifically, the supplicant wants God to be moved to intervene as legal advocate against God himself (cf. ibid., 329).

78. Gross, "Gott als Feind?"; idem, "Ein Schwerkranker betet," 111–12.

79. See 219 above.

80. Gross, "Gott als Feind?," 165; idem, "Ein Schwerkranker betet," 104.

3. The Dead Do Not Praise YHWH

Psalm 88 distinguishes itself from other Psalms of Lament, as we have seen, in that the process of praying consistently moves away from the first invocation, "YHWH, God of my salvation" (אֱלֹהֵי יְשׁוּעָתִי, v. 1/2a), and toward an accusation of God, so that what is found at the end is only the removal of the supplicant from one's social environment and one's God, who has brought about this removal: "You have removed from me friend and companion, my close friends—[there is a place of] darkness!" (v. 18/19, cf. v. 8/9). In Psalm 13, the process of praying takes the exact opposite direction: from the complaint (vv. 1–2 [2–3]), on to the petition (3–4 [4–5]), and then to the affirmation of trust and promise of praise (v. 5–6/6), which extols the accomplished act of salvation.[81]

However, if one takes into consideration verses 10–12 (11–13), the middle section of Psalm 88, there is a certain shift of emphases. In this section, which constitutes the psalm's axis of meaning,[82] the supplicant does not speak about self but about the dead[83] in general and about YHWH's relation to them. The supplicant has already compared self to the dead and slain in verse 5/6, "whom you [YHWH] no longer remember; they are cut off from your hand." This absence of relation between YHWH and supplicant is generalized in verses 10–12 (11–13) and stylistically expressed through three rhetorical questions, which are to be answered with "No":

> Should you work miracles among the dead,
> or shall the spirits of the dead rise to praise you? *Selah.*
> (Ps. 88:10/11)
> Is your **goodness** spoken of in the grave,
> your **faithfulness** in the place of doom? (v. 11/12)
> Are your **miracles** proclaimed in the darkness
> and your **righteousness** in the land of forgetfulness?[84] (v. 12/13)

Moreover, only positive actions and qualities of YHWH are mentioned here, which are expressed in verses 11–12 (12–13) through the weighty nouns "your goodness" and "your faithfulness," "your miracles" and "your righteousness":

10/11	Dead (← YHWH) עָשָׂה־פֶלֶא, "work miracles"	//	Spirits of the dead (→ YHWH) ידה Hiphil, "praise"
11/12	Grave (קֶבֶר) חֶסֶד, (YHWH's) "goodness"	//	place of doom (אֲבַדּוֹן) אֱמוּנָה, (YHWH's) "faithfulness"
12/13	Darkness (חֹשֶׁךְ) פֶּלֶה, (YHWH's) "miracles"	//	Land of forgetfulness (אֶרֶץ נְשִׁיָּה) צְדָקָה, (YHWH's) "righteousness"

These nouns are lined up in such a way as to yield a tight structure of *persons* (v. 10/11, dead // spirits of the dead) and *places* (v. 11/12, grave // place of doom; v. 12/13, darkness // land of forgetfulness). Of note here is the change

81. See 82ff. above.
82. See 220 above.
83. Cf. 88:5/6 (מֵתִים, "dead" // חֲלָלִים, "slain"); see Illman, *Formulas about Death*, 141ff.
84. The emphases are intended to facilitate the comparison with Ps. 40:5/6ff.; see below.

from *active* (v. 10/11) to *passive* verbs (vv. 11–12 [12–13]), which is especially significant in view of the thematic inclusio of verses 10/11a ("Should you work [עָשָׂה] *miracles* among the dead?") and 12/13a ("Are your miracles proclaimed [ידע Niphal] in the darkness?").

Against the background of Psalm 40:5–10 (6–11), it also becomes clear that the terms "goodness," "faithfulness," "miracles," and "righteousness" refer to human life through and before God:

> YHWH my God, you have multiplied
> your **miracles** [נִפְלְאֹת] and your **plans** [מַחְשְׁבֹת] among us;
> nothing compares to you;
> should I proclaim and speak of them,
> they are too mighty to count them.
> (Ps. 40:5/6)
> You have no pleasure in sacrifice and food offerings,
> but you have opened ears for me,
> burnt offerings and sin offerings you have not required. (v. 6/7)
> Then I said: "See, I am coming;
> in the scroll is written that which applies to me. (v. 7/8)
> To do your will, my God, is my joy,
> and your instruction is within me." (v. 8/9)
> Gladly I proclaim your **justice** [צֶדֶק] in the great assembly;
> see, I do not close my lips.
> You know it, YHWH. (v. 9/10)
> I have not hidden your **righteousness** [צְדָקָה] in my heart;
> I have spoken of your **faithfulness** [אֱמוּנָה] and your **assistance** [תְשׁוּעָה].
> I have not withheld your **goodness** [חֶסֶד] and your **truth** [אֱמֶת]
> before the great assembly. (v. 10/11)

A "miracle," that which defies the expectable, is especially hoped for in the hour of death. According to C. Hardmeier, the nouns נִפְלָאוֹת and פֶּלֶא, which are usually translated as "miracle," should be rendered as "acts [of God] that exceed the expectable" (נִפְלָאוֹת) and "acts [of God] that are contrary to expectation" (פֶּלֶא),[85] to clear the term "miracle" of its supernatural associations. Thus "פלא in the Niphal describes events that cannot be classified, grasped, or understood and which therefore appear to be unexpected, surprising, or wondrous, so that one does not know how to respond to them (cf. Deut. 17:8–9; 2 Sam. 1:26; 13:2; Prov. 30:18–19; [etc.])."[86]

Among the Thanksgiving Psalms, in Psalm 107 different groups of people are named—desert wanderers (vv. 4–9), prisoners (vv. 10–16), sick people (vv. 17–22), and sailors (vv. 23–32)—who have all been saved from respective existential crises and who should testify to this as proof of their wondrous salvation by YHWH (vv. 8, 15, 21–22, 31–32):

> [Some were languishing] because of wicked ways,
> suffering because of their transgressions.
> (Ps. 107:17)

85. Hardmeier, "Tod des Menschen," 304–5; see also Conrad, "פֶּלֶא," 572–73, 76.
86. Hardmeier, "Tod des Menschen," 304 n. 55.

Their throat despised all food;
already they knocked on the gates of death. (v. 18)
Then they cried out to YHWH in their distress;
he saved them from their anguish; (v. 19)
he sent his word and healed them
and let them escape [unharmed] from the Pit— (v. 20)
Let them thank [ידה Hiphil] YHWH for his kindness [חֶסֶד]
and for his miracles [נִפְלָאוֹת] among human beings! (v. 21)
Let them bring offerings of thanksgiving [זִבְחֵי תוֹדָה]
and joyfully proclaim [ספר Piel] his deeds. (v. 22)[87]

In the telling of the concrete experience of salvation within the context of the cult,[88] which is how Psalm 107:21–22[89] can be understood, the individual hope for salvation is integrated into the community's knowledge of salvation and thereby passed on to the surrounding world as to the next generation, keeping the name of YHWH alive in this way.[90] This transmission across generations "of the concrete experience of salvation and the collective knowledge of salvation,"[91] is a basic fundamental part of Israel's cultural memory. Especially the Psalms of Thanksgiving demonstrate that the narrative transmission of concrete experiences of salvation ("salvation from death") is the specific answer of the YHWH religion to ancestor worship and its premise of community between the living and the dead.[92]

Also in the case of Psalm 88, the "miracle" expected of YHWH (vv. 10/11a, 12/13a)—an act of God transcending the expectable (fate of death) of which the saved can tell while the dead cannot—likely refers to the unexplainable acts of salvation that YHWH has performed for the people and that belong to every one of YHWH's followers.[93] Likewise the terms "goodness" and "faithfulness" (v. 11/12)—as well as the hendiadys חֶסֶד וֶאֱמֶת, "reliable goodness"[94]—should refer to the God-human relationship, specifically to the salvific guidance of human life by God, to that which preserves a human being, toward which one orients self, and which the recipient praises gratefully and publicly, as in Psalm 40:9–10 (10–11): "in/before the great assembly."[95] Having been saved, the supplicant—according to this thanksgiving psalm (Ps. 40)—passes on the "joyful and liberating message of YHWH's order of salvation (*ṣedeq*),"[96] which is denied to the petitioner in Psalm 88. For the supplicant of Psalm 88, there are no longer friends and companions, but—in contrast to the jubilation of Psalm 30:5/6[97]—only darkness (v. 18/19; cf. v. 8/9).[98]

87. Based on the translation by Kraus, *Psalmen*, 2:908.

88. On the telling of YHWH's wondrous acts of salvation, see Conrad, "פָּלָא," 577, 579–80; Hardmeier, "Tod des Menschen," 303ff.

89. Cf. Pss. 30:4–5 (5–6), 6–11 (7–12); and 116:10–19; see 260ff. and 282ff. below.

90. Cf. Hardmeier, "Tod des Menschen," 305ff.

91. Ibid., 307.

92. See also 214ff. above.

93. For supporting passages, see Conrad, "פָּלָא," 576–77, 580–81.

94. Cf. Pss. 26:3; 115:1; 138:2; etc.

95. Cf. Pss. 22:25/26 and 35:18.

96. Hossfeld and Zenger, *Die Psalmen*, 1:256.

97. "In the evening—crying, in the morning—jubilation"; see 261–62 below.

98. The antithesis of "morning" (בֹּקֶר, 88:13/14) and "place of darkness" (מַחְשָׁךְ, v. 18/19; see 220–21 above) frames another description of affliction, with vv. 13/14 and 14–18 (15–19) as an inclusio.

In light of this fate, the question about the function of the middle portion, verses 10–12 (11–13), is all the more pressing. As we have seen, the supplicant does not speak of self here, but about the dead in general. Yet the supplicant does not describe their suffering in the underworld, but uses the distance of Sheol and its denizens from YHWH to develop an *argumentum ad deum*.[99] YHWH should recognize that it is not in YHWH's own best interest to banish the supplicant to Sheol before that person's time, since that would deprive YHWH of a valuable witness and worshiper of YHWH's goodness and faithfulness. YHWH is to be moved to act by the rhetorical questions of verses 10–12 (11–13), which therefore have an *appellatory* quality.

Let me expand this idea a little further. The theme of "cessation of God's praise in death" is found a total of five times in the Old Testament: in the laments of Psalms 6 and 88, in Psalm 30 among the Thanksgiving Psalms, in Isaiah 38, in Psalm 115—as also in Sirach 17:27–28.[100]

For in death there is no **remembrance** of you;
who shall **praise** [ידה Hiphil] you in Sheol?
(Ps. 6:5/6)

Should you work miracles among the dead,
or shall the spirits of the dead rise to **praise** [ידה Hiphil] you?
(Ps. 88:10/11)

What gain is there in my blood, if I should go down to the Pit?
Does the dust praise [ידה Hiphil] you?
Does it proclaim [נגד Hiphil] your faithfulness?
(Ps. 30:9/10)

For the underworld does not **praise** [ידה Hiphil] you;
death does not **exalt** [הלל Piel] you.
Those who go down into the Pit
do not **bear witness** to [שׂבר Piel] your faithfulness.
(Isa. 38:18)
The living, the living, they **praise** [ידה Hiphil] you, as I [do] today.
A father **makes known** [ידע Hiphil] to his children your faithfulness. (v. 19)

It is not the **dead** [הלל Piel] who praise Yah,
not those who descend into silence. (Ps. 115:17)
We, we **praise/bless** [ברך Piel] Yah,
from now to eternity. Hallelujah. (v. 18)

Who can **praise** the Most High in the realm of the dead,
in the place of the living who **offer their songs of praise**?
(Sir. 17:27)

99. Cf. Kraus, *Psalmen*, 2:775; Wächter, "שְׁאוֹל," 908; and esp. Gross, "Gott als Feind?"

100. See Westermann, *Lob und Klage*, 120ff.; cf. Hardmeier, "Tod des Menschen," 296; also Seybold, *Poetik*, 267ff; and Janowski, "Die Kostbarkeit des Lebens." Against F. Crüsemann's thesis ("Rhetorische Fragen!?"; and F. Crüsemann and M. Crüsemann, "Tod," here esp. 588), the idea found in Ps. 88:10–12 (11–13) of YHWH's overcoming the distance to the dead is not the result of late apocalyptic-visionary speculations, but already existed earlier as a "divine possibility"; see the critique by Schlegel, *Psalm 88*, 65–66; Eberhardt, *JHWH und die Unterwelt*, 5ff.; Schnocks, *Rettung*, 75 with n. 203; 102ff.; and Wälchli, *Gottes Zorn*, 67ff.

Among the dead, [with one] who lives no more,
the songs of praise have come to an end;
only the one who is alive and healthy **praises** the Lord. (v. 28)

Thematically related to Psalm 115:17–18 are Psalms 118:17 and 119:175, which are also expressions of a life-focused perspective:

I shall not die, but live,
and **recount** [ספר Piel] Yah's works.
(Ps. 118:17)

Let my *nepeš* live and **praise** [פלל Piel] you,
and let your judgments help me.
(Ps. 119:175)

The idea that the dead do not praise God or that dead dust is of no benefit for the deity is also found in Mesopotamian prayers, as in the bilingual (Old Babylonian / Neo-Babylonian) Prayer to Marduk (*AfO* 19:57, 67–69 / / *CT* 44:21.II.4–6), which, like its Old Testament parallel, refers to the master-servant relationship:

Ša tī[ṭṭiš] īmu mīnû nēmelšu
bal[tum-m]a ardu bēlašu ipallaḫ
ep[ru mī]tu ana ili mīnâ uṣṣap

67 What is gained, if one has turned to mud?
68 Only a servant who is alive praises his master!
69 Dead dust, what benefit is it to the god?

Resources

Translation of the Neo-Babylonian version is based on W. Mayer, *"Gebetsbeschwörungen,"* 314; cf. ibid., 312ff.; Sommerfeld, *Aufstieg Marduks*, 133; Seux, *Hymnes et prières*, 172ff., and 175 n. 28 (with allusion to Ps. 30:9/10 as a parallel); Foster, "Ghost's Entreaty," esp. 99 n. 13; Loretz, *Psalmstudien*, 304; idem, *Götter*, 281; Zgoll, "Für Sinne, Geist und Seele," here esp. 36–37. On the self-identification of the supplicant as "servant" (*ardu*) in Babylonian prayers, see W. Mayer, *"Gebetsbeschwörungen,"* 49–50. A similar argument is made in the Etana Epic by the eagle with regard to the sun-god Šamaš (*Bab* 12.31.26–28; cf. the translation by W. Mayer, *"Gebetsbeschwörungen,"* 314):

Should I die in the Pit,
who would know that a punishment was inflicted upon me?
Grant life to me, the eagle, so that I may proclaim your name forever.

The theme of "cessation of God's praise in death" has been treated primarily as a topic of Old Testament anthropology. According to H. W. Wolff, "This contrasts the definition of the dead (one who is cut off from the praise of God) with a characterization of the living, as the man who can praise Yahweh's works and word."[101] The threat of death has, however, also implications for the divinity of God, as von Rad has already seen: "Ancient people were obviously disturbed by the fact that there was a dimension—nay more, a form of diminished human existence—in which praise was no longer possible. With death the individual's participation in the cult was extinguished: The dead stood outside the orbit of the worship of Jahweh, and were therefore also debarred from glorifying his deeds."[102]

Here we have come across an unusual element of Old Testament theology, where God himself experiences loss or defeat in relinquishing a supplicant to death—or as Psalm 30:9/10 puts it: "What gain [בֶּצַע] is there in my blood, if I should go down to the Pit?"[103] What von Rad did not see, however, is what Martin Luther, in his *Operationes in psalmos* (1519–21), had already expressed—in the context of interpreting Psalm 6:5/6 (Vulgate):[104]

> Quoniam non est in morte, qui memor sit tui,
> in inferno autem quis confitebur tibi?[105]

> Because there is no one in death who would be mindful of you;
> in hell—who shall profess you [there]?

—the same idea of a "shameless" borderline statement by the supplicants of Psalm 6:5/6 and Psalm 88:10–12 (11–13), which stands in contrast to the tradition of prayer in the early and medieval church. God, according to the interpretation of Psalm 6:5/6, "does not permit human beings to praise him in death. But as God—God remains who God is, whether praised or not."[106]

For Luther, however, the idea of a substantial link between the silence of human beings and the existence of God was so shocking that he concludes his interpretation of Psalm 6:5/6 at the end of the scholion with an elaborate explanation (WA 55/II:92, 1–9). Under the ninth point he writes:

> Quoniam non est in morte, qui memor sit tui,
> id est qui clarificet te coram aliis. (WA 55/II:92, 1–2)

> Because there is no one in death who would be mindful of you,
> that is, who may bear witness to you before others.

This interpretation shows that Luther was not afraid of hell in itself, but rather of the termination or the impossibility of a true connection to God.[107] The cessation of the *coram-Deo* relationship in death, because one can no longer remember God and profess God publicly, is the true sting of death. For

101. H. W. Wolff, *Anthropology*, 106, including a reference to C. Barth, *Errettung vom Tode*, 151: "One should note, however, that the praise of Yahweh also has the function of being a token of vitality." Cf. also von Rad, *Old Testament Theology*, 1:121ff.; H. W. Wolff, *Anthropology*, 226ff.; Janowski, "Die 'Kleine Biblia,'" 144ff.

102. Von Rad, *Old Testament Theology*, 1:369; cf. Hardmeier, "Tod des Menschen," 293ff.

103. See 261–62 below.

104. See references in Janowski, "Die Toten loben JHWH nicht," 31 n. 81.

105. See references in ibid., 31 n. 82.

106. Knuth, *Psalm 6*, 174.

107. Cf. also the marginal gloss to Ps. 88:12/13, where Luther takes up this idea again (WA 4:34, 23ff.).

with every death of a sick person who pleads for mercy, God loses an especially valuable witness to God's saving acts on behalf of human beings and thus to salvation history, the efficacy of which is inextricably tied to the living, collective memory of the community, which must be constantly renewed. This would be the "defeat of God," which God would suffer through the death of such a valuable witness, which is implied by Luther.[108]

Against this backdrop, we can arrive at the following conclusion regarding the interpretation of Psalm 88. It appears as if the questions in the middle section, verses 10–12 (11–13), which escalate the supplicant's affliction to the extreme, go unheard and have no effect. One could, however, also and perhaps better understand them in the sense of an *argumentum ad deum*, as an appeal by the supplicant, who takes the accusation of YHWH as the cause of the petitioner's suffering (vv. 3–9a [4–10a] and 14–18 [15–19]) to the extreme and demonstrates, in the form of a "shameless" borderline statement, that God is dependent on those who receive divine grace in their lifetime and who in response can testify publicly to YHWH's saving acts. Their future is also God's future, and their death is God's defeat. This is a radical form of theology, but it is a theology that is deeply rooted in the religious traditions of Israel because it does not deny the question of God, especially in light of death.

Another, sapiential solution to the problem of transience and of God's wrath, different from Psalm 88, is found in the Prayer of Moses, Psalm 90. After the complaint about mortality in verses 3–10 is first a double question (v. 11) at the center of the psalm, which "calls into question the 'logic of death' presented in the first two parts and views of God and of humanity on which it is based."[109] This is followed by an appeal to God as the "teacher of life" (v. 12), who instructs human beings in the right response to the knowledge of one's own death:

> Who discerns the power of your wrath
> and your anger, according to the fear that is your due? (Ps. 90:11)
> Teach us to number our days,
> that we may obtain a wise heart. (v. 12)

The point here is not hope for salvation from death or even immortality, but rather "to accept with wonder each moment as a gift of the good Creator God and to persevere in its challenge."[110] This solution of the *conditio humana* problem is no more superficial than the one found in Psalm 88, but it is different:

> It is precisely through the awareness of the limitations of their lives that the faithful are called to recognize the value of each day. The knowledge of the temporal transcendence of God in contrast to one's own condition of being bound in time invites trust in the caring presence of this God and turns the focus of human beings away from anxious worry toward joy over life and the successful "work of one's hands."[111]

108. Hardmeier, "Tod des Menschen," 307; cf. Knuth, *Psalm 6*, 173–74.
109. Hossfeld and Zenger, *Psalmen 51–100*, 611.
110. Ibid., 612. On Ps. 90, see T. Krüger, "Psalm 90"; Irsigler, "Psalm 90"; Schnocks, "Die Gegenwart Gottes"; Forster, *Begrenztes Leben*, 137ff., etc.
111. Schnocks, "Die Gegenwart Gottes," 169.

To sum up: one searches in vain for Psalm 88 in the German Protestant hymnal (*Evangelisches Gesangbuch*), since it was simply left out. The wisdom of this decision need not be revisited here since it speaks for itself. While offending passages in other Psalms of Lament have been cut out[112]—presumably to spare the congregations—Psalm 88 was treated in a distinctly uncompromising manner. Those who preserved this psalm and integrated it into the second collection of Korah Psalms (Pss. 84–85; 87–88)[113] were wiser in this respect. The church should respect this decision not only theoretically, but also in practice, for "such an act of prayer and the official transmission of such a prayer test says more about a community's view of God (and the view of humanity) than an entire dogmatic tractate."[114]

At stake is the *hope for the saving God*, a hope that is kept alive by the rhetorical questions of the middle section, Psalm 88:10–12 (11–13). The supplicant "does not want to give up this hope, even if it is contrary to everything else."[115]

Psalm 88 thus represents a radical prayer, which is nevertheless rooted in the religious traditions of Israel. The place of this text in the history of Old Testament views on death will be explored below.[116]

γ. *Death Metaphors in the I-Complaint*

In my analysis of Psalm 59, I extensively discussed the animal similes in the enemy-complaint.[117] Already mentioned there were the contrasting depictions of death in the I-complaint, in which the supplicant compares self to various birds in order to convey the experience of the growing power of "death in the midst of life."[118]

Using Psalm 88:4–5 (5–6) as a starting point, we can sort the similes and metaphors used in the I-complaint into different categories,[119] from which the images are derived. Thus the following outline emerges from the Psalms:

Comparison with objects

Nature		*Culture*	
22:14/15	poured-out water	22:14/15	melted wax
69:1/2	waters [of death]	22:15/16	dried-up potsherd
69:2/3	deep mire, floods of water	31:12/13	broken vessel
102:11/12	long shadows	38:4/5	heavy burden
109:23	declining shadow	102:3/4	smoke, fire
143:6	land thirsting for water		

Comparison with human beings

28:1	those who go down to the Pit
31:12/13	dead person
38:14	deaf person, mute person

112. See Zenger, *Ein Gott der Rache*, 11ff.; Janowski, "'Dem Löwen gleich.'" On the use of the Psalms in the German Protestant Hymnal, see Nitsche, "Die Psalmenrezeption."

113. See 221 above.

114. Gross, "Gott als Feind?," 170; cf. idem, "Ein Schwerkranker betet," 112, 115ff.

115. Zenger, *Dein Angesicht suche ich*, 73; cf. 77–78.

116. See 315ff. below.

117. On the animal similes in the enemy-complaint (animal species: lion, bull, dog, snake, bee), see 114ff. above.

118. See 33ff. above.

119. See Westermann, *Vergleiche und Gleichnisse*, 228ff.

38:15	person who is unable to speak
88:4/5	those who go down to the Pit
88:5/6	those slain, lying in the grave

Comparison with animals

22:6/7	worm
42:1/2	deer longing for water
102:6/7	bird (in the desert), owl (among ruins)
102:7/8	bird (lonely on the rooftop)
109:23	locust

Comparison with plants

102:4/5	withered grass
102:11/12	dried-up grass

Conceptual comparisons

31:11/12	reproach, terror
39:5/6	nothingness, breath
39:6/7	shadow, breath (cf. v. 11/12)
62:9–10 (10–11)	breath, deception
109:23	shadow
144:4	breath, vanishing shadow

The common element in these similes and metaphors is the *transience of human beings*, whose suffering is being expressed as their "decline toward death through the empowerment of death in the midst of life,"[120] albeit with various different nuances.[121] The images used here are not aesthetic ornamentations of reality, but expressions of an understanding of reality that, following H.-P. Müller, I have called *religious appropriation of being* [*religiöse Daseinsaneignung*].[122] "Religious appropriation of being" means that, through metaphorical language, the supplicant's fate is tied so closely to the external lived-in reality (people, objects, animals, plants) that the object of comparison—the lamenting supplicant—appropriates part of the nature of the respective subject of comparison, as illustrated here:

Comparison with objects
Like **water** I am poured out;
my limbs are out of joint;
my heart has become like **wax**,
melted within my bowels.
(Ps. 22:14/15)

Comparison with human beings / objects
I have been forgotten like **one who is dead**—gone from the heart.
I have become like a **broken vessel**.
(Ps. 31:12/13)

120. Ibid., 81. Particularly significant in this context is the image of human beings or of human life as "breath," הֶבֶל (Pss. 39:5/6, 6/7, 11/12; 62:9/10, 10/11; 144:4), which also appears in Ecclesiastes (3:19; 6:12; 9:9; etc.); see Schwienhorst-Schönberger, *Kohelet im Spannungsfeld*, 14ff.; Zimmer, *Zwischen Tod und Lebensglück*, 25ff.; T. Krüger, *Kohelet*, 14–15, 101ff.; etc.

121. Ps. 39:5–6 (6–7), e.g., does not deal with an untimely ("bad") death but with the temporal limitation of life; see Forster, *Begrenztes Leben*, 35ff., 41ff.; and Schnocks, Review of *Begrenztes Leben*.

122. Cf. H.-P. Müller, *Vergleich und Metapher*, 49ff.; see 34–35 above.

Comparison with animals
As the **deer** cries over [dried up] riverbeds,
so my *nepeš* cries for you, O God.
(Ps. 42:1/2)

Comparison with plants
Withered like **grass** and dried up is my heart.
Indeed, I forgot to eat my bread.
(Ps. 102:4/5; cf. v. 11/12)

Conceptual comparisons
See, you have made my days mere handbreadths,
and my lifetime is like **nothing** before you.
Indeed, each human being standing upright is a **breath**.
(Ps. 39:5/6)

Although the semantic content of the comparison is unmistakable at its core—the subject is always the *empowerment of death in the midst of life*—Old Testament scholarship has taken a relatively long time to recognize this also theologically. For a long time, this *thinking in images* was explained on the basis of the "vivid imagination of the Semites" (Bertholet) or the "burning passion of the orientals" (Gunkel)[123] and corresponding statements about salvation from death (images or water, mire, grave/pit) as "especially fantastic expressions" for an event that would be rendered "objectively and prosaically as 'preservation from an untimely death.'"[124] Christoph Barth was the first to formulate a coherent alternative position that does justice to the intention of the text.

C. Barth opens his argument by pointing to the widespread misunderstanding of image-based language in the Psalms as "exaggeration or poetic fantasy." The question is this: Are the statements in the Psalms of Lament and Thanksgiving intended figuratively or concretely? Further: To what extent is the *dead* different from the *afflicted*, who sees self in the underworld with a living body and who therefore calls oneself "dead" or "like one who is dead"?

According to C. Barth, the situation of the afflicted is comparable but not identical to that of the dead (in the physical sense). Comparability is based on the sinister aspects of the affliction by death. This commonality has a stark contrast: "The afflicted seems to have experienced only the closeness of death, but not death itself."[125] However,

> in the thinking of ancient Near Eastern peoples, this closeness of death is equivalent to the actual experience of death. The afflicted comes in contact with the reality of death only to a limited extent, perhaps only partially, but this is precisely sufficient to allow for the experience of the entire reality of death. . . . The afflicted calls self dead only by way of comparison; this idea has its origin in the real, if only partial, equivalence of affliction and death. . . . The afflicted is neither dead nor alive in the full sense, being situated somewhere in the middle. The important point for the afflicted is not being still alive, but being close to the realm of death.[126]

123. See C. Barth, *Errettung vom Tode*, 11ff., with corresponding references.
124. Ibid., 14.
125. Ibid., 92.
126. Ibid., 92–93.

Excursus 7: Life and Death

Human beings have always known about the presence of death in life and have expressed this knowledge through words and images—with remarkable cultural and religious differences. These differences are based at least in part on the fact that the separation between life and death is not always found in the same place, but varies according to respective ontological assumptions (see Theunissen, *Negative Theologie*, 197ff.; Schütz and Luckmann, *Strukturen*, 171ff.; Macho, *Todesmetaphern*, 408ff.).

The question of what the boundaries of the world are would have been answered, for example, by an Egyptian with reference to the "boundless," meaning the primordial darkness, the primordial ocean, and the bottomless abyss of the earth. In Egyptian thought these three primordial entities are designations for the unformed, the unordered, and the unlimited, from which the ordered, delimited, and living world was created at the beginning. "For the Egyptian, existence in its spatial and temporal extent is embedded on all sides in the boundlessness of nonbeing; this nonbeing does not stop, however, at the boundaries of being, but permeates all of creation" (Hornung, *Der Eine und die Vielen*, 174; cf. idem, "Von zweierlei," 419–20; Janowski, *Rettungsgewissheit*, 145ff.). For this reason, there are "chaotic realms within the ordered world": the desert, the tomb, the night. An astronomical-cosmological text speaks of the boundaries of the primordial darkness as unknown and that neither gods nor spirits know its land: "There are no rays of light, and it [the land of the primordial darkness] extends under every place" (Hornung, *Der Eine und die Vielen*, 162).

Nonexistence is omnipresent: one encounters it with every step: *sleeping*, as the temporary descent into the bottomless abyss of the earth; *in the desert*, with its terrifying mythical creatures; and in *sickness*, as the entryway to the underworld (cf. Janowski, *Rettungsgewissheit*, 121–22, 131, etc.). In the context of personal piety in the New Kingdom (1550–1070 BCE), healing of the sick is therefore praised as "salvation from the underworld" as in the prayer:

21 "You are Amun-Re, Lord of Thebes.
22 You save the one who is in the underworld,
23 for it is you [who is merciful] when called upon;
24 it is you, who come from far away!"

(J. Assmann, *Ägyptische*, 372, no. 148;
cf. Janowski, *Rettungsgewissheit*, 121–22)

The boundary between life and death is also a central theme in the Psalms. Since death is part of life, and a human being can be "dead" while still alive, the realm of death is not restricted to a special assigned space. Part of its nature is a constant "bursting-of-its-banks," a capture of territories that should belong to the realm of life (cf. C. Barth, *Errettung vom Tode*, 42ff.). In this sense, depictions of death in the Psalms that do not directly describe the act of dying belong to the "category of descriptions of the boundary of death moved far into the territory of life" (Krieg, *Schmetterlingsweisheit*, 29). There is only a relative difference between life and death, for "not everything 'living' is truly alive and not everything 'dead' is truly dead. A sick or cursed person is already 'partly' among the dead and not only figuratively speaking" (C. Barth, "Leben und Tod," in *Errettung vom Tode*, 141). Through this presence of "death in the midst of life," an important dimension is added to life. (Compare H. W. Wolff, *Anthropology*, 110ff.) On the motif *media vita in morte sumus*, see above, 47. See also Johnston, *Shades of Sheol*; Werlitz, "Scheol und sonst nichts?"; Spronk, "Good Death"; A. Fischer, *Tod und Jenseits*; Hieke, *Tod*; Janowski, "Gott, Mensch und Raum," 18ff.; as well as the contributions in the themed volume *Jenseitsvorstellungen im Alten Testament*, ed. Leicht; and allusions above, 22ff. and 120ff.

We have seen[127] that the images of death in the Psalms of the Individual are all taken from the realm of life: the realm of nature and culture, animals and plants. Through the knowledge of the presence of "death in the midst of life," they were, however, transformed into images of death.[128] We are thus confronted with a *particular conception of* space in the death metaphor of the I-complaint, which depicts the supplicant's fate "not as figuratively exaggerated or as theological fiction, but quite realistically."[129] The particularity of this spatial conception is even more clearly marked against the background of ancient Near Eastern and Greek views of life/afterlife.

b. Anthropological Keyword 5: This Life and Afterlife

The cloud fades and vanishes,
  so those who go down to the underworld do not come up again.
They do not return to their house,
  and soon their place does not know them anymore.
Job 7:9–10

YHWH brings death and life;
  [YHWH] brings down to the underworld and up [again].
1 Samuel 2:6

Resources

Artemov, "The Elusive Beyond"; J. Assmann, "Diesseits-Jenseits-Beziehungen"; idem, *Tod und Jenseits*, 285–318; C. Barth, *Diesseits und Jenseits*, 465–502; idem, *Errettung vom Tode*, 59–97; Berlejung, "Unterwelt"; idem, "Wüste/Steppe"; Burkert, *Griechische Religion*, 300–306; Dietrich and Link, *Allmacht und Ohnmacht*, 160–67; Dietrich and Vollenweider, "Tod II," 585–88; Eberhardt,

127. See 236ff. above.
128. Cf. Krieg, *Schmetterlingsweisheit*, 29; idem, *Todesbilder*, 351ff., 612ff.; and Dietrich and Vollenweider, "Tod II," 582–83; etc. On the motif *media vita in morte sumus*, see 47 n. 57 above.
129. Von Rad, "'Gerechtigkeit' und 'Leben,'" 237; cf. idem, *Theologie*, 1:399ff.

"Gottesferne der Unterwelt"; Görg, *Ein Haus;* Graf, "Jenseitsvorstellungen"; Groneberg, *Unterweltsvorstellungen*, 244–61; Healey and Niehr, "Land ohne Wiederkehr"; Hoheisel et al., "Jenseits"; Hornung, "Schwarze Löcher"; Houtman, "Hölle"; Hutter, *Religionen*, 65–71, 149–54, 220–22; idem, "Jenseitsvorstellungen"; Janowski, "Gott, Mensch und Raum," 12ff., 18ff.; Keel, *Die Welt*, 53–68; Lang, "Leben nach dem Tod"; idem, "Leibliche Auferstehung?"; idem, "Reise ins Jenseits"; Liess, "Lokalisierung des Totenreichs"; Lundström, "Aussagekraft schriftlicher Quellen"; idem, "Ordnung der Unterwelt"; idem, "Unterwelt"; Pezzoli-Olgiati, "Gegenwelt des Todes"; Podella, "Totenrituale"; Selz, "'Brunnen der Vergangenheit'"; Stolz, "Paradiese und Gegenwelten"; idem, *Religionswissenschaft*, 94–100; idem, *Weltbilder der Religionen*, 9–15; Wilcke, "Tod im Leben."

Notions regarding what awaits human beings after their death are found in most cultures. The respective views generally correspond to the concepts "this life" and "afterlife" and their mutual relationship. This relationship can designate a *spatial* (here/beyond, below/above) or *temporal* (before/after, temporal/eternal) contrast or even a *qualitative* contrast (visible/invisible, physical/metaphysical). Already the two leading quotations from Job's second speech (Job 6:1–7:21) and the Song of Hannah (1 Sam. 2:1–10) present very different interpretations of death: the former with the idea of "land of no return"[130] and the latter with the theme of "salvation from death" characteristic of the Psalms of Lament and Thanksgiving.[131]

In the history of religions[132] the realm of death is frequently and intensively conceived of as a counterworld or nonworld, as a world that does not simply offset but also transforms this life. As the elements "counter-" or "non-" in the above terminology suggest, the deceased enters a realm with conditions and forms of being that are characteristically dissimilar from those found in the world of the living. This dissimilarity manifests itself first of all in the *position of the world beyond.*[133] This position can refer to the following:

- a grave (oval or rectangular tomb structures, vulva carved into the walls of burial places, etc.)
- a marked area on the earth surface (mountains, islands, edge of the world, extreme end of the earth, etc.)
- a region below the earth (water holes, caves, crevices, bottom of lakes, bottom of the sea, etc.)

130. This idea is found esp. in Mesopotamian texts (*ašar / erṣet lā târi*, "place/land of no return"), see Groneberg, *Unterweltsvorstellungen*, 258–59; also Healey and Niehr, "Land ohne Wiederkehr," 95ff.; Berlejung, "Tod und Leben," 466ff.; and Lundström, "Ordnung der Unterwelt." A later echo of this understanding of death is found in Shakespeare's *Hamlet* (act 3, scene 1, lines 79–80): "The undiscover'd country from whose bourn / No traveller returns."

131. See 245ff. below.

132. See the following collections: Klimkeit, *Tod und Jenseits;* Stephenson, *Leben und Tod;* von Barloewen, *Der Tod in den Weltkulturen.* A comprehensive collection of source materials is found in Eliade and Lanczkowski, *Geschichte der Religiösen Ideen: Quellentexte*, 250ff.

133. Cf. Hoheisel et al., "Jenseits," 320–21.

- a region above the earth (ascension of the soul into the heavens, deceased as stars, etc.)
- a community with the gods of deified ancestors
- a world beyond, not tied to any particular locale

Second, the counterworldly character of realm beyond is *embellished with regard to its content,*[134] such as these features:

- deterioration or diminishing of earthly existence (Tuat, Sheol, Hades, shadow-like existence of the dead, semiconscious state, etc.)
- intensification of earthly existence (paradise, Elysium, "field of rushes," immortality, etc.)
- double afterlife: as place of blessed existence (heaven), and as abyss of torment with eternal punishment (purgatory, hell)

Notions of the afterlife do not only differ between cultures; they can also vary within one and the same culture. In ancient Greece, for example,

> it was assumed on the one hand that the dead remain in the vicinity of their graves; they receive their gifts, and they come to the living in particular on their anniversaries in order to receive food and honors. On the other hand, there existed an elaborate mythology of the afterlife. The dead enter the realm of Hades, where they lead an adverse existence as shadows. Finally, one knew of an "island of the blessed," where certain select of the dead led a joyful existence. Over time, religious systems develop that offer the individuals prospects of a beautiful afterlife; the counterworld depicted in this way thereby assumes the position of an orienting force, which relativizes existence. The realm of death thus becomes a manifold counterworld, through which life receives its contours.[135]

This example demonstrates that ideas about the afterlife can be derived indirectly via this life because they represent its corollary. As the metalinguistic term "counterworld" suggests, this appears to be a structuring element of the life-afterlife relationship.

α. From This Life to the Afterlife

The experience of death is not exclusively tied to the biological end of life.[136] Important transitions within social life—such as birth, entry into adulthood, treatment of young women, or marriage—are ritualized (rites of passage) and are frequently symbolized by means of life/afterlife terminology.[137] Similarly, crisis-like events in personal life, such as illnesses, can be experienced as death that is impending or has already partially occurred and is dealt with through corresponding (figurative) language. In these transitions—from one social role to another, or from health to illness (and back again)—the relationship between this

134. Cf. ibid., 321–22.
135. Stolz, *Religionswissenschaft*, 98–99.
136. See 46–47 above.
137. For ancient Greece, e.g., see Zaidman and Pantel, *Die Religion der Griechen*, 66ff.

life and the afterlife, or between life and death, is organized on the basis of certain assumptions that are culturally conditioned and that facilitate an orientation in "social space."[138] An example for this is found in Egyptian beliefs about death and the corresponding typology of relations between this life and the afterlife.

Aside from specific questions about ritual communication with the world of the afterlife in the form of sacrifices/feasts for the dead, the relationship between this life and the afterlife in the cult of the dead and the veneration of ancestors includes three different aspects: *prospective, transitory,* and *retrospective.*[139] The prospective aspect relates to *concern for the afterlife,* measures to be taken in this life in order to arrive in the afterlife (proper behavior, position of gravesite, securing of provisions, study of literature about the afterlife). The transitory aspect pertains to the *departure from this world* and the *transition to the afterlife.* A constitutive important element here is the overcoming of certain intermediate stages, such as the crossing of waters of death (Mesopotamian Hubur, Greek Acheron, Styx, etc.)[140] or the judgment of the dead in Egypt.[141] At the end of this stage are images of hope, depicting the joyful reception of the dead into the world of the afterlife.[142]

The afterlife represents an inversion of this life. Everything that is found here is turned into its opposite there. The ancient Egyptian idea that death is the transition to another and more intensive form of life is particularly important for the third, *retrospective aspect* of the relationship between this life and the afterlife. It is based on the conviction that this life does not end for the deceased with death. Rather, the deceased builds on the previous life in various ways: before the judges of the afterlife, the person may invoke the merits gained while alive or the performance in certain cultic acts (participation in processional festivals, life according to maʿat, etc.). The continuation of the deceased's previous life culminates in the theme of *return to this life,* which dominated Egyptian beliefs about death since the time of the New Kingdom. This return includes a "reunion with one's family, benevolent care for one's household and descendants, visiting temples and participation in the festivals of the city's deity as well as other festivals"[143] (cf. fig. 28).

Jan Assmann has explained this idea by referring to the theme of "going forth by day" (*pr .t m hrw*), which depicts the "existence" of the deceased in images from the afterlife of the grave's occupant. This does not imply that the

138. This orientation in the natural and social world is achieved by the religious symbol system through certain binary pairs like pure/impure, sacred/profane, ordered/chaotic, or central/peripheral, and the corresponding experiences on which they are based. On the basis of this *symbolic order of space and time,* the social boundaries of space and time that enable such an orientation are established and defined; see esp. Leach, *Culture and Communication*; Douglas, *Purity and Danger*; also Stolz, *Religionswissenschaft,* 101ff.; and Malina, *The New Testament World.*

139. On the following discussion, see J. Assmann, "Diesseits-Jenseits-Beziehungen"; cf. also Hoheisel et al., "Jenseits," 324–25.

140. On the Greek geography of death (Acheron, Pyriphlegeton, Cocytus, Styx, etc.), see Burkert, *Griechische Religion,* 302–3.

141. See 161–62 above.

142. The interpenetration of this life and the afterlife is most pronounced at the moment of death, as the ambivalent role of the grave demonstrates in signifying both realms: "It marks a place in the afterlife, so that the deceased knows where to go when the messenger of death calls one from this life—as well as marking a place in this life, representing the grave's occupant to posterity, with the wish that memory of the deceased will live on through the 'name'" (J. Assmann, "Diesseits-Jenseits-Beziehungen," 1085–86).

143. Ibid., 1087. For a more detailed account, see J. Assmann, *Tod und Jenseits,* 285ff.

Figure. 28. Visit by the deceased in this life
(Egypt, New Kingdom)

deceased has free mobility in the afterlife, but rather describes a particular form of life after death, which is conceptualized as "return to this life." Is this concept analogous to the idea of "salvation from death" in the individual Psalms of Lament and Thanksgiving?

β. Return to This Life

The idea of a "return to this life" requires further explanation in view of the Egyptian context, since the deceased leaves the underworld "neither as a mummy nor as a spirit. The deceased is also not born again to a new life on earth. The medium of one's freedom of movement between the worlds is one's transformation."[144]

In addition to the so-called false door, *the* contact- and entry-point between this life and the afterlife,[145] the transformation of the transfigured spirit of the deceased into the *Ba*-bird or another manifestation of the *Ba* also plays a crucial role.[146] The goal of this transformation is reunion with family and friends. This is an essential development in the Egyptian beliefs about death, because it implies a "shift of views about the afterlife to this life," which corresponds inversely to a "shift to the afterlife or a sacralization of this life: "The more the dead return to this life, the more intensive becomes the sacral significance of this life. . . . The dead do not simply stay in an underworld intended for the

144. Ibid., 293.

145. See ibid., 286ff.

146. *Ba* is concept of power that refers to the ability to assume different forms (falcon, crocodile, snake, a deity, statues in the funerary chapel, etc.) and to animate them; see ibid., 293ff., etc. A useful definition is provided by Kurth (*Edfu*, 64): "*Ba* and *ka* are untranslatable concepts. Both can be explained to some extent by comparison to a plant: *Ka* corresponds to the root, *ba* to the stem, leaves, and flower. *Ka* provides stability for a living creature and embodies its vital force, which must be perpetually nourished; *ka* is its trunk, which continually gives rise to new life. *Ba* embodies the ability of a living being to show itself, to move about. Thus, e.g., the *ba* of a human being has the form of a bird with a human head, the sun is called the *ba* of the sun-god Ra, and someone who dies returns to his *ka*. The body of a living being is also used to create its *ka*, like a second body. The *ka* accompanies its owner and protects it."

afterlife, in which the sun wakes them temporarily during its nightly course; rather, they rest in a grave, which they leave in the morning like the living, to go about in this life in the form of their *Ba*."[147]

The innovation in Egyptian beliefs about death characteristic for the New Kingdom (1552–1070 BCE) was a complete orientation of hopes for an afterlife toward the world of this life and hence the expansion of this life as a "realm of the afterlife in addition to heaven and underworld."[148] There are, so to speak, "domains of the afterlife in the world of this life," analogous to the "chaotic domains within the ordered world," which Hornung has discussed in an earlier essay.[149] This includes the striking images of the deceased as strolling about in a garden, with pond near one's grave, and participating in the festival of the city's deity or the major religious festivals.[150]

The form of the regained community and divine closeness, as it appears in the texts and images of this-life-focused Egyptian expectations regarding the afterlife, is reminiscent of the polarity of this life/afterlife in the Psalms of Lament and Thanksgiving. Here too the afterlife is apparently a realm that almost literally protrudes spatially into the world of this life, thereby creating a space of death or a *domain of the afterlife in the world of this life*. The critical difference from Egypt is that in Israel the deceased (and later one's transfigured spirit) does not return to this life, but only the supplicant who has been saved from death by YHWH. This is experienced in *this life*—not only after one's death[151]—that which Christoph Barth has defined as the topos of "salvation from death."[152] Areas that are associated with the afterlife in this context include grave, dust, prison, cistern, pit, flood, sea, desert, steppe, foothills, and—as a temporal domain—darkness of night.[153] These constitute the narrow and dangerous boundary between life and death,[154] on which the supplicant finds self.

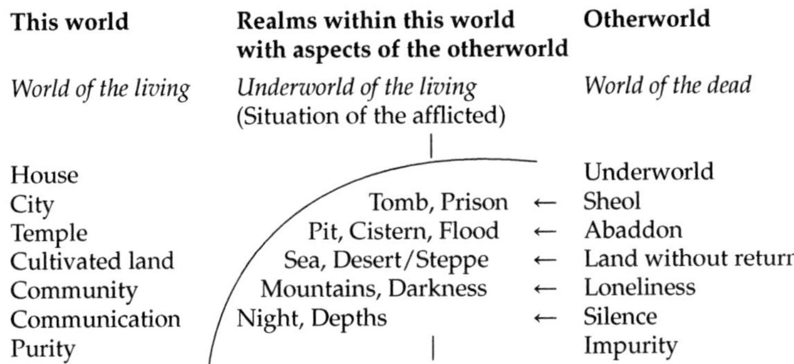

Figure 29. The boundary between life and death, according to the Psalms

147. J. Assmann, *Tod und Jenseits*, 295.
148. Ibid., 297.
149. Ibid., 297. For this thesis, see Hornung, "Chaotische Bereiche"; and see 239–40 above.
150. See references in J. Assmann, *Tod und Jenseits*, 299ff.
151. This idea is a later development; see 318ff. below.
152. See 250ff. above.
153. See Keel, *Die Welt*, 53ff.; Janowski, *Rettungsgewissheit*, 23ff.; Podella, "Jenseitsvorstellungen," 80–81; Berlejung, "Tod und Leben," 485ff.
154. See "Excursus 7: Life and Death," above, 239–40.

Let us look at an example: among the Thanksgiving Psalms, in Psalm 107 four groups that have been saved are called to proclaim YHWH's praise in the temple. The four areas from which the afflicted have called to God in their distress are the desert (vv. 4–9), the dungeon (vv. 10–16), sickness (vv. 17–22), and the sea (vv. 23–32). Burning hot deserts without paths, roaring seas, and locked dungeons are areas that can represent and depict human misery as well as the sickness that has brought the supplicant to the "gates of death" (v. 18) or into the "Pits" (v. 20), from which YHWH can deliver the supplicant by divine word:

> [Some were languishing] because of wicked ways,
> suffering because of their transgressions;
> (Ps. 107:17)
> their throat despised all food;
> already they knocked on the gates of death; (v. 18)
> then they cried out to YHWH in their distress,
> and he saved them from their anguish; (v. 19)
> [YHWH] sent his word and healed them,
> and let them escape [unharmed] from the Pit— (v. 20)
> let them thank YHWH for his kindness,
> and for his miracles among human beings! (v. 21)
> Let them bring offerings of thanksgiving
> and joyfully proclaim his deeds. (v. 22)[155]

As in Psalm 88:3–8 (4–9)—especially in verse 3/4: "For my life [*nepeš*] is full of troubles, and my life has touched the underworld"[156]—the boundary between this life and the afterlife is defined in Psalm 107:4–32 in such a way that death protrudes into life, even though in Israel's cosmological imagination the underworld is located in the outermost, inaccessible depths (cf. Job. 38:16–18).[157] The *anthropological* boundary is different from the *cosmological* boundary, or in the words of Christoph Barth:

> Coming under the influence of Sheol even in the most insignificant way is in effect to be completely in its power. If someone's foot begins to slip, there is by human estimation no stopping. If he considers his inescapable end, he is already lost from the beginning. The pars pro toto way of thinking seen here is as characteristic for ancient Near Eastern peoples as it is foreign to us today.[158]

Despite the expansion of YHWH's responsibilities that gradually occurred in Judah between the eighth and the sixth/fifth centuries BCE,[159] YHWH became neither a master of the underworld nor a god of death. He was and remained a

155. See 239–40 above.
156. See 223ff. above.
157. According to Job. 38:17, all human life and knowledge come to a halt before the "gates of the underworld" // "gates of darkness." See Strauss, "Tod (Todeswunsch; 'Jenseits'?) im Buch Hiob," 246–47, G. Fuchs, *Mythos und Hiobdichtung*, 206–7; Egger-Wenzel, *Von der Freiheit Gottes, anders zu sein*, 139, etc.
158. C. Barth, *Errettung vom Tode*, 93.
159. See 214ff. above.

God of life, who did not however save from the underworld as such, but rather "from the underworld insofar as it extended into his domain."[160] Psalm 30, one of the Thanksgiving Psalms, will show us how this saving act was experienced by the one who has been saved and the implications of this experience for the religion of YHWH.

160. Podella, "Jenseitsvorstellungen," 79.

8. "You have girded me with gladness" (Ps. 30:11/12)
The Praising Human Being

a. The Presence of Salvation

> The only relation of consciousness to happiness is gratitude: this constitutes its universal dignity.
>
> Theodor W. Adorno, *Minima moralia*, 144

α. *The Meaning of Life*

H. W. Wolff dedicated the last paragraph of his *Anthropology of the Old Testament* to the question "What is [hu]man's actual destiny?"[1] Despite changes in language, differences in point of view, and an abundance of idioms, the important answers given in the Old Testament all point in the same direction, according to Wolff. Human beings are intended to live and to praise God, the Creator and Savior. Precisely because "nothing is further from the Old Testament intention than a systematic anthropology," this point must be called "an outstanding phenomenon in the history of thought."[2]

According to H. W. Wolff, four basic objectives appear repeatedly in various traditions within the Old Testament. These are the objectives to live in the world, to love one's fellow human beings, to rule creation, and to praise God:

Living in the world. The elementary objective is the objective to live in the world: human beings are "destined to live and not to fall victim to death."[3] Wolff develops this objective, beginning with the nonpriestly primordial history (Gen. 2:4b–8:22) and follows its contours and motifs up to Psalm 16:10–11.[4] "In a world in which survival is threatening to become increasingly improbable, the biblical insight into [hu]man's destiny is ground for a new expectation of life."[5]

Loving one's fellow human beings. According to Wolff, the answer given by the Old Testament to the question of the purpose of human life is that they "are destined to love and to overcome hate."[6] Beginning again with the nonpriestly creation story, Wolff develops this objective through the example of loving

1. H. W. Wolff, *Anthropology*, 223
2. Ibid., 223.
3. Ibid.
4. Ibid., 223–25.
5. Ibid., 225.
6. Ibid.

one's enemies and neighbors.[7] Already in the Old Testament, the ultimate goal of love among human beings includes all the peoples of the world. "Guided by YHWH's edicts from Zion, they are all to cease from learning the techniques of war (Isa. 2.2–4)."[8]

Ruling over creation. In view of this anthropological objective, Wolff also begins with the priestly (and nonpriestly) primordial history and develops on the basis of wisdom texts the specific relationship of human beings in the Old Testament to the world. Ruling over creation is always ruling within the limitation of creation (priestly parts of Gen. 1:1–9:29) or ruling that is limited insofar that wisdom cannot discover "the meaning implanted in creation,"[9] because only God understands the way to it (Job 28).

Praising God. The fourth and most comprehensive objective for human beings is to *praise God.* As a basic theme of hymns in the Old Testament, the praise of God is

> a fundamental epistemological category of the God-human-world relationship. The text group of Old Testament hymns rests on this basis. It is recognizable as a speech-act and language form in the interaction of certain formal characteristics with entirely different contents, united by the experience of salvation for human beings and Israel and of being pardoned and being endowed by God as impulses to praise.[10]

Von Rad has called this form "Israel's answer." According to him the Psalms are the manifestation of a dialogue with God, in which Israel "responds" to the words and deeds of its God in order to find itself in this answer:

> It [Israel's answer] shows us how these acts affected Israel, and how Israel on its side accepted and understood this existence in immediacy with Jahweh and in proximity to him, that is, the steps that in this proximity to Jahweh, Israel took to justify or to be ashamed of itself in its own eyes and before Jahweh. But it also shows how, in this intercourse with Jahweh, Israel was revealed to itself and how Israel pictured itself when coming before Jahweh to speak to him. Here then, if anywhere, we can hope that the basic features of a theological doctrine of [the hu]man will become clear.[11]

Adopting and developing this position further, recent Psalms research has emphasized the basic genres "Psalm of Lament," "hymn/psalm of praise," and "Thanksgiving Psalms" as the *twofold significance* inherent in the Psalter through the conceptual categories of praise and lament.[12] The reason why the book of Psalms, despite its numerous laments, is a monumentally heightened

7. See 122ff. above.
8. H. W. Wolff, *Anthropology*, 226.
9. Ibid., 227.
10. Spieckermann, "Alttestamentliche 'Hymnen,'" 103; Hardmeier, "Systematische Elemente," 127. On the genre of "hymn," see the recent contribution by A. Wagner, "Der Lobaufruf"; et al.
11. Von Rad, *Old Testament Theology* 1:355–56; Zenger, *Einleitung*, 323–24; Rendtorff, *Theologie*, 293; Janowski, "Die 'Kleine Biblia,'" 144ff.; Janowski, "Die Antwort Israels."
12. Cf. Zenger, "Das Buch der Psalmen," 324; Hossfeld, "Von der Klage zum Lob"; idem, "Lob I"; also H.-P. Müller, "Gottesfrage und Psalmenexegese," 287; Rendtorff, *Theologie*, 302ff.; et al.

praise of God expanded to include all of creation[13]—as its name, Book of Praises (תְּהִלִּים [סֵפֶר]), and its concluding doxology formulas[14] also suggest—is that the praise of God is a fundamental expression of theology and is, according to the Old Testament, even the reason for human existence.[15] The praise of God, which relativizes human self-importance and self-absolutization, gives expression to the core of the relation with God: the *care of a compassionate God*, who saves from death and leads into life.

Even individual Psalms of Lament keep alive the burning questions of "Why?" and "How long?" with regard to the existence of God amid fundamentally different experiences. As "conflict dialogues with God," they draw on the belief that human life can only succeed as life *coram Deo* (in God's presence). These psalms are spoken in situations of being separated from God, but the supplicants resist the temptation to dismiss God—as Job's wife suggests to the afflicted (Job 2:9–10).[16] For this reason, they not only conclude with a confession of trust; their compositional structure (complaint with invocation, petition, expression of trust, pledge of praise)[17] also indicates that the complaint is oriented toward the praise of God and reaches its turning point here. "The goal of the complaint is not the depiction of one's own suffering and self-pity, but the turning around of suffering. The complaint is an appeal to the One who can change the suffering."[18] A Psalm of Lament—whose motifs are based on elements of trust and whose structure possesses an inclination toward the change of suffering—is to be understood as a "goal-oriented paradigm of trust"[19] and is therefore one of the strongest testimonies to God's saving action in the Old Testament.

If the complaint assumes that silence would be blasphemous,[20] the same is true for the praise of God. Praising God brings into view assumptions about life, over which the one who thanks and praises God has no control.[21] The Thanksgiving Psalms of the Individual uncover this dimension of life and make it the basis of their "theology of gratitude." A key text for this is Psalm 30.

13. The first three books of the Psalter (I: Pss. 3–41; II: Pss. 42–72; III: Pss. 73–89) are dominated by Individual Psalms of Lament and Thanksgiving, but they are repeatedly interspersed by hymns (Pss. 8; 19; 29; 33; et al.). Their respective context is important for their interpretation, as recent Psalms research has shown; see Zenger, "Der Psalter als Buch." From the fourth book onward (IV: Pss. 90–106; V: Pss. 107–145, and the concluding *Hallel* Pss. 146–150), the lament recedes while the hymns dominate and move into the foreground; cf. Hossfeld, "Von der Klage zum Lob"; and idem, "Lob I."

14. Pss. 41:13/14; 72:18–19; 89:52/53; and 106:48.

15. Cf. Ps. 34:1/2. On the subject, see H. W. Wolff, *Anthropology*, 228–29; Hossfeld, "Lob I," 476; for a discussion in reference to ancient Judaism, see Limbeck, "Der Lobpreis Gottes."

16. "[9] Then his wife said to him: 'Even now you hold on to your faith. "Praise" God and die!' [10] Then he said to her: 'You speak as a foolish woman speaks. We accept from God what is good; should we not also accept what is bad?' In all this Job did not sin with his lips." Translation based on Ebach, *Streiten mit Gott*, 1:32.

17. See 39ff. above.

18. Westermann, "Die Rolle der Klage," 255.

19. Markschies, "Vertrauensäusserungen." On the subject, also see 77 and 81 above.

20. Cf. Jüngel, "Offenbarung der Verborgenheit Gottes," 168–69: "God is not dishonored but glorified if human beings speak with God in such a way as to make him the addressee of their complaint or accusation. On the contrary, God would be dishonored if we were to deny him the glory that is his due by not making him the addressee of our complaints and accusations in such cases. Silence would be blasphemous. We would then deny him the truth. God cannot be dishonored any more than by denying him the truth."

21. On the basic structure of gratitude, see "Anthropological Keyword 6: Gratitude," 275ff. below in this chapter.

β. Psalm 30 as a Case Study

A Psalm. A song at the dedication of the (temple-) house.
By David.

I shall extol you, YHWH,
for you have lifted me up,
and have not let my enemies rejoice over me.
(Ps. 30:1/2)
YHWH my God, I have cried to you,
and you have healed me. (v. 2/3)
YHWH, you have raised up my life [*nepeš*] from the underworld;
you have revived me from among those
who go down into the Pit. (v. 3/4)
Make music for YHWH, you faithful ones,
and give thanks to the memory of his holiness. (v. 4/5)
For one moment, in his anger;
a life long, in his goodwill.
In the evening, crying;
in the morning, jubilation. (v. 5/6)
But I, in my carelessness I thought,
"I shall not stumble, not in all eternity!" (v. 6/7)
YHWH, in your goodwill you have placed [me] on firm mountains;
then you hid your face—I was petrified by fear. (v. 7/8)
I have called to you, YHWH [again and again],
and to my Lord I pleaded for mercy [without ceasing]. (v. 8/9)
"What gain is there in my blood,
if I should go down to the Pit?
Does the dust praise you?
Does it proclaim your faithfulness? (v. 9/10)
Hear, YHWH, and have mercy on me!
YHWH, be my helper!" (v. 10/11)
You have turned my mourning into a round dance—for me;
you have loosened my sackcloth
and clothed me with [a garment of] gladness, (v. 11/12)
so that [my] honor shall make music for you
and shall not be silent. (v. 12/13a)

YHWH my God, I shall praise you forever. (v. 12/13b)

Textual Notes

3/4. In v. 4b, read the Kethib, מִיּוֹרְדֵי־בוֹר, "from among those who go down into the Pit"; cf. *BHS* apparatus; Kraus, *Psalmen,* 1:386; H.-P. Müller, "Psalm 30," 192 n. 3; et al.

4/5. On the expression "to the memory of his holiness," see Hardmeier, "Der Tod des Menschen," 308 n. 65.

5/6. The MT's יָלִין, "he spent the night" is usually disregarded *metri causa* (so Kraus, *Psalmen,* 1:386; Hardmeier, "Systematische Elemente," 115 n. 11; et al.) or because of metaphorical aesthetics (so H.-P. Müller, "Psalm 30," 194).

6/7. The MT's שַׁלְוִי is a contraction or a scribal error based on שַׁלְוָתִי; see H.-P. Müller, "Psalm 30," 195–96.

7/8. Instead of the expression "you have made my mountain stand strong," the Targum's לְהַרְרֵי עֹז, "on a firm mountain," is to be preferred; see ibid., 196 n. 33.

8/9. The two imperfect forms are to be read as preterite iteratives, referring to the retrospective context of v. 7/8 (see 253 below); cf. Ps. 116:3b, 4a; etc.

11/12. On account of the corresponding verb אזר Piel, "to gird, clothe," and the contrasting שַׂק, "sackcloth," שִׂמְחָה likely also refers to a garment; cf. H.-P. Müller, "Psalm 30," 198.

12/13. On the meaning of the MT's כָּבוֹד, "honor," see 260ff. below, under "Theology of Gratitude."

In verses 1–5 (2–6), the text of Psalm 30 contains the usual elements of an individual Thanksgiving Psalm, with a *invitation to oneself to praise God*, yet directly addressed to YHWH (v. 1/2), a *retrospect of past affliction* (vv. 2–3 [3–4]), as well as an *invitation to the community* to a musical praise of God (vv. 4–5 [5–6]).[22] In verse 6/7, the supplicant begins again with a *retrospect of earlier carelessness* (vv. 6–7 [7–8]), as וַאֲנִי, "but I," at the beginning of the sentence emphasizes, which contrasts with the *retrospect of past affliction* with extensive citation of direct speech (vv. 9–10 [10–11]). The second part concludes in verses 11–12a (12–13a) with a *report of experienced salvation*, and in verse 12/13b with a *pledge of praise*, which forms an inclusio with verse 1/2a also in regard to the temporal dimension "present/future":[23]

I. Individual song of thanksgiving

1/2 Opening invitation to praise God
  (a) Invitation to oneself to praise God (→ 12/13b)
  (bc) Twofold rationale
    (b) Positive: salvation of supplicant
    (c) Negative: powerlessness of enemies
2–3 (3–4) Retrospect of past affliction (report of salvation)
  2/3 (a) Cry for help and (b) to be healed
  3/4 Salvation from death: (a) Sheol // (b) the Pit
4–5 (5–6) Invitation to others to praise God (hymn)
  4/5 Twofold invitation: (a) make music // (b) give thanks
  5/6 Rationale: binary statements on existence before God
    (a) moment :: a life long // anger :: goodwill
    (b) evening :: morning // crying :: jubilation

II. Retrospect of past affliction

6–7 (7–8) Retrospect of earlier carelessness
  6/7 (a) self-examination and (b) self-referential quotation

22. On the form-critical elements of Individual Thanksgiving Psalms, see the review in Gunkel and Begrich, *Introduction to Psalms*, 199–221; also Westermann, *Lob und Klage*, 76ff.; Gerstenberger, *Psalms, Part 1*, 14ff.; Krieg, *Todesbilder*, 360ff., 401ff., etc. See also Janowski, "Die Kostbarkeit des Lebens," 257ff. (for Ps. 30:9/10); Jenni, "Psalm 30, 6a" (for Ps. 30:5/6); Weber, *Werkbuch*, 3:72ff.; Hieke, "Orientierung," 273ff.; and Wälchli, *Gottes Zorn*, 49–50.

23. See 254ff. below.

7/8	Survival of separation from YHWH
8–10 (9–11)	Retrospect of lament
8/9	Introduction: (a) call // (b) plead
9–10 (10–11)	Quotation of lament
9/10	Questions: Motivation for YHWH's intervention
10/11	Imperatives: Plea for YHWH's attention
12–13a	Report of experienced salvation
12/13b	Concluding pledge of praise (→ 1/2a)

Each of the two "reports of salvation" (vv. 2–3 [3–4] and 6–12 [7–13]) has its own profile: the first report is concerned with the *outward* process of salvation; the second report describes the *inward* position of the supplicant (self-examination) that has prompted a sudden onset of affliction and the experience of new life as a gift.[24] As we shall see, the element of a *multilayered past*[25] is significant here. The recapitulation of past events is arranged in such a way that in a retrospect the supplicant moves "forward" through the different layers of time, beginning with the most distant layer of the past as I (vv. 6–7 [7–8]), over layer II (vv. 8–10 [9–11]), to the most recent layer of the past as III (vv. 11–12a [12–13a]), in order to pronounce in the present the supplicant's pledge of praise for the future (v. 12/13b).

The two situations of affliction presupposed in verses 1–3 (2–4) and 6–7 (7–8) are also accentuated differently: The first situation involves a grave illness[26] and the triumph of enemies;[27] the second relates the affliction to the supplicant's arrogant carelessness. The difference between these two sections is also underscored by the unusual language of verses 6–11 (7–12) and its self-referential quotation in verse 6/7b; the argumentative struggle in verses 9–10 (10–11), with questions and imperatives; as well as the binary metaphors for the turning point in verse 11/12 (mourning → round dance // sackcloth → [garment of] gladness).[28] One may wonder whether verses 6–12a (7–13a) are to be understood as a "continuation" of the "main psalm" of verses 1–5 (2–6),[29] but this question is of secondary importance for our analysis. For the following discussion, we shall use the psalm in its final form, in which the second retrospect of affliction (vv. 6–12a [7–13a]) represents a theological amplification of the thanksgiving song in verses 1–5 (2–6), which is "introduced by means of quotation,"[30] so to speak.

Thematic Analysis

Psalm 30 is an Individual Thanksgiving Psalm that describes *the supplicant's dramatic passage from hardship to salvation*, on the basis of various spatial (Sheol, temple) and temporal spheres (past, present, future); in doing so, it looks back on multilayered experiences of the relation to YHWH.

24. Cf. Hossfeld and Zenger, *Die Psalmen*, 1:186.
25. See 254ff. below; cf. also Hardmeier, "Systematische Elemente," 114ff.
26. See Seybold, *Gebet des Kranken*, 123ff.
27. On the motif of the enemies' triumph, as in Ps. 13:4/5, see 72ff. above.
28. See 261ff. below.
29. So Hossfeld and Zenger, *Die Psalmen*, 1:186; and H.-P. Müller, "Psalm 30."
30. Weber, *Werkbuch*, 1:150.

Like other Individual Thanksgiving Psalms, this text is also formulated from the *perspective of overcome affliction*, which the supplicant can now literally "leave behind" because YHWH has "raised up" the petitioner's life from the underworld (Ps. 30:3/4). Let us begin by turning to the elements of interlaced layers of time:

1. *Interlaced Layers of Time*

The temporal layers past, present and future in Psalm 30 can be distinguished by means of different fonts:[31]

I shall extol you, YHWH,	Pr
for you have lifted me up	Pa_1
and have not let my enemies rejoice over me. (v. 1/2)	Pa_1
YHWH my God, I have cried to you,	Pa_2
and you have healed me. (v. 2/3)	Pa_1
YHWH, you have raised up my life [*nepeš*] *from the underworld,*	Pa_1
you have revived me from among those	
who go down into the Pit. (v. 3/4)	Pa_1
Make music for YHWH, you faithful ones,	Pr
and give thanks to the memory of his holiness. (v. 4/5)	Pr
For one moment, in his anger; a life long, in his goodwill.	Pr
In the evening, crying; in the morning, jubilation. (v. 5/6)	Pr
But I, in my carelessness I thought,	Pa_3
"I shall not stumble, not in all eternity!" (v. 6/7)	Pa_3
YHWH, in your goodwill you have placed [me] on firm mountains,	Pa_3
then you hid your face—I was petrified by fear. (v. 7/8)	Pa_3
I have called to you, YHWH [again and again],	Pa_2
and to my Lord I pleaded for mercy [without ceasing]. (v. 8/9)	Pa_2
"What gain is there in my blood,	Pa_2
if I should go down to the Pit?	Pa_2
Does the dust praise you?	Pa_2
Does it proclaim your faithfulness? (v. 9/10)	Pa_2
Hear, YHWH, and have mercy on me!	Pa_2
YHWH, be my helper!" (v. 10/11)	Pa_2
You have turned my mourning into a round dance—for me,	Pa_1
you have loosened my sackcloth	Pa_1
and have clothed me with [a garment of] gladness, (v. 11/12)	Pa_1
so that [my] honor shall make music for you	Pa_1
and shall not be silent. (v. 12/13a)	Pa_1
YHWH my God, I shall praise you forever. (v. 12/13b)	Pr/Fu

The structure of these layers can be represented by a diagram (fig. 30): The first temporal layer is that of the present, in which the supplicant executes the performative speech-act of praising God (vv. 1/2a, 4–5 [5–6], and 12/13b). With

31. The abbreviations Pr, Pa_{1-3}, and Fu represent the layers of present, multilayered past, and future; on this representation, cf. Hardmeier, "Systematische Elemente," 114ff.

the conclusion "I shall praise you forever" (v. 12/13b), the supplicant not only gives expression to the continuation of the relation to God, but also ascribes perpetuity to it,[32] so that the temporal horizon of the individual's existence is expanded from the present to the future. The supplicant now stands before this new horizon and from there looks back into the abyss of his affliction, from which YHWH has "lifted" and "raised" him up (v. 1/2a, 3/4).

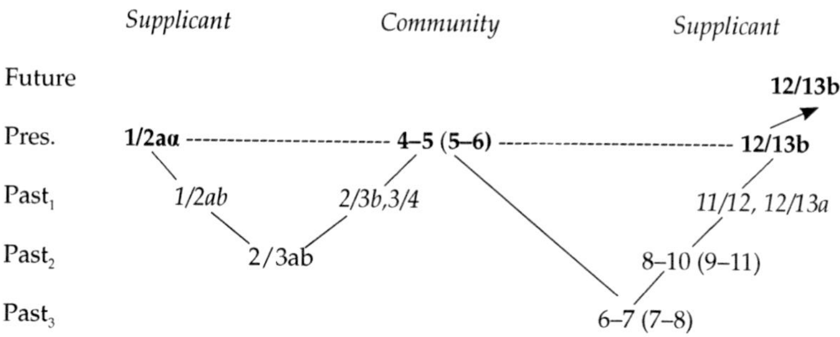

Figure 30. Diagram of temporal layers in Psalm 30

Framed by elements relating to the present (and future)—the opening invitation to oneself to extol (v. 1/2a), the invitation to others to praise God (4–5 [5–6]), and the concluding pledge of praise (v. 12/13b)—the remaining parts of Psalm 30 relate to various temporal layers representing different times of the past.[33] These layers of the past provide the necessary existential depth for the statements pertaining to the present (vv. 1/2a, 4–5 [5–6], 12/13b).

Past I

The first temporal layer of the past (Pa_1) deals with the retrospect and the recently experienced salvation:

> . . . For you have lifted me up,
> and have not let my enemies rejoice over me. (v. 1/2bc)
> YHWH my God, I have cried to you,
> and you have healed me. (v. 2/3)
> YHWH, you have raised up my life [*nepeš*)] from the underworld;
> you have revived me from among those who go down into the Pit. (v. 3/4)
>
> You have turned my mourning into a round dance—for me;
> you have loosened my sackcloth
> and clothed me with [a garment of] gladness, (v. 11/12)
> so that [my] honor shall make music for you
> and shall not be silent. (v. 12/13a)

32. Cf. H.-P. Müller, "Psalm 30," 199. Accordingly, the moment of the pledge is "once and for all." The positive לְעוֹלָם ("forever") of praising God in v. 12/13 contrasts the negative לְעוֹלָם of self-importance in v. 6/7b; cf. Weber, *Werkbuch*, 1:151.

33. Regarding the following discussion, see also Hardmeier, "Systematische Elemente,"115ff.

Past II

The second layer of the past (Pa_2) reaches behind the experience of salvation, which is spoken of in verses 1b–3 (2b–4) and 11–12a (12–13a), whereby the supplicant's pleading in the distress is called to mind again:

YHWH my God, I have cried to you,
  and you have healed me. (v. 2/3)

I have called to you, YHWH [again and again],
  and to my Lord I pleaded for mercy [without ceasing]. (v. 8/9)
"What gain is there in my blood,
  if I should go down to the Pit?
Does the dust praise you?
  Does it proclaim your faithfulness? (v. 9/10)
Hear, YHWH, and have mercy on me!
  YHWH, be my helper!" (v. 10/11)

Past III

The third layer of the past (Pa_3) reaches further back behind the pleading of verses 3 and 8–10 (9–11), first to a time in which the supplicant apparently enjoyed comfortable safety (v. 6/7), then to a time in which YHWH hid his face[34] and mortal danger befell the petitioner (v. 7/8):

But I, in my carelessness I thought,
  "I shall not stumble, not in all eternity!" (v. 6/7)
YHWH, in your goodwill you have placed [me] on firm mountains;
  then you hid your face—I was petrified by fear. (v. 7/8)

The structure of the psalm as a whole thus exhibits a *reverse interlacing of temporal layers*. The supplicant begins with the immediate present in verses 1–5 (2–6), from there looks back to the experienced salvation and calls to mind the urgent pleading before returning to the present of a public confession (Pr: v. 1/2a → $Pa_{2/1}$: vv. 1b–3 [2b–4] → Pr: vv. 4–5 [5–6]). In verses 6–11 (7–12), on the other hand, the supplicant begins with the most distant layer of the past and from there moves "forward," so to speak, toward the most recent layer of the past (Pa_3: vv. 6–7 [7–8] → Pa_2: vv. 8–10 [9–11] → Pa_1: vv. 11–12a [12–13a]). The multilayered retrospective is kept "consistently in the second-person address of YHWH."[35] The supplicant thus confirms for self, e contrario, the enduring continuity of the relation to God.

Finally, for the discursive event of the *tôdâ*, the invitation to others to praise God in verses 4–5 (5–6) is of crucial significance.[36] Here the "faithful of YHWH" are addressed, a group that itself is called upon to give praise to God:

Make music for YHWH, you faithful ones,
  and give thanks to the memory of his holiness. (v. 4/5)
For one moment, in his anger;
  a life long, in his goodwill,

34. On the motif of "YHWH's hidden face," see Ps. 13:1/2, etc., and the discussion on 64ff. above.
35. Hardmeier, "Systematische Elemente," 116.
36. Cf. ibid., 117.

In the evening, crying;
  in the morning, jubilation. (v. 5/6)

This group has the responsibility to mediate the individually experienced disruption in the supplicant-God relation through general religious knowledge: through the knowledge that YHWH's "goodwill" outlasts YHWH's "anger" for the duration of a lifetime. Before pursuing this idea further,[37] let us consider the report of salvation more closely with regard to its *spatial dimension*.

2. From Sheol to the Temple

The report of salvation in Psalm 30:2–3 (3–4), which looks back on the supplicant's distress now overcome, possesses in addition to its temporal dimension (multilayered past) also a significant spatial dimension, which graphically depicts the chasm of this affliction and its overcoming: YHWH has *"raised up"* the supplicant's *nepeš* from Sheol and has thereby led the petitioner back to life "from among those who *go down* into the Pit" (v. 3/4). In Psalm 116:3–9,[38] the supplicant's salvation is also depicted as a spatial event:

The snares of death have surrounded me,
  and the troubles of the underworld have found me.
  Trouble and grief I have found [again and again].
(Ps. 116:3)
I have called upon the name of YHWH [without ceasing],
  "O YHWH, let my life [*nepeš*] escape!" (v. 4)
YHWH is gracious and just;
  our God is a merciful one, (v. 5)
a preserver of the simple is YHWH;
  I was low and he saved me. (v. 6)
Return, my *nepeš*, to your rest,
  for YHWH has acted on your behalf. (v. 7)
Yes, you have [pulled up =] freed my soul [*nepeš*] from death,
  my eyes from tears and my foot from stumbling. (v. 8)
I shall go about before YHWH
  in the lands of the living. (v. 9)

In view of the linguistic characteristics of this passage, one could speak of a "sacred topography," as the psalm follows a general movement from Sheol (v. 3), through the *lands of the living* (v. 9), to the *courts of the house of YHWH* (v. 19), whereby step by step the supplicant follows a dramatic course from misfortune to salvation.[39] In this process, verses 3–9 constitute a line of movement that begins deep down in the (prison) area of *Sheol* (vv. 3–4) and leads to the *presence of the merciful God* (v. 5),[40] who overcomes (v. 6b;

37. See 261 below.
38. Cf. Ps. 18:3–6 (4–7); Jonah 2:3–7 (4–8); and see 258 n. 43 below.
39. Regarding the Psalms of the Individual, Hauge (*Between Sheol and Temple*, 281ff.) also speaks of a "sacred topography of contrast localities: 'Sheol,' 'temple,' and 'course' (between Sheol and temple, or from Sheol to the temple)." See Oeming, "Quelle des Gebets," 372–73.
40. The description of YHWH's attributes in v. 4/5 takes up the *Gnadenformel* (grace formula) of Exod. 34:6–7; Ps. 103:8; etc., with characteristic modifications; on the *Gnadenformel*, see 261 n. 64 below.

cf. v. 8)[41] the distance to the "lowly" supplicant (v. 6b) through his saving intervention from above (= temple) and who enables the petitioner to go about before YHWH in the *lands of the living* (v. 9).[42] The account of salvation in verses 3–6 refers to the past and verbalizes this movement as a *vertical process*,[43] with the double orientation from *below* (Sheol) to *above* (vv. 3–4), and from *above* (temple) to *below* (vv. 5–6):

Temple	YHWH	(4)	(5)	YHWH's response
	↑			↓
Sheol	Supplicant's complaint	(3)	(6)	Supplicant

Following the ensuing salvation (vv. 7–8), the supplicant's course moves in a *horizontal direction* from the place of "rest" (v. 7) / from the "lands of the living" (v. 9), to the courts of the house of YHWH (v. 19), whereby the gradual return to communion with YHWH is spatially represented by three concentric circles: *lands of the living → Jerusalem → temple courts*.[44] The goal is the thanksgiving sacrifice of the saved person in the presence of YHWH and before the entire people, as described in the second part, verses 12–19.[45]

In general, the Sheol motif appears to be typical for the genre of Thanksgiving Psalms. While the term "underworld" (שְׁאוֹל)[46] is frequently found in the Thanksgiving Psalms,[47] it is relatively rare in the laments.[48] Gunkel was the first to notice this and explained it as follows:

> If one looks more closely, one can see that this designation for the underworld only appears where the one praying believes he is close to entering the underworld or where he petitions not to be abandoned to the underworld. As soon as the pious one says that he has fallen into Sheol, with all its horrors, the clarity disappears. Suggestive images like grave, cistern, well, or individual references like the dust of death or torrents of water appear in place of clearer statements. Why does this difference happen? Apparently the background lies in trepidation before the underworld and belief in the sinister power of the name when expressed. Thus it becomes characteristic that the moment

41. Expressed through חלץ Piel, "pull out" (Ps. 116:8a; cf. 18:16/17; etc.) and three partitive ocurrences of מִן. The association of Ps. 118:8 and v. 9 underscores the *thematic association of land and temple*; cf. the contrasting use of this thematic association in Ps. 52:5/7 (uprooting of foreign heroes from the "land of the living") :: 8–9 (10–11; the righteous as olive tree in the "house of God"). On the subject see Hauge, *Between Sheol and Temple*, 34–35 with n. 67.

42. Cf. Tita, *Gelübde als Bekenntnis*, 112–13, 122–23. On the expression "land/lands of the living" as characteristic of temple theology (Isa. 38:11; 53:8; Jer. 11:19; Ezek. 26:20; 32:23, 24, 25, 27, 32; Pss. 52:5/7; 116:9; 142:5/6; Job 28:13), see Spieckermann, "Psalm 116," 273 n. 24; Raymond Jacques Tournay, *Seeing and Hearing God*, 125–26; and esp. Hartenstein, *Das Angesicht JHWHs*, 80ff.

43. A vertically oriented conceptualization of space is also found in Ps. 18:3–6 (4–7; cf. v. 16/17) and Jonah 2:3–7 (4–8); see Lux, *Jona*, 171ff.; Janowski, "Dankbarkeit." On Jonah 2:3–7 (4–8), see Jeremias, "Psalm des Jona."

44. Cf. Tita, *Gelübde als Bekenntnis*, 123.

45. See 278ff. below. On sacrifice and cult in ancient Israel, see Janowski and Zenger, "Jenseits des Alltags"; Marx, *Les systèmes sacrificiels*; and contributions to Hölscher, *Opfer*; and to Ego, *Altes Testament: Opfer und Kult*. The definition of a cultic *Sitz im Leben* for the Psalms has become extremely difficult since the time of Gunkel and Mowinckel, and any general hypotheses should be avoided. For recent discussion of the subject, see Hossfeld, "Festtraditionen"; and Janowski, "Buchreligion."

46. See C. Barth, *Errettung vom Tode*, 59ff.; Wächter, "שְׁאוֹל"; Healey and Niehr, "Land ohne Wiederkehr," 101ff.; Berlejung, "Tod und Leben," 485ff.; Rudman, "Water Imagery"; and "Anthropological Keyword 5: This Life and Afterlife," 240ff. above.

47. Cf. Pss. 9:13/14; 18:4–5 (5–6); 30:3/4; 86:13; 116:3, also Jonah 2:2/3; Jer. 38:10; Sir. 51:2, 6, 9; etc.

48. Cf. Pss. 6:5/6; 88:3/4; and 141:7.

> the poet wants to express the deepest distress of the throbbing pain, he is confronted in horror by the specific expression that he has to use. The situation is very different with the poet of the thanksgiving song. For him, the underworld has lost all of its horror in the context of the joyous thanksgiving festival. He can speak unhampered about his past mortal distress and does not need to shy away from the word "Sheol."[49]

This is a remarkable situation: Looking back at the distress, this "trepidation before the underworld" can apparently be put into words because the crisis has now been overcome. The fact that the supplicant can *look back* at the distress and *does not need to face it anymore* is linguistically reflected in the metaphors for a turning point in life.[50] This stylistic device is a basic characteristic not only of the Old Testament but also of Egyptian songs of thanksgiving.

A representative example for such a prayer of thanksgiving is the votive stela of the artisan Neb-Re,[51] whose text contains several formal elements: The superscription of the supplication scene (**A**) contains the *invocation* (lines 1–5) and the *affirmation* of Amun-Ra's power (lines 6–11); on the other hand, the text of the stela (**B**) contains the *hymn* to Amun-Ra (lines 1–24),[52] the *description* of the reason for the dedication (lines 25–45),[53] and the *conclusions* (lines 46–66).[54]

The content is as follows: Neb-Re, whose son Nachtamun "was lying ill and in a state of death" (B, line 37),[55] turned to the god, "who hears the prayer, comes at the voice of the poor and distressed, and gives breath [to] him who is weak" (A, lines 3–5). His prayer was heard and his son was called back to life (cf. B, line 41). For this salvation from death, the grateful father erects a limestone stela, thereby fulfilling his vow (B, lines 55–66). The middle of the prayer is constituted by an *aretalogy of the savior god* (B, lines 15–24), which speaks of salvation from the underworld, as does Psalm 30:1a–3 (2a–4). Here is text translated from the votive stela of the artisan Neb-Re:

> 15 You are Amun, the lord of the silent ones,
> 16 who comes at the voice of the poor!
> 17 I called to you when I was sad,
> 18 and you came and rescued me.
> 19 You gave air to the one who was afflicted;
> 20 you rescued me, who was in bondage.
> 21 You are Amun-Re, Lord of Thebes.
> 22 You rescue the one who is in the underworld:
> 23 for it is you [who is gracious] when one calls to him;
> 24 it is you who comes from afar![56]

49. Gunkel and Begrich, *Introduction to Psalms*, 133–34.

50. See 261ff. below.

51. See the picture in Keel, *Die Welt*, plate XXV. The text of the stela is cited from *ÄHG* 371ff.; see also Janowski, *Rettungsgewissheit*, 121–22, with further bibliographic references.

52. To proclaim proofs of divine power (lines 1–14) and an aretalogy of the savior god (lines 15–24).

53. To identify the author (lines 25–31), describe the affliction (lines 32–38), and report the salvation (lines 39–45).

54. Giving a general interpretation of the divine-human relationship through Nachtamun (lines 46–54) and of Neb-Re's vow (lines 55–66).

55. Line 38 alludes to Nachtamun's transgression, which is probably the cause of his illness; see Janowski, *Rettungsgewissheit*, 121 n. 583.

56. Translation based on *ÄHG* 372.

The idea that God rescues from the "underworld"—*šdj.k wnm mdʿt*, "You rescue the one who is in the underworld" (B, line 22)—is found especially in texts of personal piety, as in the famous chapter 70 of the Hymns to Amun of Papyrus Leiden (19th Dynasty):

5 He [Amun] rescues whom he wants,
even if he is in the underworld (*dʿt*),
6 who preserves from fate,
as the heart tells him.[57]

Since line 6 seems to refer to a death that has not yet occurred—Amun is able to preserve from "fate," from death, by extending the time of life—the expression "underworld" (*dʿt*) in line 5 is probably also a metaphor for affliction and illness.[58] This metaphorical representation of "underworld" as "death" is corroborated by the votive stela of the artisan Neb-Re, which refers to the fate of death of Nachtamun (Neb-Re's son) in its description of affliction (B, lines 32–38):

32 Hymns have been composed to his name,
33 because his power is so great;
34 prayers have been offered before his face,
35 in the presence of all the land,
36 on behalf of the outline draftsman Nachtamun, justified
37 when he lay ill at the edge of death,
38 when he was in Amun's power because of his cow.[59]

This is the emergency situation (mortal illness) to which the aretalogy of the savior god (lines 15–24) responds. Interestingly, the concluding interpretation of the divine-human relationship through Nachtamun (B, lines 46–54) contains a passage in lines 48–50 that corresponds to the asymmetry of wrath and mercy in Psalm 30:5/6:[60]

46 He [Nachtamun] says: "Although your servant is ready to commit sin,
47 the Lord is ready to be merciful!
48 The Lord of Thebes is angry
49 not for a whole day—
50 when he is angry it is for a moment and nothing remains.
51 The breeze has turned for us into mercy;
52 Amun came with his breath of air.
53 As long as your Ka remains, you will be merciful,
54 and we will not do it again!"

3. *Theology of Gratitude*

Let us return to Psalm 30! This thanksgiving song is not only characterized by a system of spatial and temporal layers, but also by a correlation of *individual* (v. 1/2a, 12/13b) and *collective* (vv. 4–5 [5–6]) praise of God, through which the

57. Ibid., 427; on this text see also Janowski, *Rettungsgewissheit*, 131–32.
58. See the references in Janowski, *Rettungsgewissheit*, 131.
59. Translation based on *ÄHG* 373.
60. See 261 below. Other Egyptian texts on the subject of "mercy vs. wrath" are in *ÄHG* 374.

individual's as well as the community's relation to God is reactualized and reconstituted.[61] Three elements are to be especially emphasized here: the *public nature of thanksgiving*, the *turning point in life*, and the *supplicant's future*. These three elements constitute the cornerstones of an Old Testament "theology of gratitude."

The public nature of thanksgiving. The thanksgiving praise before the assembled community by the one who has been saved (vv. 1–5 [2–6]) is primarily a *public proclamation* of the experience the supplicant had with this God.[62] The one who has been saved thereby becomes an important "witness,"[63] who authentically confirms, through continued existence, the traditional knowledge of the imbalance between YHWH's "short-lived" anger and YHWH's "lifelong" goodwill (v. 5/6; cf. Exod. 34:6–7; etc.),[64] which can thereby be newly reinforced in the community's collective memory. This situation is highlighted in verses 6–12 (7–13) through the complaint citation of verses 9–10 (10–11), which asks about the "gain" (בֶּצַע)[65] that YHWH would have as the result of the death of one of the faithful ones. The answer is the same as in Psalm 88:10–12 (11–13) or in 6:5/6: with every human being falling victim to an untimely death, YHWH would lose a valuable witness to YHWH's power, so that the former's death would also be a defeat of the latter.[66]

The motivation for YHWH to intervene as expressed in Psalm 30:9/10—"What gain is there in my blood, if I should go down to the Pit? Does the dust praise you? Does it proclaim your faithfulness?"—is anything but "naive."[67] Like Psalm 88:10–12 (11–13), it is rather a "shameless" borderline statement, with which the supplicant appeals to YHWH not to abandon to death the confessor of YHWH's goodness, faithfulness, wonders, and justice. As we have already seen above, the text offers an *argumentum ad deum* for YHWH, who is distant from Sheol: YHWH should recognize that self-interest should forbid the deity from abandoning the supplicant to Sheol before the petitioner's time since that would deprive deity of a valuable witness and worshiper of YHWH's goodness and faithfulness. YHWH is thus to be moved to intervene by the rhetorical questions of Psalm 88:10–12 (11–13), which do not have a naive but an appellatory character.[68] The same is true for Psalm 30:9/10.

The turning point in life. Through the publicly recited retrospect by the supplicant of the distress, *boundary experiences are made public*.[69] Such boundary

61. Cf. Hardmeier, "Systematische Elemente," 121ff.
62. See Bornkamm, "Lobpreis, Bekenntnis und Opfer."
63. Cf. Hardmeier, "Systematische Elemente," 118.
64. On the so-called grace formula of Exod. 34:6–7; Ps. 103:8; etc., see Spieckermann, "'Barmherzig und gnädig'"; Scoralick, *Gottes Güte*, 194ff., etc.
65. See Janowski, "Die Toten loben JHWH nicht," 24 n. 78.
66. See 232ff. above. On the "costliness of human life," see also Ps. 116:15; and 280 below.
67. As argued by H.-P. Müller, "Psalm 30," 195 n. 18. The arguments that the dead do not praise God and that dust is no gain for the Deity (cf. Pss. 6:5/6; 88:10–12 (11–13); 115:17–18; Isa. 38:18–19; Sir. 17:28–29; and 232–33 above) are also found in Mesopotamian religious literature, as in the bilingual (Old Babylonian / Neo-Babylonian) prayer to Marduk, *AfO* 19:57, 67–69: "[67] Wer zu Staub wurde—was ist sein Gewinn? [68] Nur ein lebendiger Diener kann seinen Herrn verehren. [69] Was kann toter Staub / ein toter Gefährte für den Gott vermehren?" "Only a living servant can worship the master, What can dead dust / a dead person add for the deity?" On this text, see the references in Janowski, "Dankbarkeit."
68. See 229ff. above.
69. Cf. Hardmeier, "Systematische Elemente," 118.

experiences were surrounded by a zone of silence and speechlessness, as they are today, which heightens their danger to an extreme. The public acknowledgments in hymns of praise return them to the "space of liveability"[70] and also make them accessible for others. Forms of articulation are thereby opened up to the community, which enables people to articulate linguistically and conceptually their own experiences of distress and suffering. Through the testimony of the one who has been saved, the religious knowledge of God's saving care gains "a new, embodied relevance for the present—in spite of the most bitter experience to the contrary in a situation of mortal anguish."[71]

The drama of this act of salvation is linguistically represented by *polar metaphor for a turning point in life*. This stylistic feature appears to be characteristic of the Psalms of Thanksgiving, which after all attempt to put into words the "miracle" of salvation.[72] It appears not only in negative form as a *turn from life to death* (Ps. 30:7/8: "placed on high mountains" :: "petrified by fear"), but primarily in positive form as a *turn from death to life* or *from mourning to joy*:

From death to life

- YHWH raises the supplicant's *nepeš* // he revives the supplicant from among those who go down to the Pit (Ps. 30:3/4; cf. Ps. 18:16/17; Jonah 2:1/2, 6–7 [7–8]).
- YHWH pulls up the supplicant's life from death.

From mourning to joy

- "In the evening, crying; in the morning, jubilation" (Ps. 30:5/6).
- YHWH turns the supplicant's mourning into a round dance; // YHWH loosens the petitioner's sackcloth and clothes that one with "[a garment of] gladness" (Ps. 30:11/12).

The turning point in the distressed supplicant takes place as a *spatial transition from Sheol to the temple* (Ps. 116:3, 8, 9, 19),[73] as a *temporal change from evening to morning* (30:5/6), and as an *emotional change from crying to jubilation* (30:5/6) or *from mourning to dancing* (30:11/12). This interplay of spatial and temporal layers shows that praying is a *transitory act*, which for the supplicant linguistically enables the "transition to a new life."[74]

The supplicant's future. Through the public acknowledgment of experienced salvation, the religious knowledge of God's goodwill (v. 5/6b) attains a *relevance supported by experience*. In the invitation to praise God (with music)—"Make music for YHWH, you faithful ones" (vv. 4–5 [5–6])—the community has the responsibility to connect the individual experience of salvation to the general religious knowledge, according to which YHWH persists but a moment

70. Ibid., 119.
71. Ibid.
72. On the concept of miracle, see 230ff. above.
73. See 257ff. above.
74. Within the book of Psalms, cf. also 18:19/20: "He brought me out into a spacious place; / he set me free, for he is pleased with me" (cf. v. 36/37); Ps. 31:8/9: "You have not left me in the hand of the enemy; / you have set my feet in a spacious place"; and 118:5: "In distress I called out to Yah; / the one who answered me [and set me] in a spacious place was Yah." See Bartelmus, "רָחָב," 453ff., 458; Mark, *Psalm 118*, 380ff.; and Bail, "Von zerstörten Räumen."

in anger, but a life long in goodwill (v. 5ab/6ab). The final verse (12/13a), "So that [my] honor shall make music for you and shall not be silent," takes up this invitation with the help of the term זמר Piel, "sing, make music." Together with the concluding pledge of praise (v. 12/13b), it becomes a basic motive for the future life of the supplicant, which shall continually be characterized by gratitude: "YHWH my God, I shall praise you forever!"

The honor (כָּבוֹד) of the supplicant, which makes music for YHWH and shall not be silent (v. 12/13a) evidently refers to the "restored prestige of the one who was saved, which was called into question by the derision of the enemies to which verse 1/2b referred."[75] The idea that the supplicant's "honor" would be diminished or was even threatened to be destroyed by the aggression of the enemies is also found in Psalms of Lament of the Individual:

YHWH my God, if I had done this,
  if there is guilt in my hands,
        (Ps. 7:3/4)
if I have done something to the one who [now] repays me with evil,
  or have robbed the one who [now] troubles me without cause, (v. 4/5)
then let the enemy pursue and overtake my life / me [*nepeš*]
  and trample my life to the ground, (v. 5/6)
  and lay my honor [כָּבוֹד] into the dust. *Selah.* (v. 6/7)[76]

In contrast to this, in the affirmation of confidence the supplicant knows that the restoration or preservation of one's "honor" rests with God, as seen in Psalm 73:23–24:

But I am always with you;
  you have taken hold of my right hand. (Ps. 73:23)
You guide me according to your counsel,
  and will receive me to honor [/glory; אַחַר כָּבוֹד]. (v. 24)[77]

The supplicant of Psalm 73:23–24 will suffer death and—in an innovation when compared to traditional laments of the individual—will nevertheless hope for salvation by God, who establishes relationship to the supplicant as final beyond death. The statement that YHWH "receives" the supplicant expresses the expectation of "eternal life" in the sense of a "blessed and fulfilled conclusion to life, which includes further hopes and expectations, as the supplicant hopes for an unending continuation of relationship to God at the end of one's life, which has already been recognized and established in the individual's life thus far (73:23–24a)."[78] The syntactic construction אַחַר כָּבוֹד + לָקַח, "receive someone to honor" (73:24b), thereby signifies the supplicant's lost "honor"—lost on account of the arrogance of the godless (73:3–12)—which

75. H.-P. Müller, "Psalm 30," 199.
76. On this text, see 137ff. above.
77. On the syntactic and semantic problems of this verse, see Irsigler, *Psalm 73*, 41ff., 247–48, 266ff.; and Janowski, "Die Toten loben JHWH nicht," 39ff. A different reading has been suggested more recently by Witte, "Leben nach dem Tod," who understands כָּבוֹד as a terminal accusative: "According to your plan you shall guide me and in the end receive me into [your] glory." A discussion of Irsigler's thorough analysis is not offered here.
78. A. Schmitt, *Wende des Lebens*, 229; cf. Irsigler, *Psalm 73*, 41ff.

is recovered when YHWH receives the petitioner. "The 'receiving' is God's bestowing 'honor' on the supplicant."[79]

The concept of "honor" (כָּבוֹד) in Psalm 30:12/13 is thus shown to be a *basic social-anthropological concept*. As elsewhere in ancient (as well as modern) Mediterranean cultures, also in the Old Testament "honor/prestige" and "shame/contempt"[80] are values that regulate *social cooperation and antagonism* by defining social boundaries.[81] Honor is "the value of a person in his or her own eyes (that is, one's claim to worth) *plus* that person's value in the eyes of his or her social group. Honor is a claim to worth along with the social acknowledgment of worth."[82]

If the purpose of honor is "to serve as a sort of social rating which entitles a person to interact in specific ways with his or her equals, superiors and subordinates according to the prescribed cultural cues of the society,"[83] then the psalms that speak of "honor" and "shame" describe the fragmentation of this sensitive balance. In the book of Psalms we frequently come across cases of enemies' giving *injuries to the honor* of the supplicant, even a humiliation or disgrace, which can only be ended and offset by the intervention of YHWH as judge:

Supplicant's Honor		**Supplicant's Humiliation**	
Impairment by enemies	*Restoration by God*	*Supplicant's plea for recognition*	*Plea to shame enemies*
4:2/3	3:3/4	31:1/2	83:17/18
7:5/6	16:9	69:19/20	
	30:12/13		
	62:7/8		
	73:24		
	84:11/12		
	91:14/15 (כבד Piel)		

Furthermore, we notice the idea of YHWH as the supplicant's "honor" (Pss. 3:3/4; 62:7/8) and as the provider of "honor" (8:5/6; 84:11/12).[84]

Against this background the formulation of Psalm 30:12/13a is to be understood in such a way that, with regard to the enemies, the supplicant is "honored" again because of receiving salvation from YHWH. Having been "honored" in this way, the supplicant can and will give thanks to "my God . . . forever" (v. 12/13b).

"So that [my] honor shall make music for you and shall not be silent"—this is the conclusion in Psalm 30:12/13a of the second retrospect on distress (vv. 6–12a [7–13a]). According to the segments relating to the present in 30:1/2a, 4–5

79. Irsigler, *Psalm 73*, 49.

80. On the concept of honor in the Mediterranean world, see Malina, *The New Testament World*, 28–54; and contributions in Vogt and Zingerle, *Ehre*.

81. Cf. Prov. 11:16; 29:23; etc.; see Westermann, "כָּבֵד," 800; Lamp and Tilly, "Öffentlichkeit als Bedrohung," 52; Klopfenstein, "Ehre und Schande"; H.-P. Müller, "Psalm 30," 199; and Liess, *Der Weg des Lebens*, 331–32. On social contempt in ancient Israel, see 183ff. above.

82. Malina, *The New Testament World*, 31.

83. Ibid., 52.

84. Cf. Eccl. 6:2 and 1 Chr. 29:12.

Figure 31. Lyre depicted on a scarab from Jerusalem (?) (7th c. BCE)

[5–6], 12/13b, the supplicant who has been delivered from death gives thanks to "my God" and calls on the cultic community to praise God musically with the lyre (fig. 31)[85] and to offer hymns of praise:

> I shall **extol** you, YHWH.
> (Ps. 30:1/2a)
>
> **Make music** for YHWH, you faithful ones,
> and **give thanks** to the memory of his holiness. (v. 4/5)
> for one moment, in his anger;
> a life long, in his goodwill.
> In the evening, crying; in the morning, jubilation. (v. 5/6)
>
> YHWH my God, I shall **praise** you forever! (v. 12/13b)

The cult was the primary place of hymnic speech in ancient Israel.[86] In light of YHWH's presence in the temple, the supplicant rejoices (הלל Piel) as one rejoices after a sumptuous feast.[87] A similarly spontaneous expression of exuberant joy as (cultic) rejoicing is *dance*. This calls to mind not only the round dance of women following the events at the Sea of Reeds (Exod. 15:20) or David's dance at the transfer of the ark to Zion (2 Sam. 6:14, 16, 20),[88] but also dance in the context of hymnic praise of YHWH.[89] Also according to Psalm 30:11/12, the supplicant performs a round dance, giving expression to the joy over salvation received. Through confrontation with death, the supplicant of Psalm 30 "has

85. On stringed instruments in ancient Israel, see Keel, *Die Welt*, 323ff.; and Braun, *Musikkultur*, 39ff., 44ff.

86. It was different in Egypt, where tombs, in addition to the temple cult, were among the recorded spheres of hymnic speech; see *ÄHG* 2ff.

87. Cf. Ps. 63:5–7 (6–8); etc.

88. Cf. Keel, *Die Welt*, 314–15; Keel, "Davids 'Tanz'"; and S. Schroer and Staubli, *Körpersymbolik der Bibel*, 165ff.

89. Cf. Pss. 87:7; 150:4; etc.

experienced physically that life means being allowed to live and being able to live. [The supplicant] is allowed to live, even though death is constantly trying to pull self into the depths of Sheol."[90] The supplicant accepts this gift of new life in deep gratitude and with exuberant joy—joy in which YHWH's faithful ones participate in the context of a thanksgiving sacrifice (cf. vv. 4–5 [5–6]).[91] At this point the question of the significance of the cult for the anthropology of the Old Testament[92] is essential.

γ. *Sacrifice and Cult in Ancient Israel*

In the course of our discussion, we have repeatedly come across the phenomenon of the cult, either in the context of a divine vision in the temple[93] or, as in the previous section, connected with the question of the cultic implications of Thanksgiving Psalms. Since the topic of "cult" is something of an embarrassment to many Christians, because it *executes materially* that which should *function spiritually*—the encounter with the Holy—we inevitably need to discuss it at a more fundamental level. From the complex topic, central to the Old (and New) Testament, I shall focus on the two aspects of "sacrifice" and "feast."

The Logic of Sacrifice

In traditional religions, sacrifice[94] is the sacred act as such. The word inherently signifies a religious act through which human beings attempt to establish relations with the world of gods/ancestors in order to regulate or prompt their influence on the human realm. The most important elements of sacrifice characteristic of the ancient Near East are depicted in a visually descriptive scene on the White Obelisk, an artifact from Nineveh dating to the beginning of the Neo-Assyrian Empire (fig. 32).

Figure 32. Cultic scene from Nineveh (11th c. BCE)

90. Hossfeld and Zenger, *Die Psalmen*, 1:190.

91. Cf. Pss. 22:25–26 (26–27); 66:13–15; 116:13–19; etc.; see 278ff. below.

92. In H. W. Wolff's *Anthropology*, the cult unfortunately remains a marginal phenomenon.

93. See 90ff. above.

94. The German word *Opfer* is ambiguous since it can refer to the execution of the respective act (*sacrificium*) as well as its object (*victima*). Etymologically it is derived from the Latin *operari*, "to act / be concerned with [ritual matters]"; cf. French/English *sacrifice*, from the Latin *sacrificium*, *sacrificare*, "to sanctify, make sacred." On sacrifice in ancient Israel, see Willi-Plein, *Opfer und Kult*; Janowski, "Opfer I"; idem, "Tieropfer"; Staubli, *Levitikus, Numeri*, 42ff.; Seebass, "Opfer II"; Eberhart, *Bedeutung der Opfer*, 332ff.; as well as contributions by Marx, Rentdorff, and Willi-Plein in Janowski and Welker, *Opfer*.

Figure 33. Altar for burnt offerings from Tell es-Seba'
(Beersheba, 8th c. BCE)

On a hill is the sanctuary, the entry (?) to which is framed by two doors. The deity sits on a throne with a footstool. Before him stands a worshiper with extended finger. In front of the temple is a presentation table, an incense burner with flames, and a basin for libations. The king is offering a libation. Behind him is a servant with a larger bowl. Another servant is bringing the sacrificial bull.[95]

The preferred place on which the animal sacrifice is offered is the altar, the place at which slaughtering (מִזְבֵּחַ)[96] is done, according to the Old Testament. The horned altar from Tell es-Seba' (fig. 33) provides a good impression of such a place of slaughter, as prescribed by Exodus 27:1ff.

What an altar is and the meaning of the sacrificial rite performed on it are described in the so-called altar law (Exod. 20:22–26 [19–23]), which introduces the covenant code of 20:22/19–23:33 (or 23:19):

YHWH said to Moses:
"Thus you shall speak to the Israelites:
You yourselves have seen
that I have spoken to you from the heavens.
(Exod. 20:22/19)
You shall not make gods of silver in my presence,
and gods of gold you shall not make for yourselves. (v. 23/20)
An altar of earth you shall make for me,
and sacrifice on it your burnt offerings and your peace offerings,
your sheep and your cattle.
At the place where I make my name known to you,
I shall come to you and bless you. (v. 24/21)

95. Keel, *Die Welt*, 252.
96. See Dohmen, "מִזְבֵּחַ."

> But if you make an altar of stones for me,
> you shall not build it of hewn stones;
> for then you had wielded a tool over it
> and defiled it. (v. 25/22)
> You shall not go on my altar on steps,
> so that you do not uncover your nakedness over it." (v. 26/23)[97]

The initial impression here is one of a jumble of ritual regulations. On closer examination, however, a concentric structure emerges for Exodus 20:24–26 (21–23), with verse 24b/21b at its center, according to which the emphasis is on YHWH and the divine reaction to the sacrifice:

YHWH's speech from the heavens (Exod. 20:22/19)
No gods of silver or gold (v. 23/20)

Altar of earth (v. 24/21)	
Burnt offerings and peace offerings	**Israel**
Sheep and cattle	
God's response and blessing	**Yahweh**
Altar of stones (25–26 [22–23])	
No hewn stones (defilement)	**Israel**
No steps (exposure)	

Following A. Marx,[98] we can identify three important ideas for a theology of sacrifice:

The place to which God comes. The altar is the place to which God comes. The sacrifice brings about "this most astounding and unexpected development, that God, of whom it was said a few verses before that he had spoken to his people from the heavens, thereby demonstrating his transcendence, now announces his willingness to come down to earth in order to come to his people and to do this every time somebody asks him to do so by offering a sacrifice."[99]

The visible aspect of God. The fire lit by the ones who are offering sacrifice, which now consumes the pieces of the sacrificial offering, is the visible aspect of God. In this sense, what occurs at the sacrifice is a mimesis of what occurred in the theophany at Sinai (Exod. 19:9): "At the same moment in which God declares Israel to be his people and reveals himself in thunder and lightning, he also declares his willingness to come to them every time they ask him by offering a sacrifice."[100]

Hospitality toward God. Sacrifice is a sign of hospitality toward God. The animals that are offered to God as sacrifice are the main products of livestock farming. They are slaughtered and consumed at festivals (1 Sam. 25:2–11; etc.) or a festive meal (Gen. 18:1–8; etc.). God, who is present at these occasions, is presented with the sacrificial gifts not in their raw condition, but as prepared for a meal: skinned, roasted or boiled (animal sacrifice), and ground and baked or fermented (vegetable offering).

97. On this text, see Schwienhorst-Schönberger, *Das Bundesbuch*, 287ff.
98. Marx, "Opferlogik," 131ff.
99. Ibid., 133.
100. Ibid.

In response to a sacrifice, God comes not in anger, so that he has to be appeased, as is often claimed; instead, God comes in order to accept the hospitality of his people and to bless them (Exod. 20:24–25 [21–22]). In the context of sacrifice, Yahweh is not seen as a wrathful God but as a blessing God and, as the priestly theology of atonement posits, a forgiving God.[101]

Based on the evidence provided by the Old Testament, only domestic and working animals were offered, thus animals that were of basic importance to agricultural subsistence.[102] Since gazelles, donkeys, horses, camels, pigs, and dogs[103] were excluded from sacrifice in ancient Israel on account of their uncleanness, cattle, sheep, goats, and in special cases of "poverty" also domestic pigeons and turtledoves—these constituted the only sacrificial objects of the cult. The physical flawlessness of the sacrificial animal was indispensable.[104] What counted as a "flaw" was specified in the so-called Holiness Code, Leviticus 17–26:

> A blind, lame, maimed, mutilated, mangy, or scurfy animal
> you shall not bring to YHWH.
> Of such animals you shall present none to YHWH on the altar.
> (Lev. 22:22)

At the center of the animal sacrifice is the ritual slaughter and burning, which consist essentially of the following elements: After the *presentation* of the flawless sacrificial animal,[105] the ritual began with the *binding* of the animal (cf. Gen. 22:9). This was followed by its *killing*: because of the significance of blood as the seat of life,[106] one can assume a specific procedure for the killing, the ritual slaughter (cf. שָׁחַט, "cut [the throat]"), which is only implied in the Old Testament but fully regulated in the Mishnah and Talmud.[107] As a relief from Sennacherib's Southwestern palace in Nineveh shows (fig. 34), this ritual was also known in Assyria: lying on its back on the offering table, the bound animal—a ram—is held by its front legs by a servant, while the slaughterer overstretches the animal's neck, in order to sever the carotid artery with a single, long cut. The blood could then drain into a vessel placed below.

The ritual slaughter is followed by a *blood ritual*: the blood was either poured out at the altar in order to return it to YHWH and to prevent human consumption (cf. Deut. 12:16, 27) or it was sprinkled against the altar or the curtain of the Holy of Holies. The next ritual act, the *dissection* of the sacrificial animal (Lev. 1:6), is comprised of several elements, such as the removal (and washing) of the entrails (Lev. 3:3–4) and the removal of the thighs, especially of the right joint. The *complete burning* of the sacrificial pieces (excluding the skin) concluded the procedure of ritual slaughter and burning. The sacrificial pieces that were

101. The Deuteronomic theology of blessing corresponds by way of contrast to the priestly theology of atonement; see Willi-Plein, *Opfer und Kult*, 96ff.; and Janowski, *Sühne als Heilsgeschehen*, 355ff., 452ff. On the Deuteronomic theology of sacrifice, see 271ff. below.

102. See Janowski and Neumann-Gorsolke, "Haustiere und Arbeitstiere."

103. Cf. Isa. 65:4; 66:3, 17; etc.

104. Cf. Lev. 1:3; 3:1; 22:17–25; Deut. 15:21; 17:1; etc.

105. Cf. Lev. 1:2–3; 3:1; etc.

106. Lev. 17:11; Deut. 12:16, 23b; cf. Gen. 9:4.

107. See Clements, "שָׁחַט."

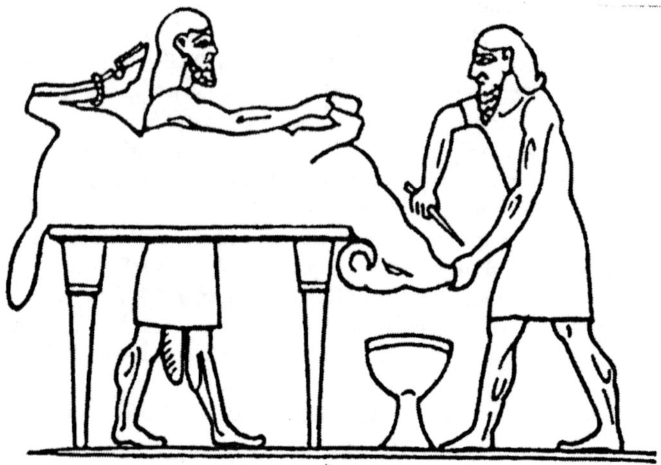

Figure 34. Assyrian sacrificial scene (7th c. BCE)

not presented to YHWH served as provisions for the priests, who frequently enjoyed the highly prized right joint.[108]

After this list of ritual elements, let us return to the original observation that sacrifice is something of an embarrassment to modern people because it executes materially that which should function spiritually. Even for renowned Old Testament scholars of the nineteenth and twentieth centuries, sacrifice was "a shocking absurdity," "a useless and inferior rite," "the epitome of nonsense"—in short, a "heathen element in Israelite religion."[109] In view of such misjudgments, which are still accepted in theology and in the church, albeit in less drastic form, it is important to understand that the point of the cult is the encounter with the Holy, something *spiritual*, but in the *context of space and time*.[110] Sacrifice theology is therefore a fundamental form of theology.

> God reveals himself in sacrifice. In other words, from the human perspective, Israel becomes acquainted with its God. It recognizes him *in very concrete ways* as a God who, although transcendent and other, is at the same time close and humanlike, who comes down to his people, even dwelling in their midst and accepting their hospitality, but who is nevertheless the Holy One. This God is a blessing God for them.[111]

The idea of a blessing God is found especially in the Deuteronomic understanding of the cult. This view of the cult, which represents the oldest biblical-festival

108. Cf. Lev. 7:32ff.; 9:21; 10:14; etc. The ritual elements identified above represent different levels of ritual development; see the overview in Janowski, "Opfer I," 37–38.

109. Julius Wellhausen, *Prolegomena to the History of Israel*; tr. J. Sutherland Black & Allan Menzies (Edinburgh: Adam & Charles Black, 1885), p. 422. For references, see Marx, "Opferlogik," 129–30.

110. A particularly illustrative example for this encounter structure within the cult is the Priestly Sinai pericope, with its focus on the "dwelling of YHWH amid the Israelites" (Exod. 29:42b–46); see Janowski, "'Ich will,'" 138ff.; Marx, "Opferlogik," 139ff., etc.

111. Marx, "Opferlogik," 146–47, emphasis added; on the subject, see also Müllner and Dschulnigg, *Feste*, 52ff., with references.

theory,[112] is especially revelant because it relates again to the larger topic of "gratitude."

The Joy of the Feast

Like (animal) sacrifice, the feast is a religious counterpoint to the quotidian and invests life with meaning and direction. The feast, according to J. Assmann's definition from the perspective of cultural studies, is "the place of the Other"[113]—the Other as the embodiment of all that a culture needs in order to function on a daily basis.

Several characteristics mark the feast as a place of transcending the mundane: the *order of rites*, the *fullness of gifts*, and the *solemnity of participants*. All these characteristics are "aesthetic categories or phenomena of *beauty*: order, fullness, and solemnity. The feast is a place of staging beauty and wholeness, on which human beings are dependent, without being able to realize them in their daily lives."[114]

The term "staging" is intended to signify the element of the formed and fixed, in other words, an act that is not oriented "toward the attainment of specific goals, but toward the 'how' of performance, toward style."[115] The category of form or "ritual coherence"[116] is fundamental here, also for the feast in ancient Israel.[117] Let us consider the example of the "little historical creed" of Deuteronomy 26:5–10, which represents a late summary[118] of the tradition of Israel's oldest history and refers to the context of the annual presentation of firstfruits. Following their deposit in a basket, the head of the family ("you") shall go to the chosen place (vv. 1–2) and recite before YHWH the creed that interprets the blessing of the harvest as the fruit of the ancestors' liberation from Egypt:[119]

Ritual Framework

When you come to the land that YHWH your God is giving you as an inheritance,
take possession of it and live in it.
(Deut. 26:1)

Then you shall take of the first crop of the fruits of the field,
which you have harvested in the land that YHWH your God is giving you,
and place it into a basket.
Then you shall go to the place that YHWH your God will choose
by making his name dwell there. (v. 2)
. . .
And you shall recite the following confession before YHWH your God: (v. 5a)

112. Braulik, "Die Freude des Festes."
113. J. Assmann, "Der zweidimensionale Mensch," 13.
114. Ibid., 17.
115. Ibid., 15.
116. On this expression, see J. Assmann, *Das kulturelle Gedächtnis*, 17–18.
117. On the festivals of ancient Israel, see the overview in W. Schmidt, *Alttestamentlicher Glaube*, 175ff.; and Müllner and Dschulnigg, *Feste*, 7ff.
118. On the interpretation of this passage, see Braulik, *Deuteronomium*, 191ff.; and more recently, Gertz, "Redaktionsgeschichte."
119. Deut. 26:3–4 and v. 10a are probably a later editorial layer; see Gertz, "Redaktionsgeschichte," 36ff.

Prayer Formula

"My father was a homeless Aramaean.[120]
He went to Egypt, lived there as a sojourner with few people
and became there a great, mighty, and numerous people. (v. 5bcd)
The Egyptians treated us badly, afflicted us,
and imposed hard labor on us. (v. 6)
We cried out to YHWH, the God of our fathers,
and YHWH heard our cries and saw our affliction,
the burden of our labor and our oppression. (v. 7)
YHWH led us with strong hand and raised arm out of Egypt,
with great terror, signs, and wonders. (v. 8)
He brought us to this place and gave us this land,
a land in which milk and honey flow." (v. 9)

Ritual Framework

When you have placed the basket before YHWH your God,
you shall prostrate yourself before YHWH your God. (v. 10b)
Then you shall be glad and rejoice over all the good things
that YHWH your God has given you and your family:
you, the Levites, and the sojourner in your midst. (v. 11)

The feast described in this text rests on two pillars: the pillar of "repetition" and the pillar of "recollection." *Repetition* ensures that every observance, the annual presentation of firstfruits, connects chronologically to the previous observance, last year's feast, and thereby establishes a "ritual coherence." *Recollection* brings an event of the distant past, such as the exodus from Egypt, to the present and thus imparts to it a fundamental horizon. This horizon is the foundational salvation history, in the remembrance of which Israel confirms its identity as the people of God.

To be glad and rejoice over God's good gifts (cf. Deut. 26:11)—this is the center of Deuteronomic festival theology: "Israel as a whole is to attain pure joy before its God with the festival sacrifice in the central sanctuary."[121] This is expressed especially in those texts in Deuteronomy that Lohfink has grouped under the rubric of "pilgrimage schema."[122] These also include the great Passover/Matzoth (Unleavened Bread) ordinance in Deuteronomy 16:1–8,[123] within the festival calendar of 16:1–17.

Excursus 8: The Beautiful Day

"The pressures imposed on human beings in their daily lives demand a prioritization of that which is closest at hand and thus a constriction of scope

120. Or "an Aramaean close to ruin"; cf. ibid., 36–44.

121. Lohfink, "Opferzentralisation," 239. Joy and rejoicing (Deut. 12:7, 12, 18; 14:26; 16:11, 14; 26:11; etc.), but not orgy-like celebration, are central motifs in Deuteronomic festival theory; see esp. Braulik, "Die Freude des Festes," 171ff.

122. See Lohfink, "Opferzentralisation," 232ff.; and Braulik, "Durften auch Frauen in Israel opfern?," 236ff.

123. On this text, see Braulik, *Deuteronomium*, 116ff.; and more recently Gertz, "Die Passa-Massot-Ordnung."

that is apparently intolerable. The feast must offer a counterbalance here and provide spaces in which the Other, which is masked in daily life, can occur. This Other does not, however, take place by itself, but has to be staged" (J. Assmann, "Zweidimensionale Mensch," 15). It is characteristic of the feast in probably all cultures that it is the primary place and the primary time for staging the Other: a religious counterpoint to the quotidian and its characteristics of "contingency," "scarcity," and "routine" (cf. ibid., 14ff.). While the categories of *contingency* and *routine* are contrasted in the feast with the categories of *staging* and *reflection* (on the great cosmic/historical connections) or with an *upsurge* (of emotions), the feast in contrast to the quotidian is the place and time of *fullness*, in which the "lack of meaning" (category of *scarcity*) is lifted and the monotony of the quotidian is overcome.

This idea finds a literary application in the topos of the "beautiful day," which plays a significant role in Egypt as well as in Israel. In the tombs of officials from the eighteenth dynasty, we find inscriptions with images of banquets that provide a summarizing caption for the depicted scenes, such as "To make the heart glad, to see a beautiful thing, to receive gifts in the house" (see J. Assmann, "Der schöne Tag," 209; idem, "Glück und Weisheit"). This usually involves the spheres of seeing and hearing, smelling and tasting (see also Kügler, Bechmann, and Wünsche, eds., *Die Macht der Nase*, 25ff.). In addition it involves "'lingering in the moment' into which eternity flows" (J. Assmann, "Zweidimensionale Mensch," 210) as well as the experience of the deity's emanation, which bestows a special atmosphere to the feast, as in this text (see ibid., 211):

O beautiful day, on which the beauty of Amun is remembered—
how the heart rejoices—
and praises you to the highest heavens.
"Glorious!" our hearts exclaim over that which they see.

The overwhelming present of God is also a basic motif of the Zion-Psalms (Pss. 46; 48; 76; 84; 87; etc.), according to which "one day in your [YHWH's] courts is better than a thousand of my own choosing" (84:10/11a) and "to stand at the threshold to the house of my God" is contrasted with "to dwell in the tents of wickedness" (84:10/11b). Thus, according to the so-called Enemy Psalms, the "beautiful day" is contrasted with the "day of distress," which is robbed of its terror by the saving God "in the morning."

Finally, in the book of Ecclesiastes, the call to rejoicing on the "day of joy" stands in direct connection to the thought of the "day of disaster" (Eccl. 7:14). In this way the Preacher/Teacher shows "that death, as a limitation imposed by *God* on human beings, also enables God in his goodness to accept the good day, since the evil day (= day of death) is also ordained by God" (Schwienhorst-Schönberger, *Kohelet im Spannungsfeld*, 168.)

Chronological frame
Observe the new moon in Abib,
and celebrate the Passover to YHWH your God;
(Deut. 16:1a)

Passover frame
for on the new moon of Abib,
  YHWH your God has led you out of Egypt by night. (v. 1b)
As Passover animals for YHWH your God,
  you shall slaughter sheep, goats, or cattle
  at the place that YHWH will choose by making his name dwell there. (v. 2)

Passover/Matzoth ordinance
You shall not eat anything that is leavened.
  For seven days you shall eat unleavened bread, the food of affliction,
so that for your whole life you remember
  the day on which you have come out of Egypt.
  For you came out of Egypt in haste. (v. 3)
In all your territory no leaven shall be found,
  and of the meat from the animal which you slaughter
  on the evening of the first day,
  none shall remain until the next morning. (v. 4)
You shall not slaughter the Passover animals in any of the cities
  that YHWH your God is giving you, (v. 5)
but only in the place that YHWH your God will choose
  by letting his name dwell there.
There you shall slaughter the Passover animals in the evening at sundown,
  at the hour on which you came out of Egypt. (v. 6)

Passover frame
You shall cook it and consume it in the place
  that YHWH your God has chosen,
  and in the morning you may return to your tents. (v. 7)

Chronological frame
For six days you shall eat unleavened bread;
  on the seventh day there shall be a solemn assembly for YHWH your God;
  you shall do no work on that day. (v. 8)

Passover and Matzoth are united here and assigned to the new moon of the month Abib (Nisan 14), so that the Passover now only constitutes the beginning of the entire festival (with the nocturnal exodus remembrance). On the next day the people return home ("to your tents," v. 7b), where the eating of unleavened bread continues for seven days. Pivotal for the Deuteronomic understanding of the cult is not only the eating of Matzoth, the "food of affliction" that commemorates the original exodus (v. 3a),[124] but also the communal consumption of the Passover animal, which restores once again the unity of the people and the *communion* with their God. "It allows every Israelite at the same time to experience personally that oneself too is included in the liberation encountered in the exodus. Whoever performs the exodus liturgically in this way can also remember it in daily life, thus letting this saving act of God become a defining act for one's own life."[125]

124. The "food of affliction [לֶחֶם עֹנִי]" (Deut. 16:3b), which consists of unleavened flatbread, is "bread for the journey, when prepared and leavened dough is not available" (Braulik, *Deuteronomium*, 117). The eating of this food, which symbolizes the hasty departure from Egypt, keeps the memory of that day alive for "your whole life" (v. 3d).

125. Ibid., 117; see also Braulik, "Durften auch Frauen in Israel opfern?," 238ff.

Accordingly, the reality of the feast takes over all of life and endows everyday existence with direction and meaning. This meaning is summarized once more under the rubric of "blessing," at the end of the festival calendar in Deuteronomy 16:1–17, which is itself the religious root of the joy of the feast:

> One shall not [enter] with empty hands [in order to] [see] YHWH's face, (v. 16b)
> but everyone with one's gift,
> according to the blessing that YHWH your God has given you. (v. 17)[126]

Success cannot be taken for granted, nor can a collective joy over such success.[127] If it takes place, however, the appropriate response to success is gratitude. The joy demanded by Deuteronomy ("You shall be glad . . .")[128] is therefore an expression of gratitude—*for the blessing given by YHWH.*[129] With the keyword "gratitude" we come to another basic anthropological concept, which is also of great significance in the Psalms.

b. Anthropological Keyword 6: Gratitude

> Praise YHWH, my *nepeš*,
> and do not forget his benefits.
> Ps. 103:2

> I shall not die, but live,
> and recount Yah's works.
> Ps. 118:17

Resources

J. Assmann, "Vergeltung und Erinnerung"; idem, *Maʿat: Gerechtigkeit*, 58–91; Benveniste, *Indo-European Language*, 156–59; Bornkamm, "Lobpreis, Bekenntnis und Opfer"; Burkert, *Kulte des Altertums*, 158–88; Gerstenberger, *Leviticus*, 6–9, 20–21; Gese, "Zum Herrenmahl"; Godelier, *Rätsel der Gabe*; Hardmeier, "Systematische Elemente," 117–22; Henrich, "Gedanken zur Dankbarkeit"; W. Herrmann, "תודה"; Hermisson, *Sprache und Ritus*, 31–64; Hodel-Hoenes, "Betrachtungen zum Dank"; Hossfeld, "Von der Klage zum Lob"; Janowski, "Dankbarkeit"; idem, "Das Dankopfer"; idem, "Opfer I"; idem, "Die Tat"; Keel, *Die Welt*, 292–97; Kellermann, *Gotteslob der Auferweckten*, 101–31; Mark, *Psalm 118*, 118–33; Mauss, *Die Gabe*; G. Mayer, J. Bergman, and von Soden, "יָדָה"; Reiner, "Dankbarkeit"; Simmel, *Sociology*, 652–70; Tita, *Gelübde als Bekenntnis*; Wannenwetsch and Betz, "Dank"; Westermann, "יָדָה";

126. On the Qal form of ראה, "see" + direct object "YHWH's face" (instead of MT's Niphal form, "be seen," with YHWH as subject), see 92, n. 169 above.

127. Cf. Braulik, "Die Freude des Festes," 186.

128. On the Deuteronomic exhortation to rejoice, see ibid., 179ff.

129. Cf. Willi-Plein, *Opfer und Kult*, 131: "The goal of the Deuteronomic liturgy at the central sanctuary is sacrifice in gratitude for received blessings and the experience of blessing in the grateful consumption of the sacrifice as the collective experience of life (which is primarily based on eating, drinking, and common celebration) before God."

Willi-Plein, *Opfer und Kult*, 25–70, 153–58; Zenger, "Das Buch der Psalmen," 323–25; idem, "'Das alles Fleisch.'" For use of the term "gratitude" in philosophical anthropology, see Haeffner, *Wege in die Freiheit*, 201ff.

Does the extraordinary have to occur—perhaps even a miracle—for us to be grateful? Is it not enough to be thankful simply for existing, having enough to eat, and living in functioning social relationships? We all know that these "simple things" are not as self-evident as it may appear, that not all may enjoy them, and that many are deprived of them. Furthermore, gratitude does not have the same significance everywhere as it does in Judaism, Christianity, and Islam. What then is "gratitude," and what does the Old Testament say about it? To answer this question, I shall begin with a social-anthropological definition of the term "gratitude" (α), which will then be theologically expanded on the basis of the *Tôdâ*-Psalms (β).

α. Acting for One Another

The history of gratitude is as old as the history of humankind,[130] yet it has different emphases in the various religions and cultures. Classical Greece, which initially lacked a comprehensive concept for gratitude, nevertheless had the word χάρις, a term signifying both "thanks" as well as "[freely given] kindness" or "favor." Not to be unappreciative toward a benefactor but friendly—including "repayment" with gifts in return—was a widely recognized and practiced moral obligation.[131] Counted as an unwritten law by Socrates,[132] gratitude, according to Aristotle, was a form of proportional equivalence, of *recompense* (τὸ ἀντιπεπονθός), the "intended goal of which, the experience of return, was generally viewed as a basic principle of justice."[133] For gratitude (χάρις), according to Aristotle, is

> [the] duty not only to repay a service done one, but another time to take the initiative in doing a service oneself.
>
> 
>
>
> Now proportionate repayment [ἀντίδοσις] is effected by diagonal conjunction. For example, let A be a builder, B a shoemaker, C a house, and D a

130. See the brief surveys in Reiner, "Dankbarkeit"; and Wannenwetsch and Betz, "Dank." On the history of the Latin terms *gratia* and *gratis*, see Benveniste, *Indo-European Language*, 160ff. The act termed *gratia* consisted initially in "rendering a service for free and without any service in return. This service, literally offered 'gratis,' brings about in return a phenomenon that we call 'gratitude.' This understanding of a service that does not call for anything in return is the origin of the two-sided concept of 'favor' [*Gunst*] and 'gratitude' [*Dankbarkeit*], which is experienced by the giver as well as the receiver. It is a reciprocal concept: the act effects the experience, and the experience effects a behavior" (ibid., 161; here, trans. of Janowski's German citation).

131. Cf. Pindar, *Pythian Odes* II, lines 21–24.

132. Cf. Xenophon, *Memorabilia* 4.19–24.

133. Reiner, "Dankbarkeit," 9. On the principle of *gratiam referre* as a retributive obligation with regard to a received favor, see also Wannenwetsch and Betz, "Dank," 562.

> shoe. It is required that the builder shall receive from the shoemaker a portion of the product of his labor, and give a portion of the product of his own [μεταδιδόναι].[134]

Without knowledge of the context presented here, the sociologist G. Simmel in his 1908 study *Soziologie* analyzed the concept of "gratitude" as a basic form of social life.[135] According to Simmel, all human associations are based on the "pattern of *devotedness* and *equivalency*."[136] In countless instances of devotedness and services such as economic exchanges, pledges of service, or commitments in a legally regulated relationship, the legal order necessitates equivalency. The gratitude resulting from such equivalencies is at the same time the "moral memory of humanity."[137] Finally, it is characteristic of gratitude that it assumes the continuation of the relation between giving and receiving beyond the moment of its origin:

> Gratitude is such a continuing existence in a most particular sense, an ideal survival of a relationship, even after it was somewhat broken off for a long time and the act of giving and receiving has been long completed. Although gratitude is a purely personal or, if one will, lyric emotion, it turns into one of the strongest bonds through its thousandfold intermeshing within the society; it is the fertile emotional foundation from which not only are individual actions stimulated toward each other, but also through its fundamental existence, even though often unconscious and interwoven with countless other motives, it adds a particular modification or intensity to actions, a linkage to them, a giving of continuity into the personality amid the vicissitudes of life. In regard to an earlier action, if every thankful response still remaining in the hearts were to be wiped out with one blow, society, at least as we know it, would disintegrate.[138]

Let us return to the history of gratitude in antiquity! A principle of action that can be termed "acting for one another," and that is fundamental to *connective justice*,[139] is found not only in Greece and Rome, but already in Egypt. This idea of a connection between actions and consequences, according to which everything that happens is tied either as reward or punishment to previous actions and to the workings of an all-inclusive justice, constitutes the "connective" aspect of justice (*iustitia connectiva*). Since connective justice links consequence to action, it ties together the course of events and through it the world as a whole into a coherent whole.

134. Aristotle, *Nicomachean Ethics* 1133a.4–9 (trans. H. Rackham, in LCL [Cambridge, MA: Harvard University Press, 1982], 281–83). Although occasionally employed by Hippocrates, the word εὐχαριστία was widely used after Aristotle. In its twofold meaning of "favorable inclination" and "giving thanks," it found its way into the New Testament; see references in Janowski, "Dankbarkeit."

135. Simmel, *Sociology*, 2:517ff., esp. 523ff.

136. Ibid., 523, emphasis added.

137. Ibid., 524.

138. Ibid. Simmel understands "giving" as "one of the strongest sociological functions" (ibid., 524 n. 1). Following Simmel, a "theory of the gift" was developed by the French anthropologist M. Mauss in his famous *Essai sur le don*, first published in a journal in 1925, then as a book in 1950; see Mauss, *Die Gabe* (ET, *The Gift*). On the later development of this discussion in enthology and social anthropology, see references in Janowski, "Dankbarkeit."

139. See "Excursus 5: Connective Justice," 132 above, and references cited there.

As J. Assmann has shown regarding connective justice with reference to the *interpretatio aegyptica*, all actions are connected to each other and in this sense "just" or "faithful to the community," in such a way that a passive ("idle") person disrupts the continuity of reality, which is based on the connectedness of all actions. In the Instruction for King Merikare (9th/10th Dynasty, ca. 2075 BCE), this theory is expressed as follows: "He is a wretch and one who has no advantage, who reconsolidates what he has brought to naught, who demolishes what he has built, or who improves what has been *damaged*. Be on guard against it. A blow is to be repaid with its [own] like. That is the *application* [lit., connectedness] of all that has been done."[140]

Acting with the interest of the community in mind presupposes not only an individual but also a "social memory," that reaches back into the past as a time-transcending horizon and ties the past to the present. This aspect of "memory" is used a central motif in the Tale of the Eloquent Peasant:

> Do not cover your face before one whom you have known,
> do not be blind to one whom you have regarded.
> Do not reject one who comes to you with pleas,
> but end this hesitation to let your judgment be heard.
> Act on behalf of him who acts on your behalf!

It continues in an equally categorical manner:

> A good person returns to the place of yesterday,
> for he is commanded: Act on behalf of him who acts,
> in order to give him cause to continue to act.
> This means, to thank him for what he has done.[141]

For the ancient Egyptian, the concept of responsible action is therefore developed from the concept of gratitude.[142] But even in ancient Egypt, gratitude is not only a form of *social* but also of *religious* practice; in other words, it is not only an anthropological and sociological but also a religious and theological topic.[143] Illustrative examples of this are not only the votive stelae of the artist Neb-Re[144] but also the Old Testament Thanksgiving Hymns, to which we shall now return.

β. Thanksgiving Song and Thanksgiving Sacrifice

Connected to the "thanksgiving song" (תּוֹדָה),[145] the most important expression of gratitude in the Old Testament is the "thanksgiving sacrifice" (זֶבַח תּוֹדָה or זֶבַח תּוֹדָה שְׁלָמִים), which was offered as a communal meal at the local

140. Instruction for King Merikare (116–122), trans. John A. Wilson in *ANET*, 417; cf. Janowski, "Die Tat," 167–91; idem, "Dank," 179 with n. 60 and references cited there.

141. Tale of the Eloquent Peasant, Papyrus B2, 105–8, based on the translation by J. Assmann, *Ma'at: Gerechtigkeit*, 63ff.; cf. *ANET* 410; Janowski, "Die Tat," 180.

142. Cf. Assmann, *Ma'at: Gerechtigkeit*, 63.

143. Hodel-Hoenes, "Betrachtungen zum Dank," 119ff.

144. See 258ff. above.

145. On form-critical aspects, see 258ff. above.

sanctuary or at the temple in Jerusalem.[146] In a situation of distress, the person giving thanks had offered a pledge (נֶדֶר/נֵדֶר), which is now solemnly redeemed in the context of a communal sacrifice,[147] a central element of which is a confession or *tôdâ*. Typical for this pledge is the verb ידה Hiphil: its basic meaning, "to confess," characterizes the two typical situations of "praise/thanks" and "confession (of sins)."[148]

Let us take Psalm 116 as an example. This individual psalm of thanksgiving had its place in the temple cult and was there recited by one who had been saved "before [YHWH's] entire people" (vv. 14b, 18b), recited in the context of a *tôdâ*-celebration (vv. 13–19). The psalm consists of two parts, verses 1–11 as a *thanksgiving song* (= expression of gratitude) and 12–19 as a *thanksgiving sacrifice* (= carrying out of gratitude),[149] and is translated as follows:

I Expression of Gratitude
I love,
  for YHWH hears my voice, my plea for mercy.
                    (Ps. 116:1)
Indeed, he has inclined his ear to me,
  and in my lifetime I shall call. (v. 2)

The snares of death have surrounded me,
  and the troubles of the underworld have found me.
  Trouble and grief I have found [again and again]. (v. 3)
I have called upon the name of YHWH [without ceasing]:
  "O YHWH, let my life [*nepeš*] escape!" (v. 4)
YHWH is gracious and just;
  our God is merciful, (v. 5)
a preserver of the simple is YHWH;
  I was low and he saved me. (v. 6)

Return, my *nepeš*, to your rest,
  for YHWH has acted on your behalf. (v. 7)
Yes, you have [pulled up =] freed my soul [*nepeš*] from death,
  my eyes from tears, and my feet from stumbling. (v. 8)
I shall go about before YHWH
  in the lands of the living. (v. 9)

I believe,
  even if I say / have to say,
  "I am bowed down low." (v. 10)

146. Cf. Pss. 22:25–26 (26–27); 66:13–15; 116:13–19; also Amos 4:5; Lev. 7:11–15; 22:29–30; 2 Chr. 29:31; 33:16; see Hermisson, *Sprache und Ritus*, 32ff.; Mayer, Bergman, and von Soden, "יָדָה," 465ff.

147. Cf. Pss. 50:14; 56:12/13; 116:17–18; also 22:22–26 (23–27); 61:8/9; 65:1/2; 116:14, 18; Jonah 2:9/10; see also Tita, *Gelübde als Bekenntnis*, 105ff.

148. See Gunkel and Begrich, *Introduction to Psalms*, 205; Bornkamm, "Lobpreis, Bekenntnis und Opfer"; Mayer, Bergman, and von Soden, "יָדָה," 456–58, 460ff.; Mark, *Psalm 118*, 124ff.; and Tita, *Gelübde als Bekenntnis*, 106–7, 136–37. A different interpretation is found in Westermann, *Lob und Klage*, 20ff. Westermann renders ידה Hiphil as "praise" and תּוֹדָה as "praise-sacrifice, praise, song of praise." Cf. Westermann, "יָדָה."

149. See also Tita, *Gelübde als Bekenntnis*, 109ff, 117ff.; and for a different interpretation, Seybold, *Die Psalmen*, 454; and Spieckermann, "Psalm 116," 268. Seybold and Spieckermann support—in part with different arguments—a two-part division of vv. 1–9 and 10–19, which is already reflected in the Septuagint; see Tita, *Gelübde als Bekenntnis*, 118ff.

I said myself / hereby say with shaking,
"All human beings are liars." (v. 11)

II Thanksgiving Sacrifice
How can I repay YHWH,
for all his benefits to me? (v. 12)

The cup of salvation I shall raise,
and I shall call out/to the name of YHWH. (v. 13)
I shall pay my vow to YHWH,
indeed, before all his people. (v. 14)

Precious / costly in the eyes of YHWH
is the death of his faithful ones. (v. 15)
YHWH, I am your servant;
I am your servant, the son of your maidservant;
you have loosened my bonds! (v. 16)

I shall sacrifice a *tôdâ*-sacrifice to you,
and call out/to the name of YHWH. (v. 17)
I shall pay my vow to YHWH,
indeed, before all his people, (v. 18)
in the courts of the house of YHWH,
in your midst, Jerusalem! (v. 19)

Hallelujah!

In view of the overall structure of the text,[150] it is clear that the question of an appropriate expression of gratitude in verse 12 introduces a new thematic section, which depicts the fulfillment of the vow made during the affliction (vv. 14a, 18a) and represents the execution of thanksgiving (vv. 13–19). Verses 13–19 function as the answer to this question, whereby verses 13–14 and 17–19 have a framing function, while 15–16 cites the "costliness" of the "faithful one" // "servant" of YHWH as the reason for this salvation from death.[151] The framing verses 13–14 and 17–18 in part exhibit correspondence in vocabulary and emphasize the main elements of the *tôdâ*-sacrifice: *raising the "cup of salvation"* (v. 13a) and completing the *tôdâ*-sacrifice (v. 17a):

A The cup of salvation I shall raise,
and I shall call out/to the name of YHWH.
(Ps. 116:13)
I shall pay my vow to YHWH,
indeed, before all his people. (v. 14)

A' I shall sacrifice a *tôdâ*-sacrifice to you,
and call out/to the name of YHWH. (v. 17)
I shall pay my vow to YHWH,
indeed, before all his people, (v. 18)
in the courts of the house of YHWH,
in your midst, Jerusalem! (v. 19)

150. On text-critical issues, see Janowski, "Dankbarkeit."
151. On the motif of "costliness of human life," see 261 above.

Both ritual elements are connected to calling upon or calling out the name of YHWH (vv. 13b, 17b; cf. 4a). According to verses 14 and 18, the *tôdâ*-sacrifice constitutes fulfillment of the vow, which the one who has been saved from affliction has made and now honors with a sacrificial thanksgiving meal. The expression of gratitude thus consists of the celebration of a sacrificial thanksgiving meal "before YHWH's entire people" by the one who has been saved, so that the thanksgiving sacrifice is the *cultic execution of the thanksgiving praise.* The process of this thanksgiving ritual is then described in Psalm 118, probably in the sense of a "fictitious liturgy."[152]

The sacrificial thanksgiving meal—which the one who has been saved celebrates, according to Psalm 116:12–19, in the forecourts of the Jerusalem temple (v. 19), together with others of the social circle—differs from a regular meal sacrifice (זֶבַח) on account of its two ritual elements: *raising (and drinking?) the cup of salvation* (vv. 13–14) and *sacrificing (and eating?) the tôdâ-sacrifice* (vv. 17–18).[153] The cup ritual has a special significance here because it involves the confessing assertion, the "proclamation" of YHWH's demonstration of power.

While Seybold interprets this cup ritual as the "ritual conclusion of a divine lawsuit"[154] and sees in this act its concrete substance, Kraus[155] understands it rather as a thanksgiving ritual: "the one giving thanks raises the cup, . . . perhaps also as a libation (or at least it was once originally such an offering)."[156] For a corresponding parallel, Kraus points to the limestone stela of Yeḥawmelek of Byblos (*KAI* 10; 5th c. BCE), which has in its upper portion an iconic depiction—the standing king hands the seated "mistress of Byblos" a drinking bowl (see fig. 37)—and below it an inscription with sixteen lines.[157] The text specifies that the process depicted here is the thanksgiving of the king of Byblos for "being heard" (*šmʿ*; *KAI* 10.3, 8) by the goddess and her establishing "goodness/joy" (*nʿm*; *KAI* 10.8) for him.[158] Although as in Psalm 116 the act of thanksgiving proceeds from human (king of Byblos) to deity (Mistress of Byblos), the image of the Phoenician votive stela is not immediately transferable to Psalm 116, since it should be interpreted, according to Hartenstein, as a scene depicting an audience or the act of adoration: "the king does not come 'empty-handed,' but his offering of the bowl represents a 'gift' in the wider sense, which emphasizes his role as servant with regard to the deity."[159]

152. See Mark, *Psalm 118*, 487ff., 500ff.

153. According to Lev. 7:11–15; 22:29–30; Amos 4:5, the *tôdâ*-sacrifice is a special form of the זֶבַח שְׁלָמִים, "meal sacrifice of salvation"; see Rendtorff, *Geschichte des Opfers*, 135ff., 52–53; Marx, "Heilsopfer"; etc. In addition to the animals for the *tôdâ*-sacrifice and the "cup of salvation" (Ps. 116:13), it included four different bread offerings: unleavened ring-bread made with oil, unleavened flatbread brushed with oil, cereal mixed with oil, as well as regular unleavened ring-bread; see Gese, "Herkunft des Herrenmahls," 117ff., esp. 119.

154. Seybold, *Die Psalmen*, 456.

155. Kraus, *Psalmen*, 2:972.

156. Ibid.

157. See the image in Keel, *Die Welt*, plate XXVI.

158. For a more detailed description, see Hartenstein, *Das Angesicht JHWHs*, 98ff.

159. Ibid., 105. For an alternative interpretation, see Janowski, "Dankbarkeit," 98ff.

Regardless of how one explains the singular (?)[160] occurrence of the cup ritual in Psalm 116:13—the association of *raising the cup*, the subsequent *drinking* (?), and the *continued existence of the one who has been saved*—all underscore the symbolic quality of the "cup of salvation," which can therefore be understood as an *elementary symbol of salvation from death and the continued existence of the one who has been saved*. It is apparently called "cup of salvation" (כּוֹס־יְשׁוּעוֹת) because YHWH has heard (116:1–2) and "saved" (ישׁע Hiphil, Ps. 116:6), the supplicant who then gives visible and audible expression to this salvation before everyone by raising this cup, sacrificing the *tôdâ*-sacrifice, and calling out YHWH's name before all of YHWH's people (vv. 14b–18b).

The second part of Psalm 116 (vv. 12–19) contains two further elements that are as central for the interpretation as a whole as the ritual elements of the *tôdâ*-sacrifice: one is the reference to the Jerusalem temple, specifically the "courts of the house of YHWH" (v. 19), as the place where the thanksgiving sacrifice is offered. Here, in the "midst of Jerusalem" (v. 19), "the movement in which YHWH and the person of the psalm approach each other . . . culminates in an intimate communion."[161] The other element is the confession of verses 15–16, according to which YHWH does not acquiesce to the loss of faithful ones // "your servant," but saves them/supplicant from death, as verse 8 reports. This defines the inner logic of the act of thanksgiving.

Equally constitutive as the *spatiality*[162] are the temporal layers of Psalm 116:1–11, which can again be emphasized by the use of different fonts:[163]

A	**I love,**	Pr
	for YHWH hears my voice, my plea for mercy. (Ps. 116:1)	Pr
	Indeed, he has inclined his ear to me,	Pa_1
	and in my lifetime I shall call. (v. 2)	Pr/Fu
B	The snares of death have surrounded me,	Pa_2
	and the troubles of the underworld have found me.	Pa_2
	Trouble and grief I have found [again and again]. (v. 3)	Pa_1
	I have called upon the name of YHWH [without ceasing],	Pa_1
	"O YHWH, let my life [nepeš] *escape!"* (v. 4)	Pa_1/Quote
	YHWH is gracious and just;	Pr
	our God is merciful, (v. 5)	Pr
	a preserver of the simple is YHWH;	Pr
	I was low *and he saved me.* (v. 6)	Pa_2/Pa_1
B'	**Return, my** *nepeš*, **to your rest,**	Pr/Fu
	for YHWH has acted on your behalf. (v. 7)	Pa_1
	Yes, you have [pulled up =] freed my soul [nepeš] *from death,*	Pa_1

160. According to Spieckermann ("Psalm 116," 272 n. 20), a similarity in content to Ps. 116:13 is found "at best in the overflowing cup in Ps. 23:5. Here too the difference is, however, also evident. While the cup in Ps. 23 is an image of God's all-encompassing care, in Ps. 116 it is evidence of the salvation experienced by the supplicant." The two are, however, not necessarily mutually exclusive since YHWH's all-encompassing care in Ps. 23:5 refers to *protection from enemies* and thus *anticipated salvation from mortal danger*; see 286ff. below.

161. Tita, *Gelübde als Bekenntnis*, 122.

162. See 234ff. above.

163. The abbreviations Pr, Pa_{1-2}, and Fu represent the layers of present, multilayered past, and future.

	my eyes from tears, and my feet from stumbling. (v. 8)	Pa_1
	I shall go about before YHWH,	Pr/Fu
	in the lands of the living. (v. 9)	Pr/Fu
A'	**I believe,**	Pr
	even if I say / have to say,	Pr
	"I am bowed down low." (v. 10)	Pr/Quote
	I said myself / ***hereby say*** *with shaking,*	Pa_1/Pr?
	"All human beings are liars." (v. 11)	Pr/Quote

The temporal layers of this text (Ps. 116) can interpreted as follows:

A / A'. *The framework.* Verses 1–2 and 10–11 represent the supplicant's present situation (and in part also the future: v. 2b), whereby the supplicant's love of YHWH (v. 1) is explained by the memory of YHWH's earlier inclination toward the supplicant, prompting the latter to call upon God for the rest of life / in the future.[164]

B. *The report of salvation.* In contrast, verses 3–6 begin with a retrospect on past affliction and the experience of salvation through YHWH (v. 3a, 6b), thus reaching far behind the present time of verses 1–2 / 10(–11) with their images of death. A second layer of the past (Pa_1) inserts itself with verbs in the imperfect in verses 3b, 4a, 6b,[165] between the present and the most distant past (Pa_2), citing the plea for salvation from death in verse 4b. This citation presents a contrast to the self-exhortation of verse 7a, which also uses the catchword נֶפֶשׁ, "life (-force), vitality,"[166] and speaks of the return of the *nepeš* to a place of "rest."

The grace formula. Essential to the act of thanksgiving of Psalm 116:1–11 is finally the fact that the multilayered retrospect on affliction in verses 5–6a is interrupted by three nominal sentences, which call to mind, through the modified use of the grace formula of Psalm 103:8 (etc.),[167] the central characteristics of the gracious and merciful God YHWH.

B'. *The report of salvation.* In verses 7–9 the second part of the salvation report (B/B') begins not with the past, but with the present situation of the one who has been saved, and also returns to the present after a second retrospect on the past affliction (Pa_1: vv. 7b–8). This inclusion gives particular weight to the prospect expressed in verse 9 of "the freedom and expanse of an unchallenged life in the presence of God."[168]

In a summarizing characterization of the intention of the *Tôdâ*-Psalms, the praise of God pushes outward in joy, gratitude, and confession.[169] In the recounting the *good news of God's saving power* is passed on to family, community, and the entire world, thus transcending generations, social strata, and nations.[170] Yet the point of departure lies with God, the Creator of the world and Savior of the individual. Confessing (ידה Hiphil) in its twofold meaning of "praising,

164. Ps. 116:11, however, seems to refer to the past affliction and to emphasize the present affirmation of faith, "I believe" (v. 10a), with the contrasting statement, "All human beings are liars" (v. 11b).
165. The imperfect forms are to be understood as preterite iteratives; see 252 above.
166. See "Anthropological Keyword 4: Vitality," 188ff. above.
167. See 261 n. 64 above.
168. Tita, *Gelübde als Bekenntnis*, 114.
169. Cf. Pss. 30:1/2a, 4–5 (5–6), 11–12 (12–13); 116:12–19; etc.
170. Cf. Hossfeld, "Von der Klage zum Lob," 17.

worshiping (God)" and "confession (guilt)"[171] always relates to God, according to the New Testament scholar G. Bornkamm: "It occurs whenever people have experienced evidence of God's power and always has the purpose of confirming this evidence of God's power. Every praise is preceded by a manifestation of God. It determines the content of the confession, which must be appropriate to the affirmation of God's power, by way of summary or expansion."[172]

This correlation between *evidence of divine power* and *public confession* has the purpose of presenting the "miracle" of salvation[173] experienced by the supplicant, making it into a paradigm of YHWH's saving power, and proclaiming it publicly before the community, the people, and the entire world.[174] The confession does not arise from a self-concern of the human person, but from the *encounter of a saving and*—in the case of the confession of sin—*judging God*.[175] It is therefore not an act of self-justification, but a response to the saving acts of God. The person who pleads begins from one's own position and that of the surrounding world. The person who praises, characteristic of the credo of gratitude, begins with God and God's good gifts.[176] What these good gifts are can be seen (e.g.) in Psalm 16 and metaphor of the "path of life" (v. 11).[177]

171. See 279 above.
172. Bornkamm, "Lobpreis, Bekenntnis und Opfer," 123.
173. On the concept of "miracle," see 229ff. above.
174. Cf. Bornkamm, "Lobpreis, Bekenntnis und Opfer," 124; and Hossfeld, "Lob I."
175. Cf. Bornkamm, "Lobpreis, Bekenntnis und Opfer," 124ff.
176. Cf. Ballhorn, *Das Telos des Psalters;* and the corresponding reference in Hossfeld, "Von der Klage zum Lob," 19.
177. See 301ff. below.

9. "You show me the path of life" (Ps. 16:11)
The Gifted Human Being

a. The God of Life

In the midst
of a station of suffering
possessed by a smile
you give answer
to those
who ask in the shadows
the mouth full of God-distorted words
pounded open
since the prehistory of pain.
Nelly Sachs, *Fahrt ins Staublose*, 317

α. The Happiness of Nearness to God

What is happiness, and what is the happiness of nearness to God? Happiness in the sense of "being happy"—not in the sense of being lucky—is "not a direct object of human endeavor, but a by-product in case of success: the quality of a satisfying life, because it is a meaningful life, in other words a *good life*."[1] Happiness in the end is a question of wisdom, since wisdom knows the limitations of human existence.[2]

One cannot resolve to be happy. Yet a person can choose a lifestyle that promises a meaningful and happy life. Such happiness is constituted "neither by a state of well-being nor by an outstanding, singular achievement, but rather by a quality attained for one's biography as a whole."[3] According to the biblical understanding, human beings do not attain this happiness apart from God, but in nearness to God; indeed, nearness to God *is* happiness or "goodness" (cf. Ps. 16:2),[4] which gives meaning and permanence to life.

1. Höffe, "Glück," 110, emphasis original. A remarkable collection of texts on the subject is found in Wetz, *Glück*.

2. A special position on the question of happiness in the sense of "satisfaction in life" is found in Qohelet; see Eccl. 2:24–25 as a key text. On the subject see Schwienhorst-Schönberger, *Kohelet im Spannungsfeld*, 80ff., 274ff.; also Zimmer, *Zwischen Tod und Lebensglück*, 65ff., 94ff., 112ff., 42ff., 56ff., 219ff.; and T. Krüger, *Kohelet*, 147ff. On the concept of happiness in antiquity, see Hossenfelder, *Antike Glückslehren*, xiiiff.

3. Höffe, "Glück," 110.

4. See 295ff. below.

An important text for the concept of happiness is Psalm 23. It shows very graphically that trust is the counterforce to confrontation, just as the "paths of righteousness" (v. 3b) are the counterpart to the "valley of darkness" (v. 4a).

A Psalm of David.

YHWH is my shepherd;
  I lack nothing.
(Ps. 23:1/1bc)
He makes me lie down in [lush] green pastures;
  he leads me to waters at resting places; (v. 2)
  he restores my life-force [*nepeš*].
He guides me in paths of righteousness,
  for the sake of his name. (v. 3)
Even though I go through the valley of darkness,
  I fear no evil,
    for you are with me;
  your rod and your staff,
    they give me confidence. (v. 4)

You prepare a table for me
  in the presence of my enemies.
You have [always] refreshed my head with oil;
  my cup is overflowing. (v. 5)
Only goodness and mercy pursue me
  all the days of my life;
I shall return to the house of YHWH [again and again],
  for the length of days / all the days of [my] life. (v. 6)

Textual Notes

1. Regarding the question which of the two words of the (identifying) nominal phrase in v. 1b is to be seen as the predicate—"YHWH" or "my shepherd"—Zenger argues for YHWH: "My shepherd is YHWH [and no one else]" (Hossfeld and Zenger, *Die Psalmen*, 1:153). For another position, see A. Müller ("Psalm 23," 32–33, with n. 33), who sees—in my opinion correctly—"my shepherd" as the predicate. Also notice the semantic parallels "YHWH is my strength" (Ps. 18:1/2), "YHWH is my light and my salvation" (27:1), "YHWH is our refuge and strength" (46:1/2), "God is my fortress" (59:9/10, 17/18; etc.).

3. Literally יְשׁוֹבֵב means "he brings back" (שׁוּב Pilel); see Mittmann, "Psalm 23," 5–6. The restoration of the supplicant's life-force is brought about, according to the context, through a refreshing drink from the "waters at resting places" (v. 2b), to which the good shepherd leads his flock; on this idea and for further semantic parallels, see J. Becker, "Elliptisches *hēšîb*," 45ff. In contrast to the *nomen unitatis* צְדָקָה, "demonstration of justice, good deed, benevolent act"—צֶדֶק, "justice, community loyalty" is a *nomen collectivum*, which expresses the totality of the phenomena of justice; see Michel, "Gerechtigkeit I." The *genitivus qualitatis* "paths of justice" refers to paths as they should be, right and correct paths of life; cf. Prov. 4:11; Spieckermann, *Heilsgegenwart*, 270.

4. On צַלְמָוֶת (< צלמות, "darkness, *nomen abstractum* of צלם II, "be/ become dark"), see Niehr, "צַלְמָוֶת," 1057–58; Gzella, *Lebenszeit und Ewigkeit*, 157ff. The juxtaposition of "valley of darkness" (v. 4a) vs. "paths of justice" gives expression to the antithesis of *happiness in life* and *mortal danger*; cf. Mittmann, "Psalm 23," 9–10.

5. On. v. 5b see A. Müller ("Psalm 23," 33), who correctly assumes the meaning of "make fat > refresh, revive" for דשן; cf. also Liess, "Bechermotiv," 49–50. On רְוָיָה as an expression of exuberant care and blessing, see A. Müller, "Psalm 23," 33; Liess, "Bechermotiv," 49–50.

6. This translation is based on Knauf, "Psalm XXIII, 6." A different reading is offered by Zenger, who reads the Masoretic וְשַׁבְתִּי, "and I shall return," as an "actualization" that "refers to the hope of return to Jerusalem and especially the reconstruction of the temple that was destroyed in 70 CE" (Hossfeld and Zenger, *Die Psalmen*, 1:153; cf. Spieckermann, *Heilsgegenwart*, 263 n. 2). While Hunziker-Rodewald (*Hirt und Herde*, 172ff.) accepts the Masoretic Text, she interprets vv. 4–6—in my opinion incorrectly—as a reference to the supplicant's continued existence after death.[5] The text assumed by the Septuagint, וְשִׁבְתִּי, "and my dwelling," appears to be based on an etymological interpretation of צַלְמָוֶת as "shadow of death" (σκιὰ θανάτου = צל, "shadow" + מָוֶת, "death") and implies an eschatological hope for YHWH's hospitality beyond the boundary of death; see Gzella, *Lebenszeit und Ewigkeit*, 151ff.

In the familiar translation of the KJV, Psalm 23 reads as follows:

A Psalm of David.

The Lord is my shepherd;
  I shall not want.
      (Ps. 23:1 KJV)
He maketh me to lie down in green pastures;
  he leadeth me beside the still waters. (v. 2)
He restoreth my soul;
  he leadeth me in the paths of righteousness for his name's sake. (v. 3)
Yea, though I walk through the valley of the shadow of death,
  I will fear no evil:
  for thou art with me;
  thy rod and thy staff they comfort me. (v. 4)
Thou preparest a table before me in the presence of mine enemies:
  thou anointest my head with oil; my cup runneth over. (v. 5)
Surely goodness and mercy shall follow me all the days of my life,
  and I will dwell in the house of the Lord forever. (v. 6)

5. What also speaks against the idea of a continued existence after the supplicant's death in Ps. 23:4–6 is the succession of the three psalms: Ps. 22:1–21 (2–22; individual lament), 22–31 (23–32; individual thanksgiving), Ps. 23 (song of confidence), and Ps. 24 (everyday ethics); see 296 and 329 n. 29 below.

This short and beautiful text consists of a *graphic section* and a *descriptive section*, which portray YHWH as shepherd (vv. 1b–4) and host (5–6) respectively. Each of the two sections forms a tension-filled unity:

- *Graphic section*. The graphic sections contain individual images of *sustenance* (vv. 1–3a: "[lush] green pastures" // "waters at resting places" and *conduct of life* (vv. 3b–4a: "paths of righteousness" // "valley of darkness") *of the flock animal by the "good shepherd."*
- *Descriptive section*. The descriptive section has corresponding statements of *sustenance provided by the divine host* (v. 5: prepares table, refreshed head, full cup) and *the supplicant's conduct of life* (v. 6: return to the house of YHWH).

Because of its overall structure, the psalm exhibits a progressive movement, which comes to rest at the end. It begins "with the image of traveling . . . , indicates the dangers of a journey, and pushes ahead to the arrival in a protective house,"[6] then concludes with the knowledge of a repeated return to YHWH's house. In between the graphic and descriptive sections is the poetically highlighted expression of trust of verse 4 (2+2+2 accents), which concludes the shepherd metaphor of the graphic section (vv. 1b–4) and at the same time effects, by means of the stylistic form of a second-person address, the transition to the metaphor of YHWH as host in the descriptive section:

I. YHWH as shepherd

1b–3a	*Sustenance*	3+2 | 3+2 accents
	(lush) green pastures	
	waters at resting places	
3b–4a	*Conduct of life*	3+2 | 3+2
	Paths of righteousness	
	Valley of darkness	
4ab	*Presence of God*	2+2+2

II. YHWH as host

5	*Sustenance*	3+2 | 3+2
	prepared table	
	refreshed head	
6	*Conduct of life*	3+2 | 3+2
	pursuit by goodness // mercy	
	return to YHWH's house	

The expression of trust of verse 4—"For you are with me; your rod and your staff, they give me confidence"—constitute the center of the psalm. It underscores that the text has expanded a motif from the laments of the individual—the affirmation of faith—into an entire psalm.[7] All six verses contain expressions of trust, and the genre of Psalm 23 is classified as a "Song of Confidence."[8] Yet the original background of the lament emerges more clearly in this central verse as *trust in the presence of God* (v. 4bcd), in contrast with the image of the

6. Hossfeld and Zenger, *Die Psalmen*, 1:152.
7. Cf. in contrast Ps. 13:5/6ab; see 75–76 above.
8. On the question of genre (song of confidence in the form of prayer), see the references in Spieckermann, *Heilsgegenwart*, 264; and Gzella, *Lebenszeit und Ewigkeit*, 154.

supplicant's moving through the "*valley of darkness*" (v. 4a). The text and the supplicant's situation in life have thus literally arrived at a "lowest point" in v. 4a. This shows clearly that Psalm 23 does not paint an idyllic picture, but assumes quite realistically that trust in God prevails in situations of conflict and mortal danger. This theme of "YHWH's providence *in the midst of* experienced injustice"[9] is characteristic of Psalm 23 as a whole.

According to A. Müller, Psalm 23 is a text of personal piety based on the *motif of trust*. Trust is defined as the stance

> that arises from a situation of conflict and is the counterweight necessary to overcome it. Psalm 23 is not a text that deals primarily with the selfless care of the good shepherd for his sheep. "The Lord is my shepherd, I shall not want" is not the confession of a human being who is not feeling lack, but rather the word of a person suffering lack and resisting that lack; one who seeks to overcome lack with such an expression. . . . Trust arises from a situation of conflict, not happiness. Psalm 23 is the prayer of a person who has not left the valley of darkness behind but who has to pass through it, the prayer of a person who strengthens one's own heart on a path that is uncertain or has become uncertain.[10]

The individual elements of the image of the shepherd in verses 1b–4 do not paint an idyllic picture but reveal the "often-dramatic struggle for survival by the seminomad and his flock."[11] One has only to look at ancient Near Eastern images on the motif of the "good shepherd" (fig. 35)[12] or read descriptions of the work of a shepherd, full of deprivation, as Jacob describes them in Genesis 31:38–40 to his father-in-law Laban:

> These twenty years I have been with you,
> your ewes and your goats have not miscarried,
> and I have not consumed the rams of your flock.
> (Gen. 31:38)
> I have not brought to you those torn by wild beasts,
> but have had to replace them myself;
> you have demanded from my hand
> that which was stolen by day and by night. (v. 39)
> By day I was consumed by heat, at night by cold,
> and sleep fled from my eyes. (v. 40)

The divine shepherd YHWH also offers his flock all they need to live:[13] pastures with fresh grass, watering places where the animals can find rest, and

9. Gzella, *Lebenszeit und Ewigkeit*, 155, emphasis original.
10. A. Müller, "Psalm 23," 31; cf. Gzella, *Lebenszeit und Ewigkeit*, 154–55.
11. Zenger, *Mit meinem Gott*, 229.
12. See Janowski and Neumann-Gorsolke, "Der 'gute Hirte' und seine Herde."
13. On the background to the imagery, see Mittmann, "Psalm 23," 4. According to Westermann, the special characteristic of shepherd metaphors is that they originally refer to the people; see, e.g., the communal lament of Ps. 80; Westermann, *Ausgewählte Psalmen*, 96. On this subject see also Spieckermann, *Heilsgegenwart*, 266ff.; and Hieke, *Psalm 80*, 334ff., esp. 339ff. See also Diesel and A. Wagner, "'Jahwe ist mein Hirte'"; Couffignal, "De la bête à l'ange"; Auffret, "Ma coupe est comble"; Arterbury and Bellinger, "Hospitality of the Lord"; Cardellini, "La metafora del 'pastore'"; Diller, "Der Becher als Zeichen der Gastfreundschaft"; van Hecke, "Pastoral Metaphors"; Zenger, *Der Psalter als biblisches Buch*; A. Müller, "Nominalsatz"; Koenen and Mell, "Hirte/Hirtin"; Riede, "Zum Tischmotiv in den Psalmen 23 und 69"; Schnocks, "Metaphern für Leben und Tod"; Janowski, "Der gute Hirte"; and the contributions in Coulot et al., *"Le Seigneur est mon berger."*

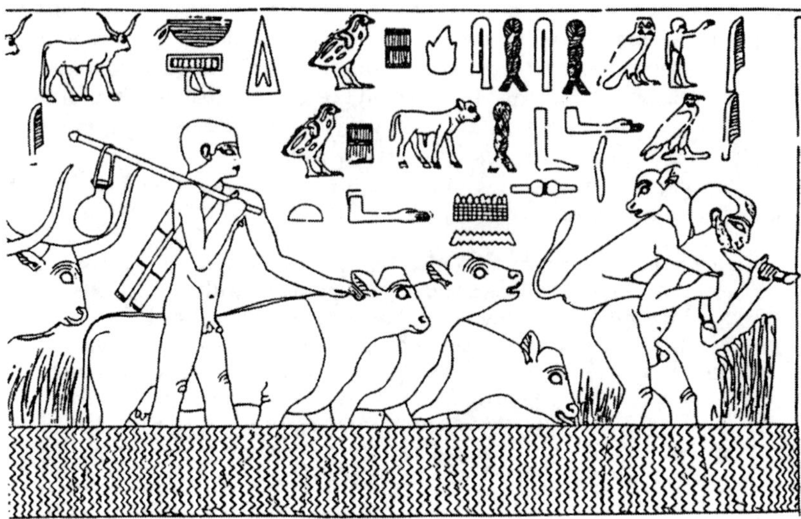

Figure 35. The good shepherd and his flock (Egypt, 5th Dynasty, 25th–24th c. BCE)

paths that have been secured by the good shepherd through his guidance (with club-like rod and long staff for support).

Like the first verse couplet of the graphic section (vv. 1–3a), the first verse couplet of the descriptive section (v. 5) deals with the *place of well-being*: the former the "[lush] green pastures" // "waters at resting places"; the latter the protective house:

YHWH is my shepherd,
  I lack nothing.
      (Ps. 23:1)
He makes me lie down in (lush) green pastures;
  he leads me to waters at resting places; (v. 2)
he restores my life-force [*nepeš*]. (v. 3a)

You prepare a table for me
  in the presence of my enemies.
You have [always] refreshed my head with oil;
  my cup is overflowing. (v. 5)

The banquet is prepared by YHWH for the supplicant—not privately, but publicly in the presence of the "enemies." Duhm, who regrets that "even in this idyll a reference to the enemies is not absent,"[14] has overlooked the fact that the enemies of verse 5a, like the "darkness" of verse 4a, represent a necessary contrast, which gives the entire scene a sense of realism. "Idyll" is simply the wrong word. Not only that: the prepared table "in the presence of my enemies" is the *symbol of reality for the nearness of God*, in which—looking at the subsection

14. Duhm, *Die Psalmen*, 100. Hunziker-Rodewald (*Hirt und Herde*, 179) also speaks of an "idyll."

Psalm 15–24—the supplicant of Psalm 16[15] has placed complete confidence. In Psalm 23 this confidence has achieved its goal.

The second verse couplet of the graphic section (vv. 3b–4a) has as its theme the course of the flock along "paths of righteousness" or through "the valley of darkness." Then the second verse couplet of the descriptive section depicts the supplicant on the path of life. Thereby the parallel expressions "all the days of my life" and "length of days [= as long as there are days in my life]" refer to life as it continues into the supplicant's future:

He guides me in paths of righteousness,
for the sake of his name.
(Ps. 23:3bc)
Even though I go through the valley of darkness,
I fear no evil. (v. 4a)

Only goodness and mercy pursue me
all the days of my life;
I shall return to the house of YHWH [again and again],
for the length of days / all the days of [my] life. (v. 6)

Neither evil (רַע, v. 4b) nor enemies (v. 5a) pursue (רָדַף),[16] but only "goodness and mercy" (טוֹב וָחֶסֶד, v. 6a; cf. Ps. 5:7/8). The last line then indicates the origin and goal of this happiness in life: it is the "house of YHWH," the Jerusalem temple, to which the supplicant will return again and again for the rest of life (v. 6b).[17] This *inviolability of God's nearness* is also the theme of Psalm 16, which corresponds thematically to Psalm 23 within the second subsection of the first Psalter of David (Pss. 15–24).[18]

β. Psalm 16 as a Case Study

A Miktām of David.

Preserve me, God,
for I have found refuge in you!
(Ps. 16:1/1b)

I [hereby] speak to YHWH:
"You are my Lord;
my goodness/happiness is only with you." (v. 2)

15. See 291ff. below.

16. The רדף (pursuit) statement of Ps. 23:6a is a characteristic complement to the רדף petitions of Ps. 7:1/2b, 5/6a.

17. On the textual problems of this verse, see 286–87 above. According to Hunziker-Rodewald (*Hirt und Herde*, 176 n. 724; cf. 179), Ps. 23:5 documents "the attempt to envision a place of continued existence after death—in reference to Pss. 27:5; 31:20/21; and 61:4/5?—as a heavenly temple analogous to the earthly temple (cf. 73:25); cf. the divine throne in Isa. 66:1. The still very abstract hopes in Pss. 49:15/16 and 73:24 of a taking away (לקח) or taking up (לקח, to YHWH) are thereby localized, so to speak." Hunziker-Rodewald arrives at this interpretation despite keeping the MT of 23:6b; see 286–87 above. Why the expectations of Pss. 49:15/16 and 73:24 should be "still very abstract hopes" is not clear to me; on Ps. 73:24, see 319 below.

18. On the correlation of Ps. 16 and Ps. 23 within the subsection Pss. 15–24, see 296 below. On Ps. 16 in general, see Liess, *Der Weg des Lebens*; Weber, "Notizen zu Form, Pragmatik"; and Schnocks, *Rettung*, 139–49, etc.

As for the saints in the land:
 [they are] the glorious ones in whom is all my delight. (v. 3)
Many are the troubles of those who have courted another [god];
 I do not pour out libations of blood for them,
 and I do not take their names on my lips. (v. 4)

YHWH is the portion of my [land] allotment and my cup;
 it is you who holds my lot. (v. 5)
The measuring lines have fallen on pleasant land for me;
 indeed, I am pleased with my inheritance. (v. 6)

I bless YHWH, who has [always] counseled me;
 even at night my kidneys have instructed me. (v. 7)
I have set YHWH always before me;
 indeed, he is to my right, so that I do not stumble. (v. 8)
Therefore my heart is glad, and my honor rejoices;
 even my flesh dwells securely. (v. 9)

Indeed, you will not abandon me / my life to the underworld;
 you do not allow your faithful one to see the Pit. (v. 10)
You show me the path of life:
 filled with joy before your face,
 pleasures in your right hand forevermore. (v. 11)

Textual Notes

2. With אָמַרְתְּ the MT may have in mind "Israel as a woman or maidservant of God" (Hossfeld and Zenger, *Die Psalmen*, 1:110); corresponding, however, to Pss. 31:14/15 and 140:6/7 (etc.), the text is to be emended to a first-person singular form or may be assumed to be an Aramaism (אָמְרֵת, first-person singular).

2. The MT may be retained if one assumes the meaning of "beyond, more than" for the preposition עַל; cf. Brockelmann, *Hebräische Syntax*, §§110–11, with parallel evidence in Gen. 48:22 and Eccl. 1:16; the translation is therefore "my happiness is not beyond you" = "only with you."

3–4. The difficult textual problems of these two verses can only be explained together. In v. 4, literally, "numerous/great are the troubles [= the troubles of those who] have gone after/have courted another [god]." Here מהרו is derived either from מהר I Piel, "hasten"; or from II, מָהַר, "to obtain someone's favor through gifts" = i.e., "to court someone"; see the discussion in Baethgen, *Die Psalmen*, 42; Craigie, *Psalms 1–50*, 155; etc. Since v. 4b speaks of drink offerings (of blood, probably blood libations as contrast to the cup motif in v. 5a (cf. Liess, "Bechermotiv," 59 n. 85) and of calling up the names, presumably of other gods, אַחֵר in v. 4a probably means "other god," i.e., the cult of a foreign god; cf. Exod. 34:14; Isa. 42:8; 48:11. A contrast is provided by v. 3: without changing the text, v. 3b can be understood as a *construct* form and can be translated: "the glorious ones all my delight in them = the glorious ones, in whom is all my delight"; cf. GKC §130d. If this interpretation is correct, the "saints" = "glorious ones" represent the community of the righteous (cf. חָסִיד, v. 10), among whom the supplicant wishes to live; cf. Baethgen, *Die Psalmen*, 41–42 (etc.).

5. Instead of the incorrect plene form תּוֹמִיךְ, we should read the Qal participle of תמך, i.e., תּוֹמֵךְ (masculine-singular active participle); see GKC §50e; Ruppert, "תָּמַךְ," 684, 686–87.

6. Instead of נַחֲלָת, "inheritance," either נַחֲלָתִי, "my inheritance," should be read, or the MT is to be retained as a special form. This form is possibly an intended graphic correlation to the construct מְנָת־ in v. 5a (chiasm!)

8. Here שִׁוִּיתִי is probably derived from שׁוה II Piel, "set, place"; see *HALOT* 1334–35 and Pss. 21:5/6; 89:19/20.

9. The MT's כְּבוֹדִי, "my honor," is in my opinion to be retained; see the exegesis of the verse.[19]

Using the striking textual markers[20] as orientation for analyzing the composition, the following structure emerges for Psalm 16 (without the superscript):[21]

Plea for preservation by God
1a Plea
1b Explanation: Refuge in God

Affirmation of faith I
2 Formulation of affirmation
3 ┌ Belonging to the YHWH community
Expansion
4 └ Distancing from foreign cults

Characterization of God
5 [Land] allotment // cup ← lot
6 Measuring lines → inheritance

Affirmation of faith II
7 ┌ Presence of YHWH (kidneys: inside)
Reason
8 └ Protection by YHWH (right side: outside)
9 *Consequence*: Joy // security

Knowledge of nearness of God
10 Not abandoned to death
11 Path of life: joy // pleasures

Several observations support this structure:

19. For a detailed text-critical analysis, see Liess, *Der Weg des Lebens*, 27ff.

20. Notice the praising with a YHWH-confession and opening with a first-person-singular verbal form ("I hereby speak," "I bless") in 16:2 and v. 7; two occurrences of nouns of the root נעם in vv. 6a and 11b; semantic connection between "preserve" in v. 1b and "not abandon // not allow" in v. 10; accumulation of the negative בַּל, "not, none," in vv. 2–4 (3x; also in v. 8b); the particle אַף, "indeed," in vv. 7–9 (2x; also in v. 6b); etc.; see also Weber, *Werkbuch*, 1:97–98.

21. Cf. ibid., 1:97; see the monocolon of v. 1b, two parts (vv. 2–6 and 7–11) of 11 lines each, which in turn contain three stanzas (vv. 2–3, 4, 5–6 / vv. 7–8, 9, 10–11) and are apparently chiastically arranged around the middle sections v. 4 and v. 9. Another structure is suggested by Hossfeld and Zenger, *Die Psalmen*, 1:108–9.

- Verses 3–4, which explicate the YHWH-confession in two ways (commitment to the community of the YHWH-faithful and renunciation of foreign cult) connect thematically, syntactically, and semantically very closely to verses 1b–2: the adjective אַחֵר, "another [god]" (v. 4a), refers antithetically to the identification of God, אֵל, in verse 1b; and טוֹבָתִי, "my goodness/happiness" (v. 2b), is a contrast to עַצְּבוֹתָם, "their troubles" (v. 4a).
- The opening position of YHWH's name and the direct address of YHWH in contrast to the supplicant's I-statements in verses 2–4 and 7–9 show that verses 5–6 represent their own stanza. The semantic field "land" is underscored thematically by the terms חֵלֶק, "[land] allotment"; גּוֹרָל, "lot"; חֶבֶל, "measuring line"; and נַחֲלָה, "inheritance"; and stylistically by the chiastic arrangement of these terms.[22]
- Verses 7–8, like verses 2–4, are introduced by a finite verb in the first-person singular ("I" of the supplicant). The verses are held together stylistically by the fact that the second stich of each verse is introduced by an emphatic particle (אַף in vv. 7, 9; כִּי in v. 8). The stanza is closed by a constitutive לָכֵן, "therefore" (= consequence of the affirmation of faith in vv. 7–8), which explains the reason for the supplicant's joy. The cohesion of verses 7–9 is also underscored by the (socio)anthropological terms "kidneys," "heart," "honor," and "flesh."
- The particle כִּי in verse 10 does not refer to the לָכֵן of verse 9, so that there is direct correspondence between the two verses.[23] It is rather to be understood deictically ("yes, indeed") and thus refers to what follows, introducing verses 10–11. This is confirmed by the direct address toYHWH ("you") in contrast to the supplicant's I-statements in verses 7–9. The stylistic change corresponds to a conceptual break: the theme is the antithesis of *death* (v. 10) and *life* (v. 11).

Verses 5–6 are located between the affirmations of faith I (vv. 2–4) and II (vv. 7–9) and linked by the term נְעִמִים, "pleasant land" (v. 6a), to verses 2–4 (טוֹבָתִי, "my goodness/happiness," v. 2b)[24] and to verses 10–11 (נְעִמוֹת, "pleasures," v. 11b):

I [hereby] speak to YHWH:
  "You are my Lord;
  my goodness [טוֹבָתִי] is only with you."
(Ps. 16:2)

YHWH is the portion of my [land] allotment and my cup;
  it is you who holds my lot. (v. 5)
The measuring lines have fallen on **pleasant land** [נְעִמִים] for me;
  indeed, I am pleased with my inheritance. (v. 6)

You show me the path of life:
  filled with joy before your face,
  pleasures [נְעִמוֹת] in your right hand forevermore. (v. 11)

22. See 297 below.
23. As suggested by Hossfeld and Zenger, *Die Psalmen*, 1:108–9.
24. On טוֹב / טוּב יהוה, "YHWH's goodness," and טוֹבָה, "goodness / טוֹב, "good," as an epithet of YHWH, see Höver-Johag, "טוֹב," 335ff.; and Hartenstein, *Das Angesicht JHWHs*, 80ff.

Significant are the two different plural forms נְעִמִים, "pleasant land" (v. 6a); and נְעִמוֹת, "pleasures"—both from the adjective נָעִים, "pleasant, comfortable, lovely,"[25] which is rooted in the language of love (Song 7:7–10) and is used metaphorically in Jacob's blessing (Gen. 49:15) for the beauty and appeal of the land of Israel:

How beautiful you are and pleasant [נָעַמְתְּ], beloved,
  daughter of all pleasures.
(Song 7:6/7)
Your figure is like that of a palm tree,
  and your breasts like clusters [of dates]. (v. 7/8)
I think: I shall climb the palm tree,
  lay hold of its fruits.
Then your breasts shall be like grapes,
  the breath of your nose like the scent of apples, (v. 8/9)
and your mouth like the finest wine,
  when it responds to [my caresses],
  and [still] brushes the lips of those asleep. (v. 9/10)[26]

Issachar is a bony ass,
  lying down between the sheepfolds.
(Gen. 49:14)
He saw that rest was good [טוֹב] and the land pleasant [נָעֵמָה],
  and he bowed his back to bear a burden,
  and became a servant. (v. 15)

In addition to Genesis 49:15,[27] the legitimacy of associating טוֹבָתִי, "my goodness/happiness" (v. 2b), and the plural forms of נָעִים, "pleasant, pleasing," is shown also by Job 36:11, where the righteous are described as follows:

If they listen and serve [him],
  they shall complete their days in goodness [טוֹב]
  and their years in pleasure[נְעִימִים].[28]

The comparison of this passage with Psalm 16:1, 6, 11 shows that the experience of God's closeness constitutes something elating for the supplicant—in contrast to Psalm 88:3–9a, 13–18 (4–10a, 14–19) and the topos of "God as enemy of the supplicant."[29] This brings us to the theme of Psalm 16.

Thematic Aspects

The theme of Psalm 16 is best defined by the expressions in verse 11: "path of life," "filled with joy before your face," and "pleasures in your right hand." The

25. See Kronholm, "נָעֵם," 503–4; Hartenstein, *Das Angesicht JHWHs*, 91–92, 94ff.; and Liess, *Der Weg des Lebens*, 246ff.

26. Translation based on Keel, *Das Hohelied*, 221; cf. also Song 1:15–17 and 2 Sam. 1:17–27; also Kronholm, "נָעֵם," 503.

27. Cf. Ezek. 32:19.

28. Cf. Ps. 133:1 (of brotherly unity) and Ps. 135:3 (of YHWH or rather of his name); Ps. 147:1 (of the service to YHWH); see Kronholm, "נָעֵם," 503–4.

29. See 226ff. above.

subject is therefore the *life*, which the supplicant can enjoy *in YHWH's presence* ("face of God")[30] *in perpetuity* ("forevermore") as *fulfilled* ("filled with joy") and *secure goodness* ("pleasures in your right hand"). As we shall see in our analysis of the tricolon in verse 11, the expression "path of life" in the first stich is explicated further in the following two stichs, which allude to the experience of God's closeness in the temple.

If one keeps in mind Psalm 23,[31] the connection between a *successful path of life* and *cultic closeness to God* is no surprise. According to Psalm 23:6, the supplicant's relation to God is heightened by a perpetual communion with YHWH, into whose "house" the petitioner will return for the rest of that person's life:

> Only goodness [טוֹב] and mercy [חֶסֶד] pursue me
> all the days of my life;
> I shall return to the house of YHWH [again and again]
> for the length of days / all the days of [my] life.

Even besides this, the terminological and thematic connections between the two psalms within the subsection Psalms 15–24 are striking:

Psalm 16	**Psalm 23**
my goodness (v. 2)	goodness (6)
my cup (5)	my cup (5)
You show me the path of life. (11)	He guides me in paths of righteousness. (3)
the path of life (11)	all the days of my life (6)
full (11)	overflowing (5)
forevermore (11)	all the days of my life (6)

Both psalms are placed in deliberate correspondence to each other within the concentrically structured subsection of Psalms 15–24 (fig. 36). Like the two framing Psalms 15 and 24, the Trust Psalms 16 and 23, the Lament and Thanksgiving Psalms 17 and 22, and the royal prayers of Psalm 18 (David's prayer of thanksgiving) and 20 (the people's plea on behalf of the king) plus 21 (the people's thanksgiving for the king)—all correspond to each other. At the apex of this structure is the creation-and-Torah Psalm 19.[32]

The subsection Psalms 15–24 develops "the ideal of 'the righteous' and asserts that he shall receive help and indeed salvation from YHWH."[33] How much this salvation characterizes the life of the "righteous" before God is shown by Psalm 16 in three large images of YHWH as "living space" (vv. 5–6a), as "one who directs life" (6b–9), and as "fullness of life" (10–11).

30. On the concept of the face of God, see 64ff. above.

31. See 286ff. above.

32. See Hossfeld and Zenger, *Die Psalmen*, 1:12–13, 105, 109, 121–22, 130, 140–41, 145, 152–53, 158; also Gianni Barbiero, *Das erste Psalmenbuch*, 323–24; Adam, *Der königliche Held*, 145ff.; Grund, *Psalm 19*, 314ff.; Liess, *Der Weg des Lebens*, 381ff.

33. Hossfeld and Zenger, *Die Psalmen*, 1:13.

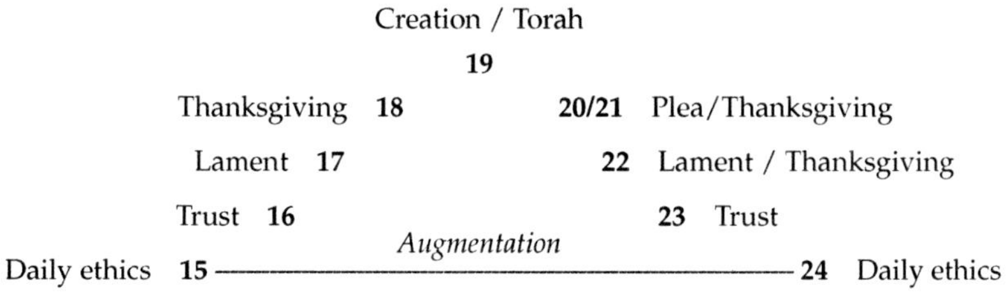

Creation / Torah

19

Thanksgiving **18** **20/21** Plea/Thanksgiving

Lament **17** **22** Lament / Thanksgiving

Trust **16** **23** Trust

Augmentation

Daily ethics **15** ———————————— **24** Daily ethics

Figure 36. Structure of the subsection Psalms 15–24

1. *God as Living Space*

In the middle of Psalm 16 (vv. 5–6) is a singular description of God, which characterizes YHWH as the supplicant's "living space"[34] through four terms taken from the context of Old Testament land distribution: חֵלֶק, property, (land) allotment; גּוֹרָל, lot; חֶבֶל, (measuring) line; and נַחֲלָה, inheritance, property.[35] These terms appear in chiastic order:

כּוֹסִי // מְנָת־חֶלְקִי ← גּוֹרָלִי	**5**	allotment // cup	←	lot
חֲבָלִים → נַחֲלָת	**6**	measuring lines	→	inheritance

What is peculiar about this passage is that YHWH is the subject as well as the object of the process of land distribution by lot. The *subjective* aspect is expressed in verse 5b, the *objective* in 5a:

> YHWH is the portion of my [land] allotment and my cup;
> it is you who holds my lot.
> (Ps. 16:5)
> The measuring lines have fallen on pleasant land for me;
> indeed, I am pleased with my inheritance. (v. 6)

Verses 5–6 are followed by a concrete process, which is metaphorized here.[36] The process itself is described in Joshua 18:1–10, where Joshua gives the following instructions to the remaining tribes of Israel:

> [3] Joshua said to the Israelites: . . . [4] "Appoint three men from each tribe. I will send them and they shall set out and go about the land and describe it according to their inheritance, then they shall come to me. [5] You shall divide it into seven parts. Judah shall remain in its territory in the South. The house of Joseph shall remain in its territory in the North. [6] But you shall describe the land according to seven divisions and bring it here; then I shall cast lots for you here, before YHWH our God. [7] But the Levites shall have no portion

34. Ibid., 111ff. (Zenger); see also Liess, "Bechermotiv," 54ff.; and more extensively in idem, *Der Weg des Lebens*, 152ff.

35. On these expressions, see Hossfeld and Zenger, *Die Psalmen*, 1:111ff.

36. The expression "metaphorization" is more appropriate than the traditional term "theologization," since metaphorization achieves a *transformation of the material without negating the concrete*; see Hossfeld, "Metaphorisierung," 21ff.

in your midst, for the priesthood of YHWH is his [*sic*] inheritance. Gad, Reuben, and the half-tribe of Manasseh [already] have their inheritance beyond the Jordan in the East, which Moses the servant of YHWH has appointed for them." [8] Then the men arose and set out, but Joshua had commanded those who went out to describe the land: "Go about in the land, describe it, and return to me. Here I shall cast lots for you before YHWH in Shiloh."[37]

The process of land distribution includes several steps: "First, the land in individual divisions (חֵלֶק) is recorded in documents over which lots (גּוֹרָל) are then cast as a cup (כּוֹס) with lottery tokens is shaken so that these fall on the documents. Then the measuring survey of the land is carried out, namely, by casting the measuring lines."[38]

The concept of land allotment also includes the specification that Levi is not considered, because YHWH is his "inheritance" (Deut. 10:9) or his "portion" (Num. 18:20):[39]

> Therefore Levi did not receive a portion of the land and an inheritance like his brothers. YHWH is his inheritance [נַחֲלָה], as YHWH your God has promised him. (Deut. 10:9)

> [20] YHWH said to Aaron: "In their land you shall have no inheritance [נחל Qal], and a portion of land [חֵלֶק] you shall not possess in their midst. I myself am your portion [חֵלֶק] and your inheritance [נַחֲלָה] in the midst of the Israelites. [21] But to the sons of Levi I hereby transfer every tenth in Israel as an inheritance [נַחֲלָה], as reward for their work; it is they who perform the work at the tent of meeting." (Num. 18:20–21)

In addition to Numbers 18:20, the meaning of the statement "I, YHWH, am their [the Levites'] portion" is also explained in Ezekiel 44:28, according to which the Levites are to receive the sacrificial portions and offerings of the Israelites as their provisions:[40]

> [28] And they [the Levites] shall possess no land. I am their property. [Also] possession you shall not give to them in Israel. I am their possession. [29] They shall eat the grain offering, the sin offering, and the guilt offering, and every dedicated offering in Israel shall be theirs.

In Psalm 16:5a the concept and practice of land distribution has been transformed into the statement that *YHWH is the land portion of the supplicant* and that YHWH holds the corresponding "lot" in his hands: "YHWH is the living

37. Translation based on Fritz, *Das Buch Josua*, 178.

38. Hossfeld and Zenger, *Die Psalmen*, 1:111–12; cf. Dommershausen, "גּוֹרָל"; Fritz, *Das Buch Josua*, 151–52, 179; and Welten, "Los." The cup motif of Ps. 16:5 is, however, not to be connected to the "concrete process of land distribution through a cup ritual" (so Hossfeld and Zenger, *Die Psalmen*, 1:111), since cups or cup-like vessels are not mentioned anywhere in the context of land distribution; see Liess, "Bechermotiv," 55. The *cup motif* of Ps. 16:5a, however, correlates closely with the *fullness motif* of v. 11b, so that "in connection to the allusion to a banquet in the sanctuary in v. 11c, . . . the cup of v. 5a could also be understood as a cup for a banquet and feast" (ibid., 57); cf. Liess, *Der Weg des Lebens*, 172ff.

39. Cf. also Deut. 12:12; 14:27; Ezek. 44:28–29; Josh. 13:14; etc.

40. Cf. Hermisson, *Sprache und Ritus*, 109; see already von Rad, "'Gerechtigkeit' und 'Leben,'" 234ff., 242–43.

space, meaning the inheritance and the arable land, which YHWH himself has appointed for the supplicant."[41]

But what is the concrete meaning of the statement? Nothing is said here of being supplied with offerings or sacrificial portions, as is the case for the Levites (cf. Ezek. 44:28–29; Num. 18:21). However, if one considers the term נְעִמִים, "pleasant land"—"the measuring lines have fallen on pleasant land for me" (Ps. 16:6a)—which is mirrored in verse 11 by the term נְעִמוֹת, "pleasures," it becomes clear that verse 11 is apparently to be read as an elaboration on what verses 5–6 express through the motif of "YHWH as living space."[42]

The interpretation of verses 5–6 has frequently posed difficulties in the past. Thus H. Schmidt[43] wanted to see "primitive, almost childish images" in these metaphors. This interpretation ignores that land distribution is a *legal act*, according to which a legitimately appointed portion of land represents an inheritance that can no longer be reappropriated.[44] In the context of the statements about land distribution in Joshua 13–21, the land distributed among the tribes was understood as an inheritance (נַחֲלָה) given by YHWH. Israel can see itself as an entitled heir, but its inheritance can also be revoked (cf. Jer. 3:19). This idea is especially to be considered in light of Psalm 16:10: "Indeed, you will not abandon my *nepeš* to the underworld." Since land law was so fundamental to life in ancient Israel that "its terminology developed into fateful concepts,"[45] one can hardly speak of "naive childishness."

In view of Psalm 16:5–6, on the other hand, von Rad has spoken of a "peculiar life-mysticism:"[46]

> Protection from death, life, and repletion in the presence of Yahweh—all this is merely an expansion of that which the previous psalm has expressed with "Yahweh is my portion" [cf. Ps. 16:5]. The goods of which verses 9–11 speak are all very vaguely defined. What exactly is the "path of life" and "repletion in your presence"? The point here is at least primarily protection from death.[47]

What is meant by this "protection" is to be explained in the context of the exegesis of verses 10–11.[48]

It appears that the entire human existence is shifted from the material realm to the presence of God. In this sense it is also more appropriate to speak in regard to verses 5–6 of *land metaphors*[49] rather than land motifs. The image of home as connected to the land is transformed here, so that no particular piece of land, but rather YHWH himself and YHWH alone is the "inheritance" allot-

41. Hossfeld, "Metaphorisierung," 29; cf. Hossfeld and Zenger, *Die Psalmen*, 1:112; and Liess, "Bechermotiv," 58.
42. Cf. von Rad, "'Gerechtigkeit' und 'Leben,'" 243.
43. H. Schmidt, *Die Psalmen*, 13.
44. Cf. Liess, "Bechermotiv," 55. "Just as the land, the נַחֲלָה, is counted as an inalienable possession, so also the speaker of the psalm's relation to God cannot be lost." On ancient Israelite land law, see Ebach, "Bodenrecht."
45. Ebach, "Bodenrecht," 313.
46. Von Rad, "'Gerechtigkeit' und 'Leben,'" 243.
47. Ibid., 243.
48. See 301ff. and 319ff. below.
49. I am taking up a suggestion by Hossfeld, "Metaphorisierung," 28ff.; see also Liess, *Der Weg des Lebens*, 136ff.

ted to the supplicant: "Preserve me, God, for I have found refuge in you!" (Ps. 16:1).[50] YHWH himself is the "portion" (v. 5), the *foundation of life* for the supplicant, both literally and metaphorically.[51]

The expression of YHWH as "portion" (חֵלֶק) as an affirmation of trust within a lament is also found in Psalm 142:4–5 (5–6):

> Look to the right and see:
>   no friend is there for me;
> [all] refuge is lost to me;
>   there is no one who cares about me. (v. 4/5)
> I have cried to you, YHWH;
>   I said: "You are my refuge,
>   my portion [חֶלְקִי] in the land of the living!" (v. 5/6)

The subject here is also the basis of life, no longer with respect to normal sustenance, but rather in the sense that the supplicant's life is to be saved from pursuers. In this salvation, the goodness of God is experienced:

> Listen to my cry,
>   for I am very weak!
> Save me from my pursuers,
>   for they are stronger than I!
>   (Ps. 142:6/7)
> Lead me / my life [*nepeš*] out of prison,
>   so that I shall praise your name!
> The righteous shall gather around me,
>   for you have acted upon me. (v. 7/8)

The most comprehensive version of the affirmation of trust as "YHWH is my portion" is found, however, in Psalm 73:25–28:[52]

> Who is there for me in the heavens?—
>   And besides you, there is no joy for me on earth. (v. 25)
> My flesh and heart may fail me,
>   [the rock of my heart (and)]
>   but my portion [חֵלֶק] is God forever. (v. 26)
> Indeed, see that those who distance themselves from you perish,
>   you have [still] destroyed all who shamefully fall away from you. (v. 27)
> But for me—to be near to God is happiness to me;
>   I have taken my refuge with Adonai (YHWH)—
>   (with the intention) to proclaim all your deeds. (v. 28)

Here the supplicant also sees in YHWH the happiness of that one's "eternal" life.[53] What this happiness in life means for the supplicant of Psalm 16 can only be understood within the context of this psalm through verses 10–11.

50. The expression חָסָה בְּ, "find refuge," has an unmistakable spatial connotation; see Gamberoni, "חָסָה," 75–76.

51. Cf. Conrad, "מָנָה," *ThWAT* 4:976–980; Hossfeld, "Metaphorisierung," 29; Hartenstein, *Das Angesicht JHWHs*, 96; and Liess, "Bechermotiv," 58.

52. See also 319–20 below.

53. On hopes for an afterlife in Ps. 73, see 318ff. below.

2. The Path to Life

From the idea of YHWH as living space (Ps. 16:5–6) comes the supplicant's trust that God will enable for self a life in happiness and security (v. 9). It is to this that the affirmation of trust II (vv. 7–9) refers, in which the accumulation of (socio)anthropological concepts heart (לֵב), honor (כָּבוֹד), and flesh (בָּשָׂר) is striking:

> Therefore my *heart* is glad, and my *honor* rejoices;
> even my *flesh* dwells securely.
> (Ps. 16:9)

While the "heart" represents what is *inside a human being*,[54] the "flesh" signifies the body or the *external form of a human being*.[55] To this the word "honor" adds the aspect of esteem, which the supplicant experiences in the presence of YHWH in contrast to the worship of other gods (v. 4).[56] Thus verse 9 focuses on the "human being as a whole"[57] as sustained by YHWH, the human whose heart rejoices and whose flesh—despite its frailness—dwells securely. The type of closeness to God signified by the image of "dwelling securely" will be of concern to us later.

The aspects of "inside" and "outside" characteristic of verse 9 are also found in verses 7–8, which identify the reason for the result described in verse 9: the supplicant blesses YHWH as "counselor" of the petitioner's interior (v. 7) and makes YHWH the constant "counterpart":

> I bless YHWH, who has [always] counseled me;
> even at night my kidneys have instructed me.
> (Ps. 16:7)
> I have set YHWH always before me;
> indeed, he is to my right, so that I do not stumble. (v. 8)
> Therefore my heart is glad, and my honor rejoices;
> even my flesh dwells securely. (v. 9)

The counsel for which the supplicant thanks God in the form of a blessing is "the plan for the future, which God has and realizes for the life of the individual. That the supplicant accepts this plan is the result of "being instructed . . . by my 'kidneys' as my nocturnal teachers."[58] The *kidneys*, as the seat of the innermost emotions, are like the *heart* in being the place where God acts upon human beings.[59] Next to this introspective is the outside perspective: YHWH is the constant *counterpart* (נֶגֶד) for the supplicant, who is at the petitioner's "right hand" (יָמִין), so that "I do not stumble."[60]

The main themes of Psalm 16:7–9—YHWH as the provident guide of life and as the helpful counterpart of the supplicant (vv. 7–8), who can therefore

54. See "Anthropological Keyword 3: Heart and Kidneys," 155ff. above.
55. See H. W. Wolff, *Anthropology*, 26ff.; Bratsiotis, "בָּשָׂר," 858ff.; Albertz, "Mensch," 465; and S. Schroer and Staubli, *Körpersymbolik der Bibel*, 231ff.
56. On the concept of "honor" in the Psalms, see 263–64 above.
57. See "Excursus 2: The Whole Human Being," in 43–44 above .
58. Hossfeld and Zenger, *Die Psalmen*, 1:112.
59. See "Anthropological Keyword 3: Heart and Kidneys," 155ff. above.
60. On the motif of "stumbling" (מוט), see 73–74 above.

exist joyfully and trustingly (v. 9)—are bundled together in verse 11 and solidified as *images of life*:

> You show me the path of life:
> filled with joy before your face,
> pleasures in your right hand forevermore.

This is the central statement of the entire psalm. It achieves its significance not only in contrast to the *images of death* in verse 10:

> Indeed, you will not abandon me / my life [*nepeš*] to the underworld;
> you do not allow your faithful one to see the Pit.[61]

This central statement also gains significance in the juxtaposition of the *image of longing* in Psalm 27:4,[62] according to which the supplicant hopes to see the "kindness" (נֹעַם)[63] and "goodness" (טוֹב)[64] of God (27:13), especially in the "house of YHWH," the place with the greatest fullness of life:[65]

> One thing I have asked of YHWH,
> therefore I ask it again:
> to dwell in the house of YHWH all the days of my life,
> to see the kindness [נֹעַם] of YHWH,
> and to look upon his temple.
> (Ps. 27:4)

The antithesis of death and life, which constitutes the foundational structure of Psalm 16:10–11, is resolved in favor of life in 16:11 with the help of the phrase "path of life" (v. 11a) and further specified through the two final stichs: "filled with joy before your face" (v. 11b) and "pleasures in your right hand forevermore" (v. 11c). In a detailed study, Seybold[66] has shown that the expression אֹרַח/דֶּרֶךְ חַיִּים, "path/way of life," is at home in the Wisdom literature and has a specific meaning in the relevant passages there. The locus classicus is Proverbs 15:24:[67]

> The path of life leads upward for one with insight,
> so that one may escape the realm of death below.

The "path of life" in Psalm 16:11 thus signifies a way of life that leads away from the powers of death toward *fullness of life in the spatial and at the same time personal closeness to YHWH*. It is possible that the image behind this is the "introduction" of the supplicant to an audience with the royal Deity,

61. The expression "not allowing to see the Pit" is a direct idiom for "not dying"; see Fuhs, "רָאָה," 242.

62. On this text and on Ps. 27:13, see 94 above.

63. On the root נעם, see the references in 295 n. 95 above.

64. Cf. Ps. 16:2b, in which YHWH is called "my goodness / happiness"; see 294 above.

65. Cf. Hartenstein, *Das Angesicht JHWHs*, 84, etc.

66. Seybold, "Der Weg des Lebens," 75ff.; cf. also Hossfeld and Zenger, *Die Psalmen*, 1:112; Hartenstein, *Das Angesicht JHWHs*, 97 n. 3; for an extensive treatment of the unique significance of Ps. 16:11a, see Liess, *Der Weg des Lebens*, 202ff.

67. Cf. Prov. 2:19; 5:6; 6:23; and Jer. 21:8.

YHWH,[68] whose presence ("face") fills[69] the worshiper with joys and whose right hand grants the worshiper the gift of "pleasures." In contrast to the hand motif of Psalms 18:16/17; 144:7 (etc.),[70] the hand motif of 16:11 expresses not *salvation from death* but *granting fullness of life*. The "pleasures" are found "in" YHWH's right hand, "from which" the supplicant hopes to receive them for the duration of that one's life.[71]

From numerous Phoenician texts and images, Hartenstein has assembled evidence for this vision of an audience,[72] thus shedding new light on Psalm 16:11 as well as 27:4. It includes the stela of Yeḥawmelek of Byblos (*KAI* 10), which was already mentioned in reference to Psalm 116:13 and contains the lexeme *n'm*, "goodness, pleasure," in the context of an answered prayer. The background image behind this is an audience of the king of Byblos with the patron deity of the city ("Mistress of Byblos"), with the expectation that blessings would be bestowed on the regent, as the upper image of the stela (fig. 37) shows. The king of Byblos appears reverently before the welcoming/blessing deity. The iconographically well-attested constellation of "deity granting access [and] human being appearing 'before' deity"[73] is also to be assumed for the audience described by Psalm 16:11. As in the Yeḥawmelek stela, the central theme here is access to the enthroned deity, which receives the supplicant with blessings and favors.

The message of Psalm 16 is that life does not end with death, but finds fulfillment in the spatial, and at the same time personal, closeness to God,[74] which invests life with a new quality, *thereby* overcoming death.[75] Just as Psalm 23 develops a "blueprint of life on the basis of inherited or metahistorical primordial images of Jewish tradition,"[76] such as wandering (in the desert), salvation from danger, hospitality and personal communion with God, so does Psalm 16 do so on the basis of images of God as "living space" (vv. 5–6), as "one who directs life" (7–9), and as "fullness of life" (10–11).[77] Both psalms represent magnificent high points in biblical anthropology because they give expression to the conviction that true happiness in life is not found in an ecstatic moment nor in an outstanding personal achievement, but in the "quality that one achieves for one's entire biography."[78]

68. Cf. Hossfeld and Zenger, *Die Psalmen*, 1:112–13; and in greater detail now, Hartenstein, *Das Angesicht JHWHs*, 94ff.

69. If it is true that Ps. 16 and Ps. 17 are deliberately arranged sequentially within the subsection Pss. 15–24 (see 296–97 above; Hossfeld and Zenger, *Die Psalmen*, 1:109), the "fullness with joys before your face" (Ps. 16:11b) could have as its goal the "satisfaction" that the supplicant of Ps. 17:15b has in "your [YHWH's] likeness" when he awakes; see 94ff. above; and on the topos of "fullness," see Liess, *Der Weg des Lebens*, 240ff.

70. See 49 above.

71. On the motif of the "right hand" of God, see Liess, *Der Weg des Lebens*, 252ff., with references to ancient Near Eastern parallels.

72. Hartenstein, *Das Angesicht JHWHs*, 98ff.

73. Cf. ibid., 103.

74. Comparable to this kind of community with God in Ps. 16:11 is the quality of divine closeness experienced by the supplicant according to Ps. 63 and Ps. 84; see Hossfeld and Zenger, *Psalmen 51–100*, 195ff., 518ff.; and see 196–97 above.

75. On the question whether this constitutes hope for this life or the next, see 318ff. below.

76. Gzella, *Lebenszeit und Ewigkeit*, 155.

77. On these qualifications, see 297 n. 35 above.

78. Höffe, "Glück," 110; cf. 285 above.

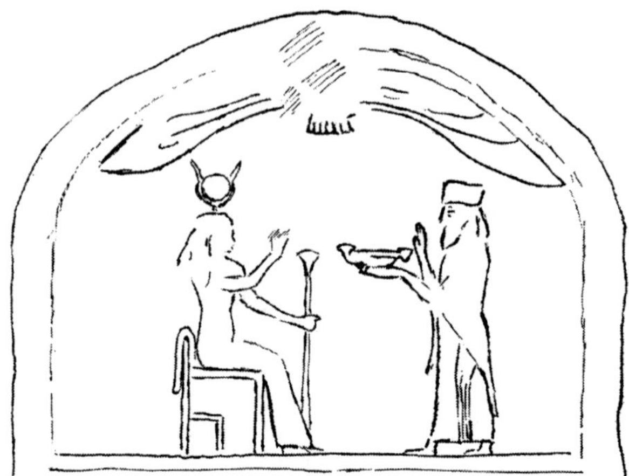

Figure 37. Stela of Yeḥawmelek of Byblos (5th/4th c. BCE)

Excursus 9: Closeness to God

The sense of the divine has always been unevenly distributed among human beings. While it is evident to some, it is angrily denied by others. "But anyone who has," according to the classicist Paul Veyne, "encountered the divine even once (and if it was only in dreams), has experienced it all at once as something incontrovertible and is no longer willing to deny the essential core of the historical religions. He will henceforth resist any reduction of the divine. It is astounding to see the overwhelming majesty, the terror, and the gentleness that proceeds from certain concrete or imaginary objects in emotionally charged moments. . . . I know very well that it is only a simple emotion, but one that is unlike any other" (Veyne, *Brot und Spiele*, 487).

In ancient religions this sense of the divine was characterized by the concept of "closeness to God." This can hardly mean just a culturally constituted and specifically dimensioned *realm of experience* in which gods and human beings are assigned to specific realms and roles in order to interact with each other—with "roles such as priests, prophets, shamans, pilgrims, hermits, mystics, magicians, dream interpreters, diviners, scribes, and so forth; and realms such as cult, nature, cosmos, history, myth, city, and so forth—but also forms of the extramundane (transcendence) and supernatural (miracle)" (J. Assmann, *Ägypten*, 15). Of all these possibilities, only some are realized in any given culture while others are excluded. It holds true, however, that "through selection and negation, the realm we call 'closeness to God' is invested with the culturally specific form and structure of the world of the senses" (ibid., 15; cf. 16ff., 25ff.; Brunner, "Gottesnähe"). It is only with the horizon of the world of the senses that action and experience are possible.

In the Old Testament, the idea of closeness to God is expressed in various ways. In addition to the idea of YHWH's presence in the holy of holies, "enthroned upon the cherubim" (Pss. 80:1/2; 99:1; etc.), there is the priestly notion of his dynamic "dwelling in the midst of the Israelites" (Exod. 29:43–46; etc.). Deuteronomistic theology, on the other hand, distinguishes between YHWH's "throne" in the heavens and the dwelling of his "name" in a named cultic site (1 Kgs. 8:14ff.; see Görg, "Gegenwart Gottes"; Janowski, "'Ich will,'" 134ff.). A unique statement about the closeness of God is found in the late Deuteronomistic text of Deut. 4:7, in which the YHWH-Israel relation is expressed as a call-hear-answer contact, which is possible at all times (Braulik, "Weisheit, Gottesnähe," 75ff., 53ff.).

Since YHWH resides in the temple, it is the focal point of the pursuit of closeness to God. There are numerous Psalms of the Individual (Pss. 17; 27; 42–43; 63; 84; etc.) that poetically establish the aura of the temple and the Deity present there "in order to convey, to those reciting these psalms far away from the temple, participation in the power of the temple God" (Zenger, "'Ich liebe den Ort,'" 182). Their longing finds fulfillment in prayer, in entering the temple, and above all in the vision of God, which is its own form of "nourishment" for body and soul (cf. Ps. 17:15). The expression "to see God / the face of God" describes a particularly intensive form of contact with God, which includes extensive blessings and favors (see Hartenstein, *Das Angesicht JHWHs*, 87ff., 90ff.; and the contributions in Eberhardt and Liess, *Gottes Nähe*).

γ. *Old Testament Metaphors for Life*

As we have seen in the example of Psalm 13:3bc/4bc—"Let my eyes shine, so that I will not sleep the sleep of death"—the individual laments and songs of thanksgiving often express the contrast of life and death through the antithesis of light and darkness or repletion and lack, thereby equating light and life, darkness and death.[79] These *homologies of light and life* are connected to the biblical understanding of seeing. Like hearing, seeing[80] is the other chief sense with which human beings perceive the world, for YHWH has indeed created both "the hearing ear and the seeing eye" (cf. Prov. 20:12).[81]

Every conscious perception begins with seeing. That which is seen must be real or figuratively "before one's eyes": it must be "visible:" "Seeing is the chief sense of the perceiving human being. *r'(h)* means 'perceiving' in general, and only one who perceives is an existing being, just as that which is exists as that which is perceived. Light is constitutive for the living, receiving being: light constitutes the essence of life, and one speaks of the 'light of life' (Ps. 56:13/14; Job 33:30)."[82]

Let us now turn to this light/life symbolism in the Old Testament.[83]

79. See "Excursus 3: Light and Darkness," 69–70 above; and "Excursus 7: Life and Death," 239–40 above; also Keel, *Die Welt*, 164ff.; Liess, *Der Weg des Lebens*, 135–36; and Janowski, "Licht und Finsternis II."

80. See "Anthropological Keyword 1: Hearing and Seeing," 85ff. above.

81. See 96 above.

82. Gese, "Johannesprolog," 191; on the subject, see also Fuhs, "רָאָה," 232ff.

83. See Janowski, *"De profundis"*; idem, "Gott, Mensch und Raum," 30ff.; and references in 1b 46ff. and 6b 188ff.

The "Light of Life"

Since the biblical concept of life means not mere existence, but the "living" or salvific and fulfilled life, the concept of light is used accordingly. Light images are metaphors of life and fulfillment, such as the following:

> Indeed, you light [אוֹר Hiphil] my lamp [נֵר], YHWH;
>   my God enlightens [נגה Hiphil] my darkness [חֹשֶׁךְ].
> (Ps. 18:28/29)

Outside of the Psalms, the association of light and life is found especially in Wisdom literature. Thus *not to see the light* means "to be dead" (Job 3:16), and *to give light* means "to give life" (3:20). Especially the first speech by Elihu (32:6–33:33) is characterized by light/life metaphors. Elihu speaks to Job about the way God answers human beings, warns them, and brings them back to the right path (33:8–22). If the underworld reaches out for the suffering, he continues, an "advocate" can be found who intercedes before God on behalf of the suffering, so that the afflicted may return from the "Pit" and see again the "light of life":

> If there is a messenger with him,
>   an advocate, one of a thousand,
>   to proclaim a person's righteousness,
> (Job 33:23)
> who has mercy and says,
>   "Let him go, so that he does not go down to the Pit,
>   I have found a ransom!," (v. 24)
> then his flesh is fresh with youthful vigor;
>   he returns to the days of his youth. (v. 25)
> He prays to God, who is inclined toward him;
>   he may see his face with joy.
> <He proclaims> his salvation to human beings, (v. 26)
>   <he sings> before the people and says:
> "I had sinned and perverted what is right,
>   but he has not <repaid> me. (v. 27)
> He has redeemed my soul from the descent to the Pit,
>   and my life sees the light." (v. 28)
> See, all this God does,
>   twice, three times for a human, (v. 29)
> to bring back that soul from the Pit,
>   <so that one may see> the life of life [אוֹר הַחַיִּים]. (v. 30)[84]

Conversely, death and dying are equivalent to the extinguishing of the light. To depart from life means to slip from the brightness of day into the darkness of night and distance from God.[85] In Bildad's speech (Job 18:1–21) the wicked is depicted as one whose light is extinguished:

84. Translation based on Ebach, *Streiten mit Gott*, 2:97–98. On the interpretation, see Strauss, *Hiob*, 283ff. For Job 33:30b, Strauss (ibid., 247, 250, 291) offers a different translation: "so that he (the one brought back from the Pit by YHWH) shines in the light of the living." On the expression "light of life," see also Ps. 56:13/14: "For you have saved my life from death and my feet from falling, so that I walk before God in the light of life." See Hossfeld and Zenger, *Psalmen 51–100*, 116.

85. See 69–70 above.

The light [אוֹר] of the wicked is also extinguished,
and the flame of his fire [שְׁבִיב אִשּׁוֹ] does not shine.
(Job 18:5)
The light [אוֹר] grows dark over his tent,
and the lamp [נֵר] above him is put out. (v. 6)
His strong steps become short,
and his own plan casts him down. (v. 7)[86]

"Anyone who has found oneself in a great darkness knows the significance of a small lamp. It can lift the whole pressure of darkness."[87] As a *metaphor for (happiness in) life*, light can signify the vital as well as the spiritual aspect of life, or—in modern terms—existence as well as consciousness.[88] For this reason light is also a *metaphor for truth*,[89] which guides the human being on his path of life:

Send out your light [אוֹר] and your truth [אֱמֶת],
they shall guide me,
[and] bring me to your holy mountain,
and to your dwelling place.
(Ps. 43:3)

Your word is a lamp [נֵר] to my feet,
and a light [אוֹר] to my path.
(Ps. 119:105)

My child, keep your father's commandment,
and do not disregard your mother's instruction!
(Prov. 6:20)
Bind them always on your heart;
tie them around your neck! (v. 21)
When you walk about, it guides you;
when you lie down, it watches over you;
and when you wake up, it greets you. (v. 22)
For the commandment is a lamp [נֵר] and the instruction a light [אוֹר],
and the reproofs of discipline are the path of life. (v. 23)[90]

This wisdom commandment is accorded the same quality here as the divine word in Psalm 119:105: it "shines light" on the path of the righteous and makes it the "path of life" (Prov. 6:23b).[91] This "enlightenment" is not a matter of reason, but a gift from God for the benefit of life.[92]

The "Source of Life"

The association between light and life described here can be further detailed on the basis of Psalm 36. This sapiential reflection on God's all-encompassing

86. Translation based on Ebach, *Streiten mit Gott*, 1:145. It is real light that is put out for the wicked: the "flame of his fire" and the "(oil) lamp in his tent" (which hung high under the roof of the tent); see Kellermann, "נֵר," 622. On the "extinguished light" of the wicked, see also ibid., 623–24; Prov. 13:9; 20:20; 24:20; Job 21:17; Egger-Wenzel, *Von der Freiheit Gottes, anders zu sein*, 129, 142, etc.
87. Keel, *Die Welt*, 168.
88. Cf. Gese, "Johannesprolog," 192.
89. On the semantic history of this idea, see Blumenberg, "Licht als Metapher."
90. Translation based on Meinhold, *Die Sprüche*, 116; see also Kellermann, "נֵר," 625–26.
91. On the expression "path/way of life," see 307 above.
92. Cf. Deut. 30:15–20 (about Torah); etc.

justice begins after a *superscription* with a unique *description of the sinner* (vv. 1–4 [2–5]), which is counterpoised by an equally unique *hymn* (5–9 [6–10]). The text concludes with a *petition* for God's goodness and help against sinners as well as a statement about the latter's fate (11–13):

For the choirmaster. By YHWH's servant, by David.

Murmurs of treachery to the wicked—within my [own] heart;
fear of God is never before their eyes.
(Ps. 36:1/2)
For they have flattered themselves [too much] in their [own] eyes,
to uncover their own sin, so as to hate it. (v. 2/3)
The words of their mouths are trouble and deception;
they are unable to be good from insight. (v. 3/4)
They devise [further] trouble on their beds;
[again and again] they go down a path that is not good;
evil they do not shun. (v. 4/5)

YHWH, your goodness [reaches] to the heavens,
your faithfulness to the clouds! (v. 5/6)
Your justice is like the mountains of God;
your judgment like the great primordial flood;
human and animal you preserve [forevermore], YHWH! (v. 6/7)

How precious is your goodness, God;
human beings can find refuge in the shadows of your wings! (v. 7/8)
They feast on the fat of your house,
and you let them drink [from] the river of your delights. (v. 8/9)
For with you is the source of life;
in your light we perceive the light! (v. 9/10)

Let your goodness continue for those who know you,
and your justice for those with upright hearts. (v. 10/11)
Let not the foot of pride reach me,
and let the hand of the wicked not drive me away! (v. 11/12)
There the evildoers have fallen;
they were pushed over and can no longer rise.[93] (v. 12/13)

The supplicant who speaks here listens within self and hears the "murmurs of treachery" (v. 1/2a), which are intent on turning the petitioner toward evil. Sin, the supplicant considers, is a possibility that can occupy space in "my [own] heart" (v. 1/2b). What constitutes this possibility? According to verses

93. On this translation, see also Lohfink, "Innenschau und Kosmosmystik," 173–74; Weber, *Werkbuch*, 1:173; Sticher, *Die Rettung der Guten*, 123–24. For text-critical issues, which cannot be addressed here, see the commentaries. Regarding the structure, it is noteworthy that (1) Ps. 36:2–4 (3–5) contains four different terms for "sin" (guilty, trouble, deception, evil), which are contrasted in vv. 5–6 (6–7) with four terms for God's goodness (goodness, faithfulness, justice, judgment; see Lohfink, "Innenschau und Kosmosmystik," 178–79); (2) the name of YHWH forms an inclusio in vv. 5–6 (6–7); and (3) the expression "your goodness" (vv. 5/6a, 7/8a, 10/11a) apparently has the function of closing a section. On the poetic structure, see the references in Weber, *Werkbuch*, 1:174–75 (who, however, groups v. 9/10 and vv. 10–12 [11–13] together); and Sticher, *Die Rettung der Guten*, 124ff.

2–4 (3–5), it is the sinners' representation of a world that is entangled in itself,[94] but that is not consistently constructed: they have eyes but cannot see, so as to hate their own guilt (v. 2/3), mouths but do not speak, so as to do good arising from insight (v. 3/4). Therefore they devise trouble "on their beds" (v. 4/5a)[95] and carry it out—as classical prophecy and ancient wisdom have known—by embarking on a *path* that is *not good* and by *not shunning evil* (v. 4ab/5ab).[96]

While the supplicant's view in verses 1–4 (2–5) is directed *inward* on the self, the hymn in verses 5–9 (6–10) is oriented *outward* toward God's creation. The change in direction occurs abruptly in the text. The supplicant first observes the world in verses 5–6 (6–7) in its spatial extent: from the heavens // the clouds (vertical: above); over the mountains of God (horizontal); to the great primordial flood (vertical: below; fig. 38).[97] In these phenomena of the created world, the supplicant sees signs of God's goodness, faithfulness, justice, and judgment, which effect the preservation of humans and animals and thus overcome the power of sin (vv. 1–4 [2–5]).[98]

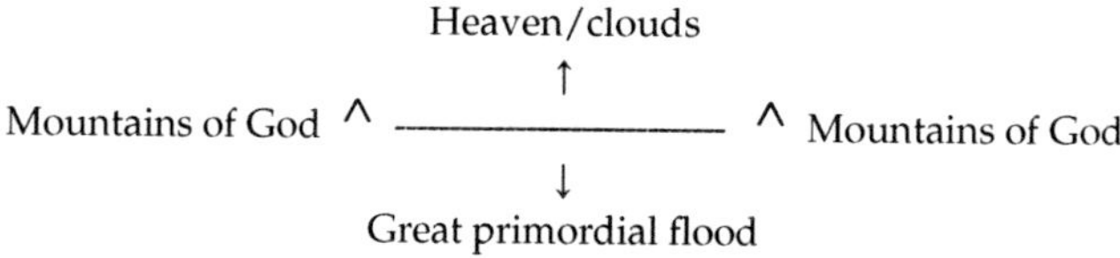

Figure 38. Diagram of the cosmic metaphor of Psalm 36:5–6 (6–7)

With the third stich—"human and animal [= the entirety of all creatures] you preserve [forevermore], YHWH!" (v. 6/7b)—the first part of the hymn (vv. 5–6 [6–7]) introduces the theme of the second part (vv. 7–9 [8–10]), which praises the human participation in the divine presence and the gifts of God. The word "goodness" (חֶסֶד), which introduces the cosmic metaphor in verse 5/6, is now developed with regard to its significance for humanity and is expanded to the YHWH-faithful in verse 10/11:

94. Ps. 36:1–4 (2–5) reads like a classic description of the *homo incurvatus in se ipsum* (the person turned in on oneself).

95. Cf. the woe-statement in Mic. 2:1: "Woe to those who devise injustice / and who who do evil on their beds: / In the morning they perform it / for it is in the power of their hands." See Kessler, *Micha*, 144–45. Kessler correctly notes that the linguistic closeness of Ps. 36:4/5 to Mic. 2:1 "shows that the social critique by the prophets often criticized conditions about which the supplicant in the laments of the individual complains as one who is affected by them" (ibid., 115). Ps. 36:4/5 thus provides an *inside view* of the events whose *outward effects* are shown in Mic. 2:1–3. This agrees with the remark by Lohfink ("Innenschau und Kosmosmystik," 178–79) that the words for "sin" in Ps. 36:2–4 (3–5; see 308, n. 93 above) all have a social dimension and that the wicked of vv. 1–4 (2–5) "disturb human society through their actions and especially through their speech."

96. Cf. Isa. 1:16–17; Amos 5:14–15; etc.; see Jeremias, *Der Prophet Amos*, 71–72.

97. Lohfink ("Innenschau und Kosmosmystik," 180) speaks of a *cosmic metaphor*: "The immense space of the entire creation is . . . filled with God's goodness. The world in its vastness is the space of divine presence and thus also of possible divine encounter."

98. "The idea of the creatures being 'preserved' by the God who governs the entire universe also makes an important statement about God without mentioning the word: He is king. For preserving is what rulers do" (ibid., 181).

YHWH, *your goodness* [reaches] to the heavens,
your faithfulness to the clouds!
(Ps. 36:5/6)

How precious is *your goodness*, God;
human beings can find refuge in the shadows of your wings! (v. 7/8)

Let *your goodness* continue for those who know you,
and your justice for those with upright hearts. (v. 10/11)

Two basic images are employed for this purpose in Psalm 36:7–8 (8–9):

- **Image 1**: "In the shadow of your wings." Verse 7/8 evokes the *image of a saving space*, in whose "shadow" (צֵל) *human beings find* refuge.[99] According to Hartenstein, the background for this image is not so much the image of a mother bird's wings covering her young[100] but rather of a "winged sun with the function of a canopy, . . . which designates the space of most intensive protection (by the 'shadow' of God) and YHWH's royal 'light of life.'"[101]
- **Image 2**: "The river of your delights." With the two components of *eating and drinking*, verse 8/9 evokes the *image of a delicious meal* that is prepared at a sacred place by YHWH the host.[102] The temple is the place of paradise-like fullness of life, where the "river of your delights" (נַחַל עֲדָנֶיךָ) originates.[103] "Here the cultic perspective with its cosmic origins extends into the primordial-eschatological world."[104]

Both images are united in verse 9/10 and given a categorical quality through an enigmatic and beautiful verse:

For with you is the source of life;
in your light we perceive the light!
(Ps. 36:9/10)

It is "with you," meaning in the temple, that the life-giving presence of God is experienced. The second part of the verse (9/10b) expands this statement through a *double light-metaphor*: The first light appears to be

> the "light of his [God's] face" (cf. [Pss. 4:6/7; 44:3/4; 89:15/16). Here "his face" (i.e., his care: *pnym* [פָּנִים], "attention, face") is an epexegetical genitive. It equates "light" with God's "care." The second light signifies nothing other than "life" itself, as the expression "light of life" ([Ps.] 56:13/14) suggests. Like "of his face," "of life" is an epexegetical genitive, which equates light and life. . . . The meaning in [Ps.] 36:9/10b is therefore: "We live by your kindness!" This meaning fits very well with the first half of the verse: "With you is the source of life" ([Ps.] 36:9/10a).[105]

99. Cf. Pss. 17:8; 57:1/2; 63:7/8; etc.
100. So Hossfeld and Zenger, *Psalmen 51–100*, 124; see the entire argument on 123ff.; and S. Schroer in Keel and Staubli, *Tiere in der Bible*, 11.
101. Hartenstein, *Das Angesicht JHWHs*, 157 n. 1; cf. 158–59.
102. Cf. Pss. 23:5; 63:1–2 (2–3), 5/6; 65:4/5; etc.
103. Cf. Pss. 46:4/5; 65:9/10; Ezek. 47:1–12; etc. On the motif of the paradisiac river of God, see Janowski, "Die heilige Wohnung," 42ff.
104. Lohfink, "Innenschau und Kosmosmystik," 184.
105. Keel, *Die Welt*, 166; cf. Hartenstein, *Das Angesicht JHWHs*, 81, 157ff.

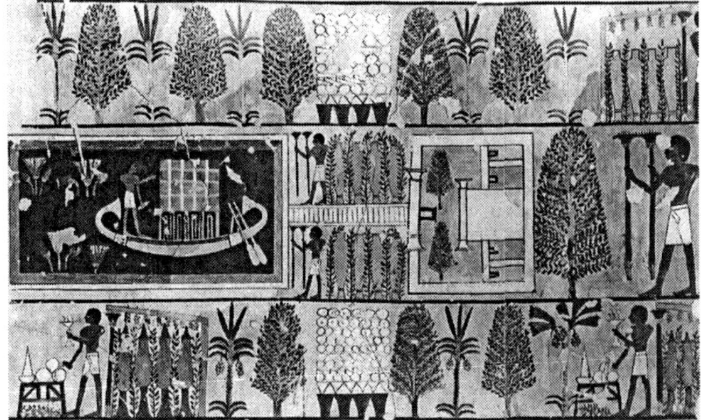

Figure 39. Painting in the tomb of Nakhtmin (Egypt, 15th c. BCE)

According to Psalm 36:7–9 (8–10), human beings (v. 7/8) experience the closeness of the living God most intensively.[106] For it is in the temple courts with its trees[107] and in the waters of the "sea of cast metal" (1 Kgs. 7:23–26) and the cauldrons (1 Kgs. 7:27–39) where the life that proceeds from the God of Zion manifests itself.[108] Therefore "one day in your courts is better than a thousand in the courts of the wicked" (Ps. 84:10/11)[109] and "a relationship characterized by faithfulness and love and more important to him than life itself ([Pss. 63:3/4; 73:23–28)."[110] The tradition of ancient Near Eastern temple gardens and sacred gardens (figs. 39–40),[111] which seem to constitute the background to this "image of paradise" in Psalm 36:8/9b, is unambiguous in this regard.

The reference to light in Psalm 36:9/10 closes the circle of describing the universal and all-pervasive[112] justice of God at the center of the psalm (vv. 5–6 [6–7]). At the same time it sets up a contrast to the hidden and dark[113] world of the wicked, whose demise is described in verse 12/13. "There the evildoers have fallen; they were pushed over and can no longer rise."[114]

106. See also Excursus 9: Closeness to God, above, 304–305.

107. See Keel, *Die Welt*, 118ff. The experience of temple as paradisiac fullness of life has also had an impact on biblical anthropology and its imagery. In Pss. 1:3; 52:8/10; 92:12–15 (13–16); and Jer. 17:7–8, the righteous are compared to a (palm, olive, or cedar) tree, planted in the house of YHWH or near water; see Janowski, "Frucht der Gerechtigkeit," 125ff.

108. On the cosmological implications of the the Jerusalem temple theology, see Janowski, "Die heilige Wohnung," 26ff.

109. On this text, see 91ff. above.

110. Keel, *Die Welt*, 166.

111. See J. Assmann, *Tod und Jenseits*, 299ff. (a this-wordly paradise as "realm of the afterlife" in addition to heaven and underworld); Janowski, "Die heilige Wohnung," 50ff.; and Neumann-Gorsolke and Riede, "Garten und Paradies."

112. According to Lohfink ("Innenschau und Kosmosmystik," 181), without making use of the term "sunlight," the background to the cosmic metaphor of Ps. 36:5–6 (6–7) is the image of sunlight: "For what fills the space between heaven and earth from one horizon to the other? Only the precious and all-illuminating light of the sun."

113. Cf. esp. 36:4/5a; see 309 n. 94 above.

114. On what is meant by "there" (the temple or the afterlife?), see Sticher, *Die Rettung der Guten*, 130ff.

Figure 40. Relief from Ashurbanipal's northern palace (Nineveh, 7th c. BCE)

The central idea of Psalm 36:5–9 (6–10) is that in praising God, the human being is outside of self,[115] entirely with the One who is the "source of life" (v. 9/10).[116] This is a form of theology that makes *createdness the benchmark for the human being's humanity* and does not lose sight of the fundamental dependence of life on everything that has been granted by God. Only in this way, Psalm 36 teaches, can the *happiness of closeness to God* be achieved: from the hand of the Creator, who bestows on his creatures—human and animal—the gift of divine presence.

Let us return to our original question of happiness. The answer given by Psalm 16 is unequivocal: A human beings finds happiness in life in the spatial and also personal closeness to God, whose blessings and favors endow human life as a whole with a new quality and thereby overcome death. We shall further ask below in what manner death is overcome through this closeness to God: in this life or the afterlife?

b. Anthropological Keyword 7: Immortality

But I am always with you;
  you have taken hold of my right hand;
you guide me according to your counsel,
  and will receive me to glory.
Psalm 73:23–24

115. In this context, Bayer ("Der Schöpfungsmorgen," 117) speaks of an "externalness of human existence."
116. Cf. Jer. 2:13; Prov. 13:14; 14:27; etc.

For who knows if the spirit of human beings rises up,
and if the spirit of animals goes down into the earth?
Ecclesiastes 3:21

Resources

J. Assmann, *Tod und Jenseits*, 496–525; idem, "Unsterblichkeit"; C. Barth, *Errettung vom Tode*, 121–32; Dietrich and Vollenweider, "Tod II," 583–95; Gese, "Der Tod"; Görg, "Auferstehung"; Janowski, "Die Toten loben JHWH nicht," 33–45; Kaiser, "Tod, Auferstehung"; idem, "Zukunft der Toten"; Kittel, *Befreit aus dem Rachen des Todes*, 73–102; Lang, "Leben nach dem Tod"; idem, "Leibliche Auferstehung?"; idem, "Reise ins Jenseits"; Lang and McDannell, *Der Himmel*, 17–43; Liess, *Der Weg des Lebens*, 265–90; Michel, "Ich aber bin immer bei dir"; Karlheinz Müller, "Weltbild der jüdischen Apokalyptik"; A. Schmitt, *Wende des Lebens*, 212–40; Spronk, *Beatific Afterlife*, 915–16; Witte, "Leben nach dem Tod"; H. W. Wolff, *Anthropology*, 107–13; Zenger, "Israel und seine Toten."

For a brief survey on the subject of "Immortality in the Old Testament," see Janowski, "Sehnsucht nach Unsterblichkeit: Zur Jenseitshoffnung." On the topic of immortality in Egypt and Mesopotamia, see idem, "Sehnsucht nach Unsterblichkeit: Zu J. Assmann"; Zgoll, "Sehnsucht nach Unsterblichkeit."

Is death the end of all things? Or does the religion of the Old Testament include a hope beyond death? In the Old Testament one can "observe the process of recognition, by which individuals praying the Psalms and teachers of wisdom gradually attained an increasingly deeper insight into the nature and truth of the God who overcomes death."[117]

At the basis of this is, as we have seen, the experience preserved in the individual laments and songs of thanksgiving that the person pursued by enemies, troubled by legal problems, or afflicted by sickness—this afflicted one—has come in contact with the reality of death (cf. Ps. 88:3/4),[118] "but that this is sufficient for the individual to experience the entire reality of death."[119] This corresponds to the opposite experience of being saved through YHWH's intervention "not only in cases of mortal danger, but also in death, from within the realm of death and from the power of death."[120] Thus ground was broken for the idea that death was not the end of all things. This relationship of YHWH to the dead introduced a new development in the Old Testament understanding of death, as Psalm 88 strikingly shows. For as D. Michel points out, "If death is the end of all things, it represents a limitation to God's power, for although he is 'God of the living,' he is not 'God of the dead.' If the deceased lead a shadow-like existence in Sheol, where they are cut off from the hand of YHWH (Ps. 88:5/6), there would be a realm in which Yahweh, the God of Israel, is no longer the sole ruler."[121]

117. Kittel, *Befreit aus dem Rachen des Todes*, 92.
118. See 223ff. above.
119. C. Barth, *Errettung vom Tode*, 92.
120. Ibid., 93.
121. Michel, "Ich aber bin immer bei dir," 156–57.

Only in the Hellenistic era, beginning in the second half of the fourth/third century BCE, do we come across voices that explicitly address crossing the threshold of death.[122] Isaiah 25:8; 26:19; Psalm 22:27–31 (28–32);[123] and Daniel 12:2–3 speak of God's defeating death and of the resurrection of the dead. At the end of the great prayer regarding the final judgment in Isaiah 26:7–21,[124] which passes along the apocalyptic motif of God's people's birth when the God-king YHWH arrives at Zion, we find a lament that this birth cannot be the result of human power:

> Like a woman in labor who is about to give birth,
> who is writhing and crying out in her labor pains,
> so we are before you, YHWH.
> (Isa. 26:17)
> We are pregnant and are writhing like her,
> giving birth to wind;
> we do not bring salvation to the earth,
> and the inhabitants of the world do not fall. (v. 18)[125]

This lament is answered by a salvation oracle in verses 19–21, with the message that suffering is transformed by a salvation that transcends all earthly limitations:

> Your [YHWH's] dead shall live,
> my [Israel's] dead bodies[126] shall rise!
> Those who dwell in the dust shall awake and rejoice:
> Truly! Your dew is dew of light!
> And you shall let [it] fall on the land of the shadows.
> (Isa. 26:19)
> Come, my people, go to your chambers,
> and close the doors behind you!
> Hide for a little while,
> until the anger has passed! (v. 20)
> See, YHWH sets out from his place/sanctuary,
> to visit upon the sin of those who dwell on the earth;
> and the earth shall uncover their blood,
> and shall no longer cover their slain. (v. 21)[127]

Unlike in traditional views of the underworld in the Old Testament, Sheol[128] here is not to be understood as a realm outside of YHWH's power. If this were the case, YHWH would not be the only God, besides whom there is no power, but would "only" be the Lord of the living, who finds that the boundary of death is the limit of his power. Yet in the context of acknowledging the unity

122. For recent discussions, see Spronk, *Beatific Afterlife*; also H. W. Wolff, *Anthropology*, 107ff.; Gese, "Der Tod," 43ff.; Preuss, *Theologie*, 2:156ff.; Waschke, "Auferstehung I/2," 916; Kittel, *Befreit aus dem Rachen des Todes*, 20ff., 90ff.; Dietrich and Vollenweider, "Tod II," 583ff.; etc.

123. See 327ff. below. On Isa. 25:8, see Hieke, "'Er verschlingt den Tod für immer.'"

124. Scholl, *Die Elenden in Gottes Thronrat*, 118ff.

125. Translation based on ibid., 121, 123.

126. On the difference in personal suffixes ("my/your" dead), see ibid., 132ff.

127. On the translation, see ibid., 123.

128. See the overview in Wächter, "שְׁאוֹל," 901ff.; and the references at 258–59 above.

and uniqueness of God,[129] it is anything but surprising that we first find in later texts like Isaiah 25:8; 26:19; Psalm 22:27–31 (28–32); and Daniel 12:2–3 references to the death of death (Isa. 25:8) and to the resurrection of the dead, and thus to a "final overcoming of this boundary."[130] It is rather surprising that this development occurred so late.

α. Crossing the Boundary of Death

As we have seen, the hope for salvation from death or preservation from an untimely and terrifying death is articulated in the individual laments (and retrospectively in the songs of thanksgiving). The statement that the dead do not praise YHWH[131] implies that there is no salvation in death, because YHWH is a God of life. Nevertheless, these texts speak of the experience of a salvation from death effected by God:

> No matter how powerfully the reviving of a sick person was understood and experienced in Israel as a radical act of salvation by God on an individual, we must see it as most peculiar and idiosyncratic to Israel that a human person in the experience of death, in the most extreme existential crisis, appeals only to the God of life, the Creator of all life, the founder and Savior of Israel, who cannot be a God of the dead. The human person that stands before this sacred vacuum of death is hindered from resigning, from abandoning self to death, and from entering the otherworldly realm of mythical humanity.[132]

This "hindrance," which was built up to an insurmountable barrier in the wake of monotheism, prompted a realization in Israel's understanding of death. From the knowledge that there was no hope of salvation beyond the boundary of death for the YHWH religion, the experience gradually developed—under the significant impact of sapiential thought—that the dead participate in the reality of God by entering a new form of existence ("eternal life," "persistence of the relation with God"). According to Michel, this influence manifests itself in two ways:[133]

Sociopolitical Aspects

As changes in the social and political conditions increased in the fifth and fourth centuries BCE, more and more frequently it occurred that "people who obviously did not observe YHWH's commandments or follow general ethical demands nevertheless led a successful life."[134] Thus the question of the validity and extent of God's justice became unavoidable. This question had to result in an aporia, if the answer was sought exclusively in this world, in the "life before

129. The literature on the problem of monotheism is now legion; see the references in H.-P. Müller, "Monotheismus und Polytheismus."

130. Michel, "Ich aber bin immer bei dir," 159; cf. Dietrich and Vollenweider, "Tod II," 594–95.

131. Cf. Pss. 6:5/6; 30:9/10; 88:10/11; 115:17; Isa. 38:18–19; and Sir. 17:27–28; see 232–33 above.

132. Gese, "Der Tod im Alten Testament," 41–42.

133. On the discussion below, see Michel, "Ich aber bin immer bei dir," 159ff.; Michel, "Weisheit und Apokalyptik," 421–22, 431ff.; Gese, "Der Tod," 43ff.; Görg, "Auferstehung"; Waschke, "Auferstehung I/2."

134. Michel, "Ich aber bin immer bei dir," 159.

death." With such a limitation to this world, the belief in YHWH's justice "and thus the ultimate meaning of existence"[135] was bound to come to despair.

Theological Aspects

As YHWH was believed to be and experienced as the foundation of all reality, the YHWH religion now also had to cross the boundary to the world beyond, the realm of death. Yet this boundary crossing did not occur as the result of an escape from the deficiencies of this world. Nevertheless, the insufficiency of this world prepared the way for what had long been recognized by religion as necessary. For if it was in fact true that YHWH was the only God, there could be no realm that was beyond YHWH's grasp: "Then finally, finally the religion had to usurp the realm beyond death on behalf of its God."[136]

Thus there were several factors that contributed to the advancement of this new insight that not "all accounts of justice . . . were resolved in this life:"[137] the *development of monotheism*, the *crisis of the connection between deeds and consequences*, and the *symbolism of death in the individual songs of lament and thanksgiving*.[138] The entire development hardly proceeded in clearly defined but rather interwoven and overlapping stages. Highly schematized, it can be sketched as follows:

Late preexilic/exilic/ postexilic period (from 7th c. BCE)	*Laments/Songs of Thanksgiving* Ps. 3ff.[139]	**"Salvation from death"**
		← Ps. 16?[140]
Persian period (539–333 BCE) (etc.)	*Wisdom literature* Job 19:25–26; Ps. 49 (?); 73[141] (etc.)	**"Eternal life"/ "Immortality"**
		← Ps. 16?
Hellenistic period (4th/3rd c. BCE)	*Apocalyptic literature* Ezek. 37:1ff.; Isa. 25:8; 26:19; Ps. 22:27/28ff. (etc.)	**"Resurrection of the dead"**
(3rd/2nd c. BCE)	Isa. 25:8; Dan. 12:2–3	Skepticism: Eccl. 3:19ff.; 9:4ff (2nd half of 3rd c. BCE)

This new insight of the connection between YHWH and the dead was not evident to everyone in Israel, such as Qohelet.[142] Regarding the hope for immortality and resurrection, the Teacher remarks, apparently in terms of a skeptical commentary:

135. Ibid.

136. Ibid., 160.

137. Assmann, *Tod und Jenseits*, 18.

138. The latter factor is not considered in the model presented by Lang, "Leben nach dem Tod."

139. The relevant texts here are those discussed in C. Barth, *Errettung vom Tode*, 72ff., 98ff.

140. On Ps. 16, see 291ff. above.

141. The question whether Ps. 49:15/16 ("God alone redeems my life, from the hand of Sheol, surely, he takes [לָקַח] me!") belongs here or rather in the context of the traditional concept "salvation from death" must remain open at this point; the latter is argued by Grimm, "Menschen mit und ohne Geld," 48ff., 52–53; see also Irsigler, "Suche nach Gerechtigkeit," 92ff.; Witte, "'Aber Gott wird meine Seele erlösen'"; Liess, *Der Weg des Lebens*, 336ff. See also Delkurt, *Tod und Hoffnung*; Schnocks, *Rettung*, 136ff.

142. The list of texts in which Qohelet speaks directly about death is long; see Zimmer, *Zwischen Tod und Lebensglück*, 45ff. This is the beginning of a discourse about death and resurrection/afterlife, which was carried on intensively in ancient Judaism by Sadducees and Pharisees as well as in early Christianity (cf. Jesus' debate with the Saduccees in Mark 12:18–27 and its Synoptic parallels); see Maier, *Zwischen den Testamenten*, 257ff., 68ff.

As for the fate of human beings
and the fate of animals:
they have the same fate.
As one dies, so dies the other;
both have the "spirit,"
and human beings have no advantage over animals.
(Eccl. 3:19)
All go to the same place.
All come from dust,
and all return to dust. (v. 20)
Who knows if the spirit of human beings rises up,
and if the spirit of animals goes down to the earth? (v. 21)
And I considered that there is nothing better
than for human beings to rejoice in their works:
indeed, this is their portion [חֵלֶק].
For who can bring him [them] there,
that he [they] may see [with joy],
what comes after him [them] [אַחֲרָיו]. (v. 22)[143]

No one and nothing—says Qohelet, for human beings cannot for certain know anything about "what comes after."[144] Thus the Teacher does not deny the new insight[145] but considers it skeptically. Therefore he observes, in contrast to the new ideas, that it is best for human beings—best for their portion—to enjoy this life and to find joy in one's works:

Now: whoever is still joined to all the living
has hope indeed,
for "a living dog
is better than a dead lion."
(Eccl. 9:4)
Now: the living know at least,
that they have to die,
but the dead know nothing.
And there is no more reward for them,
for their memory is forgotten. (v. 5)
Even their love, their strife, and their hatred
is long forgotten,
and there is never a portion [חֵלֶק] for them
in all that happens. (v. 6)[146]

143. Translation based on Michel, *Qohelet*, 139. On the interpretation of this fundamental text, see ibid., 138ff.; Michel, "Weisheit und Apokalyptik," 415ff.; Schwienhorst-Schönberger, *Kohelet im Spannungsfeld*, 112ff.; Backhaus, *Buch Kohelet*, 63ff.; Vonach, *Kohelethbuch*, 121ff., 128ff.; Zimmer, *Zwischen Tod und Lebensglück*, 50ff. See also Schwienhorst-Schönberger, *Kohelet*.

144. Cf. Vonach, *Kohelethbuch*, 122–23; and Zimmer, *Zwischen Tod und Lebensglück*, 50ff.

145. In Eccl. 3:22, אַחֲרָיו, "after him/afterward," "does not point to a time after the death of the human being in this world, but to one's fate in a 'world beyond'" (Vonach, *Kohelethbuch*, 123; cf. 121); cf. Schwienhorst-Schönberger, *Kohelet im Spannungsfeld*, 120ff., 198ff.

146. Translation based on Michel, *Qohelet*, 158. On the interpretation, see ibid., 158; Schwienhorst-Schönberger, *Kohelet im Spannungsfeld*, 196ff.; and Vonach, *Kohelethbuch*, 123ff., 128ff. However, the translation of Eccl. 9:6b should be (*pace* Michel) "in all that happens under the sun"; Qohelet therefore does not speak of a portion of the dead with God but instead polemicizes the idea "that the dead still partake of life in any form" (Schwienhorst-Schönberger, *Kohelet im Spannungsfeld*, 199).

A portion (חֵלֶק)[147] in the totality of reality—"in all that happens"—no longer exists for the dead. The highest good is therefore joy (שִׂמְחָה) over the present situation (Eccl. 3:22). A comparison, especially with Psalm 73:23–28, shows that Qohelet presents this question in the context of a critical discourse within Old Testament Wisdom literature.

β. The Immortality of the Relation with God

According to Michel, the counterposition, against which Qohelet argues and which he cites, is in Ecclesiastes 9:1:

> Indeed, to all this
>   I have devoted my mind.
>   <and my mind considered> all this:
> "The righteous and the wise and their works
>   are in the hand of God."
> Whether love or hatred,
>   human beings do not know them.[148]

This counterview is developed in Psalm 73,[149] a wisdom psalm that poses the question of theodicy. In verse 17 the psalm enigmatically articulates how the righteous arrive at their insight regarding the "end" of the wicked:

> For [only] in vain I have kept my heart pure
>   and washed my hands in innocence.
>   (Ps. 73:13)
> I was [indeed] plagued all day,
>   and rebuked every morning. (v. 14)
> If I had thought:
>   "I shall [count and] proclaim [these things]"—
>   I would have betrayed the generation of your children. (v. 15)
> So I reflected in order to understand:
>   it was a burden in my eyes, (v. 16)
> until I entered God's [exalted] sanctuary,[150]
>   [and] perceived their final fate [אַחֲרִיתָם]. (v. 17)[151]

The "fortune of the godless" (v. 3; cf. the characterization in vv. 2–12)[152] loses its sting for the supplicant because this wise person has looked at the "end"

147. On the meaning of חֵלֶק in Qohelet (as in 3:22), see Zimmer, *Zwischen Tod und Lebensglück*, 58ff.
148. See Michel, *Qohelet*, 158–59. A similar statement is found in Wis. 3:1ff.; see the references in Janowski, "Die Toten loben JHWH nicht," 39 n. 157.
149. On the discussion below, see Irsigler, *Psalm 73*; idem, "Suche nach Gerechtigkeit," 82ff.; Michel, "Ich aber bin immer bei dir," 162ff.; Michel, "Weisheit und Apokalyptik," 415ff.; Zenger, *Ich will die Morgenröte wecken*, 222ff.; A. Schmitt, *Wende des Lebens*, 212ff.; and Liess, *Der Weg des Lebens*, 309ff. See also Loretz, "'Gerechtigkeit und Unsterblichkeit'"; idem., *Götter*, 597ff.; Janowski and Liess, "Gerechtigkeit"; Schnocks, *Rettung*, 143ff.; and Schwienhorst-Schönberger, "'Bis ich eintrat.'"
150. On the grammatical and semantic meaning of the expression מִקְדְּשֵׁי־אֵל ("sanctuary of God") in Ps. 73:17a, see Irsigler, *Psalm 73*, 36–37, 163, 246, 266; idem, "Suche nach Gerechtigkeit," 89–90; Hossfeld and Zenger, *Psalmen 51–100*, 343ff.; and Liess, *Der Weg des Lebens*, 317ff. For a different reading, see Michel, "Ich aber bin immer bei dir," 162ff., esp. 167, 173.
151. Translation based on Irsigler, *Psalm 73*, 372–73.
152. On this text, see Hossfeld and Zenger, *Psalmen 51–100*, 339ff.

(אַחֲרִיתָם)[153] that God imposes on them (vv. 17b–20). The insight that the supplicant gains from this is expressed in verses 23–28:

Yet I am always with you;
you have taken hold of my right hand.
(Ps. 73:23)[154]
You guide me according to your counsel,
and will receive me to honor[155] [אַחַר כָּבוֹד]. (v. 24)[156]
Who is there for me in the heavens?—
And besides you, there is no joy for me on earth. (v. 25)
My flesh and heart may fail me,
[the rock of my heart (and)]
but my portion [חֶלֶק] is God forever. (v. 26)
Indeed, see that those who distance themselves from you perish;
you have [still] destroyed all who shamefully fall away from you. (v. 27)
But for me—to be near to God is happiness to me,
I have taken my refuge with Adonai (YHWH)—
[with the intention] to proclaim all your deeds. (v. 28)[157]

There is no longer a differentiation between the afflicted and the dead as in the individual laments and songs of thanksgiving. The supplicant of Psalm 73:23–24 will suffer death—and yet will hope for salvation from God, as God finalizes the relationship to the supplicant beyond that death. This idea, that YHWH "takes" (לָקַח, v. 24) the supplicant to YHWH does not refer to a rapture, "the physical transition into a different form of existence via bypassing death,"[158] as posited by Genesis 5:24 or 2 Kings 2:3, 5, 9–11. It rather articulates the "expectation of 'eternal life'"[159] in the sense of a "blessed and fulfilled conclusion of life, which includes continued hopes and expectations" insofar as the supplicant at the end of life "hopes for a permanent continuation of the relation with God, which has already been evident and proven in one's life until now (vv. 23–24a)."[160] Here the *idea of eternal life* finds a certain high point within the literature of the Old Testament.[161]

Where then do we situate Psalm 16? Should it be on the side of the traditional individual laments and songs of thanksgiving? Or rather on the side of Psalm 73? Does it articulate a hope in salvation from death comparable to the traditional Psalms of the Individual? *Or* does it like Psalm 73 advance to the hope that YHWH will not abandon YHWH's faithful ones even in death, by

153. In Ps. 73:17b, אַחֲרִיתָם, "result, end," seems to refers to the end of the life of the wicked and points ahead contrastingly to the אַחַר formulation in v. 24b; see Irsigler, *Psalm 73*, 246, 260–61; idem, "Suche nach Gerechtigkeit," 89ff.; A. Schmitt, *Wende des Lebens*, 223, 228–29.

154. On the idiom of "taking hold of the right hand" in the sense of guidance and protection by God, see Irsigler, *Psalm 73*, 247–48.

155. Or: "and take me [will take me?] afterward [?] in glory [up? away?]." Cf. Michel, "Ich aber bin immer bei dir," 167; idem, "Weisheit und Apokalyptik," 420.

156. On the meaning of Ps. 73:23–24, see Irsigler, *Psalm 73*, 41ff., 247ff., 266ff.; Michel, "Ich aber bin immer bei dir," 169ff.; and A. Schmitt, *Wende des Lebens*, 226ff. On the meaning of כָּבוֹד in 73:24b, see Irsigler, *Psalm 73*, 48ff., 264–65; Liess, *Der Weg des Lebens*, 329ff.

157. Translation based on Irsigler, *Psalm 73*, 373.

158. Grimm, "Menschen mit und ohne Geld," 49; cf. Dietrich and Vollenweider, "Tod II," 591–92.

159. Gese, "Der Tod," 46; cf. Zenger, *Ich will die Morgenröte wecken*, 228, etc.

160. A. Schmitt, *Wende des Lebens*, 229; cf. Irsigler, *Psalm 73*, 41ff.; idem, "Suche nach Gerechtigkeit," 91–92.

161. See the overview in Janowski, "Ewiges Leben III."

finalizing with them the relation that has grown in their lifetimes?[162] This question is to be asked of Psalm 16:10–11 and its *juxtaposition of death and life*:

> Indeed, you will not abandon me / my life [נֶפֶשׁ] to the underworld;
> you do not allow your faithful one to see the Pit.
> (Ps. 16:10)
>
> You show me the path of life:
> filled with joy before your face,
> pleasures in your right hand forevermore. (v. 11)

Does the sapiential recognition of the path of life, which the supplicant is certain to be shown by YHWH (v. 11), "contain a communion with God that transcends the boundaries of human life?"[163]

If this transcendence signifies a postmortem situation ("eternal life"), it would not do justice to Psalm 16:10–11, in my opinion. Rather, with its belief in the success of life through the permanence of the relation to God, it stands between the traditional songs of lament and thanksgiving on the one hand, and the wisdom texts of Job 19:25–26 and Psalm 73 (etc.) on the other. It thereby reconfigures the *individual* experience of salvation into a *permanent* experience, which characterizes the supplicant's life in new ways ("new life in this world"), thus as a life "before your [YHWH's] face" // "in your right hand forevermore" (Ps. 16:11b).[164]

The traditional songs of lament and thanksgiving, which in some ways also include Psalm 88, do not contain expressions of hope for immortality or resurrection because death again stands at the end of the life granted through YHWH's saving actions. Therefore the theological position of Psalm 88 in comparison to Psalms 16 and 73 can be described as follows:

- **Psalm 88**: Individual salvation from death and reintegration into the cultic and social community (*Hope for life in this world* I)
- **Psalm 16**: Permanent communion with God in a life characterized by closeness with God (*Hope for life in this world* II)
- **Psalm 73**: Finalization of the relation with God, which has grown in life, beyond death (*Hope for an afterlife*)

These three texts, used here as examples for the late preexilic and postexilic history of the Old Testament understanding of death, reflect *death* against the horizon of different views of time, all of which point to *life*: (1) during the time of finite human life, which can be temporarily saved from death, according

162. So Hossfeld and Zenger, *Die Psalmen*, 1:109: Psalm 16 "reaches its culminating conclusion in v. 11 with the vision of a life in the salvific presence of the good king YHWH. Whether in vv. 9–11 this psalm, like numerous other psalms, expresses 'only' hope in salvation from mortal danger or preservation from untimely death, or whether it advances like Psalms 49 and 73 to the message of hope that YHWH will not abandon his faithful ones even in death, via making the relation with God that has grown in life final and full of reality—this is a controversy among exegetes; our interpretation favors the latter reading." Cf. ibid., 112–13.

163. Gese, "Der Tod," 47.

164. The this-worldly character of hope for life in Ps. 16 is not only the result of the certainty of v. 9. In contrast to Ps. 73:26a ("My flesh and my heart fail me . . ."), Ps. 16 does not speak of the transience of flesh and heart! (v. 9), but also juxtaposes death symbolism (v. 10) and life symbolism (v. 11), as well as using the expression "path of life" (v. 11a); see 301ff. above.

to the traditional Psalms of the Individual (Ps. 88; etc.; "this world I" above); and (2) the time of eternal life in God, or—as in later wisdom texts (Ps. 73; etc.)—with God eternally (*aeternitatis*; "afterlife" above).[165] Intermediate stages between these two views of time, such as the hope for a permanent communion with God in a newly constituted existence in this world (Ps. 16; etc.; "this world II" above), have always been employed in the Old Testament. In this way perspectives were developed—albeit visible to us only as outlines—which led beyond the Old Testament and also to Christian reflections about life and death.

Let us pause for a moment: To search for the "path to life" and in doing so to trust completely in the presence of the living God is, according to Psalms 16 and 73, the goal of faithful existence in contrast to the designs for life by those who worship a foreign god (Ps. 16:3–4) and the wicked (73:2–12). If we can accept the witness of these texts, we can recognize that Jesus of Nazareth has sought this "path to life" with more confidence than any other supplicant before him, even up to his final hour: according to Mark 15:34, he dies with the opening words of the Psalm 22 on his lips.[166] This "son of God" as the Roman centurion confessed under the cross (Mark 15:39)[167] was in the hour of his death *the true man of God*.

The Synoptic traditions, led by the Markan passion account (Mark 14:1–16:8), formulated their crucifixion accounts with recourse to the Psalms of Israel in order to elucidate the paradigmatic nature of this event and to explain its theological meaning. At the same time they showed that the Psalms are not simply an illustration of the passion of Jesus, but also belong to the origin of Christian theology as its foundational linguistic and interpretative horizon. This Jewish heritage of Christianity shall be the subject of our conclusion.

165. On the distinction of the two views of time, see Luhmann and Kieserling, *Die Religion der Gesellschaft*, 47ff.

166. See 334ff. below.

167. See 336–37 below.

10. "My God, my God, why have you forsaken me?" (Ps. 22:1/2)

God's Human Being

a. Disputes with God

> We learn from the prayer of the Psalms what we should pray. Certain as it is that the scope of the prayer of the Psalms ranges far beyond the experience of the individual, nevertheless the individual prays in faith the whole prayer of Christ, the prayer of him who was true Man and who alone possesses the full range of experiences expressed in this prayer.
>
> Dietrich Bonhoeffer, *Life Together*, 47

a. Paradigmatic Experiences of Suffering

"My God, my God, why have you forsaken me?" (Ps. 22:1/2 = Mark 15:34; cf. Matt. 27:46).[1] With this complaint begins the most famous of all of Israel's Psalms of Lament and Thanksgiving. Because of its reception in the Markan crucifixion account (Mark 15:20b–41 // Matt. 27:45–56), it occupies a place of prominence in the two-part Christian Bible. It can be seen quite clearly that it does not have a biographical situation of an individual at its center, but a *paradigmatic experience of suffering*.[2] It therefore expresses, according to von Rad's description of the account, "the subjective experience, that which has been suffered, pointing strongly toward what is primordial and exemplary."[3]

This aspect, important for understanding the Psalms of the Individual and their language, has a correlation in the so-called Davidization of the Psalter. Thirteen (16 in LXX) superscriptions of certain psalms[4] commemorate a specific critical situation in the life of David,[5] which portrays the messianic king not

1. On the "Why?"-question, see 334 n. 56 below. On Ps. 22, see Bauks, *Die Feinde des Psalmisten*, 14ff., 95ff., 150ff.; Lescow, "Psalm 22, 2–22 und Psalm 88"; Marttila, *Reinterpretation in the Psalms*; Grohmann, "Geburt in Psalm 22"; idem, *Fruchtbarkeit*, 50ff., 142ff., 259ff. (on Ps. 22:9–10 [10–11], 29–31 [30–32]); Bester, *Psalm 22*; Weber, *Werkbuch*, 3:75ff.; Zernecke, *Gott und Mensch*, 242ff., 258ff.; and Rechberger, *Von der Klage zum Lob*, 148ff. Without offering a convincing reason (to note that something is "difficult to understand" is hardly a counterargument), Zernecke (*Gott und Mensch*, 258ff.) changes the MT's עֲנִיתָנִי, "You have answered me" (Ps. 22:21/22b), to a Aramaic adjective-derived noun + first-person-singular suffix, ענוותני, "my humility," and assumes that the change of mood occurs only *after* v. 21/22b.

2. Cf. Gese, "Psalm 22," 185, 192; also Kraus, *Psalmen*, 1:185.

3. Von Rad, "'Gerechtigkeit' und 'Leben,'" 236.

4. Pss. 3; 7; 18; 34; 51; 52; 54; 56; 57; 59; 60; 63; and 142. On concept of Davidization, see esp. Füglister, "Verständnis der Psalmen," 368ff.; also idem, "Verwendung des Psalters," 206–8; Ballhorn, "'Um deines Knechtes Davids Willen'"; Kleer, *David als Dichter und Beter*; Janowski, "Die 'Kleine Biblia,'" 153–54.

5. See Millard, *Komposition des Psalters*, 127ff., 251ff.; also Kleer, *David als Dichter und Beter*, 87ff., 94ff., 115ff.; and the literature cited in Kratz, "Die Tora Davids," 18 n. 41.

as triumphant ruler, but as *exemplary sufferer*.[6] In this way, the Psalms become "models for individual response to the conflicts, crises, and victories of life before YHWH."[7] In this context, Delitzsch also called attention to Psalm 22, which describes how David

> descends with his complaints to a depth that lies beyond the depth of his suffering and rises with his hopes to a height that lies beyond the height of the reward of his suffering. In other words, the figure of speech, hyperbole . . . , without which poetical diction would be tame and dull in the eyes of the Semite, is here taken into the service of God's Spirit. The hyperbolical element is thereby changed into the prophetical.[8]

This basic feature of the individual songs of lament and thanksgiving constitutes their linguistic form but also their repeatability. Let us approach this idea through a recapitulation of the structure of Psalm 22 and the relationship between its two parts: the lament in verses 1–21 (2–22), and the thanksgiving song in verses 22–31 (23–32).

β. Psalm 22 as a Paradigmatic Prayer

Cited in the Markan crucifixion account (Mark 15:34; cf. Matt. 27:46),[9] Psalm 22:1/2 is an exceptionally rich and powerful text. It begins as an individual lament (vv. 1–21 [2–22]), which at its apex passes into an individual song of thanksgiving (vv. 22–31 [23–32]). The textual boundary between lament and praise (from v. 21/22 to v. 22/23) is identical to the conceptual boundary between death and life.

In the two parts, the supplicant of Psalm 22 traverses the twofold way *from life to death* and *from death to life*, so that, following A. Deissler, we can identify the basic structure of this psalm as the "archetype of all prayer."[10] It begins with the deepest God-forsakenness and culminates in an apocalyptic vision of the eschatological reign of YHWH as King.

The Cry of God-Forsakenness (vv. 1–21 [2–22])

For the choirmaster. To the tune of Doe of the Dawn. A Psalm of David.

My God, my God, why have you forsaken me,
  [you who are] far from my salvation,
  from the words of my groaning?
        (Ps. 22:1/2)
I call by day, "My God!," but you do not answer,
  and by night, but I find no rest. (v. 2/3)

6. The transition from individual to type, from the concrete to the abstract, is related to the specific perception of reality and its linguistic realization in the Psalms. According to Steck's description of this process, "the extent, but not the specific type of suffering, is emphasized with the full force available to language" (*Friedensvorstellungen*, 36 n. 84).

7. Wilson, *Hebrew Psalter*, 172.

8. Delitzsch, *Book of Psalms*, 376.

9. See 334ff. below.

10. Deissler, "'Mein Gott,'" 119; cf. Irsigler, "Psalm 22," 224–25.

But you are holy,
  enthroned on the praises of Israel! (v. 3/4)
In you our ancestors placed their trust;
  they trusted and you saved them. (v. 4/5)
To you they called and were saved;
  in you they trusted,
  and they were not put to shame. (v. 5/6)

But I am a worm and no [longer a] human,
  the reproach of others, despised by the people! (v. 6/7)
All who see me laugh about me;
  they curl their lips and shake their heads. (v. 7/8)
"Place [it] on YHWH!" "Let him save him;
  let him deliver him, for he delights in him!" (v. 8/9)

Yes, it is you who pulled me from my mother's womb,
  who fed me with hope at my mother's breasts! (v. 9/10)
On you I was cast ever since my mother's womb;
  since my mother's womb, you have been my God. (v. 10/11)
Do not be far from me,
  for affliction is near;
  indeed, there is no helper! (v. 11/12)

Many bulls surround me;
  the "strong of Bashan" encircle me. (v. 12/13)
They have [already] opened their mouths wide against me,
  [like] a lion, raving and roaring. (v. 13/14)
Like water I am poured out,
  and my limbs are out of joint;
my heart has become like wax,
  melted within my bowels. (v. 14/15)
Dried up like a potsherd is my (life-)force,
  and my tongue cleaves to the roof of my mouth;
  you have laid me down in the dust of death. (v. 15/16)
Indeed, dogs have surrounded me;
  a pack of evildoers has encircled me!
[Too short are] my hands and feet; (v. 16/17)
  I can count all of my bones.
But they look at me [again and again],
  stare at me; (v. 17/18)
they divide my clothes among themselves,
  and for my coat they cast lots. (v. 18/19)

But you, YHWH, do not be distant;
  my strength, hasten to my help! (v. 19/20)
Wrest my life [*nepeš*] from the dagger,
  "my only one" from the power of the dogs. (v. 20/21)
Save me from the lion's mouth,
  from the horns of wild bulls—
  you have answered me! (v. 21/22)

Textual Notes

1/2. On the meaning of לָמָה, "why," see below, 334 n. 56. Because of the parallel expression "the words of my groaning," the pointing of the MT is generally emended to מִשַּׁוְעָתִי, "[far] from my pleading"; cf. Gese, "Psalm 22," 182; Irsigler, "Psalm 22," 229; et al. A different reading is offered by Hossfeld and Zenger (*Psalmen*, 1:148), who correctly keep the MT: "It is an elliptic expression for God's failure to help him: '[You are] far from my help!' I.e., God refrains from helping the supplicant." Also possible is the translation "Far from my salvation are the words of my groaning"; cf. Weber, *Werkbuch*, 1:120.

3/4. In my opinion, the MT and its word divisions are also to be kept here; cf. Hossfeld and Zenger, *Die Psalmen*, 1:148. The predication "enthroned on the praises of Israel" (יוֹשֵׁב תְּהִלּוֹת יִשְׂרָאֵל) is read as corresponding to the YHWH epithet "he who is enthroned on the cherubim" (יוֹשֵׁב הַכְּרוּבִים, as in 1 Sam. 4:4; 2 Sam. 6:2 = 1 Chr. 13:6; 2 Kgs. 19:15 = Isa. 37:16; Pss. 80:1/2; 99:1); cf. Janowski, "Die 'Kleine Biblia,'" 149 n. 116; and Zenger, "Psalmenforschung," 435.

8/9. Instead of the MT's גֹּל, "roll/commit" (masculine-singular imperative), LXX reads the perfect, גַּל, "he rolled/committed"; cf. Weber, *Werkbuch*, 1:120; Riede, *Im Netz des Jägers*, 307 n. 246.

9/10. Contrary to GB[18] 138–39, in my opinion, מַבְטִיחִי is not to be derived from בטח II, with the (supposed) meaning "to be round, swollen" ("You let me thrive at my mother's breast"). YHWH as "midwife" delivers the supplicant from the mother's womb and then imparts trust in God to the infant along with the mother's milk (suggestion by D. Bester-Twele, Tübingen).

15/16. According to the parallelism, one would expect חִכִּי, "my throat," instead of כֹּחִי, "my (life-)force"; but see Riede, *Im Netz des Jägers*, 221 n. 74.

16/17. The MT's כָּאֲרִי is a *crux interpretum*; see the discussion in Gese, "Psalm 22," 182–83 (who assumes a third-person plural perfect of the Aramaic *krj*, "to be short"); cf. Riede, *Im Netz des Jägers*, 221 n. 76; Strawn, "Psalm 22:17b." A remarkable solution for vv. 16b–17a (17b–18a) is offered by Weber, *Werkbuch*, 1:121: "A gang of villains has encircled me like a lion! / My hands and feet, I am able to count all my bones."

21/22. On the interpretation of עֲנִיתָנִי, "you have answered me," see 81ff., above

As we have seen, Psalm 22:1–21 (2–22) contains three laments: I, verses 1–5 (2–6); II, verses 6–11 (7–12); and III, verses 12–21 (13–22).[11] The first two laments are structured in such a way that an opening complaint (vv. 1–2 [2–3] / 6–8 [7–9]) is followed each time by an expression of trust (3–5 [4–6] / 9–11 [10–12], with a concluding plea in v. 11/12). The key that connects these two laments is God's distance (in the opening complaint, v. 1/2b, and in the concluding plea, v. 11/12). While the first expression of trust describes YHWH as royal Deity as well as the God of the ancestors and of the exodus (vv. 3–5 [4–6]), the second

11. See 79ff. above.

expression of trust changes from salvation history to an individual level, as YHWH is addressed as a *personal God*, who has protected the supplicant since birth (vv. 9–11 [10–12]). The supplicant, by confronting YHWH as God of Israel *and* as personal God with the present affliction, holds on to God despite the experience of suffering.

The third lament, on the other hand, contains a new element: the detailed complaint concludes not with another expression of faith but with a petition (vv. 19–21 [20–22]). As in verse 11/12, we find here a plea for removing the distance to God and—beyond verse 11/12—YHWH's "answer" to the supplicant's laments. Verse 21/22 represents also semantically the antithesis to verses 1–2 (2–3):

> My God, my God, why have you forsaken me,
> [you who are] far from my salvation,
> from the words of my groaning?
> (Ps. 22:1/2)
> I call by day, "My God!," but *you do not answer* [לֹא תַעֲנֶה],
> and by night, but I find no rest. (v. 2/3)
>
> But you, YHWH, do not be distant;
> my strength, hasten to my help! (v. 19/20)
> Wrest my life [*nepeš*] from the dagger,
> "my only one" from the power of the dogs. (v. 20/21)
> Save me from the lion's mouth,
> from the horns of wild bulls—
> you have answered me [עֲנִיתָנִי]! (v. 21/22)

As we have seen, the force of the expression of being heard (v. 21/22) is based on the fact that עֲנִיתָנִי ("You have answered me") still belongs in form to the lament-and-plea portion, but in content it has already crossed the boundary to a regained trust. For the interpretation of this text, I have made use of speech-act theory and have connected this transformation, from complaint to trust, to the process of praying, which began with the double invocation "my God, my God!" in verse 1/2. This prayer progresses throughout the lament up to verse 21/22.[12] The lament is therefore not simply followed by a petition, but rather the moments of trust continue to grow beyond verses 3–5 (4–6) and 9–11 (10–12) and are transformed into a trusting plea via the speech-act of verses 19–21 (20–22), which conclude the lament portion. The supplicant is now ready again to assure self of God's closeness and, with the expression "You have answered me!" (vv. 21/22b; cf. v. 24/25), return to the language of trust. In this transition from complaint to trusting confidence, we see the basic structure of the biblical lament, which is primarily "not a question of whether the affliction has been removed, but that the crisis of trust . . . , which had prompted the experience of distress, has been overcome: the trust is that God will carry out the salvation decided in faith, even if it has not yet occurred."[13] This dialectic between

12. See 80ff. above.
13. O. Fuchs, "Klage," 491. With this idea, O. Fuchs seeks to solve the problem of "change in mood." See 77ff. above.

complaint and trust is also crucial for the interpretation of Jesus' lament in the passion story of Mark 15:20b–41.[14]

The Praise of the Saved

Beginning with Psalm 22:22/23, the lament in verses 1–21 (2–22) is followed by an individual song of thanksgiving, which commences with a self-exhortation by the supplicant to praise God (v. 22/23)[15] and calls on all the "seed of Jacob/ Israel" to join in praising God (vv. 23–24 [24–25]) and to feast (25–26 [26–27]),[16] because YHWH has "heard" the afflicted (v. 24/25b).[17] In verses 27–31 (28–32) the circle of invited guests is expanded beyond Israel to universal dimensions: to the entire known world, meaning those currently *alive* (vv. 27–29a [28–30a]), those who have come before and thus are already *dead*, and those who are yet to come and thus are not yet born (vv. 30–31 [31–32]):[18]

> I will tell my brothers of your name,
> in the midst of my congregation I will praise you.
> (Ps. 22:22/23)
> You who fear YHWH, praise him;
> all of Jacob's seed, give glory to him,
> and tremble before him, all seed of Israel! (v. 23/24)
> For he has not despised me or reviled the misery of the afflicted;
> he has not hidden his face
> and has listened to the cries before him. (v. 24/25)
> From you [comes] my praise in the great assembly;
> I fulfill my vow before those who fear him. (v. 25/26)
> The afflicted shall eat and be satisfied;
> those who seek him shall praise YHWH;
> let your heart be revived forever. (v. 26/27)
> All the ends of the earth shall remember and return to YHWH,
> and all generations of the nations shall fall down before your face; (v. 27/28)
> for the kingdom is YHWH's,
> and he rules over the nations! (v. 28/29)
> Indeed, all the fat of the earth ate and fell down in supplication;
> before him bow down all who go down / have gone down to the dust,
> and whoever has not kept his life [*nepeš*]. (v. 29/30)
> Descendants shall serve him [YHWH];
> it shall be told about Adonai to the generation that is to come, (v. 30/31)
> and his justice shall be proclaimed to the people yet to be born,
> that he has executed it [justice]. (v. 31/32)

14. See 334ff. below.

15. Together with 22:25/26, likewise v. 22/23 states that praising YHWH "in the midst of the congregation" (v. 22/23b) / "in the large assembly" (v. 25/26a) constitutes the fulfillment of the vow in v. 25/26b. According to Irsigler ("Psalm 22," 200ff.), the lament extends to v. 26/27, thus encompassing vv. 1–26 (2–27), so that the promise of praise near the lament's end (v. 22/23) leads into a concluding citation of praise (vv. 23–26 [24–27]); see the critique by Tita, *Gelübde als Bekenntnis*, 140, 144ff.; on the subject, see also Gese, "Psalm 22," 190 n. 17.

16. On the subject of the *tôdâ*, see Gese, "Psalm 22," 190–91; Tita, *Gelübde als Bekenntnis*, 141, 146–47; and 278ff. above.

17. Note references to 22:21/22b ("You have answered") and v. 2/3a ("You do not answer").

18. See Gese, "Psalm 22," 191; Hossfeld and Zenger, *Die Psalmen*, 1:151; Tita, *Gelübde als Bekenntnis*, 143; and 328–29 below.

Textual Notes

29/30. The usual conjecture of יְשֵׁנֵי אֶרֶץ, "those who sleep in the earth" (see *BHS* apparatus; Gese, "Psalm 22," 183; et al.) is unnecessary. The "fat of the earth" describes "those who have vital energy" (דִּשְׁנִים < דשן Piel, "to make fat"), who are full of vigor. From an intertextual point of view, the connection to Ps. 23:5[19] is to be noted. According to the MT, v. 29/30b, "and whoever has not kept his life," appears to be semantically comparable to v. 29/30a, "all who go down / have gone down to the dust." On this topic, see Irsigler, "Psalm 22," 196ff.; Tita, *Gelübde als Bekenntnis*, 143 with n. 130; on the LXX reading, see Schaper, *Eschatology*, 50ff.

Although Psalm 22:27–29a (28–30a) anticipate the conversion of the entire world, justifying this expectation on the basis of God's universal rule as king (cf. v. 3/4!),[20] verse 29ab/30ab assumes—contrary to Psalms 6:5/6; 30:9/10; 88:10/11; 115:17; and Isaiah 38:18[21]—that the dead do indeed praise YHWH. From a theological-historical point of view, this is of extraordinary significance.[22] Not only those who have already died, but even those who are not yet born shall proclaim, to future generations, YHWH's demonstration of justice: the salvation of the supplicant from death (Ps. 22:30–31 [31–32]).

This sequence of generations—from the "fathers/ancestors" (Ps. 22:4/5, in the context of vv. 3–5 [4–6]) to "brothers [and sisters]" (v. 22/23) and "all of Jacob's/Israel's seed" (v. 23/24 in the context of vv. 22–26 [23–27]), including the present, past, and future world of the "living," the "dead" and "those to come" (vv. 27–31 [28–32])—is woven as tightly as possible by the *chain of tradition*. This produces a *continuation of trust in God and praise of God*, reaching from Israel's past to the future of the nations,[23] if it is not interrupted and dissolved by the death of the supplicant. This explains the urgency of the threefold complaint (vv. 1–2 [2–3] / 6–8 [7–9] / 12–18 [13–19]),[24] which is ended only in verse 21/22b by YHWH's answer. Only now, but all the more joyfully, can the supplicant tell others of the experienced salvation.[25] Psalm 22:22–31 (23–32) thus shows

> that the *tôdâ*-vow with its emphasis on confession is a point of departure for a living transmission of faith. The witness giving thanks in the midst of the community becomes an essential link in the chain of tradition: With his confession he confirms and gives life to the tradition of the ancients, and through the new experience he provides the impulse for passing on the tradition to future generations.[26]

19. See 286 above. On the sequence of Pss. 22–23, see 329 n. 29 below.
20. On the singular YHWH epithet "enthroned on the praises of Israel," see 325 above.
21. See 232–33 above.
22. See 229ff. above.
23. See esp. Tita, *Gelübde als Bekenntnis*, 147ff.
24. See 79ff. above.
25. Notice ספר Piel in 22:22/23a and ספר Pual in v. 30/31b; cf. נגד Hiphil, "proclaim," in v. 31/32a. On the subject "proclamation of YHWH's saving actions," see 230ff. above.
26. Tita, *Gelübde als Bekenntnis*, 149. On the subject, see also 260ff. above.

Verses 27–31 (28–32) place this "living transmission of faith" into a universal context. Since H. Gunkel, these verses have often been dismissed as pious wishes and enthusiastic expressions and have accordingly been neutralized.[27] The contextualization of this passage in the thanksgiving song of verses 22–31 (23–32) as well as the references in verses 30–31 (31–32) to themes in the lament portion of verses 1–21 (2–22) speak against such an interpretation. In contrast, H. Gese suggests the presence of an "apocalyptic theology"[28] here, which sees *in the salvation of the individual from death the coming of the royal reign of YHWH.*

The Psalms of the Individual inherently place the analogy of the individual and Israel in the foreground. In this kind of apocalyptic theology, it thus is possible "for individual piety to assume apocalyptic structures," so that "the eschatological kingship of God [is revealed] . . . in the salvation of the individual from death."[29]

According to Mark 15:20b–41, the oldest report of Jesus' death on the cross, Psalm 22 was the dying prayer of the crucified Son of God.[30] The fact that only the opening verse of Psalm 22 (Ps. 22:1 [2] = Mark 15:34; cf. Matt. 27:46) is cited does not invalidate this; rather, the contrary is true. We must therefore ask what this quotation means for the understanding of this death in a Christian hermeneutics of the Psalms.

γ. *Jesus and the Psalms of Israel*

The Psalms are the Old Testament texts that are most often quoted and linguistically/thematically invoked in the New Testament. With a total of 110 literal quotations and allusions (esp. from Pss. 2; 22; 110; 118), the Psalter constitutes about one-third of all Scripture citations in the New Testament.[31] Psalms are especially characteristic in the Markan passion account (Mark 14:1–16:8), which

27. See, e.g., Gunkel and Begrich, *Introduction to Psalms*, 25.

28. Gese, "Psalm 22," 192.

29. Ibid., 192; cf. Deissler, "'Mein Gott,'" 119–20; and Vanoni and Heininger, *Das Reich Gottes*, 30–31. Within the context of the subsection Pss. 15–24 (see 296–97 above), this idea attains further significance. Thus Ps. 23 continues the expression of trust in Ps. 22 and lets the hopeful supplicant, while alive, repeatedly return to the house of YHWH (Ps. 23:6; see 287 above). From the perspective of Ps. 22, then, Ps. 23 reads "like a commentary on the lament process and the way of the afflicted. Both supplicants face death (22:15/16; 23:4) and hope that their life is saved (22:20/21; 23:3a). The praise of YHWH's name promised in 22:22/23 is fulfilled (23:3). Especially the banquet of the poor in 22:26/27 is further developed 23:5" (Hossfeld and Zenger, *Die Psalmen*, 1:146). See also Lohfink, "Psalmengebet," 15ff. Then Ps. 22:27–31 (28–32) provides an additional perspective for Ps. 23, which now is "to be read as a prayer of trust by those who set out for the 'pilgrimage of the nations' to the house of YHWH . . . , in order to enter there together with the 'King of glory' (Ps. 24) and to receive from him blessing and 'salvation' (*ṣĕdāqâ*, 24:5!)" (Hossfeld and Zenger, *Die Psalmen*, 1:153).

30. On the reception of Ps. 22 in ancient Judaism, in the New Testament, and in patristic literature, see the references in Irsigler, "Psalm 22," 225 n. 52.

31. Cf. Löning, "Funktion des Psalters," 269 with n. 1; on the subject, see also Kraus, *Psalmen*, 3:223ff. On the reception of the Psalms in the Gospel of Mark, see Watts, "Psalms in Mark's Gospel"; idem, "The Lord's House"; idem, "Mark"; Ahearne-Kroll, "Challenging the Divine"; idem, *Psalms of Lament*; Eckey, "Verwendung des Alten Testaments"; Ådna, *Gebetbuch Jesu*, 384ff.; and Vesco, *Psautier de Jésus*, 1:276ff. On the use of Pss. 42–43 in Mark 14:32–42, see Schaper, *Studien zu Ps 42/43*, 92ff. On the use of Ps. 22 in Mark 15:20b–41, see Janowski, "Die Klage des Gekreuzigten"; Sänger, *Psalm 22*; Watts, "Mark," 235ff.; Klumbies, *Hinrichtung*, 25ff., 53ff., 72ff., 149ff., etc.; Theobald, "Tod Jesu"; and Wypadlo, "Funktion des Centuriobekenntnisses." On the question of whether Jesus "broke down" on the cross (so R. Bultmann; cf. 335 above), see Niemand, *Jesus und sein Weg zum Kreuz*, 497ff.: "One must of course point out that it is still *his* God to whom he calls out of his experience of being forsaken by God! A 'breaking down' of Jesus, if it is to be taken seriously as such, would have to be cast quite differently within the narrative!" (502 n. 423, emphasis original). Less helpful on this point is Kammler, "Verständnis der Passion Jesu," here 481ff.

contains nine passages citing the Psalter (without an introductory citation formula) or alluding to it:

Markan Passion		**Psalms**
14:18	"the one who is eating with me"	41:9/10
14:34	"my soul is sorrowful unto death"	42:5/6, 11/12; 43:5; 55:1–5 (2–6)
14:38	"the spirit is willing"	51:12/14
14:62	"sitting on the right hand of the Power"	110:1[32]
15:24	division of clothes	22:18/19
15:29	passersby shaking their heads	22:7/8
15:30–31	the righteous one mocked	22:8/9; 55:22/23
15:34	"My God, my God . . ."	22:1/2
15:36	sponge soaked with vinegar	69:21/22

Added to this are the linguistic and thematic allusions[33] in Mark 14:1 to the "deception" of the high priests and scribes,[34] in 14:41 to the Son of Man being delivered into the hands of sinners,[35] in 14:55 to the search for a witness against Jesus,[36] in 14:57 to giving false witness against Jesus,[37] in 14:61 and 15:4–5 to Jesus' silence in the face of his accusation,[38] and outside the Passion story Mark 11:9–10 quotes from Psalm 118:25–26.[39] The cited or linguistically/thematically invoked Psalms—22 (5x); 41 (1x); 42–43 (3x); 51 (1x); 55 (1x); 69 (1x); and 110 (1x)—are distributed over three scenes in the Markan passion story:[40] the account of *Jesus' Last Supper with his disciples* in Mark 14:12–25 (v. 18: Ps. 41:9/10;[41] cf. 1QH 13 [*olim* 5]. 23–24);[42] *Jesus' prayer in Gethsemane* in Mark 14:32–42 (v. 34: Ps. 42:5/6, 11/12; 43:5; v. 38: Ps. 51:12/14), with a reference pointing ahead to *Jesus' confession* in Mark 14:53–65 (v. 62: Ps. 110:1 [and Dan. 7:13]); and the *account of Jesus' crucifixion* in Mark 15:20b–41 (vv. 23, 24, 29, 30–31, 34, 36: Pss. 22:18/19, 7/8, 8/9, 1/2; 55:22/23; 69:21/22). This distribution already suggests that the Psalms used here are incorporated into the dramatic high points of the passion story. At the same time, as individual songs of lament and thanksgiving, they underscore that the fate of Jesus represents "the experience of being afflicted by the power of death as the fate of the just and righteous, suffered as violence by human hands and as scorn of the wicked."[43] Let us begin with the account of Jesus' prayer in Gethsemane.

32. Here Ps. 110:1 in combination with Dan. 7:13; cf. Luke 22:69, where only Ps. 110:1 is cited; see Ellen Flessemann-van Leer, "Passionsgeschichte," 90–91; Kraus, *Psalmen*, 3:233ff., etc.

33. See also Marcus, *Christological Exegesis*, 172–73; cf. Ruppert, *Eine motivgeschichtliche Untersuchung*, 55 with n. 43.

34. Cf. Ps. 10:7–8; also Pss. 35:20; 36:3/4; 52:2/4; and 55:11/12.

35. Cf. Ps. 140:8/9.

36. Cf. Pss. 37:32 and 54:3/4.

37. Cf. Pss. 27:12 and 35:11.

38. Cf. Ps. 38:12–14 (13–15); on the trial scene in Mark 14:55–65, see the references in 332 n. 44 below.

39. See Kraus, *Psalmen*, 3:243–44; also Löning, "Funktion des Psalters," 274 nn. 15–16.

40. The Psalm texts used here stand in promixity to citations from and allusions to Deutero-Isaiah and Trito-Isaiah; see Marcus, *Christological Exegesis*, 186ff.; and Löning, "Funktion des Psalters," 274 n. 15.

41. See Flessemann-van Leer, "Passionsgeschichte," 83–84; Ruppert, *Eine motivgeschichtliche Untersuchung*, 50; Gnilka, *Markus (Mk 8, 27–16, 20)*, 236–38; and Marcus, *Christological Exegesis*, 172–73, 183. This quotation-like allusion is esp. revealing since Ps. 41 is a thanksgiving song that incorporates a description of affliction characteristic of a lament (vv. 4–10 [5–11]; see 174ff. above).

42. See 181–82 above.

43. Löning, "Funktion des Psalters," 271.

Excursus 10: *Ecce homo*

In the Johannine Passion and resurrection, the trial of Jesus is depicted in a dramatic sequence of seven scenes (John 18:28–19:16a). The fifth scene, in 19:4–7, contains the famous *Ecce homo* expression of the Roman governor Pilate:

> [John 19:4] And Pilate came out again and said to them: "Here, I am bringing him out to you, that you may see that I find no fault in him." [5] Then Jesus came out with the crown of thorns and the purple robe. And he said to them: "See, there he is: the human being!" [Vulgate: *et dicit eis ecce homo*] [6] Now when the Pharisees and the servants saw him, they cried out and said: "Crucify him, crucify him!" Pilate said to them: "You take him and crucify him yourselves, for I find no fault in him!" [7] The Jews answered: "We have a law, and according to this law he must die, for he has made himself the Son of God."

The evangelist describes the appearance of Jesus so shockingly and graphically that he deeply touches his readers with this view of their Lord. "As faithful Christians, they are to see this abused person, robbed of all human dignity, as the Son of God and true King of Israel (1:49)!" (Wilckens, *Johannes*, 284). The horror that the evangelist prompts in his readers is to "test their faith, whether they are able to see . . . in this Jesus the Son of God, in the reality of his suffering the Lamb of God (1:29). At the same time, conversely, whether they are willing to see the Son of God in this suffering state; the Lamb, that victoriously takes away the sin of the world in the powerlessness of 'this human being' . . . and the fulfillment of the mission of the Son of God into the world at the cross!" (ibid.).

Because of its poignancy, the *Ecce homo* scene has also often been painted, for example, by Honoré Daumier and Lovis Corinth, but also by Paul Klee. His 1940 drawing in black chalk on paper *Ecce* . . . shows the face of Christ crowned with thorns and worn out by pain (fig. 41). "Traced by one line, the wrinkles of the forehead, eyebrows, nose, and drooping corners of the mouth appear pained; the nostrils, beads of sweat, and the eyes staring straight ahead in agony have a penetrating quality. . . . Even the wreath of thorns that appears crown-like here evokes the image of a king who has lost his kingdom: for example, the gloomy Saul or King Lear. Is he suffering despite being a king, or is he king precisely because he is suffering? . . . All this is expressed by the highly sensitive drawing of lines, which (without any dimension of depth) mark the painful suffering. Despite the closed, simplistic form as a whole, the sharp corners and deliberate, open lines achieve a mobility, which is read as a trace of suffering and the progression of illness: mournful, worn out, and a weak, final trace of self-irony: See, this is I" (Ringleben, *Dornenkrone und Purpurmantel*, 76).

The *Ecce homo* in John 19:5, which refers to the condemned Son of God, can also be seen in the history of reception as referring to the crucified, as in Hilde Domin's poem (in *Gedichte*, 345) by the same name:

Figure 41. Paul Klee, *Ecce . . .* (1940)

Ecce Homo
Less than the hope in him
that is the human being
one-armed
always
only the crucified
both arms
wide open
the here-am-I.

The Gethsemane Story: Mark 14:32–42

The references to the Psalter in the Markan passion account are more than an attempt to add color through the use of biblical language. Since the language of the Psalms expresses a particular understanding of God, the world, and humanity, the Markan reception of the songs of lament and thanksgiving rather intends to remove the incidental from the suffering of Jesus and anchor it—with significant accents pointing to the singularity of Jesus and his fate—in the motif tradition of the *passio iusti*.[44] The motif of suffering found in the Psalms

44. See esp. Ruppert, *Eine motivgeschichtliche Untersuchung*, 42ff.; also Flessemann-van Leer, "Passionsgeschichte," 82–83; Lührmann, *Das Markusevangelium*, 43–44, 230, 245, 250, 260, 269, etc.; G. Barth,

of Lament and Thanksgiving is found in explicit form first in the account of Jesus' prayer in Gethsemane, in Mark 14:32–42,[45] with its citation-like allusions in verse 34 to Psalms 42–43 and/or 55.

> And they came to a place called Gethsemane,
> and he said to his disciples:
> "Sit here until I have finished praying."
> (Mark 14:32)
> And he took Peter and James and John with him,
> and began to shake and to be apprehensive. (v. 33)
> And he said to them:
> "My soul is sorrowful unto death.
> Stay here and watch!"[46] (v. 34)

Already in verse 33b, the introductory account of Jesus' strong emotions, which is connected to Jesus' admonition to his disciples in verse 34 in allusion to Psalms 42–43, two verbs are used that belong to the semantic field of emotional agitation: ἐκθαμβεῖσθαι, "to be horrified," and ἀδημονεῖν, "to become afraid."[47] Verse 34 makes possible allusion to the refrain of Psalms 42–43,[48] in which the supplicant asks his *nepeš* of the cause of its anguish in order to underscore his certainty of salvation.

> Why do you melt away, my life,
> and who do you desire against me?
> Wait for God,
> for I will yet thank him
> for the salvation of my face.
> (Ps. 42:5/6; cf. 42:11/12; 43:5)[49]

A striking structural and thematic closeness to the Gethsemane narrative is also found in Psalm 55,[50] although one cannot speak of a true citation or direct allusion here. The supplicant's terror of death is caused here (Ps. 55:12–14 [13–15]),[51] as in the Gethsemane scene, by a familiar person—the "betrayer," Judas (Mark 14:42; cf. 14:18, 20–21, 44)[52]—who takes his place in the multitude of enemies and the godless, who are harassing the supplicant:

Tod Jesu Christi, 28ff.; Marcus, *Christological Exegesis*, 172ff.; et al. The classic example of the suffering righteous, which probably had a significant influence on the form of the Markan trial scene in Mark 14:55–65, is Wis. 2:12–20; 5:1–7; see Ruppert, *Eine motivgeschichtliche Untersuchung*, 53ff.; Lührmann, *Das Markusevangelium*, 248ff.; et al.

45. On the function of the Gethsemane scene in the context of the Passion story, see Feldmeier, *Krisis des Gottessohnes*, 128ff., 237ff.; and Herzer, "Freund und Feind," 118ff.

46. Translation based on Lührmann, *Das Markusevangelium*, 241.

47. On these two verbs, see Feldmeier, *Krisis des Gottessohnes*, 146ff.

48. The refrain in Pss. 42:5/6, 11/12; 43:5 divides Pss. 42–43 into three stanzas, which characterize the psalm as an individual lament with the elements of complaint (42:1–5 [2–6]), accusation (42:6–11 [7–12]), and petition with vow of praise (43:1–5); see Hossfeld and Zenger, *Die Psalmen*, 1:265ff.; Dockner, *Psalm 42 und 43*, 98ff., 181–82, 221, etc.; and 193–94 above. Herzer ("Freund und Feind," 120ff.) supports the idea that Mark 14:32–42 draws not only on Pss. 42–43, but also on other Psalms of Lament, such as Ps. 55. Noteworthy also is Herzer's reference (in 122–23) to lament prayers from Qumran, such as 1QH 16 (*olim* 8). 27–35 (esp. line 32); cf. Feldmeier, *Krisis des Gottessohnes*, 161.

49. Cf. also the translation by Dockner, *Psalm 42 und 43*, 261.

50. See Herzer, "Freund und Feind," 126ff.

51. On this "friend complaint," see 176–77 above.

52. See Herzer, "Freund und Feind," 127ff. Mark 14:18 alludes to Ps. 41:9/10; see 181ff. above.

Hear my prayer, O God,
and do not hide from my pleas.
(Ps. 55:1/2)
Consider me and hear me.
I wander about in desperation, and I am distraught (v. 2/3)
because of the shouts of the enemy,
because of the oppression by the wicked.
Indeed, they bring down trouble on me,
and in anger they accuse me. (v. 3/4)
My heart trembles inside me,
and fear of death has fallen on me. (v. 4/5)
Fear and trembling come to me,
and terror has overwhelmed me. (v. 5/6)[53]

The reception of the refrain of Psalms 42–43 in Mark 14:32–42 and—in conjunction with it (?)—the intertextual reference of the Gethsemane narrative to Psalm 55 establish a correlation between the situation of the supplicant in the Psalms and that of the Son of God, which exhibits a similar model of action, involving *the friend who becomes an enemy*.[54] In this way, the account of Jesus' last prayer before his death yields an insightful clue to "the wide applicability of Israel's Psalms traditions: They have carried the prayer of the Son of God, Jesus, in times of his strongest affliction."[55] This line of reception of the Psalms is continued in the crucifixion account.

The Crucifixion Account: Mark 15:20b–41

The actual report of Jesus' death begins, according to Mark 15:33–41, with the description of a cosmic darkness in the sixth hour.

> [33] And when the sixth hour had come, a darkness came over the land until the ninth hour. [34] And in the ninth hour Jesus cried out in a loud voice: "*Eloi, Eloi, lema sabachtani*," which is translated as "*My God, my God, why*[56] *have you forsaken me?*" [Ps. 22:1/2]. [35] And some of the bystanders heard it and said: "See, he is calling Elijah!" [36] One went, however, and filled a sponge with *vinegar*, put it on a reed, and *gave him to drink* [cf. Ps. 69:21/22b], while he said: "Wait, let us see if Elijah will come to take him down." [37] But Jesus uttered a loud cry and died. [38] And the curtain of the temple was torn in two from top to bottom. [39] When the centurion facing him saw that he died

53. Translation based on Hossfeld and Zenger, *Psalmen 51–100*, 93–94.
54. See 174ff. above; on the concept of "model of action" (*Handlungsmodell*), see Herzer, "Freund und Feind," 126, 133–34.
55. Ibid., 134; cf. 135–36.
56. The author of the Gospel of Mark correctly translated the Aramaic interrogative particle *lĕmâ* (לָמָּה) with εἰς τί; cf. Ebner, *Auferweckungshoffnung*, 78 n. 12. According to Michel, the לָמָּה question ("Why? < For what?," as in Ps. 22:1/2), in contrast to the מַדּוּעַ question ("Why? < What is known?"), does not ask about the present reason, but rather the intended purpose, which is seen as the cause of something. Thus מַדּוּעַ asks about the past, and לָמָּה asks about the future. This orientation toward the purpose or the meaning of divine actions is characteristic of לָמָּה questions in the Psalter (which incidentally does not contain any מַדּוּעַ questions!) and esp. also for Ps. 22:1/2: "The supplicant assumes that Yahweh's actions have a meaning, a goal according to which he acts and about which one can inquire, even if human beings see it as being abandoned and cannot see any meaning. In short, the *lāmâ* question does not leave the realm of faith" (Michel, "'Warum' und 'wozu'?," 22). See also G. Barth, *Tod Jesu Christi*, 130–31; and Schwemer, "Passion des Messias," 156 n. 109.

in this manner, he said: "Truly, this man was a son of God." [40] But there were also women who watched from a distance; among them were Mary the Magdalene and Mary the mother of the younger James and of Joses, and Salome. [41] They had followed him when he was in Galilee and had served him, and many other (women), who had gone up to Jerusalem with him.[57]

The question is whether in this account the entire Psalm 22 is being recited, including the thanksgiving song of verses 22–31 (23–32), or only Psalm 22:1/2—so that essentially nothing remains except a cry of being abandoned by God. The latter thesis has a long history from Hermann Samuel Reimarus over Jürgen Moltmann to Theodor Gut.[58] In taking up this thesis, Rudolf Bultmann—as is well known—did not exclude the possibility that Jesus died on the cross broken and in despair.[59]

On the other hand, H. Gese[60] has argued that not only Psalm 22:1/2 but also the entire psalm constitutes the connecting point for the report about Jesus' death and the representation of this event. This is done in two ways:

- Mark 15:20b–32 cites the beginning and the end of the enemy complaints of Psalm 22:[61] Psalm 22:7/8 (inside the second enemy complaint of vv. 6–8 [7–9]) in Mark 15:29 (passersby shaking their heads) and Psalm 22:18/19 (inside the third enemy complaint of verses 12–18 [13–19]) in Mark 15:24 (division of clothes). The *sequence* of textual elements from Psalm 22 cited in Mark 15:20b–32 reverses the order in the original text and points toward the beginning of Psalm 22, the invocation in verse 1/2.[62]
- Mark 15:33–40 reports that Jesus cries out "in a loud voice": *"Eloi, Eloi, lema sabachtani . . ."* (v. 34).[63] This cry is misunderstood by some bystanders who take the invocation of *"Eloi, Eloi, . . ."* as referring to Elijah (vv. 34–35). Next is the scene where the crucified One is given vinegar to drink (v. 36; cf. v. 23),[64] after which Jesus dies with a loud cry (v. 37). Then the temple curtain is torn

57. Translation based on Lührmann, *Das Markusevangelium*, 258, emphases and parentheses added.

58. See Gut, *Schrei der Gottverlassenheit*. On the history of interpretation of Matt. 27:46, see also Luz, *Nach Matthäus*, 335ff. On the history of artistic representations of Mark 15:34 // Matt. 27:46, see Günther Lange, *Bilder zum Glauben*, 177ff.

59. Bultmann, *Christusbotschaft*, 12; see also Gut, *Schrei der Gottverlassenheit*, 25–26.

60. Gese, "Psalm 22," 193ff.

61. As a reminder: The lament portion of Ps. 22:1–21 (2–22) is divided into three complaint sections, each of which ends in an affirmation of trust or a petition: Complaint I: vv. 1–5 (2–6) (God complaint + invocation in vv. 1–2 [2–3], affirmation of trust in vv. 3–5 [4–6]); Complaint II: vv. 6–11 (7–12) (enemy complaint in vv. 6–8 [7–9], affirmation of trust and petition in vv. 9–11 [10–12]); and Complaint III: vv. 12–21 (13–22) (enemy and God complaint in vv. 12–18 [13–19], petition + invocation in vv. 19–21 [20–22]); see 79ff. above.

62. See 336–37 below.

63. Cf. Matt. 27:46 (with Hebrew invocation *"Eli, Eli, . . ."*); see Luz, *Nach Matthäus*, 342ff. Luke 23:46 replaces Ps. 22:1/2 with Ps. 31:5/6; see Gese, "Psalm 22," 194–95; and Löning, "Funktion des Psalters," 270 n. 3.

64. By giving him vinegar to drink (following Ps. 69:21/22 in parallelism with poison), Jesus' suffering is painfully intensified immediately before the occurrence of his death (Mark 15:36–37). Immediately before the act of crucifixion (15:24), Jesus is offered a narcotic drink ("wine spiced with myrrh"), which he refuses, however (15:23); Löning ("Funktion des Psalters," 269 n. 2) sees here also an allusion to Ps. 69:21/22b. In the Matthean crucifixion account of Matt. 27:31b–56, both scenes allude to Ps. 69:21/22b (Matt. 27:34, wine mixed with gall; v. 48, vinegar); see Lührmann, *Das Markusevangelium*, 260, etc.

(v. 38). The officer who sees that Jesus dies while crying out in this manner confesses the crucified person to be "a son of God" (v. 39).

The statement that the officer acknowledges the crucified because he saw "that he died crying out in this way" (v. 39) refers to the statement that Jesus died while uttering a loud cry (v. 37). Between these two statements is the reference to the tearing of the temple curtain. In the same way, the passage of verses 35–36 stands between verses 34 and 37, so that one now "no longer immediately notices that the φωνὴ μεγάλη of Jesus' death refers to the φωνὴ μεγάλη of the citation of Psalm 22."[65] This thesis that Jesus died while calling out loudly, with Psalm 22 on his lips, is confirmed, according to Gese,[66] by the officer's reaction. "When the centurion facing him saw that he died in this manner, he said: 'Truly, this man was a son of God'" (v. 39). On the basis of these considerations, Gese comes to the "conclusion that the entire original report of Jesus' death refers to the citation of Psalm 22"[67] and at the same time is "hidden under the veil of Psalm 22."[68]

We cannot know what the crucified One felt in the hour of his death—even if Mark 15:20b–41 were a historical account. What we can adhere to, however, is the literary representation of this event by the narrator Mark, who has woven the quotation of Psalm 22:1/2, as well as other references to the same psalm, into critical passages. In view of this representation, in my opinion it still is impossible to speak of a citation of the entire Psalm 22 (Gese; et al.) or of a naked cry of desperation of the dying Son of God (Bultmann; et al.).[69] Considering the sequence of text elements from Psalm 22 used in Mark 15:20b–41, a comparison of the two texts reveals arrangements with opposite directions.[70]

Mark 15		**Psalm 22**	**Features**
v. 24	←	vv. 18/19	Division of clothes
29	←	7/8	Passersby shake their heads
30–31	←	8/9	The righteous being mocked
34	←	1/2	Invocation and "Why?" question

Division of clothes

They divide my clothes among themselves,
and for my coat they cast lots
(Ps. 22:18/19)

And they crucified him and divided his clothes by casting dice,
to see who should take them.
(Mark 15:24)

65. Gese, "Psalm 22," 195.
66. Ibid.
67. Ibid., 196.
68. Ibid.
69. With the following considerations, I correct my earlier view of these issues; see Janowski, "'Verstehst du auch?,'" 166ff. and the notes.
70. Cf. already Zenger, who assumes that "Mark wants to mask precisely the optimistic conclusion of Ps. 22. Against the background of the image of Jesus as the 'suffering righteous' person characteristic of Mark 15, here Psalm 22:1/2 on the lips of Jesus is accusing [God] yet keeping open the question of theodicy: In the accusatory holding fast to God, when everything speaks *against* this God, 'this man is truly God's Son' (Mark 15:39)" (Zenger, *Ein Gott der Rache*, 151–52, emphasis original). See also Oeming, *Psalm 1–41*, 150ff.; Lescow, *Theodizee*, 121ff.; and Luz, *Nach Matthäus*, 342ff.

Passersby shake their heads / the righteous being mocked
All who see me laugh about me;
they curl their lips and shake their heads.
"Place [it] on YHWH!" "Let him save him;
let him deliver him, for he delights in him!"
(Ps. 22:7–8 [8–9])

[29] And the passersby derided him by shaking their heads and saying, "You, who destroys the temple and rebuilds it in three days, [30] save yourself by coming down from the cross!" [31] Similarly the high priests mocked him among each other along with the scribes and said: "He has saved others, but he cannot save himself!" (Mark 15:29–31)

Invocation and "Why?" question
My God, my God, why have you forsaken me . . .
(Ps. 22:1/2)

And in the ninth hour Jesus cried out in a loud voice,
"Eloi, Eloi, lema sabachtani,"
which is translated as
"My God, my God, why have you forsaken me?"
(Mark 15:34)

In this sequence of scenes, it is apparent that the lament of Psalm 22:1–21 (2–22) is "unrolled from the back"[71] in the Markan passion: first, the elements of the enemy complaint are taken up before the invocation of Psalm 22:1/2 is cited. The counterdirection described here results from the fact that in the narrative chronology of the crucifixion account, the description of affliction by the enemies—division of clothes (Mark 15:24), passersby shaking their heads (v. 29), and their mocking the righteous One (vv. 30–31)—stand at the beginning as the factor that sets the actions of the event in motion; then the complaining "Why?" question (v. 34) follows at the end of the narrative. After the misunderstanding regarding Elijah (vv. 35–36), it only says: "but Jesus uttered a loud cry and died" (v. 37). Then the temple curtain is torn, and the centurion facing him sees that he died in this manner, with Psalm 22:1/2 on his lips, and utters his confession: "Truly, this man was a son of God" (v. 39). No further element that goes beyond the lament portion (Ps. 22:1–21 [2–22]) is given after Mark 15:34.

But God, who is addressed (as "you") by the crucified One with the question "Why?," is silent. The narrator Mark also gives no indication at first how and when God responds. In the crucifixion account, there is "no hidden light shining":[72] all is darkness. All the more urgent is the question of what meaning there could be in the *focus on the lament of the crucified One*—is it after all the meaning identified by Rudolf Bultmann?[73] The answer should be the same as in the case of the Old Testament laments of the individual. There, as can be seen with the paradigmatic example of Psalm 13,[74] the lament is neither a naked cry of despair, nor an insignificant transitory phenomenon to ascertain salvation,

71. Ebner, *Auferweckungshoffnung*, 77.
72. Luz, *Nach Matthäus*, 347 (in reference to the parallel account in Matt. 27:45–50).
73. See 335 above.
74. See 59ff. above.

but on the contrary the "attempt of a renewed 'assurance of trust,' by posing the question of the meaning of affliction and at the same time expressing the hope of a possible change."[75] In this sense, the "Why?" question of Mark 15:34, which is concerned with the meaning of divine action, does not leave the realm of faith, even if it remains unanswered. It is "addressed to God, even in the hour of death. He alone can save him [Jesus]."[76]

In conclusion we can say that the crucifixion account is no historical protocol, but has always been an interpreted event. For the interpretation, Psalms 22 and 69 are used, whereby textual/thematic allusions are operative, with the exception of the citation of Psalm 22:1/2a in Mark 15:34b. These allusions function on different textual levels:[77] on the *level of the narrator of the Gospel*, who appropriates the language of the Psalms as his own (Mark 15:24, 29, 30–31, 34b [translation formula], 36); and on the *level of the protagonist* (Jesus), who like the narrator also appropriates the language of the Psalms as his own (Mark 15:34b; cf. 14:18, 34, 38, 62); and finally on the *level of secondary characters*, who speak the Psalms on their own authority (Mark 11:9–10). Characteristic for the use of the Psalms in the Markan passion account is the fact that the Old Testament texts are never "identified as partial texts, and are therefore [never treated] as texts of a different origin," but function "always as integral elements of the texts offered by the author of Mark,"[78] which enter the narrative and interpret it from the perspective of Israel's religious experience. Thus, by taking recourse to the Psalms of Israel, the early community could

> "capture" in language that which was incomprehensible about Jesus' life and death. . . . The first interpretative reaction to the fate of Jesus was evoked by that Jewish lament-spirituality, which the dying man as well as those who survived him not only knew from their own Jewish tradition, but which they also lived. Jesus was the afflicted and righteous person who trustingly complains to God, who is heard by God, and who will be saved from affliction by God, despite appearances to the contrary.[79]

When seen in this way, the citation of Psalm 22:1/2 in the Markan crucifixion account is a significant hermeneutic element. Because the reference to the Psalms, which is not accidental but is intended by Mark or by the pre-Markan tradition, and which represents the framework for the formulation of the belief in resurrection, shows that "the New Testament Christology . . . [is] largely a Psalms-Christology."[80] The significance of the Old Testament lament-spirituality for the Christian understanding of Jesus' death and resurrection is therefore the basis for the inclusion of the Psalms of Lament as an integral component

75. Ebner, *Auferweckungshoffnung*, 79.

76. Berger, *Jesus*, 149; see also 145ff. on the subject. Within the context of the Gospel of Mark, Jesus' lament does not go unheard. However, an intervention by God is not mentioned until the tomb pericope Mark 16:1–8, when the narrator of Mark has the women who visit the tomb see the stone already rolled away and hear the message of resurrection from the angel; cf. Ebner, *Auferweckungshoffnung*, 79 with n. 14.

77. Cf. Löning, "Funktion des Psalters," 270ff.

78. Ibid., 271.

79. O. Fuchs, "Klage," 492; cf. Löning, "Memoria des Todes Jesu," 146.

80. Zenger, "Das Buch der Psalmen," 326; cf. idem, "'Du thronst,'" 24–25; and Janowski, "'Verstehst du auch?,'" 171–72.

of Christian prayer. It is time that this insight—which is hardly new—takes its place again in theology and in the church.

b. Anthropological Keyword 8: Psalm-Prayer

> But you are holy,
> enthroned on the praises of Israel!
> Psalm 22:3/4

> For I say: Christ has become a servant to the circumcised for the sake of God's truthfulness, in order to confirm the promise made to the fathers; the Gentiles however shall praise God for the sake of his mercy—as it says in the Scriptures: "Therefore I shall praise you among the Gentiles and sing to your name." [Ps. 18:49/50]
>
> Romans 15:8–9

Resources

Bader, *Psalterium affectuum palaestra*; Baldermann, *Wer hört mein Weinen?*; idem, *Ich werde nicht sterben*; Bieler, "Psalmengottesdienste"; D. Bonhoeffer, *Gemeinsames Leben; Das Gebetbuch der Bibel*, 38–43, 105–32; Dohmen, "'Mein Gott, mein Gott'"; Erbele-Küster, *Lesen als Akt des Betens*; O. Fuchs, *Klage als Gebet*, 854–66; idem, "Klage"; O. Fuchs and Janowski, *Klage*; Gese, "Bemerkungen zum Vaterunser"; Heschel, *Mensch fragt nach Gott*; Hossfeld, "Lob I"; idem, "Von der Klage zum Lob"; Janowski, "Die Antwort Israels"; idem, "Klage II"; idem, "Die 'Kleine Biblia'"; Lohfink, "Psalmengebet"; Metz, "Gotteskrise"; Miller, *They Cried to the Lord*; Oeming, "Quelle des Gebets"; Petuchowski, *Gottesdienst des Herzens*; Schneider-Flume, *Glaubenserfahrung in den Psalmen*; Spieckermann, *Heilsgegenwart*, 137–53; Steins, *Schweigen wäre gotteslästerlich*; Stolt, *Rhetorik des Herzens*, 42–61; Wiesel, *Macht Gebete*, 24–44; Zenger, "'Du thronst'"; idem, *Ein Gott der Rache*; idem, "'Ich aber sage.'"

On the subject of a "theology of accusation," see Schönemann, *Der untreue Gott*, 463ff. There are several new collections with Psalm-prayers/meditations, such as the *Münsterschwarzacher Psalter*; Zenger, *Stuttgarter Psalter*; Hugger, *Kunst des Psalmenbetens*; Nachama and Gardei, *Psalmen lesen*. See also Ballhorn, "Gefährliche Doxologie"; Deselaers, "Psalmen predigen"; Lohfink, "Münsterschwarzacher Psalter"; Reemts, "Das Psalmengebet"; Saur, "Mensch und Gebet"; Sauter, "Selbstwahrnehmung in Psalmengebeten"; Schneider-Flume, "Leben in Gottes Geschichte"; A. Wagner, "Strukturen des Gebets"; Weber, *Werkbuch*, 3:55ff.; Zenger, "Gebetbuch der Bibel." On the theology of prayer, see Tietz, "Gott erhört Gebet?" Although Tietz is a systematic theologian and focuses on the prayers of petition and lament, she does not mention the Psalms of Lament and Thanksgiving in the Old Testament: prayer appears to begin for her only in the New Testament!

Speaking of God, as J. B. Metz wrote in his essay "Gotteskrise: Versuch zur 'geistigen Situation der Zeit,'" always has its origin in "speaking to God, and theology in the language of prayer."[81] This language is "much more resilient, less smooth and adaptable, much less forgetful than the Platonic or idealistic language through which theology strives to be compatible with modernity and with which it examines its resistance to being confounded by every disaster and every experience of nonidentity."[82]

Not all judgments passed by Metz in his diagnosis of our time ought to be accepted.[83] He did, however, recognize the sign of a crisis that he called "God-crisis," since it is the crisis of our discourse about God. This discourse about God has "the most peculiar and yet the most widespread language of the children of humanity,"[84] the language of prayer, too often neglected because it does not correspond to the usual standards of speech and thought. In response, Metz speaks of the "sensitivity to suffering"[85] of the Christian discourse about God, which has largely been lost and which must be regained.

One way in which this could be done is to rediscover the book of Psalms, with E. Lévinas, as the "book of 'pure spirituality,'"[86] and to reformulate this spiritually mediated speech to and about God as an indispensible element of Christian theology. It is well known that such an attempt of reformulation meets with deeply ingrained prejudices, which are connected to the act of praying and which, beyond Christian "griping about the 'Jewish' Psalms,"[87] have blocked any access to their spirituality. Modern critiques of prayer have created the normative framework for this and have denied its legitimacy, especially through I. Kant's moralization of all that pertains to religion. According to Kant, anyone who has advanced in doing what is morally good will cease to pray or at least to complain or plead. Persistent pleading is self-deception and useless: "whatever, over and above good life-conduct, [the hu]man fancies that he [or she] can do to become well-pleasing to God is mere religious illusion and pseudo-service of God."[88]

Following this philosophical critique of prayer, the realization has been lost to modernity that the individual songs of lament and thanksgiving are foundational anthropological texts: the view of the human being found in these texts obviously did not fit the axioms of the Enlightenment and Idealism. The difficulties and prejudices that have accumulated here and have downright piled up at times do not resolve themselves. They turn up in ecclesial practices and theological reflections of today as unresolved problems and continue to have a paralyzing effect. This can be seen in the example of the widespread difficulties regarding the Enemy Psalms and their unsettling if not offensive representations of God and human beings.[89]

81. Metz, "Gotteskrise," 79.

82. Ibid., 80.

83. I find it problematic, e.g., to make soteriology the subject of negotiation. This creates alternatives that are not productive.

84. Metz, "Gotteskrise," 81.

85. Ibid., 76ff.

86. Lévinas, *Outside the Subject*, 131; see 342ff. below.

87. Zenger, *Das Erste Testament*, 38; cf. Zenger, *Ein Gott Der Rache*, 11ff., 165ff.

88. Kant, *Religion within the Limits*, 156–63, esp. 158 (4.2.1–2); see Bayer, "Wann hat das Böse endlich ein Ende?," 200–201. On the subject, see also Reventlow, *Gebet im Alten Testament*, 14ff.; Cullmann, *Das Gebet im Neuen Testament*, 12ff.; and Luibl, "Beten Begreifen," 41ff.

89. See 97ff. above.

α. The "Little Biblia"

Yet there have been and still are other voices. For example, that of Rainer Maria Rilke, who wrote to his publisher S. Fischer on January 4, 1915: "I spent the night in solitude with many an inner settling of accounts and finally, by the light of my Christmas-tree, which I had lit once more, read the Psalms, one of the few books in which one can bring every bit of oneself under shelter, however distraught and disordered and bothered one may be."[90]

The Psalter—a book "in which one can bring every bit of oneself under shelter," in which, as Luther judged four hundred years earlier, "you shall find . . . the right *Gnōthi seauton* as well as God and all his creatures."[91] From the beginning, Christian interpretations of the Psalms[92] have highlighted the existential quality of the Psalter in addition to the christological; in fact, the emotional and tangible language of the Jewish Psalms has early on made them into source texts for Christian spirituality. This process intensified after the fourth century, when the Psalter was adopted by Egyptian monks as the official book for prayer and meditation and eventually became the chief component of the monastic liturgy of the hours.[93] Benedict of Nursia (d. ca. 550), for example, assigned the 150 Psalms to the daily prayer times in such a way that the entire Psalter was prayed or sung once every week (Rule 18). The Rule of Benedict even considers this as little: "We read that our holy Fathers strenuously fulfilled in one day what we lukewarm monks should, please God, perform at least in a whole week!"[94] This tradition of spirituality also includes Luther, who was introduced into the practice of meditating on the Psalms by the Augustinian hermits of Erfurt.

Luther's reformation impulse owes no more to any biblical book than to the Psalter.[95] His understanding finds expression especially in the *Dicta super Psalterium* (1513–15), in the *Summaries of the Psalms* (1531–33), and in the three prefaces to the Psalter of 1524, 1528, and 1545. In the famous preface of 1528, he calls the Psalter

> a little Bible. In it is contained most beautifully and briefly everything that is in the entire Bible. It is really a fine enchiridion, or handbook. In fact, I have a notion that the Holy Spirit wanted to take the trouble himself to compile a short Bible and book of examples of all Christendom or all saints, so that anyone who could not read the whole Bible would here have anyway almost an entire summary of it, comprised in one little booklet.[96]

Luther bases this unique quality on three characteristics: First, the Psalter contains the *words of the saints*, through which they appear to us as *speaking*

90. Rilke, *Letters*, 126.

91. Luther, "Zweite Vorrede auf den Psalter (1528)," 69. For the original text see WA.DB 10/1:98–104. Here Luther quotes a famous slogan from Socrates, who appropriated words written in the forecourt of the temple of Apollo at Delphi: *Gnōthi seauton*, "Know yourself."

92. See Raeder, "Psalmen/Psalmenbuch II"; a condensed summary of Christian interpretations appears in Seybold, *Psalmen: Eine Einführung*, 174ff., 193ff.

93. See references in Janowski, "Die 'Kleine Biblia,'" 125 n. 4.

94. Rule of Benedict 18, http://www.osb.org/rb/text/rbefjo3.html#18.

95. See Raeder, "Psalmen/Psalmenbuch II," 629ff.; also Bader, *Psalterium affectuum palaestra*, 155ff.; Reventlow, *Epochen der Bibelauslegung*, 3:68ff., etc.

96. Luther, "Preface to the Psalter: 1545 (1528)," 26.

and therefore *living* human beings; second, these words are a *mirror of the soul,* which opens the way to the human heart more than other work; third, these words are of a special quality, which *universalizes subjective experience* like joy and affliction. As impressive as the description of Luther's second characteristic is—one need only read the famous simile of the human heart as a "ship on the wild sea"[97]—central to our subject is the third characteristic, which I will call *universalizing tendency*: The Psalms universalize a subjective experience and thus bestow on it a superindividual and, according to Luther, even an ecclesiological quality:

> And that they [the Psalms] speak these words to God and with God, this, I repeat, is the best thing of all. This gives the words *double earnestness and life.* For when humans speak with humans about these matters, what they say does not come powerfully from the heart; it does not burn and live, is not so urgent. Hence it is that the Psalter is the *book of all the saints*; and *everyone, in whatever situation they may be,* finds in that situation psalms and *words that fit their case,* that suit *them* as if the words were put there *just for their sake,* so that they could not put it better themselves, or find or wish for anything better. This also serves well another purpose. When these words please a human and fit the case, that person becomes sure of being in the *community of saints,* and that it has gone with *all the saints* as it goes with oneself, since they *all* sing with *self* one little song.[98]

The Psalter—a source text of *personal* spirituality and "book of all saints," a mirror of human *existence* and a testimony to the "*community* of the saints," "summa"—in this way Luther concludes his preface: "If you would see the holy Christian church painted in living color and shape, comprehended in one little picture, them take up the Psalter. There you have a fine, bright, pure mirror that will show you what Christendom is. Indeed, you will find in it also yourself and the true *Gnōthi seauton*, as well as God himself and all creatures."[99]

"The true *Gnōthi seauton* . . . as well as God himself and all his creatures"—this aspect of the Psalter cannot be demonstrated better than by the Psalter itself. Thus the "anthropology of Israel's *coram Deo* [in God's presence]"[100] culminates in the final Hallel Psalms, 146–150, which has grown out of Psalm 145 with a praise refusing to end, a praise of the royal God, who as savior of the poor executes the eschatological judgment (149:5–9) and thus brings about the new heaven and the new earth (Ps. 150).[101] To this royal God is due the praise to which Psalm 150 calls the new cosmos—"all that breathes" (v. 6)—and which has as its motivation the goodness and mercy of this royal God, as Psalm 145 expounds its corresponding subsection:[102]

97. See 347ff. below.

98. Luther, "Preface to the Psalter 1545 (1528)," 27–28, alt. to be inclusive, emphasis added.

99. Ibid., 28. In Calvin's preface to his commentary on the Psalms, he also calls the Psalter a "mirror": "I have been accustomed to call this book, not inappropriately, an anatomy of all the parts of the soul, for there is not an emotion of which anyone can be conscious that is not there represented as in a mirror" (Calvin, *Der Psalmenkommentar: Eine Auswahl*).

100. Zenger, "'Du Thronst,'" 20; cf. Zenger, "'Ich aber Sage,'" 16ff.

101. See Zenger, "'Das alles Fleisch,'" 7ff.; Janowski, "Der Barmherzige Richter," 71ff.; Vanoni and Heininger, *Das Reich Gottes*, 39ff.

102. The two antithetically arranged discursive directions of Ps. 145, *supplicant* → *YHWH* (vv. 3–9) and *YHWH* → *supplicant* (vv. 14–20), are emphasized here by means of different fonts (bold roman

Superscript and theme
A praise of/for David.

I shall **raise** you up, my God, O king,
I shall **bless** your name forever and ever.
(Ps. 145:1)

Frame (blessing // praising)
Each day I shall **bless** you,
and I shall **praise** your name forever and ever. (v. 2)

Praise of YHWH's greatness and power
Great is YHWH and greatly to be **praised**;
his greatness is unsearchable. (v. 3)
One generation shall **extol** your works to another,
and your mighty deeds they shall **proclaim**. (v. 4)
Of the glorious splendor of your majesty
and of your wondrous works I shall **sing**. (v. 5)
Of the power of your awe-inspiring deeds they shall **speak**,
and of your mighty deeds I shall **tell**. (v. 6)

Praise of YHWH's goodness and mercy
The memory of your great goodness they shall **proclaim**,
and in your justice they shall **rejoice**: (v. 7)
Gracious and ***merciful*** is YHWH,
slow to anger and ***abounding*** in love. (v. 8)
YHWH is ***good*** to all,
and his ***compassion*** [is] over [governs] all his works. (v. 9)

Center: YHWH's royal dominion and praise
I shall **praise** you, YHWH, all your works,
and your faithful shall **bless** you. (v. 10)
Of the splendor of your kingdom they shall **speak**,
and of your mighty deeds they shall **tell,** (v. 11)
to **proclaim** his ***mighty deeds*** to the children of humanity, (v. 12a)

---

and the ***glorious splendor*** of his kingdom. (v. 12b)
Your ***kingdom*** is a kingdom of eternity,
and your ***royal dominion*** is over all generations. (v. 13a)
<YHWH is ***faithful*** in all his words,
and he is ***true*** in all his works.> (v. 13b)

Demonstration of YHWH's goodness and mercy
YHWH ***supports*** all who have fallen down,
and ***raises up*** all who are bowed down. (v. 14)
The eyes of all wait upon you,
and you ***give*** them their food in due time. (v. 15)
[You] ***open*** your hand
and ***satisfy*** the desire of every living thing. (v. 16)

and bold italics). They meet directly at the center of the Psalm: ". . . in order to proclaim his mighty deeds and the glory of his kingdom to the children of humanity" (v. 12). This shows clearly that the motivation for praising God is constituted by the demonstrations of this God's power, which are to be "proclaimed" (ידע Hiphil, v. 12a) to all people.

Demonstration of YHWH's greatness and power
YHWH is ***just*** in all his ways,
and he is ***true*** in all his works. (v. 17)
YHWH is ***close*** to all who call on him,
all who call him in faithfulness. (v. 18)
He ***fulfills the desires*** of those who fear him;
he ***hears their*** cries and ***saves*** them. (v. 19)
YHWH ***preserves*** all who love him,
and all the wicked he shall ***destroy***. (v. 20)

Frame (blessing // praising)
My mouth shall **speak** the **praise** of YHWH,
and all flesh shall **bless** his holy name forever and ever. (v. 21)[103]

Thus the subject of "gratitude"[104] has achieved a further dimension of depth at the end of the "little Biblia," while maintaining its original sense as the "epitome of the most elementary 'attribute of being alive,'"[105] indeed as the signature of entire creation.

β. The "Book of Pure Spirituality"

How then is one to speak of God and of human beings so that the "pure spirituality" (E. Lévinas)[106] of the Psalms of Lament and Thanksgiving regains its rightful position? And "what heuristic speaking does theology need to practice, so that neither humanity nor God disappears in this?"[107] The point of departure for the theological and liturgical reappropriation of the Psalms of Lament and Thanksgiving is primarily the fact that the Psalms of Israel have always been the prayer book of the church, as they still are today, because they unite a *small degree of historical contextualization* with a *high degree of situational contextualization*. Or in the words of Lévinas, "To seek a presence-absolute-at the center of a silence, to despair in the heart of hope, but to quench one's thirst with the very infinity of its fire, to proclaim that beneath the protection of an Invisible Pastor I shall not want: religious adventure, paradox, and lyricism find in the Psalms their expression and model."[108]

When we as Christians read or pray the Psalms, we not only allow the history of revelation and faith found in them to apply to us; we also enter the "great school of prayer,"[109] which teaches us always anew who God is and what God does, and which tells us who we are and where we are going. Who God

103. Ps. 145:13cd is supplied from LXX; cf. v. 17. On the translation see also Zenger, "'Du Thronst,'" 8–9.

104. See 275ff. above.

105. Von Rad, *Theologie*, 1:381; cf. C. Barth, *Errettung vom Tode*, 120. On the "praise of God" in ancient Judaism, see Limbeck, "Der Lobpreis Gottes"; and Kellermann, *Gotteslob der Auferweckten*.

106. See 340 above. In contrast to Lévinas, Sloterdijk (*Zorn und Zeit*, 110–69, esp. 129ff.) fails to recognize the intended meaning of the so-called Enemy Psalms and indulges in trite, anti-Jewish clichés. Habermas (*Glauben und Wissen*, 20ff.), on the other hand, shows that a philosopher can also offer a different evaluation of difficult biblical texts.

107. Metz, "Gotteskrise," 82.

108. Lévinas, *Outside the Subject*, 131.

109. D. Bonhoeffer, *Gemeinsames Leben; Das Gebetbuch der Bibel*, 40.

is and who we are—this is what the Psalter tells us, along with bringing an awareness of the dangers in creation, and an equally strong awareness of the Creator's love for the creation.

- YHWH is a *God of life*, who "preserves (always anew) human and animal" (Ps. 36:6/7) and does not let the cry for justice go unheard. In YHWH's execution of justice, there is no irrational revenge or hateful vengeance, but the establishment of righteousness and justice in a world full of injustice.
- The songs of lament and thanksgiving relentlessly uncover the *mechanisms of violence* as actions of social disregard and disgrace, proceeding from specific human beings and institutions, and they develop countervisions of hope. With their sharp light/darkness contrasts, they are a necessary sting against a possible underestimation of violence.
- In light of the dominance of suffering that the supplicant faces, the songs of lament and thanksgiving prevent victims from losing their voice or becoming apathetic. There is literally nothing that the supplicant encounters in life in terms of affliction and suffering that lies outside the relation to God. Everything is included here and is problematized.
- The laments in the Psalms of the Individual always deal with a specific situation. They are therefore to be taken as literally as possible, albeit not too literally in the sense of biographical documents. The lament unfolds an *archetype of suffering*, in which every suffering—no matter how unique—can be seen reflected.
- While the lament proceeds from the supplicant and the local world, praise begins with God and God's good gifts. Just like the lament, the praise of God is a *basic form of theology*, because it expresses what is at the core of the relation to God: the care of the compassionate God, who saves from death and leads into life.

As the condensation of a dialogue with God, in which Israel responds to YHWH's words and deeds and finds itself *coram Deo* (in God's presence), the Psalms are, as this book has attempted to show, "conflict dialogues with God," and the Psalter is "the book of pure spirituality." Its language is *truthful* because it does not beautify the dark sides of God and the chasms of human existence, but expresses them in an unadorned and sometimes harsh manner (*high degree of reality*). The Psalter is *poetic* because it thinks in images and thereby breaks up that which is reified and closed in order to enable a liberating experience of God and self (*picture language*).[110] And the Psalter is *meditative* because through the multidimensionality of meaning resulting from the superimposition of images and motifs, it opens up linguistic and existential spaces in which understanding has room to move about (*stereometry*).[111]

110. See "The Language of Human Beings," 14ff. above.

111. See 14ff. above. On the concatenation of the Psalms as a meditative aid, see esp. Lohfink, "Psalmengebet," 7ff.; Zenger, "Psalmenforschung," 419ff.; Janowski, "Die 'Kleine Biblia,'" 128ff.; and Weber, *Werkbuch*, 1:45–46.

The Psalter's incomparable potential for expressiveness transcends history and helps to put into words that which leaves human beings speechless.[112] Theology and the church should not leave this potential untapped, which is "much more unsettling, much more uncomfortable, and much less harmonious"[113] than the usual language for weekdays or Sundays. The conviction that every human being possesses dignity, and "the knowledge that this conviction can neither be gained nor maintained without an understanding of the human person as 'child of God'"[114]—all this is lastingly strengthened by the biblical Psalms of Lament and Thanksgiving.

112. Thus, after the terror attacks on the World Trade Center on September 11, 2001, and after the school massacre in Erfurt on April 26, 2002, it was not least of all the Psalms—such as Pss. 23; 102; or 130—that assumed this role in public church services or vigils. It is thought provoking that the secular public sphere needs to be reminded of the "sense of expresiveness of religious languages" by a "religiously unskilled" person like Jürgen Habermas (sociologist, philosopher; see his *Glauben und Wissen*, 22, 30).

113. Metz, "Gotteskrise," 79.

114. Härle, "Der Mensch Gottes," 543.

Postscript
The Way toward Life

> It is indeed possible to live or at least to exist without hope, perhaps even without truth, but not without prayer; for prayer, as an urgent movement inward and outward, is a way toward life.
>
> Elie Wiesel, *Macht Gebete aus meinen Geschichten*, 33

Elie Wiesel's words about prayer from his collection of biographical essays[1] have been similarly expressed again and again also by Christian theologians. The idea that the Psalter is a "mirror" in which a human being can recognize self "as well as God and all of God's creatures"[2] runs like a thread through the history of Christianity. The organ through which this understanding is perceived is the human heart, which Luther, in a famous passage from his second preface to the Psalms (1528), compared to a ship on a wild sea. This comparison illustrates once more why the Psalter, Israel's prayer book, became the church's prayer book and textbook, which it remains to this day:

> A human heart *is* like a ship on a wild sea, tossed about by stormy winds from the four corners of the earth. From here comes fear and sorrow about future misfortune; from there comes grief and sorrow about the present evil. Here blows hope and confidence regarding future happiness; there blows security and joy over present possessions. Such stormy winds, however, teach us to speak in earnest and to open the heart and pour out what is at its bottom. Whoever is stuck in fear and affliction speaks of misfortune quite differently than one who floats on joy. Whoever is floating on joy speaks and sings of joy quite differently than one who is stuck in fear. (It is said that) it is not from the heart when a sad man laughs or when a happy man weeps; that is, what is at the bottom of the heart is not laid open and does not come out.
>
> But what is most distinct about the Psalter compared to such earnest speech amid such various stormy winds? Where do you find finer words of joy than those in the Psalms of Praise and Thanksgiving? There you look into the hearts of all the saints as into beautiful and pleasant gardens, indeed as into the heavens themselves, where fine and pleasant flowers of the heart spring up from all kinds of beautiful, happy thoughts about God and God's blessings. On the other hand, where do you find deeper, sadder, more sorrowful words of sadness that those in the Psalms of Lament. Again you look into the hearts of all the saints as into death. How gloomy and dark it is there, from all kinds of somber thought about God's wrath! So also, when they

1. Wiesel, *Macht Gebete*; cf. 204–205 above.
2. Luther, "Preface to the Psalter: 1545 (1528)," 27; cf. 341–42 above.

> speak of fear or hope, they use such words that no painter could depict fear or hope for you and no Cicero or orator could describe them.[3]

In the Psalms, human life finds itself, because they are the "mirror of the soul" and a "treasury of the Scriptures."[4] They are this mirror and this treasury because they literally contain the "saving, sheltering, comforting, and forgiving presence of God."[5] In an unmistakable way, the Psalms offer testimony to the encounter of the complaining and praising human being with this presence of God: no other form of speech leads deeper into the darkness of death, and no other is a way to life as they are.

"God can bear reality. So can the Psalms."[6] That is the simple but poignant insight that offers itself anew with every of reading of the Psalms. For this reason, the Psalms are book for living [*Lebensbuch*] rather than a book for reading [*Lesebuch*]. Thus Zenger observes:

> With the Psalms, it is as with bread and wine: only those who eat bread experience that bread is nourishing, and only those who drink wine experience that wine is invigorating. Those who speak the Psalms inwardly to themselves, who recite the Psalms together with others, or who sing them with great musical talent—in short, those who make the Psalms their own words will learn a language that offers strength and joy—like bread and wine.[7]

The Psalms also encounter a dimension of reality that only they can unlock with such poetic density, as K. Seybold claims:[8] the dimension of *breadth*, which includes everything that breathes (cf. Ps. 150); the dimension of *height*, which speaks of God and God's creation in incomparable images (cf. Ps. 36); and the dimension of *depth*, the profundity of which defies all reason (cf. Ps. 88). But what remains in the end is the dimension of *closeness* of the living God (cf. Ps. 1), who shows the way to life (cf. Ps. 16) and lets embattled human beings partake of the divine presence in their lifetime (cf. Ps. 23). Therein lies the spiritual power of the Psalms, which are like a *templum spirituale*, a temple not of stones but of words, with the proem of Psalm 1–2 as a wide "entrance portal" and the final Hallel of Psalms 146–150 as a resounding "keystone."[9] The image of the Psalms as a "large house" (*magna domus*), with Psalms 1 and 2 as the entrance portal and Psalms 3–150 as individual rooms, was proposed already by Jerome (ca. 347–419/420) in the introduction to his commentary on the Psalms.[10] There he calls Psalm 1 the main entrance (*grandis porta*) leading into the "great house" (*magna domus*) of the Psalms:[11]

3. Luther, "Zweite Vorrede auf den Psalter (1528)," 69. On the origin and significance of the ship metaphor, see Bader, *Psalterium affectuum palaestra*, 170ff.; Stolt, *Rhetorik des Herzens*, 52–53.

4. On the metaphors of the Psalter as the "mirror of the soul" and "treasury of the holy Scriptures," see 341 n. 96 and 342 n. 99 above.

5. Zenger, "Psalmenforschung," 435; cf. Knauf, "Fundamentale Einheit," 26–27.

6. Hugger, *Kunst des Psalmenbetens*, 10.

7. Zenger, *Stuttgarter Psalter*, 6.

8. Seybold, *Poetik*, 371ff., 375ff.

9. See Zenger, "'Aller Atem lobe JHWH!'"

10. Jerome, *Tractatus in Psalmos*.

11. Cf. Reemts, *Schriftauslegung*, 23, 34; Janowski, "Ein Tempel aus Worten."

> The Psalms in a sense are a great house, which has one key for the outside door, but individual keys for the various inner rooms. The key to the main door—the Holy Spirit—may be larger, but each room has its own little key. If someone should toss all the keys of the house into a pile and would like to open a room, that person would not be able to do so without finding the [specific] key. Thus the individual Psalms are in a sense individual rooms with their own keys. The main door of this house is the First Psalm.

Anyone who enters this "temple of words" and travels while meditating on the 150 individual texts, experiences the long and tiring journey from lament to praise, and on this journey encounters the King and Savior-God of Zion, who offers salvation to Israel and to the nations, indeed for all creation (cf. Ps. 150:6). One who leaves this "temple of words" through a different door than the main entrance, yet absorbs with understanding everything encountered on the way, finds life. That makes the book of Psalms into a book of life and, as Lévinas said, a book of "pure spirituality.[12]

12. See 344ff. above; Janowski, "Wie ein Baum," 216–17; and Hartenstein and Janowski, *Psalmen*, 50ff. (by Janowski).

Reviews of Editions 1–3

F. J. Backhaus and M. Hartmann, *Bibel und Kirche* 67 (2012): 50; E. Dafni, *Orthodoxes Forum* 19 (2005): 317–21; G. Fischer, *Zeitschrift für katholische Theologie* 126 (2004): 160–61; F. Hartenstein, *Marburger Jahrbuch für Theologie* 17 (2005): 227–30; H. M. Niemann, *Jahrbuch für Liturgik und Hymnologie* 44 (2005): 91–92; M. Oeming, *Theologische Literaturzeitung* 130 (2005): 759–62; A. Renker, *Freiburger Rundbrief* 11 (2004): 57–58; J. W. Rogerson, *Journal for the Study of the Old Testament* 29, no. 5 (Book List 2005): 70–71; G. Sauter, *Evangelische Theologie* 66 (2006): 317–19; W. Schoberth, *Verkündigung und Forschung* 51 (2006): 38–55, esp. 55; A. Schüle, *Theologische Zeitschrift* 61 (2005): 172–73; B. Weber, *Jahrbuch für Evangelikale Theologie* 17 (2003): 224–25; F. Hartenstein, *Verkündigung und Forschung* 54 (2009): 31–42, esp. 34–35.

Bibliography

Achenbach, Reinhard. "Zum Sitz im Leben mesopotamischer und altisraelitischer Klagegebete: Teil I, Zum rituellen Umgang mit Unheilsdrohungen in Mesopotamien." *Zeitschrift für die alttestamentliche Wissenschaft* 116 (2004): 364–78. "Teil II, Klagegebete des Einzelnen im Psalter." *ZAW* 116 (2004): 581–94.

Achenbach, Reinhard, Martin Arneth, and Eckart Otto, eds. *"Gerechtigkeit und Recht zu üben" (Gen 18, 19): Studien zur altorientalischen und biblischen Rechtsgeschichte, zur Religionsgeschichte Israels und zur Religionssoziologie; Festschrift für Eckart Otto zum 65. Geburtstag*. Wiesbaden: O. Harrassowitz, 2009.

Ackroyd, Peter. "Hand." In *NBL* 2:25–27.

———. "יָד." In *ThWAT* 3:421–55.

Adam, Klaus Peter. *Der königliche Held: Die Entsprechung von kämpfendem Gott und kämpfendem König in Psalm 18*. Neukirchen-Vluyn: Neukirchener Verlag, 2001.

Adler, Leo. *Der Mensch in der Sicht der Bibel*. Munich: E. Reinhardt, 1965.

Ådna, Jostein. "Der Psalter als Gebetbuch Jesu nach der Darstellung des Markus- und des Matthäusevangeliums." *Theologische Beiträge* 6 (2010): 384–400.

Adorno, Theodor W. *Minima moralia: Reflexionen aus dem beschädigten Leben*. Frankfurt am Main: Suhrkamp, 1964.

———. "Schubert (1928)." Translated by Jonathan Dunsby and Beate Perrey. *19th-Century Music* 29, no. 1 (Summer 2005): 3–14.

Aejmelaeus, Anneli. *The Traditional Prayer in the Psalms*. Berlin and New York: Walter de Gruyter, 1986.

Agus, Aharon R. E., and Jan Assmann, eds. *Ocular Desire = Sehnsucht des Auges*. Yearbook for Religious Anthropology. Berlin: Akademie Verlag, 1994.

Ahearne-Kroll, Stephen P. "Challenging the Divine: LXX Ps 21 in the Passion Narrative of the Gospel of Mark." In *The Trial and Death of Jesus: Essays on the Passion Narrative in Mark*, edited by Geert Van Oyen and Tom Shepherd, 119–48. Leuven and Dudley, MA: Peeters, 2006.

———. *The Psalms of Lament in Mark's Passion: Jesus' Davidic Suffering*. Cambridge: Cambridge University Press, 2007.

Albani, Matthias. "'Die Verständigen werden leuchten wie der Glanz der Himmelsfeste' (Dan 12, 3): Die postmortale Hoffnungsperspektive der Weisheit in der frühen Apokalyptik." In Berlejung and Heckl, *Ex Oriente lux*, 547–70.

Albertz, Rainer. "Gebet." In *TRE* 12:34–42.

———. "Mensch." In *TRE* 22:464–74.

———. *Persönliche Frömmigkeit und offizielle Religion: Religionsinterner Pluralismus in Israel und Babylon*. Stuttgart: Calwer Verlag, 1978.

———. *Religionsgeschichte Israels in alttestamentlicher Zeit*. Göttingen: Vandenhoeck & Ruprecht, 1992.

———. "Die Theologisierung des Rechts im Alten Israel." In *Religion und Gesellschaft: Studien zu ihrer Wechselbeziehung in der Kulturen des antiken Vorderen Orients*, edited by Rainer Albertz, 115–32. Münster: Ugarit-Verlag, 1997.

———. "Warum 'Wozu'? Zur Pragmatik der an Gott gerichteten Fragen in den Klagegebeten der Hebräischen Bibel." In *Fragen wider die Antworten: Festschrift für Jürgen Ebach zum 65. Geburtstag*, edited by Kerstin Schiffner et al., 318–40. Gütersloh: Gütersloher Verlagshaus, 2010.

Alter, Robert. *The Book of Psalms: A Translation with Commentary*. New York: Norton, 2007.

Altes Testament: Opfer und Kult. Themed volume of *Verkündigung und Forschung* 56, no. 2. Gütersloh: Christian Kaiser, 2011.

Anderegg, Johannes. *Sprache und Verwandlung: Zur literarischen Ästhetik*. Göttingen: Vandenhoeck & Ruprecht, 1985.

———. "Zum Ort der Klage: Literaturwissenschaftliche Erkundungen." *Jahrbuch für biblische Theologie* 16 (2001): 185–208.

Arambarri, Jesús. *Der Wortstamm "hören" im Alten Testament: Semantik und Syntax eines hebräischen Verbs*. Stuttgart: Verlag Katholisches Bibelwerk, 1990.

Arenhoevel, Heinrich, Gerhard Barth, Christoph Wezel, et al. *Die grosse Bibel der Moderne: Einheitsübersetzung der Heiligen Schrift*. Stuttgart: Verlag Katholisches Bildwerk, 1999.

Ariès, Philippe. *Studien zur Geschichte des Todes im Abendland*. Munich: Hanser Verlag, 1976.

———. *Western Attitudes toward Death: From the Middle Ages to the Present*. Baltimore: Johns Hopkins University Press, 1974.

Arlt, Gerhard. *Philosophische Anthropologie*. Stuttgart: Metzler, 2001.

Arneth, Martin. *"Sonne der Gerechtigkeit": Studien zur Solarisierung der Jahweh-Religion im Lichte von Psalm 72*. Wiesbaden: O. Harrassowitz Verlag, 2000.

Artemov, Nikita. "The Elusive Beyond: Some Notes on the Netherworld Geography in Sumerian Tradition." In *Altorientalische Studien zu Ehren von Pascal Attinger*, edited by Catherine Mittermayer und Sabine Ecklin, 1–30. Fribourg, Switzerland: Academic Press; Göttingen: Vandenhoeck & Ruprecht, 2012.

Arterbury, Andrew E., and William H. Bellinger Jr. "'Returning' to the Hospitality of the Lord: A Reconsideration of Psalm 23, 5–6." *Biblica* 86 (2005): 387–95.

Assmann, Aleida. "Auge und Ohr: Bemerkungen zur Kulturgeschichte der Sinne in der Neuzeit." In Agus and J. Assmann, *Ocular Desire*, 142–60.

———. *Einführung in die Kulturwissenschaft: Grundbegriffe, Themen, Fragestellungen*. Berlin: Schmidt, 2006.

Assmann, Jan. *Ägypten: Eine Sinngeschichte*. Munich: Hanser Verlag, 1996.

———. *Ägypten: Theologie und Frömmigkeit einer frühen Hochkultur*. Stuttgart: W. Kohlhammer, 1984.

———, trans. *Ägyptische Hymnen und Gebete: übersetzt, kommentiert und eingeleitet* [*ÄHG*]. 2nd ed. Göttingen: Vandenhoeck & Ruprecht, 1999.

———. "Aton." In *Lexikon der Ägyptologie*, 1:526–40. Wiesbaden: O. Harrassowitz, 1975.

———. "Diesseits-Jenseits-Beziehungen." In *Lexikon der Ägyptologie*, edited by Wolfgang Helck and Eberhard Otto, 1:1085–93. Wiesbaden: O. Harrassowitz, 1975.

———. "'Der Eine lebt, wenn der Andere ihn leitet': Altägyptische Konzepte konnektiven Lebens." In *Individuum und System: Für Helm Stierlin*, edited by Hans Rudi Fischer and Gunthard Weber, 147–61. Frankfurt am Main: Suhrkamp, 2000.

———. *Das Fest und das Heilige: Religiöse Kontrapunkte zur Alltagswelt*. Gütersloh: Gütersloher Verlagshaus G. Mohn, 1991.

———. "Glück und Weisheit." In *Vom guten Leben: Glücksvorstellungen in Hochkulturen*, edited by Alfred Bellebaum, 17–54. Berlin: Akademie Verlag, 1994.

———. *Herrschaft und Heil: Politische Theologie in Altägypten, Israel und Europa*. Munich: Hanser Verlag, 2000.

———. "Konstellative Anthropologie: Zum Bild des Menschen im Alten Ägypten." In Janowski, Liess, and Zaft, *Der Mensch*, 95–120.

———. *Das kulturelle Gedächtnis: Schrift, Erinnerung und politische Identität in frühen Hochkulturen*. Munich: C. H. Beck, 1992.

———. "Ma'at." In *RGG*[4] 5 (2002): 633–34.

———. "Ma'at—Gemeinschaftskunst im alten Ägypten." In *Ma'at—Konfuzius—Goethe: Drei Lehren für das richtige Leben*, by Jan Assmann, Helwig Schmidt-Glintzer, and Ekkehardt Krippendorff, 23–69. Frankfurt am Main: Insel Verlag, 2006.

———. *Ma'at: Gerechtigkeit und Unsterblichkeit im alten Ägypten*. Munich: C. H. Beck, 1990.

———. "Ocular Desire in a Time of Darkness: Urban Festivals and Divine Visibility in Ancient Egypt." In Agus and J. Assmann, *Ocular Desire*, 13–29.

———. "Der schöne Tag." In *Stein und Zeit: Mensch und Gesellschaft im alten Ägypten*, edited by Jan Assmann, 200–237. Munich: W. Fink, 1991.

———. "Die Theologisierung der Gerechtigkeit." In *Moral und Weltreligionen*, edited by Christof Gestrich, 129–46. Berlin: Wichern-Verlag, 2000.

———. *Der Tod als Thema der Kulturtheorie: Todesbilder und Totenriten im alten Ägypten*. Frankfurt am Main: Suhrkamp, 2000.

———. *Tod und Jenseits im alten Ägypten*. Munich: C. H. Beck, 2001.

———. "Todesbefallenheit im alten Ägypten." In J. Assmann and Trauzettel, *Tod, Jenseits*, 230–51.

———. "Unsterblichkeit." In *HWP* 11:275–94.

———. "Vergeltung und Erinnerung." In *Studien zu Sprache und Religion Ägyptens*, edited by Wolfhart Westendorf, 2:687–701. Göttingen: F. Junge, 1984.

———. *Weisheit, Loyalismus und Frömmigkeit*. Freiburg im Breisgau: Herder Verlag, 1979.

———. "Zur Geschichte des Herzens im alten Ägypten." In *Die Erfindung des inneren Menschen: Studien zur religiösen Anthropologie*, 81–113. Gütersloh: Gütersloher Verlagshaus G. Mohn, 1993.

———. "Der zweidimensionale Mensch." In *Das Fest und das Heilige: Religiöse Kontrapunkte zur Alltagswelt*, edited by Jan Assmann, 13–30. Gütersloh: Gütersloher Verlagshaus G. Mohn, 1991.

Assmann, Jan, Bernd Janowski, and Michael Welker. "Richten und Retten: Zur Aktualität der altorientalischen und biblischen Gerechtigkeitskonzeption." In *Gerechtigkeit: Richten und Retten in der abendländischen Tradition und ihren altorientalischen Ursprüngen*, edited by Jan Assmann, Bernd Janowski, and Michael Welker, 9–35. Munich: Fink, 1998.

Assmann, Jan, and Rolf Trauzettel, eds. *Tod, Jenseits und Identität: Perspektiven einer kulturwissenschaftlichen Thanatologie*. Freiburg im Breisgau: Alber, 2002.

Athanasius. "The Letter of St. Athanasius to Marcellinus on the Interpretation of the Psalms." In *On the Incarnation: The Treatise "De incarnatione Verbi Dei,"* 97–119. Crestwood, NY: St. Vladimir's Seminary Press, 1996.

Auffret, Pierre. "Ma coupe est comble: Étude structurelle du psaume 23." *Biblische Notitzen* 126 (2005): 37–43.

Austin, John Langshaw. *How to Do Things with Words*. 2nd ed. Cambridge: Harvard University Press, 1978.

Bachmann, Ingeborg. *Gedichte, hörspiele, libretti, übersetzungen*. Vol. 1 of *Werke*. 3rd ed. Munich: Piper, 1993.

Bachmann, Ingeborg, and Hans Höller. *Letzte, unveröffentlichte Gedichte, Entwürfe und Fassungen*. Frankfurt am Main: Suhrkamp, 1998.

Backhaus, Franz Josef. *"Es gibt nichts besseres für den Menschen" (Koh. 3, 22): Studien zur Komposition und zur Weisheitskritik im Buch Kohelet*. Bodenheim: Philo Verlagsgesellschaft, 1998.

———. "'JHWH, mein Gott, rette mich!'": Menschliche Gewalt und göttliche Gerechtigkeit in Psalm 7." *Bibel und Kirche* 66 (2011): 150–58.

Bader, Günter. *Psalterium affectuum palaestra: Prolegomena zu einer Theologie des Psalters*. Tübingen: Mohr, 1996.

Baethgen, Friedrich. *Die Psalmen*. Göttingen: Vandenhoeck & Ruprecht, 1904.

Bail, Ulrike. *Gegen das Schweigen klagen: Eine intertextuelle Studie zu den Klagepsalmen Ps. 6 und Ps. 55 und der Erzählung von der Vergewaltigung Tamars*. Gütersloh: Christian Kaiser / Gütersloher Verlagshaus, 1998.

———. "Hautritzen als Körperinszenierungen der Trauer und des Verlustes im Alten Testament." *Jabboq* 6 (2006): 54–80.

———. "Von zerstörten Räumen und Barfussgehen: Anmerkungen zu Text-Räumen der Enge in der hebräischen Bibel." *Evangelische Theologie* 61, no. 2 (2001): 92–101.

Baldermann, Ingo. *Einführung in die Bibel*. Göttingen: Vandenhoeck & Ruprecht, 1988.

———. *Ich werde nicht sterben, sondern leben: Psalmen als Gebrauchstexte*. Neukirchen-Vluyn: Neukirchener Verlag, 1990.

———. "Klage IV." In *RGG*[4] 4 (2001): 1392–93.

———."Psalmen." In *Von Hiob bis Thomas von Kempen*, edited by Christian Möller, 23–34. Vol. 1 of *Geschichte der Seelsorge in Einzelportraits*. Göttingen: Vandenhoeck & Ruprecht, 1994.

———. *Wer hört mein Weinen? Kinder entdecken sich selbst in den Psalmen*. Neukirchen-Vluyn: Neukirchener Verlag, 1989.

Ballhorn, Egbert. "Gefährliche Doxologie: Eine Theologie des Gotteslobs in den Psalmen." *Bibel und Liturgie* 77 (2004): 11–19.

———. "'Glücklich der Mensch . . .': Weisung und Gebrauchsanweisung für das Psalmenbuch." *Pastoralblatt für die Diözesen Aachen, Berlin, Essen, Hamburg, Hildesheim, Köln, Osnabrück* 55 (2003): 12–16.

———. *Das Telos des Psalters: Der Textzusammenhang des vierten und fünften Psalmenbuches (Ps 90–150)*. Diss., Universität Bonn, 2000. Reprint, Berlin: Philo, 2004.

———. "'Um deines Knechtes Davids Willen' (Ps 132, 10): Die Gestalt Davids im Psalter." *Biblische Notizen*, no. 76 (1995): 16–31.

———. *Zum Telos des Psalters: Der Textzusammenhang des Vierten und Fünften Psalmenbuches (Ps 90–150)*. Berlin: Philo, 2004.

Baltzer, Klaus. *Deutero-Jesaja: Kommentar zum Alten Testament*. Gütersloh: Gütersloher Verlagshaus, 1999.

Barbiero, Gianni. *Das erste Psalmenbuch als Einheit: Eine synchrone Analyse von Psalm 1–41*. Frankfurt am Main: Peter Lang, 1999.

Barkay, Gabriel, Marilyn J. Lundberg, Andrew G. Vaughn, and Bruce Zuckermann. "The Amulets from Ketef Hinnom: A New Edition and Evaluation." *Bulletin of the American Schools of Oriental Research*, no. 334 (May 2004): 41–71.

Barkhaus, Annette, Matthias Mayer, Neil Roughley, and Donatus Thürnau. *Identität, Leiblichkeit, Normativität: Neue Horizonte anthropologischen Denkens*. Frankfurt: Suhrkamp, 1996.

Barloewen, Constantin von. *Der Tod in den Weltkulturen und Weltreligionen*. Munich: Diederichs, 1996.

Barr, James. *Bibelexegese und moderne Semantik: Theologische und linguistische Methode in der Bibelwissenschaft*. Munich: Christian Kaiser, 1965.

———. *The Garden of Eden and the Hope of Immortality: The Read-Tuckwell Lectures for 1990*. London: SCM Press, 1992.

Barré, Michael L. "'Wandering About' as a Topos of Depression in Ancient Near Eastern Literature and in the Bible." *Journal of Near Eastern Studies* 60, no. 3 (2001): 177–87.

Barta, Heinz, Robert Rollinger, and Martin Lang, eds. *Recht und Religion: Menschliche und göttliche Gerechtigkeitsvorstellungen in den antiken Welten*. Wiesbaden: O. Harrassowitz, 2008.

Bartelmus, Rüdiger. "רָחָב." In *ThWAT* 7:449–60.

———. "שָׁמַיִם." In *ThWAT* 7:204–39.

———. "Tempus als Strukturprinzip: Anmerkungen zur stilistischen und theologischen Relevanz des Tempusgebrauchs im 'Lied der Hanna' (1 Sam 2:1–10)." *Biblische Zeitschrift* 31, no. 1 (1987): 15–35.

Barth, Christoph. *Diesseits und Jenseits im Glauben des späten Israel*. Stuttgart: KBW Verlag, 1974.

———. *Die Errettung vom Tode: Leben und Tod in den Klage- und Dankliedern des Alten Testaments*. Edited by Bernd Janowski. 3rd ed. Stuttgart: W. Kohlhammer, 1997.

———. "Leben und Tod." In C. Barth, *Die Errettung vom Tode*.

Barth, Gerhard. *Der Tod Jesu Christi im Verständnis des Neuen Testaments*. Neukirchen-Vluyn: Neukirchener Verlag, 1992.

Barth, Karl. *Der Römerbrief*. 10th ed. Zurich: EVZ-Verlag, 1967.

Basson, Alec. *Divine Metaphors in Selected Hebrew Psalms of Lamentation*. Tübingen: Mohr Siebeck, 2006.

Bauer, Uwe F. W. *Rachgier—Lohnsucht—Aberwitz: Eine Analyse antijudaistischer Interpretationen und Sprachmuster in Psalmenkommentaren des deutschen Protestantismus im 19. und 20. Jahrhundert*. Münster: LIT Verlag, 2009.

Bauks, Michaela. *Die Feinde des Psalmisten und die Freunde Ijobs: Untersuchungen zur Freund-Klage im Alten Testament am Beispiel von Psalm 22*. Stuttgart: Verlag Katholisches Bibelwerk, 2004.

Bayer, Oswald. *Aus Glauben Leben: Über Rechtfertigung und Heiligung*. Stuttgart: Calwer Verlag, 1984.

———. "Erhörte Klage." In *Leibliches Wort: Reformation und Neuzeit im Konflikt*, 334–48. Tübingen: J. C. B. Mohr, 1992.

———. "Klage III." In *RGG*[4] 4 (2001): 1391–92.

———. "Schöpfungslehre als Rechtfertigungsontologie." In *Word—Gift—Being: Justification—Economy—Ontology*, edited by Bo Kristian Holm and Peter Widmann, 17–41. Tübingen: Mohr Siebeck, 2009.

———. "Der Schöpfungsmorgen." In *Schöpfung als Anrede: Zu einer Hermeneutik der Schöpfung*, 109–27. Tübingen: J. C. B. Mohr (Paul Siebeck), 1990.

———. "Wann hat das Böse endlich ein Ende?" In *Gott als Autor: Zu einer poietologischen Theologie*, 198–205. Tübingen: Mohr Siebeck, 1999.

———. "Zur Theologie der Klage." *Jahrbuch für biblische Theologie* 16 (2001): 298–305.

Beale, Gregory K., and Donald A. Carson. *Commentary on the New Testament Use of the Old Testament*. Grand Rapids: Baker Academic, 2007.

Bechmann, Ulrike. "Frau I." In *NBL* 1:693–99.

Beck, Matthias. *Seele und Krankheit: Psychosomatische Medizin und theologische Anthropologie*. Paderborn: Schöningh, 2000.

Becker, Hansjakob. "Aus tiefer Not schrei ich zu dir." In *Geistliches Wunderhorn: Grosse deutsche Kirchenlieder*, 124–34. Munich: C. H. Beck, 2001.

Becker, Joachim. "Elliptisches *hēšîb* (*nœpœš*) [*nepeš*] in Ps 68, 23 und 73, 10." *Biblische Notizen*, no. 103 (2000): 43–52.

———. "Das priesterliche Heilsorakel." In *Gesammelte Studien zum Alten Testament*, edited by Walther Zimmerli, 217–31. Munich: Christian Kaiser, 1964.

———. *Wege der Psalmenexegese*. Stuttgart: KBW Verlag, 1975.

Begrich, Joachim. "Das priesterliche Heilsorakel." In *Gesammelte Studien zum Alten Testament*, edited by Walther Zimmerli, 217–31. Munich: Christian Kaiser, 1964.

Belting, Hans. "Das Körperbild als Menschenbild: Eine Repräsentation in der Krise." In *Bild-Anthropologie: Entwürfe für eine Bildwissenschaft*, 87–113. Munich: W. Fink, 2001.

Benthien, Claudia, Anne Fleig, and Ingrid Kasten. *Emotionalität: Zur Geschichte der Gefühle*. Cologne: Böhlau, 2000.

Benveniste, Émile. *Indo-European Language and Society*. Translation of *Le Vocabulaire des institutions indo-européennes* (1969) by Elizabeth Palmer. Miami: University of Miami Press, 1973. In German, *Indoeuropäische Institutionen: Wortschatz, Geschichte, Funktionen*. Translated by Wolfram Bayer. Frankfurt am Main: Campus-Verlag, 1993.

Berger, Klaus. *Historische Psychologie des Neuen Testaments*. Stuttgart: Verlag Katholisches Bibelwerk, 1991.

———. *Jesus*. Munich: Pattloch, 2004.

———. *Psalmen aus Qumran*. Stuttgart: Quell, 1994.

Berges, Ulrich. *Klagelieder*. Freiburg im Breisgau, 2002.

———. *Schweigen ist Silber, Klagen ist Gold: Das Drama der Gottesbeziehung aus alttestamentlicher Sicht mit einer Auslegung zu Ps 88*. Münster: LIT Verlag, 2003.

Berlejung, Angelika. "Geschichte und Religionsgeschichte des antiken Israel." In *Grundinformation Altes Testament: Eine Einführung in Literatur, Religion und Geschichte des Alten Testaments*, edited by Jan Christian Gertz and Angelika Berlejung, 59–192. 3rd ed. Göttingen: Vandenhoeck & Ruprecht, 2009.

———. "Körperkonzepte und Geschlechterdifferenz in der physiognomischen Tradition des Alten Orients und des Alten Testaments." In Janowski, Liess, and Zaft, *Der Mensch*, 299–337.

———. "Licht/Finsternis." In *HGANT*² 303–4.

———. "Ein Programm fürs Leben: Theologisches Wort und anthropologischer Ort der Silberamulette von Ketef Hinnom." *Zeitschrift für die alttestamentliche Wissenschaft* 120 (2008): 204–30.

———. *Die Theologie der Bilder: Herstellung und Einweihung von Kultbildern in Mesopotamien und die alttestamentliche Bilderpolemik*. Göttingen: Vandenhoeck & Ruprecht, 1998.

———. "Tod und Leben nach den Vorstellungen der Israeliten: Ein ausgewählter Aspekt zu einer Metapher im Spannungsfeld von Leben und Tod." In *Das biblische Weltbild und seine altorientalischen Kontexte*, edited by Bernd Janowski and Beate Ego, 465–502. Tübingen: Mohr Siebeck, 2001.

———. "Unterwelt." In *HGANT*² 400–401.

———. "Weltbild/Kosmologie." In *HGANT*² 65–72.

———. "Wüste/Steppe." In *HGANT*² 427–28.

Berlejung, Angelika, and Raik Heckl, eds. *Ex Oriente lux: Studien zur Theologie des Alten Testaments; Festschrift für Rüdiger Lux zum 65. Geburtstag*. Leipzig: Evangelische Verlagsanstalt, 2012.

Berlejung, Angelika, and Bernd Janowski, eds. *Tod und Jenseits im alten Israel und in seiner Umwelt: Theologische, religionsgeschichtliche, archäologische und ikonographische Aspekte*. Tübingen: Mohr Siebeck, 2009.

Berlejung, Angelika, and Annette Merz. "Feind." In *HGANT*² 182–84.

Berlin, Adele. *The Dynamics of Biblical Parallelism*. Bloomington: Indiana University Press, 1985.

———. "On Reading Biblical Poetry: The Role of Metaphor." In *Congress Volume*, edited by J. A. Emerton, 25–36. Leiden: E. J. Brill, 1997.

Bernhardt, Karl-Heinz. "אָוֶן." In *ThWAT* 1:151–59.

Bester, Dörte. *Körperbilder in den Psalmen: Studien zu Psalm 22 und verwandten Texten*. Tübingen: Mohr Siebeck, 2007.

Beyerle, Stefan. "'Medizin'—Phänomene im Alten Israel und im antiken Judentum." In *Gesundheit: Humanwissenschaftliche, historische und theologische Aspekte*, edited by Michael Roth and Jochen Schmidt, 45–78. Leipzig: Evangelische Verlagsanstalt, 2008.

Beyerlin, Walter. *Die Rettung der Bedrängten in den Feindpsalmen der Einzelnen auf institutionelle Zusammenhänge Untersucht.* Göttingen: Vandenhoeck & Ruprecht, 1970.

———. *Weisheitlich-Kultische Heilsordnung: Studien zum 15. Psalm.* Neukirchen-Vluyn: Neukirchener Verlag, 1985.

———. *Weisheitliche Vergewisserung mit Bezug auf den Zionskult: Studien zum 125. Psalm.* Göttingen: Vandenhoeck & Ruprecht, 1985.

Beyse, Karl-Martin. "עֶצֶם." In *ThWAT* 6:310–32.

Biberger, Bernd. Review of *JHWH und die Unterwelt: Spuren einer Kompetenzausweitung JHWHs im Alten Testament,* by Gönke D. Eberhardt. *Orientalistische Literaturzeitung* 104 (2009): 194–98.

Bickel, Susanne, et al., eds. *Bilder als Quellen—Images as Sources: Studies on Ancient Near Eastern Artefacts and the Bible Inspired by the Work of Othmar Keel.* Freiburg, Switzerland: Academic Press; Göttingen: Vandenhoeck & Ruprecht, 2007.

Bieberstein, Klaus, and Sabine Bieberstein. "Auferweckt gemäß der Schrift: Das Ringen um Gottes Gerechtigkeit und die Hoffnung auf Auferweckung der Toten." *Bibel und Kirche* 64 (2009): 70–77.

Bieberstein, Klaus, and Lukas Bormann. "Gerechtigkeit/Recht." *SWB* 197–203.

Bieberstein, Sabine. "Der lange Weg zur Auferstehung der Toten: Eine Skizze zur Entstehung der Eschatologie im Alten Testament." In *Auferstehung hat einen Namen: Biblische Anstösse zum Christsein heute; Festschrift für Hermann-Josef Venetz,* edited by Sabine Bieberstein and Daniel Kosch, 3–16. Lucerne: Edition Exodus, 1998.

Bieler, Andrea. "Psalmengottesdienste als Klageräume für Überlebende sexueller Gewalt: Poimenische und liturgische Überlegungen." *Evangelische Theologie* 60, no. 2 (2000): 117–30.

Biesinger, Albert, and Joachim Hänle. "Zwischen Horror und Erlösung: Gerichtsvorstellungen Jugendlicher als Herausforderung an religionspädagogische Theorie und Praxis." *Theologische Quartalschrift* 178, no. 3 (1998): 209–28.

Bird, Phyllis A. "The Place of Women in the Israelite Cultus." In *Missing Persons and Mistaken Identities: Women and Gender in Ancient Israel,* edited by Phyllis A. Bird, 81–102. Minneapolis: Fortress Press, 1997.

Blenkinsopp, Joseph. "Deuteronomy and the Politics of Post-mortem Existence." *Vetus Testamentum* 45, no. 1 (1995): 1–16.

———. "Life Expectancy in Ancient Palestine." *Scandinavian Journal of the Old Testament* 11, no. 1 (1997): 44–55.

Blum, Erhard. *Studien zur Komposition des Pentateuch.* Berlin: Walter de Gruyter, 1990.

Blum, Erhard, and Heinz-Josef Fabry. "רִב." In *ThWAT* 7:294–320.

Blumenberg, Hans. *Beschreibung des Menschen.* Frankfurt am Main: Suhrkamp, 2006.

———. "Licht als Metapher der Wahrheit: Im Vorfeld der philosophischen Begriffsbildung." In *Ästhetische und Metaphorologische Schriften,* edited by Hans Blumenberg and Anselm Haverkamp, 139–71. Frankfurt am Main: Suhrkamp, 2001.

———. *Schiffbruch mit Zuschauer: Paradigma einer Daseinsmetapher.* Frankfurt am Main: Suhrkamp 1979.

Bödeker, Heinz. "Anthropologie." In *Lexikon der Aufklärung: Deutschland und Europa,* edited by Werner Schneiders, 38–39. Munich: C. H. Beck, 1995.

———. "Mensch." In *Lexikon der Aufklärung: Deutschland und Europa,* edited by Werner Schneiders. Munich: C. H. Beck 1995.

Boecker, Hans Jochen. "'Feindesliebe' im alttestamentlichen Recht? Überlegungen zu Exodus 23, 4–5." In *Verbindungslinien,* edited by Axel Graupner, Holger Delkurt, and Alexander Ernst, 19–25. Neukirchen-Vluyn: Neukirchener Verlag, 2000.

———. "Psalmen." In *Altes Testament*, edited by Hans Jochen Boecker et al., 179–99. Neukirchen-Vluyn: Neukirchener Verlag, 1996.

———. *Recht und Gesetz im Alten Testament und im Alten Orient*. 2nd ed. Neukirchen-Vluyn: Neukirchener Verlag, 1984.

———. *Redeformen des Rechtslebens im Alten Testament*. Neukirchen-Vluyn: Neukirchener Verlag, 1964.

Bohlken, Eike, and Christian Thies, eds. *Handbuch Anthropologie: Der Mensch zwischen Natur, Kultur und Technik*. Stuttgart: Metzler, 2009.

Böhme, Gernot. *Ethik leiblicher Existenz: Über unseren moralischen Umgang mit der eigenen Natur*. Frankfurt am Main: Suhrkamp, 2008.

———. *Ich-Selbst: Über die Formation des Subjekts*. Munich: Fink, 2012.

———. "Umriss einer Kulturgeschichte des Wassers: Eine Einleitung." In *Anthropologie in pragmatischer Hinsicht: Darmstädter Vorlesungen*, 7–42. Frankfurt am Main: Suhrkamp, 1985.

Böhme, Hartmut. "Leibliche und kulturelle Codierungen der Angst." In *Große Gefühle: Bausteine menschlichen Verhaltens*, edited by ZDF-Nachtstudio, 214–40. Frankfurt am Main: Suhrkamp, 2000.

Böhme, Hartmut, Peter Matussek, and Lothar Müller. *Orientierung Kulturwissenschaft: Was sie kann, was sie will*. Reinbek bei Hamburg: Rowohlt, 2000. 2nd ed., 2002.

Boman, Thorleif. *Das hebräische Denken im Vergleich mit dem griechischen*. Göttingen: Vandenhoeck & Ruprecht, 1983.

Bonhoeffer, Dietrich. *Gemeinsames Leben; Das Gebetbuch der Bibel*. Edited by Gerhard Ludwig Müller and Albrecht Schönherr. Vol. 5 of *Werke*. Munich: Christian Kaiser, 1987.

———. *Life Together*. Translated by John W. Doberstein. San Francisco: Harper & Row, 1954.

———. *Widerstand und Ergebung: Briefe und Aufzeichnungen aus der Haft*. Gütersloh: Christian Kaiser, 1998.

Bonhoeffer, Thomas. *Ursprung und Wesen der christlichen Seelsorge*. Munich: Christian Kaiser, 1985.

Bons, Eberhard. "Le Psaume 7 dans la version de la Septante." *Revue des sciences religieuses* 77 (2003): 512–28.

Bornkamm, Günther. "Lobpreis, Bekenntnis und Opfer." In *Das Ende des Gesetzes: Paulusstudien*, 122–39. Munich: Christian Kaiser, 1952.

———. "Das überlebensgrosse Ich: Der messianische Typos der altestamentlichen Confessio." In *Schuld, Gewissen und Person: Studien zur Geschichte des inneren Menschen*, edited by Jan Assmann and Theodor Sundermeier, 102–17. Gütersloh: Gütersloher Verlagshaus, 1997.

Botterweck, G. Johannes. "אֲרִי." In *ThWAT* 1:416–18.

Bratsiotis, N. P. "בָּשָׂר." In *ThWAT* 1:850–67.

Braulik, Georg. *Deuteronomium*. Würzburg: Echter Verlag, 1986.

———. "Durften auch Frauen in Israel opfern? Beobachtungen zur Sinn- und Festgestalt des Opfers im Deuteronomium." *Jahrbuch für Liturgie* 48 (1988): 222–48.

———. "Die Freude des Festes: Das Kultverständnis des Deuteronomiums—die älteste biblische Festtheorie." 1980. Reprinted in *Studien zur Theologie des Deuteronomiums*, edited by Georg Braulik, 161–218. Stuttgart: Verlag Katholisches Bibelwerk, 1988.

———. "Rezeptionsästhetik, kanonische Intertextualität und unsere Meditation des Psalters." *Heiliger Dienst* 57 (2003): 38–56.

———. "Spuren einer Neubearbeitung des deuteronomistischen Geschichtswerkes in 1 Kön 8, 52–53.59–60." *Biblica* 52 (1971): 20–33.

———. "Weisheit, Gottesnähe und Gesetz: Zum Kerygma von Deuteronomium 4:5–8." In *Studien zur Theologie des Deuteronomiums*, edited by Georg Braulik, 53–93. Stuttgart: Verlag Katholisches Bibelwerk, 1988.

———. "'Weisheit' im Buch Deuteronomium." In *Studien zum Buch Deuteronomium*, edited by Georg Braulik, 225–71. Stuttgart: Verlag Katholisches Bibelwerk, 1997.

Braun, Joachim. *Die Musikkultur Altisraels/Palästinas: Studien zu archäologischen, schriftlichen und vergleichenden Quellen*. Göttingen: Vandenhoeck & Ruprecht, 1999. Revised in ET, *Music in Ancient Israel/Palestine: Archaeological, Written, and Comparative Sources*. Translated by Douglas W. Stott. Grand Rapids: Eerdmans, 2002.

Bremmer, Jan N. "Die Karriere der Seele: Vom antiken Griechenland ins moderne Europa." In Janowski, *Der ganze Mensch*, 173–98.

Briend, Jacques. "Krankheit und Heilung im Alten Testament." *Welt und Umwelt der Bibel: Archäologie, Kunst, Geschichte* 18 (2000): 84.

Brockelmann, Carl. *Hebräische Syntax*. Neukirchen-Vluyn: Neukirchener Verlag, 1956.

Brown, Peter. *Society and the Holy in Late Antiquity*. Berkeley and Los Angeles: University of California Press, 1982.

Brown, William P. *Psalms*. Nashville: Abingdon Press, 2010.

———. *Seeing the Psalms: A Theology of Metaphor*. Louisville, KY: Westminster John Knox, 2002.

Brueggemann, Walter. *Theology of the Old Testament: Testimony, Dispute, Advocacy*. Minneapolis: Fortress Press, 1997.

Bruit Zaidman, Louise, and Pauline Schmitt Pantel. *Die Religion der Griechen: Kult und Mythos*. Munich: C. H. Beck, 1994.

Brünenberg, Esther. "Wenn Jahwes Widerstand sich regt: Überlegungen zum alttestamentlichen Verständnis von Strafe." In *Textarbeit: Studien zu Texten und ihrer Rezeption aus dem Alten Testament und der Umwelt Israels; Festschrift für Peter Weimar zur Vollendung seines 60. Lebensjahres*, edited by von Klaus Kiesow and Thomas Meurer, 53–74. Münster: Ugarit-Verlag, 2003.

Brunert, Gunild. *Psalm 102 im Kontext des vierten Psalmenbuches*. Stuttgart: Verlag Katholisches Bibelwerk, 1996.

Brüning, Christian. "'Gott möge ihnen einen Blitz ins Gesäß jagen!' Zu den Feindaussagen in den Psalmen." *Erbe und Auftrag* 82 (2006): 128–38.

Brunner, Hellmut. *Altägyptische Weisheit: Lehren für das Leben*. Zurich: Artemis Verlag, 1988.

———. "Blindheit." In *Lexikon der Ägyptologie*, edited by Wolfgang Helck, 1:828–33. Wiesbaden: O. Harrassowitz, 1975.

———. "Gottesnähe und -ferne." In *Lexikon der Ägyptologie*, edited by Wolfgang Helck, 2:817–19. Wiesbaden: O. Harrassowitz, 1977.

———. *Grundzüge der altägyptischen Religion*. Darmstadt: Wissenschaftliche Buchgesellschaft, 1983.

———. "Das hörende Herz." In *Das hörende Herz: Kleine Schriften zur Religions- und Geistesgeschichte Ägyptens*, edited by Hellmut Brunner and Wolfgang Röllig, 3–5. Göttingen: Vandenhoeck & Ruprecht, 1988.

Brunner-Traut, Emma. "Aspektive." In *Lexikon der Ägyptologie*, edited by Wolfgang Helck, 1:474–88. Wiesbaden: O. Harrassowitz, 1975.

———. *Frühformen des Erkennens: Am Beispiel Altägyptens*. 2nd ed. Darmstadt: Wissenschaftliche Buchgesellschaft, 1992.

Budde, Kai. "Der sezierte Tote—ein schreckliches Bild? Über das Verhältnis der Lebenden zum toten präparierten Körper." In *Körperwelten: Einblicke in den menschlichen Körper*, edited by Landesmuseum für Technik und Arbeit in Mannheim, 11–28. Mannheim: Landesmuseum für Technik und Arbeit, 1997.

Buggle, Franz. *Denn sie wissen nicht, was sie glauben oder warum man redlicherweise nicht mehr Christ sein kann: Eine Streitschrift*. Reinbek bei Hamburg: Rowohlt, 1997.

Bukowski, Peter. *Die Bibel ins Gespräch bringen: Erwägungen zu einer Grundfrage der Seelsorge*. Neukirchen-Vlyun: Neukirchener Verlag, 1994.

Bultmann, Rudolf. *Das Verhältnis der urchristlichen Christusbotschaft zum historischen Jesus*. Heidelberg: C. Winter, 1960.

Burke, Peter. "The Rise of Literal-Mindedness." *Common Knowledge* 2, no. 2 (1993): 108–21.

———. *Was ist Kulturgeschichte?* Frankfurt am Main: Suhrkamp, 2005.

Burkert, Walter. *Griechische Religion der archaischen und klassischen Epoche*. Stuttgart: W. Kohlhammer, 1977.

———. *Kulte des Altertums: Biologische Grundlagen der Religion*. Munich: C. H. Beck, 1994.

———. "Mikroskopie der Geistesgeschichte: Bruno Snells 'Entdeckung des Geistes' im kritischen Rückblick." *Philologus* 148 (2004): 168–82.

Burns, Lori. *Bach's Modal Chorales*. Stuyvesant, NY: Pendragon Press, 1995.

Calvin, John. *Calvin-Studienausgabe*. Vol. 6, *Der Psalmenkommentar: Eine Auswahl*, edited by Eberhard Busch et al. Neukirchen-Vluyn: Neukirchener Verlag, 2008.

Cardellini, Innocenzo. "La metafora del 'pastore' nell'antico testamento alla luce del retroterra culturale mesopotamico." *Lateranum* 71 (2005): 249–78.

Cassin, Elena M. *La spendeur divine: Introduction à l'étude de la mentalité mésopotamienne*. Paris: La Haye, Mouton & Co., 1968.

Celan, Paul, Beda Allemann, and Stefan Reichert. *Gesammelte Werke in fünf Bänden*. Frankfurt am Main: Suhrkamp, 1983.

Claessens, Dieter. *Das Konkrete und das Abstrakte: Soziologische Skizzen zur Anthropologie*. Frankfurt am Main: Suhrkamp, 1980.

Claussen, Johann Hinrich, ed. *Spiegelungen: Biblische Texte und moderne Lyrik*. Zurich: Pano Verlag, 2004.

Clements, Ronald E. "שָׁחַט." In *ThWAT* 7:1214–18.

Colpe, Carsten, and Wilhelm Schmidt-Biggemann. *Das Böse: Eine historische Phänomenologie des Unerklärlichen*. Frankfurt am Main: Suhrkamp, 1993.

Conrad, J. "מָנָה." In *ThWAT* (1989): 4:976–980.

——. "פָּלָא." In *ThWAT* 6:569–83.

Conzelmann, Hans. *Zur Bedeutung des Todes Jesu: Exegetische Beiträge*. Gütersloh: Gütersloher Verlagshaus, 1967.

Cornelius, Izak. "The Sun Epiphany in Job 38:12–15 and the Iconography of the Gods in the Ancient Near East—The Palestinian Connection." *Journal of Northwest Semitic Languages* 16 (1990): 25–43.

Couffignal, Robert. "De la bête à l'ange: Le Psaume 23, miroir de l'aventure spirituelle." *Zeitschrift für die alttestamentliche Wissenschaft* 115 (2003): 557–77.

Coulot, Claude, René Heyer, and Jacques Joubert, eds. *"Le Seigneur est mon berger," Ps 23 (22): Exégèse et patristique*. Themed volume of *Revue des sciences religieuses* 83, no. 3. Strasbourg: Presses Universitaires Strasbourg, 2009.

Craigie, Peter C. *Psalms 1–50*. Word Biblical Commentary. Waco: Word Books, 1983.

Crüsemann, Frank. *Das Alte Testament als Wahrheitsraum des Neuen: Die neue Sicht der Bibel*. Gütersloh: Gütersloher Verlagshaus, 2011.

———. "Der Gewalt nicht glauben: Hiobbuch und Klagepsalmen—zwei Modell theologischer Verarbeitung traumatischer Gewalterfahrungen." In *Dem Tod nicht glauben: Sozialgeschichte der Bibel; Festschrift für Luise Schottroff zum 70. Geburtstag*, edited by Frank Crüsemann et al., 251–68. Gütersloh: Gütersloher Verlagshaus, 2004.

———. "Im Netz: Zur Frage nach der 'eigentlichen Not' in den Klagen des Einzelnen." In *Schöpfung und Befreiung: Für Claus Westermann zum 80. Geburtstag*, edited by Rainer Albertz, Friedemann W. Golka, and Jürgen Kegler, 139–48. Stuttgart: Calwer Verlag, 1989.

———. "Rhetorische Fragen!? Eine Aufkündigung des Konsenses über Psalm 88:11–13 und seine Bedeutung für das alttestamentliche Reden von Gott und Tod." *BibInt* 11 (2003): 345–60.

———. *Die Tora: Theologie und Sozialgeschichte des alttestamentlichen Gesetzes*. Munich: Christian Kaiser, 1992.

Crüsemann, Frank, and Marlene Crüsemann. "Tod." *SWB* 586–89.

Crüsemann, Frank, Christof Hardmeier, and Rainer Kessler, eds. *Was ist der Mensch . . . ? Beiträge zur Anthropologie des Alten Testaments; Hans Walter Wolff zum 80. Geburtstag*. Munich: Christian Kaiser, 1992.

Cullmann, Oscar. *Das Gebet im Neuen Testament: Zugleich Versuch einer vom Neuen Testament aus zu erteilenden Antwort auf heutige Fragen*. 2nd ed. Tübingen: J. C. B. Mohr, 1997.

Dahood, Mitchell J. *Psalms I: 1–50*. Anchor Bible. Garden City, NY: Doubleday, 1966.

———. *Psalms II: 51–100*. Anchor Bible. Garden City, NY: Doubleday, 1968.

———. *Psalms III: 101–150*. Anchor Bible. Garden City, NY: Doubleday, 1970.

Dalferth, Ingolf. "In Bildern denken: Die Sprache der Glaubenserfahrung." *Evangelische Kommentare* 30 (1997): 165–67.

———. *Das Böse: Essay über die Denkform des Unbegreiflichen*. Tübingen: Mohr Siebeck, 2006.

———. *Leiden und Böses: Vom schwierigen Umgang mit Widersinnigem*. Leipzig: Evangelische Verlagsanstalt, 2006.

Daniel, Ute. *Kompendium Kulturgeschichte: Theorien, Praxis, Schlüsselwörter*. Frankfurt am Main: Suhrkamp, 2001.

Degenhardt, Johannes Joachim, ed. *Die Freude an Gott, unsere Kraft: Festschrift für Otto Bernhard Knoch zum 65. Geburtstag*. Stuttgart: Verlag Katholisches Bildwerk, 1991.

Deissler, Alfons. "'Mein Gott, warum hast du mich verlassen . . . !'" In *Ich will euer Gott werden*, edited by Norbert Lohfink, 97–121. Stuttgart: Verlag Katholisches Bibelwerk, 1981.

Delitzsch, Franz. *A Commentary on the Book of Psalms*. Translated by David Eaton and James E. Duguid. New York: Funk & Wagnalls, 1983.

Delkurt, Holger. *Ethische Einsichten in der alttestamentlichen Spruchweisheit*. Neukirchen-Vluyn: Neukirchener Verlag, 1993.

———. *"Der Mensch ist dem Vieh gleich, das vertilgt wird": Tod und Hoffnung gegen den Tod in Ps 49 und bei Kohelet*. Neukirchen-Vluyn: Neukirchener Verlag, 2005.

Deselaers, Paul. "Psalmen predigen: Ermutigung aus der neuen Psalmenforschung." In *Das Manna fällt auch heute noch: Beiträge zur Geschichte und Theologie des Alten, Ersten Testaments; Festschrift für Erich Zenger*, edited by Frank-Lothar Hossfeld and Ludger Schwienhorst-Schönberger, 158–73. Freiburg im Breisgau: Herder Verlag, 2004.

Di Vito, Robert A. "Anthropology II." *EBR* 2 (2009): 117–26.

———. "Anthropology, OT Theological." *The New Interpreter's Dictionary of the Bible*, 1:171–74. Nashville: Abingdon, 2006.

———. "Old Testament Anthropology and the Construction of Personal Identity." *Catholic Biblical Quarterly* 61 (1999): 217–38. Trans. as "Alttestamentliche Anthropologie und die Konstruktion personaler Identität." In Janowski, Liess, and Zaft, *Der Mensch*, 213–41.

Diesel, Anja A., and Andreas Wagner. "'Jahwe ist mein Hirte': Zum Verständnis der Nominalen Behauptung in Ps 23, 1." In A. Wagner, *Beten und Bekennen*, 197–215.

Dietrich, Walter. "Im Zeichen Kains: Gewalt und Gewaltüberwindung in der Hebräischen Bibel." *Evangelische Theologie* 64 (2004): 252–67.

———. "Rache: Erwägungen zu einem alttestamentlichen Thema." *Evangelische Theologie* 36 (1976): 450–72.

———. "Unheil." In *NBL* 3:959–64.

Dietrich, Walter, and Christoph Link. *Die dunklen Seiten Gottes*. Vol. 1, *Willkür und Gewalt*. Vol. 2, *Allmacht und Ohnmacht*. Neukirchen-Vluyn: Neukirchener Verlag, 1995–2000.

Dietrich, Walter, and Moisés Mayordomo. *Gewalt und Gewaltüberwindung in der Bibel*. Zurich: Theologischer Verlag, 2005.

Dietrich, Walter, and Samuel Vollenweider. "Tod II: Altes und Neues Testament." In *TRE* 33:582–600.

Diller, Carmen. "'Du füllst mir reichlich den Becher . . .': Der Becher als Zeichen der Gastfreundschaft am Beispiel von Ps 23." In Diller, *Syntax, Sprechaktanalyse und Metaphorik*, 81–104.

———, ed. *"Erforsche mich, Gott, und erkenne mein Herz!": Beiträge zur Syntax, Sprechaktanalyse und Metaphorik im Alten Testament; Schülerfestschrift für Hubert Irsigler zum 60. Geburtstag*. St. Ottilien: EOS-Verlag, 2005.

Dirscherl, Erwin. *Grundriß theologischer Anthropologie: Die Entschiedenheit des Menschen angesichts des Anderen*. Regensburg: Pustet, 2006.

———. "Über spannende Beziehungen nachdenken: Der Mensch als Geschöpf, als Ebenbild Gottes und seine Ambivalenz als Sünder." In *Beziehung leben: Theologische Anthropologie*, by Erwin Dirscherl et al., 46–89. Freiburg im Breisgau: Herder Verlag, 2008.

Dockner, Thomas. *"Sicut cerva—": Text, Struktur und Bedeutung von Psalm 42 und 43*. St. Ottilien: EOS Verlag, 2001.

Doeker, Andrea. *Die Funktion der Gottesrede in den Psalmen: Eine poetologische Untersuchung*. Berlin: Philo, 2002.

Dohmen, Christoph. *Das Bilderverbot: Seine Entstehung und seine Entwicklung im Alten Testament*. Frankfurt am Main: Athenäum, 1987.

———. "'Mein Gott, mein Gott, wozu hast du mich verlassen?' (Ps. 22, 2): Wie die Bibel die Warum-Frage im Leid überwindet." In *Warum, Gott . . . ? Der fragende Mensch vor dem Geheimnis Gottes; Ralph Sauer zum 65. Geburtstag*, edited by Karl Josef Lesch and Margot Saller, 12–18. Kevelaer: Verlag Butzon & Bercker, 1993.

———. "מִזְבֵּחַ." In *ThWAT* 4:787–801.

———. "'Nicht sieht mich der Mensch und lebt' (Ex 33, 20): Aspekte einer Gottesschau im Alten Testament." *Jahrbuch für biblische Theologie* 13 (1998): 31–51.

———. *Vom Umgang mit dem Alten Testament*. Stuttgart: Verlag Katholisches Bibelwerk, 1995.

———. "Von Gott zu Gott sprechen: Wenn die Theologie ins Gebet genommen wird." *Geist und Leben* 74 (2001): 326–35.

Domin, Hilde. *Ausgewählte Gedichte*. Frankfurt am Main: Fischer Taschenbuch-Verlag, 2000.

Dommershausen, Werner. "גּוֹרָל." In *ThWAT* 1:991–98.

Douglas, Mary. *Purity and Danger: An Analysis of Concepts of Pollution and Taboo*. New York: Praeger, 1966.

Doyle, Brian. "God as a Dog: Metaphorical Allusions in Psalm 59." In van Hecke, *Metaphor in the Hebrew Bible*, 41–54.

Duhm, Bernhard. *Die Psalmen*. 2nd ed. Tübingen: J. C. B. Mohr, 1922.

Dülmen, Richard van. *Historische Anthropologie: Entwicklung, Probleme, Aufgaben*. Cologne: Böhlau, 2000.

Düsing, Edith, and Hans-Dieter Klein, eds. *Geist und Psyche: Klassische Modelle von Platon bis Freud und Damasio*. Würzburg: Königshausen & Neumann, 2008.

Dux, Günter. *Die Logik der Weltbilder: Sinnstrukturen im Wandel der Geschichte*. Frankfurt am Main: Suhrkamp, 1982.

Dyma, Oliver. "'Gottes Angesicht schauen' oder 'vor ihm erscheinen' als Wallfahrtsterminologie?" In Steingrimsson and Ólason, *Literatur- und sprachwissenschaftliche Beiträge*, 23–36.

Ebach, Jürgen. "Bodenrecht." In *NBL* 1:313–14.

———. "Der Gott des Alten Testaments—Ein Gott der Rache?" In *Biblische Erinnerungen: Theologische Reden zur Zeit*, edited by Jürgen Ebach, 81–93. Bochum: SWI Verlag, 1993.

———. "Licht." *SWB* 353–56.

———. "Die Poesie der Bibel: Über Parallelismus und Widersprüche, 'unspezifische Genauigkeiten' sowie Antworten, die zu Fragen werden." In *Theopoesie: Theologie und Poesie in Hermeneutischer Sicht*, edited by Henning Schroer, Gotthard Fermor, and Harald Schroeter, 13–41. Rheinbach: CMZ-Verlag, 1998.

———. *Streiten mit Gott*. Part 1, *Hiob 1–20*. Part 2, *Hiob 21–42*. Neukirchen-Vluyn: Neukirchener Verlag, 1995–96.

———. "Weltbild." *SWB* 646–48.

Eberhardt, Gönke D. "Die Gottesferne der Unterwelt in der JHWH-Religion." In Berlejung and Janowski, *Tod und Jenseits*, 373–95.

———. *JHWH und die Unterwelt: Spuren einer Kompetenzausweitung JHWHs im Alten Testament*. Tübingen: Mohr Siebeck, 2007. [Review by Biberger, listed above.]

Eberhardt, Gönke D., and Kathrin Liess, eds. *Gottes Nähe im Alten Testament*. Stuttgart: Verlag Katholisches Bibelwerk, 2004.

Eberhart, Christian. *Studien zur Bedeutung der Opfer im Alten Testament: Die Signifikanz von Blut- und Verbrennungsriten im kultischen Rahmen*. Neukirchen-Vluyn: Neukirchener Verlag, 2002.

Ebner, Martin. *Klage und Auferweckungshoffnung im Neuen Testament*. Neukirchen-Vluyn: Neukirchener Verlag, 2001.

Ebner, Martin, Irmtraud Fischer, Jörg Frey, Ottmar Fuchs, Berndt Hamm, and Bernd Janowski. "Das Böse." *Jahrbuch für biblische Theologie* 26 (2011). Published as *Das Böse*. Neukirchen-Vluyn: Neukirchener Verlagsgesellschaft, 2012.

Eckey, Wilfried. "Die Verwendung des Alten Testaments im Markusevangelium." In *Kontexte: Biografische und forschungsgeschichtliche Schnittpunkte der alttestamentlichen Wissenschaft; Festschrift für Hans Jochen Boecker zum 80. Geburtstag*, edited by Thomas Wagner et al., 3–22. Neukirchen-Vluyn: Neukirchener Verlag, 2008.

Eder, Sigrid, and Irmtraud Fischer, eds. *". . . männlich und weiblich schuf er sie . . ." (Gen 1,27): Zur Brisanz der Geschlechterfrage in Religion und Gesellschaft*. Innsbruck: Tyrolia-Verlag, 2009.

Egger-Wenzel, Renate. *Von der Freiheit Gottes, anders zu sein: Die zentrale Rolle der Kapitel 9 und 10 für das Ijobbuch*. Würzburg: Echter Verlag, 1998.

Ego, Beate, ed. *Altes Testament: Opfer und Kult*. Themed volume of *Verkündigung und Forschung* 56, no. 2. Gütersloh: Christian Kaiser, 2011.

———. "'Seine Tage gehen dahin wie ein Schatten': Zur Vergänglichkeitsmotivik in den Psalmen." In *FS Janowski*, 77–91.

———. "Wasser, Fels und preisende Sterne: Aspekte der Relation von Weltbild und Lebenswelt am Beispiel der Psalmen." *Biblische Zeitschrift* 46 (2002): 222–39.

Ehrmann, Michael. *Klagephänomene in zwischentestamentlicher Literatur*. Frankfurt am Main: Peter Lang, 1997.

Eidevall, Göran. "Images of God, Self, and the Enemy in the Psalms: On the Role of Metaphor in Identity Construction." In van Hecke, *Metaphor in the Hebrew Bible*, 55–66.

Eliade, Mircea, and Günter Lanczkowski. *Geschichte der Religiösen Ideen: Quellentexte.* Freiburg im Breisgau: Herder Verlag, 1981.

Elias, Norbert. *Über die Einsamkeit der Sterbenden in unseren Tagen.* Frankfurt am Main: Suhrkamp, 1982.

Emmendörffer, Michael. *Der ferne Gott: Eine Untersuchung der alttestamentlichen Volksklagelieder vor dem Hintergrund der mesopotamischen Literatur.* Tübingen: Mohr Siebeck, 1998.

Emmerich, Wolfgang. *Paul Celan.* Reinbek: Rowohlt, 1999.

Engels, Eve-Marie. "Natur- und Menschenbilder in der Bioethik des 20. Jahrhunderts." In *Biologie und Ethik,* edited by Eve-Marie Engels, 7–42. Stuttgart: Reclam, 1999.

Erbele-Küster, Dorothea. "Gender Trouble in the Old Testament: Three Models of the Relation between Sex and Gender." *Scandinavian Journal of the Old Testament* 13, no. 1 (1999): 131–41.

———. *Lesen als Akt des Betens: Eine Rezeptionsästhetik der Psalmen.* Neukirchen-Vluyn: Neukirchener Verlag, 2001.

Etzelmüller, Gregor. "Der kranke Mensch als Thema theologischer Anthropologie." *Zeitschrift für evangelische Ethik* 53 (2009): 163–76.

Fabry, Heinz-Josef. "'Gedenken' im Alten Testament." In *Freude am Gottesdienst: Aspekte ursprünglicher Liturgie; Festschrift für Josef G. Plöger,* edited by Josef Schreiner, 177–87. Stuttgart: Verlag Katholisches Bibelwerk, 1983.

———. "Leiden II." In *RGG*[4] 5 (2002): 235–37. Tübingen: Mohr Siebeck, 2002.

———. "לֵבָב/לֵב." In *ThWAT* 4:413–51.

———. "מַיִם." In *ThWAT* 4:843–66.

Falkenstein, Adam, and Wolfram von Soden, eds. *Sumerische und akkadische Hymnen und Gebete.* Zurich: Artemis Verlag, 1953.

Farmer, Kathleen A. "Psalms." In *The Women's Bible Commentary,* edited by Carol A. Newsom and Sharon H. Ringe, 137–44. Louisville, KY: Westminster/John Knox Press, 1992.

Fath, Manfred. *Paul Klee—die Zeit der Reife: Werke aus der Sammlung der Familie Klee.* Munich: Prestel, 1996.

Faust, P. U., ed. *Die Benediktsregel: Lateinisch/Deutsch.* Stuttgart: Reclam, 2009.

Feldmann, Klaus, and Werner Fuchs-Heinritz. *Der Tod ist ein Problem der Lebenden: Beiträge zur Soziologie des Todes.* Frankfurt am Main: Suhrkamp, 1995.

Feldmeier, Reinhard. *Die Krisis des Gottessohnes: Die Gethsemaneerzählung als Schlüssel der Markuspassion.* Tübingen: J. C. B. Mohr, 1987.

Feldmeier, Reinhard, and Hermann Spieckermann. *Der Gott der Lebendigen: Eine biblische Gotteslehre.* Tübingen: Mohr Siebeck, 2011.

Felstiner, John. *Paul Celan: Poet, Survivor, Jew.* New Haven: Yale University Press, 1995.

Firmage, Edwin Brown, Jacob Milgrom, and Ulrich Dahmen. "רוּם." In *ThWAT* 7:425–34.

Fischer, Alexander A. *Tod und Jenseits im Alten Orient und im Alten Testament.* Neukirchen-Vluyn: Neukirchener, 2005.

Fischer, Irmtraud. "Egalitär entworfen—hierarchisch gelebt: Zur Problematik des Geschlechterverhältnisses und einer genderfairen Anthropologie im Alten Testamen." In Janowski, Liess, and Zaft, *Der Mensch,* 265–98.

———. *Rut.* Freiburg im Breisgau: Herder Verlag, 2001.

———. "Zwischen Kahlschlag, Durchforstung und neuer Pflanzung: Zu einigen Aspekten Feministischer Exegese und ihrer Relevanz für eine Theologie des Alten Testaments." In *Theologie und Exegese des Alten Testaments, der Hebräischen Bibel: Zwischenbilanz und Zukunftsperspektiven,* edited by Bernd Janowski, 41–72. Stuttgart: Verlag Katholisches Bibelwerk, 2005.

Fischer, Joachim. *Philosophische Anthropologie: Eine Denkrichtung des 20. Jahrhunderts.* Freiburg im Breisgau: Alber, 2008.
Fischer-Elfert, H.-W. "Herkunft, Wesen und Grenzen des Menschen nach altägyptischer Vorstellung." In Stagl and Reinhard, *Grenzen des Menschseins*, 217–34.
Flaig, Egon. *Ödipus: Tragischer Vatermord im klassischen Athen*. Munich: C. H. Beck, 1998.
Flessemann-van Leer, Ellen. "Die Interpretation der Passionsgeschichte vom Alten Testament aus." In *Zur Bedeutung des Todes Jesu: Exegetische Beiträge*, edited by Hans Conzelmann, 79–96. Gütersloh: Gütersloher Verlagshaus, 1967.
Flint, Peter W., and Patrick D. Miller, eds. *The Book of Psalms: Composition and Reception*. Leiden and Boston: E. J. Brill, 2005.
Fohrer, Georg. *Das Buch Hiob*. Gütersloh: Gütersloher Verlagshaus G. Mohn, 1963.
Forster, Christine. *Begrenztes Leben als Herausforderung: Das Vergänglichkeitsmotiv in weisheitlichen Psalmen*. Leipzig: Evangelische Verlagsanstalt, 2000.
Foster, Benjamin R."Letters and Literature: A Ghost's Entreaty." In *The Tablet and the Scroll: Near Eastern Studies in Honor of William W. Hallo*, edited by Mark E. Cohen, Daniel C. Snell, and David B. Weisberg, 98–102. Bethesda, MD: CDL Press, 1993.
Frankfort, Henri, and Peter Dülberg. *Alter Orient: Mythos und Wirklichkeit*. 2nd ed. Stuttgart: W. Kohlhammer, 1981.
Franz, Ansgar, and Hansjakob Becker. "Mitten wir im Leben sind." In *Geistliches Wunderhorn: Grosse deutsche Kirchenlieder*, 84–93. Munich: C. H. Beck, 2001.
Freuling, Georg. *"Wer eine Grube gräbt . . .": Der Tun-Ergehen-Zusammenhang und sein Wandel in der alttestamentlichen Weisheitsliteratur*. Neukirchen-Vluyn: Neukirchener Verlag, 2004.
Frevel, Christian. "Altes Testament." In *Menschsein: Perspektiven des Alten und des Neuen Testaments*, edited by Christian Frevel and Oda Wischmeyer, 7–60, 121–25, 129–31. Würzburg: Echter Verlag, 2003.
———. "Anthropologie." In *HGANT*[2] 1–7.
———, ed. *Biblische Anthropologie: Neue Einsichten aus dem Alten Testament*. Freiburg in Breisgau: Herder Verlag, 2010.
———. "Eine kleine Theologie der Menschwürde: Ps 8 und seine Rezeption im Buch Ijob." In *Das Manna fällt auch heute noch: Beiträge zur Geschichte und Theologie des Alten, Ersten Testaments; Festschrift für Erich Zenger*, edited by Frank-Lothar Hossfeld and Ludger Schwienhorst-Schönberger, 244–72. Freiburg im Breisgau: Herder Verlag, 2004.
———. "Fleisch und Geist I." In *RGG*[4] 3 (2000): 155–56.
———. "Herz." In *HGANT*[2] 250–52.
———. "Körper." In *HGANT*[2] 280–83.
———. "Leben." In *HGANT*[2] 295–98.
———. "'Mögen sie fluchen—du wirst segnen' (Ps 109, 16): Gewalt in den Psalmen." *Wort und Antwort* 45 (2004): 184–88.
———. "Tod." In *HGANT*[2] 389–92.
———. "Würde." In *HGANT*[2] 426–27.
Fritz, Volkmar. *Das Buch Josua*. Tübingen: Mohr Siebeck, 1994.
Fuchs, Gisela. "Die Klage des Propheten: Beobachtungen zu den Konfessionen Jeremias im Vergleich mit den Klagen Hiobs (Erster Teil)." *Biblische Zeitschrift* 41 (1997): 212–28.
———. "'Du bist mir zum Trugbach geworden': Verwandte Motive in den Konfessionen Jeremias und den Klagen Hiobs (Zweiter Teil)." *Biblische Zeitschrift* 42, no. 1 (1998): 19–38.
———. *Mythos und Hiobdichtung: Aufnahme und Umdeutung altorientalischer Vorstellungen*. Stuttgart: W. Kohlhammer, 1993.

Fuchs, Ottmar. "Fluch und Klage als biblische Herausforderung: Zur spirituellen und sozialen Praxis der Christen." *Bibel und Kirche* 47 (1995): 201–8.

———. "Gott in Dunkelheit erahnen: Die biblische Verbindung von Lob und Klage." *Bibel und Kirche* 63 (2008): 22–27.

———. "Die Herausforderung Israels an die spirituelle und soziale Praxis der Christen." *Jahrbuch für biblische Theologie* 6 (1991): 89–113.

———. "Klage." In *NBL* 2:489–93.

———. *Die Klage als Gebet: Eine theologische Besinnung am Beispiel des Psalms 22.* Munich: Kösel, 1982.

———. "Klage: Eine vergessene Gebetsform." In *Im Angesicht des Todes: Ein interdisziplinäres Kompendium*, edited by Hansjakob Ullrich Becker, Bernhard Einig, and Peter Otto Ulrich, 939–1024. St. Ottilien: EOS Verlag, 1987.

———. "Sprachliche Begegnung mit Gott." *Katechetische Blätter* 104 (1979): 854–66.

Fuchs, Ottmar, and Bernd Janowski, eds. *Klage*. Jahrbuch für biblische Theologie 16. Neukirchen-Vluyn: Neukirchener Verlag, 2001.

Fuchs-Heinritz, Werner. *Todesbilder in der modernen Gesellschaft*. Frankfurt am Main: Suhrkamp, 1973.

Füglister, Notker. "Die Verwendung des Psalters zur Zeit Jesu: Der Psalter as Lehr- und Lebensbuch." *Bibel und Kirche* 47 (1992): 201–8.

———. "Die Verwendung und das Verständnis der Psalmen und des Psalters um die Zeitwende." In *Beiträge zur Psalmenforschung: Psalm 2 und 22*, edited by Josef Schreiner, 319–84. Würzburg: Echter Verlag, 1988.

Fuhs, Hans Ferdinand. "רָאָה." In *ThWAT* 7:225–66.

———. *Sehen und Schauen: Die Wurzel* ḥzh *im Alten Orient und im Alten Testament; Ein Beitrag zum prophetischen Offenbarungsempfang*. Würzburg: Echter Verlag, 1978.

Gadamer, Hans-Georg. "Die Erfahrung des Todes." In *Über die Verborgenheit der Gesundheit: Aufsätze und Vorträge*, 84–94. Frankfurt am Main: Suhrkamp, 1993.

———. *Wahrheit und Methode: Grundzüge einer philosophischen Hermeneutik*. Tübingen: Mohr Siebeck, 1990.

Gadamer, Hans-Georg, and Paul Vogler, eds. *Neue Anthropologie*. 7 vols. Munich: DTV; Stuttgart: Thieme, 1972–75.

Gamberoni, Johann. "חָסָה." In *ThWAT* 3:71–83.

Gamper, Arnold. *Gott als Richter in Mesopotamien und im Alten Testament: Zum Verständnis einer Gebetsbitte*. Innsbruch: Universitätsverlag Wagner, 1966.

García Martínez, Florentino. *The Dead Sea Scrolls Translated: The Qumran Texts in English.* Translated by Wilfred G. E. Watson. 2nd ed. Leiden: E. J. Brill; Grand Rapids: Wm. B. Eerdmans Publishing Co., 1996.

Gebauer, Gunter. *Anthropologie*. Leipzig: Reclam, 1998.

———. *Historische Anthropologie: Zum Problem der Humanwissenschaften heute, oder, Versuche einer Neubegründung*. Reinbek bei Hamburg: Rowohlt, 1989.

Geertz, Clifford. "Religion as a Cultural System." In *The Interpretation of Cultures*, 87–125. New York: Basic Books, 1973.

Gellner, Christoph. "'Geheiligt werde dein zugefrorener Name . . .': Moderne Psalmgedichte—spirituell gelesen." *Bibel und Kirche* 56 (2001): 46–51.

Gerleman, Gillis. "Der Sinnbereich 'fest-los(e)' im hebräischen." *Zeitschrift für die alttestamentliche Wissenschaft* 92, no. 3 (1980): 404–15.

Gerstenberger, Erhard S. *Der bittende Mensch: Bittritual und Klagelied des Einzelnen im Alten Testament*. Neukirchen-Vluyn: Neukirchener Verlag, 1980.

———. *Das dritte Buch Mose: Leviticus*. Göttingen: Vandenhoeck & Ruprecht, 1993.

———. "Enemies and Evildoers in the Psalms: A Challenge to Christian Preaching." *Horizons in Biblical Theology* 4–5 (1982–83): 61–77.

———. *Festschrift für Erhard S. Gerstenberger. See* Kessler, Rainer.
———. "Frau und Mann im Alten Testament." In *Frau und Mann*, edited by Erhard S. Gerstenberger and Wolfgang Schrage, 9–91. Stuttgart: W. Kohlhammer, 1980.
———. "'Höre mein Volk, lass mich reden!' (Ps 50, 7)." *Bibel und Kirche* 56 (2001): 21–25.
———. *Israel in der Perserzeit. 5. und 4. Jahrhundert v. Chr.* Stuttgart: W. Kohlhammer, 2005.
———. "Der klagende Mensch: Anmerkungen zu den Klagegattungen in Israel." In *Probleme biblischer Theologie: Gerhard von Rad zum 70. Geburtstag*, edited by Hans Walter Wolff, 64–72. Munich: Christian Kaiser, 1971.
———. "Krankheit." In *NBL* 2:542–44.
———. "Lebenslauf und Lebensphasen im Alten Testament: 'dass wir leben und nicht sterben' (1. Mose 42, 2)." *Der evangelische Erzieher* 40, no. 3 (1990): 254–65.
———. "Leiden im Alten Testament." In *Leiden*, edited by Erhard Gerstenberger and Wolfgang Schrage, 9–117. Stuttgart: W. Kohlhammer, 1977.
———. "מות." In *THAT* 1:893–97.
———. "Psalmen (Buch)." In *NBL* 3:209–13.
———. *Psalms, Part 1, with an Introduction to Cultic Poetry*. Grand Rapids: Wm. B. Eerdmans Publishing Co., 1988.
———. *Psalms, Part 2, and Lamentations*. Grand Rapids: Wm. B. Eerdmans Publishing Co., 2001.
———. "שְׁאוֹל." In *ThWAT* 2:837–41.
———. "Weibliche Spiritualität in Psalmen und Hauskult." In *Ein Gott allein? JHWH-Verehrung und biblischer Monotheismus im Kontext der israelitischen und altorientalischen Religionsgeschichte*, edited by Walter Dietrich and Martin A. Klopfenstein, 349–63. Göttingen: Vandenhoeck & Ruprecht, 1994.
Gertz, Jan Christian. "Die Passa-Massot-Ordnung im deuteronomischen Festkalender." In *Das Deuteronomium und seine Querbeziehungen*, edited by Timo Veijola, 56–80. Göttingen: Vandenhoeck & Ruprecht, 1996.
———. "Die Stellung des kleinen geschichtlichen Credos in der Redaktionsgeschichte von Deuteronomium und Pentateuch." In *Liebe und Gebot: Studien zum Deuteronomium; Festschrift zum 70. Geburtstag von Lothar Perlit*, edited by Reinhard Gregor Kratz and Hermann Spieckermann, 30–45. Göttingen: Vandenhoeck & Ruprecht, 2000.
———. "Der zerbrechliche und zugleich königliche Mensch: Anmerkungen zum Menschenbild des Alten Testaments." In *Theologie und Menschenbild: Beiträge zum interdisziplinären Gespräch*, edited by Frank Martin Brunn, 19–31. Leipzig: Evangelische Verlagsanstalt, 2007.
Gese, Hartmut. "Bemerkungen zum Vaterunser unter dem Gesichtspunkt alttestamentlicher Gebetsformen." In *Jesus Christus als die Mitte der Schrift: Studien zur Hermeneutik des Evangeliums; Festschrift für Otfried Hofius zum 70. Geburtstag*, edited by Christof Landmesser and Hans-Joachim Echstein, 405–37. Berlin: Walter de Gruyter, 1997.
———. "Der Dekalog als Ganzheit betrachtet." In *Vom Sinai zum Zion*, edited by Hartmut Gese, 63–80. Munich: Christian Kaiser, 1989.
———. "Die Frage des Weltbildes." In *Zur biblischen Theologie: Alttestamentliche Vorträge*, edited by Hartmut Gese, 202–22. Tübingen: J. C. B. Mohr, 1989.
———. "Die Frage nach dem Lebenssinn." In *Zur biblischen Theologie: Alttestamentliche Vorträge*, edited by Hartmut Gese, 170–88. Tübingen: J. C. B. Mohr, 1989.
———. "Die Herkunft des Herrenmahls." In *Zur biblischen Theologie: Alttestamentliche Vorträge*, edited by Hartmut Gese, 107–27. Tübingen: J. C. B. Mohr, 1989.

———. "Der Johannesprolog." In *Zur biblischen Theologie: Alttestamentliche Vorträge*, edited by Hartmut Gese, 152–201. Tübingen: J. C. B. Mohr, 1989.

———. "Psalm 22 und das Neue Testament: Der älteste Bericht vom Tode Jesu und die Entstehung des Herrenmahles." In *Vom Sinai zum Zion*, edited by Hartmut Gese, 180–201. Munich: Christian Kaiser, 1989.

———. "Psalm 50 und das alttestamentliche Gesetzesverständnis." In *Alttesament-liche Studien*, edited by Hartmut Gese, 149–69. Tübingen: Mohr, 1991.

———. "Der Tod im Alten Testament." In *Zur biblischen Theologie: Alttestamentliche Vorträge*, edited by Hartmut Gese, 31–54. Tübingen: J. C. B. Mohr (Paul Siebeck), 1989.

———. "Zum Herrenmahl." In *Zur biblischen Theologie: Alttestamentliche Vorträge*, 117–22. Tübingen: J. C. B. Mohr, 1989.

Gillmayr-Bucher, Susanne. "Body Images in the Psalms." *Journal for the Study of the Old Testament* 28 (2004): 301–26.

———. "Meine Zunge—ein Griffel eines geschickten Schreibers: Der kommunikative Aspekt der Körpermetaphern in den Psalmen." In van Hecke, *Metaphor in the Hebrew Bible*, 197–214.

———. *Die Psalmen im Spiegel der Lyrik Thomas Bernhards*. Stuttgart: Verlag Katholisches Bibelwerk, 2002.

———. "Rauchende Nase, bebendes Herz: Gefühle zur Sprache bringen." *Bibel und Kirche* 67 (2012): 21–25.

———. "Wenn die Dichter verstummen: Das Schweigen in den Psalmen." *Theologie und Glaube* 93 (2003): 316–32.

Gnilka, Joachim. *Das Evangelium nach Markus (Mk 8, 27–16, 20)*. Zurich: Benziger, 1979.

Godelier, Maurice. *Das Rätsel der Gabe: Geld, Geschenke, heilige Objekte*. Munich: C. H. Beck, 1999.

Görg, Manfred. "Auferstehung." In *NBL* 1:199–202.

———. "'Aus der Tiefe' und 'Halleluja': Kontroverse Bildsprache in der Psalmen." *Religionsunterricht an höheren Schulen* 36 (1993): 149–53.

———. "Begräbnis." In *NBL* 1:262–64.

———. "Bildsprache." In *NBL* 1:298–99.

———. "גָּזַר." In *ThWAT* 1:1001–4.

———. *Ein Haus im Totenreich: Jenseitsvorstellungen in Israel und Ägypten*. Düsseldorf: Patmos Verlag, 1998.

———. "Ge-Ben-Hinnom." In *NBL* 1:738–39.

———. "Gegenwart Gottes." In *NBL* 1:758–59.

———. *Der un-heile Gott: Die Bibel im Bann der Gewalt*. Düsseldorf: Patmos, 1995.

Görner, Rüdiger. *Unerhörte Klagen: Deutsche Elegien des 20. Jahrhunderts*. Frankfurt am Main: Insel Verlag, 2000.

Graf, Fritz. "Jenseitsvorstellungen." In *Der neue Pauly* [*DNP*]: *Enzyklopädie der Antike*, edited by Hubert Cancik, Helmuth Schneider, and August Friedrich von Pauly, 5:897–99. Stuttgart: J. B. Metzler, 1998.

Grapow, Hermann. *Die bildlichen Ausdrücke des Ägyptischen: Vom Denken und Dichten einer altorientalischen Sprache*. Leipzig: J. C. Hinrichs, 1924. Facsimile, Darmstadt: Wissenschaftliche Buchgesellschaft, 1983.

Greiner, Bernhard, Barbara Thums, Wolfgang Vitzthum, and Julia Kertscher, eds. *Recht und Literatur: Interdisziplinäre Bezüge*. Heidelberg: Winter, 2010.

Gressmann, Hugo. *Altorientalische Bilder zum Alten Testament*. 2nd ed. Berlin, Leipzig: Walter de Gruyter, 1927.

Grimm, Markus. *"Dies Leben ist der Tod": Vergänglichkeit in den Reden Ijobs; Entwurf einer Textsemantik*. St. Ottilien: EOS Verlag, 1998.

———. "Menschen mit und ohne Geld: Wovon spricht Ps 49?" *Biblische Notizen*, no. 96 (1999): 38–55.

Grohmann, Marianne. "Ambivalent Images of Birth in Psalm 7, 15." *Vetus Testamentum* 55 (2005): 439–49.

———. "Der Anfang des Lebens: Anthropologische Aspekte der Rede von Geburt im Alten Testament." In Janowski, Liess, and Zaft, *Der Mensch*, 365–99.

———. "'Du hast mich aus meiner Mutter Leib gezogen': Geburt in Psalm 22." In *"Du hast mich aus meiner Mutter Leib gezogen": Beiträge zur Geburt im Alten Testament*, edited by Detlef Dieckmann and Dorothea Erbele-Küster, 73–97. Neukirchen-Vluyn: Neukirchener Verlag, 2006.

———. *Fruchtbarkeit und Geburt in den Psalmen*. Tübingen: Mohr Siebeck, 2007.

Groneberg, Brigitte. *Zu den mesopotamischen Unterweltsvorstellungen: Das Jenseits als Fortsetzung des Diesseits*. Berlin: Akademie Verlag, 1990.

Gross, Walter, ed. *Bibelübersetzung heute: Geschichtliche Entwicklungen und aktuelle Herausforderungen; Stuttgarter Symposion 2000, in Memoriam Siegfried Meurer*. Stuttgart: Deutsche Bibelgesellschaft, 2001.

———. *Doppelt besetztes Vorfeld: Syntaktische, pragmatische und übersetzungstechnische Studien aum Althebräischen Verbalsatz*. Berlin and New York: Walter de Gruyter, 2001.

———. "Ein Schwerkranker betet: Psalm 88 als Paradigma." In *Angesichts des Leids an Gott Glauben? Zur Theologie der Klage*, edited by Gotthard Fuchs, 101–18. Frankfurt am Main: Verlag J. Knecht, 1996.

———. "Gott als Feind des einzelnen? Psalm 88." In *Studien zur Priesterschrift und zu alttestamentlichen Gottesbildern*, 159–71. Stuttgart: Verlag Katholisches Bibelwerk, 1999.

———. "Otto Rössler und die Diskussion um das althebräische Verbalsystem." *Biblische Notizen*, no. 18 (1982): 28–78.

———. "Das verborgene Gesicht Gottes: Eine alttestamentliche Grunderfahrung und die heutige religiöse Krise." In *Studien zur Priesterschrift und zu alttestamentlichen Gottesbildern*, edited by Walter Gross, 185–97. Stuttgart: Verlag Katholisches Bibelwerk, 1999.

———. "Zorn Gottes: Ein biblisches Theologumenon." In *Studien zur Priesterschrift und zu alttestamentlichen Gottesbildern*, edited by Walter Gross, 199–238. Stuttgart: Verlag Katholisches Bibelwerk, 1999.

———. *Zukunft für Israel: Alttestamentliche Bundeskonzepte und die aktuelle Debatte um den Neuen Bund*. Stuttgart: Verlag Katholisches Bibelwerk, 1998.

Gruber, Margareta, and Andreas Michel. "Individualität." *SWB* 270–74.

———. "Körper." *SWB* 307–12.

Gruber, Mayer I. *Aspects of Nonverbal Communication in the Ancient Near East*. Rome: Pontifical Biblical Institute Press, 1980.

Grund, Alexandra Stephanie. "'Aus der Schönheit Vollendung strahlt Gott auf' (Ps 50, 2): Bemerkungen zur Wahrnehmung des Schönen in den Psalmen." In *"Wie schön sind deine Zelte, Jakob!": Beiträge zur Ästhetik des Alten Testaments*, edited by Alexandra Grund, 100–129. Neukirchen-Vluyn: Neukirchener Verlag, 2003.

———. *"Der Himmel erzählt die Herrlichkeit Gottes": Psalm 19 im Kontext der nachexilischen Toraweisheit*. Diss., Universität Tübingen, 2002. Reprint, Neukirchen-Vluyn: Neukirchener Verlag, 2004.

———. "'Schmähungen der dich Schmähenden sind auf mich gefallen': Kulturanthropologische und sozialpsychologische Aspekte von Ehre und Scham in Ps 69." *Evangelische Theologie* 72 (2012): 174–93.

———. "'. . . So sollst du geben Auge für Auge, Zahn für Zahn': Vergeltung als Prinzip der Strafe im Alten Testament?" In Sünker and Berner, *Vergeltung ohne Ende?*, 39–81.

———. "Tun-Ergehens-Zusammenhang." *RGG*[4] 8 (2005): 654–56.

Grünwaldt, Klaus. *Auge um Auge, Zahn um Zahn? Das Recht im Alten Testament.* Mainz: Matthias Grünewald Verlag, 2002.

———. "Loblied und Laienlyrik: Zum exegetischen Verständnis der Psalmen." *Der evangelische Erzieher* 47 (1995): 12–27.

Gryphius, Andreas. *Gedichte: Eine Auswahl.* Stuttgart: Reclam, 1996.

Guglielmi, Waltraud. "Zur Bedeutung von Symbolen der persönlichen Frömmigkeit: Die verschiedenfarbigen Ohren und das Ka-Zeichen." *Zeitschrift für ägyptische Sprache und Altertumskunde* 118 (1991): 116–27.

Guglielmi, Waltraud, and Johanna Dittmar. "Anrufungen der persönlichen Frömmigkeit auf Gans- und Widder-Darstellungen des Amun." In *Gegengabe: Festschrift für Emma Brunner-Traut,* edited by Ingrid Gamer-Wallert and Wolfgang Helck, 119–42. Tübingen: Attempto Verlag, 1992.

Gunkel, Hermann. *Die Psalmen.* 6th ed. Göttingen: Vandenhoeck & Ruprecht, 1986.

Gunkel, Hermann, and Joachim Begrich. *Introduction to Psalms: The Genres of the Religious Lyric of Israel.* Translated by James D. Nogalski. Macon, GA: Mercer University Press, 1985.

Gut, Theodor. *Der Schrei der Gottverlassenheit: Fragen an die Theologie.* Zurich: Theologischer Verlag, 1994.

Gzella, Holger. *Lebenszeit und Ewigkeit: Studien zur Eschatologie und Anthropologie des Septuaginta-Psalters.* Berlin: Philo, 2002.

Ha, Kyung-Taek. *Frage und Antwort: Studien zu Hiob 3 im Kontext des Hiobbuches.* Freiburg im Breisgau: Herder Verlag, 2005.

Haag, Ernst. "Psalm 88." In *Freude an der Weisung des Herrn: Beiträge zur Theologie der Psalmen; Festgabe zum 70. Geburtstag von Heinrich Gross,* edited by Ernst Haag and Frank-Lothar Hossfeld, 149–70. Stuttgart: Verlag Katholisches Bibelwerk, 1986.

———. "Seele IV." In *Lexikon für Theologie und Kirche,* edited by Michael Buchberger and Walter Kasper, 9:373–75. 3rd ed. Freiburg im Breisgau: Herder Verlag, 2000.

———. "Seele und Unsterblichkeit in biblischer Sicht." In *Seele: Problembegriff christlicher Eschatologie,* edited by Richard Friedli and Wilhelm Breuning, 31–93. Freiburg im Breisgau: Herder Verlag, 1986.

———, Ernst Lohfink, ed. *Gewalt und Gewaltlosigkeit im Alten Testament.* Freiburg im Breisgau: Herder Verlag, 1983.

Habermas, Jürgen. *Glauben und Wissen: Friedenspreis des Deutschen Buchhandels 2001.* Frankfurt am Main: Suhrkamp 2001.

———. *Die Zukunft der menschlichen Natur: Auf dem Weg zu einer liberalen Eugenik?* Frankfurt am Main: Suhrkamp 2001.

Habermas, Jürgen, and Angela Krebs. "Die Herausforderung der ökologischen Ethik für eine anthropozentrisch ansetzende Konzeption." In *Naturethik: Grundtexte der gegenwärtigen Tier- und ökoethischen Diskussion,* 92–99. Frankfurt am Main: Suhrkamp, 1997.

Haeffner, Gerd. *Wege in die Freiheit: Philosophische Meditationen über das Menschein.* Stuttgart: W. Kohlhammer, 2006.

Hager, Fritz-Peter, H. Huhn, and Andreas Speer. "Selbsterkenntnis." In *HWP* 9:406–40.

Hahn, Alois, and Rüdiger Jacob. "Der Körper als soziales Bedeutungssystem." In *Der Mensch, das Medium der Gesellschaft?,* edited by Rüdiger Jacob, Peter Fuchs, and Andreas Göbel, 146–88. Frankfurt am Main: Suhrkamp, 1994.

Hahn, Eberhard. "Vergeltung." In *CBL* 2:1408–9.

Halfwassen, Jens. "Die Seele und ihr Verhältnis zum Geist bei Plotin." In Düsing and Klein, *Geist und Psyche,* 65–80.

Hampe, Michael. "Anthropologie." In *RGG*[4] 1 (1998): 521ff.

Harasta, Eva. *Lob und Bitte: Eine systematisch-theologische Untersuchung über das Gebet*. Neukirchen-Vluyn: Neukirchener Verlag, 2005.

———, ed. *Mit Gott klagen: Eine theologische Diskussion; Mit Beiträgen von Jonas Bauer*. Neukirchen-Vluyn: Neukirchener Verlag, 2008.

Hardmeier, Christof. "'Denn im Tod ist kein Gedenken an dich . . .' (Psalm 6:6): Der Tod des Menschen—Gottes Tod?" *Evangelische Theologie* 48, no. 4 (1988): 292–311.

———. "Der Lobpreis des verborgenen Gottes in Psalm 13: Paradigma einer performativen Theologie der Klagepsalmen." In Berlejung and Heckl, *Ex oriente Lux*, 227–46.

———. "'Stark wie der Tod ist die Liebe': Der Mensch und sein Tod in den Schriften des Alten Testaments." In *Der Mensch und sein Tod: Grundsätze der ärztlichen Sterbebegleitung*, edited by Michael Herbst, 209–27. Frankfurt and New York: Peter Lang, 2001.

———. "Systematische Elemente der Theo-logie in der hebräischen Bibel: Das Loben Gottes—ein Kristallisationsmoment biblischer Theo-logie." *Jahrbuch für biblische Theologie* 10 (1995): 111–27.

Härle, Wilfried. "Der Mensch Gottes: Die öffentliche Orientierungsleistung des christlichen Menschenverständnisses." In *Menschenbild und Menschenwürde*, edited by Eilert Herms, 529–43. Gütersloh: Christian Kaiser, Gütersloher Verlagshaus, 2001.

Harnack, Adolf von. *Marcion, das Evangelium vom fremden Gott: Eine Monographie zur Geschichte der Grundlegung der katholischen Kirche*. Darmstadt: Wissenschaftliche Buchgesellschaft, 1985.

Hartenstein, Friedhelm. "Das 'Angesicht JHWHs' in Exodus 32–34." In *Gottes Volk am Sinai: Untersuchungen zu Ex 32–34 und Dtn 9–10*, edited by Matthias Köckert and Erhard Blum, 157–83. Gütersloh: Christian Kaiser / Gütersloher Verlagshaus, 2001.

———. *Das Angesicht JHWHs: Studien zu seinem höfischen und kultischen Bedeutungshintergrund in den Psalmen und in Exodus 32–34*. Tübingen: Mohr Siebeck, 2008.

———. "'Damit nicht spricht mein Feind: Ich habe ihn überwältigt!' (Psalm 13, 5): Zur theologischen Funktion der Feindbilder in den Psalmen Israels." In *Feindschaft: Theologische und philosophische Perspektiven*, edited by Michael Moxter and Markus Firchow, 19–40. Leipzig: Evangelische Verlagsanstalt, 2012.

———. "Kulturwissenschaften und Altes Testament: Themen und Perspektiven." *Verkündigung und Forschung* 54 (2009): 31–42.

———. "'Schaffe mir Recht, JHWH!' (Psalm 7, 9): Zum theologischen und anthropologischen Profil der Teilkomposition Psalm 3–14." In *The Composition of the Book of Psalms*, edited by Erich Zenger, 229–58. Leuven and Walpole, MA: Peeters, 2010.

———. "Die unvergleichliche Gestalt JHWHs: Israels Geschichte mit den Bildern im Licht von Dtn 4, 1–40." In *Die Sichtbarkeit des Unsichtbaren: Zur Korrelation von Text und Bild im Wirkungskreis der Bibel (Tübinger Symposion 1999)*, edited by Bernd Janowski and Nino M. Zchomelidze, 49–77. Stuttgart: Deutsche Bibelgesellschaft, 2003.

———. *Die Unzugänglichkeit Gottes im Heiligtum: Jesaja 6 und der Wohnort JHWHs in der Jerusalemer Kulttradition*. Neukirchen-Vluyn: Neukirchener Verlag, 1997.

———. "Vom Sehen und Schauen Gottes: Überlegungen zu einer theologischen Ästhetik aus der Sicht des Alten Testaments." In *Ästhetik*, edited by Elisabeth Gräb-Schmidt and Reiner Preul, 15–37. Leipzig: Evangelische Verlagsanstalt, 2010.

———. "Weltbild und Bilderverbot." In *Die Welt als Bild: Interdisziplinäre Beiträge zur Visualität von Weltbildern*, edited by Christoph Markschies and Johannes Zachhuber, 15–37. Berlin and New York: Walter de Gruyter, 2008.

———. "Wolkendunkel und Himmelsfeste: Zur Genese und Kosmologie der Vorstellung des himmlischen Heiligtums JHWHs." In *Das biblische Weltbild und seine Altorientalischen Kontexte*, edited by Bernd Janowski and Beate Ego, 125–79. Tübingen: Mohr Siebeck, 2001.

Hartenstein, Friedhelm, and Bernd Janowski. *Psalmen*. Vol. 15/1 of Biblischer Kommentar, Altes Testament. Neukirchen-Vluyn: Neukirchener Verlag, 2012.

Hartung, Gerald. *Philosophische Anthropologie*. Stuttgart: Reclam, 2008.

Hasenfratz, Hans-Peter. *Die Seele: Einführung in ein religiöses Grundphänomen (mit Ausgewählten Texten)*. Zurich: Theologischer Verlag, 1986.

———. "Tod und Leben: Der unselige Tod und der soziale Tod." In J. Assmann and Trauzettel, *Tod, Jenseits*, 223–29.

———. *Die toten Lebenden: Eine Religionsphänomenologische Studie zum sozialen Tod in Archaischen Gesellschaften: Zugleich ein kritischer Beitrag zur Sogenannten Strafopfertheorie*. Leiden: E. J. Brill, 1982.

———. "Zum sozialen Tod in archaischen Gesellschaften." *Saeculum* 34 (1983): 126–37.

Hastedt, Heiner. *Das Leib-Seele-Problem: Zwischen Naturwissenschaft des Geistes und kultureller Eindimensionalität*. Frankfurt am Main: Suhrkamp, 1988.

Hauge, Martin Ravndal. *Between Sheol and Temple: Motif Structure and Function in the I-Psalms*. Sheffield, UK: Sheffield Academic Press, 1995.

Häusl, Maria. "Verkörpertes Leben: Körperbilder und -konzepte im Alten Testament." *Bibel und Kirche* 67 (2012): 10–15.

———. "Zuraten, zurechtweisen und sich zurückhalten: Sprüche zur Sprache aus der älteren Weisheit (Spr 10–22 und 25–29)." *Biblische Zeitschrift* 49 (2005): 26–45.

Häussling, Angelun Albert. "Die Psalmen des Alten Testaments in der Liturgie des Neuen Bundes." In *Christologie der Liturgie: Der Gottesdienst der Kirche—Christusbekenntnis und Sinaibund*, edited by Klemens Richter and Benedikt Kranemann, 87–102. Freiburg im Breisgau: Herder Verlag, 1995.

Haverkamp, Anselm. *Theorie der Metapher*. Darmstadt: Wissenschaftliche Buchgesellschaft, 1996.

Healey, John F., and Herbert Niehr. "Das Land ohne Wiederkehr: Die Unterwelt im antiken Ugarit und im Alten Testament." *Theologische Quartalschrift* 177, no. 2 (1997): 94–104.

Hecke, Pierre Jacques Paul van, ed. *Metaphor in the Hebrew Bible*. Leuven: Leuven University Press, 2005.

———. "Pastoral Metaphors in the Hebrew Bible and in Its Ancient Near Eastern Context." In *The Old Testament in Its World*, edited by Robert P. Gordon and Johannes C. de Moor, 200–217. Leiden and New York: E. J. Brill, 2005.

Hecke, Pierre Jacques Paul van, and Antje Labahn, eds. *Metaphors in the Psalms*. Leuven and Walpole, MA: Peeters, 2010.

Hedwig-Jahnow-Forschungsprojekt and Ulrike Bail, eds. *Körperkonzepte im Ersten Testament: Aspekte einer Feministischen Anthropologie*. Stuttgart: W. Kohlhammer, 2003.

Helck, Wolfgang, and Eberhard Otto, eds. *Lexikon der Ägyptologie*. Wiesbaden: O. Harrassowitz, 1975–92.

Hell, Heinrich M., Wolfgang Wiesmüller, and Heinrich M. Schmidinger. "Die Psalmen: Rezeption biblischer Lyrik in Gedichten." In *Die Bibel in der deutschsprachigen Literatur des 20. Jahrhunderts*, 158–204. Mainz: Matthias-Grünewald-Verlag, 1999.

Hennig, Gerhard. "Wie redet die Bibel von der Seelsorge?" *Theologische Beiträge* 32 (2001): 181–98.

Henrich, Dieter. "Gedanken zur Dankbarkeit." In *Bewusstes Leben: Untersuchungen zum Verhältnis von Subjektivität und Metaphysik*, edited by Dieter Henrich, 152–93. Stuttgart: Reclam, 1999.

Herder, Johann Gottfried. *The Spirit of Hebrew Poetry*. Translated by James Marsh. 2 vols. Burlington, VT: Edward Smith, 1833.

———. "Vom Geist der ebräischen Poesie." 1782. In *Johann Gottfried Herder: Schriften zum Alten Testament*, 661–1309. Frankfurt am Main: Deutscher Klassiker Verlag, 1993.

Hermisson, Hans-Jürgen. *Alttestamentliche Theologie und Religionsgeschichte Israels.* Leipzig: Evangelische Verlagsanstalt, 2000.

———. "Glauben." In *Glauben*, edited by Hans-Jürgen Hermisson and Eduard Lohse. Stuttgart: W. Kohlhammer, 1978.

———. "Jahwehs und Jeremias Rechtstreit: Zum Thema der Konfessionen Jeremias." In *Studien zu Prophetie und Weisheit: Gesammelte Aufsätze*, edited by Jörg Barthel, 5–36. Tübingen: Mohr Siebeck, 1998.

———. *Sprache und Ritus im altisraelitischen Kult: Zur "Spiritualisierung" der Kultbegriffe im Alten Testament.* Neukirchen-Vluyn: Neukirchener Verlag des Erziehungsvereins, 1965.

———. "Der verborgene Gott im Buch Jesaja." In *Studien zu Prophetie und Weisheit: Gesammelte Aufsätze*, edited by Jörg Barthel, 105–16. Tübingen: Mohr Siebeck, 1998.

———. "Zur Schöpfungestheologie der Weisheit." In *Studien zu Prophetie und Weisheit: Gesammelte Aufsätze*, 269–85. Tübingen: Mohr Siebeck, 1998.

Herms, Eilert, ed. *Leben: Verständnis, Wissenschaft, Technik; Kongreßband des XI. Europäischen Kongresses für Theologie, 15.–19. September 2002 in Zürich.* Gütersloh: Gütersloher Verlagshaus, 2005.

Herrmann, Steffen K., Sybille Krämer, and Hannes Kuch, eds. *Verletzende Worte: Die Grammatik sprachlicher Mißachtung.* Bielefeld: Transcript Verlag, 2007.

Herrmann, Wolfram. "Die Rede von göttlichem Schlafen im Alten Testament." *Ugarit-Forschungen* 36 (2004): 185–93.

———. "תודה: Ein Kapitel alttestamentlicher Theologie." *Zeitschrift für die alttestamentliche Wissenschaft* 119 (2007): 90–99.

Herzer, Jens. "Freund und Feind: Beobachtungen zum alttestamentlich-frühjüdischen Hintergrund und zum impliziten Handlungsmodell der Gethsemane-Perikope Mk 14, 32–42." *Leqach: Mitteilungen und Beiträge* 1 (2001): 107–36.

Heschel, Abraham Joshua. *Der Mensch fragt nach Gott: Untersuchungen zum Gebet und zur Symbolik.* Neukirchen-Vluyn: Neukirchener Verlag, 1982.

Hieke, Thomas. "'Er verschlingt den Tod für immer' (Jes 25,8a): Eine unerfüllte Verheißung im Alten und Neuen Testament." *Biblische Zeitschrift* 50 (2006): 31–50.

———. "Orientierung—Desorientierung—Neuorientierung: Gebetsprozesse im Alten Testament anhand der Psalmen 103; 13 und 30." In *Sophia—Paideia: Sapienza e eduzione (Sir 1, 27); Miscellanea di studi offerti in onore del prof. Don Mario Cimosa*, edited by Gillian Bonney and Rafael Vicent, 259–81. Rome: Libreria Ateneo Salesiano, 2012.

———. "Psalm 7." In Diller, *Syntax, Sprechaktanalyse und Metaphorik*, 37–60.

———. *Psalm 80—Praxis eines Methodenprogramms: Eine Literaturwissenschaftliche Untersuchung mit einem gattungskritischen Beitrag zum Klagelied des Volkes.* St. Ottilien: EOS, 1997.

———. "'Schon zähle ich zu denen, die in die Grube fahren . . .' (Ps 88, 5): Einige Sichtweisen des Todes im Alten Testament." *Lebendiges Zeugnis* 57 (2002): 164–77.

———. *Tod—Ende oder Anfang? Was die Bibel sagt.* Stuttgart: Verlag Katholisches Bibelwerk, 2005.

Hilgert, Marcus, and Michael Wink, eds. *Menschenbilder: Darstellungen des Humanen in der Wissenschaft.* Heidelberg: Springer Verlag, 2012.

Hodel-Hoenes, Sigrid. "Betrachtungen zum Dank im alten Ägypten." In *Festschrift Jürgen von Beckerath: Zum 70. Geburtstag am 19. Februar 1990*, edited by Bettina Schmitz and Arne Eggebrecht, 119–38. Hildesheim: Gerstenberg, 1990.

Höffe, Otfried. "Ehre." In *Lexikon der Ethik*, edited by Otfried Höffe, 50–51. Munich: C. H. Beck, 1997.

———. "Gerechtigkeit." In *Lexikon der Ethik*, edited by Otfried Höffe, 91–95. Munich: C. H. Beck, 1997.

———. *Gerechtigkeit: Eine philosophische Einführung*. Munich: C. H. Beck, 2001.

———. "Glück." In *Lexikon der Ethik*, edited by Otfried Höffe, 110–13. Munich: C. H. Beck, 1997.

Hoheisel, Karl, Hubert Cancik, Burkhard Gladigow, and Matthias Samuel Laubscher. "Jenseits." In *Handbuch religionswissenschaftlicher Grundbegriffe*, 3:318–26. Stuttgart: W. Kohlhammer, 1993.

Hölscher, Andreas, ed. *Opfer*. Themed volume of *Bibel und Kirche* 64, no. 3. Stuttgart: Verlag Katholisches Bibelwerk, 2009.

Honneth, Axel. *Kampf um Anerkennung: Zur moralischen Grammatik sozialer Konflikte*. Frankfurt am Main: Suhrkamp, 1994. Translated as *The Struggle for Recognition: The Moral Grammar of Social Conflicts*. Cambridge: Polity Press, 1995.

Hörisch, Jochen. "Die Poesie der Medien: Die Niemandsrose." In *Theopoesie: Theologie und Poesie in hermeneutischer Sicht*, edited by Henning Schröer, Gotthard Fermor, and Harald Schroeter, 103–12. Rheinbach: CMZ-Verlag, 1998.

Hornung, Erik. "Chaotische Bereiche in der geordneten Welt." *Zeitschrift für Ägyptische Sprache* 81 (1956): 28–32.

———. *Der Eine und die Vielen: Ägyptische Gottesvorstellungen*. Darmstadt: Wissenschaftliche Buchgesellschaft, 1993.

———. *Geist der Pharaonenzeit*. Zurich: Artemis Verlag, 1989.

———. "Schwarze Löcher von innen betrachtet: Die ägyptische Hölle." *Eranos Jahrbuch*, NF 2 (1994): 227–62.

———. *Das Totenbuch der Ägypter*. Zurich: Artemis Verlag, 1979.

———. "Von zweierlei Grenzen im alten Ägypten." *Eranos Jahrbuch* 49 (1980): 393–427.

Hossenfelder, Malte. *Antike Glückslehren: Kynismus und Kyrenaismus, Stoa, Epikureismus und Skepsis; Quellen in deutscher Übersetzung mit Einführungen*. Stuttgart: A. Kröner, 1998.

Hossfeld, Frank-Lothar. "Die Aufwertung Hannas durch ihren Lobgesang 1 Sam 2, 1–10." In *"Gott bin ich, kein Mann": Beiträge zur Hermeneutik der biblischen Gottesrede; Festschrift für Helen Schüngel-Straumann zum 65. Geburtstag*, edited by Ilona Riedel-Spangenberger and Erich Zenger, 246–58. Paderborn: Schöningh, 2006.

———. "David als exemplarischer Mensch: Literarische Biographie und Anthropologie am Beispiel Davids." In *Biblische Anthropologie: Neue Einsichten aus dem Alten Testament*, edited by Christian Frevel, 243–55. Freiburg in Breisgau: Herder Verlag, 2010.

———. "Festtraditionen im Psalter." In *Festtraditionen in Israel und im Alten Orient*, edited by Erhard Blum and Rüdiger Lux, 157–73. Gütersloh: Gütersloher Verlagshaus, 2006.

———. "Das göttliche Strafgericht in Feind- und Fluchpsalmen: Der Psalmenbeter zwischen eigener Ohnmacht und dem Schrei nach göttlicher Parteilichkeit." In *Krieg und Christentum: Religiöse Gewalttheorien in der Kriegserfahrung des Westens*, edited by Andreas Holzem, 128–36. Paderborn: Schöningh, 2009.

———. "Lob I." In *RGG*[4] 5 (2002): 476–77.

———. "Die Metaphorisierung der Beziehung Israels zum Land im Frühjudentum und im Christentum." In *Zion—Ort der Begegnung: Festschrift für Laurentius Klein zur Vollendung des 65. Lebensjahres*, edited by Ferdinand Hahn, Frank-Lothar Hossfeld, Hans Jorissen, and Angelika Neuwirth, 19–33. Bodenheim: Athenäum, 1993.

———. "Musik und Gebet im Alten Testament." In *Musik im Raum der Kirche: Fragen und Perspektiven; Ein ökumenisches Handbuch zur Kirchenmusik*, edited by Winfried Böing and Wolfgang Bretschneider, 44–50. Stuttgart: Carus-Verlag, 2007.

———. "Rechtfertigung." In *Lexikon für Theologie und Kirche*, edited by Michael Buchberger and Walter Kasper, 8:882–84. 3rd ed. Freiburg im Breisgau: Herder Verlag, 1999.

———. "Von der Klage zum Lob: Die Dynamik des Gebets in den Psalmen." *Bibel und Kirche* 56 (2001): 16–20.

Hossfeld, Frank-Lothar, and Erich Zenger. *Die Psalmen*. Vol. 1, *Psalm 1–50*. Vol. 2, *Psalm 51–100*. Vol. 3, *Psalm 101–150*. Die Neue Echter Bibel. Würzburg: Echter Verlag, 1993, 2002, 2012.

———. *Psalmen 1–50* (2004). *Psalmen 51–100* (2000). *Psalmen 101–150* (2008). Herders theologischer Kommentar zum Alten Testament. Freiburg im Breisgau: Herder Verlag, 2000–2008.

———. "'Selig, wer auf die Armen achtet' (Ps 41, 2): Beobachtungen zur Gottesvolk-Theologie des ersten Davidpsalters." *Jahrbuch für biblische Theologie* 7 (1992): 21–50.

Houtman, Cees. *Der Himmel im Alten Testament: Israels Weltbild und Weltanschauung*. Leiden and New York: E. J. Brill, 1993.

———. "Hölle." In *RGG*[4] 3 (2000): 1846–47.

Höver-Johag, I. "טוֹב." In *ThWAT* 3:315–39.

Hugger, Pirmin. *Jahwe meine Zuflucht: Gestalt und Theologie des 91. Psalms*. Münsterschwarzach: Vier-Türme, 1971.

———. *Die Kunst des Psalmenbetens*. Münsterschwarzach: Vier-Türme-Verlag, 2006.

Human, Dirk. "Psalm 82: God Presides in a Deflated Pantheon to Remain the Sole Just Ruler." In *"From Ebla to Stellenbosch": Syro-Palestinian Religions and the Hebrew Bible*, edited by Izak Cornelius and Louis Jonker, 154–68. Wiesbaden: O. Harrassowitz, 2008.

Hunziker-Rodewald, Regine. *Hirt und Herde: Ein Beitrag zum alttestamentlichen Gottesverständnis*. Stuttgart: W. Kohlhammer, 2001.

Hutter, Manfred. "Jenseitsvorstellungen." In *RGG*[4] 4 (2001): 404–6.

———. *Religionen in der Umwelt des Alten Testaments*. Stuttgart: W. Kohlhammer, 1996.

Illman, Karl-Johan. *Old Testament Formulas about Death*. Åbo: Åbo Akademi Forskningsinstitut, 1979.

Irsigler, Hubert. *Einführung in das biblische Hebräisch*. St. Ottilien: EOS Verlag, 1978.

———. "Die Frage nach dem Menschen in Psalm 8: Zu Bedeutung und Horizont eines kontroversen Menschenbildes im Alten Testament." In *Vom Adamssohn zum Immanuel: Gastvorträge Pretoria 1996*, edited by Hubert Irsigler, 1–48. St. Ottilien: EOS Verlag, 1997.

———. "Psalm 22: Endgestalt, Bedeutung und Funktion." In *Beiträge zur Psalmenforschung*, edited by Josef Schreiner, 193–237. Würzburg: Echter Verlag, 1988.

———. *Psalm 73: Monolog eines Weisen: Text, Programm, Struktur*. St. Ottilien: EOS Verlag, 1984.

———. "Psalm 90: Der vergängliche Mensch vor dem ewigen Gott." In *Vom Adamssohn zum Immanuel: Gastvorträge Pretoria 1996*, 49–69. St. Ottilien: EOS Verlag, 1997.

———. "Psalm-Rede als Handlungs-, Wirk- und Aussageprozess: Sprechaktanalyse und Psalmeninterpretation am Beispiel von Psalm 13." In *Neue Wege der Psalmenforschung: Für Walter Beyerlin*, edited by Klaus Seybold and Erich Zenger, 63–104. Freiburg im Breisgau: Herder Verlag, 1994.

———. "Die Suche nach Gerechtigkeit in den Psalmen 37, 49 und 73." In *Vom Adamssohn zum Immanuel: Gastvorträge Pretoria 1996*, edited by Hubert Irsigler, 71–100. St. Ottilien: EOS Verlag, 1997.

———. "Zur Interdependenz von Gottes- und Menschenbildern im Kontext alttestamentlicher Anthropologie." In *Biblische Anthropologie: Neue Einsichten aus dem Alten Testament*, edited by Christian Frevel, 350–89. Freiburg in Breisgau, Herder Verlag, 2010.

Ishikawa, Ritsu. *Der Hymnus im Alten Testament und seine kritische Funktion*. Diss., Universität Munich, 1995.

Jacob, Edmond. "Die Anthropologie des Alten Testaments." In *Theologisches Wörterbuch zum Neuen Testament*, edited by Gerhard Kittel, 9:614–29. Stuttgart: W. Kohlhammer, 1973.

Jaeger, Friedrich, and Jürgen Straub, eds. *Was ist der Mensch, was Geschichte? Annäherungen an eine kulturwissenschaftliche Anthropologie; Jörn Rüsen zum 65. Geburtstag*. Bielefeld: Transcript, 2005.

Janowski, Bernd. "Anerkennung und Gegenseitigkeit: Zum konstellativen Personbegriff des Alten Testaments." In Janowski, Liess, and Zaft, *Der Mensch*, 181–211.

———. "Angesicht/Schauen Gottes." In *HGANT*[2] 89–90.

———. "Die Antwort Israels: Theologische Einführung in die Psalmen." *Bibel und Kirche* 56 (2001): 2–7.

———. "Auf dem Weg zur Buchreligion: Transformationen des Kultischen im Psalter." In *Trägerkreise in den Psalmen*, edited by J. Bremer, F.-L. Hossfeld, and T. M. Steiner, 2013.

———. "Der barmherzige Richter: Zur Einheit von Gerechtigkeit und Barmherzigkeit im Gottesbild des Alten Orients und des Alten Testaments." In *Drama der Barmherzigkeit Gottes: Studien zur biblischen Gottesrede und ihrer Wirkungsgeschichte in Judentum und Christentum*, edited by Ruth Scoralick, 33–91. Stuttgart: W. Kohlhammer, 2000.

———. "Das biblische Weltbild: Eine methodologische Skizze." In *Das biblische Weltbild und seine altorientalischen Kontexte*, edited by Bernd Janowski and Beate Ego, 3–26. Tübingen: Mohr Siebeck, 2001.

———. "Das Buch der unverfälschten Spiritualität: Zum neuen Psalmenkommentar von F.-L. Hossfeld und E. Zenger." *Biblische Zeitschrift* 47 (2003): 43–65.

———. "Dankbarkeit: Ein anthropologischer Grundbegriff im Spiegel der Toda-Psalmen." In *Ritual und Poesie: Formen und Orte religiöser Dichtung im Alten Orient, im Judentum und im Christentum*, edited by Erich Zenger, 90–136. Freiburg im Breisgau: Herder Verlag, 2003.

———. "Das Dankopfer." In *Le repas de Dieu / Das Mahl Gottes*, edited by Christian Grappe, 51–58. Tübingen: Mohr Siebeck, 2004.

———. "*De profundis*: Tod und Leben in der Bildsprache der Psalmen." In *Der Mensch vor Gott: Forschungen zum Menschenbild in Bibel, antikem Judentum und Koran: Festschrift für Hermann Lichtenberger zum 60. Geburtstag*, edited by Ulrike Mittmann-Richert, Friedrich Avemarie, and Gerbern S. Oegema, 41–64. Neukirchen-Vluyn: Neukirchener Verlag, 2003. Reprinted in *Der Gott des Lebens*, 244–66.

———. "'Du stellst meine Füße auf weiten Raum' (Ps 31, 9): Gott, Mensch und Raum im Alten Testament." In *Die Welt als Schöpfung*, 3–38.

———. "Ein Gott der Gewalt? Perspektiven des Alten Testaments." In *Gottes Name(n): Zum Gedenken an Erich Zenger*, edited by I. Müllner, L. Schwienhorst-Schönberger, and R. Scoralick, 11–33. Freiburg im Breisgau: Herder Verlag, 2012.

———. "Der eine Gott der beiden Testamente: Grundfragen einer biblischen Theologie." In *Die rettende Gerechtigkeit*, 249–84.

———. "'Die Erde ist in die Hand eines Frevlers gegeben' (Hi 9, 24): Die Frage nach der Gerechtigkeit Gottes im Hiobbuch." In *Wo ist Gott? Die Theodizee-Frage und die Theologie im Pfarramt*, edited by Hermann Lichtenberger and Hartmut Zweigle, 1–18. Neukirchen-Vluyn: Neukirchener Verlag, 2009.

———. "Ewiges Leben III." In *RGG*^{4} 2 (1999): 1762–63.

———. "Die Frucht der Gerechtigkeit: Psalm 72 und die judäische Königsideologie." In *"Mein Sohn bist Du" (Ps 2, 7): Studien zu den Königspsalmen*, edited by Eckart Otto and Erich Zenger, 94–134. Stuttgart: Verlag Katholisches Bibelwerk, 2002.

———, ed. *Der ganze Mensch: Zur Anthropologie der Antike und ihrer europäischen Nachgeschichte*. Berlin: Akademie-Verlag, 2012.

———. "Der 'ganze Mensch': Zur Geschichte und Absicht einer integrativen Formel." In Janowski, *Der ganze Mensch*, 9–21.

———. *Der Gott des Lebens*. Vol. 3 of *Beiträge zur Theologie des Alten Testaments*. Neukirchen-Vluyn: Neukirchener Verlag, 2003.

———. "Der Gott Israels und die Toten: Eine religions- und theologiegeschichtliche Skizze." In *Die Welt als Schöpfung*, 266–304.

———. "Gottebenbildlichkeit." In *RGG*^{4} 3 (2000): 1159–60.

———. *Gottes Gegenwart in Israel*. Vol. 1 of *Beiträge zur Theologie des Alten Testaments*. Neukirchen-Vluyn: Neukirchener Verlag, 1993.

———. "Der gute Hirte: Psalm 23 und das biblische Gottesbild." In Berlejung and Heckl, *Ex Oriente lux*, 247–71.

——— "Hans Walter Wolff und die alttestamentliche Anthropologie." In *"Neu aufbrechen, den Menschen zu suchen und zu erkennen": Symposion anlässlich des 100. Geburtstages von H. W. Wolff*, edited by Jan Christian Gertz and Manfred Oeming, 85–125. Neukirchen-Vluyn: Neukirchener Verlag, 2013.

———. "'Heile mich, denn ich habe an dir gesündigt!' (Ps 41, 5): Zum Konzept von Krankheit und Heilung im Alten Testament." In *Krankheitsdeutung in der postsäkularen Gesellschaft: Theologische Ansätze im interdisziplinären Gespräch*, edited by Günter Thomas and Isolde Karle, 47–66. Stuttgart: W. Kohlhammer, 2009.

———. "Die heilige Wohnung des Höchsten: Kosmologische Implikationen der Jerusalemer Tempeltheologie." In *Gottesstadt und Gottesgarten: Zu Geschichte und Theologie des Jerusalemer Tempels*, edited by Othmar Keel and Erich Zenger, 24–68. Freiburg im Breisgau: Herder Verlag, 2002.

———. "Herrschaft über die Tiere: Gen 1, 26–28 und die Semantik von *radâ* [רָדָה]." In *Biblische Theologie und gesellschaftlicher Wandel: Festschrift für Norbert Lohfink SJ*, edited by Georg Braulik, Walter Gross, and Sean E. McEvenue, 183–98. Freiburg im Breisgau: Herder Verlag, 1993. Reprinted in *Die rettende Gerechtigkeit*, 33–48.

———. "'Hingabe' oder 'Opfer'? Zur gegenwärtigen Kontroverse um die Deutung des Todes Jesu." In *Das Kreuz Jesu: Gewalt-Opfer-Sühne*, edited by Rudolf Weth, 13–43. Neukirchen-Vluyn: Neukirchener Verlag, 2001.

———. "'Ich will in eurer Mitte wohnen': Struktur und Genese der exilischen Schekina-Theologie." In *Gottes Gegenwart in Israel*, 119–47.

———. "Jenseits von Eden: Gen 4:1–16 und die nichtpriesterliche Urgeschichte." In *Die Dämonen: Die Dämonologie der israelitisch-jüdischen und frühchristlichen Literatur im Kontext ihrer Umwelt = Demons: The Demonology of Israelite-Jewish and Early Christian Literature in Context of Their Environment*, edited by Armin Lange and Hermann Lichtenberger, 137–59. Tübingen: Mohr Siebeck, 2003.

———. "Jenseitsvorstellungen II/2." In *RGG*^{4} 4 (2001): 406–7.

———. "JHWH der Richter—ein rettender Gott: Psalm 7 und das Motiv des Gottesgerichts." In *Die rettende Gerechtigkeit*, 92–124.

———. "JHWH und der Sonnengott: Aspekte der Solarisierung JHWHs in vorexilischer Zeit." In *Die rettende Gerechtigkeit*, 192–219.

———. "Klage II." In *RGG*^{4} 4 (2001): 1389–91.

———. "Die Klage des Gekreuzigten: Psalm 22 und der markinische Kreuzigungsbericht." In *Kreuzestheologie—kontrovers und erhellend; Prof. Dr. Volker Weymann zur Verabschiedung in den Ruhestand*, edited by Klaus Grünwaldt and Udo Hahn, 11–28. Hannover: Amt der VELKD, 2007.

———. "Die 'Kleine Biblia': Die Bedeutung der Psalmen für eine Theologie des Alten Testaments." In *Die rettende Gerechtigkeit*, 125–64.

———. "Das Königtum Gottes in den Psalmen: Bemerkungen zu einem neuen Gesamtentwurf." In *Gottes Gegenwart in Israel*, 148–213.

———. "Die Kostbarkeit des Lebens: Zur Theologie und Semantik eines Psalmenmotivs." In *Die Welt als Schöpfung*, 249–65.

———. "Die lebendige *næpæš* [*nepeš*]: Das Alte Testament und die Frage nach der 'Seele.'" In *Gott—Seele—Welt: Interdisziplinäre Beiträge zur Rede von der Seele*, edited by Bernd Janowski and Christoph Schwöbel, 25–53. Neukirchen-Vluyn: Neukirchener Theologie, 2013.

———. "Die lebendige Statue Gottes: Zur Anthropologie der priesterlichen Urgeschichte." In *Die Welt als Schöpfung*, 140–71.

———. "Das Licht des Lebens: Zur Lichtmetaphorik in den Psalmen." In *Die Welt als Schöpfung*, 221–48.

———. "Licht und Finsternis II." In *RGG*[4] 5 (2002): 330–31.

———. "'Dem Löwen gleich, gierig nach Raub' (Ps 17, 12): Zum Feindbild in den Psalmen." In *Die rettende Gerechtigkeit*, 49–77.

———. "Mensch IV." In *RGG*[4] 5 (2002): 1057–58.

———. "Der Mensch im alten Israel: Grundfragen alttestamentlicher Anthropologie." In *Die Welt als Schöpfung*, 107–39.

———. "Opfer I." In *NBL* 3:36–40.

———. "Opfermahl." In *NBL* 3:43–46.

———. "Der Ort des Lebens: Zur Kultsymbolik des Jerusalemer Tempels." In *Tempelbau und Tempelkult: Zur Architektur und kultischen Ausstattung von Tempeln in der Levante (2.–1. Jt. v. Chr.)*, edited by Jens Kamlah, 369–97. Wiesbaden: O. Harrassowitz, 2012.

———. *Die rettende Gerechtigkeit*. Vol. 2 of *Beiträge zur Theologie des Alten Testaments*. Neukirchen-Vluyn: Neukirchener Verlag, 1999.

———. "Die rettende Gerechtigkeit: Zum Gerechtigkeitsdiskurs in den Psalmen." In Achenbach, Arneth, and Otto, *Rechtsgeschichte*, 362–76.

———. *Rettungsgewissheit und Epiphanie des Heils: Das Motiv der Hilfe Gottes "am Morgen" im Alten Orient und im Alten Testament*. Neukirchen-Vluyn: Neukirchener Verlag, 1989.

———. "Schöpferische Erinnerung: Zum 'Gedenken Gottes' in der priesterlichen Fluterzählung." In *Die Welt als Schöpfung*, 172–98.

———. "Sehnsucht nach Unsterblichkeit: Zu J. Assmann, *Tod und Jenseits im Alten Ägypten*." In *Die Welt als Schöpfung*, 305–19.

———. "Sehnsucht nach Unsterblichkeit: Zur Jenseitshoffnung in der weisheitlichen Literatur." *Bibel und Kirche* 61 (2006): 34–39.

———. *Stellvertretung: Alttestamentliche Studien zu einem theologischen Grundbegriff*. Stuttgart: Verlag Katholisches Bibelwerk, 1997.

———. *Sühne als Heilsgeschehen: Traditions- und religionsgeschichtliche Studien zur Sühnetheologie der Priesterschrift*. Neukirchen-Vluyn: Neukirchener Verlag, 2000.

———. "Die Tat kehrt zum Täter zurück: Offene Fragen im Umkreis des Tun-Ergehen-Zusammenhangs." In *Die rettende Gerechtigkeit*, 167–91.

———. "Ein Tempel aus Worten: Zur theologischen Architektur des Psalters." In Zenger, *The Composition of the Book of Psalms*, 279–306.

———. "Tieropfer." *Religionsunterricht an höheren Schulen* 44 (2001): 339–44.

———. "Die Toten loben JHWH nicht: Psalm 88 und das alttestamentliche Todesverständnis." Paper presented at the Auferstehung—Resurrection: The Fourth

Durham-Tübingen Research Symposium; Resurrection, Transfiguration and Exaltation in Old Testament, Ancient Judaism and Early Christianity, Tübingen, 1999. In *Auferstehung—Resurrection*, edited by Friedrich Avemarie and Hermann Lichtenberger, 3–45. Tübingen: Mohr Siebeck, 2001.
———. "Das verborgene Angesicht Gottes: Psalm 13 als Muster eines Klagelieds des einzelnen." *Jahrbuch für biblische Theologie* 16 (2001): 25–53.
———. "Vergeltung II." *RGG*[4] 8 (2005): 1000.
———. "'Verstehst du auch, was du liest?' Reflexionen auf die Leserichtung der christlichen Bibel." In *Wieviel Systematik erlaubt die Schrift? Auf der Suche nach einer gesamtbiblischen Theologie*, edited by Frank-Lothar Hossfeld, 150–91. Freiburg im Breisgau: Herder Verlag, 2001.
———. "Was ist der Mensch? Grundzüge einer biblischen Sicht des Menschen." *Bibel und Kirche* 67 (2012): 4–9.
———. *Die Welt als Schöpfung*. Vol. 4 of *Beiträge zur Theologie des Alten Testaments*. Neukirchen-Vluyn: Neukirchener Verlag, 2008.
———. "Weltbild III." *RGG*[4] 8 (2005): 1409–14.
———. "Wie ein Baum an Wasserkanälen: Psalm 1 als Tor zum Psalter." In *Die Welt als Schöpfung*, 199–218.
Janowski, Bernd, and Dörte Bester. "Anthropologie des Alten Testaments: Ein forschungsgeschichtlicher Überblick." In Janowski, Liess, and Zaft, *Der Mensch*, 3–40.
Janowski, Bernd, and Alexandra Stephanie Grund. "'Solange die Erde steht . . .': Zur Erfahrung von Raum und Zeit im alten Israel." In Janowski, Liess, and Zaft, *Der Mensch*, 487–535.
Janowski, Bernd, and Friedhelm Hartenstein. "Psalmen/Psalter I–III." *RGG*[4] 6 (2003): 1762–77.
Janowski, Bernd, and Kathrin Liess. "Gerechtigkeit und Unsterblichkeit: Psalm 73 und die Frage nach dem 'ewigen Leben.'" In *Alles in allem: Eschatologische Anstöße; J. Christine Janowski zum 60. Geburtstag*, edited by Ruth Hess and Martin Leiner, 69–92. Neukirchen-Vluyn: Neukirchener Verlag, 2005.
Janowski, Bernd, Kathrin Liess, and Niko Zaft, eds. *Der Mensch im alten Israel: Neue Forschungen zur alttestamentlichen Anthropologie*. Freiburg im Breisgau: Herder Verlag, 2009.
Janowski, Bernd, and Ute Neumann-Gorsolke. "Der 'gute Hirte' und seine Herde." In *Gefährten und Feinde des Menschen: Das Tier in der Lebenswelt des alten Israel*, edited by Bernd Janowski, Ute Neumann-Gorsolke, and Uwe Glessmer, 85–89. Neukirchen-Vluyn: Neukirchener Verlag, 1993.
———. "Haustiere und Arbeitstiere." In *Gefährten und Feinde des Menschen: Das Tier in der Lebenswelt des alten Israel*, edited by Bernd Janowski, Ute Neumann-Gorsolke, and Uwe Glessmer, 62–66. Neukirchen-Vluyn: Neukirchener Verlag, 1993.
———. "Motive und Materialien 7: Reine und unreine Tiere." In *Gefährten und Feinde des Menschen: Das Tier in der Lebenswelt des alten Israel*, edited by Bernd Janowski, Ute Neumann-Gorsolke, and Uwe Glessmer, 214–18. Neukirchen-Vluyn: Neukirchener Verlag, 1993.
———. "Opfertiere und Tieropfer." In *Gefährten und Feinde des Menschen: Das Tier in der Lebenswelt des alten Israel*, edited by Bernd Janowski, Ute Neumann-Gorsolke, and Uwe Glessmer, 240–44. Neukirchen-Vluyn: Neukirchener Verlag, 1993.
———. "Das Tier als Exponent dämonischer Mächte." In *Gefährten und Feinde des Menschen: Das Tier in der Lebenswelt des alten Israel*, edited by Bernd Janowski, Ute Neumann-Gorsolke, and Uwe Glessmer, 278–82. Neukirchen-Vluyn: Neukirchener Verlag, 1993.
———. "Tierbezeichnungen und Tiervergleiche." In *Gefährten und Feinde des Menschen: Das Tier in der Lebenswelt des alten Israel*, edited by Bernd Janowski, Ute

Neumann-Gorsolke, and Uwe Glessmer, 194–98. Neukirchen-Vluyn: Neukirchener Verlag, 1993.

Janowski, Bernd, and Daniel Schwemer, eds. *Hymnen, Klagelieder und Gebete*. Vol. 7 of *Texte aus der Umwelt des Alten Testaments: Neue Folge*. Gütersloh: Gütersloher Verlagshaus, 2013.

Janowski, Bernd, and Michael Welker. *Opfer: Theologische und kulturelle Kontexte*. Frankfurt am Main: Suhrkamp, 2000.

Janowski, Bernd, and Erich Zenger. "Jenseits des Alltags: Fest und Opfer als religiöse Kontrapunkte zur Alltagswelt im alten Israel." *Jahrbuch für biblische Theologie* 18 (2003): 63–102.

Janssen, Claudia, and Rainer Kessler. "Trauer." *SWB* 597–98.

Jaques, Margaret, ed. *Klagetraditionen: Form und Funktion der Klage in den Kulturen der Antike*. Fribourg, Switzerland: Academic Press; Göttingen: Vandenhoeck & Ruprecht, 2011.

Jaroš, Karl. *Die ältesten Fragmente eines biblischen Textes: Zu den Silberamuletten von Jerusalem*. Mainz am Rhein: P. von Zabern, 1997.

———. "Die Vorstellung Altisraels über Tod und Fortleben nach dem Tod." *Bibel und Liturgie* 51 (1978): 219–82.

Jauss, Hannlore. "Fluchpsalmen beten? Zum Problem der Feind- und Fluchpsalmen." *Bibel und Kirche* 51 (1996): 107–15.

Jenni, Ernst. *Die Präposition Beth*. Vol. 1 of *Die hebräischen Präpositionen*. Stuttgart: W. Kohlhammer, 1992.

———. *Die Präposition Kaph*. Vol. 2 of *Die hebräischen Präpositionen*. Stuttgart: W. Kohlhammer, 1994.

———. "Psalm 30, 6a—eine ungewöhnliche Sentenz." In *Wege zur Hebräischen Bibel: Denken—Sprache—Kultur; In memoriam Hans-Peter Müller*, edited by Armin Lange and K. F. Diethard Römheld, 13–28. Göttingen: Vandenhoeck & Ruprecht, 2009.

———. "יוֹם." In *THAT* 1:707–26.

———. "Verba gesticulationis im Hebräischen." In *Studien zur Sprachwelt des Alten Testaments*, edited by Ernst Jenni, Beat Huwyler, and Klaus Seybold, 150–61. Stuttgart: W. Kohlhammer, 1991.

———. "Zur Semantik der hebräischen Personen-, Tier- und Dingvergleiche." *Zeitschrift für Althebraistik* 3, no. 2 (1990): 133–66.

Jeremias, Jörg. "Die Erde 'wankt.'" In *"Ihr Völker all, klatscht in die Hände": Festschrift für Erhard S. Gerstenberger zum 65. Geburtstag*, edited by Rainer Kessler, 166–80. Münster: LIT Verlag, 1997.

———. *Das Königtum Gottes in den Psalmen: Israels Begegnung mit dem kanaanäischen Mythos in den Jahwe-König-Psalmen*. Göttingen: Vandenhoeck & Ruprecht, 1987.

———. *Der Prophet Amos*. Göttingen: Vandenhoeck & Ruprecht, 1995.

———. *Der Prophet Hosea*. Göttingen: Vandenhoeck & Ruprecht, 1983.

———. "Der Psalm des Jona (Jona 2, 3–10)." In *FS Janowski*, 203–14.

———. "Psalm 130 im alttestamentlichen Kontext und in Luthers Nachdichtung." *Theologische Beiträge* 20 (1989): 284–97.

———. *Die Reue Gottes: Aspekte alttestamentlicher Gottesvorstellung*. 2nd ed. Neukirchen-Vluyn: Neukirchener Verlag, 1997.

———. *Theophanie: Die Geschichte einer alttestamentlichen Gattung*. Neukirchen-Vluyn: Neukirchener Verlag, 1977.

Jeremias, Jörg, and Friedhelm Hartenstein. "'JHWH und seine Aschera': 'Offizielle Religion' und 'Volksreligion' zur Zeit der klassischen Propheten." In *Religionsgeschichte Israels: Formale und Materiale Aspekte*, 79–138. Gütersloh: Christian Kaiser, 1999.

Jerome, Obiorah Mary. *"How Lovely Is Your Dwelling Place": The Desire for God's House in Psalm 84*. St. Ottilien: EOS-Verlag, 2004.

Johnson, Aubrey Rodway. *The Vitality of the Individual in the Thought of Ancient Israel*. Cardiff: University of Wales Press, 1964.

Johnston, Philip. *Shades of Sheol: Death and Afterlife in the Old Testament*. Downers Grove, IL: InterVarsity, 2002.

Joüon, Paul. *Syntax: Paradigms and Indices*. Part 3 of vol. 2 of *A Grammar of Biblical Hebrew*. Rome: Editrice Pontificio Istituto Biblio, 1991.

Jüngel, Eberhard. "Böse, das, V." In *RGG*[4] 1 (1998): 1707–8.

———. *Das Evangelium von der Rechtfertigung des Gottlosen als Zentrum des christlichen Glaubens: Eine theologische Studie in ökumenischer Absicht*. Tübingen: Mohr Siebeck, 1998.

———. "Die Offenbarung der Verborgenheit Gottes: Ein Beitrag zum evangelischen Verständnis der Verborgenheit des göttlichen Wirkens." In *Wertlose Wahrheit: Zur Identität und Relevanz des christlichen Glaubens*, 163–82. Vol. 3 of *Theologische Erörterungen*. Munich: Christian Kaiser, 1990.

———. "Was heisst beten?" In *Wertlose Wahrheit: Zur Identität und Relevanz des christlichen Glaubens*, 397–405. Vol. 3 of *Theologische Erörterungen*. Munich: Christian Kaiser, 1990.

Jüttemann, Gerd, Michael Sonntag, and Christoph Wulf, eds. *Die Seele: Ihre Geschichte im Abendland*. Göttingen: Vandenhoeck & Ruprecht, 2005.

Kaelin, Oskar. "Pazuzu, Lamaschtu-Reliefs und Horus-Stelen—Ägypten als Modell im 1. Jt. v. Chr." In Bickel et al., *Bilder als Quellen*, 365–78.

Kaiser, Otto. *Einleitung in das Alte Testament: Eine Einführung in ihre Ergebnisse und Probleme*. 5th ed. Gütersloh: Gütersloher Verlagshaus G. Mohn, 1984.

———. *Der Gott des Alten Testaments*. 3 vols. Göttingen: Vandenhoeck & Ruprecht, 1993, 1998, 2003.

———. "Tod, Auferstehung und Unsterblichkeit im Alten Testament und im frühen Judentum—in religionsgeschichtlichen Zusammenhang bedacht." In *Tod und Leben*, edited by Otto Kaiser and Eduard Lohse, 7–80. Stuttgart: W. Kohlhammer, 1977.

———. "Die Zukunft der Toten nach den Zeugnissen der alttestamentlich-frühjüdischen Religion." In *Der Mensch unter dem Schicksal: Studien zur Geschichte, Theologie und Gegenwartsbedeutung der Weisheit*, edited by Otto Kaiser, 182–95. Berlin: Walter de Gruyter, 1985.

Kamlah, Jens. "Grab und Begräbnis in Israel/Juda." In Berlejung and Janowski, *Tod und Jenseits*, 257–97.

Kammler, Hans-Christian. "Das Verständnis der Passion Jesu im Markusevangelium." *Zeitschrift für Theologie und Kirche* 103 (2006): 461–91.

Kamper, Dietmar, and Christoph Wulf. *Anthropologie nach dem Tode des Menschen: Vervollkommnung und Unverbesserlichkeit*. Frankfurt am Main: Suhrkamp, 1994.

Kant, Immanuel. *Die Religion innerhalb der Grenzen der blossen Vernunft*. 1793. Edited by Karl Vorländer. Hamburg: F. Meiner, 1956. ET, *Religion within the Limits of Reason Alone*. Translated by Theodore M. Greene and Hoyt H. Hudson. New York: Harper, 1960.

Kantorowicz, Ernst Hartwig. *Die zwei Körper des Königs: Eine Studie zur politischen Theologie des Mittelalters*. Munich: Deutscher Taschenbuch Verlag, 1990.

Karle, Isolde. "Chancen der Seelsorge unter den Bedingungen der Moderne." In *Was hat die Kirche heute zu sagen? Auftrag und Freiheit der Kirche in der pluralistischen Gesellschaft*, edited by Rudolf Weth, 58–66. Neukirchen-Vluyn: Neukirchener Verlag, 1998.

Kedar-Kopfstein, Benjamin. *Biblische Semantik: Eine Einführung*. Stuttgart: W. Kohlhammer, 1981.

Keel, Othmar. "Altägyptische und biblische Weltbilder, die Anfänge der vorsokratischen Philosophie und das ἀρχή-Problem in späten biblischen Schriften." In *Das biblische Weltbild und seine altorientalischen Kontexte*, edited by Bernd Janowski and Beate Ego, 27–63. Tübingen: Mohr Siebeck, 2001.

———. "Der bedrängte Beter: Wer sind die Feinde in den Psalmen?" *Bibel und Kirche* 26 (1971): 103–7.

———. "Davids 'Tanz' vor der Lade." *Bibel und Kirche* 51 (1996): 11–14.

———. *Deine Blicke sind Tauben: Zur Metaphorik des Hohen Liedes*. Stuttgart: Verlag Katholisches Bibelwerk, 1984.

———. "Die Erde als Mutterschoss in der hebräischen Bibel." In *Studien zu den Stempelsiegeln aus Palästina/Israel*, edited by Othmar Keel, Silvia Schroer, and Hildi Keel-Leu, 2:70–75. Göttingen: Vandenhoeck & Ruprecht, 1985.

———. "Die 'Feinde' in den Psalmen." *Brennpunkt Gemeinde: Missionarische Impulse für Verkündigung und Gemeindeaufbau* 50 (1997): 56–60.

———. *Feinde und Gottesleugner: Studien zum Image der Widersacher in den Individualpsalmen*. Stuttgart: Verlag Katholisches Bibelwerk, 1969.

———. "Fern von Jerusalem: Frühe Jerusalemer Kulttraditionen und ihre Träger und Trägerinnen." In *Zion—Ort der Begegnung: Festschrift für Laurentius Klein zur Vollendung des 65. Lebensjahres*, edited by Ferdinand Hahn, Frank-Lothar Hossfeld, Hans Jorissen, and Angelika Neuwirth, 439–502. Bodenheim: Athenäum, 1993.

———. *Das Hohelied*. Zurich: Theologischer Verlag, 1986. 2nd ed., 1992.

———. "Das je verschiedene theologische Profil der Klagelieder und der Volksklagen." In *L'Écrit et l'esprit: Études d'histoire du texte de théologie biblique en hommage à Adrian Schenker*, edited by Dieter Böhler, Innocent Himbaza, and Philippe Hugo, 128–42. Freiburg, Switzerland: Academic Press, 2005.

———. *Das Recht der Bilder gesehen zu Werden: Drei Fallstudien zur Methode der Interpretation altorientalischer Bilder*. Göttingen: Vandenhoeck & Ruprecht, 1992.

———. *Schöne, schwierige Welt—Leben mit Klagen und Loben: Ausgewählte Psalmen*. Berlin: Evanglische Haupt-Bibelgesellschaft, 1991.

———. "Das sogenannte altorientalische Weltbild." *Bibel und Kirche* 40 (1985): 157–65.

———. "Warum im Jerusalemer Tempel kein anthropomorphes Kultbild gestanden haben dürfte." In *Homo Pictor*, edited by Gottfried Boehm and Stephan E. Hauser, 244–82. Munich: Saur, 2001.

———. "Die Welt der altorientalischen Bildsymbolik und das Alte Testament, am Beispiel der Psalmen." *Bibel und Kirche* 26 (1971): 103–7.

———. *Die Welt der altorientalischen Bildsymbolik und das Alte Testament: Am Beispiel der Psalmen*. Göttingen: Vandenhoeck & Ruprecht, 1996.

Keel, Othmar, and Detlef Puttkammer. *Ausdrücklich Leben: Psalmen; Einführung, Materialien und Vorschläge zur Gestaltung [zur 54. Bibelwoche 1991/92]*. Neukirchen-Vluyn: Aussaat Verlag, 1991.

Keel, Othmar, and Silvia Schroer. *Schöpfung: Biblische Theologien im Kontext altorientalischer Religionen*. Göttingen: Vandenhoeck & Ruprecht, 2002. 2nd ed., 2008.

Keel, Othmar, Thomas Staubli, et al. *"Im Schatten deiner Flügel": Tiere in der Bibel und im Alten Orient*. Edited by Thomas Staubli. Freiburg, Switzerland: Universitätsverlag, 2001.

Keel, Othmar, and Christoph Uehlinger. *Göttinnen, Götter und Gottessymbole: Neue Erkenntnisse zur Religionsgeschichte Kanaans und Israels aufgrund bislang unerschlossener Ikonographischer Quellen*. Freiburg im Breisgau: Herder Verlag, 2001. 6th ed., with an epilogue by Florian Lippke, 2010.

———. "Jahwe und die Sonnengottheit von Jerusalem." In *Ein Gott allein? JHWH-Verehrung und biblischer Monotheismus im Kontext der israelitischen und altorientalischen Religionsgeschichte*, edited by Walter Dietrich and Martin A. Klopfenstein, 269–306. Göttingen: Vandenhoeck & Ruprecht, 1994.

Kegler, Jürgen. "Beobachtungen zur Körpererfahrung in der hebräischen Bibel." In F. Crüsemann, Hardmeier, and Kessler, *Was ist der Mensch . . . ?*, 28–41.

———. "Mensch." In *CBL* 2:897f.

Kellermann, Dieter. "כִּלְיוֹת." In *ThWAT* 4:185–92.

———. *Das Gotteslob der Auferweckten: Motivgeschichtliche Beobachtungen in Texten des Alten Testaments, des frühen Judentums und Urchristentums*. Neukirchen-Vluyn: Neukirchener Verlag, 2001.

———. "Niere." In *NBL* 2:925.

———. "נֵר." In *ThWAT* 5:616–26.

———. "Überwindung des Todesgeschicks in der alttestamentlichen Frömmigkeit vor und neben dem Auferstehungsglauben." *Zeitschrift für Theologie und Kirche* 73, no. 3 (1976): 259–82.

Kessler, Rainer. "Der antwortende Gott." *Wort und Dienst* 21 (1991): 43–57.

———. *Micha*. Freiburg im Breisgau: Herder Verlag, 1999.

Kessler, Rainer, et al., eds. *"Ihr Völker alle, klatscht in die Hände!": Festschrift für Erhard S. Gerstenberger zum 65. Geburtstag*. Münster: LIT Verlag, 1997.

Keupp, Heiner, ed. *Lust an der Erkenntnis: Der Mensch als soziales Wesen; Sozialpsychologisches Denken im 20. Jahrhundert; Ein Lesebuch*. Munich: Piper, 1995.

Kilian, Rudolf. "Ps 22 und das priesterliche Heilsorakel." *Biblische Zeitschrift* 12 (1968): 172–85.

King, L. W. *The Seven Tablets of Creation*. 2 vols. London: Luzac, 1902.

Kittel, Gisela. *Befreit aus dem Rachen des Todes: Tod und Todesüberwindung im Alten und Neuen Testament*. Göttingen: Vandenhoeck & Ruprecht, 1999.

Klee, Paul. *Gedichte*. Edited by Felix Klee. Zurich: Arche, 2001.

———. *Tagebücher von Paul Klee, 1898–1918*. Edited by Felix Klee. Cologne: M. Dumont Schauberg, 1957.

Kleer, Martin. *"Der liebliche Sänger der Psalmen Israels": Untersuchungen zu David als Dichter und Beter der Psalmen*. Bodenheim: Philo Verlagsgesellschaft, 1996.

Klein, Rebekka A. "Die Inhumanität des Animal Sociale: Vier Thesen zum interdisziplinären Beitrag der theologischen Anthropologie." *Neue Zeitschrift für Systematische Theologie und Religionsphilosophie* 51 (2009): 427–44.

Kleinknecht, Karl Theodor. *Der leidende Gerechtfertigte: Die alttestamentlich-jüdische Tradition vom "leidenden Gerechten" und ihre Rezeption bei Paulus*. 2nd ed. Tübingen: J. C. B. Mohr, 1988.

Klimkeit, Hans-Joachim. *Tod und Jenseits im Glauben der Völker*. Wiesbaden: O. Harrassowitz, 1978.

Klinger, Elmar, Stephanie Böhm, and Theodor Seidl, eds. *Der Körper und die Religion: Das Problem der Konstruktion von Geschlechterrollen*. Würzburg: Echter Verlag, 2000.

Klopfenstein, Martin A. "Ehre und Schande." In *NBL* 1:485–86.

Klumbies, Paul-Gerhard. *Von der Hinrichtung zur Himmelfahrt: Der Schluss der Jesuserzählung nach Markus und Lukas*. Neukirchen-Vluyn: Neukirchener Theologie, 2010.

Knauf, Ernst Axel. "Fundamentale Einheit—Faszinierende Vielfalt." Paper presented at the Jahrestagung des Vereins der Religionslehrerinnen und Religionslehrer an Gymnasien des Bistums Trier, Trier, 1999.

———. "Psalm XXIII, 6." *Vetus Testamentum* 51 (2001): 556.

Knuth, Hans Christian. *Zur Auslegungsgeschichte von Psalm 6*. Tübingen: Mohr Siebeck, 1971.

Koch, Klaus. "Die Entstehung der sozialen Kritik bei den Profeten." In *Spuren des hebräischen Denkens: Beiträge zur alttestamentlichen Theologie*, edited by Klaus Koch, 146–66. Neukirchen-Vluyn: Neukirchener Verlag, 1991.

———. "Gibt es ein hebräisches Denken?" In *Spuren des hebräischen Denkens: Beiträge zur alttestamentlichen Theologie*, edited by Klaus Koch, 3–24. Neukirchen-Vluyn: Neukirchener Verlag, 1991.

———. "Strafe." In *Reclams Bibellexikon*, edited by Klaus Koch, 481–82. Stuttgart: Reclam, 1987.

———. "צָדַק." In *THAT* 2:507–30.

———. "קֶבֶר." In *ThWAT* 6:1149–56.

———. *Was ist Formgeschichte? Methoden der Bibelexegese*. 5th ed. Neukirchen-Vluyn: Neukirchener Verlag, 1989.

———. "Weltbild." In *Reclams Bibellexikon*, edited by Klaus Koch, 586–87. Stuttgart: Reclam, 1987.

Koch, Klaus, and Jürgen Roloff. "Tat-Ergehen-Zusammenhang." In *Reclams Bibellexikon*, edited by Klaus Koch, 493–95. Stuttgart: Reclam, 1987.

Köckert, Matthias. "Die Theophanie des Wettergottes Jahweh in Psalm 18." In *Kulturgeschichten: Altorientalistische Studien für Volkert Haas zum 65. Geburtstag*, edited by Thomas Richter, Doris Prechel, and Jörg Klinger, 209–26. Saarbrücken: SDV, Saarbrücker Druckerei und Verlag, 2001.

———. "Wandlungen Gottes im alten Israel." *Berliner Theologische Zeitschrift* 22 (2005): 3–36.

Koenen, Klaus. *Gottesworte in den Psalmen: Eine formgeschichtliche Untersuchung*. Neukirchen-Vluyn: Neukirchener Verlag, 1996.

———. "שָׂכַל." In *ThWAT* 7:781–95.

Koenen, Klaus, and Ulrich Mell. "Hirte/Hirtin." *SWB* 264–66.

Köhler, Ludwig. *Der hebräische Mensch: Eine Skizze*. Darmstadt: Wissenschaftliche Buchgesellschaft, 1976.

———. *Theologie des Alten Testaments*. 4th ed. Tübingen: Mohr Siebeck, 1966.

Köhlmoos, Melanie. *Das Auge Gottes: Textstrategie im Hiobbuch*. Tübingen: Mohr Siebeck, 1999.

Konersmann, Ralf. "Die Augen der Philosophen: Zur historischen Semantik und Kritik des Sehens." In *Kritik des Sehens*, edited by Ralf Konersman, 9–47. Leipzig: Reclam, 1997.

———. "Sehen." In *HWP* 9:121–61.

Konstan, David, et al. *Émotions*. Special issue of *Mètis: Anthropologie des mondes grecs anciens*, n.s., 9 (2011). Paris and Athens: Daedalus, 2011.

Korff, Malte von. *Franz Schubert*. Munich: Deutscher Taschenbuch-Verlag, 2003.

Korpel, Marjo C. A. *A Rift in the Clouds: Ugaritic and Hebrew Descriptions of the Divine*. Münster: Ugarit Verlag, 1990.

Körtner, Ulrich H. J. "Mit Krankheit leben: Der Krankheitsbegriff in der medizinischen Diskussion." *Theologische Literaturzeitung* 130 (2005): 1273–90.

———. *Wie lange noch, wie lange? Über das Böse, Leid und Tod*. Neukirchen-Vluyn: Neukirchener Verlag, 1998.

Koselleck, Reinhart. *Zeitschichten: Studien zur Historik*. Frankfurt am Main: Suhrkamp, 2000.

Krammer, Ingrid. "'Wer anderen eine Grube gräbt, fällt selbst hinein': Ben Sira als Tradent eines bekannten Sprichwortes." In *Einzelne und seine Gemeinschaft bei Ben Sira*, edited by Ingrid Krammer and Renate Egger-Wenzel, 239–60. Berlin: Walter de Gruyter, 1998.

Kratz, Reinhard Gregor. "Die Gnade des täglichen Brots: Späte Psalmen auf dem Weg zum Vaterunser." *Zeitschrift für Theologie und Kirche* 89, no. 1 (1992): 1–40.

———. "Klage." In *HGANT*[2] 273–75.

———. "Lob/Dank." In *HGANT*[2] 308–9.

———. *Reste hebräischen Heidentums am Beispiel der Psalmen*. Göttingen: Vandenhoeck & Ruprecht, 2004.

———. "Die Tora Davids: Psalm 1 und die doxologische Fünfteilung des Psalters." *Zeitschrift für Theologie und Kirche* 93, no. 1 (1996): 1–34.

———. "Trauer." In *HGANT*[2] 396–98.

Kraus, Hans-Joachim. "Hören und Sehen in der althebräischen Tradition." In *Biblisch-theologische Aufsätze*, edited by Hans-Joachim Kraus, 84–101. Neukirchen-Vluyn: Neukirchener Verlag, 1972.

———. *Psalmen*. 6th ed. of vol. 1, *Psalmen 1–59* (pp. 1–584); and vol. 2, *Psalmen 60–150* (pp. 585–1179). 2nd ed. of vol. 3, *Theologie der Psalmen*. Neukirchen-Vluyn: Neukirchener Verlag, 1989.

———. "Vom Tod und Leben in den Psalmen: Eine Studie zu Calvins Psalmenkommentar." In *Biblisch-theologische Aufsätze*, edited by Hans-Joachim Kraus, 258–77. Neukirchen-Vluyn: Neukirchener Verlag, 1972.

Krawczack, Peter. *"Es gibt einen Gott, der Richter ist auf Erden!" (Ps 58, 12b): Ein exegetischer Beitrag zum Verständnis von Psalm 58*. Berlin: Philo, 2001.

Krebernik, Manfred. "Sonnengott. A. I. In Mesopotamien: Philologisch." *Reallexikon der Assyriologie* 12 (2011): 599–611.

Krieg, Matthias. "Leiblichkeit im Alten Testament." In *Leiblichkeit*, edited by Matthias Krieg, 7–29. Zurich: Theologischer Verlag, 1983.

———. *Schmetterlingsweisheit: Die Todesbilder der Nelly Sachs*. Berlin: Selbstverlag Institut Kirche und Judentum, 1983.

———. *Todesbilder im Alten Testament, oder, "Wie die Alten den Tod gebildet."* Zurich: Theologischer Verlag, 1988.

Kronholm, Tryggve. "נָעֵם." In *ThWAT* 5:500–506.

Kruck, Günter, and Claudia Sticher, eds. *"Deine Bilder stehn vor dir wie Namen": Zur Rede von Zorn und Erbarmen Gottes in der Heiligen Schrift*. Mainz: Grünewald, 2005.

Krüger, Annette. *Das Lob des Schöpfers: Studien zu Sprache, Motivik und Theologie von Psalm 104*. Neukirchen-Vluyn: Neukirchener Verlag, 2010.

Krüger, Hans-Peter, and Gesa Lindemann, eds. *Philosophische Anthropologie im 21. Jahrhundert*. Berlin: Akademie Verlag, 2006.

Kruger, Paul A. "Depression in the Hebrew Bible: An Update." *Journal of Near Eastern Studies* 64 (2005): 187–92.

———. "The Inverse World of Mourning in the Hebrew Bible." *Biblische Notizen*, no. 124 (2005): 41–49.

———. "On Emotions and the Expression of Emotions in the Old Testament: A Few Introductory Remarks." *Biblische Zeitschrift* 48 (2004): 213–28. Reprinted in Janowski, Liess, and Zaft, *Der Mensch*, 243–62.

Krüger, Thomas. "*ach ja die seele*: Der Verlust der Seele—ein Gewinn für die theologische Anthropologie?" *Hermeneutische Blätter* 1, no. 2 (2005): 34–41.

———. "Das 'Herz' in der alttestamentlichen Anthropologie." In A. Wagner, *Anthropologische Aufbrüche*, 103–18.

———. *Kohelet (Prediger)*. Neukirchen-Vluyn: Neukirchener Verlag, 2000.

———. "Das menschliche Herz und die Weisung Gottes: Elemente einer Diskussion über Möglichkeiten und Grenzen der Tora-Rezeption im Alten Testament." In *Rezeption und Auslegung im Alten Testament und in seinem Umfeld: Ein Symposion aus Anlass des 60. Geburtstags von Odil Hannes Steck*, edited by Reinhard Gregor Kratz and Thomas Krüger, 65–92. Göttingen: Vandenhoeck & Ruprecht, 1997.

———. "Ohr/Hören." In *HGANT*[2] 329–31.

———. "Psalm 90 und die 'Vergänglichkeit des Menschen.'" In *Kritische Weisheit: Studien zur weisheitlichen Traditionskritik im Alten Testament*, edited by Thomas Krüger, 67–89. Zurich: Pano Verlag, 1997.

Kselman, John S. "Double Entendre in Psalm 59." In Flint and Miller, *Book of Psalms*, 184–89.

Kselman, John S., and Michael L. Barré. "Psalm 55: Problems and Proposals." *Catholic Biblical Quarterly* 60, no. 3 (1998): 440–62.

Kuckhoff, Antonius. *Psalm 6 und die Bitten im Psalter: Ein paradigmatisches Bitt- und Klagegebet im Horizont des Gesamtpsalters*. Göttingen: V&R Unipress / Bonn University Press, 2011.

Kugel, James L. *The Idea of Biblical Poetry: Parallelism and Its History*. New Haven: Yale University Press, 1981.

Kügler, Joachim. *Der andere König: Religionsgeschichtliche Perspektiven auf die Christologie des Johannesevangeliums*. Stuttgart: Verlag Katholisches Bibelwerk, 1999.

———. "Gerechtigkeit." In *HGANT*[2] 211–12.

Kügler, Joachim, Ulrike Bechmann, and Peter Wünsche, eds. *Die Macht der Nase: Zur religiösen Bedeutung des Duftes; Religionsgeschichte—Bibel—Liturgie*. Stuttgart: Verlag Katholisches Bibelwerk, 2000.

Kühn, Dagmar. *Totengedenken bei den Nabatäern und im Alten Testament: Eine religionsgeschichtliche und exegetische Studie*. Münster: Ugarit-Verlag, 2005.

Kunz, Andreas. "Der Mensch auf der Waage: Die Vorstellung vom Gerichtshandeln Gottes im ägyptischen Totenbuch (Tb 125) und bei Hiob (Ijob 31)." *Biblische Zeitschrift* 45, no. 2 (2001): 235–50.

Kurth, Dieter. *Edfu: Ein ägyptischer Tempel, gesehen mit den Augen der alten Ägypter*. Darmstadt: Wissenschaftliche Buchgesellschaft, 1994.

Kurz, Paul Konrad. *Höre Gott! Psalmen des Jahrhunderts*. Zurich: Benziger, 1997.

———. *Psalmen vom Expressionismus bis zur Gegenwart*. Freiburg im Breisgau: Herder Verlag, 1978.

Kurzke, Hermann. "Säkularisation oder Realisation? Zur Wirkungsgeschichte von Psalm 130." In *Liturgie und Dichtung: Ein interdisziplinäres Kompendium*, edited by Hansjakob Becker and Reiner Kacczinski, 2:67–89. St. Ottilien: EOS Verlag, 1983.

Kutsch, Ernst. "'Trauerbräuche' und 'Selbstminderungsriten' im Alten Testament." In *Kleine Schriften zum Alten Testament: Zum 65. Geburtstag*, edited by Ludwig Schmidt and Karl Eberlein, 78–95. Berlin: Walter de Gruyter, 1986.

Kwakkel, Gert [Gerrit]. *According to My Righteousness: Upright Behaviour as Grounds for Deliverance in Psalms 7, 17, 18, 26 and 44*. Leiden: E. J. Brill, 2002.

Kytzler, Bernhard, Jürgen Ebach, and Richard Faber. "Moderne Psalmen." In *Bibel und Literatur*, 157–81. Munich: W. Fink, 1995.

Labisch, Alfons. *Homo hygienicus: Gesundheit und Medizin in der Neuzeit*. Frankfurt am Main: Campus Verlag, 1992.

Lachmann, Rolf. *Susanne K. Langer: Die lebendige Form menschlichen Fühlens und Verstehens*. Munich: W. Fink, 2000.

Lactantius, Lucius Caecilius Firmianus. *A Treatise on the Anger of God*. In *The Ante-Nicene Fathers*, edited by Alexander Roberts, James Donaldson, and Arthur C. Coxe, 7:259–80. New York: Cosimo, 2004.

Lamp, Erich, and Michael Tilly. "Öffentlichkeit als Bedrohung: Ein Beitrag zur Deutung des 'Feindes' im Klagepsalm des Einzelnen." *Biblische Notizen*, no. 50 (1989): 46–57.

Lanckau, Jörg. *Der Herr der Träume: Eine Studie zur Funktion des Traumes in der Josefsgeschichte der Hebräischen Bibel*. Zurich: Theologischer Verlag, 2006.

Landsberger, Benno. "Die Eigenbegrifflichkeit der babylonischen Welt." In *Die Eigenbegrifflichkeit der babylonischen Welt und Leistung und Grenze sumerischer und babylonischer Wissenschaft*, edited by Benno Landsberger and Wolfram von Soden, 1–18. Darmstadt: Wissenschaftliche Buchgesellschaft, 1965. Reprint of *Islamica* 2 (1926): 355–72.

Lang, Bernhard, ed. *Anthropological Approaches to the Old Testament*. Philadelphia: Fortress Press, 1985.

———. "Feind." In *NBL* 1:663.

———. *Jahwe der biblische Gott: Ein Porträt*. Munich: C. H. Beck, 2002.

———. "Ein Kranker sieht seinen Gott." In *Wie wird man Prophet in Israel? Aufsätze zum Alten Testament*, edited by Bernhard Lang, 137–48. Düsseldorf: Patmos, 1980.

———. "Leben nach dem Tod." In *NBL* 2:599–602.

———. "Leibliche Auferstehung und ewiges Leben? Das biblische Jenseits in neuer Sicht." *Bibel und Kirche* 49 (1994): 2–10.

———. "Das Loben Gottes und die Verwünschung der Feinde: Kleine Einführung in die Psalmen." *Religionsunterricht an höheren Schulen* 36 (1993): 141–48.

———. "Rachepsalmen." In *NBL* 3:270.

———. "Reise ins Jenseits." In *NBL* 2:322–34.

———. "Religion und glückliche Menschenerfahrung: Zur alttestamentlichen Theorie des Glücks." In *Vom Guten Leben: Glücksvorstellungen in Hochkulturen*, edited by Alfred Bellebaum, 59–110. Berlin: Akademie Verlag, 1994.

———. "Sehen und Schauen." In *NBL* 3:555–61.

———. "Weltbild." In *NBL* 3:1098–1105.

Lang, Bernhard, and Colleen McDannell. *Der Himmel: Eine Kulturgeschichte des ewigen Lebens*. Frankfurt am Main: Insel Verlag, 1996.

Lange, Günther. *Bilder zum Glauben: Christliche Kunst sehen und verstehen*. Munich: Kösel, 2002.

Langenhorst, Georg, and Arnold Stadler. "Neue Sicht auf die Psalmen." Themenheft, *RHS* [*Religionsunterricht an höheren Schulen*] 49 (2006): Heft 6:371–76.

Langer, Birgit. *Gott als "Licht" in Israel und Mesopotamien: Eine Studie zu Jes 60, 1–3.19f*. Klosterneuburg: Österreichisches Katholische Bibelwerk, 1989.

Langer, Susanne Katherina Knauth. *Philosophie auf neuem Wege: Das Symbol im Denken, im Ritus, und in der Kunst*. Berlin: S. Fischer, 1965.

Lauha, Risto. *Psychophysischer Sprachgebrauch im Alten Testament: Eine Struktursemantische Analyse von לֵב, נֶפֶשׁ, und רוּחַ*. Helsinki: Suomalainen tiedeakatemia, 1983.

Leach, Edmund. *Culture and Communication: The Logic by Which Symbols Are Connected: An Introduction to the Use of Structuralist Analysis in Social Anthropology*. Cambridge: Cambridge University Press, 1976.

Leicht, Barbara D., ed. *Jenseitsvorstellungen im Alten Testament*. Stuttgart: Verlag Katholisches Bibelwerk, 2006.

Lescow, Theodor. *Das hadernde Wort: Paul Celans Todesfuge und Blasphemische Gedichte*. Münster: LIT Verlag, 2005.

———. "'Mein Herz schwimmt im Blut': Die Solokantate BW 199 von J. S. Bach als individuelles Klagelied in der Tradition der alttestamentlichen Klagepsalmen." *Biblische Notizen*, no. 121 (2004): 95–102.

———. "Psalm 22, 2–22 und Psalm 88: Komposition und Dramaturgie." *Zeitschrift für die alttestamentliche Wissenschaft* 177 (2005): 217–31.

———. *Theodizee: Christa Wolf, Altes Testament, Neues Testament, Paul Celan*. Malente: Books on Demand, 2002.

Leuenberger, Martin. "'Deine Gnade ist besser als Leben' (Ps 63, 4): Ausformungen der Grundkonstellation von Leben und Tod im alten Israel." *Biblica* 86 (2005): 343–68.

———. *Gott in Bewegung: Religions- und theologiegeschichtliche Beiträge zu Gottesvorstellungen im alten Israel*. Tübingen: Mohr Siebeck, 2011.

———. *Konzeptionen des Königtums Gottes im Psalter: Untersuchungen zu Komposition und Redaktion der theokratischen Bücher IV–V im Psalter*. Zurich: Theologischer Verlag Zürich, 2004.

Levin, Christoph. "Klagelieder Jeremias." In *RGG*[4] 4 (2001): 1394–96.

Lévinas, Emmanuel. *Ausser Sich: Meditationen über Religion und Philosophie*. Wien: Hanser Verlag, 1991. ET, *Outside the Subject*. Translated by Michael B. Smith. Stanford, CA: Stanford University Press, 1993.

Lewis, T. J. "Dead, Abode of." In *ABD* 2 (1992): 101–5.

Lichtenberger, Hermann. "Mensch V." In *RGG*[4] 5 (2002): 1058–61.

———. *Studien zum Menschenbild in Texten der Qumrangemeinde*. Göttingen: Vandenhoeck & Ruprecht, 1980.

Liess, Kathrin. "'Hast du die Tore der Finsternis gesehen?': Zur Lokalisierung des Totenreichs im Alten Testament." In Berlejung and Janowski, *Tod und Jenseits*, 397–422.

———. "'JHWH ist mein Becheranteil': Zum Bechermotiv in den Psalmen 16; 23 und 116." In *Gott, Mensch, Sprache: Schülerfestschrift für Walter Gross zum 60. Geburtstag*, edited by Andreas Michel and Herrmann-Josef Stipp, 45–63. St. Ottilien: EOS-Verlag, 2001.

———. "Sättigung mit langem Leben: Vergänglichkeit, Lebenszeit und Alter in den Psalmen 90–92." In *FS Janowski*, 329–42.

———. "Tod II." *RGG*[4] 8 (2005): 429–31.

———. "Von der Gottesferne zur Gottesnähe: Zur Todes- und Lebensmetaphorik in den Psalmen." In van Hecke and Labahn, *Metaphors in the Psalms*, 167–95.

———. *Der Weg des Lebens: Psalm 16 und das Lebens- und Todesverständnis der Individualpsalmen*. Diss., Universität Tübingen, 2002. Reprint, Tübingen: Mohr Siebeck, 2004.

———. "Wege aus der Vergessenheit: Zu einem neuen Sammelband zum Thema 'Klage.'" *Jahrbuch für biblische Theologie* 16 (2001): 383–96.

Limbeck, Meinrad. "Der Beter, die Wahrheit, das Böse." *Bibel und Kirche* 35 (1980): 70.

———. "Die Klage—eine verschwundene Gebetsgattung." *Theologische Quartalschrift* 157 (1977): 3–16.

———. "Der Lobpreis Gottes als Sinn des Daseins." *Theologische Quartalschrift* 150 (1970): 349–57.

Lindström, Fredrik. *Suffering and Sin: Interpretations of Illness in the Individual Complaint Psalms*. Stockholm: Almqvist & Wiksell International, 1994.

Lindström, Fredrik, and Meinrad Limbeck. "Das Böse I–II." In *NBL* 1:314–16.

Link, Christoph. "Menschenbild—Theologische Grundlegung aus evangelischer Sicht." In *Bioethik und Menschenbild bei Juden und Christen: Bewährungsfeld Anthropologie*, edited by Wolfgang Kraus, 57–71. Neukirchen-Vluyn: Neukirchener Verlag, 1999.

Lipiński, Edward. "נָקַם . . . ." In *ThWAT* 5:602–12.

Liwak, Rüdiger. "שָׁפַךְ." In *ThWAT* 8:428–38.

Lohfink, Norbert. "Das Alte Testament und der christliche Tageslauf." *Bibel und Kirche* 56 (2001): 26–34.

———. "Enthielten die im Alten Testament bezeugten Klageriten eine Phase des Schweigens?" *Vetus Testamentum* 12 (1962): 260–77.

———. "'Ich bin Jahweh, dein Arzt' (Ex 15, 26): Gott, Gesellschaft und menschliche Gesundheit in einer nachexilischen Pentateuchbearbeitung." In *Studien zum Pentateuch*, edited by Norbert Lohfink, 91–155. Stuttgart: Verlag Katholisches Bibelwerk, 1988.

———. "Innenschau und Kosmosmystik: Zu Psalm 36." In *Im Schatten deiner Flügel: Große Bibeltexte neu erschlossen*, edited by Norbert Lohfink, 172–87. Freiburg im Breisgau: Herder Verlag, 2000.

———. *Lobgesänge der Armen: Studien zum Magnifikat, den Hodajot von Qumran und einigen späten Psalmen*. Stuttgart: Verlag Katholisches Bibelwerk, 1990.

———. "Der Münsterschwarzacher Psalter." *Bibel und Liturgie* 76 (2003): 71–81.

———. "Opferzentralisation, Säkularisierungsthese und mimetische Theorie." In *Studien zum Deuteronomium und zur Deuteronomistischen Literatur*, edited by Norbert Lohfink, 3:219–60. Stuttgart: Verlag Katholisches Bibelwerk, 1995.

———. "Ps 7, 2–6—vom Löwen gejagt." In *Die Freude an Gott, unsere Kraft: Festschrift für Otto Bernhard Knoch zum 65. Geburtstag*, edited by Johannes Joachim Degenhardt, Eleonore Beck, and Eugen Sitarz, 60–67. Stuttgart: Verlag Katholisches Bibelwerk, 1991.

———. "Psalmen im Neuen Testament: Die Lieder der Kindheitsgeschichte bei Lukas." In *Neue Wege der Psalmenforschung*, edited by Klaus Seybold and Erich Zenger, 105–25. Freiburg im Breisgau: Herder Verlag, 1995.

———. "Psalmengebet und Psalterredaktion." *Archiv für Liturgiewissenschaft* 34, nos. 1–2 (1992): 1–22.

———. "Der Psalter und die christliche Meditation: Die Bedeutung der Endredaktion für das Verständnis der Psalmen." *Bibel und Kirche* 4 (1992): 195–200.

———. "Über die Feinde des Kranken im alten Orient und in den Psalmen." In *Unsere grossen Wörter: Das Alte Testament zu Themen dieser Jahre*, edited by Norbert Lohfink, 145–55. Freiburg im Breisgau: Herder Verlag, 1985.

———. "Von der 'Anawim-Partei' zur 'Kirche der Armen': Die bibelwissenschaftliche Ahnentafel eines Hauptbegriffs der 'Theologie der Befreiung.'" *Biblica* 67, no. 2 (1986): 153–76.

———. "Das vorpersonale Böse: Das Alte Testament und der Begriff der Erbsünde." In *Das jüdische am Christentum: Die verlorene Dimension*, edited by Norbert Lohfink, 167–99. Freiburg im Breisgau: Herder Verlag, 1987.

———. "Was wird anders bei kanonischer Schriftauslegung? Beobachtungen am Beispiel von Ps. 6." *Jahrbuch für biblische Theologie* 3 (1988): 29–53.

Lohfink, Norbert, and Georg Fischer. "'Diese Worte sollst du summen': Dtn 6, 7 *wĕdibbartā bām*—ein verlorener Schlüssel zur meditativen Kultur in Israel." In *Studien zum Deuteronomium und zur Deuteronomistischen Literatur*, edited by Norbert Lohfink, 3:181–203. Stuttgart: Verlag Katholisches Bibelwerk, 1995.

Lohfink, Norbert, and Erich Zenger. *Der Gott Israels und die Völker: Untersuchungen zum Jesajabuch und zu den Psalmen*. Stuttgart: Verlag Katholisches Bibelwerk, 1994.

Löning, Karl. "Die Funktion des Psalters im Neuen Testament." In *Der Psalter in Judentum und Christentum*, edited by Erich Zenger and Norbert Lohfink, 269–95. Freiburg im Breisgau: Herder Verlag, 1998.

———. "Die Memoria des Todes Jesu als Zugang zur Schrift im Urchristentum." In *Christologie der Liturgie: Der Gottesdienst der Kirche—Christusbekenntnis und Sinaibund*, edited by Klemens Richter and Benedikt Kranemann, 138–49. Freiburg im Breisgau: Herder Verlag, 1995.

Loretz, Oswald. "Akkadisch-ugaritisch *ḫalbu/ḫlb*—hebräisch *ḥlb* (Ps 81, 17): Ein Beitrag zur Sozialgeschichte Altsyrien-Palästinas." In *Dubsar Anta-Men: Studien zur Altorientalistik; Festschrift für Willem H. Ph. Römer zur Vollendung seines 70. Lebensjahres, mit Beiträgen von Freunden, Schülern und Kollegen*, edited by Thomas E. Balke, Manfried Dietrich, and Oswald Loretz, 223–44. Münster: Ugarit-Verlag, 1998.

———. "'Gerechtigkeit und Unsterblichkeit': In ägyptischer und westsemitischer Sicht." In *Ägypten—Münster: Kulturwissenschaftliche Studien zu Ägypten, dem Vorderen Orient und verwandten Gebieten*, edited by Anke Ilona Blöbaum et al., 187–95. Wiesbaden: O. Harrassowitz, 2003.

———. *Götter—Ahnen—Könige als gerechte Richter: Der "Rechtsfall" des Menschen vor Gott nach altorientalischen und biblischen Texten*. Münster: Ugarit-Verlag, 2003.

———. "Mythische Götterrebellion und königliche Sozialpflichten als gemeinsamer altorientalischer Hintergrund von Ps 82." In *Berührungspunkte: Studien zur Sozial- und Religionsgeschichte Israels und seiner Umwelt; Festschrift für Rainer Albertz zu seinem 65. Geburtstag*, edited by Ingo Kottsieper et al., 393–408. Münster: Ugarit-Verlag, 2008.

———. "Nekromantie und Totenevokation in Mesopotamien, Ugarit und Israel." In *Religionsgeschichtliche Beziehungen zwischen Kleinasien, Nordsyrien und dem Alten Testament: Internationales Symposion Hamburg, 17.–21. März 1990*, edited by Bernd Janowski, Klaus Koch, and Gernot Wilhelm, 285–318. Göttingen: Vandenhoeck & Ruprecht, 1993.

———. "Die postmortale (himmlische) Theoxenie der *npš* 'Seele, Totenseele' in ugaritisch-biblischer Sicht nach Psalm 16, 10–11." *Ugarit-Forschungen* 38 (2006): 445–97.

———. *Psalmstudien: Kolometrie, Strophik und Theologie ausgewählter Psalmen*. Berlin and New York, 2002.

———. *Ugarit und die Bibel kanaanäische Götter und Religion im Alten Testament*. 2nd ed. Darmstadt: Wissenschaftliche Buchgesellschaft, 1996.

———. "Vom kanaanäischen Totenkult zur jüdischen Patriarchen- und Elternverehrung." *Jahrbuch für Anthropologie und Religionsgeschichte* 3 (1978): 149–204.

Lugt, Peter van der. *Cantos and Strophes in Biblical Hebrew Poetry with Special Reference to the First Book of the Psalter*. Leiden and Boston: E. J. Brill, 2006.

Luhmann, Niklas, and André Kieserling. *Die Religion der Gesellschaft*. Frankfurt am Main: Suhrkamp, 2000.

Lührmann, Dieter. *Das Markusevangelium*. Tübingen: Mohr, 1987.

Luibl, Hans Jürgen. "Beten begreifen: Über die seltsame Lust der Philosophie am Gebet." In *Die Vernunft ins Gebet nehmen: Philosophisch-theologische Betrachtungen*, edited by Elmar Salmann and Joachim Hake, 31–58. Stuttgart: W. Kohlhammer, 2000.

Lundström, Steven. "Unterwelt." In *Der neue Pauly*, edited by Hubert Cancik, Helmuth Schneider, and August Friedrich von Pauly, 12/1:1012–19. Stuttgart: J. B. Metzler, 2002.

———. "'Wenn du in die Unterwelt hinabsteigen willst': Mesopotamische Vorstellungen von der Ordnung der Unterwelt." In *Kulturgeschichten: Altorientalistische Studien für Volkert Haas zum 65. Geburtstag*, edited by Thomas Richter, Doris Prechel, and Jörg Klinger, 245–53. Saarbrücken: SDV, Saarbrücker Druckerei & Verlag, 2001.

———. "Zur Aussagekraft schriftlicher Quellen hinsichtlich der Vorstellungen vom Leben nach dem Tod in Mesopotamien." *Altorientalische Forschungen* 30 (2003): 30–50.

Lüpke, Johannes von. "Herz." In *RGG*[4] 3 (2000): 1695–97.

Luther, Martin. "Preface to the Psalter: 1545 (1528)." In *Faith and Freedom: An Invitation to the Writings of Martin Luther*, edited by John F. Thornton and Susanne B. Varenne, 25–29. New York: Random House, 2002.

———. *Von wahrer und falscher Frömmigkeit: Auslegungen des 5. und 22. Psalms*. Gütersloh: Gütersloher Verlagshaus Gerd Mohn, 1977.

———. "Zweite Vorrede auf den Psalter (1528)." In *Luthers Vorreden zur Bibel*, edited by Heinrich Bornkamm, 64–69. Frankfurt am Main: Insel Verlag, 1983.

Lux, Rüdiger. "Die Bibel—Lehrerin der Menschheit: Anmerkungen zur biblischen Anthropologie." *Die Zeichen der Zeit* 4 (1996): 122–29.

———. *Jona, Prophet zwischen "Verweigerung" und "Gehorsam": Eine erzählanalytische Studie*. Göttingen: Vandenhoeck & Ruprecht, 1994.

———. *Josef: Der Auserwählte unter seinen Brüdern*. Leipzig: Evangelische Verlagsanstalt, 2001.

Luz, Ulrich. *Das Evangelium nach Matthäus.* Neukirchen-Vlyun: Neukirchener Verlag, 1985.

Maag, Viktor. "Tod und Jenseits nach dem Alten Testament." In *Kultur, Kulturkontakt und Religion: Gesammelte Studien zur allgemeinen und alttestamentlichen Religionsgeschichte zum 70. Geburtstag herausgegeben,* edited by Hans Heinrich Schmid and Odil Hannes Steck, 181–202. Göttingen: Vandenhoeck & Ruprecht, 1980.

Macho, Thomas H. *Todesmetaphern: Zur Logik der Grenzerfahrung.* Frankfurt am Main: Suhrkamp, 1987.

Macholz, Christian. "Bemerkungen zu Ps 7, 4–6." *Zeitschrift für die alttestamentliche Wissenschaft* 91 (1979): 127–29.

Maier, Johann. *Zwischen den Testamenten: Geschichte und Religion in der Zeit des zweiten Tempels.* Würzburg: Echter Verlag, 1990.

Malina, Bruce J. *The New Testament World: Insights from Cultural Anthropology.* 3rd ed. Louisville, KY: Westminster John Knox Press, 2001.

Marcus, Joel. *The Way of the Lord: Christological Exegesis of the Old Testament in the Gospel of Mark.* Louisville, KY: Westminster/John Knox Press, 1992.

Mark, Martin. *Meine Stärke und mein Schutz ist der Herr: Poetologisch-theologische Studie zu Psalm 118.* Würzburg: Echter Verlag, 1999.

Markschies, Christoph. "'Ich aber vertraue auf dich, Herr!': Vertrauensäusserungen als Grundmotiv in den Klageliedern des Einzelnen." *Zeitschrift für die alttestamentliche Wissenschaft* 103, no. 3 (1991): 386–98.

Markschies, Christoph, et al. *Atlas der Weltbilder.* Berlin: Akademie Verlag, 2011.

Marquard, Odo. "Anthropologie." In *HWP* 1:362–74.

Marttila, Marko. *Collective Reinterpretation in the Psalms: A Study of the Redaction History of the Psalter.* Tübingen: Mohr Siebeck, 2006.

Marx, Alfred. "Heilsopfer." In *NBL* 2:108–9.

———. "Opferlogik im alten Israel." In *Opfer: Theologische und kulturelle Kontexte,* edited by Bernd Janowski and Michael Welker, 129–49. Frankfurt am Main: Suhrkamp, 2000.

———. *Les systèmes sacrificiels de l'Ancien Testament: Formes et fonctions du culte sacrificiel à Yhwh.* Leiden and Boston: E. J. Brill, 2005.

Mathys, Hans-Peter. *Liebe deinen Nächsten wie dich selbst: Untersuchungen zum alttestamentlichen Gebot der Nächstenliebe (Lev 19, 18).* 2nd ed. Freiburg, Switzerland: Universitätsverlag, 1990.

Maul, Stefan M. "Altorientalische Trauerriten." In *Der Abschied von den Toten: Trauerrituale im Kulturvergleich,* edited by Jan Assmann, Franz Maciejewski, and Axel Michaels, 359–72. Göttingen: Wallstein Verlag, 2005.

———. "Der assyrische König—Hüter der Weltordnung." In *Priests and Officials in the Ancient Near East: Papers of the Second Colloquium on the Ancient Near East—the City and Its Life, Held at the Middle Eastern Culture Center in Japan (Mitaka, Tokyo), March 22–24, 1996,* edited by Kazuko Watanabe, 201–14. Heidelberg: Universitätsverlag C. Winter, 1999.

———. "'Auf meinen Rechtsfall werde doch aufmerksam!': Wie sich die Babylonier und Assyrer vor Unheil schützten, das sich durch ein Vorzeichen angekündigt hatte." *Mitteilungen der Deutschen Orient-Gesellschaft* 124 (1992): 131–42.

———. "Die 'Lösung vom Bann': Überlegungen zu altorientalischen Konzeptionen von Krankheit und Heilskunst." In *Magic and Rationality in Ancient Near Eastern and Graeco-Roman Medicine,* edited by Herman F. J. Horstmanshoff and Marten Stol, 79–95. Leiden and Boston: E. J. Brill, 2004.

———. "Der Sieg über die Mächte des Bösen: Götterkampf, Triumpgrituale und Torarchitektur in Assyrien." In *Gegenwelten: Zu den Kulturen Griechenlands und Roms in der Antike,* edited by Tonio Hölscher, 19–46. Munich: Saur, 2000.

———. "'Wenn der Held (zum Kampfe) auszieht . . .': Ein Ninurta-Ersemma." *Orientalia* 60, no. 4 (1991): 312–34.

———. *Zukunftsbewältigung: Eine Untersuchung altorientalischen Denkens anhand der Babylonisch-Assyrischen Löserituale (Namburbi)*. Mainz am Rhein: Verlag Philipp von Zabern, 1994.

Mauss, Marcel. *Die Gabe: Form und Funktion des Austauschs in archaischen Gesellschaften*. Frankfurt am Main: Suhrkamp, 1990. Translation of *Essai sur le don* (1925, 1950). ET, *The Gift: Forms and Functions of Exchange in Archaic Societies*. Glencoe, IL: Free Press, 1954.

Mayer, Günter, Jan Bergman, and Wolfram von Soden. "יָדָה." In *ThWAT* 3:455–74.

Mayer, Werner R. "'Ich rufe dich von ferne, höre mich von nahe!': Zu einer babylonischen Gebetsformel." In *Werden und Wirken des Alten Testaments: Festschrift für Claus Westermann*, edited by Rainer Albertz, 302–17. Göttingen: Vandenhoeck & Ruprecht, 1980.

———. *Untersuchungen zur Formensprache der babylonischen "Gebetsbeschwörungen."* Rome: Pontifical Biblical Institute Press, 1976.

Meinhold, Arndt. "Bewertung und Beginn des Greisenalters." In *Zur weisheitlichen Sicht des Menschen: Gesammelte Aufsätze*, edited by Arndt Meinhold and Thomas Neumann, 99–116. Leipzig: Evangelische Verlagsanstalt, 2002.

———. "Der Gewaltmensch als abschreckendes Beispiel in Proverbien 1–9." In *Zur weisheitlichen Sicht des Menschen: Gesammelte Aufsätze*, edited by Arndt Meinhold and Thomas Neumann, 151–64. Leipzig: Evangelische Verlagsanstalt, 2002.

———. "Menschsein in der Welt vor Gott: Alttestamentliche Perspektiven." In *Zur weisheitlichen Sicht des Menschen: Gesammelte Aufsätze*, edited by Arndt Meinhold and Thomas Neumann, 13–34. Leipzig: Evangelische Verlagsanstalt, 2002.

———. *Die Sprüche*. Zurich: Theologischer Verlag, 1991.

———. "Der Umgang mit dem Feind nach Spr 25, 21f. als Massstab für das Menschsein." In *Zur weisheitlichen Sicht des Menschen: Gesammelte Aufsätze*, edited by Arndt Meinhold and Thomas Neumann, 189–97. Leipzig: Evangelische Verlagsanstalt, 2002.

Mettinger, Tryggve N. D. *In Search of God: The Meaning and Message of the Everlasting Names*. Philadelphia: Fortress Press, 1988.

Metz, Johannes Baptist. "Gotteskrise: Versuch zur 'geistigen Situation der Zeit.'" In *Diagnosen zur Zeit*, edited by Johannes Baptist Metz, 76–92. Düsseldorf: Patmos, 1994.

Metzger, Mendel. *Himmlische und irdische Wohnstatt Jahwes*. Kevelaer: Butzon & Bercker, 1970.

Meyer, Martin F. "Der Wandel des Psyche-Begriffs im frühgriechischen Denken von Homer bis Heraklit." *Arbeiten zur Bibel und ihrer Geschichte* 50 (2008): 9–28.

Meyer-Dietrich, Erika. *Senebi und Selbst: Personenkonstituenten zur rituellen Wiedergeburt in einem Frauensarg des Mittleren Reiches*. Freiburg, Switzerland: Academic Press, 2006.

Michel, Diethelm. "Armut II." In *TRE* 4:72–76.

———. "Gericht Gottes." In *NBL* 1 (1991): 801–3, 807.

———. "Gerechtigkeit I." In *NBL* 1 (1991): 795–98.

———. *Grundlegung einer hebräischen Syntax*. Neukirchen-Vluyn: Neukirchener Verlag, 1977.

———. "Ich aber bin immer bei dir: Von der Unsterblichkeit der Gottesbeziehung." In *Studien zur Überlieferungsgeschichte alttestamentlicher Texte*, edited by Diethelm Michel and Andreas Wagner, 155–79. Gütersloh: Christian Kaiser, 1997.

———. "*Næpæš* [*Nepeš*] als Leichnam." *Zeitschrift für Althebraistik* 7 (1994): 81–84.

———. *Qohelet*. Darmstadt: Wissenschaftliche Buchgesellschaft, 1988.

———. *Tempora und Satzstellung in den Psalmen*. Bonn: H. Bouvier, 1960.

———. "'Warum' und 'wozu'? Eine bisher übersehene Eigentümlichkeit des Hebräischen und ihre Konsequenz für das alttestamentliche Geschichtsverständnis." In *Studien zur Überlieferungsgeschichte alttestamentlicher Texte*, edited by Diethelm Michel and Andreas Wagner, 13–34. Gütersloh: Christian Kaiser, 1997.

———. "Weisheit und Apokalyptik." In *The Book of Daniel in the Light of New Findings*, edited by A. S. van der Woude, 413–34. Leuven: Leuven University Press, 1993.

Mieth, Irene, and Dietmar Mieth. "'Im Eisverhau': Psalmen finden in Gedichten." *Bibel und Kirche* 47 (1992): 209–13.

Millard, Matthias. *Die Komposition des Psalters: Ein formgeschichtlicher Ansatz*. Tübingen: J. C. B. Mohr, 1994.

Miller, Patrick D. "Deuteronomy and Psalms: Evoking a Biblical Conversation." *Journal of Biblical Literature* 118, no. 1 (1999): 3–18.

———. *They Cried to the Lord: The Form and Theology of Biblical Prayer*. Minneapolis: Fortress Press, 1994.

Mitscherlich, Alexander. *Krankheit als Konflikt*. Frankfurt am Main: Suhrkamp, 1966.

Mitscherlich, Alexander, and Margarete Mitscherlich. *Die Unfähigkeit zu Trauern: Grundlagen kollektiven Verhaltens*. Munich: Piper, 1967.

Mittmann, Siegfried. "Aufbau und Einheit des Danklieds Psalm 23." *Zeitschrift für Theologie und Kirche* 77, no. 1 (1980): 1–23.

———. "Das Symbol der Hand in der altorientalistischen Ikonographie." In *La main de Dieu = Die Hand Gottes*, edited by René Kieffer and Jan Bergman, 19–47. Tübingen: Mohr Siebeck, 1997.

Moltmann, Jürgen. *Der gekreuzigte Gott: Das Kreuz Christi als Grund und Kritik christlicher Theologie*. Munich: Christian Kaiser, 1972.

———. "Die Rechtfertigung Gottes." In *Das Kreuz Jesu: Gewalt, Opfer, Sühne*, edited by Rudolf Weth, 120–41. Neukirchen-Vluyn: Neukirchener Verlag, 2001.

———. *"Sein Name ist Gerechtigkeit": Neue Beiträge zur christlichen Gotteslehre*. Gütersloh: Gütersloher Verlagshaus, 2008.

———. "Sonne der Gerechtigkeit: Das Evangelium vom Gericht und der Neuschöpfung aller Dinge." In *Neue Beiträge zur christlichen Gotteslehre*, 118–36.

Mowinckel, Sigmund. *Åwän und die individuellen Klagepsalmen*. Vol. 1 of *Psalmenstudien*. Kristiania: Jacob Dybwad, 1921.

Müller, Augustin R. "Psalm 23 als Text persönlicher Frömmigkeit." In *In Würde leben: Interdisziplinäre Studien zu Ehren von Ernst Ludwig Grasmück*, edited by Rainer Bucher, Ottmar Fuchs, and Joachim Kügler, 24–34. Lucerne: Edition Exodus, 1998.

———. "Psalm 23, 1 und der identifizierende Nominalsatz." In Steingrimsson and Ólason, *Literatur- und sprachwissenschaftliche Beiträge*, 137–53.

———. "Stimmungsumschwung im Klagepsalm: Zu O. Fuchs, *Die Klage als Gebet*." *Archiv für Liturgiewissenschaft* 28 (1986): 416–26.

Müller, Hans-Peter. "Formgeschichtliche und sprachliche Beobachtungen zu Psalm 30." *Zeitschrift für Althebraistik* 12 (1999): 192–201.

———. "Gottesfrage und Psalmenexegese: Zur Hermeneutik der Klagepsalmen des einzelnen." In *Neue Wege der Psalmenforschung: Für Walter Beyerlin*, edited by Klaus Seybold and Erich Zenger, 279–99. Freiburg im Breisgau: Herder Verlag, 1994.

———. *Das Hohelied, Klagelieder, Das Buch Ester*. Göttingen: Vandenhoeck & Ruprecht, 1992.

———. "Menschen, Landschaften und religiöse Erinnerungsreste." *Zeitschrift für Theologie und Kirche* 91 (1994): 375–95.

———. "Monotheismus und Polytheismus." In *RGG*[4] 5 (2002): 1459–62.

———. "Mythische Elemente in der jahwistischen Schöpfungserzählung." In *Mythos, Kerygma, Wahrheit: Gesammelte Aufsätze zum Alten Testament in seiner Umwelt und zur biblischen Theologie*, edited by Hans-Peter Müller, 3–42. Berlin: Walter de Gruyter, 1991.

———. "Psalmen und frühgriechische Lyrik: Drei Beispiele." *Biblische Zeitschrift* 47 (2003): 23–42.

———. Review of *Anthropologie des Alten Testaments*, by Hans Walter Wolff. *Theologische Literaturzeitung* 100 (1975): 501–4.

———. "Rückzug Gottes ins Namenlose: Zu einem Gedicht Paul Celans." In *Glauben, Denken und Hoffen: Alttestamentliche Botschaften in den Auseinandersetzungen unserer Zeit*, 311–19. Münster: LIT Verlag, 1998.

———. *Vergleich und Metapher im Hohenlied*. Freiburg, Switzerland: Universitätsverlag, 1984.

———. "Was der Akzeptanz einer biblischen Anthropologie entgegensteht und wie wir mit der Herausforderung umgehen." In *Der Mensch vor Gott: Forschungen zum Menschenbild in Bibel, antikem Judentum und Koran; Festschrift für Hermann Lichtenberger zum 60. Geburtstag*, edited by Ulrike Mittmann-Richert, Friedrich Avemarie, and Gerbern S. Oegema, 3–13. Neukirchen-Vluyn: Neukirchener Verlag, 2003.

Müller, Hans-Peter, Otto Kaiser, and James Alfred Loader. *Das Hohelied, Klagelieder, Das Buch Ester*. Göttingen: Vandenhoeck & Ruprecht, 1992.

Müller, Karlheinz. "Das Weltbild der jüdischen Apokalyptik und die Rede von Jesu Auferstehung." *Bibel und Kirche* 52 (1997): 8–18.

Müller, Klaus E. "Perspektiven der Historischen Anthropologie." In *Westliches Geschichtsdenken: Eine interkulturelle Debatte*, edited by Jörn Rüsen, 55–80. Göttingen: Vandenhoeck & Ruprecht, 1999. ET, "Perspectives in Historical Anthropology." In *Western Historical Thinking: An Intercultural Debate*, edited by Jörn Rüsen, 33–52. New York: Berghahn Books, 2002.

Müllner, Ilse, and Peter Dschulnigg. *Jüdische und christliche Feste*. Würzburg: Echter Verlag, 2002.

Münsterschwarzacher Psalter: Die Psalmen. Münsterschwarzach: Vier-Türme-Verlag, 2003.

Nachama, Andreas, and Marion Gardei. *Du bist mein Gott, den ich suche: Psalmen lesen im jüdisch-christlichen Dialog*. Gütersloh: Gütersloher Verlagshaus, 2012.

Nentel, Jochen. *Trägerschaft und Intentionen des deuteronomistischen Geschichtswerks: Untersuchungen zu den Reflexionsreden Jos 1; 23; 24; 1 Sam 12 und 1 Kön 8*. Berlin: Walter de Gruyter, 2000.

Neumann, Klaus. "Kultur und Mentalität." In *HGANT*² 35–42.

———. "Person." In *HGANT*² 339–40.

Neumann, P. H. A. "Weltbild." In *CBL* 2:1454–57.

Neumann-Gorsolke, Ute. "'Alt und lebenssatt . . .'—der Tod zur rechten Zeit." In Berlejung and Janowski, *Tod und Jenseits*, 111–36.

———. *Herrschen in den Grenzen der Schöpfung: Ein Beitrag zur alttestamentlichen Anthropologie am Beispiel von Psalm 8, Genesis 1 und Verwandten Texten*. Diss., Universität Tübingen, 2002–3. Reprint, Neukirchen-Vluyn: Neukirchener Verlag, 2004.

———. "'Mit Ehre und Hoheit has Du ihn gekrönt' (Ps 8, 6): Alttestamentliche Aspekte zum Thema Menschenwürde." *Jahrbuch für biblische Theologie* 15 (2000): 39–65.

Neumann-Gorsolke, Ute, and Peter Riede. "Garten und Paradies." In *Das Kleid der Erde: Pflanzen in der Lebenswelt des alten Israel*, edited by Ute Neumann-Gorsolke and Peter Riede, 108–13. Stuttgart: Calwer Verlag, 2002.

Niehr, Herbert. "Aspekte des Totengedenkens im Juda der Königszeit: Eine Problemskizze." *Theologische Quartalschrift* 178, no. 1 (1998): 1–13.

———. *Herrschen und Richten: Die Wurzel špṭ im Alten Orient und im Alten Testament*. Würzburg: Echter Verlag, 1986.

———. "Himmel, Hölle, Fegefeuer: Die biblischen Grundlagen." In *Himmel—Hölle—Fegefeuer: Theologisches Kontaktstudium 1995*, edited by Albert Biesinger and Michael Kessler, 55–74. Tübingen: Francke, 1995.

———. *Rechtsprechung in Israel: Untersuchungen zur Geschichte der Gerichtsorganisation im Alten Testament*. Stuttgart: Verlag Katholisches Bibelwerk, 1987.

———. *Religionen in Israels Umwelt: Einführung in die Nordwestsemitischen Religionen Syrien-Palästinas*. Würzburg: Echter Verlag, 1998.

———. "צַלְמָוֶת." In *ThWAT* 6:1056–59.

Niemand, Christoph. *Jesus und sein Weg zum Kreuz: Ein historisch-rekonstruktives und theologisches Modellbild*. Stuttgart: Kohlhammer, 2007.

Nitsche, Stefan Ark. "Vor der Antwort käme der Frage: Die Psalmenrezeption im Evangelischen Gesangbuch." In *Schweigen wäre gotteslästerlich: Die heilende Kraft der Klage*, edited by Georg Steins, 133–53. Würzburg: Echter Verlag, 2000.

Noort, Edward. "JHWH und das Böse: Bemerkungen zu einer Verhältnisbestimmung." In *Prophets, Worship and Theodicy*, edited by John Barton, Robert Carroll, and Jan P. Fokkelman, 120–36. Leiden: E. J. Brill, 1984.

———. "Der Tod und die Gerechtigkeit im alten Israel: Zwei Rollenspiele." In *Berührungspunkte: Studien zur Sozial- und Religionsgeschichte Israels und seiner Umwelt; Festschrift für Rainer Albertz zu seinem 65. Geburtstag*, edited by I. Kottsieper, Rüdiger Schmitt, and Jakob Wöhrle, 369–81. Münster: Ugarit-Verlag, 2008.

Norin, Stig. "Die Hand Gottes im Alten Testament." In *La main de Dieu = Die Hand Gottes*, edited by René Kieffer and Jan Bergman, 49–63. Tübingen: Mohr Siebeck, 1997.

North, Christopher R. *The Second Isaiah*. Oxford: Clarendon Press, 1964.

North, Robert Grady. "Did Ancient Israelites Have a Heart?" In *Medicine in the Biblical Background and Other Essays on the Origins of Hebrew*, edited by Robert Grady North, 69–72. Rome: Pontificio Istituto Biblico, 2000.

———. "Medicine and Healing in the Old Testament Background." In *Medicine in the Biblical Background and Other Essays on the Origins of Hebrew*, edited by Robert Grady North, 9–34. Rome: Pontificio Istituto Biblico, 2000.

Oeming, Manfred. "An der Quelle des Gebets: Neuere Untersuchungen zu den Psalmen." *Theologische Literaturzeitung* 127, no. 4 (2002): 367–84.

———. *Das Buch der Psalmen: Psalm 1–41*. Stuttgart: Verlag Katholisches Bibelwerk, 2000.

———. "'Mein Herz ist durchbohrt in meinem Innern' (Ps 109, 22): Krankheit und Leid in alttestamentlicher Sicht." In *Krankheit und Leid in der Sicht der Religionen*, edited by Manfred Oeming and Friedhelm Krüger, 5–28. Osnabrück: Universität Osnabrück, Fachbereich Erziehungs- und Kulturwissenschaft, 1994.

———. "Welt/Weltanschauung/Weltbild IV/2." *TRE* 35 (2003): 569–81.

Oeming, Manfred, and Joachim Vette. *Das Buch der Psalmen: Psalm 42–89*. Stuttgart: Verlag Katholisches Bibelwerk, 2010.

Ogushi, Motosuke. "Ist nur das Herz die Mitte des Menschen?" In F. Crüsemann, Hardmeier, and Kessler, *Was ist der Mensch . . . ?*, 42–47.

Oorschot, Jürgen van. "Der ferne *deus praesens* des Tempels: Die Korachpsalmen und der Wandel israelitischer Tempeltheologie." In *Wer ist wie du, Herr, unter den Göttern? Studien zur Theologie und Religionsgeschichte Israels; Für Otto Kaiser zum 70. Geburtstag*, edited by Ingo Kottsieper, 416–30. Göttingen: Vandenhoeck & Ruprecht, 1994.

———. "Menschenbild, Gottesbild und Menschenwürde: Ein Beitrag des Hiobbuches." In *Menschenbild und Menschenwürde*, edited by Eilert Herms, 320–43. Gütersloh: Christian Kaiser, Gütersloher Verlagshaus, 2001.

———. "Zur Grundlegung alttestamentlicher Anthropologie: Orientierung und Zwischenruf." In *Der Mensch als Thema theologischer Anthropologie: Beiträge in interdisziplinärer Perspektive; Kurt Seidel zum 80. Geburtstag*, edited by Markus Iff, 1–41. Neukirchen-Vluyn: Neukirchener Verlag, 2010.

Otto, Eckart. "Die Bedeutung der altorientalischen Rechtsgeschichte für das Verständnis des Alten Testaments." *Zeitschrift für Theologie und Kirche* 88, no. 2 (1991): 139–68.

———. *Das Deuteronomium: Politische Theologie und Rechtsreform in Juda und Assyrien*. Berlin: Walter de Gruyter, 1999.

———. "Gerechtigkeit und Erbarmen im Recht des Alten Testaments und seiner christlichen Rezeption." In *Gerechtigkeit: Richten und Retten in der Abendländischen Tradition und ihren Altorientalischen Ursprüngen*, edited by Jan Assmann, Bernd Janowski, and Michael Welker, 79–95. Munich: Fink, 1998.

———. *Krieg und Frieden in der hebräischen Bibel und im Alten Orient: Aspekte für eine Friedensordnung in der Moderne*. Stuttgart: W. Kohlhammer, 1999.

———. "Magie—Dämonen—göttliche Kräfte: Krankheit und Heilung im Alten Orient und im Alten Testament." In *Heilung—Energie—Geist: Heilung zwischen Wissenschaft, Religion und Geschäft*, edited by Werner H. Ritter and Bernhard Wolf, 209–25. Göttingen: Vandenhoeck & Ruprecht, 2005.

———. "Recht/Rechtstheologie/Rechtsphilosophie." In *TRE* 28:197–209.

———. *Theologische Ethik des Alten Testaments*. Stuttgart: W. Kohlhammer, 1994.

———. "'Um Gerechtigkeit im Land sichtbar werden zu lassen . . .': Zur Vermittlung von Recht und Gerechtigkeit im Alten Orient, in der hebräischen Bibel und in der Moderne." In *Recht—Macht—Gerechtigkeit*, edited by Joachim Mehlhausen, 107–45. Gütersloh: Christian Kaiser / Gütersloher Verlagshaus, 1998.

Otzen, Benedikt. "בָּהַל." In *ThWAT* 1:520–23.

———. "בְּלִיַּעַל." In *ThWAT* 1:654–58.

Pannenberg, Wolfhart. *Anthropologie in theologischer Perspektive*. Göttingen: Vandenhoeck & Ruprecht, 1983.

———. *Systematische Theologie*. Vol. 2. Göttingen: Vandenhoeck & Ruprecht, 1988.

———. *Was ist der Mensch? Die Anthropologie der Gegenwart im Lichte der Theologie*. 2nd ed. Göttingen: Vandenhoeck & Ruprecht, 1964.

Paris, Rainer. *Stachel und Speer: Machtstudien*. Frankfurt am Main: Suhrkamp, 1998.

Parker, Simon B. "The Use of Similes in Ugaritic Literature." *Ugarit-Forschungen* 36 (2004): 357–69.

Paul, Axel T. "Die Rache und das Rätsel der Gabe." *Leviathan* 33 (2005): 240–56.

Pedersen, Johannes. *Israel, Its Life and Culture*. Vol. 1/2. London: Oxford University Press, 1926.

———. *Israel, Its Life and Culture*. Vol. 3/4. London: Oxford University Press, 1940.

Peil, Dietmar. "Metapherntheorien." In *Metzler Lexikon Literatur- und Kulturtheorie: Ansätze, Personen, Grundbegriffe*, edited by Ansgar Nünning, 364–66. Stuttgart: J. B. Metzler, 1998.

———. "Symbol." In *Metzler Lexikon Literatur- und Kulturtheorie: Ansätze, Personen, Grundbegriffe*, edited by Ansgar Nünning, 518–19. Stuttgart: J. B. Metzler, 1998.

Perlitt, Lothar. "Anklage und Freispruch Gottes: Theologische Motive in der Zeit des Exils." In *Deuteronomium-Studien*, edited by Lothar Perlitt, 20–31. Tübingen: Mohr, 1994.

———. *Bundestheologie im Alten Testament*. Neukirchen-Vluyn: Neukirchener Verlag, 1969.

———. "Die Verborgenheit Gottes." In *Allein mit dem Wort: Theologische Studien*, edited by Hermann Spieckermann, 11–25. Göttingen: Vandenhoeck & Ruprecht, 1995.

Pesch, Rudolf. *Das Markusevangelium*. Freiburg im Breisgau: Herder Verlag, 1977.
Petuchowski, Jakob Josef. *Gottesdienst des Herzens: Eine Auswahl aus dem Gebetsschatz des Judentums*. Freiburg im Breisgau: Herder Verlag, 1981.
Pezzoli-Olgiati, Daria. "Die Gegenwelt des Todes in Bild und Text: Ein religionswissenschaftlicher Blick auf mesopotamische Beispiele." In Bickel et al., *Bilder als Quellen*, 379–401.
Philonenko, Marc. *Das Vaterunser: Vom Gebet Jesu zum Gebet der Jünger*. Tübingen: Mohr Siebeck, 2002.
Pleister, Wolfgang, Wolfgang Schild, and Hans Latz. "Der Mythos des Rechts." In *Recht und Gerechtigkeit im Spiegel der europäischen Kunst*, 8–43. Cologne: DuMont, 1988.
Plessner, Helmuth. "Anthropologie II." In *Die Religion in Geschichte und Gegenwart: Handwörterbuch für Theologie und Religionswissenschaft*, edited by Kurt Galling and Hans von Campenhausen, 1:410–14. 3rd ed. Tübingen: Mohr, 1957.
Podella, Thomas. "Ahnen/Ahnenverehrung III." In *RGG*[4] 1 (1998): 227–28.
———. "Grundzüge alttestamentlicher Jenseitsvorstellungen." *Biblische Notizen*, no. 43 (1988): 70–89.
———. *Das Lichtkleid JHWHs: Untersuchungen zur Gestalthaftigkeit Gottes im Alten Testament und seiner altorientalischen Umwelt*. Tübingen: J. C. B. Mohr, 1996.
———. "Nekromantie." *Theologische Quartalschrift* 177, no. 2 (1997): 121–33.
———. "Sich zeigen und gesehen werden: Bemerkungen zu *r'h* N-Stamm." *Zeitschrift für Althebraistik* 2 (1989): 160–87.
———. "Totenrituale und Jenseitsbeschreibungen: Zur anamnetischen Struktur der Religionsgeschichte Israels." In Assmann and Trauzettel, *Tod, Jenseits*, 530–61.
———. "Transformationen kultischer Darstellungen: Toraliturgien in Ps 15 und 24." *Scandinavian Journal of the Old Testament* 13 (1999): 95–130.
———. "Trauerbräuche II." *RGG*[4] 8 (2005): 559–60.
Pola, Thomas. "Was ist 'Leben' im Alten Testament?" *Zeitschrift für die alttestamentliche Wissenschaft* 116 (2004): 251–52.
Pongratz-Leisten, Beate. "Anthropology I." *EBR* 2 (2009): 114–17.
———. *Ina šulmi īrub: Die kulttopographische und ideologische Programmatik der Akitu-Prozession in Babylonien und Assyrien im 1. Jahrtausend v. Chr.* Mainz am Rhein: P. von Zabern, 1994.
Popitz, Heinrich. "Gewalt." In *Phänomene der Macht: Autorität—Herrschaft—Gewalt—Technik*, 43–78. (1986.) 2nd ed. Tübingen: J. C. B. Mohr (P. Siebeck), 1992.
Preuss, Horst Dietrich. "שָׁבַח." In *ThWAT* 7:1318–23.
———. *Theologie des Alten Testaments*. 2 vols. Stuttgart: W. Kohlhammer, 1991–92.
———. "תּוֹעֵבָה." In *ThWAT* 9:580–92.
Puech, Émile. "Palestinian Funerary Inscriptions." In *ABD* 5 (1992): 126–35.
Rad, Gerhard von. "'Gerechtigkeit' und 'Leben' in der Kultsprache der Psalmen." In *Gesammelte Studien zum Alten Testament*, 225–47. Munich: Christian Kaiser, 1965.
———. *Old Testament Theology*. 2 vols. New York: Harper & Row, 1962–65.
———. *Theologie des Alten Testaments*. 10th ed. 2 vols. Munich: Christian Kaiser, 1992–93.
———. *Wisdom in Israel*. Nashville: Abingdon, 1972.
———. "Die Wirklichkeit Gottes." In *Gottes Wirken in Israel: Vorträge zum Alten Testament*, edited by Odil Hannes Steck, 141–62. Neukirchen-Vluyn: Neukirchener Verlag des Erziehungsvereins, 1974.
Raeder, Siegfried. "Psalmen/Psalmenbuch II." In *TRE* 27:624–34.
Raible, W. "Zur Begriffsgeschichte von 'Mensch': Skizze einer kognitiven Landkarte." In Stagl and Reinhard, *Grenzen des Menschseins*, 155–73.
Rechberger, Uwe. *Von der Klage zum Lob: Studien zum "Stimmungsumschwung" in den Psalmen*. Neukirchen-Vluyn: Neukirchener Verlag, 2012.

Rechenmacher, Hans. *Personennamen als theologische Aussagen: Die syntaktischen und semantischen Strukturen der satzhaften theophoren Personennamen in der hebräischen Bibel*. St. Ottilien: EOS Verlag, 1997.

Reemts, Christiana. "Christus begegnen: Das Psalmengebet bei den Vätern der Kirche." *Erbe und Auftrag* 82 (2006): 139–49.

———. *Schriftauslegung: Die Psalmen bei den Kirchenvätern*. Stuttgart: Verlag Katholisches Bibelwerk, 2000.

Reindl, Joseph. *Das Angesicht Gottes im Sprachgebrauch des Alten Testaments*. Leipzig: St. Benno Verlag, 1970.

Reiner, Hans. "Dankbarkeit." In *HWP* 2:9–11.

Reiterer, Friedrich Vinzenz. "שָׁוְא." In *ThWAT* 7:1104–17.

Rendtorff, Rolf. *Studien zur Geschichte des Opfers in alten Israel*. Neukirchen-Vluyn: Neukirchener Verlag, 1967.

———. "Die sündige *næfæš* [*nepeš*]." In F. Crüsemann, Hardmeier, and Kessler, *Was ist der Mensch . . . ?*, 211–20.

———. *Theologie des Alten Testaments: Ein kanonischer Entwurf*. Neukirchen-Vluyn: Neukirchener Verlag, 1999.

Renz, Johannes, and Wolfgang Röllig. *Handbuch der althebräischen Epigraphik*. Darmstadt: Wissenschaftliche Buchgesellschaft, 1995.

Reventlow, Henning. "Gebet II." In *RGG*[4] 3 (2000): 485–88.

———. *Gebet im Alten Testament*. Stuttgart: W. Kohlhammer, 1986.

———. *Rechtfertigung im Horizont des Alten Testaments*. Munich: Christian Kaiser, 1971.

———. *Renaissance, Reformation, Humanismus*. Vol. 3 of *Epochen der Bibelauslegung*. Munich: C. H. Beck, 1997.

———. *Vom Alten Testament bis Origenes*. Vol. 1 of *Epochen der Bibelauslegung*. Munich: C. H. Beck, 1990.

Ricken, Norbert. "Menschen—Zur Struktur anthropologischer Reflexionen als einer unverzichtbaren kulturwissenschaftlichen Dimension." In *Handbuch der Kulturwissenschaften*, edited by Friedrich Jaeger and Burkhard Liebsch, 1:152–72. Stuttgart: Metzler, 2004.

Ricoeur, Paul. *Das Böse: Eine Herausforderung für Philosophie und Theologie*. Zurich: Theologischer Verlag, 2006.

———. *Das Rätsel der Vergangenheit: Erinnern—Vergessen—Verzeihen*. Göttingen: Wallstein Verlag, 1998.

Riede, Peter. "'Die auf JHWH vertrauen, sind wie der Berg Zion, der nicht ins Wanken gerät' (Psalm 125, 1): Zur Verbindung von Anthropologie und Kosmologie in Ps 125." In *FS Janowski*, 421–34.

———. "'Du bereitest vor mir einen Tisch': Zum Tischmotiv in den Psalmen 23 und 69." In van Hecke and Labahn, *Metaphors in the Psalms*, 217–33.

———. *Im Netz des Jägers: Studien zur Feindmetaphorik der Individualpsalmen*. Neukirchen-Vluyn: Neukirchener Verlag, 2000.

———. "Noch einmal: Was ist 'Leben' im Alten Testament?" In *Schöpfung und Lebenswelt: Studien zur Theologie und Anthropologie des Alten Testaments*, 131–36. Leipzig: Evangelische Verlagsanstalt, 2009.

———. "Die Sprache der Bilder: Zur Bedeutung und Funktion der Metaphorik in den Feindpsalmen des Alten Testaments am Beispiel der Psalmen 57 und 59." In van Hecke, *Metaphor in the Hebrew Bible*, 19–40.

Rilke, Rainer Maria. *Letters of Rainer Maria Rilke*. Translated by Jane Bannard Greene and Mary Dows Herter Norton. New York: Norton, 1972.

Ringgren, Helmer. "הָיָה." In *ThWAT* 2:874–98.

———. "חֹשֶׁךְ." In *ThWAT* 3:261–77.

———. "מָסַס." In *ThWAT* 4:1016–18.

Ringleben, Joachim. *Dornenkrone und Purpurmantel: Theologische Betrachtungen zu Bildern von Grünewald bis Paul Klee*. Frankfurt am Main: Insel Verlag, 1996.

———. "Was ist der Mensch, daß du seiner gedenkst?": Grundgedanken evangelischer Anthropologie im Anschluß an Psalm 8, 5." In *Was ist der Mensch?*, edited by N. Elsner and H.-L. Schreiber, 271–87. Göttingen: Wallstein Verlag, 2002.

Riniker, Christian, ed. *Gericht und Zorn Gottes*. Vol. 9 of *ZNT*. Tübingen: Franke, 2002.

Risse, Siegfried. "'Wohl dem, der deine Kinder packt und sie am Felsen zerschmettert': Zur Auslegungsgeschichte von Ps 137, 9." *BibInt* 14 (2006): 364–84.

Ro, Johannes Un-Sok. *Die sogenannte "Armenfrömmigkeit" im nachexilischen Israel*. Berlin: Walter de Gryuter, 2002.

Ro, Johannes Un-Sok, Karl-Johan Illman, and Heinz-Josef Fabry. "מוּת." In *ThWAT* 4:763–87.

Rogerson, John W. "The Enemy in the Old Testament." In *Understanding Poets and Prophets: Essays in Honour of George Wishart Anderson*, edited by A. Graeme Auld, 284–93. Sheffield, England: JSOT Press, 1993.

———. "The World-View of the Old Testament." In *Beginning Old Testament Study*, 55–73. London: SPCK, 1983. New ed., 1998.

Rohde, Michael. *Der Knecht Hiob im Gespräch mit Mose: Eine traditions- und redaktionsgeschichtliche Studie zum Hiobbuch*. Leipzig: Evangelische Verlagsanstalt, 2007.

Röllig, Wolfgang. "Begegnungen mit Göttern und Dämonen der Levante." In *Gegenwelten: Zu den Kulturen Griechenlands und Roms in der Antike*, edited by Tonio Hölscher, 47–66. Munich: Saur, 2000.

———. "Der den Schwachen vom Starken nicht entrechten lässt, der der Waise Recht verschafft . . . : Gleich und ungleich im religiösen Denken des Alten Orients." In *"Vor Gott sind alle gleich": Soziale Gleichheit, Soziale Ungleichheit und die Religionen*, edited by Günter Kehrer and Hubert Cancik, 42–52. Düsseldorf: Patmos, 1983.

Rösel, Christoph. "'Ein Prüfer der Herzen ist JHWH' (Spr 17, 3b): Gott und das menschliche Herz im Alten Testament." *Biblische Zeitung* 56 (2012): 286–98.

Rösel, Martin. "Die Geburt der Seele in der Übersetzung: Von der hebräischen *näfäsch* [*nepeš*] über die *psychē* der LXX zur deutschen Seele." In A. Wagner, *Anthropologische Aufbrüche*, 151–70.

———. "Der hebräische Mensch im griechischen Gewand: Anthropologische Akzentsetzungen in der Septuaginta." In Herms, *Leben: Verständnis*, 237–54. Expanded in Janowski, Liess, and Zaft, *Der Mensch*, 69–92.

———. "Tun-Ergehen-Zusammenhang." In *NBL* 3:931–34.

———. "Von der Kehle zur Seele: Neue Akzente im Menschenbild der Septuaginta." *Bibel und Kirche* 67 (2012): 30–35.

Rössler, Dietrich. "Mensch, ganzer." In *HWP* 5:1106–11.

Rössner, Hans. *Der ganze Mensch: Aspekte einer pragmatischen Anthropologie*. Munich: DTV, 1986.

Rudman, Dominic. "The Use of Water Imagery in Descriptions of Sheol." *Zeitschrift für die alttestamentliche Wissenschaft* 113, no. 2 (2001): 240–44.

Rüegger, Hans-Ulrich, and Annelies Hämmig. "'Mein gott: varzuo hastu [hast du] mich gelassen?': Philologische Annäherung an eine theologische Frage (Mk 15, 34)." *Zeitschrift für die neutestamentliche Wissenschaft und die Kunde der älteren Kirche* 102 (2011): 40–58.

Ruppert, Lothar. "Dürsten nach Gott: Ein psalmistisches Motiv im religionsphänomenologischen Vergleich." In *Studien zur Literaturgeschichte des Alten Testaments*, edited by Lothar Ruppert, 211–26. Stuttgart: Verlag Katholisches Bibelwerk, 1994.

———. "Fluch- und Rachepsalmen." In *NBL* 1 (1991): 685–86.

———. *Jesus als der leidende Gerechte? Der Weg Jesu im Lichte eines alt- und zwischentestamentlichen Motivs*. Stuttgart: Verlag Katholisches Bibelwerk, 1972.

———. "Klage oder Bitte: Zu einer neuen Sicht der individuellen Klagelieder." *Biblische Zeitschrift* 33, no. 2 (1989): 252–55.

———. *Der leidende Gerechte: Eine motivgeschichtliche Untersuchung zum Alten Testament und zwischentestamentlichen Judentum*. Würzburg: Echter Verlag, 1972.

———. *Der leidende Gerechte und seine Feinde: Eine Wortfelduntersuchung*. Würzburg: Echter Verlag, 1973.

———. "תָּמַךְ." In *ThWAT* 8 (1995): 683–88.

Rüsen, Jörn, and Klaus E. Müller. "Was heisst: Sinn der Geschichte?" In *Historische Sinnbildung: Problemstellungen, Zeitkonzepte, Wahrnehmungshorizonte, Darstellungsstrategien*, 17–47. Reinbek bei Hamburg: Rowohlt, 1997.

Rüterswörden, Udo. "שָׁמַע." In *ThWAT* 8:255–79.

Ruwe, Andreas, and Felix Facklam. *Die Psalmen zum Betrachten, Studieren und Vorlesen: Eine textanalytische Übersetzung*. Zurich: Theologischer Verlag, 2012.

Ruwe, Andreas, and Dierk Starnitzke. "Krankheit/Heilung." *SWB* 315–20.

Sachs, Nelly. *Fahrt ins Staublose: Die Gedichte der Nelly Sachs*. Frankfurt am Main: Suhrkamp, 1986.

Safranski, Rüdiger. *Das Böse, oder, das Drama der Freiheit*. Munich: Hanser Verlag, 1997.

Sänger, Dieter, ed. *Psalm 22 und die Passionsgeschichten der Evangelien*. Neukirchen-Vluyn: Neukirchener Verlag, 2007.

Särkiö, Pekka. "Hilferuf zu Jahwe aus dem Versteck: Eine neue Deutung der Inschrift *yšr mḥr* aus Ḫirbet Bēt Lēy." *Zeitschrift des Deutschen Palästina-Vereins* 113 (1997): 39–60.

Sauer, Ralph. *Warum, Gott . . . ?* Kevelaer: Verlag Butzon & Bercker, 1993.

Saur, Markus. *Einführung in die alttestamentliche Weisheitsliteratur*. Darmstadt: Wissenschaftliche Buchgesellschaft, 2012.

———. "'Herr, höre meine Worte, merke auf mein Reden!' (Ps 5, 2): Mensch und Gebet in den Psalmen." In *Menschsein denken: Anthropologien in theologischen Perspektiven*, edited by Christina Aus der Au, 9–21. Neukirchen-Vluyn: Neukirchener Verlag, 2005.

Sauter, Gerhard. *Das verborgene Leben: Eine theologische Anthropologie*. Gütersloh: Gütersloher Verlagshaus, 2011.

———. "'Was ist der Mensch, daß Du seiner gedenkst?': Selbstwahrnehmung in Psalmengebeten." *Evangelische Theologie* 66 (2006): 317–19.

Savran, George W. "Seeing Is Believing: On the Relative Priority of Visual and Verbal Perception of the Divine." *BibInt* 17 (2009): 320–61.

Schäfer, Heinrich. "Weltgebäude der alten Ägypter." In *Ägyptische und heutige Kunst und Weltgebäude der alten Ägypter*, edited by Heinrich Schäfer, 83–128. Berlin: Walter de Gruyter, 1928.

Schäfer, Rolf. *Die Poesie der Weisen: Dichotomie als Grundstruktur der Lehr- und Weisheitsgedichte in Proverbien 1–9*. Neukirchen-Vluyn: Neukirchener Verlag, 1999.

Schaper, Joachim. *Eschatology in the Greek Psalter*. Tübingen: Mohr-Siebeck, 1995.

———. *"Wie der Hirsch lechzt nach frischem Wasser . . .": Studien zu Ps 42/43; Religionsgeschichte, Theologie und kirchlicher Praxis*. Neukirchen-Vluyn: Neukirchener Verlag, 2004.

Scharbert, Josef. "Gerechtigkeit I." In *TRE* 12:404–11.

Schenker, Adrian. *Alte Gerichtsbarkeit: Vom Gottesurteil bis zum Beginn der modernen Rechtsprechung*. Munich: Callwey, 1980.

———. "Die Tafel des Herzens: Eine Studie über Anthropologie und Gnade im Denken des Propheten Jeremia im Zusammenhang mit Jer 31, 31–34." In *Text und Sinn im Alten Testament: Textgeschichtliche und bibeltheologische Studien*, edited by Adrian Schenker, 68–81. Göttingen: Vandenhoeck & Ruprecht, 1991.

Schild, Wolfgang. *Alte Gerichtsbarkeit vom Gottesurteil bis zum Beginn der modernen Rechtsprechung*. Munich: Callwey, 1980.

———. "Gott als Richter." In *Recht und Gerechtigkeit im Spiegel der europäischen Kunst*, edited by Wolfgang Pleister, Wolfgang Schild, and Hans Latz, 44–85. Cologne: DuMont, 1988.

Schlegel, Juliane. *Psalm 88 als Prüfstein der Exegese: Zu Sinn und Bedeutung eines beispiellosen Psalms*. Neukirchen-Vluyn: Neukirchener Verlag, 2005.

Schmeisser, Martin. *Das Buch der Psalmen: Die 150 Psalmen in Bildern*. Eschbach: Verlag am Eschbach, 1990.

Schmid, Hans Heinrich. *Gerechtigkeit als Weltordnung: Hintergrund und Geschichte der alttestamentlichen Gerechtigkeitsbegriffes*. Tübingen: Mohr Siebeck, 1968.

Schmid, Konrad. "Fülle des Lebens oder erfülltes Leben? Religionsgeschichtliche und theologische Überlegungen zur Lebensthematik im Alten Testament." In Herms, *Leben: Verständnis*, 154–64.

———. "Was heißt Vertrauen? Biblische Erkundungen anhand von Psalm 13 und der Abrahamüberlieferung der Genesis." In *Gottvertrauen: Die ökumenische Diskussion um die fiducia*, edited by Ingolf U. Dalferth and Simon Peng-Keller, 31–47. Freiburg im Breisgau: Herder Verlag, 2012.

Schmidt, Hans. "Das Gebet der Angeklagten im Alten Testament." In *Zur neueren Psalmenforschung*, edited by Peter H. A. Neumann, 156–67. Darmstadt: Wissenschaftliche Buchgesellschaft, 1976.

———. *Die Psalmen*. Tübingen: J. C. B. Mohr, 1934.

Schmidt, Werner H. "Alttestamentliche Anthropologie." In *Evangelisches Kirchenlexikon*, edited by Erwin Fahlbusch, 3:156–58. Göttingen: Vandenhoeck & Ruprecht, 1986.

———. *Alttestamentlicher Glaube*. Neukirchen-Vluyn: Neukirchener Verlag, 1996.

———. "Anthropologische Begriffe im Alten Testament." In *Vielfalt und Einheit alttestamentlichen Glaubens*, edited by Werner H. Schmidt and Axel Graupner, 77–91. Neukirchen-Vluyn: Neukirchener Verlag, 1995.

———. "'Der du die Menschen lässest sterben': Exegetische Anmerkungen zu Ps 90." In *Vielfalt und Einheit alttestamentlichen Glaubens*, edited by Werner H. Schmidt and Axel Graupner, 31–46. Neukirchen-Vluyn: Neukirchener Verlag, 1995.

———. *Exodus*. Neukirchen-Vluyn: Neukirchener Verlag, 1988.

———. "'Was ist der Mensch?': Anthropologische Einsichten des Alten Testaments." *Bibel und Kirche* 42 (1987): 2–15.

Schmidt, Werner H., Holger Delkurt, and Axel Graupner. *Die zehn Gebote im Rahmen alttestamentlicher Ethik*. Darmstadt: Wissenschaftliche Buchgesellschaft, 1993.

Schmitt, Armin. "Entrückung." In *NBL* 1:543–47.

———. *Wende des Lebens: Untersuchungen zu einem Situations-Motiv der Bibel*. Berlin and New York: Walter de Gruyter, 1996.

Schmitt, Rüdiger. "Perspektiven und Probleme einer Anthropologie des Alten Testaments." *MARG* [*Mitteilungen für Anthropologie und Religionsgeschichte*] 20 (2010): 177–215.

Schneider-Flume, Gunda. *Glaubenserfahrung in den Psalmen: Leben in der Geschichte mit Gott*. Göttingen: Vandenhoeck & Ruprecht, 1998.

———. "Leben in Gottes Geschichte: Psalmen als Gebete des christlichen Glaubens." *Erbe und Auftrag* 82 (2006): 164–74.

Schnelle, Udo. *Neutestamentliche Anthropologie: Jesus, Paulus, Johannes*. Neukirchen-Vluyn: Neukirchener Verlag, 1991. ET, *The Human Condition: Anthropology in the Teachings of Jesus, Paul, and John*. Translated by O. C. Dean Jr. Minneapolis: Fortress Press, 1996.

Schnieringer, Helmut. *Psalm 8: Text—Gestalt—Bedeutung*. Wiesbaden: O. Harrassowitz, 2004.

Schnocks, Johannes. "'Ehe die Berge geboren wurden, bist du': Die Gegenwart Gottes im 90. Psalm." *Bibel und Kirche* 54 (1999): 163–69.

———. "Metaphern für Leben und Tod in den Psalmen 23 und 88." In van Hecke and Labahn, *Metaphors in the Psalms*, 235–49.

———. *Rettung und Neuschöpfung: Studien zur alttestamentlichen Grundlegung einer gesamtbiblischen Theologie der Auferstehung*. Göttingen: V&R Unipress et al., 2009.

———. Review of *Begrenztes Leben als Herausforderung: Das Vergänglichkeitsmotiv in weisheitlichen Psalmen*, by Christine Forster. *Theologische Revue* 97 (2001): 298–301.

Schoberth, Ingrid. "Kein bloß 'lieber Gott': Die Verharmlosung der Gottesrede als Problem der Praktischen Theologie." *ZNT* 9 (2002): 60–66.

Schoberth, Wolfgang. *Einführung in die theologische Anthropologie*. Darmstadt: Wissenschaftliche Buchgesellschaft, 2006.

———. "Wozu theologische Anthropologie?" *Verkündigung und Forschung* 51 (2006): 38–55.

Scholl, Reinhold. *Die Elenden in Gottes Thronrat: Stilistisch-kompositorische Untersuchungen zu Jesaja 24–27*. Berlin: Walter de Gruyter, 2000.

Schönemann, Hubertus. *Der untreue Gott und sein treues Volk: Anklage Gottes angesichts unschuldigen Leidens nach Psalm 44*. Göttingen: V&R Unipress et al., 2009.

Schöpf, Alfred. "Krankheit." In *Lexikon der Ethik*, edited by Otfried Höffe, 161–63. Munich: C. H. Beck, 1997.

Schöpflin, Karin. "Seele II." In *TRE* 30:737–40.

Schorch, Stefan. *Euphemismen in der Hebräischen Bibel*. Wiesbaden: O. Harrassowitz, 2000.

Schottroff, Willy. "Alter als soziales Problem in der hebräischen Bibel." In F. Crüsemann, Hardmeier, and Kessler, *Was ist der Mensch . . . ?*, 61–77.

Schramme, Thomas, ed. *Krankheitstheorien*. Berlin: Suhrkamp, 2012.

Schreiner, Josef. "Geburt und Tod in biblischer Sicht." In *Segen für die Völker: Gesammelte Schriften zur Entstehung und Theologie des Alten Testaments*, edited by Josef Schreiner and Erich Zenger, 331–57. Würzburg: Echter Verlag, 1987.

———. *Theologie des Alten Testaments*. Würzburg: Echter Verlag, 1995.

Schroeder, Christoph. "Psalm 3 und das Traumorakel des von Feinden bedrängten Beters." *Biblica* 81, no. 2 (2000): 243–51.

Schroer, Markus, ed. *Soziologie des Körpers*. Frankfurt am Main: Suhrkamp, 2005.

Schroer, Silvia. "Beobachtungen zur Aktualisierung und Transformation von Totenweltmythologie im alten Israel." In *Mythisches in biblischer Bildsprache: Gestalt und Verwandlung in Prophetie und Psalmen*, edited by Hubert Irsigler and Eberhard Bons, 290–317. Freiburg im Breisgau: Herder Verlag, 2004.

———. "Feministische Anthropologie des Ersten Testaments: Beobachtungen, Fragen, Plädoyers." *Lectio difficilior: European Electronic Journal for Feminist Exegesis* [*www.lectio.unibe.ch*], no. 1/1, 2003, 1–21, http://www.aletta.nu/ezines/web/LectioDifficilior/2003/No1/No1/schroer.pdf.

———. "Häusliche und außerhäusliche religiöse Kompetenzen israelitischer Frauen: Am Beispiel von Totenklage und Totenbefragung." In *Haushalt, Hauskult, Hauskirche: Zur Arbeitsteilung der Geschlechter in Wirtschaft und Religion*, edited by Elmar Klinger, Stefanie Böhm, and Thomas Franz, 9–34. Würzburg: Echter Verlag, 2004.

———. *In Israel gab es Bilder: Nachrichten von darstellender Kunst im Alten Testament.* Freiburg, Switzerland: Universitätsverlag, 1987.

———. "Trauerriten und Totenklage im Alten Israel." In Berlejung and Janowski, *Tod und Jenseits*, 299–321.

Schroer, Silvia, and Thomas Staubli. *Die Körpersymbolik der Bibel.* Darmstadt: Wissenschaftliche Buchgesellschaft, 1998. 2nd ed. Gütersloh: Gütersloher Verlagshaus, 2005.

Schroer, Silvia, and Ruben Zimmermann. "Mensch/Menschsein." *SWB* 368–76.

Schüle, Andreas. "Anthropologie des Alten Testaments." *Theologische Rundschau* 76 (2011): 399–414.

———. "'Call on Me in the Day of Trouble . . .': From Oral Lament to Lament Psalms." In *The Interface of Orality and Writing: Speaking, Seeing, Writing in the Shaping of New Genres*, edited by Annette Weissenrieder and Robert B. Coote, 322–34. Tübingen: Mohr Siebeck, 2010.

———. "'Denn er ist wie Du': Zu Übersetzung und Verständnis des alttestamentlichen Liebesgebots Lev 19, 18." *Zeitschrift für die alttestamentliche Wissenschaft* 113, no. 4 (2001): 515–34.

———. "Gottes Handeln als Gedächtnis: Auferstehung in kulturtheoretischer und biblisch-theologischer Perspektive." In *Die Wirklichkeit der Auferstehung*, edited by Hans-Joachim Eckstein and Michael Welker, 237–75. Neukirchen-Vluyn: Neukirchener Verlag, 2002. 4th ed., 2010.

Schult, H. "שָׁמַע." In *THAT* 2:974–82.

Schulz, Walter. "Wandlungen der Einstellungen zum Tode." In *Prüfendes Denken: Essays zur Wiederbelebung der Philosophie*, 95–113. Tübingen: Klöpfer & Meyer, 2002.

Schüssler, Werner, ed. *Philosophische Anthropologie*. Freiburg im Breisgau: Alber, 2000.

Schütz, Alfred, and Thomas Luckmann. *Strukturen der Lebenswelt*. Vol. 2. Frankfurt am Main: Suhrkamp, 1984.

Schwarz, Rudolf. *Johannes Calvins Lebenswerk in seinen Briefen: Eine Auswahl von Briefen Calvins*. Vol. 2. Tübingen: Mohr Siebeck, 1909.

Schweizer, Harald. "Metaphorik." In *NBL* 2:791–92.

Schwemer, Anna Maria. "Die Passion des Messias nach Markus und der Vorwurf des Antijudaismus." In *Der Messianische Anspruch Jesu und die Anfänge der Christologie: Vier Studien*, edited by Martin Hengel and Anna Maria Schwemer, 133–63. Tübingen: Mohr Siebeck, 2001.

Schwienhorst-Schönberger, Ludger. "'Bis ich eintrat in die Heiligtümer Gottes' (Ps 73, 17): Ps 73 im Horizont biblischer und theologischer Hermeneutik." In Achenbach, Arneth, and Otto, *Rechtsgeschichte*, 387–402.

———. *Das Bundesbuch (Ex 20, 22–23, 33): Studien zu seiner Entstehung und Theologie.* Berlin and New York: Walter de Gruyter, 1990.

———. "Gottesbilder des Alten Testaments." *Theologisch praktische Quartalsschrift* 148 (2000): 358–68.

———. *Kohelet*. Freiburg im Breisgau: Herder, 2004.

———. "נָגַע." In *ThWAT* 5:219–26.

———. *"Nicht im Menschen gründet das Glück" (Koh 2, 24): Kohelet im Spannungsfeld jüdischer Weisheit und hellenistischer Philosophie*. Freiburg im Breisgau: Herder Verlag, 1994.

———. "Sehen im Nicht-Sehen: Mose auf dem Berg Sinai." In *Gottes Wahrnehmungen: Helmut Utzschneider zum 60. Geburtstag*, edited by Stefan Gehrig and Stefan Seiler, 102–22. Stuttgart: W. Kohlhammer, 2009.

———. "Vergeltung." In *Lexikon für Theologie und Kirche*, edited by Michael Buchberger and Walter Kasper, 10:654–56. 3rd ed. Freiburg im Breisgau: Herder Verlag, 2001.

Scoralick, Ruth. *Gottes Güte und Gottes Zorn: Die Gottesprädikationen in Exodus 34, 6f und ihre intertextuellen Beziehungen zum Zwölfprophetenbuch*. Freiburg im Breisgau: Herder Verlag, 2002.

Sedlmeier, Franz. "'Vom Mutterschoß her bin ich geworfen auf dich' (Ps 22, 11): Wert und Würde des Menschen nach Texten des Alten Testaments." In Frevel, *Biblische Anthropologie*, 300–316.

Seebass, Horst. "אַחֲרִית." In *ThWAT* 1 (1973): 224–28.

———. "נֶפֶשׁ." In *ThWAT* 5:531–55.

———. "Opfer II." In *TRE* 25:258–67.

———. "Über den Beitrag des Alten Testaments zu einer theologischen Anthropologie." *Kerygma und Dogma* 22, no. 1 (1976): 41–63.

———. *Urgeschichte*. Vol. 1 of *Genesis*. Neukirchen-Vluyn: Neukirchener Verlag, 1996.

Seeligmann, Isaac Leo. "Erkenntnis Gottes und historisches Bewusstsein im alten Israel." In *Beiträge zur alttestamentlichen Theologie*, edited by Walther Zimmerli, Herbert Donner, Robert Hanhart, and Rudolf Smend, 414–45. Göttingen: Vandenhoeck & Ruprecht, 1977.

Seidel, Hans. *Auf den Spuren der Beter*. 2nd ed. Berlin: Evangelische Verlagsanstalt, 1987.

———. *Das Erlebnis der Einsamkeit im Alten Testament: Eine Untersuchung zum Menschenbild des Alten Testamentes*. Berlin: Evangelische Verlagsanstalt, 1969.

Seidl, Theodor. "'Schön bist du meine Freundin': Wahrnehmung des Körpers im Hohen Lied." In *Der Körper und die Religion: Das Problem der Konstruktion von Geschlechterrollen*, edited by Elmar Klinger, Stefanie Böhm, and Theodor Seidl, 129–57. Würzburg: Echter Verlag, 2000.

Seifert, Brigitte. *Metaphorisches Reden von Gott im Hoseabuch*. Göttingen: Vandenhoeck & Ruprecht, 1996.

Selz, Gebhard J. "'Tief ist der Brunnen der Vergangenheit': Zu 'Leben' und 'Tod' nach Quellen der mesopotamischen Frühzeit—Interaktionen zwischen Diesseits und Jenseits." In *Zwischen Euphrat und Tigris: Österreichische Forschungen zum Alten Orient*, edited by Friedrich Schipper, 39–59. Wien: Lit, 2004.

Seux, Marie-Joseph. *Hymnes et prières aux dieux de Babylonie et d'Assyrie*. Paris: Éditions du Cerf, 1976.

Seybold, Klaus. *Der Aaronitische Segen: Studien zu Numeri 6, 22–27*. Neukirchen-Vluyn: Neukirchener Verlag, 1977.

———. *Das Gebet des Kranken im Alten Testament: Untersuchungen zur Bestimmung und Zuordnung der Krankheits- und Heilungspsalmen*. Stuttgart: W. Kohlhammer, 1973.

———. "Gericht Gottes." In *TRE* 12:460–66.

———. "Hymnus I." In *NBL* 2:207–8.

———. "Krankheit als Problem und als Thema der biblischen Tradition: A. Altes Testament." In *Krankheit und Heilung*, edited by Klaus Seybold and Ulrich B. Müller, 11–78. Stuttgart: W. Kohlhammer, 1978.

———. "Krankheit und Heilung." *Bibel und Kirche* 26 (1971): 107–11.

———. "Poesie, biblische." In *TRE* 26:743–48.

———. *Poetik der Psalmen*. Stuttgart: W. Kohlhammer, 2003.

———. *Die Psalmen*. Tübingen: J. C. B. Mohr (Paul Siebeck), 1996.

———. *Die Psalmen: Eine Einführung*. Stuttgart: W. Kohlhammer, 1991.

———. "Psalmen/Psalmenbuch." In *TRE* 27:610–24.

———. "Der Weg des Lebens: Eine Studie zu Psalm 16." In *Studien zur Psalmenauslegung*, 75–84. Stuttgart: W. Kohlhammer, 1998.

———. "Zur Sprache des Hohenliedes." *Theologische Zeitschrift* 55 (1999): 112–20.

Sieben, Hermann Josef. *Schlüssel zum Psalter: Sechzehn Kirchenvätereinführungen von Hippolyt bis Cassiodor*. Paderborn: Schöningh, 2011.

Siegrist, Johannes. *Lehrbuch der Medizinischen Soziologie*. Munich: Urban & Schwarzenberg, 1977.

Sigurvinsson, Jón Ásgeir. "Ps 17, 14c–e: Vorwurf an JHWH oder Fluch über die Feinde? Die Deutung von *ṣĕpûnkā* als eine sprechaktliche crux interpretum." In Diller, *Syntax, Sprechaktanalyse und Metaphorik*, 61–79.

Simian-Yofre, Horacio. "פָּנִים." In *ThWAT* 6:629–59.

Simmel, Georg. *Soziologie: Untersuchungen über die Formen der Vergesellschaftung*. Edited by Otthein Rammstedt. Leipzig: Duncker & Humblot, 1908. Frankfurt am Main: Suhrkamp, 1992. ET, *Sociology: Inquiries into the Construction of Social Forms*. Translated by Anthony J. Blasi, Anton K. Jacobs, and Matthew Kanjirathinkal. Leiden: E. J. Brill, 2009.

Singer, Karl-Heinz. "Rache." In *NBL* 3:269–70.

Sloterdijk, Peter. *Zorn und Zeit: Politisch-psychologischer Versuch*. Frankfurt am Main: Suhrkamp, 2006.

Smend, Rudolf. "Der Entdecker des Parallelismus: Robert Lowth (1710–1787)." In *Prophetie und Psalmen: Festschrift für Klaus Seybold zum 65. Geburtstag*, edited by Beat Huwyler, Hans-Peter Mathys, and Beat Weber, 185–99. Münster: Ugarit-Verlag, 2001.

———. "Lowth in Deutschland." In *Bibel und Wissenschaft: Historische Aufsätze*, 51–70. Tübingen: Mohr Siebeck, 2004.

Smith, Mark S. "The Heart and Innards in Israelite Emotional Expressions: Notes from Anthropology and Psychobiology." *Journal of Biblical Literature* 117, no. 3 (1998): 427–36. Translated as "Herz und Innereien in israelitischen Gefühlsäußerungen: Notizen aus der Anthropologie und Psychologie." In A. Wagner, *Anthropologische Aufbrüche*, 171–81.

———. "The Near Eastern Background of Solar Language for Yahweh." *Journal of Biblical Literature* 109, no. 1 (1990): 29–39.

———. "'Seeing God' in the Psalms: The Background to the Beatific Vision in the Hebrew Bible." *Catholic Biblical Quarterly* 50, no. 2 (1988): 171–83.

Soden, Wolfram von. "Gebet II." In *Reallexikon der Assyriologie*, edited by D. O. Edzard, 3:160–70. Berlin: Walter de Gruyter, 1957–71.

Sofsky, Wolfgang. *Traktat über die Gewalt*. Frankfurt am Main: S. Fischer, 1996.

———. *Zeiten des Schreckens: Amok, Terror, Krieg*. Frankfurt am Main: S. Fischer, 2002.

Soggin, Jan Alberto. "יָמִין." In *ThWAT* 3:658–63.

Sommerfeld, Walter. *Der Aufstieg Marduks: Die Stellung Marduks in der babylonischen Religion des zweiten Jahrtausends v.Chr.* Neukirchen-Vluyn: Neukirchener Verlag, 1982.

Soosten, Joachim von. "Die 'Erfindung' der Sünde: Soziologische und semantische Aspekte zu der Rede von der Sünde im alttestamentlichen Sprachgebrauch."*Jahrbuch für biblische Theologie* 9 (1994): 87–110.

Spieckermann, Hermann. "Alttestamentliche 'Hymnen.'" In *Hymnen der Alten Welt im Kulturvergleich*, edited by Walter Burkert and Fritz Stolz, 97–108. Freiburg, Switzerland: Universitätsverlag, 1994.

———. "'Barmherzig und gnädig ist der Herr. . . .'" In *Gottes Liebe zu Israel: Studien zur Theologie des Alten Testaments*, edited by Hermann Spieckermann, 3–19. Tübingen: Mohr Siebeck, 2001.

———. "Gerechtigkeit Gottes II." In *RGG*[4] 3 (2000): 718–20.

———. *Heilsgegenwart: Eine Theologie der Psalmen*. Göttingen: Vandenhoeck & Ruprecht, 1989.

———. "Lieben und Glauben: Beobachtungen in Psalm 116." In *Meilenstein: Festgabe für Herbert Donner zum 16. Februar 1995*, edited by Manfred Weippert and Stefan Timm, 266–75. Wiesbaden: O. Harrassowitz, 1995.

———. "Rechtfertigung I." In *TRE* 28:282–86.

———. "Der Retter ist nah: Heilsverheißung und Rechtfertigung nach dem Alten Testament." In *Im Licht der Gnade Gottes: Zur Gegenwartsbedeutung der Rechtfertigungsbotschaft*, edited by Wilfried Härle and Peter Neuner, 27–51. Münster: LIT Verlag, 2004.

———. "Die Satanisierung Gottes: Zur inneren Konkordanz von Novelle, Dialog und Gottesreden im Hiobbuch." In *Wer ist wie du, Herr, unter den Göttern? Studien zur Theologie und Religionsgeschichte Israels; Für Otto Kaiser zum 70. Geburtstag*, edited by Ingo Kottsieper, 431–44. Göttingen: Vandenhoeck & Ruprecht, 1994.

———. "Schweigen und Beten: Von stillem Lobgesang und zerbrechender Rede im Psalter." In *Das Manna fällt auch heute noch: Beiträge zur Geschichte und Theologie des Alten, Ersten Testaments; Festschrift für Erich Zenger*, edited by Frank-Lothar Hossfeld and Ludger Schwienhorst-Schönberger, 567–84. Freiburg im Breisgau: Herder Verlag, 2004.

———. "Der theologische Kosmos des Psalters." *Berliner Theologische Zeitschrift* 21 (2004): 61–79.

Spronk, Klaas. *Beatific Afterlife in Ancient Israel and in the Ancient Near East*. Kevelaer: Butzon & Bercker, 1986.

———. "Good Death and Bad Death in Ancient Israel according to Biblical Lore." *Social Science and Medicine* 58 (2004): 987–95.

Stadelmann, Luis I. J. *The Hebrew Conception of the World: A Philological and Literary Study*. Rome: Pontifical Biblical Institute Press, 1970.

Stadler, Arnold, trans. *"Die Menschen lügen. Alle" und andere Psalmen*. Translated from the Hebrew. Frankfurt am Main: Insel Verlag, 1999. Expanded ed., with an essay by Wolfgang Frühwald, 2005.

Stagl, Justin, and Wolfgang Reinhard, eds. *Grenzen des Menschseins: Probleme einer Definition des Menschlichen*. Vienna: Böhlau, 2005.

Stähli, Hans-Peter. "Tod und Leben im Alten Testament." *Theologie und Glaube* 76 (1986): 172–92.

Staubli, Thomas. *Die Bücher Levitikus, Numeri*. Stuttgart: Verlag Katholisches Bibelwerk, 1996.

———. Review of *Körperbilder in den Psalmen: Studien zu Psalm 22 und verwandten Texten*, by Dörte Bester. *Orientalistische Literaturzeitung* 104 (2009): 185–92.

Steck, Odil Hannes. "Beobachtungen zur Beziehung von Klage und Bitte in Psalm 13." *Biblische Notizen*, no. 13 (1980): 57–62.

———. *Friedensvorstellungen im alten Jerusalem: Psalmen, Jesaja, Deuterojesaja*. Zurich: Theologischer Verlag, 1972.

Steinert, Ulrike. *Aspekte des Menschseins im Alten Mesopotamien: Eine Studie zu Person und Identität im 2. und 1. Jt. v. Chr*. Leiden: E. J. Brill, 2012.

———. "'Zwei Drittel Gott, ein Drittel Mensch': Überlegungen zum altmesopotamischen Menschenbild." In Janowski, *Der ganze Mensch*, 59–81.

Steingrimsson, Sigurdur Örn, and Kristinn Ólason, eds. *Literatur- und sprachwissenschaftliche Beiträge zu alttestamentlichen Texten: . . . Wolfgang Richter zum 80. Geburtstag*. St. Ottilien: Eos Verlag, 2007.

Steins, Georg, ed. *Schweigen wäre gotteslästerlich: Die heilende Kraft der Klage*. Würzburg: Echter Verlag, 2000.

Stendebach, Franz-Josef. "עַיִן." In *ThWAT* 6:31–48.

Stephenson, Gunther. *Leben und Tod in den Religionen: Symbol und Wirklichkeit*. Darmstadt: Wissenschaftliche Buchgesellschaft, 1980.

Sticher, Claudia. "'Die Gottlosen gedeihen wie Gras': Zu einigen Pflanzenmetaphern in den Psalmen; Eine kanonische Lektüre." In van Hecke and Labahn, *Metaphors in the Psalms*, 251–68.

———. *Die Rettung der Guten durch Gott und die Selbstzerstörung der Bösen: Ein theologisches Denkmuster im Psalter*. Berlin: Philo, 2002.

Stoebe, Hans-Joachim. *Das zweite Buch Samuelis*. Gütersloh: Gütersloher Verlagshaus, 1994.

Stol, Marten. "Psychosomatic Suffering in Ancient Mesopotamia." In *Mesopotamian Magic: Textual, Historical and Interpretative Perspectives*, edited by I. Tzvi Abusch and Karen van der Toorn, 57–68. Groningen: Styx Publications, 1999.

Stolt, Birgit. *Martin Luthers Rhetorik des Herzens*. Tübingen: Mohr Siebeck, 2000.

Stolz, Fritz. *Grundzüge der Religionswissenschaft*. Göttingen: Vandenhoeck & Ruprecht, 2001.

———. "Paradiese und Gegenwelten." *Zeitschrift für Religionswissenschaft* 1 (1993): 5–24.

———. *Weltbilder der Religionen: Kultur und Natur, Diesseits und Jenseits, Kontrollierbares und Unkontrollierbares*. Zurich: Pano Verlag, 2001.

Stolz, Fritz, Horst Balz, Gerhard Krause, and Robert Müller. "Rache." In *TRE* 28:82–88.

Strauss, Hans. "Die 'Freunde' Hiobs—ein Kreis frommer Weiser im Hintergrund des Hiobuches." *Biblische Notizen*, no. 95 (1998): 71–78.

———. *Hiob*. Neukirchen-Vluyn: Neukirchener Verlag, 1995.

———. "Tod (Todeswunsch; 'Jenseits'?) im Buch Hiob." In *Gottes Recht als Lebensraum: Festschrift für Hans Jochen Boecker*, edited by Peter Mommer, Werner H. Schmidt, and Hans Strauss, 239–49. Neukirchen-Vluyn: Neukirchener Verlag, 1993.

Strawn, Brent A. "Psalm 22:17b: More Guessing." *Journal of Biblical Literature* 119, no. 3 (2000): 439–51.

———. *What Is Stronger Than a Lion? Leonine Image and Metaphor in the Hebrew Bible and the Ancient Near East*. Göttingen: Vandenhoeck & Ruprecht, 2005.

Streck, Bernhard. "Weltbild." In *Wörterbuch der Ethnologie*, 291–95. 2nd ed. Wuppertal: Hammer, 2000.

Streck, Michael P. *Die Bildersprache der Akkadischen Epik*. Münster: Ugarit-Verlag, 1999.

———. "Person." *Reallexikon der Assyriologie und Vorderasiatischen Archäologie* 10:429–31. Edited by Otto Edzard Dietz. Berlin: W. de Gruyter, 2005.

Strola, Germana. *Il desiderio di Dio: Studio dei Salmi 42–43*. Assisi (Perugia): Cittadella, 2003.

Sünker, Heinz, and Knut Berner, eds. *Vergeltung ohne Ende? Über Strafe und ihre Alternativen im 21. Jahrhundert*. Lahnstein: Neue Praxis, 2012.

Szlezák, Thomas Alexander. "Psyche: Ihr Ort im Menschen, im Kosmos und im Geist nach Platon und Plotin." In Düsing and Klein, *Geist und Psyche*, 17–39.

Tacke, Helmut. *Glaubenshilfe als Lebenshilfe: Probleme und Chancen heutiger Seelsorge*. 2nd ed. Neukirchen-Vluyn: Neukirchener Verlag, 1979.

Talmon, Shemaryahu. "מִדְבָּר." In *ThWAT* 4:660–95.

———. "Die Wertung von 'Leben' in der hebräischen Bibel." In *Juden und Christen im Gespräch: Gesammelte Aufsätze*, edited by Shemaryahu Talmon, 2:48–60. Neukirchen-Vluyn: Neukirchener Verlag, 1992.

Tanner, Jakob. *Historische Anthropologie zur Einführung*. Hamburg: Junius, 2004.

Tate, Marvin E. *Psalms 51–100*. Waco, TX: Word Books, 1990.

Terrien, Samuel. *The Psalms: Strophic Structure and Theological Commentary*. Grand Rapids and Cambridge: Eerdmans, 2003.

Theobald, Michael. "Der Tod Jesu im Spiegel seiner 'letzten Worte' vom Kreuz." *Theologische Quartalschrift* 190 (2010): 1–31.
Theunissen, Michael. *Negative Theologie der Zeit*. Frankfurt am Main: Suhrkamp, 1991.
Thiel, Winfried. "שָׁק." *ThWAT* 7:849–55.
Thies, Christian. *Einführung in die philosophische Anthropologie*. 2nd ed. Darmstadt: Wissenschaftliche Buchgesellschaft, 2009.
———. "Mensch." In *Neues Handbuch philosophischer Grundbegriffe*, edited by Petra Kolmer and Armin G. Wildfeuer, 2:1515–26. Freiburg im Breisgau: Alber, 2011.
Thommen, Lukas. *Antike Körpergeschichte*. Zurich: VDF Hochschulverlag AG, 2007.
Tietz, Christiane. "Was heißt: Gott erhört Gebet?" *Zeitschrift für Theologie und Kirche* 106 (2009): 327–44.
Tillmann, Norbert. *"Das Wasser bis zum Hals!": Gestalt, Geschichte und Theologie des 69. Psalms*. Altenberge: Oros Verlag, 1993.
Tita, Hubert. *Gelübde als Bekenntnis: Eine Studie zu den Gelübden im Alten Testament*. Freiburg, Switzerland: Universitätsverlag, 2001.
Tomes, Roger. *"I Have Written to the King, My Lord": Secular Analogies for the Psalms*. Sheffield: Sheffield Phoenix Press, 2005.
Toorn, Karel van der. *Family Religion in Babylonia, Syria and Israel: Continuity and Changes in the Forms of Religious Life*. Leiden: E. J. Brill, 1996.
———. "Ordeal." In *ABD* 5 (1992): 40–42.
———. "Ordeal Procedures in the Psalms and the Passover Meal." *Vetus Testamentum* 38, no. 4 (1988): 427–45.
Toorn, Karel van der, and Herbert Niehr. "Ein verborgenes Erbe: Totenkult im frühen Israel." *Theologische Quartalschrift* 177, no. 2 (1997): 105–20.
Tournay, Raymond Jacques. *Seeing and Hearing God with the Psalms: The Prophetic Liturgy of the Second Temple in Jerusalem*. Sheffield: JSOT Press, 1991.
Tromp, Nicholas J., and Biblico Pontificio Istituto. *Primitive Conceptions of Death and the Nether World in the Old Testament*. Rome: Pontifical Biblical Institute Press, 1969.
Tropper, Josef. *Nekromantie: Totenbefragung im Alten Orient und im Alten Testament*. Kevelaer: Butzon & Bercker, 1989.
Tück, Jan Heiner. *Gelobt seist Du, Niemand: Paul Celans Dichtung, eine Theologische Provokation*. Frankfurt: Knecht, 2000.
Uehlinger, Christoph. "Achabs 'Elfenbeinhaus' und der 'Elfenbeinturm' in Hld 7, 5: Archäologie und Poetik." *Biblische Notizen*, no. 102 (2000): 95–111.
———. "Antiker Tell, lebendiges Stadtviertel: Das Psalmenbuch als Sammlung von Einzeldichtungen und als Grosskomposition." *Bibel und Kirche* 56 (2001): 174–77.
———. "Bilderverbot." In *RGG*[4] 1 (1998): 1574–77. Tübingen: Mohr Siebeck, 1998.
———. "Gab es eine joschijanische Kultreform? Plädoyer für ein begründetes Minimum." In *Jeremia und die "deuteronomistische Bewegung,"* edited by Walter Gross and Dieter Bohler, 55–89. Weinheim: Beltz Athenäum, 1995.
Utzschneider, Helmut. "Der friedvolle und der bittere Tod: Einstellungen und Horizonte gegenüber Tod und Sterben im Alten Testament." In *Kurtur, Politik, Religion, Sprache—Text: Wolfgang Stegemann zum 60. Geburtstag*, edited by Christian Strecker, 37–48. Vol. 2 of *Kontexte der Schrift*. Stuttgart: W. Kohlhammer, 2005.
———. "Zum Verständnis des Lebens im AT: Ein Glossar mit sechs Stichworten." *Glauben und Lernen* 19 (2004): 118–24.
Vanoni, Gottfried. "Psalm 22: Literarkritik." In *Beiträge zur Psalmenforschung: Psalm 2 und 22*, edited by Josef Schreiner, 153–92. Würzburg: Echter Verlag, 1988.
Vanoni, Gottfried, and Bernhard Heininger. *Das Reich Gottes*. Würzburg: Echter Verlag, 2002.
Veijola, Timo. "'Fluch des Totengeistes ist der Aufgehängte' (Dtn 21, 23)." *Ugarit-Forschungen* 32 (2000): 543–53.

———. "Das Klagegebet in Literatur und Leben der Exilsgeneration am Beispiel einiger Prosatexte." In *Moses Erben: Studien zum Dekalog, zum Deuteronomismus, und zum Schriftgelehrtentum*, edited by Timo Veijola, 176–91. Stuttgart: W. Kohlhammer, 2000.

Velden, Frank van der. *Psalm 109 und die Aussagen zur Feindschädigung in den Psalmen*. Stuttgart: Verlag Katholisches Bibelwerk, 1997.

Vernant, Jean-Pierre. "Individuum, Tod, Liebe: Das Selbst und der andere im alten Griechenland." In *Anthropologie*, edited by Gunter Gebauer, 22–48. Leipzig: Reclam, 1998.

———. *Der Mensch der griechischen Antike*. Frankfurt am Main: Campus-Verlag, 1993.

———. "Mythos und Geist im alten Griechenland." In *Anthropologie nach dem Tode des Menschen: Vervollkommnung und Unverbesserlichkeit*, edited by Dietmar Kamper and Christoph Wulf, 357–69. Frankfurt am Main: Suhrkamp, 1994.

Vesco, Jean-Luc. *Le psautier de David: Traduit et commenté*. 2 vols. Paris: Éditions du Cerf, 2006.

———. *Le psautier de Jésus: Les citations des Psaumes dans le Nouveau Testament*. 2 vols. Paris: Éditions du Cerf, 2012.

Veyne, Paul. *Brot und Spiele: Gesellschaftliche Macht und politische Herrschaft in der Antike*. Frankfurt am Main: Campus Verlag, 1988.

Villanueva, Federico G. *The "Uncertainty of a Hearing": A Study of the Sudden Change of Mood in the Psalms of Lament*. Leiden and Boston: E. J. Brill, 2008.

Vincent, Jean Marcel. *Das Auge hört: Die Erfahrbarkeit Gottes im Alten Testament*. Neukirchen-Vluyn: Neukirchener Verlag, 1998.

Vogel, Thomas, and Hermann Bausinger. *Über das Hören: Einem Phänomen auf der Spur*. Tübingen: Attempto, 1996.

Vogt, Ludgera, and Arnold Zingerle, eds. *Ehre: Archaische Momente in der Moderne*. Frankfurt am Main: Suhrkamp, 1994.

Vonach, Andreas. *Nähere dich um zu Hören: Gottesvorstellungen und Glaubensvermittlung im Kohelethbuch*. Berlin: Philo, 1999.

Vorländer, Hermann. *Mein Gott: Die Vorstellungen vom persönlichen Gott im Alten Orient und im Alten Testament*. Kevelaer: Butzon & Bercker, 1975.

Vos, Christiane de. *Klage als Gotteslob aus der Tiefe: Der Mensch vor Gott in den individuellen Klagepsalmen*. Tübingen: Mohr Siebeck, 2005.

Wächter, Ludwig. "שְׁאוֹל." In *ThWAT* 7:901–10.

———. *Der Tod im Alten Testament*. Stuttgart: Calwer Verlag, 1967.

———. "Tod im Alten Testament." *Zeichen der Zeit* 40 (1986): 35–42.

———. "Unterweltvorstellungen und Unterweltnamen in Babylonien, Israel und Ugarit." *Mitteilungen des Instituts für Orientforschung* 15 (1969): 327–36.

Wagner, Andreas, ed. *Anthropologische Aufbrüche: Alttestamentliche und interdisziplinäre Zugänge zur historischen Anthropologie*. Göttingen: Vandenhoeck & Ruprecht, 2009.

———. *Beten und Bekennen: Über Psalmen*. Neukirchen-Vluyn: Neukirchener Verlag, 2008.

———. *Emotionen, Gefühle und Sprache im Alten Testament: Vier Studien*. Waltrop: Spenner, 2006.

———. *Gottes Körper: Zur alttestamentlichen Vorstellung der Menschengestaltigkeit Gottes*. Gütersloh: Gütersloher Verlagshaus, 2010.

———. "Körperbegriffe als Stellvertreterausdrücke der Person in den Psalmen." In *Beten und Bekennen*, 289–317.

———. "Der Lobaufruf im israelitischen Hymnus als indirekter Sprechakt." In *Studien zur hebräischen Grammatik*, 143–56. Freiburg, Switzerland: Universitätsverlag, 1997.

———. "Mensch." In *Das wissenschaftliche Bibellexikon im Internet*, edited by Michaela Bauks and Klaus Koenen. www.wibilex.de, 2007.

———, ed. *Parallelismus membrorum*. Freiburg, Switzerland: Academic Press; Göttingen: Vandenhoeck & Ruprecht, 2007.

———. "Der Parallelismus zwischen poetischer Form und Denkfigur." In *Beten und Bekennen*, 235–61.

———. *Sprechakte und Sprechaktanalyse im Alten Testament: Untersuchungen im biblischen Hebräisch an der Nahtstelle zwischen Handlungsebene und Grammatik*. Berlin: Walter de Gruyter, 1997.

———. "Strukturen des Gebets im Alten Testament." In *Orakel und Gebete: Interdisziplinäre Studien zur Sprache der Religion in Ägypten, Vorderasien und Griechenland in hellenistischer Zeit*, edited by Markus Witte and Johannes F. Diehl, 197–215. Tübingen: Mohr Siebeck, 2009.

———. "Das synthetische Bedeutungsspektrum hebräischer Körperteilbezeichnungen." *Biblische Zeitschrift* 51 (2007): 257–65.

———. "Wider die Reduktion des Lebendigen: Über das Verhältnis der sog. anthropologischen Grundbegriffe und die Unmöglichkeit, mit ihnen die alttestamentliche Menschenvorstellung zu erfassen." In A. Wagner, *Anthropologische Aufbrüche*, 183–99.

Wagner, Siegfried. "יָקַר." In *ThWAT* 3:855–65.

———. "סָתַר." In *ThWAT* 5:967–77.

Wahrig, Gerhard. *DTV-Wörterbuch der deutschen Sprache*. Munich: Deutscher Taschenbuch-Verlag, 1978.

Wälchli, Stefan H. *Gottes Zorn in den Psalmen: Eine Studie zur Rede vom Zorn Gottes in den Psalmen im Kontext des Alten Testamentes und des Alten Orients*. Fribourg: Academic Press; Göttingen: Vandenhoeck & Ruprecht, 2012.

———. *Der weise König Salomo: Eine Studie zu den Erzählungen von der Weisheit Salomos in ihrem alttestamentlichen und altorientalischen Kontext*. Stuttgart: W. Kohlhammer, 1999.

Wannenwetsch, Bernd. "Dank." In *RGG*[4] 2 (1999): 561–62.

Wannenwetsch, Bernd, and Hans Dieter Betz. "Dank." In *RGG*[4] 2 (1999): 562–63.

Warmuth, Georg. "שָׂבַע." In *ThWAT* 7:693–704.

Waschke, Ernst-Joachim. "Auferstehung I/2." In *RGG*[4] 1 (1998): 915–16.

———. "תְּמוּנָה." In *ThWAT* 8:677–80.

———. "'Was ist der Mensch, dass du seiner gedenkst?' (Ps 8, 5): Theologische und anthropologische Koordinaten für die Fragen nach dem Menschen im Kontext alttestamentlicher Aussagen." *Theologische Literaturzeitung* 116, no. 11 (1991): 801–12.

Watson, Wilfred G. E. *Classical Hebrew Poetry: A Guide to Its Techniques*. Sheffield: JSOT Press, 1986.

———. "The Unnoticed Word Pair 'Eye(s)'//'Heart.'" *Zeitschrift für die alttestamentliche Wissenschaft* 101, no. 3 (1989): 398–408.

Watts, Rikk E. "The Lord's House and David's Lord: The Psalms and Mark's Perspective on Jesus and the Temple." *BibInt* 15 (2007): 307–22.

———. "Mark." In Beale and Carson, *Commentary*, 111–249.

———. "The Psalms in Mark's Gospel." In *The Psalms in the New Testament*, edited by Steve Moyise and Maarten J. J. Menken, 25–45. London and New York: T&T Clark International, 2004.

Weber, Beat. "Le caractère poétique des Psaumes et son incidence sur leur interpretation: Quelques considérations sur une approche littéraire des Psaumes." *Revue des sciences religieuses* 77 (2003): 481–96.

———. "Einige poetologische Überlegungen zur Psalmeninterpretation verbunden mit einer exemplarischen Anwendung an Psalm 130." *Old Testament Essays* 18 (2005): 891–906.

———. "Entwurf einer Poetologie der Psalmen." In *Lesarten der Bibel: Untersuchungen zu einer Theorie der Exegese des Alten Testaments*, edited by Helmut Utzschneider and Erhard Blum, 127–54. Stuttgart: W. Kohlhammer, 2006.

———. "'JHWH, Gott der Rettung' und das Schreien aus 'finsterem Ort': Klangmuster und andere Stilmittel in Psalm 88." *Old Testament Essays* 20 (2007): 471–88.

———. "'JHWH, Gott meiner Rettung!': Beobachtungen und Erwägungen zur Struktur von Psalm 88." *Vetus Testamentum* 58 (2008): 595–607.

———. "Lob und Klage in den Psalmen als Anfrage und Herausforderung an unsere Gebets- und Gottesdienstpraxis." *Jahrbuch für evangelikale Theologie* 13 (1999): 33–47.

———. "Notizen zu Form, Pragmatik und Struktur von Psalm 16." *Biblische Notizen*, no. 125 (2005): 25–38.

———. "Psalm 30 als Paradigma für einen heutigen 'Kasus der Wiederherstellung.'" *Jahrbuch für evangelikale Theologie* 21 (2007): 31–50.

———. Review of *The "Uncertainty of a Hearing": A Study of the Sudden Change of Mood in the Psalms of Lament*, by Federico G. Villanueva. *Theologische Literaturzeitung* 134 (2009): 681–83.

———. "'Wenn du Vergehen aufbewahrtest . . .': Linguistische, poetologische und theologische Notizen zu Psalm 130." *Biblische Notizen*, no. 107/108 (2001): 146–60.

———. *Werkbuch Psalmen*. Vol. 1, *Die Psalmen 1 bis 72*. Vol. 2, *Die Psalmen 73 bis 150*. Vol. 3, *Theologie und Spiritualität des Psalters und seiner Psalmen*. Stuttgart: W. Kohlhammer, 2001, 2003, 2010.

———. "Zum sogenannten 'Stimmungsumschwung' in Psalm 13." In Flint and Miller, *Book of Psalms*, 116–38.

Wehrle, Josef. "Metapher." In *NBL* 2:789–91.

———. "Ps 1—Das Tor zum Psalter: Exegese und theologische Schwerpunkte." *Münchener theologische Zeitschrift* 46 (1995): 215–29.

Wehrle, Josef, and Rainer Kampling. "Herz." In *NBL* 2:137–41.

Weippert, Helga. "Altisraelitische Welterfahrung: Die Erfahrung von Raum und Zeit nach dem Alten Testament." In *Ebenbild Gottes—Herrscher über die Welt: Studien zu Würde und Auftrag des Menschen*, edited by Hans-Peter Mathys, 9–34. Neukirchen-Vluyn: Neukirchener Verlag, 1998.

Weippert, Manfred. "Aspekte israelitischer Prophetie im Lichte verwandter Erscheinungen des Alten Orients." In *Ad bene et fideliter seminandum: Festgabe für Karlheinz Deller zum 21. Februar 1987*, edited by Gerlinde Mauer and Ursula Magen, 287–319. Kevelaer: Butzon & Bercker, 1988.

———. "Assyrische Prophetien der Zeit Asarhaddons und Assurbanipals." In *Assyrian Royal Inscriptions: New Horizons in Literary, Ideological and Historical Analysis; Papers of Symposium held in Cetona (Siena), June 26–28, 1980*, edited by Frederick Mario Fales, 71–115. Rome: Istituto per l'Oriente, Centro per le antichità e la storia dell'arte del vicino Oriente, 1980.

———. "Ecce non dormitabit neque dormiet qui custodit Israhel: Zur Erklärung von Psalm 121, 4." In *Jahwe und die anderen Götter: Studien zur Religionsgeschichte des antiken Israel in ihrem syrisch-palästinischen Kontext*, edited by Manfred Weippert, 99–107. Tübingen: Mohr Siebeck, 1997.

———. "Synkretismus und Monotheismus: Religionsinterne Konfliktbewältigung im alten Israel." In *Jahwe und die anderen Götter: Studien zur Religionsgeschichte des antiken Israel in ihrem syrisch-palästinischen Kontext*, edited by Manfred Weippert, 1–24. Tübingen: Mohr Siebeck, 1997.

Welten, Peter. "Los." In *NBL* 2:667–68.

Wenning, Robert. "Bestattungen im königszeitlichen Juda." *Theologische Quartalschrift* 177 (1997): 82–93.

———. "Grab." In *NBL* 1:942–46.

Wenning, Robert and Hans-Peter Kuhnen. "Bestattung II–III." In *RGG*[4] 1 (1998): 1363–65.

Wenning, Robert, and Erich Zenger. "Tod und Bestattung im biblischen Israel: Eine archäologische und religionsgeschichtliche Skizze." In *"Ihr alle aber seid Brüder": Festschrift für A. Th. Khoury Zum 60. Geburtstag*, edited by Ludwig Hagemann and Ernst Pulsfort, 285–303. Würzburg: Echter Verlag, 1990.

Wenzel, Horst. *Hören und Sehen, Schrift und Bild: Kultur und Gedächtnis im Mittelalter*. Munich: C. H. Beck, 1995.

Werbick, Jürgen. "Auf der Spur der Bilder." *Bibel und Kirche* 54 (1999): 2–9.

———. *Bilder sind Wege: Eine Gotteslehre*. Munich: Kösel, 1992.

———. "Metapher." In *Lexikon für Theologie und Kirche*, edited by Michael Buchberger and Walter Kasper, 6:187–90. 3rd ed. Freiburg im Breisgau: Herder Verlag, 1997.

Werbick, Jürgen, and H. L. J. Vanstiphout. *Den Glauben verantworten: Eine Fundamentaltheologie*. Freiburg im Breisgau: Herder Verlag, 2000.

Werlitz, Jürgen. "Scheol und sonst nichts? Zu den alttestamentlichen 'Jenseits'-Vorstellungen." In *Das Jenseits: Perspektiven christlicher Theologie*, edited by Stefan Schreiber and Stefan Siemons, 41–61. Darmstadt: Wissenschaftliche Buchgesellschaft, 2003.

Werner, W. "Leben I." In *NBL* 1:595–96, 598.

Westendorf, Wolfhart. *Studien zu Sprache und Religion Ägyptens*. Göttingen: F. Junge, 1984.

Westenholz, Joan Goodnick. "Symbolic Language in Akkadian Narrative Poetry: The Metaphorical Relationship between Poetical Images and the Real World." In *Mesopotamian Poetic Language: Sumerian and Akkadian*, edited by Marianna E. Vogelzang and H. L. J. Vanstiphout, 183–206. Groningen: Styx Publications, 1996.

Westermann, Claus. "Anthropologische und theologische Aspekte des Gebets in den Psalmen." In *Zur neueren Psalmenforschung*, edited by Peter H. A. Neumann, 452–68. Darmstadt: Wissenschaftliche Buchgesellschaft, 1976.

———. *Ausgewählte Psalmen: Übersetzt end erklärt*. Göttingen: Vandenhoeck & Ruprecht, 1984.

———. *Das Buch Jesaja: Kapitel 40–66*. Göttingen: Vandenhoeck & Ruprecht, 1986. ET, *Isaiah 40–66: A Commentary*. Translated by David M. G. Stalker. Philadelphia: Westminster Press, 1969.

———. *Erträge der Forschung am Alten Testament: Zu seinem 65. Geburtstag am 7. Oktober 1974*. Vol. 3 of *Gesammelte Studien*. Edited by Rainer Albertz. Munich: Christian Kaiser, 1984.

———. "Gesundheit, Leben und Tod aus der Sicht des Alten Testaments." In *Forschung am Alten Testament*, edited by Rainer Albertz, 152–65. Vol. 3 of *Gesammelte Studien*. Munich: Christian Kaiser, 1974.

———. "כָּבֵד, schwer sein." In *THAT* 1:794–812.

———. *Die Klagelieder: Forschungsgeschichte und Auslegung*. Neukirchen-Vluyn: Neukirchener Verlag, 1990.

———. *Lob und Klage in den Psalmen*. Göttingen: Vandenhoeck & Ruprecht, 1977.

———. *Der Mensch im Alten Testament*. Münster: LIT Verlag, 2000.

———. "נֶפֶשׁ." In *THAT* 2:71–96.

———. "Die Rolle der Klage in der Theologie des Alten Testaments." In *Forschung am Alten Testament: Gesammelte Studien*, edited by Claus Westermann, 250–68. Munich: Christian Kaiser, 1974.

———. "Das Schöne im Alten Testament." In *Beiträge zur alttestamentlichen Theologie: Festschrift für Walther Zimmerli zum 70. Geburtstag*, edited by Herbert Donner, Robert Hanhart, and Rudolf Smend, 479–97. Göttingen: Vandenhoeck & Ruprecht, 1977.

———. "Struktur und Geschichte der Klage im Alten Testament." In *Lob und Klage in den Psalmen*, edited by Claus Westermann, 125–64. Göttingen: Vandenhoeck & Ruprecht, 1977.

———. *Vergleiche und Gleichnisse im Alten und Neuen Testament*. Stuttgart: Calwer Verlag, 1984.

———. "יָדָה." In *THAT* 1:674–82.

Wetz, Franz Josef. *Glück*. Stuttgart: Klett-Cotta, 2002.

Weymann, Volker. "Bilder der Hoffnung angesichts von Sterben und Tod." *Evangelische Theologie* 54, no. 6 (1994): 501–19.

White, Hayden. *Tropics of Discourse: Essays in Cultural Criticism*. Baltimore: Johns Hopkins University Press, 1985.

Wichmann, Hans. *Der Mensch ohne Hand oder: Die Zerstörung der menschlichen Ganzheit; Ein Symposion des Werkbundes Bayern*. Munich: Deutscher Taschenbuch-Verlag, 1979.

Wiesel, Elie. *Macht Gebete aus meinen Geschichten: Essays eines Betroffenen*. Freiburg im Breisgau: Herder Verlag, 1986.

Wiesenhütter, Eckart, and Berthold Barend Stokvis. *Der Mensch in der Entspannung: Lehrbuch autosuggestiver und übender Verfahren der Psychotherapie und Psychosomatik*. 3rd ed. Stuttgart: Hippokrates Verlag, 1971.

Wiggermann, Frans. "Magie, Magier I." In *Der neue Pauly*, edited by Hubert Cancik, Helmuth Schneider, and August Friedrich von Pauly, 7:657–61. Stuttgart: J. B. Metzler, 1999.

Wiklander, B. "זָעַם." In *ThWAT* 2:621–26.

Wilcke, Claus. "Der Tod im Leben der Babylonier." In Assmann and Trauzettel, *Tod, Jenseits*, 252–66.

———. "Vom Wesen des Menschen in altorientalischer Mythologie." In Stagl and Reinhard, *Grenzen des Menschseins*, 235–51.

Wilckens, Ulrich. *Das Evangelium nach Johannes*. Göttingen: Vandenhoeck & Ruprecht, 1998.

Willi, Thomas. "Die Freiheit Israels: Philologische Notizen zu den Wurzeln *ḥpš*, *'zb* und *drr*." In *Beiträge zur alttestamentlichen Theologie: Festschrift für Walther Zimmerli zum 70. Geburtstag*, edited by Herbert Donner, Robert Hanhart, and Rudolf Smend, 531–46. Göttingen: Vandenhoeck & Ruprecht, 1977.

———. "Der Ort von Gen 4:1–16 innerhalb der althebräischen Geschichtsschreibung." In *Isac Leo Seeligmann Volume: Essays on the Bible and the Ancient World*, edited by Alexander Zakovitch Rofé and Yair Zakovitch, 99–113. Jerusalem: E. Rubinstein, 1983.

Willi-Plein, Ina. *Opfer und Kult im alttestamentlichen Israel: Textbefragungen und Zwischenergebnisse*. Stuttgart: Verlag Katholisches Bibelwerk, 1993.

———. "Vision." In *NBL* 14:1038–40.

Willis, John T. *Genesis*. Austin: Sweet Publishing Co., 1979.

———. "*Qûmāh* YHWH." *Journal of Northwest Semitic Languages* 16 (1990): 207–21.

Wilson, Gerald Henry. *The Editing of the Hebrew Psalter*. Chico, CA: Scholars Press, 1985.

Winterling, Aloys, ed. *Historische Anthropologie*. Stuttgart: Steiner, 2006.

Wischnowsky, Marc. *Tochter Zion: Aufnahme und Uberwindung der Stadtklage in den Prophetenschriften des Alten Testaments*. Neukirchen-Vluyn: Neukirchener Verlag, 2001.

Witte, Markus. "'Aber Gott wird meine Seele erlösen': Tod und Leben nach Psalm XLIX." *Vetus Testamentum* 50, no. 4 (2000): 540–60.

———. "Auf dem Weg in ein Leben nach dem Tod: Beobachtungen zur Traditions- und Redaktionsgeschichte von Psalm 73, 24–26." *Theologische Zeitschrift* 58 (2002): 15–30.

———. *Die biblische Urgeschichte: Redaktions- und theologiegeschichtliche Beobachtungen zu Genesis 1, 1–11, 26*. Berlin: Walter de Gruyter, 1998.

———, ed. *Gerechtigkeit*. Tübingen: Mohr Siebeck, 2012.

———. "Der Psalter." In *Grundinformation Altes Testament*, edited by Jan Christian Gertz, 414–32. 3rd ed. Göttingen: Vandenhoeck & Ruprecht, 2009.

———. "'Vom Geist der Ebräischen Poesie': Johann Gottfried Herder als Bibelwissenschaftler." In *Herder-Gedenken: Interdisziplinäre Beiträge anlässlich des 200. Todestages von Johann Gottfried Herder*, edited by Wilhelm-Ludwig Federlin and Markus Witte, 171–87. Frankfurt am Main: Lang, 2005.

Wöhrle, Jakob. "Der verborgene und der rettende Gott: Exegetische und religionsgeschichtliche Überlegungen zur Theologie der Klagepsalmen." *Biblische Zeitschrift* 55 (2011): 224–41.

Wolde, Ellen van. "Sentiments as Culturally Constructed Emotions: Anger and Love in the Hebrew Bible." *BibInt* 16 (2008): 1–24.

Wolff, Hanna. *Neuer Wein—alte Schläuche: Das Identitätsproblem des Christentums im Lichte der Tiefenpsychologie*. Stuttgart: Radius, 1981.

Wolff, Hans Walter. *Anthropologie des Alten Testaments*. 7th ed. Gütersloh: Christian Kaiser, 2002. 8th ed., with two appendixes, edited by Bernd Janowski, 2010.

———. *Anthropology of the Old Testament*. Translated by Margaret Kohl. Philadelphia: Fortress Press, 1974.

Woude, A. S. van der. "פָּנִים." In *ThWAT* 2:432–60.

Wulf, Christoph. *Anthropologie: Geschichte, Kultur, Philosophie*. Reinbek bei Hamburg: Rowohlt Taschenbuch Verlag, 2004.

———. *Vom Menschen: Handbuch historische Anthropologie*. Weinheim: Beltz, 1997.

Wypadlo, Adrian. "'Wahrhaftig, dieser Mensch war Gottes Sohn' (Mk 15, 39): Überlegungen zur Funktion des Centuriobekenntnisses im christologischen Entwurf des Markusevangeliums." *Biblische Zeitschrift* 55 (2011): 179–208.

Youens, Susan. *Retracing a Winter's Journey: Schubert's "Winterreise."* Ithaca, NY: Cornell University Press, 1991.

Zeindler, Matthias. *Gott der Richter: Zu einem unverzichtbaren Aspekt christlichen Glaubens*. Zurich: Theologischer Verlag, 2004.

Zenger, Erich. "'Aller Atem lobe JHWH!': Anthropologische Perspektiven im Hallel Ps 146–150." In *FS Janowski*, 565–79.

———. "'Das alles Fleisch den Namen seiner Heiligung segne' (Ps 145, 21): Die Komposition Ps 145–150 als Anstoss zu einer christlich-jüdischen Psalmenhermeneutik." *Biblische Zeitschrift* 41, no. 1 (1997): 1–27.

———."Das alttestamentliche Israel und seine Toten." In *Der Umgang mit den Toten: Tod und Bestattung in der christlichen Gemeinde*, edited by Monika Ausel and Klemens Richter, 132–52. Freiburg im Breisgau: Herder Verlag, 1990.

———. *Am Fuss des Sinai: Gottesbilder des Ersten Testaments*. Düsseldorf: Patmos, 1993.

———. "Das Buch der Psalmen." In *Einleitung in das Alte Testament*, edited by Erich Zenger, 309–26. Stuttgart: W. Kohlhammer, 2001.

———, ed. *The Composition of the Book of Psalms*. Leuven and Walpole, MA: Peeters, 2010.

———. *Dein Angesicht suche ich: Neue Psalmenauslegungen*. Freiburg im Breisgau: Herder Verlag, 1998.

———. "'Du thronst auf den Psalmen Israels' (Ps 22, 4): Von der Unverzichtbarkeit der jüdischen Psalmen im christlichen Wortgottesdienst." In *Wie das Wort Gottes feiern? Der Wortgottesdienst als theologische Herausforderung*, edited by Benedikt Kranemann and Thomas Sternberg, 16–40. Freiburg im Breisgau: Herder Verlag, 2002.

———. *Ein Gott der Rache: Feindespsalmen verstehen*. Freiburg im Breisgau: Herder Verlag, 1994.

———. *Einleitung in das Alte Testament*. Stuttgart: W. Kohlhammer, 1998.

———. *Das Erste Testament: Die jüdische Bibel und die Christen*. Düsseldorf: Patmos Verlag, 1991.

———. "Fluchpsalmen." In *Lexikon für Theologie und Kirche*, edited by Michael Buchberger and Walter Kasper, 3:1335–36. 3rd ed. Freiburg im Breisgau: Herder Verlag, 1995.

———. "'Gib deinem Knecht ein hörendes Herz!': Von der messianischen Kraft des rechten Hörens." In *Über das Hören: Einem Phänomen auf der Spur*, edited by Thomas Vogel, 27–43. Tübingen: Attempto, 1996.

———. "'Ich aber sage: Du bist mein Gott' (Ps 31, 14): Kirchliches Psalmengebet nach der Schoa." In *Weg und Weite: Festschrift für Karl Lehmann*, edited by Albert Raffelt and Barbara Nichtweiss, 15–31. Freiburg im Breisgau: Herder Verlag, 2001.

———. "'Ich liebe den Ort, da deine Herrlichkeit wohnt' (Ps 26, 8): Tempeltheologische Semiotisierung des Alltags im Psalter." In *Gottesstadt und Gottesgarten: Zu Geschichte und Theologie des Jerusalemer Tempels*, edited by Othmar Keel and Erich Zenger, 180–206. Freiburg im Breisgau: Herder Verlag, 2002.

———. *Ich will die Morgenröte wecken: Psalmenauslegung*. Freiburg im Breisgau: Herder Verlag, 1991.

———. "Mit Gott ums Leben kämpfen: Zur Funktion der Todesbilder in den Psalmen." *Jahrbuch für biblische Theologie* 19 (2004): 63–78. Also in *Leben trotz Tod*, edited by Martin Ebner and Paul D. Hansen, 63–78. Neukirchen-Vluyn: Neukirchener Verlag, 2005.

———. *Mit meinem Gott überspringe ich Mauern: Einführung in das Psalmenbuch*. Freiburg im Breisgau: Herder Verlag, 1987.

———. "Das Mythische in den Psalmen 84 und 85." In *Mythos im Alten Testament und seiner Umwelt: Festschrift für Hans-Peter Müller zum 65. Geburtstag*, edited by Armin Lange, Hermann Lichtenberger, and Diethard Römheld, 233–51. Berlin: Walter de Gruyter, 1999.

———. *Psalmen: Auslegungen*. 4 vols. Freiburg im Breisgau: Herder Verlag, 2003.

———. "Psalmenexegese und Psalterexegese: Eine Forschungsskizze." In Zenger, *Composition of the Book of Psalms*, 17–65.

———. "Psalmenforschung nach Hermann Gunkel und Sigmund Mowinckel." In *Congress Volume Oslo 1998*, edited by André Lemaire and Magne Sæbø, 399–435. Leiden: E. J. Brill, 2000.

———. "Der Psalter als biblisches Buch: Alte und neue Wege der Psalmenauslegung am Beispiel von Psalm 23." *RHS* [*Religionsunterricht an höheren Schulen*] 49 (2006): 324–37.

———. "Der Psalter als Buch: Beobachtungen zu seiner Entstehung, Komposition und Funktion." In *Der Psalter in Judentum und Christentum*, edited by Erich Zenger and Norbert Lohfink, 1–57. Freiburg im Breisgau: Herder Verlag, 1998.

———. "Der Psalter—das Gebetbuch der Bibel." *Internationale katholische Zeitschrift* 37 (2008): 547–59.

———. "Der Psalter im Horizont von Tora und Prophetie: Kanongeschichtliche und kanonhermeneutische Perspektiven." In *The Biblical Canons*, edited by Jean-Marie Auwers and H. J. de Jonge, 111–34. Leuven: Leuven University Press, 2003.

———. "Rache II." *RGG*[4] 7 (2004): 11–12.

———. Review of *Anthropologie des Alten Testaments*, by Hans Walter Wolff. *Theologische Revue* 70 (1974): 361–62.

———. *Stuttgarter Psalter: Mit Einleitungen und Kurzkommentaren*. Stuttgart: Verlag Katholisches Bibelwerk, 2005.

———. "Von der Psalmenexegese zur Psalterexegese: Neue Perspektiven der Forschung." *Bibel und Kirche* 56 (2001): 8–15.

———. "Zur redaktionsgeschichtlichen Bedeutung der Korachpsalmen." In *Neue Wege der Psalmenforschung: Für Walter Beyerlin*, edited by Klaus Seybold and Erich Zenger, 175–98. Freiburg im Breisgau: Herder Verlag, 1994.

Zenger, Erich, and Frank-Lothar Hossfeld. "Das Buch der Psalmen." In *Einleitung in das Alte Testament*, edited by Erich Zenger and Christian Frevel, 428–52. 8th ed. Stuttgart: W. Kohlhammer, 2012.

Zenger, Erich, and Christoph Wetzel. *Die Psalmen: Mit Meisterwerken des Mittelalters und der Renaissance; Der ökumenische Text der Einheitsübersetzung*. Stuttgart: Verlag Katholisches Bibelwerk, 1997.

Zernecke, Anna Elise. *Gott und Mensch in Klagegebeten aus Israel und Mesopotamien: Die Handerhebungsgebete Ištar 10 und Ištar 2 und die Klagepsalmen Ps 38 und Ps 22 im Vergleich*. Münster: Ugarit-Verlag, 2011.

Zgoll, Anette. "Der betende Mensch: Zur Anthropologie in Mesopotamien." In Janowski, Liess, and Zaft, *Der Mensch*, 121–40.

———. "'Einen Namen will ich mir machen!': Die Sehnsucht nach Unsterblichkeit im Alten Orient." *Saeculum: Jahrbuch für Universalgeschichte* 54 (2003): 1–11.

———. "Für Sinne, Geist und Seele: Vom konkreten Ablauf mesopotamischer Rituale zu einer generellen Systematik von Ritualfunktionen." In *Ritual und Poesie: Formen und Orte religiöser Dichtung im Alten Orient, im Judentum und im Christentum*, edited by Erich Zenger, 25–46. Freiburg im Breisgau: Herder Verlag, 2003.

———. *Die Kunst des Betens: Form und Funktion, Theologie und Psychagogik in babylonisch-assyrischen Handerhebungsgebeten zu Ištar*. Münster: Ugarit-Verlag, 2003.

Ziemer, Jürgen. "Schreie aus der Not: Überlegungen für eine Seelsorge mit den Psalmen." In *Gottes Ehre erzählen: Festschrift für Hans Seidel zum 65. Geburtstag*, edited by Matthias Albani and Timotheus Arndt, 225–35. Leipzig: Thomas Verlag, 1994.

———. *Seelsorgelehre: Eine Einführung für Studium und Praxis*. Göttingen: Vandenhoeck & Ruprecht, 2000.

Zimmer, Tilmann. *Zwischen Tod und Lebensglück: Eine Untersuchung zur Anthropologie Kohelets*. Berlin: Walter de Gruyter, 1999.

Zimmerli, Walther. *1. Mose 1–11: Urgeschichte*. Zurich: Theologischer Verlag, 1984.

———. *Das Menschenbild des Alten Testament*. Munich: Christian Kaiser, 1949.

———. "Was ist der Mensch?" In *Studien zur alttestamentlichen Theologie und Prophetie*, edited by Walther Zimmerli, 311–24. Munich: Christian Kaiser, 1974.

———. *Die Weltlichkeit des Alten Testamentes*. Göttingen: Vandenhoeck & Ruprecht, 1971.

Zimmermann, Ruben. "Metapherntheorie und biblische Bildersprache: Ein methodologischer Versuch." *Theologische Zeitschrift* 56, no. 2 (2000): 108–33.

Zwickel, Wolfgang. "Zur Symbolik der Pflanzen im salomonischen Tempel." In *Das Kleid der Erde: Pflanzen in der Lebenswelt des alten Israel*, edited by Ute Neumann-Gorsolke and Peter Riede, 194–221. Stuttgart: Calwer Verlag, 2002.

Index of Ancient Sources

Scripture index uses traditional versification of Protestant, English Bibles.